CHICAGO AND THE
OLD NORTHWEST,
1673–1835

MARQUETTE AT THE CHICAGO PORTAGE
From the bas relief by H. A. MacNeil
(By courtesy of the Chicago Historical Society)

CHICAGO AND THE OLD NORTHWEST, 1673–1835

A Study of the Evolution of the Northwestern Frontier, Together with a History of Fort Dearborn

Milo Milton Quaife

Introduction by Perry R. Duis

UNIVERSITY OF ILLINOIS PRESS
URBANA, CHICAGO, AND SPRINGFIELD

∞ This book is printed on acid-free paper.

Library of Congress Cataloging-in-Publication Data
Quaife, Milo Milton, 1880–1959.
Chicago and the Old Northwest, 1673–1835 / Milo Milton Quaife ;
introduction by Perry R. Duis.
p. cm.
Originally published: Chicago : University of Chicago Press, 1913.
Includes bibliographical references and index.
ISBN 0-252-02656-X (acid-free paper)
ISBN 0-252-06970-6 (pbk. : acid-free paper)
1. Chicago (Ill.)—History—To 1875. 2. Northwest, Old—History.
3. Frontier and pioneer life—Illinois—Chicago. 4. Frontier and
pioneer life—Northwest, Old. 5. Massacres—Illinois—Chicago—
History. I. Title.
F548.4.Q2 2001
977.3'11—dc21 00-047668

TABLE OF CONTENTS

CHAPTER PAGE

INTRODUCTION by Perry R. Duis vii

PREFACE xix

I. THE CHICAGO PORTAGE 1

II. CHICAGO IN THE SEVENTEENTH CENTURY 21

III. THE FOX WARS: A HALF-CENTURY OF CONFLICT . . . 51

IV. CHICAGO IN THE REVOLUTION 79

V. THE FIGHT FOR THE NORTHWEST 105

VI. THE FOUNDING OF FORT DEARBORN 127

VII. NINE YEARS OF GARRISON LIFE 153

VIII. THE INDIAN UTOPIA 178

IX. THE OUTBREAK OF WAR 195

X. THE BATTLE AND DEFEAT 211

XI. THE FATE OF THE SURVIVORS 232

XII. THE NEW FORT DEARBORN 262

XIII. THE INDIAN TRADE 285

XIV. WAR AND THE PLAGUE 310

XV. THE VANISHING OF THE RED MAN 340

APPENDIX I: Journal of Lieutenant James Strode Swearingen . . 373

APPENDIX II: Sources of Information for the Fort Dearborn Massacre 378

APPENDIX III: Nathan Heald's Journal 402

APPENDIX IV: Captain Heald's Official Report of the Evacuation of Fort Dearborn 406

APPENDIX V: Darius Heald's Narrative of the Chicago Massacre, as Told to Lyman C. Draper in 1868 409

APPENDIX VI: Lieutenant Helm's Account of the Massacre . . . 415

APPENDIX VII: Letter of Judge Augustus B. Woodward to Colonel Proctor concerning the Survivors of the Chicago Massacre . . 422

APPENDIX VIII: Muster-Roll of Captain Nathan Heald's Company of Infantry at Fort Dearborn 425

APPENDIX IX: The Fated Company: A Discussion of the Names and Fate of the Whites Involved in the Fort Dearborn Massacre 428

BIBLIOGRAPHY 439

INDEX 459

Illustrations follow page 210

INTRODUCTION

Perry R. Duis

What does the writing of a great book about early Chicago have to do with the production of electricity fifty miles from the city? A lot, it turns out, in the case of *Chicago and the Old Northwest, 1673–1835*, described on its title page as *A Study of the Evolution of the Northwestern Frontier.*

The story began in 1905 when the Economy Light and Power Company of Joliet obtained permission from the Illinois and Michigan Canal Company to lease and rebuild a small publicly built power dam across the Des Plaines River at a point called Dresden Heights. State and local officials objected, claiming that it would impede navigation on a proposed Lakes-to-the-Gulf Deep Waterway that would make Chicago accessible to ocean-going vessels via the Mississippi. The power company responded by bringing its own suit to seize a large tract of land surrounding the Dresden site, claiming that a private business as essential as a utility should enjoy the right of eminent domain. When the rising utilities mogul Samuel Insull and his Commonwealth Edison company took control of Economy and began construction on a new dam in 1907, the Sanitary District of Metropolitan Chicago tried to halt the construction through an act in the state legislature. The district's chairman, *Tribune* publisher Robert R. McCormick, claimed that the right to generate valuable electricity at the site should belong to the general public.[1] Local and state governments also joined in a lawsuit against Economy, basing much of their legal argument on the future navigability issue. But the Grundy County Court, the state appellate court, and then the Illinois Supreme Court in 1909 all sided with the utility and its lease of the site.[2] The following year saw the appeal process enter the federal court system, where one of the central strategies of the anti-Economy coalition was to discredit the power company's claim that the Des Plaines could be blocked because it had never throughout its history been really navigable. At that point, the company's opponents turned to a group of historians, one of them a young Chicagoan named Milo Quaife. Although at the age of thirty he was just beginning a career that would ultimately span nearly half a century, he was already one of the leading experts on the early history of the Chicago–Des Plaines–Illinois Rivers valley.

Milo Milton Quaife had been born on a farm near Nashua in northeast Iowa on October 6, 1880.[3] The product of a one-room school and a tiny prairie high school, he graduated from Iowa (later Grinnell) College in 1903. After a year of high school teaching, he entered the University of Missouri, from which he earned an M.A. in 1905. He then moved on to the University of Chicago, receiving his Ph.D. in 1908. His dissertation, "The Doctrine of Non-Intervention with Slavery in the Territories," appeared in print three years later. His work so impressed the constitutional historian Andrew C. McLaughlin that it led to the editorship of the four volumes of the presidential diaries of President James K. Polk. This massive work was published in 1910 under the auspices of the Chicago Historical Society.[4] That institution then hired Quaife as a consultant to its commemoration of the Fort Dearborn Massacre. The following year he read a paper at the Mississippi Valley Historical Association thoroughly debunking several widely held myths surrounding the massacre.[5]

Quaife plunged into intensive research on the Chicago–Des Plaines–Illinois Rivers region with an enormous sense of urgency in preparation for his appearance as one of the appellees' star experts in the Dresden case. His sixteen days of testimony—535 printed pages—demonstrated that boats of various sizes had plied the river for centuries. He brought in notes from dozens of diaries, government documents, and maps from the age of exploration, facts that wove their way into the plaintiffs' plea before the United States Supreme Court.[6] On June 22, 1914, however, Economy and Insull won their case based on riparian rights arguments and the validity of the original lease. The Des Plaines sported a power head that would prove to be very profitable to the Economy-Insull interests.[7] But Quaife's detailed court preparation was hardly in vain. By this time he had already utilized it in writing parts of *Chicago and the Old Northwest,* which had been published the previous year. The same body of research also contributed to his edited volume *The Development of Chicago, 1674–1914,* published in 1916 by the Caxton Club, a group of Chicago bibliophiles. The first documentary book about Chicago, it was a collection of travelers' accounts and reminiscences. A similar compilation about the state, *Pictures of Illinois One Hundred Years Ago,* appeared in 1918.[8]

The court case and the acclaim from his new books also had an impact on Quaife's career. In 1908 he had joined the faculty of Chicago's Lewis Institute of Technology, rising quickly through the ranks to professor. Now he was able to shed his teaching responsibilities for the world of libraries and editing that he really preferred. In 1914 he moved to the State Historical Society of Wisconsin, at first combining jobs as superintendent and editor. He located and secured numerous manuscript collections and purchased hundreds of bound volumes of newspapers for the society. He initiated a monthly clip sheet of historical stories for the press and coauthored a pamphlet meant to encourage local towns to celebrate their pasts with pageants. He edited the society's annual *Proceedings* and then in 1917 initiated and became the first editor of the quarterly *Wisconsin Magazine of History.*[9] At that point he also began what would be a forty-three-year association with the R. R. Donnelly Company, a Chicago printer and publisher, to edit the "Lakeside Classics" series of edited reprints of books about the early history of the West. Among the first in the series were new editions of the autobiography of Chief Black Hawk and the journals of explorers Meriwether Lewis and John Ordway.[10]

In 1920 the society divided the tasks he had been performing and he became its editor. Disagreements over the allocation of the institution's diminished budget prompted him to leave two years later to become a freelance writer.[11] He had already begun publishing what would become a series of a hundred brief articles in the *Milwaukee Journal* over a two-year period. Self-employment also allowed him to complete another classic of local history, *Chicago's Highways Old and New: From Indian Trail to Motor Road,* in 1923. This popular volume focused on histories and lore of the numerous non-rail land routes that led to the city. Like the WPA state guides that followed in the 1930s, this book invited readers to visit the various historic sites remaining along the routes.[12]

Quaife's last career move came in March 1924, when he accepted an offer to become secretary and editor of the Burton Historical Collection at the Detroit Public Library. Funded by a Detroit lawyer, the collection featured an extensive array of rare manuscripts, maps, and books documenting the early history of the entire Midwest. During the first three decades of the twentieth century, scholars were continuing to unearth new sources about the pre-1840 period. Most of those archival finds were logically being made in archives east of Illinois, several unearthed at the Burton itself and others in federal records housed in Washington. Although Quaife's personal interests continued to center on the region west of Detroit, the gradual eastward movement of his own career from Iowa toward Michigan was logical: he was following the trail of sources about frontier Chicago closer to their points of origin.

Quaife spent the rest of his professional life not only turning the Burton into a premier research library, but also trying to bridge the gap between scholarly history and writing for mass audiences. He became well known for working with researchers of all skills at the Burton, but he also taught graduate seminars at Wayne (later State) University and the University of Detroit (later Detroit-Mercy). From 1924 to 1931 he served as editor of the *Mississippi Valley Historical Review* (forerunner of the *Journal of American History*), where he often inserted curmudgeonly editorials encouraging his fellow historians to strive for greater objectivity and more involvement in contemporary issues of their field. He reminded readers of hoaxes; chided librarians who recommended second-rate history to patrons; and commented on textbook censorship, novelists as historians, biographers of Lincoln, and the importance of pageantry.[13] Meanwhile he produced a phenomenal amount of scholarship that served both the popular interest in the past and the emerging notion of scientific history.

Quaife's work also represents a transition toward modern attitudes regarding the role of historians in the deflation of American myths. The historical universe in which he began his career—and in which *Chicago and the Old Northwest* appeared—was still populated by legendary, heroic white frontiersmen who bravely liberated the land from "inferior" Indians and made possible the march toward modernity. The book's extensive documentation—it was one of the first footnoted books written about Chicago—represents an important shift toward more modern methods of scholarship and toward contemporary attitudes about the subject matter. He was one of the first historians to understand the role of transportation, even on foot and in canoes, in the development of the region. And he was the first to discuss the importance of the portage that linked the Chicago and Des Plaines Rivers.[14]

Although not always thoroughly modern, his attitude toward the native peoples was much more sympathetic than that of his contemporaries. He occasionally used the word "savages," but it was meant more as a translation of the French word *sauvages,* a word he encountered frequently in his documentation, than as a derogatory term. In numerous places he respectfully described the natives' attitudes toward land ownership and nature, while casting the pioneers as land-hungry invaders who ultimately won the battle of possession because of sheer strength rather than the moral superiority of their purpose. The whites were capable of as much brutality as the Indians. And land sales represented a "[white] policy of persistent abuse and a disregard of justice and treaty obligations which operated time and time again to goad the red man into impotent warfare, and this in turn became the excuse for further spoliation" (p. 179).

Quaife's later career saw him uncovering small pieces of corroborating manuscript material that supplemented *Chicago and the Old Northwest* without changing its major conclusions. Some of it concerned the so-called Fort Dearborn Massacre, a term and an event that Quaife tended to downplay in the book. It was part of "the contest with the red man for the possession of this continent and it is better that the gory details should sink into oblivion" (p. 235). He lifted some of the burden of blame from the natives by describing the preceding events from their viewpoint as well as that of the whites. He also directed the focus toward the fate of the survivors. The book tended to remove some of the onus for the massacre from Captain Nathan Heald, the fort commander, who had often been criticized for deciding to evacuate whites from the supposed safety of the garrison, and who was then vilified for surviving the bloody event. While writing the book, Quaife had literally dug up Heald's post-massacre correspondence buried under leaves and mud on the floor of an abandoned farm building in Missouri. A few years later the diary of a soldier at the fort and other corroborating evidence surfaced. The discoveries prompted Quaife to publish notes in a scholarly journal, and there was a similar update about the Black Hawk War.[15]

Another critical new piece of evidence strengthened one of the book's most significant contributions, the recognition of Jean Baptiste Point Du Sable, a trader of French and West Indian ancestry, as the first permanent resident of what would become the city of Chicago. Most Chicagoans had grown to believe the oft-repeated myth that installed the family of John Kinzie in that role. In fact, Du Sable had appeared in the region as early as 1789, fourteen years before the Kinzie family arrived from Detroit. But, because the Chicago Fire had destroyed the local depositories of the written record, historians were left to depend on two other kinds of sources: information scattered in dozens of out-of-town collections and the reminiscences of the pioneers themselves. The most influential account of the dawn of the city was *Wau-Bun,* published in 1856 by Kinzie's daughter-in-law. Although largely fictional, Chicagoans had always accepted it as fact, including its reduction of Du Sable to an insignificant role. Some later historians, including A. T. Andreas, had mentioned Du Sable but had provided little detail about his life. Quaife pointed out that perhaps Chicago's white boosters had been less than enthusiastic about admitting that a person of color had founded their city. While the Kinzie name was given to a prominent downtown street, Du Sable's name appeared only on a high school in the African American section of town.[16]

Quaife began the rehabilitation of Du Sable in *Chicago and the Old Northwest,* drawing on such sources as early travelers' accounts and the records of Fort Mackinac, where the trader had been held captive during the American Revolution. The book hints at Du Sable's business acumen and the apparent comfort of his home at the mouth of the Chicago River. Then in 1928 Quaife made a discovery in early records of Wayne County in Detroit: Du Sable's 1800 bill of sale to another French trader, Jean Lalime. The document demonstrated that Du Sable had not only built a 40′ × 22′ "wooden house," rather than the crude log cabin attributed to him, but he also owned household possessions that included mirrors, French walnut cabinets, and other furnishings that were unusually fine for life on the frontier. His complex of domestic and commercial buildings totaled nearly four thousand square feet and undoubtedly operated as a major trading post. Lalime, in turn, sold the property to Kinzie in 1804. Thus, the Kinzies were not only later arrivals, but also ended up as the third owners of the house originally built by the man they ignored. Moreover, John Kinzie had become Chicago's first recorded murderer when he stabbed Lalime to death in 1812, later claiming that the latter had always been some sort of indigent miscreant, another misstatement disproved by the inventory.

Quaife rushed news of the Du Sable discovery into the *Mississippi Valley Historical Review* and seized every opportunity to correct the story of Chicago's birth.[17] One came in 1933, when the University of Chicago Press published his *Checagou: From Indian Wigwam to Modern City, 1673–1835,* a brief and popular, yet insightful, account of the early city produced for the Century of Progress Exposition. Quaife included a sophisticated interpretation of Du Sable's importance. Thus, Century of Progress visitors who bought the book read the true story; unfortunately, the exposition's representation of the Du Sable house was merely a crude log cabin. Quaife also anticipated the revival of popular interest in *Wau-Bun* because of Chicago's centennial and the fair and published his own edition with an introduction and explanatory notes that place the work in the realm of fiction.[18]

There was great irony in the fate of *Chicago and the Old Northwest* as a publication. Although it had appeared to much acclaim and garnered positive reviews, it was pushed out of print by a new generation of popular writers who quickly assembled commercial histories that were often under-researched and overwritten. During the Roaring Twenties, marketability tended too often to displace quality as the prevailing standard in publishing. Amateur historians and publicists created new myths, such as the holiday display of Christmas trees during the early years of Fort Dearborn. This clearly upset Quaife, who believed that popular books should still be accurate and enlightening.[19] But even though *Chicago and the Old Northwest* moved from bookstore displays to dusty library shelves, later generations of academic historians continued to appreciate the book's prodigious research base, the skill of its narrative, and its many interpretive observations. Its influence was also evident in the works of Bessie Louise Pierce, who moved from the University of Iowa to the University of Chicago in 1929. Her History of Chicago Project turned out *As Others See Chicago: Impressions of Visitors, 1673–1933*, as a companion to Quaife's *Checagou* for the Century of Progress trade. Then in 1937 the first of her projected five-volume *A History of Chicago* appeared. Covering the years 1673 to 1848, she devoted only 43 of its 455 pages to the pre-1835 period. Her debt to Quaife is clear in her footnotes, however, and the review of her book in the *Wisconsin Magazine of History* noted that *Chicago and the Old Northwest* was so definitive that Pierce, in effect, saw no need to attempt an exhaustive re-researching and retelling of the very early story.[20]

Meanwhile, Quaife remained remarkably prolific. Even after he retired as secretary of the Burton in 1947, every year saw a few scholarly articles and at least one Lakeside Classics volume for which he had plucked from obscurity some early traveler's account or reminiscence and added a thoughtful introduction and detailed notes. But there were also such popular works as his historical studies of the states of Wisconsin and Michigan, the city of Detroit, and the Mormons. He also wrote an excellent history of Lake Michigan for Bobbs-Merrill's ten-volume American Lakes series, which he edited.[21] But on September 1, 1959, all of that ended tragically with his death in a traffic accident near Sault Ste. Marie, Michigan. The obituaries noted his prolific output, its quality, and his solid contribution to the professionalization of local and regional history.[22]

And what of the river controversy that had been so significant in launching Quaife's early career? The water highway of the natives and the French explorers gained a new distinction in the mid-twentieth century. Commonwealth Edison not only held on to the power-dam site and continued to generate electricity there, but it also expanded its land holdings around it. Construction began in June 1957 on a new kind of power facility that would use the waters of the Des Plaines for cooling purposes rather than to turn power heads. Tall cooling towers loomed over the historic stream, and on April 15, 1960—not long after Quaife's death—Dresden Unit 1 began producing electricity. It had the distinction of being the world's first privately financed commercial nuclear power station.[23]

NOTES

1. For conflicting views of the dam and the issues surrounding it, see Harold Platt, *Electric City: Energy and the Growth of the Chicago Area, 1880–1930* (Chicago: University of Chicago Press, 1991), 186–88, and Richard Norton Smith, *The Colonel: The Life and Legend of Robert R. McCormick* (Boston: Houghton Mifflin, 1997), 116–23. The incident turned McCormick into a lifelong critic of Insull.

2. People vs. Economy Light and Power Company 241 Ill. 290 (1909).

3. Milo M. Quaife, comp., and Joe L. Norris, ed., *Forty-six Years: The*

Published Writings of Milo M. Quaife, 1910–1955 (Detroit: Algonquin Club, 1956), contains a brief biographical sketch.

4. See Milo M. Quaife, *The Doctrine of Non-Intervention with Slavery in the Territories* (Chicago: M. C. Chamberlin, 1908); *The Diary of James K. Polk during His Presidency, 1845 to 1849,* 4 vols. (Chicago: Chicago Historical Society, 1910).

5. Milo M. Quaife, "Some Notes on the Fort Dearborn Massacre," Mississippi Valley Historical Association, *Proceedings, 1910–11,* 112–37; the contents of Quaife's paper were reported in the Chicago *Record-Herald* May 19, June 10, August 31, 1911.

6. *In the District Court of the United States For the Northern District of Illinois, Eastern Division: United States of America vs. Economy light and Power Company; In Chancery No. 29776.* 3 vols., 1912, 1:1399–1934. The 3,186 pages of testimony from historians Quaife, Clarence Alvord, Judson Lee, Reuben Gold Thwaites, and others constitute the first exhaustive look at the history of the travel through the Chicago portage, the link between the Chicago and Des Plaines Rivers systems.

7. Illinois v. Economy Light and Power Company, 234 U.S. 497 (1913).

8. Milo M. Quaife, *The Development of Chicago, 1674–1914* (Chicago: Caxton Club, 1916); Milo M. Quaife, *Pictures of Illinois One Hundred Years Ago* (Chicago: Lakeside Press, 1918). Quaife proudly proclaimed the originality of the documentary format in his review of Bessie Louise Pierce, *As Others See Chicago: Impressions of Visitors, 1673–1933* (Chicago: University of Chicago Press, 1933), in *Mississippi Valley Historical Review* 20 (Dec. 1933): 425–26.

9. Clifford L. Lord and Carl Ubbelohde, *Clio's Servant: The State Historical Society of Wisconsin, 1846–1954* (Madison: State Historical Society of Wisconsin, 1967), 201–59. See also Milo M. Quaife, "Some Memories of Forty Years," *Wisconsin Magazine of History* 38 (Summer 1955): 217–24, 250–52, which reproduces his address at the institution's semicentennial celebration. Lewis Institute of Technology merged in 1940 with Armour Institute of Technology to form the Illinois Institute of Technology.

10. Quaife and Norris, *Forty-six Years,* lists the volumes published through 1955; there were forty-three in all.

11. On Quaife's departure, see Carl Ubbelohde, "The Threshold of Possibilities: The Society, 1900–1955," *Wisconsin Magazine of History* 39 (Winter 1955–56): 80.

12. See Milo M. Quaife, *Chicago's Highways Old and New: From Indian Trail to Motor Road* (Chicago: D. F. Kellar, 1923).

13. See the "News and Comment" section of each issue of the *Mississippi Valley Historical Review,* especially 12 (Sept. 1925): 294–97; 12 (March 1926): 625–27; 13 (Dec. 1926): 454–57; 13 (March 1927): 601; 14 (June 1927): 124–26; 14 (Sept. 1927): 278–79; 14 (March 1928): 580–81; 15 (March 1929): 578–84; 16 (Dec. 1929): 435–37; 16 (March 1930): 600–602.

14. See the unsigned review of Quaife's *Chicago and the Old Northwest* in the *American Historical Review* 19 (April 1914): 647–49; and the review by Isaac Joslin Cox, *Mississippi Valley Historical Review* 1 (Sept. 1914): 305–7.

15. See Milo M. Quaife, ed., "Notes and Documents: The Fort Dearborn Massacre," *Mississippi Valley Historical Review* 1 (March 1915): 562–73; idem, "Notes and Documents: The Story of James Corbin, a Soldier of Fort Dearborn," ibid. 3 (Sept. 1916): 217–28; idem, "Documents: Journals and Reports of the Black Hawk War," ibid. 12 (Dec. 1925): 392–409.

16. The tendency to ignore Du Sable in favor of the self-promoting Kinzie family continues. Donald L. Miller, *City of the Century: The Epic of America and the Making of Chicago* (New York: Simon and Schuster, 1996), for instance, mysteriously omits Du Sable altogether but includes several pages on the Kinzies.

17. Quaife discusses Du Sable's importance in "Documents: Property of Jean Baptiste Point Sable," *Mississippi Valley Historical Review* 15 (June 1928): 89–92.

18. See Mrs. John H. Kinzie, *Wau-Bun: The "Early Day" in the North-West,* ed. Milo Milton Quaife (Chicago: Lakeside Press, 1932). Quaife notes that she "had but the vaguest comprehension of the historian's calling" (lii). *Wau-Bun* appeared in several editions, the most recent being Juliette M. Kinzie, *Wau-Bun: The "Early Day" in the North-West,* introduction by Nina Baym (Urbana: University of Illinois Press, 1992).

19. See Lloyd Lewis and Henry Justin Smith, *Chicago: The History of Its Reputation* (New York: Harcourt, Brace, 1929), which Quaife reviewed in *Mississippi Valley Historical Review* 16 (Dec. 1929): 431–32. The holiday myth began with "Christmas at Old Fort Dearborn," *Fort Dearborn Magazine* 2 (Dec. 1920): 3, 16–17, a publication of the Fort Dearborn Bank, and has been repeated for decades; the celebration of the Christmas holiday with greenery, of course, did not take place in Chicago until the arrival of German immigrants some years later.

20. Pierce's first volume was reviewed by "J.S." [Joseph Schafer] in *Wisconsin Magazine of History* 21 (Sept. 1937): 109–11; on Pierce, see Perry R. Duis, "Bessie Louise Pierce, Symbol and Scholar," *Chicago History* 5 (Fall 1976): 130–40.

21. Quaife wrote volume 1 and edited volume 2 of the four-volume *Wisconsin: Its History and Its People* (Chicago: S. J. Clarke, 1924). Other notable works by Quaife include *The Kingdom of Saint James: A Narrative of the Mormons* (New Haven: Yale University Press, 1930); *Lake Michigan* (Indianapolis: Bobbs-Merrill, 1944); *Michigan: From Primitive Wilderness to Industrial Commonwealth* (New York: Prentice-Hall, 1948); *This Is Detroit, 1701–1951: Two Hundred and Fifty Years in Pictures* (Detroit: Wayne State University Press, 1951); [with Joseph and Estelle Bayliss], *River of Destiny: The St. Mary's* (Detroit: Wayne State University Press, 1955). Quaife's prodigious production down to 1955 fills forty-two pages in Quaife and Norris, *Forty-six Years.* For items during the last four years of his life, see the 1956–60 volumes of the American Historical Association's series Writings in American History.

22. For obituaries, see *American Historical Review* 65 (Jan. 1960): 489; and F. Clever Bald, "Dr. Milo Milton Quaife, 1880–1959," *Michigan History* 44 (March 1960): 36–38.

23. John Hogan, *A Spirit Capable: The Story of Commonwealth Edison* (Chicago: Mobium Press, 1986), 265–74.

PREFACE

There are many histories of Chicago in existence, yet none of them supplies the want which has induced the preparation of the present work. It has been written under the conviction that there is ample justification for a comprehensive and scholarly treatment of the beginnings of Chicago and its place in the evolution of the old Northwest. I have endeavored to produce a readable narrative without in any way trenching upon the principles of sound scholarship. To what extent, if any, I have succeeded must be for the reader to judge. I may, however, claim the negative virtue of entire freedom from the motives of commercial gain and family partisanship, which enter so largely into our local historical literature.

In preparing the work I have made as diligent a study of the sources as practicable, at the same time availing myself freely of the studies of others in the same field. With one exception acknowledgment of my obligations to the latter is made in the footnotes. The manuscript of a lecture by the late Professor Charles W. Mann on the Fort Dearborn massacre was put at my disposal. I have used it as far as it served my purpose without attempting to cite it in the footnotes.

In many places I have broken new ground and I can scarcely expect my work to be entirely free from error. I am particularly conscious of this in connection with chap. xiii on the Indian Trade, a subject to which a volume might well be devoted. In controversial matters I have written without fear or favor from any source. If in many cases my conclusions seem to differ from those of other writers, I can only say that the words of a recent historian with reference to history writing in the Middle Ages, "Recorded events were accepted without challenge, and the sanction of tradition guaranteed the reality of the occurrence," apply with almost equal force to much of the literature pertaining to early Chicago.

I desire to express my obligation for courtesies rendered, or facilities extended, to the Chicago Historical Society, the Wisconsin State Historical Society, the Detroit Public Library, the Division of Manuscripts of the Library of Congress, the Bureau of Indian Affairs, and the War Department. I am indebted also for many favors to Miss Caroline McIlvaine, librarian, and Mr. Marius Dahl, record clerk, of the Chicago Historical Society; to Mr. C. M. Burton, of Detroit; to the descendants of Nathan Heald, Mr. and Mrs. Thomas McCluer and Mrs. Arthur McCluer, of O'Fallon, Mo., Mrs. Lillian Heald Richmond and Dr. and Mrs. Ottofy of St. Louis, and Mr. and Mrs. Wright Johnson, of Rutherford, N.J.; and to my wife and to my father-in-law, Rev. G. W. Goslin, for unwearied assistance in the preparation and revision of the manuscript. Finally I wish to record my deep obligation to Dr. Otto L. Schmidt, president of the Illinois State Historical Society, for much sympathetic advice and encouragement.

M. M. QUAIFE

CHICAGO
September, 1913

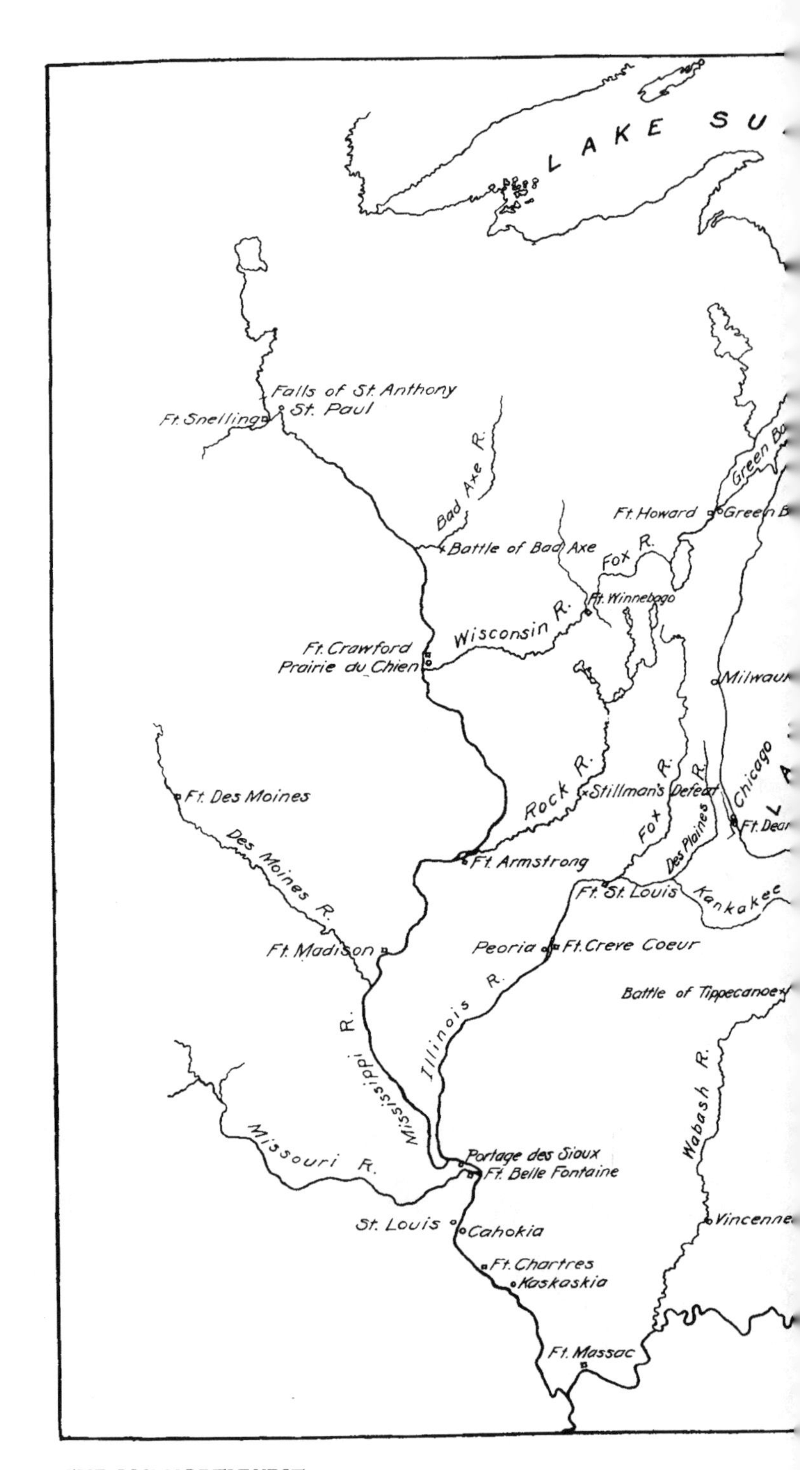

THE OLD NORTHWEST

Showing the principal waterways and places of historical interest in the early period

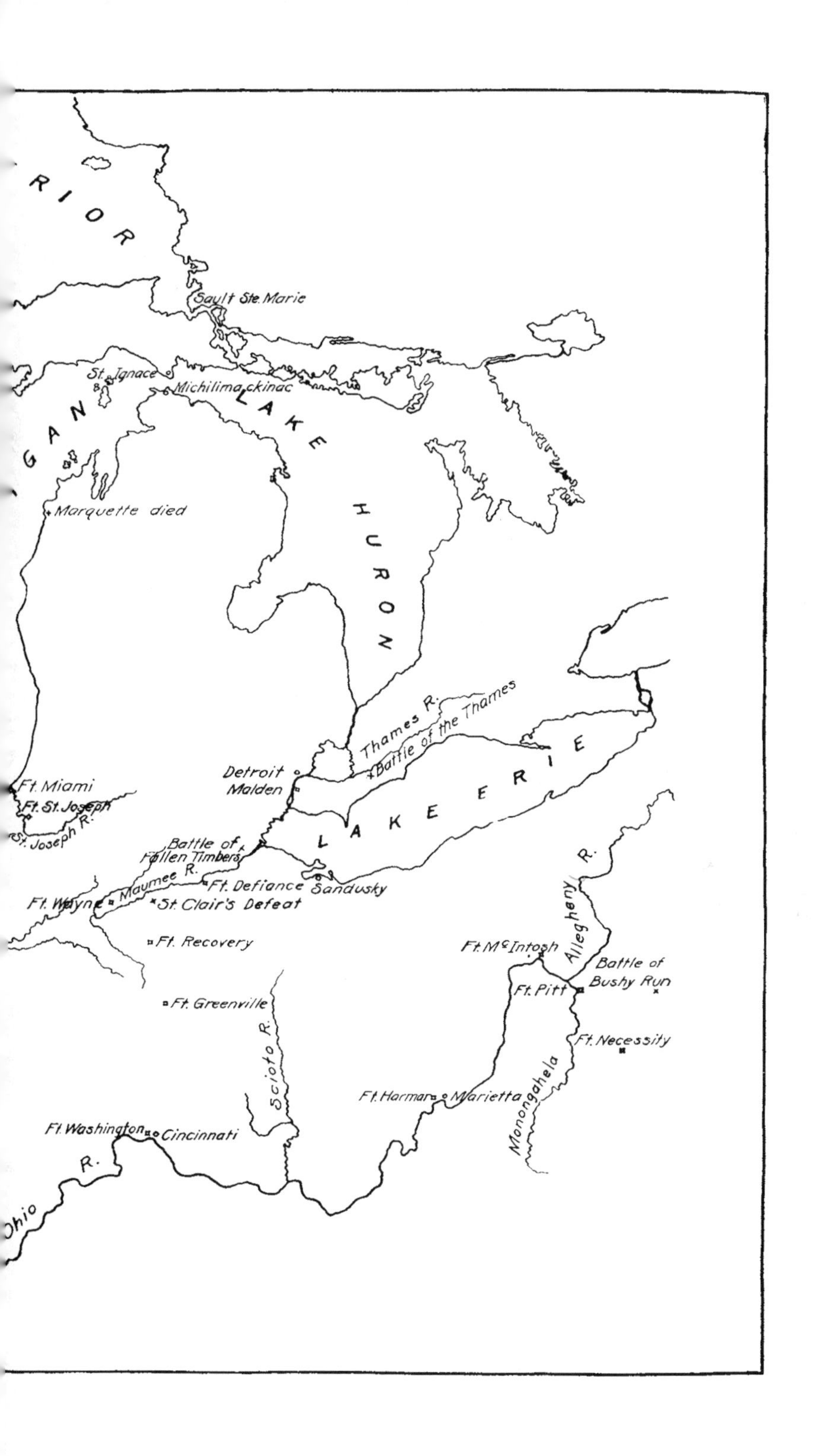
RIOR
GAN
LAKE
HURON
LAKE ERIE
Sault Ste. Marie
St. Ignace
Michilimackinac
Marquette died
Thames R.
Battle of the Thames
Detroit
Malden
Ft. Miami
Ft. St. Joseph
St. Joseph R.
Battle of Fallen Timbers
Maumee R.
Ft. Defiance
Sandusky
Ft. Wayne
St. Clair's Defeat
Ft. Recovery
Ft. Greenville
Scioto R.
Allegheny R.
Ft. McIntosh
Battle of Bushy Run
Ft. Pitt
Ft. Necessity
Monongahela
Ft. Harmar
Marietta
Ft. Washington
Cincinnati
Ohio R.

CHICAGO AND THE OLD NORTHWEST, 1673–1835

CHAPTER I

THE CHICAGO PORTAGE

The story of Chicago properly begins with an account of the city's natural surroundings. For while her citizens have striven worthily, during the three-quarters of a century that has passed since the birth of the modern city, to achieve greatness for her, it is none the less true that Nature has dealt kindly with Chicago, and is entitled to share with them the credit for the creation of the great metropolis of the present day. If in recent years the enterprise of man rather than the generosity of Nature has seemed chiefly responsible for the growth of Chicago, in the long period which preceded the birth of the modern city such was not the case; for whatever importance Chicago then possessed was due primarily to the natural advantages of her position.

Since this volume is to tell the story of early Chicago, concluding at the point where the life of the modern city begins, it is not my purpose to dwell upon the natural advantages which today contribute to the city's prosperity. Her central location with respect to population, surrounded by hundreds of thousands of square miles of country as fair, and supporting a population as progressive, as any on the face of the globe; her contiguity to the wheat fields of the great West; her situation in the heart of the corn belt of the United States; the wealth of coal fields and iron mines and forests poured out, as it were, at her feet; her unrivaled systems of transportation by lake and by rail; how all these factors, reinforced by the daring energy of her citizens, have combined to render Chicago the industrial heart of the nation is a matter of common knowledge. That in the days before the coming of the railroad or the settler, when for hundreds of miles in every direction the wilderness, monotonous and unbroken, stretched away, inhabited only by the wild beast and the wild Indian; when only at infrequent intervals were its forest paths or waterways traversed by the fur trader or the priest, the representatives of commerce and the Cross, the two mightiest forces of the civilization before the advance of which the wilderness was to give way; that even in this far-away period Nature made of Chicago a place of importance and of concourse, the rendezvous of parties bent on peaceful and on warlike projects, is not so commonly understood.

The importance of Chicago in this early period was primarily due to the fact of her strategic location, whether for the prosecution of war or of commerce, at the head of the Great Lakes on one of the principal highways of travel between the two greatest interior waterway systems of the continent, those of the Great Lakes–St. Lawrence and the Mississippi River. The two most important factors in the exploration and settlement of a country are the waterways and mountain systems—the one an assistance, the other an obstacle, to travel.[1] The early English colonists in America, settling first in Virginia and Massachusetts and gradually spreading out over the Atlantic coastal plain, were shut from the interior of the continent by the great wall presented by the Allegheny Mountains. The French, securing a foothold about the same time at the mouth of the St. Lawrence River, found themselves in possession of a highway which offered ready access into the interior. The importance of the rivers and streams as highways of travel in this early period is difficult to realize today. The dense forests which spread over the eastern half of the continent were penetrated only by the narrow Indian trail or the winding river. The former was passable only on foot, and even by pack animals but with difficulty.[2] The latter, however, afforded a ready highway into the interior, and the light canoe of the Indian a conveyance admirably adapted to the exigencies of river travel. By carrying it over the portages separating the headwaters of the great river systems the early voyageurs could penetrate into the heart of the continent.

[1] Farrand, *Basis of American History*, 23.

[2] *Ibid.*

Proceeding up the St. Lawrence, the French colonists early gained the Great Lakes. Their advance rested here for a time, but in the last quarter of the seventeenth century, by a great outburst of exploring activity, the upper waters of the Mississippi were gained and eagerly followed to their outlet in the Gulf of Mexico. Thus New France found a second outlet to the sea, and thus, even before the English had crossed the Alleghenies, the French had fairly encircled them, and planted themselves in the heart of the continent. From the basin of the Great Lakes to that of the Mississippi they early made use of five principal highways.[3] On each, of course, occurred a portage at the point where the transfer from the head of the one system of navigation to the other occurred. One of these five highways led from the foot of Lake Michigan by way of the Chicago River and Portage to and down the Illinois. The Chicago Portage thus constituted one of the "keys of the continent," as Hulbert, the historian of the portage paths, has so aptly termed them.[4]

The comparatively undeveloped state of the field of American historical research is well illustrated by the fact that despite the historical importance of the Chicago Portage, no careful study of it has ever been made. The student will seek in vain for even an adequate description of the physical characteristics of the portage. Winsor's description, a paragraph in length, is perhaps the best and most authoritative one available.[5] Yet, aside from its brevity, neither of the two sources to which he makes specific reference can be regarded as reliable authorities

[3] Winsor, *Narrative and Critical History of America*, IV, 224.

[4] Hulbert, *Portage Paths: The Keys of the Continent.*

[5] "What Herman Moll, the English cartographer, called the 'land carriage of Chekakou' is described by James Logan, in a communication which he made in 1718 to the English Board of Trade, as running from the lake three leagues up the river, then a half a league of carriage, then a mile of water, next a small carry, then two miles to the Illinois, and then one hundred and thirty leagues to the Mississippi. But descriptions varied with the seasons. It was usually called a carriage of from four to nine miles, according to the stage of the water. In dry seasons it was even farther while in wet times it might not be more than a mile; and, indeed, when the intervening lands were 'drowned,' it was quite possible to pass in a canoe amid the sedges from Lake Michigan to the Des Plaines, and so to the Illinois and the Mississippi."—Winsor, *Mississippi Basin*, 24. For similar descriptions see Hulbert, *Portage Paths*, 181; *Jesuit Relations*, LIX, 313–14, note 41.

upon the Chicago Portage. Moll, the cartographer, notable for his credulous temperament,[6] relied for his knowledge of the Great Lakes region upon the discredited maps of Lahontan.[7] James Logan, whose description of the portage is quoted,[8] was a reputable official of Pennsylvania, but, in common with the seaboard English colonists generally, his knowledge of the geography of the interior was extremely hazy. This is sufficiently shown by the fact that he located La Salle's Fort Miami, which had stood during the brief period of its existence at the mouth of the St. Joseph River, on the Chicago.

That there should be confusion and misconception in the secondary descriptions of the Chicago Portage is not surprising, in view, on the one hand, of the unusual seasonal variations in its character, and, on the other, of the dispute which very early arose concerning it. None of the other portages between the Great Lakes and the Mississippi—if indeed any in America—were subject to such changes as this one. The dispute over its character goes back to the beginning of the French exploration of this region. When Joliet returned to Canada from his famous expedition down the Mississippi in 1673, filled with enthusiasm over his discoveries, he gave out a glowing account of the country he had visited. In particular he seems to have dwelt upon the ease of communication between the Great Lakes and the Gulf of Mexico by way of the Chicago and Illinois rivers to the Mississippi. Joliet's records were lost, but both Frontenac, the governor of New France, and Father Dablon have left accounts of his verbal report.[9] Frontenac stated that a bark could go from the St. Lawrence to the Gulf of Mexico, with only a portage of half a league at Niagara. Dablon, who seems to have appreciated the situation more intelligently than Frontenac, said that a bark could go from

[6] Winsor, *Mississippi Basin*, 80, 104, 111, 163.

[7] Moll's map in his *Atlas Minor* is simply an English copy of Lahontan's map of 1703. For the latter see Lahontan, *New Voyages to North America* (Thwaites ed.), I, 156.

[8] For the substance of Logan's report see the British Board of Trade report of September 8, 1721, printed in O'Callaghan, *Documents Relative to the Colonial History of the State of New York*, V, 621. This will be cited henceforth as *New York Colonial Documents*.

[9] Winsor, *Cartier to Frontenac*, 246–47; *Jesuit Relations*, LVIII, 105.

Lake Erie to the Gulf if a canal of half a league were cut at the Chicago Portage.

Probably Dablon's report represents more nearly than that of Frontenac what Joliet actually said, for it seems unlikely that he would ignore utterly the existence of the portage at Chicago. Even so, however, his description of the ease of water communication between the Great Lakes and the Mississippi River was unduly optimistic. Its accuracy was sharply challenged by La Salle upon his visit to Chicago several years later. Joliet passed through Illinois but once, rather hurriedly, knowing nothing of the country aside from what he learned of it on this trip. He was ill-qualified, therefore, to describe accurately the Illinois-Chicago highway and portage; at the most he could describe only the conditions prevailing at the time of his hasty passage. La Salle, on the other hand, was operating in the Illinois country from 1679 to 1683, seeking to establish a colony with its capital at the modern Starved Rock, one hundred miles from Chicago. He was greatly interested in developing the trade of this region, and, while he looked forward ultimately to securing a southern outlet for it, for the present he must find such outlet by way of Canada. In the course of his Illinois career he passed between his colony and Canada several times, and from both necessity and self-interest became thoroughly familiar with the routes of communication which could be followed. He himself ordinarily came by the Great Lakes to the foot of Lake Michigan and thence by the St. Joseph River and portage or the Chicago to the Illinois, but he became convinced that it would not be practicable to carry on commerce between his Illinois colony and Canada through the upper lakes, and that a route by way of the Ohio River and thence to the lower lakes and Canada was more feasible.

In discussing this subject La Salle was led to take issue with Joliet as to the feasibility of navigation between Lake Michigan and the Illinois, and so to state explicitly what the hindrances were.[10] The goods brought to Chicago in barges must be

[10] Margry, *Découvertes et établissements des Français dans l'ouest et dans le sud de l'Amérique septentrionale*, II, 81–82. This collection will be cited henceforth as Margry.

transshipped here in canoes, for, despite Joliet's assertions, only canoes could navigate the Des Plaines for a distance of forty leagues. At a later time La Salle reverted to this subject, and in this connection gave the first detailed description we have of the Chicago Portage.[11] From the lake one passes by a channel formed by the junction of several small streams or gullies, and navigable about two leagues to the edge of the prairie. Beyond this at a distance of a quarter of a league to the westward is a little lake a league and a half in length, divided into two parts by a beaver dam. From this lake issues a little stream which, after twining in and out for half a league across the rushes, falls into the Chicago River, which in turn empties into the Illinois.

The "channel" was the main portion and south branch of the modern Chicago River. The lake has long since disappeared by reason of the artificial changes brought about by engineers; in the early period of white settlement at Chicago it was known as Mud Lake. La Salle's "Chicago River," into which Mud Lake ordinarily drained, was, of course, the modern Des Plaines.

Continuing his description of the water route by way of the Chicago and Des Plaines, La Salle pointed out that when the little lake in the prairie was full, either from great rains in summer or from the vernal floods, it discharged also into the "channel" leading to Lake Michigan, whose surface was seven feet lower than the prairie where Mud Lake lay. The Des Plaines, too, in time of spring flood, discharged a part of its waters by way of Mud Lake and the channel into Lake Michigan. La Salle granted that at this time Joliet's proposed canal of half a league across the portage would permit the passage of boats from Lake Michigan to the sea. But he denied that this would be possible in the summer, for there was then no water in the river as far down as his post of St. Louis, the modern Starved Rock, where at this season the navigation of the river began. Still other obstacles to the feasibility of Joliet's proposed canal were pointed out. The action of the waters of Lake Michigan had created a sand bank at the mouth of the Chicago River which the force

[11] Margry, pp. 166 ff.

of the current of the Des Plaines, when made to discharge into the lake, would be unable to clear away. Again, the possibility of a boat's stemming the spring floods of the Des Plaines, "much stronger than those of the Rhone," was doubtful. But if all other obstacles were surmounted, the canal would still have no practical value because the navigation of the Des Plaines would be possible for but fifteen or twenty days at most, in time of spring flood; while the navigation of the Great Lakes was rendered impossible by the ice until mid-April, or even later, by which time the flood on the Des Plaines had subsided and that stream had become unnavigable, even for canoes, except after some storm.

Thus there was initiated by La Salle a dispute over the character of the water communication from Lake Michigan to the Mississippi by way of the Chicago Portage which has been revived in our own day, and in the decision of which property interests to the value of hundreds of thousands of dollars are involved.[12] Of the essential correctness of La Salle's description there can be no question. Considering its early date and the many cares with which the mind of the busy explorer was burdened, it constitutes a significant testimonial to his ability and powers of observation. It may well be doubted whether any later writer has improved upon—if, indeed, any has equaled—La Salle's description of the Chicago–Des Plaines route. From its perusal may be gathered the clue to the fundamental defect in the descriptions of the Chicago Portage which modern historians have given us. Overlooking the fact that the Des Plaines River was subject to fluctuation to an unusual degree, they err in assuming that the portage ceased when the Des Plaines was reached. The portage was the carriage which must be made between the two water systems. Hulbert is quite right in saying, as he does, that none of the western portages varied more in length than did this one.[13] In fact his words

[12] *The United States of America* vs. *The Economy Light and Power Company.* The evidence taken in this case constitutes by far the most exhaustive study of the character and historical use of the Chicago Portage that has ever been made.

[13] Hulbert, *Portage Paths*, 181.

possess far more significance than the writer himself attaches to them; for the length of the carriage that must be made at Chicago varied from nothing at all to fifty miles or, at times, to even twice this distance. At times there was an actual union of the waters flowing into Lake Michigan with those entering the Illinois River, permitting the uninterrupted passage of boats from the one system to the other. At other times the portage which must be made extended from the south branch of the Chicago to the mouth of the Vermilion River, some fifty miles below the mouth of the Des Plaines.

It is doubtless true that "truth, crushed to earth, will rise again," but the converse proposition of the poet that error dies amid its worshipers requires qualification. Certainly in the matter under discussion La Salle as early as 1683 dealt the errors of Joliet with respect to the Chicago Portage a crushing blow. Yet these self-same errors were destined to "rise again," and in the early nineteenth century it was again commonly reported that a practicable waterway from Lake Michigan to the Mississippi could be attained by the construction of a canal a few miles in length across what for convenience may be termed the short Chicago Portage, from the south branch of the Chicago River through Mud Lake to the Des Plaines. Even capable engineers threw the weight of their opinion in support of this fallacy.[14] But the young state of Illinois learned to her cost, in the hard school of experience, the truth of La Salle's observations. The canal of half a league extended in the making to a hundred miles and required for its construction years of time and the expenditure of millions of dollars.

We may now consider the dispute between Joliet and La Salle over the character of the Chicago Portage in the light of the information afforded by the statements of later writers. It will follow from what has already been said that the secondary statements, whether of travelers or of gazetteers and other compendiums of information, made in the early part of the nineteenth century, must be subjected to critical examination.

[14] E.g., Major Stephen H. Long. For his report see the *National Register*, III, 193–98.

The only way in which this may be done is by a resort to the sources; and our conclusions concerning the Chicago-Illinois Portage and route must be based upon the testimony of those who actually used it, or were familiar with the use made of it by others. A study of these sources makes it clear that the Des Plaines River was subject to great fluctuation at different seasons, or even as between periods of drought and periods of copious rainfall, and that the length and character of the portage at any given time depended entirely upon the stage of water in the Des Plaines. During the brief period of the spring flood boats capable of carrying several tons might pass between Lake Michigan and the Des Plaines and along the latter stream without meeting with obstacles other than those incident to the high stage of the water. The extreme range of the fluctuation was many feet.[15] Its effect upon the character of the Des Plaines was to cause it to pass through all the gradations from a raging torrent to a stream with no discharge, dry except for the pools which marked its course. There were times, then, in connection with these fluctuations, when the stream might be navigable for canoes, although it would not permit the passage of boats of greater draft.

The duration of the spring flood was put by La Salle at fifteen or twenty days. At this time the flood was heavier than that of the Rhone, and a portion of it found its way through Mud Lake and the south branch of the Chicago River into Lake Michigan. The effect of this on the portage, obvious in itself, is described in many of the sources. Marquette, who was flooded out of his winter camp on the South Branch in the latter part of March, 1675, found no difficulty, aside from the obstacles presented by the floating ice, in passing from that point down the Des Plaines.[16] He reports the water as being twelve feet higher than when he passed through here in the late

[15] Schoolcraft estimated its depth in the seasons of periodica lfloods at eight to ten feet (*Summary Narrative of an Exploratory Expedition to the Sources of the Mississippi River, in 1820*, 398). See also Marquette's description of the spring flood of 1675, in *Jesuit Relations*, LIX, 181.

[16] Marquette's Journal, *Jesuit Relations*, LIX, 181.

summer of 1673. In 1821, in a time of high water, Ebenezer Childs passed up the Illinois and Des Plaines rivers to Chicago in a small canoe.[17] No month or date is given for this trip, but Childs expressly states that there had been heavy rains for several days before his arrival at the Des Plaines. He was unable to find any signs of a portage between the Des Plaines and the Chicago. When he had ascended the former to a point where he supposed the portage should begin he left it and taking a northeasterly course perceived, after traveling a few miles, the current of the Chicago. The whole intervening country was inundated, and not less than two feet of water existed all the way across the portage. Two years later Keating, the historian of Major Long's expedition to the source of the St. Peter's River, which passed through Chicago in early June, 1823, was informed by Lieutenant Hopson, an officer at Fort Dearborn, that he had crossed the portage with ease in a boat loaded with lead and flour.[18] Of similar purport to the testimony of Childs and Hopson is the account given by Gurdon S. Hubbard of his first ascent of the Des Plaines with the Illinois "brigade" of the American Fur Company in the spring of 1819.[19] The passage from Starved Rock up the river to Cache Island against the heavy current was difficult and exhausting. From this point, with a strong wind blowing from the southwest, sails were hoisted and the loaded boats passed rapidly up the Des Plaines and across the portage to the Chicago, "regardless of the course of the channel."

With the subsidence of the spring flood the Des Plaines fell to so low a stage as to become unnavigable, even by the small boats ordinarily employed by the fur traders and travelers, except at such times as the river was raised by rains. According to La Salle, it was "not even navigable for canoes" except after the spring flood, and it would be easier to transport goods

[17] *Wisconsin Hist. Colls.*, IV, 162–63.

[18] Keating, *Expedition to the Source of St. Peter's River, ... in the Year 1823*, I, 166.

[19] *Hubbard, Gurdon Saltonstall, Incidents and Events in the Life of*, 60. MS in the Chicago Historical Society library. This work will be cited henceforth as *Life*.

from Lake Michigan to Fort St. Louis by land with horses, than by the use of boats on the river.[20]

This statement of La Salle is corroborated by many other observers. St. Cosme's party of Seminary priests which passed from Chicago down the Illinois in the early part of November, 1698,[21] was compelled to portage eight leagues or more[22] along the Des Plaines, in addition to the three leagues across from the Chicago to that stream, and almost two weeks were consumed in passing from Chicago to the mouth of the Des Plaines, a distance of about fifty miles.[23] In describing the journey St. Cosme states that from Isle la Cache to Monjolly, a space of seven leagues, "you must always make a portage, there being no water in the river."

In September, 1721, Father Charlevoix, touring America for the purpose of reporting to his king the condition of New France, came to the post of St. Joseph. His ultimate destination was lower Louisiana; from St. Joseph to the Illinois River proper two alternative routes were presented for his consideration, the one by way of the St. Joseph Portage and down the Kankakee River, the other around the southern end of Lake Michigan to Chicago and thence down the Des Plaines. His first intention was to follow the latter, but this was abandoned in favor of the route by the Kankakee, partly because of a storm on Lake Michigan, but also for the additional reason that since the upper Illinois, the modern Des Plaines, was a mere brook, he was told it did not have, at this season, water enough to float a canoe.[24] In his passage down the Kankakee the traveler observed at the mouth of the Des Plaines a buffalo crossing the

[20] Margry, II, 168.

[21] Shea, *Early Voyages Up and Down the Mississippi*, 45 ff

[22] The distances given in St. Cosme's detailed account total this amount. La Source's general statement is that the party portaged fifteen leagues (*ibid.*, 83), but this, apparently, included the distance between the Chicago River and the Des Plaines.

[23] The party left Chicago October 29, and reached the mouth of the Des Plaines November 11.

[24] Charlevoix, *Histoire et description générale de la Nouvelle France, avec le journal historique d'un voyage fait par ordre du roi dans l'Amérique septentrionale*, VI, 104.

stream. Although sixty leagues from its source, Charlevoix noted that the Des Plaines was still so shallow that the water did not rise above the middle of the animal's legs.[25]

A hundred years after Charlevoix's passage down the Illinois, in midsummer, 1821, Governor Cass and Henry R. Schoolcraft came up that stream in a large canoe en route for Chicago. The observant Schoolcraft has left a careful and detailed narrative of their experiences, and a description of the Illinois River as continued in the Des Plaines.[26] The party was compelled to abandon the canoe at Starved Rock, and the remainder of the journey to Chicago was made on horseback. The route taken was in general along the banks of the river, although the actual channel was observed only occasionally. The result of this observation was the conclusion that the "long and formidable rapids" seen by the travelers completely intercepted navigation at this sultry season. This conclusion was further confirmed by meeting several traders on the plains who were transporting their goods and boats in carts from the Chicago River. They thought it practicable to enter the Des Plaines at Mount Joliet, thus necessitating a portage of about thirty miles, but Schoolcraft in recording this opinion points out that his own party had experienced difficulties far below this point. Although himself an enthusiast on the subject of the future commercial importance of Chicago, and of the utility of a canal connecting the Chicago and Illinois rivers, Schoolcraft's experience on this journey led him to call attention to the error of those who supposed a canal of only eight or ten miles in length would be sufficient to provide a navigable highway between Lake Michigan and the Illinois. This opinion was approved by Thomas Tousey of Virginia, another enthusiast on the subject of the canal, who explored the route of the Des Plaines on horseback in the autumn of 1822.[27] Although the water was uncommonly

[25] *Op. cit.*, 118.

[26] Schoolcraft, *Travels in the Central Portions of the Mississippi Valley*, 313 ff.

[27] Schoolcraft, *Personal Memoirs of a Residence of Thirty Years with the Indian Tribes on the American Frontiers*, 179–80.

high for the season, Tousey's investigation, while imbuing him with a "more exalted" opinion of the country and the proposed canal communication, convinced him that it would be attended with greater expense to open than he had formerly supposed.

The conditions encountered by John Tanner in a journey from Chicago down the Illinois River in the year 1820[28] were similar to those described by Schoolcraft the following year. Tanner was traveling from Mackinac to St. Louis in a birch-bark canoe. Some Indians who were accompanying him turned back before reaching Chicago, on receiving from others whom they met discouraging accounts of the stage of the water in the Illinois. Tanner, however, persevered in his enterprise. After a period of illness at Chicago he engaged a Frenchman, who had just returned from hauling some boats across the portage, to take him across also. The Frenchman agreed to transport Tanner sixty miles, and if his horses, which were much worn from the previous long journey, could hold out, one hundred and twenty miles, the length of the portage at the present stage of water. With his canoe in the Frenchman's cart and Tanner himself riding a horse belonging to the latter, the overland journey began. Before the first sixty-mile stage had been completed the Frenchman became ill. He turned back, therefore, and Tanner and his one companion attempted to put their canoe in the water and continue their journey. The water was so low that the members of the party themselves were compelled to walk, the men propelling the canoe by walking, one at the bow and the other at the stern. After three miles had been laboriously traversed in this fashion a Pottawatomie Indian was engaged to take the baggage and Tanner's children on horseback as far as the mouth of the Yellow Ochre River,[29] while Tanner and his companion continued to propel the now lightened

[28] *Narrative of the Captivity and Adventures of John Tanner*, 256–59. This work will be cited henceforth as *Tanner's Narrative*.

[29] The similarity of names and distance from Chicago render it probable that Tanner here refers to the Vermilion River.

canoe as before. On reaching the Yellow Ochre a sufficient depth of water was found to permit the further descent of the Illinois in the loaded canoe.

Perhaps the most interesting account of the passage of the portage in the dry season, and in some respects the most detailed, is the one contained in the autobiography of Gurdon S. Hubbard.[30] Beginning with 1818, for several years, with a single exception, Hubbard accompanied the Illinois "brigade" of the American Fur Company on its annual autumnal trip from Mackinac by way of Lake Michigan and the Chicago Portage to the lower Illinois River. Only the first crossing of the portage, in October, 1818, is described in detail. Leaving Chicago the party, comprising about a dozen boat crews, camped a day on the South Branch near the present commencement of the Illinois and Michigan Canal, preparing to pass the boats through Mud Lake to the Des Plaines. Mud Lake drained both ways, into the Des Plaines, and through a narrow, crooked channel into the South Branch, and only in very wet seasons, Hubbard states, did it contain water enough to float an empty boat. The mud was very deep and the lake was surrounded by an almost impenetrable growth of wild rice and grass.

From the South Branch the empty boats were pulled up the channel leading from Mud Lake. In many places where there was a hard bottom and absence of water they were placed on short rollers, and in this way were propelled along until the lake was reached. Here mud, thick and deep, was encountered, but only at rare intervals was there any water. Four men stayed in the boat while six or eight more waded in the mud alongside. The former were equipped with boat-poles to the ends of which forked branches of trees had been fastened. By pushing with these against the hummocks, while the men in the mud lifted and shoved, the boat was jerked along. The men in the mud frequently sank to their waists, and at times were forced to cling to the boat to prevent going over their heads. Their limbs were covered with bloodsuckers which caused intense agony

[30] Hubbard. *Life*, 39–41.

for several days, and sleep at night was rendered hopeless by the swarms of mosquitoes which assailed them. Yet three consecutive days of toil from dawn until dark under such conditions were required to pass all the boats through Mud Lake and reach the Des Plaines River.

The passage down the Des Plaines and the Illinois as far as the mouth of Fox River consumed almost three weeks more. Until Cache Island was reached the journey was comparatively easy, although even in this portion of the Des Plaines progress was frequently interrupted by the necessity of making portages or passing the boats along on rollers.[31] From Cache Island to the Illinois River the goods were carried on the men's backs most of the way, while the lightened boats were pulled over the shallow places, often being placed on poles and thus dragged over the rocks and shoals. In the autumn of 1823 Hubbard was sent to a post on the Iroquois River. To shorten his journey and "avoid the delays and hardships of the old route by way of Mud Lake and the Des Plaines" he resolved to travel to his destination by way of the St. Joseph Portage and the Kankakee River. A year later he was placed in charge of the Illinois River posts of the American Fur Company. He thereupon proceeded to execute a plan he had long urged upon his predecessor. The boats were unloaded on their return from Mackinac to Chicago, and scuttled in the swamp to insure their safety until they should be needed for the return voyage to Mackinac laden with furs the following spring. The goods and furs were transported between Chicago and the Indian hunting-grounds on pack horses. Thus "the long, tedious, and difficult passage" through Mud Lake into and down the Des Plaines was avoided.

It is evident, then, that the chief factor in determining the character and length of the Chicago Portage was the Des Plaines River, and that during a large part of the year the portage that must be made extended much farther than simply from the Chicago to the Des Plaines. Schoolcraft and Cass in 1821 were compelled to abandon their canoe at Starved Rock, almost

[31] *Ibid.*

one hundred miles from Chicago. The traders whom they met in the course of their horseback journey were apparently planning to put their boats into the Des Plaines at Mount Joliet, after a portage of thirty miles. Whether, in view of Schoolcraft's own experience, they succeeded in entering the river at this point may well be doubted. The transcript of names from the account books kept by John Kinzie at Chicago[32] contains several entries of charges for assisting traders over the portage; some of these show that the portage was made from Mount Joliet, while one, in June, 1806, shows that it extended to the "forks" of the Illinois. Tanner's experience presents the extreme example, if his statement of distances can be relied on, of a portage of one hundred and twenty miles.[33] The varying length of the portage necessary at different seasons is well described in an official report made in 1819 by Graham and Phillips.[34] At one season there is an uninterrupted water communication between Lake Michigan and the Mississippi; at another season a portage of two miles; at another a portage of seven miles, from the Chicago River to the Des Plaines; and at still another, a portage of fifty miles, extending to the mouth of the Des Plaines.

These fluctuations in the state of the Des Plaines and in the length of the portage influenced materially the plans of the traders and travelers who had occasion to traverse this route. For obvious reasons in times when the Des Plaines was known to be low and the portage correspondingly long the Chicago route would be avoided if practicable. Thus Charlevoix preferred the Kankakee to it in 1721. A hundred years later, the Indians who had set out with Tanner upon learning of the low stage of the water in the Illinois, abandoned the journey and

[32] Barry, Rev. Wm., *Transcript of Names in John Kinzie's Account Books*, MS in the Chicago Historical Society library. This will be cited henceforth as the *Barry Transcript*.

[33] If, as suggested above, the Yellow Ochre was the same stream as the Vermilion River, the distance from Chicago to its mouth was about one hundred miles.

[34] *State Papers, Doc. No. 17, 16th Congress, 1st Sess.* Senator Benton claimed in 1847 that he had written this report from data supplied him by Graham and Phillips (*Niles' Register*, LXXII, 309).

returned to their homes. St. Cosme's party in 1698 sought to reach the Illinois from Lake Michigan by the Root and Fox rivers, desisting from the effort only under the belief that this would necessitate a portage of forty leagues. Compelled to follow the Chicago route, the prospect of the long and difficult passage down the Des Plaines to navigable water on the Illinois induced them to leave all of their goods but one boat-load at Chicago in charge of a member of the party. This made necessary a return from the lower Mississippi for them the following spring, but even this was preferred to the arduous undertaking of transporting them over the long portage at Chicago in the dry season.

More significant, perhaps, is the fact that those who had occasion to cross the Chicago Portage, and were informed concerning the seasonal fluctuations of the Des Plaines, planned their business so as to take advantage, as far as possible, of the seasons of high water. Colonel Kingsbury, who in 1805 conducted a company of soldiers from Mackinac to the Mississippi by way of the Illinois River to establish Fort Belle Fontaine, was ordered to proceed to Chicago with them on the first vessel in the spring.[35] The Illinois River traders in the employ of the American Fur Company in the period from 1818 to 1824 so planned their business as to bring their boats laden with furs up the Des Plaines in the season of the spring flood.

La Salle had early contended that it was more feasible to transport goods between Chicago and Starved Rock with horses than by boats on the river. There arose very early a demand for another means of transportation between the two places at such times as the use of the Des Plaines in boats was impracticable, whether from excess or from deficiency of water. Lahontan

[35] Cushing to Lieutenant-colonel Kingsbury, February 20, 1805. This letter belongs to the collection of letter books, letters, and other papers of Jacob Kingsbury in the Chicago Historical Society library. Kingsbury was in command of Detroit, Mackinac, and other northwestern posts from 1804 on, and for a time was the superior authority in charge of a group of posts including Fort Wayne, Fort Dearborn, Mackinac, and Detroit. His letters and papers constitute a source of prime importance for this period of northwestern history. They will be cited henceforth as the *Kingsbury Papers*.

represents, in his famous narrative of his Long River expedition,[36] that he returned by way of the Illinois River and Chicago Portage. To lessen the drudgery of "a great land carriage of twelve great leagues," he engaged four hundred Indians to transport his baggage from the Illinois village to Lake Michigan, "which they did in the space of four days." Historians have long agreed in denouncing the pretended Long River discovery as fraudulent, but there is nothing improbable about the statement of the necessity of a land carriage of twelve great leagues at the Chicago Portage.

Whether Lahontan ever in fact employed four hundred Indians to transport his baggage over the Chicago Portage may well be doubted; but that other travelers employed Indians in a similar capacity is certain. The companions of Cavelier, La Salle's brother, who passed from Fort St. Louis to Lake Michigan in September, 1687, employed a dozen Shawnee Indians to carry their goods to the lake, because there was no water in the river at this season of the year.[37] Unable to make their way from Chicago to Mackinac they returned to the fort to pass the winter. In this same autumn of 1687, some Frenchmen en route from Montreal to Fort St. Louis with three canoes loaded with merchandise and ammunition were halted at Chicago on account of lack of water in the Des Plaines.[38] Upon information of this being brought to Tonty he engaged the services of forty Shawnee Indians, women and men, by whom the goods were transported to the fort.

When horses were first employed on the Chicago Portage cannot, of course, be stated. We have seen that La Salle advocated their employment, but he himself was never in a position to use them. That such use began very early, however, is indicated by a tradition preserved by Gurdon S. Hubbard of an adventure of a trader named Cerré on the Des Plaines.[39] The Indians sought to force him to pay toll to them, but he defied them;

[36] Lahontan, *Voyages*, I, 167 ff.

[37] Joutel's Journal, in Margry, III, 482, 484.

[38] *Ibid.*, 497.

[39] Hubbard, *Life*, 41–43.

the controversy ended happily, however, and the Indians transported Cerré's goods on their pack horses from Cache Island to the mouth of the Des Plaines. The date of this incident is not recorded, but Cerré first came into the Illinois country in 1756. If the Indians were accustomed thus early to use pack horses to transport the goods of travelers it is not improbable that the practice may have originated long before.

The demand for transportation facilities at the portage was thus coeval with the advent of the French in this region. In the early nineteenth century the satisfaction of this demand afforded employment and a livelihood to some of the inhabitants of Chicago. The transporting of travelers and their baggage across the portage formed part of the business of John Kinzie. That it was Ouilmette's principal occupation, at least for a considerable period, seems probable.[40] Major Stoddard stated in 1812 concerning the Chicago Portage that in the dry season boats and their cargoes were transported across it by teams kept at Chicago for this purpose.[41] Several years later Graham and Phillips reported that there was a well-beaten road from the mouth of the Des Plaines to the lake, over which boats and their loads were hauled by oxen and vehicles kept for this purpose by the French settlers at Chicago.[42] Schoolcraft and Cass procured horses to convey them to Chicago from the point near Starved Rock where they abandoned their canoe. John Tanner's narrative shows that the Frenchman who carried him a distance of sixty miles from Chicago to the Illinois River in the preceding year was commonly engaged in this business. Probably this man was Ouilmette, although Tanner does not give his name. If it was someone other than Ouilmette, it is evident that at least two Chicago residents were engaged in this business.

The project of Joliet of a canal to connect Lake Michigan with the Illinois River was revived early in the nineteenth century. After numerous investigations and reports had been

[40] See *Post*, pp. 143–44; *Tanner's Narrative*, 257; *Barry Transcript*.

[41] Stoddard, *Sketches, Historical and Descriptive, of Louisiana*, 368 ff.

[42] *State Papers, Doc. No. 17, 16th Congress, 1st Sess.*

made, the work of construction was at last begun, amid great enthusiasm, in the year 1836. Twelve years later the Illinois and Michigan Canal was completed, and therewith the Chicago Portage ceased to be. Even without the construction of the canal its old importance and use were about to terminate. The advance of white settlement sounded the death knell of the fur trade. With the advent of the railroad, trade and commerce sought other channels and another means of transportation. The waterways lost their old importance and the Chicago Portage passed into history. Ere this time, however, the New Chicago had been born and her future, with its marvelous possibilities, was secure.

CHAPTER II

CHICAGO IN THE SEVENTEENTH CENTURY

It seems quite probable that Chicago was an important meeting-place for Indian travelers long before the first white men came to the foot of Lake Michigan. The portage of the Indian preceded the canoe of the white man, and the Indian trail was the forerunner of the white man's road. Who the first white visitor to Chicago was cannot be stated with certainty. The chief incentive to the exploration of the Northwest was the prosecution of the fur trade, and it is probable that wandering coureurs de bois had visited this region in advance of any of the explorers who have left us records of their travels. Coming to the domain of recorded history we encounter, on the threshold as it were, the master dreamer and empire builder, La Salle.

Already interested in the subject of western exploration, in the summer of 1669 he set out from his estate of Lachine in search of a river which flowed to the western sea.[43] His course to the western end of Lake Ontario is known to us, but from this point his movements for the next two years are involved in mist and obscurity. It is believed by some that he descended the Ohio to the Mississippi in 1670, and that the following year he traversed Lake Michigan from north to south, crossed the Chicago Portage, and descended the Illinois River till he again reached the Mississippi. But the claim that he reached the Mississippi during these years is rejected by most historians. Probably the exact facts as to his movements at this time will never be known. We are here interested, however, primarily in the question whether he came to the site of Chicago. Even this cannot be stated with certainty, but the preponderance of

[43] For this expedition and the subsequent movements of La Salle see Winsor, *Cartier to Frontenac;* Parkman, *La Salle and the Discovery of the Great West;* Winsor, *Narrative and Critical History,* IV, 201 ff.

opinion among those best qualified to judge is that he probably did.[44]

The pages of history might be scanned in vain for a more fitting character with which to begin the annals of the great city of today. La Salle is noted, even as it is noted, for boundless energy, lofty aspiration, and daring enterprise. He combined the capacity to dream with the resolution to make his visions real. "He was the real discoverer of the Great West, for he planned its occupation and began its settlement; and he alone of the men of his time appreciated its boundless possibilities, and with prophetic eye saw in the future its wide area peopled by his own race."[45]

In strong contrast with the masterful La Salle succeeds, in the early annals of Chicago, the gentle, saintly Marquette. For a number of years vague and indefinite reports had been carried to Canada of the existence, to the west of the Great Lakes, of a "great river" flowing westwardly to the Vermillion Sea, as the Gulf of California was then known. These reports roused in the French the hope of finding an easy way to the South Sea, and thence to the golden commerce of the Indies.

Spurred on by the home government Talon, the intendant of Canada, took up the project of solving the problem of the great western river.[46] It chanced that for several years Marquette, a Jesuit missionary, had been stationed on the shore of Lake Superior. Here he heard from his dusky charges stories of the great river and of the pleasant country to the westward. In consequence he became imbued with the double ambition of solving the geographical question of the ultimate direction of the river's flow, and of seeking in this new region a more fruitful field of labor.[47] In the summer of 1672 Talon

[44] Margry was convinced of this and Parkman thought it entirely probable. Winsor thought that La Salle came to the head of Lake Michigan, but was in doubt whether he entered the Chicago River or the St. Joseph. Shea, who constantly belittles La Salle's achievements, believed he "reached the Illinois or some other affluent of the Mississippi." See the references given in note 43.

[45] Edward G. Mason, "Early Visitors to Chicago," in *New England Magazine*, New Ser., VI, 189.

[46] Winsor, *Cartier to Frontenac*, 231. [47] *Ibid.*, 199–201.

appointed Louis Joliet, a young Canadian who had already achieved something of a reputation as an explorer, to carry out the new task, and the projected exploration of the great river was launched. Joliet proceeded that autumn to Mackinac—the Michilimackinac of the French period—where he spent the winter preparing for the enterprise. Hither Marquette had come two years before, and here he had established the mission of St. Ignace. Proximity and a common interest in the projected enterprise combined to draw the two together; so that when the expedition set out from Mackinac in May, 1673, the party was composed of Joliet, Marquette, and five companions. Though Joliet was the official head of the expedition, it has come about, through the circumstance that his records were lost almost at the end of his toilsome journey, that we are chiefly indebted to the journal of Marquette for our knowledge of it, and have come insensibly to ascribe the credit for it to him.

From Mackinac the party passed, in two canoes, to the head of Green Bay, and thence by way of the Fox-Wisconsin River route to the Mississippi, which was reached a month after the departure from the mission of St. Ignace.[48] Down its broad current the voyagers paddled and floated for another month. Arrived at the mouth of the Arkansas, they were told by the natives that the sea was distant but ten days' journey, and that the intervening region was inhabited by warlike tribes, equipped with firearms, and hostile to their entertainers. This information led the explorers to take counsel concerning their further course. Deeming it established beyond doubt that the river emptied into "the Florida or Mexican Gulf," and fearful of losing the fruits of their discovery by falling into the hands of the Spaniards, they decided to turn about and begin the homeward journey.

On reaching the mouth of the Illinois they learned that they could shorten their return to Mackinac by passing up that river. A pleasing picture is drawn by Marquette of the country through

[48] Marquette's Journal of the expedition is printed in *Jesuit Relations*, Vol. LIX. For standard secondary accounts see the works of Parkman and Winsor.

which this new route led them. They had seen nothing comparable to it for fertility of soil, for prairies, woods, "cattle," and other game. The Indians received them kindly, and obliged Marquette to promise that he would return to instruct them. Under the guidance of an Indian escort the voyagers passed, probably by way of the Chicago Portage and River,[49] to Lake Michigan, whence they made their way to Green Bay by the end of September.

The following year Joliet continued on his way to Quebec to report to Count Frontenac the results of his expedition. Marquette remained at Green Bay, worn down by the illness that was shortly to terminate his career. In the autumn of 1674, the disease having temporarily abated, he undertook the fulfilment of his promise to the Illinois Indians to return and establish a mission among them. Late in October he began the journey,[50] accompanied by two voyageurs, Pierre Porteret and Jacques, one of whom had been a member of the earlier expedition. The little party was soon increased by the addition of a number of Indians, and all together made their way down Green Bay and the western shore of Lake Michigan, to the mouth of the "river of the portage"—the Chicago. Over a month had been consumed in the journey, owing to frequent delays caused by the stormy lake. The river was frozen to the depth of half a foot and snow was plentiful. Ten days were passed here, when, Marquette's malady having returned, a camp was made two leagues up the river, close to the portage, and it was decided to spend the winter there. Thus began in December, 1674, the first extended sojourn, so far as we have record, of white men on the site of the future Chicago. There has been much loose writing concerning the character of their habitation. Even

[49] It was the contention of Albert D. Hagar, a former secretary of the Chicago Historical Society, that on both this expedition and that of 1675 Marquette passed from the Des Plaines River to Lake Michigan by way of the Calumet Portage and River. (Andreas, *History of Chicago*, I, 46.) The evidence, however, seems to me to point to the route by way of the Chicago Portage and River. Hagar's argument is refuted by Hurlbut in *Chicago Antiquities*, 384–88.

[50] For Marquette's Journal of this expedition see *Jesuit Relations*, Vol. LIX. Parkman and Winsor have written standard secondary accounts.

Parkman states that they constructed a "log hut," and other writers have made similar assertions. There is no warrant for this in the original documents, and all the circumstances of the case combine to render it improbable.[51] Marquette was too sick to travel, and he had but two companions to assist him. They made two camps, one at the entrance of the river, and the other, a few days later, at the portage. It was already the dead of winter, and they could not have been equipped with heavy tools. It seems entirely probable that in place of a "log hut" they constructed the customary Indian shelter or wigwam.[52]

Marquette found that two Frenchmen had preceded him in establishing themselves in the Illinois country. He designates them as "La Taupine and the surgeon," and says that they were stationed eighteen leagues below Chicago, "in a fine place for hunting cattle, deer, and turkeys."[53] They were supplied with corn and other provisions, and were engaged in the fur trade. Apparently their location was selected either because it was "a fine place for hunting," or else because of its advantages as a trading station, for it is evident from the narrative that they were in close proximity to the Indians.

Who were these French pioneers of the upper Illinois Valley? We know concerning La Taupine—the mole—that he was a noted fur trader whose real name was Pierre Moreau;[54] that he was an adherent of Count Frontenac, the governor of New

[51] The French word used by Marquette, *cabannez*, was commonly employed, whether as a verb or a noun, to designate the ordinary temporary encampment of travelers and the wigwam of the Indian. In Marquette's Journal of his first expedition (*Jesuit Relations*, LIX, 146), the word is used to designate the cover of sailcloth erected over the voyagers' canoes to protect them from the mosquitoes and the sun while floating down the Mississippi. Later, on the second expedition, when Marquette, hastening along the eastern shore of Lake Michigan toward Mackinac, found himself at the point of death, his companions hastily landed and constructed a "wretched cabin of bark" to lay him in (*ibid.*, 194). Numerous other instances of the habitual use of the word to indicate a temporary camp might easily be cited.

[52] For a further development of this subject see H. H. Hurlbut's pamphlet, *Father Marquette at Mackinac and Chicago*, 13–14.

[53] *Jesuit Relations*, LIX, 174–76.

[54] *Ibid.*, 314; Mason, "Early Visitors to Chicago," cited in note 45.

France; and that he was accused by the intendant with being one of the Governor's agents in the prosecution of an illicit trade with the Indians. He had been with St. Lusson at the Sault Ste. Marie in 1671, and doubtless was possessed of all the information current among the French concerning the region beyond the Great Lakes. In what year he pushed out into this region and established the first habitation and business of a white man in northern Illinois will probably forever remain unknown.

The little that Marquette tells us of the companion of La Taupine serves only to whet our curiosity. Though these first residents were lawbreakers, they were not without redeeming qualities. In anticipation, apparently, of Marquette's arrival at their station they had made preparations to receive him, and had told the savages "that their cabin belonged to the black robe."[55] As soon as they learned of the priest's illness at Chicago the surgeon came, in spite of snow and bitter cold,[56] a distance of fifty miles to bring him some corn and blueberries. Marquette sent Jacques back with the surgeon to bear a message to the Indians who lived in his vicinity, and the traders loaded him, on his return, with corn and "other delicacies" for the sick priest. Furthermore, the surgeon was a devout man, for he spent some time with Marquette in order to perform his devotions. Clearly here is a character who improves with closer acquaintance. But such acquaintance is denied us. As a ship passing in the night the surgeon flashes across Chicago's early horizon; whence he came, whither he went, even his name will doubtless remain forever a mystery.

Meanwhile, how fared the winter with the three Frenchmen in their primitive camp near the portage? The picture of their life as painted in the pages of Marquette's Journal is not, on the whole, unattractive. The fraternal spirit manifested for them by the traders has already been noted. The Indians were

[55] *Jesuit Relations*, LIX, 176.

[56] The Journal records that the Indians were suffering from hunger because the cold and snow prevented them from hunting.

equally friendly. When those living in a village six leagues away learned of Marquette's plight, they were so solicitous for his welfare, and so fearful that he would suffer from hunger, that, notwithstanding the cold, Jacques had much difficulty in preventing the young men from coming to the portage to carry away to their village all Marquette's belongings.

The Indians' fears, however, proved groundless. Deer and buffalo abounded, partridges, much like those of France, were killed, and turkeys swarmed around the camp. The traders sent corn and blueberries, and the Indians brought corn, dried meat, and pumpkins. The severe winter produced its effect upon the game, some of the deer that were killed being so lean as to be worthless. But "the Blessed Virgin Immaculate," Marquette's celestial queen, took such care of them that there was no lack of provisions, and when the camp was broken up in the spring there was still on hand a large sack of corn and a supply of meat.

An intense spirit of religious devotion animated Marquette throughout the winter. It was his zeal in the service of his Heavenly Master that had led him, in his illness, to brave the rigors of a winter in the wilderness. Despite his bodily affliction, the observance of religious exercises was maintained. Mass was said every day throughout the winter, but they were able to observe Lent only on Fridays and Saturdays. On December 15 the mass of the Conception was celebrated. Early in February a novena, or nine days' devotion to the Virgin, was begun, to ask God for the restoration of Marquette's health. Shortly afterward his condition improved, in consequence, as he believed, of these devotions. An opportunity to give his religion a practical application was afforded him in the latter part of January. A deputation of Illinois Indians came bringing presents, in return for which they requested, among other things, a supply of powder. Marquette refused this, saying he had come to instruct them and to restore peace, and did not wish them to begin a war with their neighbors, the Miamis.

Toward the end of March the ice began to thaw, but on breaking up it formed a gorge, causing a rapid rise in the river. The camping-place was suddenly flooded, the occupants having barely time enough to secure their goods upon the trees. They themselves spent the night on a hillock, with the water steadily gaining upon them. The following day the gorge dissolved, the ice drifted away, and the travelers prepared to resume their journey to the village of the Illinois.

Eleven days were consumed in this journey, during which Marquette suffered much from illness and exposure.[57] According to Father Dablon he was received by the Indians "as an angel from Heaven." He preached to them and established his mission, and then, feeling the hand of death upon him, began his return journey to the distant mission of St. Ignace.

And now we come to what may be regarded as the next scene in the annals of Chicago. A crowd of the Illinois accompanied Marquette, as a mark of honor, for more than thirty leagues, vying with each other in taking charge of his slender baggage. Then, "filled with great esteem for the gospel," they took leave of him, and continuing his journey he shortly afterward reached Lake Michigan.[58] The route followed from this point was by way of the eastern side of the lake. But the missionary's life was to terminate sooner than the voyage. On May 19 he died, on the lonely shore of the lake, and was

[57] Marquette's Journal ends abruptly at this point, his last entry being made on April 6 while the little party was waiting at the Des Plaines River for the subsidence of the ice and the cold winds to permit them to descend. For the remainder of the story we are indebted to the narrative of Father Dablon, Marquette's superior, whose information was derived from the two companions of Marquette. Dablon's narrative is printed in *Jesuit Relations*, Vol. LIX.

[58] The route followed by Marquette and his escort from the Illinois village to Lake Michigan is not certainly known. From the fact that after reaching the lake Marquette sought to reach Mackinac by following around its eastern shore, it has been argued that he ascended the Kankakee to reach Lake Michigan. The evidence seems to me, however, to favor the route by the Des Plaines and Chicago. Marquette had gone this way on the return from his first expedition, and had returned to the Illinois the same way. If he now followed this route, the thirty leagues which the Indians accompanied him would have brought them to the vicinity of the portage between the Des Plaines and the Chicago. In the period when travel was chiefly by water portages were natural meeting (and parting) places. The one argument in support of the Kankakee route is the fact that the further

buried near the mouth of a small river in the state of Michigan which was long to bear his name.

A successor to Marquette at the mission of the Illinois was found in the person of Father Claude Allouez, who was then stationed at the mission of St. Francis Xavier at Green Bay. In October, 1676, with two companions he set out in a canoe for his new field of work.[59] The winter closed down early, however, and before they had proceeded far they were compelled to lie over until February with some Pottawatomie Indians. Then they proceeded once more, in a way "very extraordinary"; for instead of putting the canoe into the water, they placed it upon the ice, over which a sail and a favoring wind "made it go as on the water." When the wind failed they drew it along by means of ropes. New obstacles to their progress arose, however, so that not until April did they enter "the river which leads to the Illinois." At its entrance they were met by a band of eighty Illinois Indians who had come from their village to welcome Allouez. The ceremony of reception which ensued may well be set forth in the words of the missionary himself, in whose honor it was staged.

"The captain came about 30 steps to meet me, carrying in one hand a firebrand and in the other a Calumet adorned with feathers. Approaching me, he placed it in my mouth and himself lighted the tobacco, which obliged me to make a pretense of smoking it. Then he made me come into his Cabin, and having given me the place of honor, he spoke to me as follows:

'My Father, have pity on me; suffer me to return with thee, to bear thee company and take thee into my village. The meeting I have had today with thee will prove fatal to me if I do not

route of the party was along the eastern shore of the lake. But this fact does not obviate the possibility of a return to the lake by the Des Plaines and Chicago. Furthermore, by the Kankakee route from the point where the Indians turned back Marquette would still have to travel upward of one hundred and fifty miles to reach the lake. Yet the narrative states that he reached it "shortly after" they left him—a statement which harmonizes with the supposition that the leave-taking occurred at or near the Chicago Portage. For these reasons I have chosen to consider this an event in early Chicago history.

[59] The narrative of Allouez is printed in *Jesuit Relations*, Vol. LX. The quotations from it which follow are from the Thwaites translation there given.

use it to my advantage. Thou bearest to us the gospel and the prayer. If I lose the opportunity of listening to thee, I shall be punished by the loss of my nephews, whom thou seest in so great number; without doubt, they will be defeated by our enemies. Let us embark, then, in company, that I may profit by thy coming into our land.'"

It is not to be supposed that the exact words of the "Captain" have been preserved, though it may well be that the general tenor of his remarks is here set forth. The speech concluded, they set out together, and "shortly after" arrived at the Chief's abode. We have no clue, further than this, to the location of the Indian camp. Probably it was in the vicinity of the portage; for aside from the fact that this furnished a logical stopping-place Marquette tells us that during his sojourn here, two years before, Indians were encamped in his vicinity during a portion of the winter.

After a brief stay among the Indians on the Illinois, where his labors met with great success, Allouez left them, returning again the next year. We have no details of these journeys, however, and our next account of the presence of white men in this region involves us in the schemes and deeds of the masterful La Salle.

La Salle conceived the ambitious design of leading France and civilization together into the valley of the Mississippi.[60] But vast obstacles interposed to hinder him in its execution. Canada must be his base of operations, and Canada abounded in hostile traders and priests who jealously sought to checkmate him at every opportunity. The initiation of his design involved the establishment of a colony in the Illinois country. In 1678 he sent out in advance a party of men to engage in trade for him and ultimately to go to the Illinois country and prepare for his coming. Meanwhile he himself was busied with further preparations for the execution of his project; a sailing vessel was constructed close above Niagara Falls, and in August, 1678, its

[60] For the original documents pertaining to La Salle's work see Margry's collection. For standard secondary accounts see the works of Parkman and Winsor. I have drawn freely upon these in preparing this portion of my own narrative.

sails were spread upon Lake Erie for the voyage around the upper lakes. Arrived at Green Bay, the vessel was loaded with furs and started on its return, while La Salle and fourteen followers, in four canoes, continued their way down the western shore of Lake Michigan. The party laboriously made its way past the site of the modern cities of Milwaukee and Chicago and around the southern end of the lake to the mouth of the St. Joseph River. This had been agreed upon as the place of rendezvous with Tonty, La Salle's faithful lieutenant, who with twenty men was toiling, meanwhile, down the eastern side of the lake from Mackinac. Tonty had been delayed, and La Salle employed the period of waiting for him in building Fort Miami on an eminence near the mouth of the river. This became, therefore, the oldest fort in this region, and constituted an important base of operations for the prosecution of his designs.

At last Tonty arrived, bringing news which rendered probable the loss of La Salle's sailing vessel, the "Griffin," with her cargo of furs. Early in December the combined party ascended the St. Joseph River to the portage leading to the Kankakee, near the site of the modern city of South Bend. Down the latter river they passed and into the Illinois, until they came to the great Indian village, in the vicinity of Starved Rock, where Marquette and Allouez had labored as missionaries during the past five years. The place was deserted, however, the inhabitants having departed for their annual winter hunt. The journey was resumed, therefore, as far as Lake Peoria, near which place a village of the Illinois was found.

A parley was held with the Indians, in the course of which La Salle unfolded his design of building a fort in their midst, and a "great wooden Canoe" on the Mississippi, which would go down to the sea, and return thence with the goods they so much desired. La Salle was successful in overcoming alike the suspicions of the natives, the intrigues of his enemies, and the disloyalty of his own men. A site suitable for a fort was selected, and here in the dead of winter was constructed the first civilized habitation of a permanent character in the modern state of

Illinois; the Indians gave to the fort the name of Checagou, but by La Salle it was christened Fort Crevecoeur.

La Salle had thus established himself in the heart of the Mississippi Valley, and had initiated the work of carving out what was to become the imperial domain of French Louisiana. But the major portion of that work lay yet before him, and difficulties were to succeed one another in its prosecution until the leader's death at the hands of a hidden assassin was to terminate his life in seeming failure. It is not our purpose here to attempt a history of La Salle's career; rather our aim is to sketch such of its salient features as may be pertinent to the unfolding of the story of the genesis of Chicago. The loss of the "Griffin" imposed upon La Salle the necessity of returning to Fort Frontenac for supplies. Having urged forward the construction of his fort and arranged for the departure of Hennepin and his associates on what eventuated in their famous exploration of the upper waters of the Mississippi, La Salle left Tonty in command at Fort Crevecoeur, and himself, in March, 1680, set forth on his long and terrible journey. In its course he again paused near Starved Rock, noted the ease with which it might be defended, and passing on to Fort Miami, dispatched orders to Tonty to occupy and fortify it. He then crossed on foot the trackless waste of southern Michigan in the season of spring floods, and came at last to his destination. He spent some months in setting his affairs in order, and in August, 1680, set out on the return to Illinois, passing by way of Mackinac and thence down the eastern side of Lake Michigan to Fort Miami.

Meanwhile, what of Tonty and affairs at Fort Crevecoeur? Faithful to his orders, Tonty, on receipt of the dispatch which La Salle had sent forward from Fort Miami, set forth to occupy Starved Rock. In his absence the men left at Fort Crevecoeur, spurred on by the tales of financial disaster to La Salle related by the new arrivals, rose in mutiny. They destroyed the fort, stole its provisions, and writing on the side of the unfinished vessel the legend *Nous sommes tous sauvages*—"We are all savages"—departed. Upon the heels of this disaster succeeded a still greater menace to La Salle's designs. It was essential to their success that the Illinois Indians should retain peaceable possession of their territory. But now came against them a war party of the terrible Iroquois. They assailed and destroyed the village at the Rock and pursued the fleeing Illinois until the scattered survivors found refuge across the Mississippi.

The indomitable Tonty, almost alone in this sea of savagery, had done what he could to save the Illinois from destruction. His efforts proved vain, and with his few followers he fled from impending destruction. Their goal was distant Mackinac, and their route was up the Illinois and the Des Plaines to Lake Michigan and thence northward along its western shore. Doubtless the forlorn little party passed by Chicago, though we have no direct details as to this portion of their journey. Hardships and dangers in abundance were endured before the survivors found refuge with a band of friendly Pottawatomies at some point to the southward of Green Bay.

Shortly after the destruction of the Illinois La Salle, in ignorance of what had happened, came from Fort Miami to the relief of Tonty. In the ghastly remains of the village at Starved Rock he read the story of this new disaster to his plans. Failing to find the bodies of Tonty and his companions among them, he followed in the track of the pursued and pursuing savages until he reached the Mississippi. Concluding at last that Tonty had not come this way he retraced his steps to the junction of the Kankakee with the Des Plaines, and turning up the latter stream soon found traces of Tonty's party. It was now the dead of winter. Convinced of Tonty's escape, La Salle abandoned the canoes, which he had dragged with him on sledges thus far, and made his way overland through extreme cold and deep snow to Fort Miami, where he arrived at the end of January.

The design was now conceived by La Salle of welding the western tribes into a confederation, which, under the guidance of himself and his French followers, should oppose the marauding incursions of the Iroquois into the West. The year 1681 was devoted to the furthering of this project and to the gathering of La Salle's scattered resources for a renewal of his attempt at establishing himself in the Mississippi Valley. Late in the year he was again at Fort Miami with a considerable party of French and Indians, ready for the exploit which has given him his greatest fame—the descent of the Mississippi to its mouth.

From Fort Miami the route followed led around the foot of Lake Michigan to Chicago; thence across the portage and down the Des Plaines, the Illinois, and the Mississippi to the Gulf of Mexico. The expedition set forth in two divisions, Tonty with the first crossing over to the Chicago River in the closing days of December, 1681, where he prepared sledges for transporting the canoes and equipment on the ice, and awaited the arrival of his chief. La Salle with the second division arrived early in January, and after a detention of a few days, occasioned by unfavorable weather, the united party set out, dragging their sledges on the surface of the frozen rivers until open water was reached below Lake Peoria. There they embarked, and three months later, on April 9, 1682, at the mouth of the Great River he had descended La Salle took formal possession, under the name of Louisiana, of all the vast country drained by it and by its tributaries, stretching "from the Alleghenies to the Rocky Mountains; from the Rio Grande and the Gulf to the farthest springs of the Missouri."[61]

La Salle's discovery of the mouth of the Mississippi caused him to broaden his projects. He would establish a colony at the mouth of the Great River to serve as an outlet for his colony on the Illinois where he hoped to gather the furs on which he relied to render his whole vast enterprise commercially successful. The prosecution of his designs, therefore, depended ultimately on his ability to make the Illinois colony profitable. On his return to Mackinac from the descent of the Mississippi, in the autumn of 1682, he learned that the Iroquois were about to renew their attacks upon the West. The best efforts of himself and Tonty were now directed, therefore, to the fortification of

[61] Parkman, *La Salle*, chap. xxi.

Starved Rock, which he planned to serve as the center of his colony and its rock of defense against the invader.

Here, on a cliff which rises sheer from the water's edge to a height of one hundred and twenty-five feet, with its crest about an acre in extent, and accessible only by a narrow pathway in the rear, during the winter of 1682 and 1683 the fort was constructed. At the same time the work of alliance with the Indians went vigorously forward until from the lofty ramparts of St. Louis, the name given by La Salle to his fortress, the leader could look down upon the lodges of four thousand warriors, gathered from half a score of tribes, and a total population of upward of twenty thousand souls. The stability of the colony thus gathered depended on La Salle's ability to protect his allies against the Iroquois, and to furnish them with goods and a market for their furs.

La Salle's career shows that over natural obstacles and the wiles of the red man he could rise triumphant, but that he was no match for the intriguing enemies of his own race. By these his plans were shipwrecked once more, and for the last time, so far as his Illinois career was concerned. Count Frontenac, his staunch supporter hitherto, was recalled, and the new governor, De la Barre, pursued a policy of unscrupulous hostility toward him. His ammunition and supplies to sustain himself against the Iroquois were detained, lying reports about him were sent to the home government, and finally a force was sent to supersede him in command of Fort St. Louis.

La Salle's only remedy against such an enemy was to appeal in person to his monarch. Leaving Tonty in command of the colony he went, by way of Canada, to France, whence he embarked upon the enterprise which was to end so disastrously in the wilds of Texas. Under the guidance of others Louisiana became, in the following century, the fairest province of New France. Wrested from French control by the Anglo-Saxon, it has come in time to constitute the heart and center of our magnificent national domain. The geographical monuments to the memory of La Salle are few; a county in Texas, a city and a county in Illinois are all, aside from a few insignificant post towns, that bear his name. Yet in the eyes of history he will always be regarded as the father of Louisiana, a province as favored by Nature, as imperial in character, as any the sun ever shone upon.

Since 1678 La Salle's chief lieutenant in the prosecution of his enterprises had been the capable and valorous Tonty.[62] La Salle's mission to the French Court in 1684 had resulted in the restoration of Tonty to command at Fort St. Louis. On the death of La Salle he sought to step into his former leader's place, and to complete the establishment of the French power in the Mississippi Valley. For a dozen years longer he held his lofty post of St. Louis, seeking meanwhile to interest the French Court in the uncompleted design of his former chief. But other and more powerful interests held the ear of the distant monarch, and his efforts were in vain. Finally, in 1700 an expedition was sent out under the command of Iberville to take possession of the mouth of the Mississippi. A settlement was made at Biloxi Bay, and hither Tonty came, abandoning his fort at the Rock, and joining his efforts in support of the more powerful enterprise. After four years more of service in the cause in which he had first enlisted under La Salle's banner, he died at Biloxi of yellow fever. There in September, 1704, "was dug the grave of the most unselfish and loyal, as he was one of the most courageous and intrepid, of the many knightly men who blazed the path whence entered civilization into what later became known as the old Northwest."[63]

During Tonty's occupancy of Fort St. Louis in the period following the death of La Salle a number of travelers passed between Lake Michigan and the Mississippi by the Chicago-Illinois route the records of whose experiences are still preserved. One of the most interesting of these narratives is that of Joutel, the com-

[62] The story of Tonty is told by Parkman in connection with his account of La Salle. "Henry de Tonty," a sketch and appreciation of Tonty's career by Henry E. Legler, is printed in *Parkman Club Publications*, No. 3. For an English translation of Tonty's own modest narrative of his career to 1693 see French, *Historical Collections of Louisiana*, I, 52 ff.

[63] Legler, *op. cit.*, 37.

panion of Cavelier.[64] Their party comprised the sole survivors of La Salle's ill-fated Texan expedition who returned to France and civilization. They came, a band of five forlorn fugitives, up the Mississippi and the Illinois, arriving at Fort St. Louis in September, 1687. Carefully concealing the fact of La Salle's death, they obtained means to continue their journey, and soon set out for Lake Michigan accompanied by a dozen savages who carried their goods and baggage, because of the lack of water in the Des Plaines. On the twenty-fifth they arrived at Chicago and there found a canoe left by some Frenchmen who had recently passed down to Fort St. Louis. Their lack of experience as canoemen, together with contrary winds and bad weather, caused a delay of eight days at this place. Meanwhile the season was advancing and their scanty supply of provisions was being consumed. The state of mind to which they were reduced is naïvely shown by the record of Joutel that one of the party, having shot at some chickens and cracked his gun, "was so provoked that it gave him a fever."

Finally they embarked on the lake and advanced some eight or ten leagues along the shore to the northward, striving to come to the villages of the Pottawatomies, where they hoped to procure a fresh supply of food. The effort was a pitiful failure. Starvation lay before them; the loss of a year of time with the consequently lessened prospect of affording succor in season to the survivors of La Salle's colony in Texas, and the danger of the discovery of their guilty secret concerning their leader's fate, awaited their return to Fort St. Louis.

They decided, however, to turn back. It was a dejected party, we may well believe, which came early in October to the entrance of the Chicago River. Here they made a cache in which they concealed their goods, put their canoe upon a scaffold, and retraced their steps to Fort St. Louis. In this place they passed the winter, and from them we get our fullest description of

[64] For the story of Cavelier's party see Joutel's Journal printed in Margry, III, 89–535. An abridged and distorted English translation of the Journal was published in 1714, and this was reprinted at Albany in 1906 under the editorial direction of Henry Reed Stiles.

the fort, and of the manner of life that prevailed there. Some three weeks after their arrival at the fort Tonty returned from his participation in Denonville's famous campaign against the Iroquois. From Fort St. Louis he had led sixteen Frenchmen and two hundred Indians to share in this distant enterprise. With a baseness which is difficult to excuse the fugitives deceived him concerning the death of La Salle, and after accepting his hospitality through the winter secured from him, on the assumption that La Salle was still alive, a considerable quantity of furs and other supplies.

Taking advantage of the spring floods they set out once more for Chicago, March 21, 1688. They arrived on March 29, after a toilsome journey. Because of the swiftness of the river they were compelled to wade in the water, pulling their canoes, much of the way. Joutel avers that he suffered more on this short trip than he had done before since his departure from the Gulf of Mexico. Again bad weather compelled them to delay at Chicago, this time for ten days. There was little game and they had only corn meal to eat. But Providence furnished them "a kind of manna" to eat with their meal, which appears from the description to have consisted of maple sap. They also procured in the woods garlic and other edible plants, and Joutel records that Chicago takes its name, as they were informed, from the profusion of garlic growing in the surrounding woods.[65]

The members of Joutel's party passed on to Canada, and here we may leave them to pursue their way, burdened with their terrible secret, as best they may. Our interest meanwhile shifts to the story of Father Pinet and his mission of the Guardian Angel. We have seen that commerce and the Cross entered the upper Mississippi Valley together in 1673, in the persons of Joliet and Marquette. During the succeeding years the efforts of the servants of the Cross to gain control of this region were scarcely less zealous than were those of the devotees of trade. The missionary accompanied, sometimes even preceded, the explorer in his journeys, seeking everywhere to introduce the

[65] Margry, III, 485.

doctrine of the true faith and win the natives to the Church. The representatives of the Jesuit order were the most active agents of the Church in this work of proselyting. Under its auspices Marquette had established the Illinois Mission. Its vicissitudes of fortune were as various as those of La Salle himself, but, on the whole, it was as successful as any in all the annals of Catholic missions to the red man.[66]

We are more particularly concerned with that portion of the work of the Jesuits among the Illinois which pertains to the mission of the Guardian Angel at Chicago.[67] This was established in 1696 by Father Pierre Pinet, who had been stationed at Mackinac for a couple of years. According to the Jesuit records, however, Pinet was soon driven from Chicago and his mission broken up by no less a person than Count Frontenac, governor of New France.[68] An appeal to Bishop Laval resulted in a cessation of Frontenac's opposition, which, in the eyes of Pinet's associates, amounted to persecution. The mission of the Guardian Angel was accordingly resumed in 1698, but two years later it was permanently abandoned.

Pinet was a man of deeds rather than words, and has himself left no account of his mission. The statements of his associates show that he was successful in his work here; the adult Indians, "hardened in debauchery," paid little heed to his teachings, but the young were baptized, and even the medicine men, who were the most inveterate opponents of Christianity, manifested a desire to have their children instructed.[69] It was Pinet's practice to spend only the summer season at Chicago. The winters he spent with the missionaries lower down on the Illinois, or in following his charges on their annual hunt.[70]

[66] For the history of the Illinois Mission see Shea, *Catholic Missions among the Indian Tribes of the United States*, chaps. xxii, xxiii.

[67] For a brief biographical sketch of Pinet see *Jesuit Relations*, LXIV, 278. Various references to Pinet scattered throughout the *Jesuit Relations* have been collected by Frank R. Grover in his lecture on Pinet and his mission of the Guardian Angel of Chicago, published by the Chicago Historical Society in 1907.

[68] Letter of Gravier to Laval, September 17, 1697, *Jesuit Relations*, LXV, 52.

[69] *Ibid.*, 70; Shea, *Early Voyages Up and Down the Mississippi*, 53–54.

[70] *Jesuit Relations*, LXV, 70; Shea, *op. cit.*, 53, 59.

The site of the mission of the Guardian Angel has long been a subject of misapprehension. Aside from the general allusions to the mission as being at Chicago, the document of chief importance in determining its location is the letter of St. Cosme of January 2, 1699.[71] He had passed during the preceding autumn and early winter, in company with a party of associates, from Mackinac to the Mississippi by way of Green Bay, the Chicago Portage, and the Illinois River route, and the letter is, in fact, a report concerning this trip. The party spent some time at Pinet's mission, detained by storms and other obstacles. From a study of this letter, as printed by Shea, Grover concludes that the mission was situated above the modern Chicago on the North Shore, near the present village of Gross Point.[72]

Shea's translation of St. Cosme's letter, however, frequently departs from the original manuscript.[73] Because of this fact, reference to the latter deprives Grover's argument of whatever force it might otherwise possess.[74] It shows that St. Cosme's party left the site of the modern city of Racine on October 17, and having been detained by wind, cabined three days later "five leagues from Chikagwa." This they should have reached early on the twenty-first, but a wind suddenly springing up from the lake obliged them to land "half a league from Etpikagwa." Here the priests left their baggage with the canoemen, and went "by land" to the house of Father Pinet, which they say was built on the bank of the little river, having on one side the lake and on the other a fine large prairie. On the twenty-fourth, the wind having fallen, they had their canoes brought with all their baggage, and, the waters being extremely low, placed everything not absolutely necessary for their further journey in a cache, to be sent for the following spring. Finally on the

[71] Printed in Shea, *op. cit.*, 45 ff.

[72] Grover, *Pinet*, 167 ff.

[73] This is preserved in the archives of Laval University at Quebec. I have used an attested copy made "with the greatest possible fidelity" by Father Gosselin, archivist of Laval University, in the Chicago Historical Society library.

[74] Aside from the inaccuracy of Shea's translation of St. Cosme's letter, on which Grover bases his argument, he has made it the basis of a number of unwarranted and erroneous conclusions.

twenty-ninth they started from Chicago and encamped for the night at the portage, two leagues up the river.

It is clear from this account that "Etpikagwa" was a point on the lake not more than fifteen miles north of Chicago; that here the party landed early on October 21, and the priests, leaving the boatmen behind, went by land to Pinet's house. Grover says that this shows the mission was not on the lake shore, and that they went inland to reach it; and he further assumes that they proceeded but a short distance. In fact, it shows neither of these things, and since three days elapsed before the canoes were sent for, there is nothing in the account inconsistent with the supposition that the priests proceeded a distance of fifteen miles down the lake shore in coming to the mission.

On the contrary, the account directly supports this supposition. If the mission was inland near the Skokie marsh, as Grover supposes, they could hardly have had the canoes brought to it on the twenty-fourth. The supposition that it was located at the modern Chicago is strengthened by St. Cosme's account of the departure from Chicago. Having sent for the canoes on the twenty-fourth, the party started from Chicago on the twenty-ninth and camped for the night two leagues up the river at the beginning of the portage. They had been staying with Father Pinet, and Father Pinet was at "Chikagwa." Now they depart from "Chikagwa," and two leagues away, "where the little river loses itself in the prairies," and at the commencement of the portage they camp. Pinet's mission was, then, apparently, near the mouth of the Chicago River. Reverting to the description already given of it as "on the bank of the little river, having on one side the lake, and on the other a fine large prairie," we find nothing to conflict with this conclusion.

Finally, St. Cosme records that having made half of the portage they were delayed by the discovery that a little boy, who had joined the party, had wandered off. St. Cosme with four of the men turned back next day to look for him. Their quest was unsuccessful, and the next day being All Saints', St. Cosme was obliged to go and pass the night at Chicago. Mass having been said early, the following day was devoted to the search. Evidently the Chicago here referred to was not, as Grover supposes, located on the North Shore fifteen miles above the mouth of the river. On the contrary, it must have been within a reasonable distance of the portage where the boy was lost. From every point of view the study of St. Cosme's letter leads to the conclusion that the mission of the Guardian Angel was on the Chicago River at some point between the forks and the mouth.

The members of St. Cosme's party proceeded on their way, having left a man at Chicago in charge of some of their supplies, and without having found the lost boy. After spending the winter among the tribes along the lower Mississippi, the party retraced its steps northward.[75] St. Cosme remained among the Tamaroas at Cahokia, while his companions continued on their way to Chicago, where they arrived on "maundy Thursday." One of them records that the boy who had been lost made his way to Chicago after thirteen days, utterly exhausted and "out of his head." In the spring of 1700 Father Pinet abandoned his mission at Chicago and joined St. Cosme at Cahokia, where he died a few years later.[76] Therewith Chicago ceased to be a place of residence for white men for almost a century. Owing to causes which will be set forth in the following chapter, the frequent visits made by the French in the seventeenth century ceased, and the story of Chicago during the first half of the eighteenth century concerns itself almost wholly with the terrible Indian wars which desolated the Northwest during this period.

Much has been said and written on the subject of a fort at Chicago in the French period. In the Treaty of Greenville of 1795 one of the cessions which General Wayne extorted from the tribes was a tract of land six miles square at the mouth of the

[75] On the travels and experiences of the missionaries see their letters in Shea, *Early Voyages Up and Down the Mississippi*.

[76] Citations from the Jesuit Relations in Grover, *Pinet*, 162–64. The date of Pinet's death is variously given as 1702 and 1704.

Chicago River "where a fort formerly stood."[77] Since the English never had a fort at Chicago, the allusion is obviously to one belonging to the French. Thomas Hutchins, the first and only civil "geographer of the United States,"[78] who himself had traveled extensively in the Northwest, placed an "Indian Village and Fort" at the entrance of the Chicago River on the map which accompanied his famous *Topographical Description* of 1778. Many earlier maps might be cited to show the existence of a fort at Chicago in the French period.[79] Coming to secondary accounts, most of the local histories which treat of early Chicago with any degree of fulness credit the French fort tradition.[80] Mr. Edward G. Mason, a zealous worker in the field of Illinois history, even thought there was a fort at Chicago from 1685 until the end of French control in this region.[81]

Despite these numerous assertions, however, it is extremely doubtful whether the French ever had a regular fort at Chicago, and it can be shown conclusively that if so it existed for but a short period only. La Salle and Tonty passed by Chicago at various times and their movements are known during the entire period of La Salle's activities in Illinois. But for two exceptions, to be noted shortly, they nowhere speak of a fort at Chicago at this time, and the evidence that there was none, though negative, may be regarded as conclusive. There was no establishment at

[77] *American State Papers, Indian Affairs,* I, 562.

[78] Hutchins, *Topographical Description of Virginia, Pennsylvania, Maryland, and North Carolina,* 7.

[79] E.g., Hennepin, *Nouvelle découverte d'un très grand pays situé dans l'Amérique,* Utrecht, 1697, I, (facing) 1. This map was frequently copied by others in the years following its first appearance. Jean Baptiste Homann's map of North and South America (copy in Chicago Historical Society library), of unknown date, but probably about the year 1700; Bellin, *Carte de l'Amérique septentrionale,* 1755; Jean Roque's map of North America, 1754–61.

[80] See among others Mason, *Chapters from Illinois History,* 163–64; Hurlbut, *Chicago Antiquities,* 164, 171, 360–61, 592; Blanchard, *Discovery and Conquests of the Northwest with the History of Chicago,* I, 68 (this work will be cited henceforth as *The Northwest and Chicago*); Davidson and Stuvé, *History of Illinois,* 260. Many other works and historical articles speak more or less briefly of the supposed French fort at Chicago; see for example Andreas, *History of Chicago,* I, 79; Shea, "Chicago from 1673 to 1825," in *Historical Magazine,* V, 103.

[81] Mason, "Early Visitors to Chicago," 201–2.

Chicago in 1687 when Cavalier La Salle's party was here vainly seeking to push on to Mackinac; nor in 1688 when the same party, having wintered at Fort St. Louis, again tarried at Chicago while on its way to Canada. There is no evidence that such a fort was established in the succeeding decade; and there is negative evidence to the contrary, both in the fact that St. Cosme makes no mention of a fort at Chicago at the time of his visit and that the French government gave only a grudging permission to Tonty to continue at Fort St. Louis, limiting his yearly operations to two canoes of merchandise, and finally, by royal decree, directing the abandonment of the fort.[82]

We have thus arrived at the beginning of the eighteenth century. Did the French have a fort at Chicago between the years 1700 and 1763? James Logan's report to Governor Keith in 1718, upon the French establishment in the interior, which was used by Keith in his memorial to the Board of Trade, so asserts. By the latter the statements of Logan were incorporated in a report to the king,[83] and this, apparently, was the source of Popple's representation of a "Fort Miamis" at Chicago on his great *Map of the British Empire in America* of 1732.[84] In spite of this contemporary evidence, which has gained the approval of many historians, it may confidently be asserted that no such fort existed at Chicago in the eighteenth century. That there was no fort here in 1715 is shown by two independent sources. In November of this year, Claude de Ramezay, acting governor, and Begon, intendant of New France, in a report to the French minister dealing in part with the military situation in the region between the upper lakes and the Mississippi, recommended the establishment of several new posts.[85] Among the number a post at "Chicagou" was urged, "to facilitate access to the Illinois and the miamis, and to keep those

[82] Legler, "Henry de Tonty"; Winsor, *Cartier to Frontenac*, 340.

[83] Printed in O'Callaghan, *New York Colonial Documents*, V, 620–21.

[84] Popple states that his map was undertaken with the approbation of the Lords of Trade; and that it is based upon maps, charts, and especially the records transmitted to them by the governors of the British colonies and others.

[85] *Wisconsin Historical Collections*, XVI, 327 ff.

nations in our interests." If a fort already existed at Chicago the two highest officials in New France would have been aware of the fact, and there would have been no reason for this recommendation. In this same year, 1715, as part of an elaborately planned campaign against the Fox Indians of Wisconsin, the French arranged for the rendezvous at Chicago of forces from Detroit, from the Wabash, and from the lower Illinois River settlements.[86] A series of mishaps caused a complete miscarriage of plans for the campaign; but these very mishaps show there was at all events no garrison at Chicago. The three parties which were to effect a junction here arrived at different times, and, ignorant of the movements of the others, each in turn abandoned the expedition and retired. Obviously if there had been a garrison at Chicago it would have constituted an important factor in planning the campaign; and the various bands which were to effect a junction here would have been informed, on their arrival, of the movements of the others.

That there was no French establishment at Chicago in 1721 is evident from the journal of Father Charlevoix. In this year he was touring the interior of America on a royal commission to examine and report to his king the condition of New France. His letters and history constitute the most authoritative eighteenth-century source for the history of New France. In the very month of September, 1721, when the British Board of Trade report was made, Charlevoix passed from Fort St. Joseph, where the city of Niles, Michigan, now stands, down the Kankakee and the Illinois to Peoria, and beyond.[87] He had first intended to pass through Chicago, but a storm on the lake, together with information of the impossibility of navigating the Des Plaines in a canoe at this season, led him to follow the route by the St. Joseph Portage and the Kankakee. His journal is detailed and explicit; he carefully describes the various posts and routes of communication. He had planned to pass by

[86] *Ibid.*, 313 ff.

[87] Charlevoix, *Histoire et description générale de la Nouvelle France, avec le journal historique d'un voyage fait par ordre du roi dans l'Amérique septentrionale*, letters of September 14 and 17, 1721.

Chicago, and had informed himself concerning the portage and the Des Plaines River. Yet he gives no hint of a fort here, a thing incomprehensible if such a fort had in fact existed.

There is abundant evidence in the sources pertaining to the operations of the French in the Northwest that they had no fort at Chicago after 1721. In connection with the Fox wars numerous campaigns were waged in which the Chicago garrison, if there had been such, would have participated. Yet no such force is ever mentioned, and some of the sources make it positively evident that there was neither garrison nor fort here. In 1727 the holding of a great conference with the Foxes the following year at Starved Rock or Chicago was proposed.[88] If this were done it was deemed necessary for the French to be first on the spot appointed for the rendezvous "to erect a fort" and otherwise prepare for the council. The project never materialized, however, and so the fort was not built. In 1730, when the French succeeded in trapping and destroying a large band of the Foxes in the vicinity of Starved Rock,[89] parties came to the scene of conflict from many directions—from Ouiatanon, St. Joseph, Fort Chartres, and elsewhere; but none came from Chicago, although it was nearer the scene than any of the places from which the French forces did come—obviously because there was no garrison at Chicago. In the early winter of 1731–32 a Huron-Iroquois war party passed from Detroit to St. Joseph and thence around the southern end of Lake Michigan and on into Wisconsin to attack the Foxes.[90] The party paused at Chicago long enough to build a fort in which to leave their sick. This "fort" was evidently a temporary Indian shelter, but it is also evident that if an ungarrisoned French fort had been standing here, the construction of such a shelter would have been unnecessary. An official list of the commanders of the various western posts a dozen years later is preserved in the French colonial archives.[91] The posts at Detroit, Mackinac, Green Bay, St. Joseph, Ouiatanon, and elsewhere are mentioned, but the

[88] *Wisconsin Historical Collections*, XVII, 3–6.

[89] *Ibid.*, 109–30. [90] *Ibid.*, 148–50. [91] *Ibid.*, 432–33.

name of Chicago is not included in the list. Finally an exhaustive memoir upon the posts and trade of the interior of the continent by Bougainville in 1757 includes no mention of a post at Chicago, although the neighboring posts which are known to have existed at this time receive careful attention.[92]

It is evident, then, that the French had no fort at Chicago during the eighteenth century. Did they have one here at any time during the seventeenth? Two exceptions to the proposition that La Salle and Tonty make no mention of such a fort have been noted. In a letter written from the Chicago Portage, June 4, 1683, La Salle[93] speaks of a "fort" here, built by two of his men the preceding winter. This structure Mason describes as a "little stockade with a log house within its enclosure,"[94] and declares it to have been the first known structure of anything like a permanent character at Chicago. But a log hut constructed by two men and never garrisoned by any regular force hardly merits the designation of a fort in the ordinary acceptation of this term, even though it was surrounded by a stockade. Those who speak of a French fort at Chicago in this period refer not to this structure but to the "Fort of Chicagou" commanded by M. de la Durantaye in the winter of 1685–86.

Our information concerning this fort is very scanty, being confined to a simple mention of it with the name of its commander, in Tonty's memoir of 1693.[95] At the end of October, 1685, Tonty started from Mackinac in a canoe on Lake Michigan to go to Fort St. Louis on the Illinois River. Because of the lateness of the season his progress was rendered impossible by the formation of ice in the lake. This compelled him to return to Mackinac, whence he again set forth, this time by land, for Fort St. Louis. An earlier account of this trip than that of 1693, but of equal brevity, was written by Tonty in the summer of 1686.[96] It does not even mention Durantaye's "Fort of

[92] *Ibid.*, XVIII, 167 ff.

[93] Margry, II, 317.

[94] Mason, *Chapters from Illinois History*, 144.

[95] French, *Historical Collections of Louisiana*, I, 67.

[96] Letter of Tonty to M. Cabart de Villermont, August 24, 1686, in Margry, III, 560.

Chicagou," but it adds certain details concerning Tonty's trip which are of importance in determining the location of that establishment.

Tonty was, of course, familiar by 1686 with both sides of Lake Michigan. In view of this fact it is extremely improbable that, having to go by land from Mackinac to Fort St. Louis in the winter time, he would make the long détour around the head of Lake Michigan and Green Bay and down the western side of the lake, rather than follow the shorter route down the eastern side and around its southern end. This reasoning finds support in the statements of Tonty of the distances he traversed. The entire distance from Mackinac to Fort St. Louis he gives as two hundred leagues, and states that after traveling one hundred and twenty leagues he came to Durantaye's fort. It was, therefore, eighty leagues from Fort St. Louis. The usual estimate of French travelers of this time of the distance between Chicago and Fort St. Louis was thirty leagues;[97] while the distance overland from St. Joseph to Fort St. Louis was approximately eighty leagues. It is incredible that Tonty would estimate the distance from Mackinac to Chicago by land at one hundred and twenty leagues, and that from Chicago to Fort St. Louis at eighty leagues, a distance two-thirds as great. The supposition that Durantaye's fort was on the St. Joseph River rather than the modern Chicago harmonizes well both with the probabilities of the case and the distances given us by Tonty.

The foregoing reasoning is not, of course, absolutely conclusive of the location of Durantaye's "Fort of Chicagou." It is strengthened, however, by one other consideration. If such a fort was in fact here in January, 1686, what had happened to it in the interval between this time and Cavalier La Salle's visit in the autumn of 1687? Joutel's narrative of the adventures of his party is given with a wealth of detail. Both in the autumn of 1687 and again in the spring of 1688 the traveler stayed at Chicago for several days. Not only does the narrative show

[97] See for example St. Cosme's statement in Shea, *Early Voyages Up and Down the Mississippi*, 59.

that there was no garrison or fort here, but it contains no mention of such an establishment at any previous time.

The French had no fort at Chicago in the eighteenth century, then, and if they had one in the seventeenth century it could only have been a temporary structure which quickly disappeared. It remains to suggest an explanation of the origin of the widespread belief that there was a French fort at Chicago. It seems evident that it was due largely to the cartographers, who, residing for the most part in Europe, found themselves at a loss to interpret correctly the narratives of the explorers, which were themselves oftentimes confused and inaccurate, or lacking in detail. That the cartographers often labored in the dark, and that their work was frequently erroneous, will be apparent from a comparison of their maps with those of an authoritative modern atlas. The representations of the map-makers can no more be relied upon implicitly than can the narratives of the time; and there is as much reason in the one case as in the other for subjecting them to critical scrutiny.

In the present instance the erroneous belief in the existence of a French fort at Chicago in the eighteenth century probably originated with Father Hennepin, the garrulous companion of La Salle. He had been at La Salle's Fort Miami on the St. Joseph, and had passed thence with his leader down the Kankakee and the Illinois. Yet his *New Discovery*, first published in 1697, contains a map[98] showing "Fort des Miamis" at the mouth of a stream emptying into the southwestern corner of Lake Michigan. It is obvious from a comparison of this map with the one in Hennepin's earlier work, the *Description of Louisiana*, published in 1683,[99] that this representation is intended for the St. Joseph River and La Salle's Fort Miami, which, by a stupid blunder, have been transferred from the southeastern to the southwestern side of the lake. The *New Discovery*

[98] For a reproduction of this map see Winsor, *Narrative and Critical History*, IV, 251; Hennepin, *New Discovery* (Thwaites ed.), I, (facing) 22.

[99] For a reproduction of this map see Winsor, *op. cit.*, IV, 249; Hennepin, *op. cit.*, I, frontispiece.

enjoyed widespread popularity, and numerous editions were issued during the following years, not only in French but also in foreign languages. Hennepin's maps, too, were widely copied in other works, and so the blunder with respect to the location of Fort Miami was perpetuated. Evidently this was the source of the error of Logan and of the many who in later times repeated his statements. Ignorant alike of the fact that Fort Miami had stood at the mouth of the St. Joseph and that it had been destroyed nearly forty years before, Logan located it at Chicago in 1718, adding the interesting information that it "was not regularly garrisoned."

CHAPTER III

THE FOX WARS: A HALF-CENTURY OF CONFLICT

With the dawn of the eighteenth century the character of the annals of Chicago undergoes a radical change. The period which had just closed had been marked by great activity on the part of the French in the adjoining region. For a quarter of a century the Illinois River had constituted their chief highway from the Great Lakes to the Mississippi. Upon its placid bosom trader, priest, and warrior alike had plied their bark canoes. For the time being the Illinois realized La Salle's design for it of furnishing the connecting link between the two great river systems of New France. The Chicago River and Portage thus became an important feature in the geography of New France, although it shared with the Kankakee the sum total of travel by the Illinois River route.

But already forces were at work which were to effect a complete readjustment of the Indian map of Illinois and Wisconsin, to shift the center of French influence in this region from northern Illinois to its lower Mississippi border, and to furnish one of the interesting although much-neglected chapters in the history of the long struggle between France and England for the supremacy of the continent. An adequate understanding of the character and operation of these influences necessitates a brief review of the circumstances of their origin.

In the year after the founding of Quebec, Champlain, the "Father of New France," engaged in an enterprise which proved to be fraught with far-reaching consequences for his countrymen. To gain the favor of the dusky neighbors of the infant colony he accompanied an Algonquin war party on a foray against their ancient foes, the Iroquois.[100] The latter had never seen a fire-

[100] For this expedition and its results see Winsor, *Narrative and Critical History*, IV, 117–21; 167–68.

arm, and their warriors fled in terror before the death-dealing device of the white man. The Algonquins gained a temporary triumph, and Champlain gave his name to the beautiful lake which still bears it. But of greater moment was it that New France, almost at its birth, gained the undying enmity of the Iroquois.

Before the death of Champlain, and largely due to his zeal, the French had extended their explorations and trading-houses to the Great Lakes. In 1634 Nicolet passed through the Straits of Mackinac to Lake Michigan, traversed Green Bay, and revealed to his countrymen the region now known as Wisconsin. But now ensued a lull in the exploring activities of the French, and soon they were led to abandon their trading-posts on the lakes. The Iroquois had succeeded in establishing friendly relations with the Dutch along the Hudson, and by them were provided with guns and ammunition.[101] Thus armed they turned upon their enemies. The French had at first refrained from supplying their red allies with guns, and these now fell an easy prey to the combination of Iroquois courage and Dutch guns. In the ensuing years the Hurons were ruined, the Eries were exterminated, the region to the west, between the Ohio and the Great Lakes, was turned into a desert, and life was made a burden to the French of Canada.

The expansion of New France was shortly resumed, but the hostility of the Iroquois operated powerfully to determine its course. By their victories the Iroquois secured possession of the upper St. Lawrence and of Lakes Erie and Ontario. The French were thus prevented from expanding southward. Their natural entrance to the Great Lakes by way of the upper St. Lawrence was closed, and they were forced to seek the upper lakes by the Ottawa River route to Georgian Bay. The alliance with the Algonquins, begun by Champlain, became general, and the French control over these tribes in the Great Lakes region was firmly established. The fur trade of the great interior thus

[101] Winsor, *op. cit.*, chap. v; Turner, "Character and Influence of the Indian Trade in Wisconsin," 14.

became the chief financial support of Canada. On the other hand the English succeeded to the Dutch trade and friendship with the Iroquois, and, working through them as middlemen, competed actively with the French for the trade of the Northwest.

The effect of this combination on the execution of La Salle's designs has already been seen. The desire of the English to share in the fur trade of the Northwest furnished the principal motive for fomenting the wars between the French and the Iroquois.[102] Protection of his Indian allies against the Iroquois war parties was one of the conditions essential to the maintenance of La Salle's Illinois colony. The active competition of the English for the fur trade of the interior shortly produced another result. Before the advent of the white man in America the Indian had been economically self-sustaining.[103] Contact with civilization speedily developed in him new wants and tastes without developing the corresponding ability to satisfy them. In the fur-bearing animals of his country, however, he possessed a source of wealth greatly prized by the European peoples. Hence the basis of the barter which constituted the Indian trade. In this barter the red man should have occupied a position of equality with the white, since each possessed articles valuable in the eyes of the other. But, as always in bargaining, where the parties are unequally matched, the Indian, less intelligent and less shrewd than the white man, and dependent on the supplies of the latter for his very existence, got the worst of it. As long as the French monopolized the trade of the Northwest, so long was their control over the Indians absolute. The entrance of the English into competition for this trade, by giving the Indian another market for his furs and another source of supply of the goods needed, tended to free him from this control.

About the time of La Salle's death the Fox Indians of Wisconsin became disgruntled over the system of trade carried on

[102] Turner, "Character and Influence of the Fur Trade in Wisconsin," in *Wisconsin State Historical Society Proceedings* for 1889, 69.

[103] *American State Papers, Indian Affairs,* II, 181, 261; Turner, *Indian Trade in Wisconsin,* 32, 68.

by the French, and in particular over the attempt of the latter to establish commercial relations with the Sioux, their ancient enemy to the westward.[104] By means of their strategic position, both geographically with reference to the Fox-Wisconsin waterway which they controlled, and with respect to their relations with the various tribes to east and west, they found it possible to deal with the French on somewhat even terms. In 1687 they threatened to pillage the post at Green Bay, and before the end of the century they had effectually closed the Fox-Wisconsin highway to the Mississippi to French travel. St. Cosme's party which visited Chicago in 1698 desired to follow this route, which would have been both easier and shorter. They were forced to take the "Chicago road," however, because the Foxes would permit no one to pass the northern route for fear they would go to their enemies.[105]

The story of the wars thus opened presents a dreary succession of cruel deeds and bloody scenes, broken by intervals of inactivity, lasting for half a century.[106] The Foxes guarded with grim tenacity the Fox-Wisconsin highway; they seemed determined to block every avenue by which the French might reach the Sioux, and for many years no one might pass between Canada and Louisiana except at imminent risk of his life. In part owing to ancient relationship, in part because of the logic of the situation, the Foxes entered into friendly relations with the Iroquois and were in turn encouraged by them in their contest

[104] Turner, *op. cit.* There were two reasons for their opposition to this trade. By supplying the Sioux with firearms and goods the French enabled them to carry on their contest with the Foxes on even terms. Furthermore the Foxes desired to play the rôle of middlemen in the trade between the French and the Indians farther west. As early as 1675, according to Marquette (*Jesuit Relations*, LIX, 174), the Illinois Indians were trading in this way between the French and their own people, and already were acting "like the traders" and giving them hardly more for their furs than did the French themselves.

[105] Shea, *Early Voyages Up and Down the Mississippi*, 49.

[106] For a brief summary of the Fox wars and their results see Turner, *Indian Trade in Wisconsin*, 34-39. Fuller and more important accounts are given by Parkman, *A Half Century of Conflict*, and Hebberd, *Wisconsin under the Dominion of France*. The latter takes issue with Parkman in certain important respects. A large number of the original documents pertaining to the subject are printed in O'Callaghan, *New York Colonial Documents*, Vols. IX, X, and in *Wisconsin Historical Collections*, Vols. XVI, XVII.

with the French. For a like reason they made war upon the Illinois, the faithful allies of the French, raiding their territory again and again, sometimes even to the walls of Fort Chartres, the great French stronghold of the upper Mississippi Valley. The Foxes were fewer but no less courageous than the terrible Iroquois, and the rôle they now played in the West was curiously similar to that so long enacted on a larger scale by the Iroquois toward the French. Their opposition became so intolerable to the French that repeated attempts were made to exterminate them. The Foxes were terribly punished, and for a long time their power seemed fairly broken, the survivors being driven to abandon their homes in Wisconsin and seek refuge beyond the Mississippi. But they were not exterminated, and the French were at last compelled to give up the attempt. The dominion of France in the Northwest was itself drawing to a close; and to its downfall the long struggle with the Foxes, with its consequent drain upon the treasury of Canada and the disaffection for the French engendered by it among the northwestern tribes, materially contributed.

The first great event in the fifty-year contest occurred at Detroit in 1712. Before this post there appeared in the early summer of that year a band of a thousand Outagamies or Foxes, three hundred of them warriors, the remainder women and children. Of the siege, and the destruction of the Foxes at the hands of the French and their red allies, which ensued, two accounts differing widely from each other have come down to us.[107] The official report of Dubuisson, the French commandant at Detroit, represents that the Foxes came with hostile intent, which was manifested in their conduct from the moment of their arrival. This report has been accepted by Parkman, whose account of the siege is in effect a paraphrase of it.[108] Yet in many respects its reliability is open to question. The very fact that the Fox warriors came incumbered with seven hundred women and children suffices to show that they were not engaged

[107] For the documents see *Wisconsin Historical Collections*, XVI, 267 ff.

[108] Parkman, *Half Century of Conflict*, chap. xii.

in a hostile expedition. The other contemporary account of the affair, by DeLery, asserts it was due to a plot on the part of the French, designed to lure the obnoxious tribe to its destruction.[109] This account differs from Dubuisson's report in other respects as well; among other things DeLery represents that the Foxes evacuated their fort on the eighth day of the siege, while Dubuisson states that this occurred on the nineteenth day. It seems impossible at this day, in view of our limited information, to decide between the two conflicting versions. Concerning the main facts of the destruction of the Foxes, however, the two accounts agree fairly well; since Dubuisson's is that of an eyewitness who was at the same time the commander of the French, and moreover since it is much more detailed than DeLery's account, the following narrative of the siege is based upon it.

The Foxes constructed a fort within fifty paces of the French post and began to conduct themselves with great insolence. Since Dubuisson's allies were absent upon their hunting expedition, he felt compelled to submit to their indignities, until a party sought to kill two of the French within the fort itself. Then the commandant interfered and cleared the fort, but he was still compelled to temporize until the arrival of the Ottawa and other bands for whom he had hastily sent.

Six hundred of the allied warriors shortly arrived, burning with zeal for the destruction of the hated Foxes, whose warfare had been directed in turn against all the northwestern tribes except the Sacs, Kickapoos, and Mascoutens, their allies.[110] The French distributed arms and ammunition to the warriors and the contest was promptly joined. Their war cries "made the earth tremble," but evidently the Foxes were not similarly

[109] *Wisconsin Historical Collections*, XVI, 293–95.

[110] The story of an affair which occurred in the vicinity of Chicago affords a concrete illustration of the misdeeds by which these tribes incurred the enmity of their neighbors. Three Miami squaws who had been captured by the Iroquois had effected their escape in consequence of the defeat administered to the Senecas by Denonville's expedition in 1687. Returning to their homes, the squaws encountered at the River "Chikagou" some Mascoutens, who shortly before had assassinated two Frenchmen. The fear that the women would reveal this affair led the assassins to "break their heads." To add insult to injury they carried away the scalps of the women and gave them to the Miamis to eat, saying

affected, for they replied in kind less than a pistol shot away, and the firing began. The Foxes were badly outnumbered and in sore straits for food and water, but their ancient reputation for bravery was not belied. The French erected towers from which they fired down into the hostile camp, driving the Foxes to seek refuge in holes in the ground. In this fashion the siege was pressed for nineteen days, with alternations of hope and despair on the part of the contestants.

At one time the Foxes, perishing from thirst, adopted a ruse which smacks of the Homeric age. Covering their ramparts with scarlet blankets and erecting twelve red standards to attract attention, they addressed their opponents with taunting speeches. The great war chief of the Pottawatomies mounted one of the towers and began an eloquent reply, in which the character of the English, who were regarded as the sponsors of the Foxes, was severely handled. Meanwhile under cover of this oratorical contest the Foxes had crept out to secure a supply of water; seeing which, Dubuisson cut short the speech with an order to recommence firing and the chieftain's further opinion of the English was forever lost to the world.

The Foxes soon made overtures to surrender, but the red foe was implacable for their destruction and the French commander, reflecting that they had been set on by the English to destroy him, and that "war and pity do not well agree together," abandoned them to their fate. Taking advantage of a stormy night the survivors made their escape and fled. Dubuisson spurred on the pursuit, however, and they were brought to bay a few miles away. A second siege ensued, terminating four days later in an abject surrender. No quarter was granted to the vanquished warriors; all but a hundred were killed, and these were tied, being reserved, evidently, for future torture. This

that they were scalps of the Iroquois. For thus causing the Miamis to eat their own flesh the Great Spirit afflicted the Mascoutens with a malady which caused them and their children to die. Not satisfied with this divine vengeance, however, a party of Miamis came to Perrot in 1690 to tell him their story and obtain his assistance in a war against the Mascoutens. The French were still engrossed in their struggle with the Iroquois, however, and the Miamis were compelled to nurse their vengeance until a more opportune time (*Wisconsin Historical Collections*, XVI, 145–46).

pleasure was denied the victors, however, for all succeeded in making their escape. The conquerors returned to the fort with the enslaved women and children, where "their amusement was" to shoot four or five each day. The Hurons spared not a single one of their captives. "In this manner," concludes Dubuisson, "came to an end, Sir, these two wicked nations, who so badly afflicted and troubled all the country. Our Rev. Father chaunted a grand mass to render thanks to God for having preserved us from the enemy."

But this pious thanksgiving proved premature. The Foxes had suffered a great disaster, but only a portion of the tribe had been involved in it, and of this portion one-third of the warriors had escaped. The immediate result was that they turned on their foes with redoubled fury. Father Marest, writing only a week after Dubuisson's report was made, points out that, with their allies, the Foxes still number five hundred warriors. The French in this region will always have cause to fear an attack and travelers will always be in danger; "for the Foxes, Kickapoos, and Mascoutens are found everywhere, and they are a people without pity and without reason."[111]

The good Father's fears were amply justified. DeLery tells us that as soon as the Mascoutens and Kickapoos of the larger villages heard of the destruction of their allies, they sent out war parties to Green Bay, Detroit, and to all the routes of travel. Their Indian foes fled in terror before them, and this went on until Louvigny brought about peace four years later.[112] These are the statements of an enemy of Dubuisson, but they are amply corroborated by official sources.[113] So great was the fear of the Foxes on the part of the other tribes that they preferred death from starvation in their cabins to the risk of meeting them on their hunting expeditions. It was this interference with the prosecution of the fur trade that chiefly excited the anger of the French. Ramezay, the acting governor of Canada, observes in

[111] *Wisconsin Historical Collections*, XVI, 289.

[112] *Ibid.*, 293–95.

[113] See letters of Ramezay and Veudreuil, *ibid.*, 300–307.

a letter of September, 1714, that the merchants will this year have a gloomy confirmation of these conditions, seeing how little peltry has come down to Mackinac.

In this same year the Foxes fell upon the Illinois and killed or carried off seventy-seven of them.[114] Veudreuil, the governor, had decided the preceding year that the Foxes must be destroyed and had intrusted the task to Louvigny, the former commander at Mackinac.[115] It was planned to establish peace between the Miamis and the Illinois, who were enemies in common of the Foxes, and then to lead all the northwestern tribes friendly to the French against the Foxes and their allies.[116] This project failed of execution, however, owing to the illness of Louvigny.[117] De Lignery was therefore substituted as the leader, and a more elaborate campaign was devised. The Miamis, Ouiatanons, Illinois, and Detroit Indians were to rendezvous at Chicago under French leadership in the summer of 1715, while the coureurs de bois, the Ottawas, and the other northern tribes were to be gathered at Mackinac under De Lignery. The departure of the forces from these places was to be so timed that both would arrive at the Fox fort at the end of August. The detachment which arrived first was to invest the fort and then await the arrival of the second corps before attempting its reduction. To complete the plan, agents had been sent to the Sioux to urge them not only to refuse the Foxes an asylum, but to join the French in making war upon them.

The campaign thus elaborately projected utterly miscarried, but its story deserves a place in the history of early Chicago, none the less. The choice of Chicago as the place of rendezvous of the southern tribes was due, aside from the obvious convenience of its location, to the game of all sorts which abounded here, on which the savages could easily subsist while awaiting the arrival of the Detroit contingent.[118] An epidemic of measles assailed the Ouiatanons, and the fickle savages promptly charged

[114] Parkman, *Half Century of Conflict*, chap. xiv.

[115] *Wisconsin Historical Collections*, XVI, 298.

[116] *Ibid.*, 303–7; 319–20. [117] *Ibid.*, 312–14. [118] *Ibid.*, 319.

the deaths which resulted to the French, who had come to lead them to the place of rendezvous.[119] They were cajoled into promising, however, that such as were able would go to Chicago, and a half-dozen Frenchmen were left among them to insure their arrival by the tenth of August. The remainder of the French went on to rouse the Illinois and lead them to the meeting-place.

Meanwhile the measles continued to afflict the Ouiatanons, the death rate mounting to fifteen or twenty a day. Instead of the two hundred warriors that had been promised, the little band of Frenchmen were forced to depart on the overland march to Chicago with only one-tenth as many.[120] Their food supply was scanty, and the savages were restrained from hunting along the way by their fear of the Foxes, whose war trails leading toward Detroit were encountered. When they reached Chicago they found the Illinois and Detroit savages had not yet arrived; nor were there any signs of the canoes which were to have come from Mackinac to inform them regarding the march against the Foxes from that point. To add to their troubles two of their party were attacked by the measles, whereupon the whole band of Indians deserted the Frenchmen and returned to their homes. The latter, after waiting four or five days beyond the time set for the arrival of their comrades with the Illinois contingent, set out to meet them. In this they failed because of their ignorance of the route, and the little party found rest for the time being with the Indians at Starved Rock.

Meanwhile, what had happened to the Illinois Indians? The Frenchmen who had gone from the Ouiatanons to rouse the Illinois received a royal welcome from the Indians of the Rock, and, collecting their warriors, led a band of four hundred and fifty to Chicago, which was reached on the seventeenth of August. The leader was much mortified to find no one there and to get no news from Mackinac. To divert the savages and if possible to obtain news, scouts were sent out to a distance of

[119] *Wisconsin Historical Collections*, XVI, 322–25.

[120] *Ibid.*

thirty leagues. Their efforts were fruitless, however. On their return ten days later without any tidings, the Indians could be restrained no longer. They dispersed and the Frenchmen returned to Starved Rock, where they found their countrymen whom they had left among the Ouiatanons.

One further act remains to complete this series of misfortunes. The coureurs de bois assembled at Mackinac, but the failure of the supplies which were expected from Montreal to arrive led to the abandonment of the northern end of the expedition.[121] This explains the non-arrival of the canoes at Chicago, which had so disappointed the Ouiatanon and Illinois detachments. In ignorance of these various miscarriages the Detroit contingent arrived. From Chicago they proceeded to the Illinois village at the Rock, expecting to find there the French leaders of the enterprise.[122] They, however, were now at Kaskaskia, overcome with illness. They could only send a messenger to urge the Illinois to join the Hurons and others who composed the expedition in a foray against the Mascoutens and Kickapoos, allies of the Foxes, who were hunting "along a certain river." This was done, and in November the combined bands, accompanied by only two Frenchmen, fell upon the Mascoutens. The report of what followed must be taken with the usual allowance for statements which have an Indian origin.[123] According to their story they attacked the Mascoutens, who were stationed on a rock, and after a sharp battle forced their position, killing one hundred warriors and taking forty-seven prisoners, without counting the women and children. To conceal the route of their retreat the party went down the river

[121] *Ibid.*, 339.

[122] *Ibid.*, 341. That they came to Chicago is not directly stated, but I consider this a fair inference from this and the preceding documents.

[123] It is true there were two Frenchmen with the party, as already stated. But these had a direct interest in permitting the Indian reports to go uncorrected; one of them was, in fact, promoted for his participation in this expedition, and the other was an outlawed bushranger among the Illinois, whose "reprobate life" had been the subject of an indignant letter from the governor to the French ministry only the year before (*Wisconsin Historical Collections*, XVI, 302–3). Now, apparently, a virtue was made of necessity, and he was urged to use his influence over the Illinois to induce them to join the Hurons in the proposed expedition.

in canoes a distance of twenty-five leagues. In spite of this precaution they were overtaken on the eleventh day by four hundred men, "the elite of the Reynards." Though they numbered but eighty, and were incumbered by the prisoners and wounded, they asserted that in a battle lasting from dawn till three o'clock in the afternoon they defeated the Foxes with great loss and pursued them for several hours.

In the following year, 1716, the delayed project against the Foxes was executed. Louvigny was again intrusted with the command.[124] He left Montreal the first of May with two hundred and twenty-five Frenchmen, and two hundred more were to join him at Mackinac.[125] While en route they were joined by about four hundred Indian allies, and the whole party proceeded by way of Mackinac and Green Bay to the country of the Foxes. The latter had gathered to the number of five hundred warriors and three thousand women and children in a fort protected by three rows of oaken palisades and a ditch, located on the Fox River some distance from Green Bay. This Louvigny besieged in regular European fashion, with trenches and mining operations. The Foxes fought with spirit, although, according to Charlevoix, both besiegers and besieged believed them to be on the brink of destruction. At the end of three days, however, a surrender was arranged, terms were granted the besieged, and the invading army marched away.

The reason for this surprising outcome of the great expedition remains a matter of doubt to the present day. Louvigny asserted that the terms he imposed were so harsh that no one believed the Foxes would accede to them; and further, that his allies approved of the arrangement made.[126] The first of these statements is not worthy of serious attention, and the last the French Indians themselves indignantly denied.[127] The Fox

[124] *Wisconsin Historical Collections*, XVI, 328–30.

[125] *Ibid.*, 342. For secondary accounts of this expedition see Hebberd, *Wisconsin under the Dominion of France*, 94 ff.; Charlevoix, *History of New France* (Shea transl.), V, 305 ff.

[126] *Wisconsin Historical Collections*, XVI, 343.

[127] Charlevoix, *History of New France*, V, 306.

chieftain, Ouashala, later asserted that they could easily have escaped by means of a sortie by night, and that this had already been resolved upon. Possibly the real truth is that Louvigny was hampered by his instructions and that he feared to press the Foxes to the last extremity. It may be also that the reported approach of three hundred allies of the Foxes influenced his decision. Whatever the reason, the results from the expedition were meager. The Foxes did not fulfil the terms of their agreement with Louvigny, and although they refrained from making war on the French Indians for a time, the situation in the Northwest continued to be as intolerable to the French as ever.

The lull which followed Louvigny's expedition was soon broken, and the restless feuds between the Illinois and the Foxes and their allies were renewed. In 1719 the Foxes were again at war with the Illinois, who seem this time to have been the aggressors.[128] When Charlevoix passed down the Kankakee and Illinois rivers in 1721, he devoted a considerable portion of his journal to a description of the dangers encountered along the way.[129] At Starved Rock he was filled with horror at the spectacle of the remains of two prisoners who had been burned recently. At Lake Peoria he was informed by some Canadians that his party was in the midst of four Fox war parties. A band of Illinois had recently encountered one of them, and each party had taken a prisoner. Here as at Starved Rock the priest was horrified by the spectacle of the wretch whom the Illinois had tortured to death. Notwithstanding Charlevoix's sturdy escort, commanded by the gallant St. Ange,[130] it was considered dangerous for the party to proceed. It was strengthened somewhat and the resolution was formed to press on, but the horrors he had seen and heard so affected the good Father that for a week he was unable to sleep soundly.

[128] *Wisconsin Historical Collections*, XVIII, 381, 429, 445, 447.

[129] Charlevoix, *Histoire . . . . de la Nouvelle France*, VI, letters of September 17 and October 5, 1721.

[130] For an account of St. Ange's career in Illinois see Mason, "Illinois in the Eighteenth Century," in *Chapters from Illinois History*.

The Illinois now captured and burned the nephew of Ouashala, the principal war chief of the Foxes. The latter avenged this by laying siege the next year to the Illinois stronghold of Starved Rock. They starved the defenders into a surrender, and then, to placate the French, spared their lives.[131] Returning to their own territory the leaders hastened to Green Bay to justify to the French commandant their action in going to war. Montigny blustered and assured them that whenever Onontio[132] wished it they should "indeed die and perish without resource." To the French minister, however, Veudreuil admitted, in a report of the following year, that the Illinois directly, and indirectly the French, through their neglect to secure justice to the Foxes, were responsible for the hostilities.[133] It is evident from the reports of the French themselves that the Foxes were frequently treated unjustly by the French and their Indian allies, and that in spite of this and their natural ferocity, they at times displayed admirable patience in enduring the impositions heaped upon them.

For several years following 1725 divided counsels prevailed among the French with respect to the policy to be pursued toward the Foxes.[134] Some argued that they should be destroyed. Others agreed as to the desirability of this, but, dubious as to its practicability, counseled a policy of conciliation. The French

[131] For the original documents pertaining to this affair see *Wisconsin Historical Collections*, XVI, 418–22, 428–31.

[132] The Indian designation for the French Governor. It was later applied also to the French King.

[133] *Wisconsin Historical Collections*, XVI, 429–30. An inaccurate description of the affray at Starved Rock is given by Charlevoix (*History of New France*, VI, 71). He states that the Illinois beat off the Foxes with a loss of one hundred and twenty men, having themselves lost only twenty. He adds that the attack determined the Illinois to abandon the Rock and Lake Peoria, and join their kinsmen who had already sought refuge at Fort Chartres. No check whatever now existed to the raids of the Foxes along the Illinois River, and communication between Canada and Louisiana by this route became more impracticable than ever. It is plain, however, in spite of Charlevoix's statements, that there were Illinois at the Rock during the following years. For references to them between 1730 and 1736 see *Wisconsin Historical Collections*, XVII, 110, 183, 251. At the latter date the Illinois village numbered fifty warriors.

[134] See Parkman, *Half Century of Conflict*, chap. xiv. For the original documents see *Wisconsin Historical Collections*, Vol. XVI.

king first ordered their destruction, and then that they be let alone. A fitful peace was patched up for a time, but the receipt of information that the Foxes had promised English emissaries to kill all the French decided the latter to make war in earnest.[135]

The Foxes resisted desperately the attempt to exterminate them.[136] De Lignery led an expedition from Montreal in 1728, which on its arrival in Wisconsin numbered five hundred Frenchmen and over a thousand Indians. To this invasion of her future sister state Illinois contributed a force of twenty Frenchmen and five hundred Indians, who came by way of the Chicago Portage. The results of this great effort, however, were but slight. The Foxes abandoned their villages and retired before the French, who succeeded in capturing two squaws and an old man. The former were enslaved and the latter was roasted at a slow fire, to the scandal of Father Crespel, who expressed his surprise to the tormentors at the pleasure they derived from the performance.

Having burned the villages and ravaged the cornfields De Lignery retired, confessing his failure and placing the responsibility for it on the Illinois contingent, who should have come by way of the Wisconsin Portage instead of by Chicago, and thus have taken the Foxes in the rear. The forts upon Lake Pepin and Green Bay were evacuated, and Wisconsin was temporarily abandoned to the red man. The only recourse now before the French was to rouse against the Foxes the neighboring tribes, who by constantly harassing them might gradually wear them down.[137] This policy proved effective, and in 1729 the Foxes sued for peace. It was not granted, however, and meanwhile a chain of circumstances arising from De Lignery's humiliation of 1728 was weaving for them a disaster more terrible than that which had befallen them at Detroit in 1712.

[135] *Wisconsin Historical Collections*, XVI, 476–77.

[136] For the facts about the ensuing period see *Wisconsin Historical Collections*, Vol. XVII, editorial introduction and accompanying documents. Father Crespel's report of De Lignery's expedition is printed in Smith, *History of Wisconsin*, I, 339 ff.

[137] *Wisconsin Historical Collections*, XVIII, xiii.

When the French evacuated Fort Beauharnois[138] on Lake Pepin in 1728, they attempted to escape down the Mississippi to Fort Chartres, but were taken captive by the Kickapoos and Mascoutens, hitherto the allies of the Foxes, who had settled in eastern Iowa.[139] During the long captivity that ensued Father Guignas, one of the prisoners, succeeded in inducing their captors to desert the Foxes and sue for peace with the French.[140] Weakened by this defection the Foxes sought, by passing around the southern end of Lake Michigan and through the country of the Ouiatanons, who were well disposed toward them, to escape to the Iroquois.[141] The Kickapoos and Mascoutens reported this design to the nearest French posts, but, doubting the fidelity of their new allies, the settlers around Fort Chartres for a time declined to take the field.

Confirmation shortly arrived in the shape of information that the Foxes had captured some of the Illinois near Starved Rock and had burned the son of the great chief of the Cahokias. On this St. Ange, the commandant of Fort Chartres, conducted an expedition against them. Parties of French and of savages gathered from all directions. From Fort St. Joseph came De Villiers and his son, the latter a mere youth, destined, a quarter of a century later at Fort Necessity, to defeat and capture the youthful George Washington.

In all some twelve or thirteen hundred French and Indians surrounded the doomed Foxes. The latter had intrenched themselves in a grove on the bank of a small river, some distance to the southeast of Starved Rock.[142] Under the direction of the

[138] Named for Charles Beauharnois, governor of New France from 1726 to 1747. He was reputed to be the natural son of Louis XIV, and it has sometimes been said, though apparently incorrectly, that the Empress Josephine was descended from him.

[139] Narrative of De Boucherville, *Wisconsin Historical Collections*, XVII, 36 ff.

[140] *Ibid.*, 36 ff., 110.

[141] For the documents pertaining to this affair see *Wisconsin Historical Collections*, V, 106–7; and XVII, 100–101, 109–30.

[142] *Wisconsin Historical Collections*, XVII, 111, 115, 129. J. F. Steward (*Lost Maramech and Earliest Chicago*) locates this fort on the Fox River, in Kendall County, Illinois. This does not harmonize, however, with Hocquart's letter to the French minister, January 15, 1731, describing the place and the destruction of the Foxes.

elder De Villiers the siege was pressed with vigor. Both forces suffered from lack of food, but the necessity of the Foxes was naturally the greater. On the twenty-third day of the siege, under cover of a cold and stormy night they attempted to make their escape. Their design was revealed by the crying of the children and the besiegers promptly pursued them. As soon as daylight made it possible to distinguish friend from foe an indiscriminate slaughter began. The Fox warriors, weakened by hunger and long exertion and surrounded by overwhelming numbers, maintained their courage to the end. The women and children and old men walked in front, and the warriors stationed themselves in the rear between them and the enemy. But their line was speedily broken. Two hundred of the warriors were killed, besides an equal number of women and children. Some four or five hundred of the latter were taken prisoners and scattered as slaves among the various tribes. A few of the warriors, by throwing away their arms and ammunition, succeeded in escaping, but in such a plight that their fate was little preferable to that of the slain.

The triumph of the French over the foe that had defied them for a generation was, apparently, complete. Even their Indian allies had been moved to pity by the plight of the Foxes, but no humane sentiment animated the subjects of the Most Christian King.[143] The extirpation of the hated race was decreed, and the savage allies were spurred on to the work of destruction. By drawing in the slaves from the nations to which they had been distributed,[144] the surviving Foxes managed to assemble a village of forty-five cabins the year after their overthrow at the hands of De Villiers. The Hurons of Detroit, ancient enemies of the Foxes, assumed the task of destroying this remnant of the tribe, and sent an invitation to the band of Christian Iroquois at the Lake of the Two Mountains to join them in the work. They accepted, and in the autumn of 1731 a band of forty-seven

[143] *Wisconsin Historical Collections*, XVII, xiv, 167–69.

[144] The Illinois furnished an exception; their captives had all been put to death (*ibid.*, 163).

appeared at Detroit where they were joined by seventy-four Hurons and four Ottawas and the whole set out for Wisconsin.[145]

They followed the Indian trail to the mouth of the St. Joseph River and thence around the southern end of Lake Michigan to the Chicago Portage, where they built a fort and left in it some sick men with a guard to protect them. Some chiefs of the St. Joseph Pottawatomies came to them while here and promised if they would defer their expedition until spring they would join them. They declined to assent to this, and pushed on westward to the village of the Mascoutens and Kickapoos located on Rock River. According to the boastful report of the Indians, made on their return from the expedition, these were asked to join them but refused in terror. They were persuaded, however, to furnish guides to conduct the party to their former allies, but these prudently turned back before the village of the Foxes was reached.

Winter had now arrived and the party was suffering from hunger and the fatigue caused by the deep snow. A council was held and the old men favored turning back. The young men declined to accede to this, however, and so the party divided. The old men returned to Chicago, while the others to the number of forty Hurons and thirty Iroquois pushed on toward the Wisconsin, where they expected to find their quarry. After several days they came upon the Foxes, who promptly took to flight. For the story of what followed we have only the report of the victors, which is manifestly unreliable. It is repeated, therefore, rather as furnishing a typical illustration of an Indian report of such an encounter than because of faith in the trustworthiness of its details.

The warriors, in hot pursuit of the fleeing quarry, were astonished on reaching the top of the hill at seeing in the valley before them, on the bank of the Wisconsin, the main village of the Foxes comprising forty-six cabins. From these the men streamed forth, arms in hand, to the number of ninety, to meet them.

[145] Parkman (*Half Century of Conflict*, chap. xiv) tells the story of the expedition. For the original documents pertaining to it see *Wisconsin Historical Collections*, XVII, 148–69.

The chiefs of the attacking party exhorted their young men, volleys were exchanged, and the assailants threw aside their guns and with tomahawk and dagger drove the Foxes back into the village with great slaughter. One hundred and fifty were killed and an equal number made captive, while but ten escaped; and these, quite naked, died of cold.

This overwhelming victory is partly accounted for by the explanation that both parties to the contest fought on snowshoes, and the Foxes, being less expert in the use of these than were the Hurons and the Iroquois, were placed at a great disadvantage. Before the conflict the heathen Hurons, in spite of the remonstrance of the Christian Iroquois, "made medicine" to protect them from the hostile bullets and arrows. At the first volley the chief medicine man and four or five others of the Hurons were killed, while the Iroquois, who had prayed assiduously during the whole expedition and had placed all their reliance in the Master of Life, escaped unscathed.

After the battle the victors released a wounded Fox warrior and sent him with six of the women to carry the pleasant message to the remaining villages that their chief village had just been eaten up by the Hurons and the Iroquois, who would remain there for two days; the Foxes were welcome to follow them, but as soon as they should see them they would "break the heads" of their women and children and make a rampart of their dead bodies, and would endeavor to complete the work by piling the remainder of the nation on top of them. Strangely enough it does not appear that this invitation was accepted.

As usual the Fox version of this action was never told. We may well believe that another serious defeat was dealt them, for the war party returned to Detroit with one hundred captives and reported having killed some fifty on the way. Further than this we cannot safely go. The tribe was not exterminated, however much its power was broken. After the decisive overthrow of the Foxes in 1730 the French re-established the post of Green Bay, and hither, in 1733, came De Villiers, the leader in that conflict. In this same year Beauharnois, the governor, had again resolved that the Foxes must be exterminated.[146] De Villiers rashly attempted to seize some who had taken refuge with the Sacs and in the mêlée that ensued the commandant, together with his son and a number of the French, was slain.[147] The Sacs, retreating, were followed by the French and a drawn battle ensued.

The consequences of this embroilment were far-reaching. The Sacs were kinsmen of the Foxes, but hitherto they had held aloof from them and had submitted to French control. Together with the Foxes many now withdrew from Wisconsin and established themselves west of the Mississippi within the boundaries of the modern state of Iowa. From this time, therefore, dates the confederation of the two tribes. This migration did not end the struggle, however. The French felt that the affair at Green Bay must be avenged if they would retain their influence over the tribes of the Northwest. It was recognized that De Villiers' foolhardiness, rather than misconduct on the part of the Sacs, had occasioned his death, and it was therefore determined to pardon them on condition that they abandon the Foxes and return to their French allegiance. If they refused this reparation they were to be destroyed.

In August, 1734, sixty Frenchmen under the command of the Sieur De Noyelles set out from Montreal for a winter expedition against the distant tribes.[148] The party was to go to Detroit, and from thence either by way of Mackinac or "in a strait line overland," according to circumstances. In addition to his sixty Frenchmen De Noyelles was accompanied by bands of Iroquois from the Lake of the Two Mountains and Hurons from Detroit, and in case he decided to follow the overland route from Detroit he was to arrange a rendezvous with Celeron who was to lead a mixed force of French and Indians from Mackinac.

The ultimate failure of the expedition was decreed even before it started. The chief reliance for the punishment of the Sacs

[146] *Wisconsin Historical Collections*, XVII, 182.

[147] On this affair see *ibid.*, pp. xv, 188–91, 200–204.

[148] For the documents pertaining to this expedition see *Wisconsin Historical Collections*, XVII, 206 ff.

and Foxes was placed in the friendly Indians, who largely outnumbered the French. To provide even the small number of the latter which had been decided upon necessitated stripping Canada of one-tenth of her armed defenders.[149] The policy which had been determined upon with respect to the Sacs has already been indicated. In accordance with it De Noyelles was ordered to grant peace to them on condition that they give up the Foxes; otherwise he was to destroy both nations and to let his red allies "eat them up."[150] The expectation of enjoying this pleasure was the sole inducement for the Huron and Iroquois contingents to engage in the enterprise; yet they were deceived by De Noyelles as to the nature of his orders. When the Hurons, in council, stated that they would not march unless he had orders to destroy the Sacs as well as the Foxes, he replied, without further explanation, that he had orders "to Eat up both nations."[151] When this deception was discovered, the Hurons and Iroquois declined to assist De Noyelles further, and this, as will be seen, caused not only the failure of the expedition, but came near resulting in the complete destruction of the Frenchmen engaged in it.

When De Noyelles reached Detroit it was decided to continue overland. This involved passing around the southern end of Lake Michigan and through the tribe of the Ouiatanons, located on the upper Wabash.[152] Here it was learned that six cabins of the Sacs had established themselves on the St. Joseph River, having taken refuge here, in a region where the French influence was strongest, in token of their desire for peace. De Noyelles' Huron and Iroquois allies, however, having come out in search of Sac and Fox scalps, immediately declared their intention of going to "eat up" these six cabins. De Noyelles protested against this, explaining to them, apparently for the first time, his instructions to spare the Sacs who made their submission to the French. In spite of all he could do the Hurons

[149] *Ibid.*, 208, footnote. [150] *Ibid.*, 209–10. [151] *Ibid.*, 256–57.

[152] The French established a fort near the site of the modern city of Lafayette, Indiana, about the year 1720. For its location and history see Oscar J. Craig, "Ouiatanon," in *Indiana Historical Society Publications*, Vol. II, No. 8.

persisted in their design, and departed in a body to execute it. The Iroquois stayed with De Noyelles, but their disaffection, which in the end was to bring the expedition to naught, dates from this incident.

The documents left us do not permit a detailed statement concerning the route followed from the country of the Ouiatanons to the Mississippi. De Noyelles had planned to go by way of the Illinois, but this was given up because of the long dêtour it would necessitate. From the Ouiatanons he proceeded to the Kickapoo tribe, on leaving which five Sacs en route to the St. Joseph River were captured. Under threat of torture these were forced to guide the party to the Fox village. It is clear that the expedition rounded Lake Michigan and traveled in a general northwesterly direction. It is possible and even probable that it passed by the site of Chicago, as did the Huron-Iroquois party of 1731; but since the party was traveling overland on snowshoes, and was thus not bound to follow the river courses, the route taken by it cannot be definitely known.

From the prisoners it was learned that the Foxes had left their posts on the Pomme de Cigne River—the modern Wapsipinacon—where they had established themselves on retiring from Wisconsin after the death of the two De Villiers, in 1733, and had withdrawn to the river Des Moines. On crossing the Mississippi, the supply of provisions having become low, the party was forced to content itself with one "very inferior" meal each day. On March 12 the Fox fort was reached; it was deserted, but the intense cold compelled a halt of two days, during which the party was entirely without food. Meanwhile reconnoitering parties had been sent out, and these now returned to report that they had seen smoke. The little army moved forward by night, crossing several rivers with the water up to the men's waists. A halt was made behind a hill and the men, wrapped in their robes, tired, wet through, and hungry, awaited the dawn. They then advanced again; the Indians, believing the goal was at hand, and that the hostile village numbered only four cabins, eager to have the honor of arriving first, proceeded at a run for four or five leagues, the Frenchmen following as best they could. The race ended on the bank of a wide and rapid river, full of floating ice. On the opposite bank stood the village they had come so far to seek; but in place of four or five cabins it numbered fifty-five.

The river was the Des Moines, the largest western tributary of the Mississippi above the Missouri; and the point where the village stood was sixty leagues from its mouth, in the vicinity, probably, of the modern capital of Iowa. Nontagarouche, the Iroquois war chief, proposed to De Noyelles that the whole party should swim across. This the latter declared to be impossible, on account of the cold. He further pointed out that they had only sixty men at hand, the others having scattered in search of the village, the tracks of whose occupants they had been following; and that, even if it were possible, the enemy would kill them as fast as they landed. He proposed, therefore, to reassemble the party and, as they were still undiscovered, to go higher up the river and construct rafts on which to cross over. They would then be in a position to attack the enemy with arms in their hands, and with some prospect of success. Nontagarouche replied that De Noyelles "was no man." At this the brave Frenchman's anger blazed forth. "Dog," he cried, "if thou art so brave, swim over and let us see what Thou wilt do."

The chief did not immediately avail himself of this invitation, but his insubordination destroyed the last hope of a successful issue of the campaign. The details of the action that followed are not entirely clear, though its main features may be followed with assurance. The Iroquois, with some of the French, left the commander, who proceeded along the river about a league. Meanwhile others of the army, probably some of those who had spread out in search of the hostile village, had crossed the river on a jam of driftwood and logs, and joined battle with the enemy. The advance party, consisting of seven Frenchmen and twenty-three Indians, thus found itself confronted by two hundred and fifty Sacs and Foxes. Onorakinguiah, an Iroquois chief from the Sault St. Louis, cried out: "My French and

Indian brothers, we are dead men, but we must sell our lives very dearly and not let ourselves be captured." They fought so fiercely that the foe was at first driven back. On perceiving the small number of their opponents, however, they pressed forward with the design of surrounding them, seeing which the French and Iroquois in turn retreated, fighting as best they might. One of them ran to report the situation to De Noyelles, who had crossed the river and returned to the village which he found had been deserted. On receiving the report of the plight of the advance guard he sent forward all of the men who were with him, with word that he would join them with the main body as soon as it should arrive. A half-hour later he moved forward with such as had joined him in the meantime, and the combat was continued for several hours.

Toward nightfall the Foxes attempted to scalp the wounded on the other side. This led De Noyelles to order his force to fall back in search of a suitable spot to fortify. A detachment of fifty men was made to continue the fighting and cover the work of the remainder while constructing the fort. Meanwhile the contingent of Kickapoos observed the contest from a near-by eminence, debating, as De Noyelles feared, whether they should join forces with the enemy.

The next day through the instrumentality of the disaffected Iroquois a council was held with the Sacs. They informed De Noyelles that but for the fact that the French had attacked them, and for the small number of Frenchmen, they would have surrendered; but that as the French were inferior in number to the Iroquois they feared the latter, when they were at a distance from the Foxes, would "put them in the Kettle." According to his own story, De Noyelles adopted in reply the tone of a conqueror. The Sacs were told they might come forth in perfect safety, and were promised protection from the Iroquois. In truth, De Noyelles had so little control over his allies that he could not protect his own soldiers from being beaten by them before his face. This fear removed, however, the Sacs discovered other obstacles. The weather was too cold for their women and children to travel; if the Sacs really had any desire to join the French the project was effectually prevented by the Foxes. They informed their allies that in case they deserted to the French they would immediately "eat" their women and children.

For four days longer the French faced their foe. During this time they were sorely beset by hunger, their menu consisting of twelve dogs and a horse; this supply being exhausted, they were reduced to eating their moccasins. The Iroquois now proposed to abandon them, and De Noyelles was forced to give up the enterprise. He covered his failure as well as possible by sending a "collar"[153] to the Sacs offering to grant them their lives on condition that they desert the Foxes and return to their old homes at Green Bay. This the Sacs promised to do. The French then retired and made their way to Fort Chartres.[154]

The expedition had extended over seven months of time during which the party had traversed hundreds of miles of wilderness in the dead of winter, exposed to the inclemency of the elements, and much of the time in immediate peril of starvation. At the end, confronted by two hundred and fifty Sacs and Foxes, and with disaffection rife among his Indian allies, De Noyelles had been compelled to give up and retreat. The only immediate result was the infliction of a slight loss upon the enemy in the battle, and the promise of the Sacs to abandon the Foxes and return to Green Bay. Both the governor and the intendant joined in approval of the conduct of De Noyelles, the intendant expressing his surprise that Frenchmen should be able to endure the hardships which his party had surmounted.[155] The governor declared that the savages admitted the courage of the French to be equal to every obstacle, and that they would seek the enemy "at the end of the world."[156]

[153] A belt to accompany a formal communication of a public character.

[154] For the narrative of this expedition I have drawn chiefly upon the report of De Noyelles, printed in *Wisconsin Historical Collections*, XVII, 221–30. It differs from the report of Hocquart, the intendant, in some respects, but aside from the fact that De Noyelles was the leader of the expedition while Hocquart remained in Canada, the latter had an interest in misrepresenting the facts, in order to minimize as much as possible the failure which had occurred.

[155] *Wisconsin Historical Collections*, XVII, 232.

[156] *Ibid.*, 219.

With the failure of De Noyelles' expedition the French felt constrained to resort to a policy of conciliation. Grave fears were entertained for a time lest the failure should have a disastrous effect upon their authority throughout the Northwest generally. If the dispatches of the governor and the intendant of Canada are to be credited, however, no such result manifested itself. But scattered here and there throughout the dispatches of this period are intimations that all was not going well with the French, and the truth seems to be that the long contest with the Foxes, with its attendant consequences, had greatly weakened their hold upon the northwestern tribes. It is plain from their own dispatches that the French did not dare to attempt the extermination of the Sacs; nor, even after all the disasters which they had suffered, to prosecute further the policy of exterminating the Foxes. The latter sued for peace, but at the same time succeeded in entering into a new alliance with the Sioux who promised them an asylum in case of need.[157] Beauharnois, the governor, sagely concluding that "there Was danger in driving the Reynards to despair," offered to pardon them on condition that they disperse among the other tribes and that no mention ever be made of the name of the Reynards, "who had so often Disturbed the earth."[158]

The French found it impossible, however, to carry out even the new policy of mildness toward the obnoxious tribe. Their efforts to compel the Sacs to return to their old home near Green Bay were unsuccessful. Various excuses were given: the land had lost its fertility on account of its being stained with the blood of the French and of themselves. Probably the real reason, however, was the one given by some spokesmen of the Sacs and Foxes who had settled on Rock River, at a conference held in the spring of 1739. They stated that they had determined to return to "LaBaye" as Onontio had desired them, but they had been told by many French and savages that the French desired their return only in order that they might the more easily slaughter

[157] *Wisconsin Historical Collections*, XVII, 258-59. [158] *Ibid.*, 258, 275-76.

them, and that an army of French and their allies was already prepared for this purpose.[159]

Whatever truth there may have been in this at the time, the Foxes could hardly be blamed, in view of what had gone before, for their suspicions. Their alliance with the Sioux was continued and the tribes in common made war upon the Chippewas and the Illinois, both allies of the French.[160] The Foxes took the further precaution of entering into an understanding with the Iroquois, similar to that already entered into with the Sioux, which secured them an asylum in time of need.[161] They were thus prepared, in case of a new French attack, to retreat in either direction to safety.

That these precautions, and the suspicions of French treachery toward them, were not without reason, is shown by the dispatches of Beauharnois. In a speech to the representatives of the Sacs and Foxes at Montreal in July, 1743, the Governor assured them he had no hostile disposition toward them, and urged them not to listen to the "evil words" that came to them from the St. Joseph River.[162] He further directed that the bands located at Chicago, Milwaukee, and on Rock River should join those who had returned to their old home near Green Bay.[163] Yet he had secretly planned an expedition for the year 1742 to destroy them, and the project had been approved by his advisers on the ground that for several years the French Court had had "nothing so much at heart" as the destruction of the Foxes.[164]

That the French did not dare to execute this program is sufficiently evident. Their power in the Northwest was tottering, and in 1743 Beauharnois confessed that he was powerless to hinder the union of the Sioux with the Foxes.[165] The tribe

[159] *Ibid.*, 320.

[160] Hebberd, *Wisconsin Under the Dominion of France*, 147.

[161] *Wisconsin Historical Collections*, XVII, 339.

[162] This refers to the French who came from the St. Joseph to carry on a trade, apparently illicit, with the Foxes at Chicago and Milwaukee.

[163] *Wisconsin Historical Collections*, XVII, 404–5.

[164] *Ibid.*, 338–39.

[165] *Ibid.*, 435–38.

whose destruction had so often been decreed and so many times attempted could at last defy the French with impunity. A few years later the disaffection among the Indians for the French culminated in a widespread revolt.[166] Even the Illinois, with whom allegiance to the French had become proverbial, for a time inclined to join it. The danger was surmounted for the time being but the struggle of the French to maintain themselves was shortly transferred to a far wider field. In the upper Ohio Valley they joined in deadly combat with the English. The immediate stake was the control of the Indian trade of the Mississippi Valley, and so, appropriately enough, the contest was inaugurated by a descent on Pickawillany, the center of influence of the English traders in the Northwest, by a band of French Indians led by the young Wisconsin half-breed fur trader, Charles de Langlade.[167] The larger stake was the commercial and political supremacy of three continents and all the seas. The struggle was accordingly waged on a world-wide scale. When it ended the dominion of France in North America had passed forever. We shall have occasion still to deal with the French, whose influence long persisted in the Northwest, but henceforth the shaping of the destiny of Chicago and the tributary region rested with the Anglo-Saxon.

[166] *Wisconsin Historical Collections*, XVII, 456–69, 478–93.

[167] Turner, *Indian Trade in Wisconsin*, 40–41.

CHAPTER IV

CHICAGO IN THE REVOLUTION

The years from 1754 to 1760 witnessed the overthrow of the power of France in the new world. For the fourth time in two generations England and France had joined in deadly combat. Twice the issue ended in a drawn contest; twice France was overwhelmed, and the English gained a decisive victory. Each of these great wars had its American counterpart, and the outcome of each was reflected in the disposition made in the treaty of peace of the territories of the warring nations in America. At the close of the two drawn contests there were no territorial changes. By the Treaty of Utrecht, which closed the Spanish Succession War, however, England made substantial territorial gains in North America at the expense of her defeated rival. Finally, by the Treaty of Paris of 1763, which registered the results of the Seven Years' War, France lost all of her vast American possessions on the mainland. Canada passed into the hands of the English, while the imperial domain of Louisiana, in the establishment of which La Salle and Tonty and many another intrepid Frenchman had toiled and died, was divided; all that lay west of the Mississippi was given to Spain, while the portion drained by the eastern tributaries of that stream fell to the English.

What the dividing line between Canada and Louisiana had been in the French period is not easy to determine. Nor is it necessary to our purpose to do so, for whether it had belonged to Canada or Louisiana, the region tributary to Chicago, since known as the old Northwest, was now the property of England. Her civilized rival crushed, however, another foe arose to resist the assumption by England of possession of her new-won territory. The idea of passing under the control of the English was extremely distasteful to a large proportion of the northwestern

Indians. Under the leadership of Pontiac a conspiracy was formed in the spring of 1763 to wipe out in a day all the English posts from Pennsylvania to Lake Superior.[168] The execution of this terrible project stopped short of complete success. Fort Pitt and Detroit withstood the attacks of the savages. But Green Bay and Sault Ste. Marie were abandoned; the forts at Mackinac, Sandusky, Miami, St. Joseph, Ouiatanon, Presqu' Isle, and Venango were taken; and over two thousand frontier settlers were slain.

The storm had not broken entirely without warning, and the effort to relieve the posts that still held out and to subdue the obstreperous savages was promptly begun. In August Colonel Bouquet threw a relieving force into Fort Pitt, having beaten off the savages at Bushy Run in a bloody battle of two days' duration. The following season two armies were sent into the Indian country between the Great Lakes and the Ohio. A force under Bradstreet passed by way of Niagara and the southern shore of Lake Erie to Detroit, from which place detachments were sent out to take possession of Sault Ste. Marie, Mackinac, and Green Bay. In the fall of 1764 Bouquet with the second army crossed the Ohio River and advanced into the valley of the Muskingum where, in November, the tribes of the surrounding region were forced to subscribe to the terms of peace which the invader imposed upon them.

Not until another year had passed did the English gain possession of the country bordering on the Illinois and the Wabash.[169] A force of four hundred men with which Major Loftus attempted to ascend the Mississippi to Fort Chartres in the spring of 1764 was defeated and driven back, when only two hundred and forty miles above New Orleans. A year later Lieutenant Fraser was sent down the Ohio from Fort Pitt to warn the tribes and the French of the prospective approach of

[168] The classic account of these events is Parkman's *Conspiracy of Pontiac*. For a brief narrative see Winsor, *Mississippi Basin*, chaps. xxii, xxiii.

[169] For the facts given here I have relied on Winsor, *Mississippi Basin*. Edward G. Mason has written charmingly of these events in his *Chapters from Illinois History*.

a force of troops which was to follow after him. He succeeded in reaching the Illinois villages, but was glad to flee in disguise down the Mississippi. He owed his life to the protection of Pontiac, but before granting it that terrible chieftain had "kept him all one night in dread of being boiled alive."[170] A second herald now set out, in the person of the redoubtable George Croghan, to descend the Ohio from Fort Pitt to Fort Chartres. Near the mouth of the Wabash, however, he was seized by a band of Indians and carried prisoner to Vincennes. He was subsequently released at Ouiatanon, and made a treaty with the neighboring tribes; proceeding to Detroit he repeated his success with the savages there, and then returned to Niagara. On the receipt of Croghan's report of his success in treating with the Indians, a force of one hundred and twenty Highlanders of the famous Black Watch Regiment proceeded down the Ohio from Fort Pitt, and on October 10, 1765, at Fort Chartres of the Illinois, in the heart of the Mississippi Valley, the last banner of France east of the Mississippi was hauled down. "The lilies of France gave place to the red cross of St. George, and the long struggle was ended."[171] The control of the British over this region which was thus at last established was to continue unchallenged by a civilized power less than a decade and a half.

The old Northwest, to which Chicago belonged, did not participate actively in the Revolutionary struggle during its earlier stages. At the beginning of the war the British were, of course, in possession of all the Northwest. The vantage points from which they directed the affairs of this region were, in general, the old French posts, now occupied by British garrisons. Among these may be named Detroit, Mackinac, Fort Gage, and Cahokia. The first named of these was easily the most important center of British influence in the Northwest, being looked upon as the headquarters of the posts and the key to the fur trade and to the control of the Indian tribes of this region.[172] The fort was

[170] Mason, *op. cit.*, 234.

[171] *Ibid.*, 235.

[172] James, "Indian Diplomacy and Opening of the Revolution in the West," in *Wisconsin State Historical Society, Proceedings*, 1909, 125.

defended by a palisade of pickets and contained at the beginning of the year 1776 a garrison of one hundred and twenty men. In the town and country adjoining were three hundred and fifty men, mostly French, capable of bearing arms; and to complete the tale of Detroit's military resources, there floated in the river opposite the fort several tiny public vessels with crews aggregating thirty "seamen and servants."

The only other considerable centers of white population in the Northwest were the old French posts on the Wabash, Ouiatanon and Vincennes, and, most populous of all, the settlements along the eastern shore of the Mississippi from the mouth of the Missouri to the mouth of the Ohio, on what later came to be known as the "American Bottom." At Ouiatanon, at the beginning of the Revolution there were about a dozen French families.[173] Vincennes had, in 1776, according to the report of Lieutenant Fraser, about sixty farmers.[174] This would imply a total population of between two and three hundred, and this estimate is borne out by a "census" of Indiana of 1769. This lists the names of sixty-six "Inhabitants" and states that in addition there are fifty women and one hundred and fifty children "belonging to the Inhabitants."[175] There were, at this time, fifty men capable of bearing arms, and during the next half-dozen years the population increased somewhat.

In the Illinois settlements of the American Bottom in 1778 there was a population of about one thousand whites, and as many Indians and negroes.[176] The more populous settlements were Cahokia, with three hundred white inhabitants, and Kaskaskia, with five hundred whites and almost as many negroes.

[173] *Indiana Historical Society, Publications*, II, 338.

[174] *Ibid.*, 410.

[175] *Ibid.*, 439. Hamilton, who captured the place in 1778, states, however, that he found 621 inhabitants of whom 217 were able to bear arms (*Michigan Pioneer and Historical Society Collections*, IX, 495). This work will be cited henceforth as *Michigan Pioneer Collections*.

[176] For an account of these settlements see the introduction to the Cahokia Records, *Illinois Historical Collections*, II, pp. xiii ff.

For the rest, the vast region which now teems with a population as prosperous and as highly civilized as any on the face of the globe was a wilderness. The Indian tribes could muster, according to the usual estimates, about eight thousand warriors, which would imply a total population several times as large.[177] The Chippewas alone numbered over half of this total. Our interest, however, is concerned rather with certain of the smaller tribes. Around the southern end of Lake Michigan, with a village at Chicago but with their principal seat on the St. Joseph River, were the Pottawatomies, numbering some four hundred warriors. To the south and southeast of these, in the modern states of Indiana and Ohio, were the Miamis, Shawnees, and other tribes, who were to contest the possession of the Northwest with the Americans even more fiercely than did Great Britain herself. To the north, at Milwaukee, was located a "horrid set of refractory Indians," according to the picturesque language of Colonel De Peyster, which seems to have been composed of the off-scourings of various tribes and bands. To the west and northwest, in northern Illinois and the state of Wisconsin, were the descendants of the Sacs and Foxes, the Winnebagoes, and other tribes.

The advancing wave of English settlement pouring into the upper Ohio Valley had precipitated the French and Indian War. As yet this tidal wave of civilization had not crossed the Ohio, although it had spread out along its eastern valley as far south as Tennessee. The most important point along this extensive frontier was still, as in the days of the old war, Fort Pitt at the Forks of the Ohio.[178] It was the center, therefore, from which radiated the American efforts to control the northwestern tribes, just as, at a later date, it afforded the principal gateway through which the flood of civilization poured into this region.[179]

The Americans at first strove to secure the neutrality of the Indians in the impending contest. But the disposition of the

[177] James, *op. cit.*, 137; Walker, *The Northwest during the Revolution*, 12.

[178] James, *op. cit.*, 126.

[179] On the rival efforts to control the northwestern tribes in the early period of the Revolution see *ibid.*, 125 ff.

red man did not permit him to stand idly by while a war was going on, and the British more wisely directed their efforts to securing his active support. This policy was shortly copied by the Americans, and soon the perplexed red men were being plied with rival solicitations for alliance, accompanied by corresponding threats of punishment and prophecies of disaster which were to follow their failure to comply. The British urged them on to assail the outlying settlements of the American frontiers, counseling humanity to the vanquished, but effectually nullifying this counsel by offering rewards for all scalps brought in. Lieutenant-governor Hamilton at Detroit was particularly zealous in hounding the Indians on to the work of devastation.[180] The Americans, to their honor, offered rewards for prisoners but none for scalps.

Two courses of action were open to the Americans in view of this situation. They might endeavor to punish the hostile Indians by launching retaliatory expeditions against them; or they might by capturing Detroit, from whence issued alike the supplies for the marauders and payment for the scalps they took, destroy the opposition at its fountain-head.[181] The latter course was urged by Colonel Morgan, the Indian agent for the Middle Department, a man of much experience among the Indians of the Northwest. The reasons which he advanced in support of this policy and against the alternative one were telling,[182] but his advice went unheeded. Seeing this, and believing a general Indian war was about to be precipitated, he resigned his office; the control of the Western Department passed into incompetent hands, and it seemed probable that the western frontier was about to be overrun by the British and Indians when an important diversion occurred. The advent of the Virginia "Hannibal," George Rogers Clark, in the Illinois country, compelled the British at Detroit to turn their attention to the defense of the Northwest, and shortly of Detroit itself, against the invader.

[180] James, *op. cit.;* Thwaites, *How George Rogers Clark Won the Northwest,* 8–10. Hamilton himself vigorously denied the charges of inhumanity which the Americans preferred against him. *Michigan Pioneer Collections,* IX, 490.

[181] James, *op. cit.*, 141–42.

[182] For a statement of them, see *ibid.*

In 1776 Clark had cast in his lot with the young settlements of Kentucky.[183] These were nominally a part of Virginia, but in fact they were too remote to receive much protection from the mother colony. It was congenial, too, to the spirit of the American frontiersman to depend upon himself, and Clark, who had come to the conclusion that the only means of obtaining safety was to carry the war into the enemy's country, was one of those who favored action independently of authorization from the government of Virginia.

Other counsels prevailed, however. The protection of the parent colony was sought, and as a result the Virginia Assembly declared the extension of its authority over the region and in December, 1776, created the county of Kentucky.[184] The next summer Clark learned from spies whom he had sent into the Illinois settlements that the French settlers were lukewarm in their allegiance to Great Britain and that only a few of them were participating in the raids against the Americans, which, fomented from Detroit, made these settlements their starting-point and base of operations. Fired by these reports with the purpose to conquer the Illinois settlements, he proceeded the same summer to Virginia. Here he laid his project before Governor Henry and received his authorization to raise and equip a force of troops for the work, and with this and a scanty supply of money he returned to Kentucky and launched the enterprise.

In the spring of 1778 Clark collected a little army of about one hundred and fifty men at Redstone, now Brownsville, Pennsylvania, and dropped down the Monongahela and Ohio, taking on supplies and reinforcements at Pittsburgh and other places along the way. At the Falls of the Ohio, where the metropolis of Kentucky now stands, he paused long enough to

[183] Many of the original documents pertaining to Clark's career in the Northwest have been printed in the *Illinois Historical Collections*, Vol. I; the *Michigan Pioneer Collections;* and the *Wisconsin Historical Collections*. Among the secondary accounts may be mentioned Dunn, *Indiana;* Winsor, *Westward Movement*, chap. viii; Thwaites, *How George Rogers Clark Won the Northwest*.

[184] Winsor, *Westward Movement*, 116.

build a blockhouse on Corn Island. On June 24, while the sun was obscured by a great eclipse, the journey was renewed, the objective being Kaskaskia, the principal settlement of the Illinois country. At Fort Massac the little party landed and began the overland march of one hundred and twenty miles to Kaskaskia. On the way the hunter who had been engaged to guide them lost his bearings. This created some excitement, and caused Clark, who suspected treachery, to threaten him with death unless he found the way that evening. In this he succeeded, and accordingly the afternoon of July 4 found the party within three miles of the goal.

Clark halted his little army until nightfall, when he advanced to a farmhouse a mile from the town, and seizing the family secured information of the conditions that prevailed there. Thus armed, the party moved forward in two divisions and surrounded the place. We may safely dismiss to the limbo of myth the romantic story of Clark's appearance, alone, at the ball where garrison and villagers were disporting themselves, and his dramatic announcement to the merrymakers that the dance might go on, but it must be under the banner of Virginia.[185] The story betrays too conspicuously the handiwork of the romancer. It is clear, however, that garrison and townsmen were completely surprised, and surrendered without a blow being struck or a gun fired. By a judicious mixture of bluster and leniency Clark soon succeeded in gaining the hearty support of the villagers. One of his most effective allies was the priest, Father Gibault, who assured Clark that although, by reason of his calling, he had "nothing to do with temporal business, that he would give them such hints in the Spiritual way, that would be very conducive to the business."[186]

[185] On this see Thwaites, *op. cit*, 28-31. I have drawn freely on this reference and on Winsor, *Westward Movement*, for the facts concerning Clark's expedition.

[186] Thwaites, *op. cit.*, 33. That he kept his promise is sufficiently attested by Hamilton, who describes him as a "wretch," "who absolved the French inhabitants from their allegiance to the King of Great Britain," and "an active agent for the rebels & whose vicious & immoral conduct was sufficient to do infinite mischief in a country where ignorance & bigotry give full scope to the depravity of a licentious ecclesiastic."—*Michigan Pioneer Collections*, XIX, 487.

The Cahokians readily followed the lead of the Kaskaskians in submitting to Clark's rule; so, too, did the inhabitants of Vincennes, to whom Father Gibault went as an emissary of Clark. Thus far Clark's success had been unchecked; as far as the French settlers were concerned, the British power had crumbled. But the Indians were still to be reckoned with, and the British at Detroit to be heard from, and Clark's resources were pitifully inadequate for the task in hand. Even a large part of his Virginia troops abandoned him on the expiration of their term of enlistment. With such as consented to remain, augmented by enlistments on the part of the French whom he had come to conquer, Clark maintained his position throughout the winter. None knew better than he how to combine in the right proportions terrible energy, braggadocio, tact, and cajolery. Friendly relations were established with De Leyba, the Spanish commander at St. Louis. The Indians were handled so adroitly that an "Amazeing number" flocked in from five hundred miles around to treat for peace and learn the will of the Big Knife Chief.

Meanwhile on August 6, 1778, the news had come to Hamilton at Detroit of the capture of Kaskaskia, and he promptly began preparations for the recovery of the posts that had been lost.[187] On October 7 he set out from Detroit by boat with nearly two hundred whites, chiefly volunteers, and three hundred Indians. The destination was Vincennes, and the route followed led up the Maumee and down the Wabash River. Although expedition was all-important, the progress made was tedious and slow. Not until December 17 was Vincennes reached. On the news of Hamilton's approach the French militia of Captain Helm, Clark's representative, deserted him. Again, as in the case of the capture of Kaskaskia by Clark, a melodramatic tale is told of the capture of the fort. Helm, with his garrison dwindled to a single man, is represented as standing, lighted match in hand, by a well-charged cannon which he has placed in the fort gate,

[187] For Hamilton's own narrative of his course see *Michigan Pioneer Collections*, IX, 489 ff. His correspondence is printed in *Illinois Historical Collections*, I, 330 ff.

halting the British force, and surrendering with the honors of war. The story is without adequate historical foundation and may properly be dismissed as a pleasing bit of fiction.

Although Vincennes surrendered without resistance, the delays which had been encountered proved fatal to Hamilton's project. If he had pushed on to Kaskaskia at once it seems certain that Clark must have succumbed. But winter having now arrived, Hamilton decided to remain at Vincennes until spring, when he would not only retake the Illinois settlements but turn the tables on the invaders by sweeping the Americans from Kentucky.

Pending the arrival of spring, the greater part of Hamilton's force was dispersed. Not until the last of January did full news of the situation at Vincennes and the projected vernal attack upon Kaskaskia come to Clark. As soon as he had quelled the panic which the tidings caused among the Kaskaskians, he projected a counter-assault upon Vincennes. An armed galley was sent around by water, down the Mississippi and up the Ohio and the Wabash to a point ten leagues below Vincennes, where it was to await the arrival of Clark, who, meanwhile, would lead a force overland across Illinois. The story of the difficulties encountered and vanquished on the march of this little force across the Illinois swamps and prairies surpasses many a flight of fiction. It was February and a thaw that had set in had flooded the lowlands and driven away the game. To the fatigues and discomforts of wading swollen rivers and marching through boggy and oftentimes "drowned" land in midwinter were added the pangs of hunger. The last stage necessitated the crossing of miles of bottom land overflowed to the depth of three feet and upward by the swollen waters of the rivers. Here the sufferings of the party were such that Clark avers that the bare recital of them would be "too incredible for any Person to believe except those that are well acquainted with me."

It had been Clark's purpose to take the garrison by surprise but on learning from some villagers whom he captured that the force of British and French largely outnumbered his own, and that the villagers were not ill-disposed toward the Americans, he changed his plan. Fearing that in the fight that would doubtless ensue some of the French and Indians would be slain and that this would embitter the rest, he determined to bluff the garrison and the town into a surrender. Halting his little army in sight of the town, but concealed from the view of the garrison, he sent a menacing letter ahead, designed to awe the townsmen into submission. At nightfall, with the garrison still ignorant of his approach, Clark's men moved into the village. The creoles greeted them with enthusiasm, and the fickle Indians, who made up the larger portion of Hamilton's force, either offered to join Clark or drew aside to await the issue of the contest between the palefaces.

The British had been attracted by the commotion and the discharge of guns, but not until a sergeant received a bullet in the breast did they know whether to attribute the cause to some jollification or to the arrival of the "Virginians." Throughout the night and early morning Clark's riflemen harassed the garrison. About eight o'clock, while his men stopped for breakfast, a summons to surrender was dispatched to Hamilton. It was received by the garrison with mingled feelings of defiance and despair. According to Hamilton, the British assured him they would stick to him "as the shirt to my back," while the French "hung their heads." The firing was resumed, but later in the day Hamilton agreed to surrender. The next morning, February 25, 1779, the fort changed hands and name as well, for the Americans now christened it Fort Patrick Henry, in honor of the governor of Virginia.

Clark's ultimate goal was the capture of Detroit, but with his small force and scanty supplies he could not at once move forward. While waiting for reinforcements he applied himself vigorously to the work of governing his newly won territory, establishing satisfactory relations with the Indians, and preparing the way for the greater exploit which he was destined never to perform. To this work the ensuing spring and summer were devoted.

Meanwhile certain events were taking place in the region west of Lake Michigan and the vicinity of Chicago which now demand our attention. When Hamilton began preparations for his expedition in the autumn of 1778, he sent word to De Peyster, who commanded at Mackinac, to raise the Indians tributary to that post and co-operate with him by an expedition down the Illinois River.[188] Many of the Indians who frequented Mackinac had dispersed, however, and the lateness of the season rendered those who could be reached indisposed to engage in such an enterprise. Nevertheless De Peyster, whom Winsor describes as "a somewhat rattle-brained person, given to writing illiterate letters, but in some ways an enterprising and prudent commander,"[189] did what he could. He sent Langlade, the man who had destroyed Pickawillany in 1752, to the Ottawas and Chippewas in Michigan, and Gautier to the Pottawatomies of St. Joseph, to lead them to Hamilton's assistance. At the same time he suggested to Haldimand the project of sending an Indian party from Green Bay by way of the Fox-Wisconsin route and the Mississippi, directly against the Illinois posts. The Grand River Indians declined to start until spring, and Gautier did not reach St. Joseph until December. What few Pottawatomies could then be raised were taken on by Louis Chevalier, a trader who resided among them; Langlade returned to Green Bay and Gautier to his station on the Mississippi, carrying speeches and belts to exhort the Indians to be ready for an expedition in the spring.[190]

During the winter Hamilton sent orders to Langlade at Green Bay requiring him and Gautier to join him early in the spring in an attack upon Kaskaskia.[191] Langlade was to proceed from Green Bay down Lake Michigan, and thence by way of the Illinois River, while Gautier was to gather the Indians from the upper Mississippi and descend that stream. Thus a grand

188 *Illinois Historical Collections*, I, 364.

189 Winsor, *Westward Movement*, 130.

190 *Wisconsin Historical Collections*, XI, 122–23.

191 *Illinois Historical Collections*, I, 436–38.

converging attack from three directions would be made on the Illinois settlements. How Hamilton took and then lost Vincennes has already been seen. In ignorance of the latter occurrence, Langlade set out from Green Bay with a band of Indians, and proceeded as far as Milwaukee.[192] Here they learned the news of Hamilton's capture, which so disheartened the Indians that they refused to go farther. Clark's emissaries were in the neighborhood, purchasing horses and threatening to be at "Labaye" soon with three hundred men, but Langlade's Indians were so disaffected that he was unable to capture them.[193]

Gautier's experience was even more discouraging. With a party of two hundred Indians, made up of Foxes, Ottawas, and others, he crossed by the Fox and Wisconsin rivers to the Mississippi, and proceeded down that stream as far as the mouth of the Rock.[194] Here a party of Sacs whom he stopped to harangue not only mocked his arguments and threats but had the "insollance" to force him to release one hundred and twenty of his followers. Other bands whom he addressed replied by threatening to carry news of his measures to the "Bostonnais," as the Americans were called. Like Langlade, therefore, he was forced to return to Green Bay.

The news of Hamilton's surrender filled the British at Detroit and Mackinac with forebodings of an immediate attack. Appeals were sent to Haldimand for reinforcements, while the defenses at the two posts were put in readiness to withstand an assault.[195] The Indians reported to De Peyster that the "Virginians" were building boats near Milwaukee, and also that they were near Chicago, but it shortly developed that these statements were the inventions of some "evil minded" Indians.[196] De Peyster professed not to care how soon "Mr. Clark" might appear, provided he "come by Lake Michigan & the Indians prove staunch &

192 *Ibid.* 193 *Ibid.*

194 *Wisconsin Historical Collections*, XI, 126.

195 *Michigan Pioneer Collections*, IX, 387 *et passim;* James, "Some Problems of the Northwest in 1779," in *Essays in American History*, 62.

196 *Illinois Historical Collections*, I, 436.

above all that the Canadians do not follow the example of their brethren at the Illinois who have joined the Rebels to a man."[197] Since there was little likelihood that these conditions would be realized, it is evident his confidence was not very deep-seated.

Meanwhile Clark, as a part of his preparations for the projected attack upon Detroit, dispatched Captain Linctot, a trader who had recently joined the Americans, and who was influential with the Indians, up the Illinois River with a company of forty men to secure the neutrality of the Indians, and to cover the design of his main expedition.[198] On learning this, and that Linctot had reached Lake Peoria, De Peyster sent Gautier with a party of Indians with orders to burn the fort, hoping thus to intimidate the Americans from attempting an expedition by this route.[199] A few days after receiving this information a report came to De Peyster from St. Joseph to the effect that the Americans were about to send seven hundred men against Detroit by way of the Wabash River, and four hundred cavalry under Linctot were to come up the Illinois and thence by St. Joseph to co-operate with them.[200] In consequence of this intelligence he detached Lieutenant Bennett with twenty men from his little force to go, with sixty traders and canoemen and two hundred Indians, to intercept Linctot, or to harass the "Rebels" in any way possible.[201] At the same time Langlade was ordered, July 1, 1779, to raise the savages of l'Arbre Croche,[202] Milwaukee, and other places along the shore of Lake Michigan and join Bennett at Chicago, or if he should have passed that point, to hasten to join him before he should reach Peoria.[203]

Bennett carried a war belt a yard and a half long, containing twelve thousand wampum beads, and early reports received from

[197] *Illinois Historical Collections*, I, 437.

[198] *Michigan Pioneer Collections*, IX, 389; James, "Some Problems of the Northwest in 1779," *op. cit.*, 378

[199] *Michigan Pioneer Collections*, IX, 389.

[200] *Ibid.*, 390. [201] *Ibid.*

[202] A mission village on Little Traverse Bay, at this time occupied by a band of Ottawas. See *Wisconsin Historical Collections*, XVIII, 253, 375.

[203] *Ibid.*, 375–76.

him were to the effect that the savages were joining it "fast."[204] De Peyster himself accompanied Langlade as far as l'Arbre Croche, where, on July 4, he harangued the assembled Indians. At a later date he gave vent to his poetical propensities by turning this speech into rhymed verses which constitute one of the literary curiosities of the English language.[205] Its chief interest for the history of Chicago consists in the allusion to Baptiste Point Du Sable, who is said to have already established himself here.

From Peoria Linctot and his party crossed the country to Ouiatanon, there to join Clark in his advance. He reached there in August, accompanied by a large concourse of Indians.[206] By this time Clark had abandoned the idea of an immediate advance on Detroit. Linctot, therefore, conceived the idea of attacking St. Joseph, to which place Bennett's party had meanwhile come.[207] He sent a message to Vincennes for reinforcements, but the French refused to respond, and the projected attack was abandoned.[208]

Bennett was sufficiently involved in difficulties, however, without interference from Linctot. On reaching St. Joseph, July 23, he threw up a slight intrenchment and sent out bands of Indians toward Peoria, Ouiatanon, and the Miamis, to learn of his opponents' movements and harass them if practicable.[209] These parties shortly returned in a disaffected state without having seen the enemy. On July 26 Bennett sent a message to Detroit informing Captain Lernault of his movements and offering to co-operate with him in any practicable operation. While awaiting an answer the greater portion of his Indians, having

[204] *Michigan Pioneer Collections*, IX, 391; *Wisconsin Historical Collections*, XVIII, 390.

[205] Printed in De Peyster's *Miscellanies;* it may also be found, with editorial notes, in *Wisconsin Historical Collections*, XVIII, 377–90.

[206] Said to have numbered 6,000, but this is obviously a gross exaggeration. (*Wisconsin Historical Collections*, XVIII, 376.)

[207] *Ibid.*, 286, 398.

[208] *Wisconsin Historical Collections*, XVIII, 376; *Michigan Pioneer Collections*, XIX, 467.

[209] *Wisconsin Historical Collections*, XVIII, 398.

consumed his supplies and rum, deserted. Langlade, meanwhile, arrived with sixty Chippewas, who conducted themselves with even greater insolence than the others. Finding himself helpless to accomplish anything Bennett abandoned St. Joseph about the middle of August and returned to Mackinac.[210]

Active military operations in the Northwest for the year 1779 were now at an end. Late in the year De Peyster was sent to Detroit to take the place of Hamilton, who had been sent by his captors to languish in a Virginia prison. Lieutenant-governor Patrick Sinclair was sent by Haldimand to succeed De Peyster at Mackinac.[211] On the American side Clark had retired to the Falls of the Ohio, his first base of operations in the Northwest. Upon the declaration of war against Great Britain by Spain in 1779, the British proceeded to plan a comprehensive campaign which would sweep the whole western American frontier from Canada to Florida and result in destroying the power of both Spain and the colonists in the Mississippi Valley.[212] From Pensacola in the South and Detroit in the Northwest as centers of operation, the British forces were to converge upon lower Louisiana, having taken St. Louis en route. Meanwhile, to cover these operations, De Peyster from Detroit was to advance on Clark at the Falls of the Ohio by way of the Maumee and Wabash rivers. The execution of this comprehensive program was rendered impossible, even before its initiation, by the enterprise of Galvez, the Spanish governor at New Orleans. In a series of operations extending over two years of time, he cleared the British out of the lower Mississippi Valley, concluding the process by the capture of Pensacola in May, 1781.[213]

Meanwhile, ignorant of the successes of Galvez in the South, the British forces stationed in the Northwest began, early in the year 1780, the execution of their part of the general plan of

[210] I have drawn this narrative from Bennett's Journal, in *Wisconsin Historical Collections*, XVIII, 398–401, and the other sources cited above.

[211] Winsor, *Westward Movement*, 142.

[212] For a statement of this project see James, "Significance of the Attack on St. Louis," in *Mississippi Valley Historical Association Proceedings*, II, 199 ff.

[213] *Ibid.*, 203–4.

operations. The campaign was initiated by Sinclair, who early in February sent a body of Indians to engage the noted Sioux chief, Wabasha, to descend the Mississippi to Natchez with his two hundred warriors.[214] About the middle of the same month Sinclair ordered Emanuel Hesse, a trader who had formerly served in the British army, to assemble the Sacs, Foxes, and other Wisconsin Indians at the Fox-Wisconsin Portage and proceed with them to the mouth of the Wisconsin, where the Indians from the upper Mississippi would join them in a descent upon St. Louis.[215] The services of Matchekewis, who had massacred the garrison at Mackinac in 1763, but who now was zealously serving the British, were also enlisted,[216] and it was planned that Langlade with a chosen band of Canadians and Indians should join a party gathered at Chicago and lead them down the Illinois River. Another party was to "watch the Plains" between the Wabash and the Mississippi,[217] while still another and larger expedition from Detroit under the command of Captain Henry Bird was to descend the Wabash to "amuse" Clark at the Falls of the Ohio.[218] Sinclair believed St. Louis could easily be surprised and taken, and that the traders who would profit by the English thus gaining control of the rich "furr Trade" of the Missouri River would give their assistance to the enterprise.[219]

On May 2, 1780, the force gathered at the mouth of the Wisconsin, consisting of about a thousand men, Indians, traders, and servants, began the descent of the Mississippi.[220] The news of its approach was carried to St. Louis by a trader, and the Spaniards made hasty preparations for defense.[221] De Leyba, the governor, ordered a wooden tower to be erected at one end

[214] For a secondary account of this campaign see *ibid.* For the original documents pertaining to it see *Wisconsin Historical Collections,* III, XI, XVIII; *Michigan Pioneer Collections,* IX; *Missouri Historical Collections,* II, No. 6.

[215] *Wisconsin Historical Collections,* XI, 147–48.

[216] *Ibid.,* 151.

[217] *Ibid.*

[218] Winsor, *Westward Movement,* 171; *Michigan Pioneer Collections,* X, 372, 377, 395.

[219] *Wisconsin Historical Collections,* XI, 148.

[220] James, "Significance of the Attack on St. Louis," in *Essays in American History,* 205.

[221] *Missouri Historical Collections,* II, No. 6, 45; *Wisconsin Historical Collections,* XVIII, 407.

of the town in which he placed five cannons, and intrenchments were constructed at the other exposed places. To man these defenses he had a force of twenty-nine regular soldiers and two hundred and eighty-one countrymen. On May 26 the hostile forces appeared and a vigorous firing began, to which the besieged replied with their cannon. "Then were to be heard the confusion and the lamentable cries of the women and children who had been shut up in the house of the commandant, ... the dolorous echoes of which seemed to inspire in the besieged an extraordinary valor and spirit."[222] Finally the besiegers abandoned the assault on the town itself, and devoted their attention to ravaging the surrounding country, where they killed or captured a number of farmers and their slaves. The Spaniards reported a loss of twenty-nine dead and wounded and twenty-four prisoners at St. Louis itself, in addition to forty-six taken captive in minor forays which attended the invasion.[223] Sinclair, on the other hand, reported that sixty-eight of the enemy were killed at St. Louis and eighteen taken prisoners.[224]

The attack having failed, the British began their retreat. According to Sinclair the defeat was caused by the treachery of the traders and part of the Indians. The attempt to surprise the Spaniards was a failure, and in the actual assault the Sacs and Foxes, led by certain of the traders, proved treacherous.[225] Another, and possibly the chief, reason for the retreat of the British was the arrival of George Rogers Clark at Cahokia with a small body of men shortly before the attack on St. Louis began.[226] Although he took no part in the fight at St. Louis, his presence at Cahokia across the river was probably an important factor in determining the British to give up the enterprise, and he promptly organized an expedition to pursue and punish the retreating forces.

[222] *Wisconsin Historical Collections*, XVIII, 408.

[223] *Ibid.*, 409. The British while proceeding down the Mississippi had captured an armed boat with thirteen men near the mouth of the modern Turkey River, and in a side expedition to the lead mines seventeen more were taken (*Wisconsin Historical Collections*, XI, 151).

[224] *Wisconsin Historical Collections*, XI, 156.

[225] *Ibid.*, 155–56.

[226] James, *op. cit.*, 210–13.

The British forces retreated in two divisions, one up the Mississippi, the other overland to Lake Michigan and Mackinac.[227] Clark now learned of the advance of the force from Detroit upon Kentucky and made haste to return to its defense, having ordered Colonel Montgomery to follow and harass the forces retreating from St. Louis while the Indians were still demoralized from their recent defeat.[228] Montgomery with three hundred and fifty men advanced up the Illinois River as far as Lake Peoria,[229] and then crossed to Rock River, destroying the crops and villages of the Indians on his way. At this point he was compelled to stop through lack of provisions, and his retreat to the French settlements was attended with great hardship and suffering.

The fortunes of the party led by Langlade by way of Chicago remain to be told. While proceeding down the Illinois it learned of the advance of Montgomery's force and thereupon beat a hasty retreat.[230] At Chicago the party was rescued from threatened destruction at the hands of a band of Indians in the "Rebel" interest by a relieving party which Sinclair had sent down Lake Michigan in two small vessels. Sinclair reported to Haldimand that five days after the vessels left Chicago two hundred Illinois cavalry arrived there,[231] but this was evidently a mistaken rumor caused by the advance of Montgomery's expedition, which, as has been seen, came no farther than Lake Peoria.

The fugitives from the St. Louis expedition had no sooner gained shelter at Mackinac than Sinclair began to plan for a new attack on the Illinois settlements[232] the following year. The

[227] *Michigan Pioneer Collections*, IX, 558.

[228] *Virginia State Papers*, III, 443.

[229] Montgomery says he went "to the Lake open on the Illinois River" (*Virginia State Papers*, III, 443). Peoria was variously designated at this time as the Pee, Pey, Opie, etc. This designation is said to have originated as a corruption of the French words *au pied*, used with reference to the foot of the lake. Montgomery's "Lake open" was, apparently, but another variant of the original French form.

[230] *Wisconsin Historical Collections*, XVIII, 411; *Michigan Pioneer Collections*, XI, 558.

[231] *Michigan Pioneer Collections*, XI, 558.

[232] The settlements on both sides of the Mississippi were referred to as the settlements of the Illinois. In Navarro's official report concerning the attack on St. Louis in 1780 that place is designated "San Luis de Ylinoises" (*Wisconsin Historical Collections*, XVIII, 407).

services of Wabasha were engaged anew, and Sinclair assured Haldimand that one thousand Sioux would be in the field under his leadership by April, 1781.[233] To insure that secrecy the absence of which had proved so disastrous to the expedition of 1780, Wabasha came in person to Mackinac to make the necessary arrangements for the enterprise. But the attempt at secrecy proved futile for in December, Cruzat, the new governor at St. Louis,[234] was reporting to his superiors the news that Wabasha was returning to his tribe from "Michely Makinak" with a great quantity of merchandise to arouse his own and the neighboring tribes.[235] At the same time Cruzat announced that he had decided upon measures for checkmating the British design, but refrained from telling what they were until after they should be executed.

Whether Cruzat alluded to the mysterious project of De la Balme against Detroit, which had even then come to an unfortunate end, or to the forthcoming Spanish expedition against St. Joseph must remain a matter of conjecture. De la Balme was a French officer who appeared in the Illinois villages in the summer of 1780, and rousing the villagers with the story that their former king was coming to their assistance, announced his own purpose to lead them in an assault on Detroit and thence on Canada itself.[236] With a little band of French and Indians, about eighty in number, flying the banner of France at its head, he moved upon the British post of Miami near the modern Fort Wayne, and captured and plundered it. The Indians, however, shortly attacked De la Balme's party in turn and defeated it, the commander being numbered among the slain.[237] This occurred at the beginning of November, 1780.

[233] *Michigan Pioneer Collections*, IX, 559.

[234] De Leyba had died shortly after the British attack of 1780 and before the arrival of the news that his government had promoted him for his conduct on that occasion (*Wisconsin Historical Collections*, XVIII, 410).

[235] *Ibid.*, 414.

[236] On De la Balme's mission see Burton, "Augustin Mottin de la Balme," in *Illinois State Historical Society Transactions*, 1909, 104 ff.; *Illinois Historical Collections*, II, lxviii–xciv; *Wisconsin Historical Collections*, XVIII, 416; *Missouri Historical Review*, II, 202–3.

[237] *Michigan Pioneer Collections*, XIX, 581–82.

Thus ended De la Balme's projected invasion of Canada. But the episode of his advent in the Northwest was attended by further interesting consequences. Before his departure for Detroit he had sent a detachment from Cahokia under command of Jean Baptiste Hamelin against the post of St. Joseph.[238] There had been no regular garrison here since the massacre of the British soldiers at the time of Pontiac's war; but the post was advantageously located for trading purposes. It possessed a further importance as the gathering-place of the Pottawatomie war parties sent out to harass the Americans, while the fact that a large stock of goods had been stored here by the British traders[239] served to increase the zeal of Hamelin's men for the assault. According to a census that has been preserved, St. Joseph contained in June, 1780, a population of forty-eight French and half-breeds.[240] During the summer some of the inhabitants had been carried off to Mackinac by Sinclair's orders, so that at the time Hamelin fell upon it the post contained a smaller population than it had in June.

Hamelin's foray was so timed as to reach St. Joseph early in December, 1780, when the Indians were absent on their first hunt.[241] The party numbered only seventeen men; but they overpowered the traders, loaded their goods on packhorses, and with twenty-two prisoners beat a hasty retreat around the lake toward Chicago.[242] Their triumph, however, was short lived. In the spring of the year De Peyster, who now commanded at Detroit, had stationed Lieutenant De Quindre at St. Joseph to look after the interests of the British in that region. He was temporarily absent at the time of Hamelin's attack, but, returning shortly afterward, he assembled a party of Pottawatomies and set out to punish the audacious intruders. Hamelin was overtaken on December 5 at a place called Petite Fort, a day's

[238] *Missouri Historical Review*, II, 204.

[239] According to a memoir by the traders to Haldimand for indemnity these amounted to 62,000 livres in value (*Michigan Pioneer Collections*, X, 367).

[240] *Ibid.*, 406–7.

[241] *Ibid.*, XIX, 591.

[242] *Ibid.*; *Virginia State Papers*, I, 465.

journey beyond the River Chemin,[243] and in the fight that ensued all but three of his party were killed or taken prisoners.

This comparatively insignificant affair, which terminated at Chicago's back door, as it were, was quickly followed by a second attack upon St. Joseph, the echoes of which were heard in distant Europe. The preparations which the English were making for a new descent upon St. Louis in the spring of 1781 excited the genuine alarm of Cruzat, the new Spanish governor.[244] Profiting, possibly, by the example set by George Rogers Clark, in his attack upon Vincennes, Cruzat determined to anticipate the blow. On January 2, 1781, less than a month after the disaster to the Americans at the Petite Fort, a Spanish expedition set out from St. Louis for St. Joseph.[245] It consisted in the beginning of thirty Spaniards from St. Louis and twenty residents of Cahokia. On the way across Illinois these were joined by a dozen Spanish soldiers who had been sent up the Illinois River in the preceding November to serve as an outpost against the British in that direction.[246] In addition to this, and of greater importance doubtless, the party was joined by two hundred Indians. Included in the latter were the "runagates" from Milwaukee under the leadership of Siggenauk and Nakewoin, whose tendency to side with the Americans had long disturbed the British commanders in the Northwest.[247] In 1779 De

[243] The stream at the mouth of which Michigan City, Indiana, now stands. Petite Fort has been said to have been near the Calumet River. I have not succeeded in locating it more definitely than is indicated above.

[244] *Missouri Historical Review*, V, 223.

[245] Three detailed studies of this expedition have been made. The conclusions of the first, by Edward G. Mason, were generally accepted by scholars as valid until Professor Clarence W. Alvord's study appeared. His conclusions differ materially from those reached by Mason. More recently Frederick J. Teggart has challenged Alvord's conclusions. For his study, with references to the earlier studies and the sources, see "The Capture of St. Joseph, Michigan, by the Spaniards in 1781," in *Missouri Historical Review*, V, 214 ff.

[246] Teggart, *op. cit.*, 216.

[247] De Peyster's characterization of them as "a horrid set of refractory Indians" has already been mentioned (*Wisconsin Historical Collections*, XVIII, 384). Probably it was this band which had threatened to destroy the British force at Chicago retreating from St. Louis in the preceding summer. For a sketch of Siggenauk's career see *Wisconsin Historical Collections*, XVIII, 384.

Peyster, then at Mackinac, had bribed a chief, Chambolee, to capture Siggenauk by fair means or foul and turn him over to the English, promising that in the event of success he would be "weall rewarded."[248] This attempt to secure the obnoxious chieftain proved vain, however. At another time, whether before or after this does not appear, De Peyster tried the plan of buying off the "Runagade chiefs," but this too proved futile.[249] Some time after the St. Joseph expedition, however, Siggenauk turned against the Americans.

The expedition proceeded up the Illinois River as far as Lake Peoria.[250] Here, the river having frozen, it was found necessary to leave the boats behind and continue the journey on foot. It was midwinter, and before the Spaniards lay three hundred miles of wilderness infested with savages, who might at any moment fall upon them. At the end of their march lay the prospect of a hostile force surrounded by savages friendly to it and hostile to them, with their base of supplies, and their refuge in case of defeat, four hundred miles away. Naturally our only knowledge of the experiences of the party on the march comes from the Spaniards themselves. We may well believe, however, that they suffered "the greatest inconveniences from cold and hunger,"[251] not to mention the labor of carrying through the trackless wilderness provisions for themselves and a supply of goods to be used in placating the Indians.

Three weeks were consumed in the march from Lake Peoria to St. Joseph. On February 11 at nightfall the party was within two leagues of its destination. It had had the good fortune to secure the assistance of Louis Chevalier, who was intimately acquainted with the St. Joseph Indians, his father having been the principal trader and resident of St. Joseph for many years, until his arrest and removal by Sinclair's order in the summer

[248] *Wisconsin Historical Collections*, XI, 210.

[249] *Michigan Pioneer Collections*, X, 454–55.

[250] *Missouri Historical Review*, V, 216.

[251] *Madrid Gazette*, March 12, 1782, quoted in *Missouri Historical Review*, II, 195. For further details of the march see Teggart, *op. cit.*

of 1781.[252] While the party halted an emissary was sent on to the Indians at the post, and by promises of sharing the booty with them a pledge of neutrality on their part was secured. Early the next morning, February 12, the Spaniards crossed the river on the ice and made themselves masters of the post without a blow being struck. De Quindre was absent at the time, and all circumstances conspired to render the traders an easy prey to the invaders. The goods were divided between the St. Joseph Indians and those accompanying the expedition, and a supply of corn, gathered in expectation of the coming attack upon St. Louis, was destroyed. The party remained at St. Joseph only twenty-four hours, but during this time the Spanish flag was kept flying and formal possession was taken of the country in the name of the king of Spain. A hasty retreat was then begun, and the party arrived at St. Louis early in March without the loss of a man. On the day after its departure from St. Joseph De Quindre returned to that place. He sought to rouse the Indians, as he had done on the former occasion, to pursue the invaders, but this time without success. Their zeal for such exploits had evaporated, and they insisted on being led in the opposite direction to Detroit, to make their excuses to De Peyster for having allowed their traders to be carried off.

The importance which later came to be attached to this expedition was due to its bearing upon the political rather than upon the military situation. It has generally been supposed by historians that the expedition was inspired by the Spanish Court to furnish the basis for laying claim in the peace negotiations to the British Northwest. The latest student of the subject rejects this supposition,[253] as also the further one that when the news of the successful termination of the exploit became known in Spain the Court proceeded to turn it to political advantage by founding extravagant claims upon it. That Vergennes, the French minister, and Aranda, the representative of Spain in the negotiations for the treaty, made such use of it is admitted. In 1780,

[252] For the elder Chevalier see *Wisconsin Historical Collections*, XVIII, 372.

[253] Teggart, in *Missouri Historical Review*, V, 220–23.

the year before the expedition against St. Joseph occurred, the French minister, Luzerne, announced to Congress the view of the Spanish king that the territory east of the Mississippi and north of the Ohio belonged to Great Britain and was a proper object of Spanish conquest. Two years later, in the summer of 1782, in discussing with Jay the boundary between the possessions of Spain and the United States, the Spanish representative argued that the western country had belonged to Great Britain until by conquest during the Revolution it came into the possession of Spain. The contention was not established, but the evident design of France and Spain to advance the interests of the latter in America at the expense of the United States induced the American negotiators to conclude a separate treaty with England, in violation not only of their instructions but also of the treaty of alliance between the United States and France in 1778.

The remainder of the story of the Revolution in the Northwest can quickly be told. Clark still dreamed of an expedition against Detroit, and both Jefferson, governor of Virginia, and General Washington looked with favor upon the project and held out promises of the necessary assistance.[254] For the year 1781 a force of two thousand men was promised Clark, and Colonel Brodhead at Fort Pitt was ordered by Washington to assist him with troops and supplies. But Clark was doomed again to disappointment. Jefferson resigned the gubernatorial office, and Washington was engrossed in his contest with Clinton and Cornwallis which was to end in the capture of the latter at Yorktown. The British on their part manifested great activity during 1781 in raiding the settlements along the Ohio River. The harassed settlers, less far-sighted than Clark, were little disposed to engage in a distant expedition; a force of over one hundred men descending the Ohio to join Clark was cut to pieces in August by a combined British and Indian force sent out from Detroit by De Peyster, every man being killed or captured.

[254] Winsor, *Westward Movement*, chap. xi; James, "George Rogers Clark and Detroit, 1780–1781," in *Mississippi Valley Historical Association, Proceedings*, III, 291 ff.

The victors even considered the project of attacking Clark, who was now in his stockade fort at the Falls of the Ohio, impatiently awaiting the assembling of the forces for his projected expedition. By order of the Virginia Assembly this was again postponed. Clark's disappointment was keen, for as far as any positive action was concerned, his projects for the year had completely failed. From another point of view, however, the prospect was less dismal. If he had failed to take Detroit, the failure of the British plans for ousting the Americans from the Northwest had been no less signal. And the sequel proved that Clark's stubborn retention of the grip on this region, which he had gained in 1779, was the principal factor in securing it to the United States in the negotiations which resulted in the treaty of 1783.

CHAPTER V

THE FIGHT FOR THE NORTHWEST

Long before the issue of the military struggle a contest of another sort for the possession of the Northwest had begun. France and Spain had entered into the conflict between Great Britain and her American colonies from no love of the latter, but rather from a desire on the one hand to humble Great Britain, on the other to advance their own interests. With the opening of the peace negotiations, therefore, an effort was made by these countries to limit the boundary of the new nation on the west to the Allegheny Mountains, and to give the dominant influence over the vast territory stretching thence to the Mississippi, together with the exclusive navigation of that stream, to Spain. That the project failed, and the Mississippi was made the western boundary of the new nation, was due in part to the shrewdness and persistence of the American diplomats, in part to the complaisance of Great Britain herself. Her representatives did not hesitate to reject the temptation offered of an alliance with the two continental monarchies for the purpose of advancing their own projects at the expense of her former colonies, in favor of such a settlement with the latter as would, by making possible their future development, secure their friendship and good will. By the terms of the treaty, therefore, the Northwest was secured to the United States, its boundaries being a middle line through the Great Lakes, and on the west the Mississippi River.

The prospect thus opened for an early reconciliation between the mother country and her revolted colonies did not, unfortunately, materialize. The war had left Great Britain burdened with a vast debt, her dominion curtailed by more than a million square miles of her finest territory, her prestige no less seriously damaged, and her ancient foe across the Channel glorying in the humiliation which had overtaken her. It was, perhaps, too much to expect, in view of all these things, that the mother country should at once receive the disobedient daughter to her bosom, without attempting in any way to manifest her resentment for the humiliation she had suffered.

Furthermore, conditions in America at the close of the war were such as to breed irritation and hostility between the two countries. The Revolution had been in a very real sense a civil war. Upward of one-third of the American colonists had sided with the British, and in their ranks were to be found the major portion of the colonists who were endowed with wealth, good birth, and education. Between these loyalists, or "Tories," and the "patriots," whose cause had now triumphed, the most intense feeling of bitterness existed. Even as wise and conservative a man as Franklin shared the general feeling of resentment toward the loyalists and was ready to justify the confiscation of their estates. Yet they had risked their all for the sake of the mother country, and Great Britain's honor was involved in securing them against being punished for their loyalty and devotion to her interests. A futile attempt was made during the peace negotiations to insure their protection, and its total failure, while natural enough in view of the circumstances, furnished one of the elements making for discord later on between the two countries.

There were other causes of discord and, in fact, neither the United States nor Great Britain honestly tried to fulfil all the obligations they had entered into. One of the leading sources of trouble pertained to the situation in the Northwest. Great Britain had agreed to withdraw her armies from all places in the United States "with all convenient speed." This obligation was kept elsewhere, but it was calmly and deliberately broken as far as the northwestern posts were concerned.[255] The demands of the American government for evacuation were met by evasion and, later, by open refusal, and even an explanation of the reasons for this course was long withheld. Finally the pretense

[255] The standard study of this subject is McLaughlin's "Western Posts and the British Debts," in *American Historical Association, Annual Report*, 1894, 413 ff. See also Roosevelt, *Winning of the West*, Vol. IV.

was urged that the posts were being held as a guaranty of the fulfilment by the Americans of their own treaty obligations. That we were justly chargeable with failure in this respect is clear; but it is equally clear that the British determination to retain the posts antedated our infractions of the treaty, and that the claim that they were being held because of American violations of the treaty was a mere afterthought, put forward by way of excuse for a policy in itself indefensible.

The real reasons for the British policy with reference to the Northwest were the desire to retain control of the fur trade and of the Indian tribes of that region. In one sense these two reasons coalesce, but to some extent they may be distinguished. The fur trade constituted Canada's chief commercial asset, and the Canadians had looked upon the concessions contained in the treaty of 1783 as needlessly generous to the Americans and fatal to their own prosperity. To retain this trade the Americans must be shut out of the Northwest, and to this end the posts must be retained. Further than this, it was an obvious fact that in time of war the Indian would side with the party with whom he traded in time of peace. By her control of the Indian trade and the exclusion of the Americans from the Northwest Great Britain assured herself that in case of a future war with America or Spain the tomahawk and scalping knife might once more be called into requisition against her enemy.[256]

To these considerations was joined another, which proved potent to fill the Northwest with strife and bloodshed for a dozen years after the close of the Revolution. It shortly became the aim of Great Britain to secure to the powerful tribes in western New York and in the territory west and north of the Ohio River the retention of their lands. They would thus serve the purpose of a buffer state between the United States and Canada, and would, by proper management of the Indians, render permanent the grip which the Canadian merchants had on the fur trade. To secure these ends the British sought to keep the Indians united

[256] McLaughlin, *op. cit.*, 430.

and to influence them not to yield too readily to the blandishments or threats of the Americans. The attempt was made to establish a sort of guardianship over the Indian tribes and to require that interviews between them and the Americans be held in the presence of Canadian officials or in places where the British influence might be made manifest. In all this the home government refrained from instigating the Indians to war upon the Americans, and steadily instructed its representatives to encourage them to keep the peace. But it is none the less true that its attitude toward them was productive of a state of affairs and an attitude of mind on the part of the Indians which made war with the Americans inevitable.[257] At last the British officials lost their earlier solicitude for the preservation of peace, and in the period immediately preceding Wayne's victory of 1794 they openly encouraged the Indians to make war on the Americans, and supplied them with the guns, ammunition, and other provisions which made their long resistance possible.[258]

We may now turn to a consideration of the relations between the Americans and the Indians on the northwestern frontier in the period which falls between the close of the Revolution and the Treaty of Greenville of 1795. By the close of the Revolution two important steps had been taken in the direction of opening the Northwest to settlement. The claims of the various states to a portion or all of this region had been ceded to the national government, and by the Treaty of Paris the sovereignty of the United States as against foreign nations had been recognized. It remained to quiet the Indian title to the lands in question, and, in this connection, to overcome their opposition to their settlement by the whites.

Encouraged by the British officials, the Indians at first strenuously resisted the American claim to sovereignty north and west of the Ohio River. In the course of a few years, however, various treaties were entered into between the United States and the different tribes providing for the cession to the former of lands

[257] McLaughlin, *op. cit.*, 435.

[258] *Ibid.*, 436; Roosevelt, *Winning of the West*, Vol. IV, *passim*.

beyond the Ohio.[259] Such treaties were made at Fort McIntosh, January 21, 1785, and at Fort Finney, January 31, 1786. But only a portion of the tribes concerned participated in these treaties; those who opposed the cessions saw in them only an incitement to hostilities. In the summer of 1786 the disaffected ones gathered in council at Niagara, and an ineffectual effort was made to unite them in a war upon the Americans. Meanwhile raiding went on along the border, and Congress was impotent to protect it by waging war upon the hostile tribes.[260] Thereupon the Kentuckians to the number of twelve hundred gathered under the leadership of George Rogers Clark to chastise the tribes on their own account. But the force was poorly organized. Clark had lost the qualities of dauntless leadership for which he had been distinguished a few years before, and the expedition accomplished little or nothing.[261]

Meanwhile the rush of settlers into the lands west of the Alleghenies went on apace. Owing to the Indian menace north of the Ohio, for the first few years following the close of the Revolution this settlement was practically confined to the region south of that river. It was only a question of time, however, when the Indian barrier would be broken down. The famous ordinance of 1787 made provision for civil government and for the ultimate formation of states in the Northwest. In the same year Congress sold to the Ohio Company five million acres of land, and provision was made for a territorial government, of which General St. Clair was to become the first chief executive. In 1788 the Ohio Company formally inaugurated its enterprise by founding Marietta at the mouth of the Muskingum, and the tide of immigration into the Northwest may be said to have fairly begun.[262] The opposition of the Indians was, naturally, not conciliated by these developments. In 1789 St. Clair negotiated a

[259] For an account of these treaties see Winsor, *Westward Movement*, 267 ff. The treaties themselves are printed in *American State Papers, Indian Affairs*, Vol. I, and in the various collections of treaties between the United States and the Indian tribes.

[260] Winsor, *Westward Movement*, 274.

[261] *Ibid.*, 275.

[262] For a description of this movement see *ibid.*, chap. xiv.

treaty with certain of the tribes at Fort Harmar, which, in effect, confirmed the grants to the United States north of the Ohio which had been made by the treaties of Fort McIntosh and Fort Finney.[263] But a large portion of the tribes affected held aloof and took no part in the treaty.

It is clear today, as it was to those actually on the frontier at the time, that with both parties determined to possess the Northwest war in earnest between the red men and the white was inevitable. When once the issue was fairly joined the ultimate outcome could hardly remain a matter of doubt, yet the government entered upon the war with extreme reluctance, and only after a flood of appeals from the frontier for protection had been poured upon it.[264] Several causes operated to produce this hesitation. The new government, feeble and lacking in resources, dreaded the expense. The hostile tribes were more numerous and formidable than any combination the red race had ever yet brought into the field against the white. They gathered in bodies so large as fairly to deserve the name of armies, and fought pitched battles with American armies as large as those commanded by Washington at Trenton or by Greene at Eutaw Springs.[265] Finally the government was actuated by an honest desire to promote the welfare of the Indians and to discharge scrupulously all of its treaty obligations toward them.[266]

In 1790 the hovering war cloud burst. The Indians forced the issue by intercepting and plundering the boats conveying settlers down the Ohio, the main avenue of travel into the western country. In July St. Clair, the governor of the Northwest Territory, called upon the state of Kentucky for troops, authorized the raising of the militia of the western counties of Pennsylvania and Virginia, and set his own forces in motion. The main expedition was sent from Fort Washington against the Miamis,

[263] Winsor, *op. cit.*, 308–10.

[264] Roosevelt, *op. cit.*, IV, 9, 18, 27 *et passim*.

[265] *Ibid.*, IV, 17–18.

[266] *Ibid.*, 9, 17; see, also, documents pertaining to the establishment by the government of Indian trading houses, in *American State Papers, Indian Affairs*, Vols. I and II, *passim*.

under command of General Harmar.[267] In October he set out with fourteen hundred men for the hostile villages. Rumor going in advance multiplied the numbers of his little army, so that the Indians made no attempt at resistance. The towns at the junction of the St. Mary's and St. Joseph rivers were found deserted and were destroyed. At this point Harmar divided his force, sending out detachments in various directions. These were severely handled, though they inflicted perhaps an equal loss upon the Indians. The whole body shortly made a disorderly retreat, and the campaign was ended. No great disaster had been suffered, but the army had lost two hundred men and the net result had been a "mortifying failure."

That the Indians were not cowed by Harmar was shown by the prompt renewal of their marauding expeditions. Early in the year 1791 they raided the New England settlements near Marietta, killing a dozen persons and carrying half as many more into captivity.[268] This is but typical of further raids which continued throughout the winter. Meanwhile the Americans were preparing another expedition. Washington asked and received permission from Congress to raise three thousand troops to be placed under St. Clair's command. To protect the frontier while this army was being made ready, bodies of rangers composed of the more capable and daring bordermen were employed.[269] Moving in small parties and fighting the Indian in his own fashion, they performed much effective service. In addition to this measure the Kentuckians were authorized to conduct two raids upon the enemy. Each expedition consisted of several hundred mounted volunteers under experienced leaders. Each succeeded in harrying a number of villages, with almost no loss to the raiders themselves.

The gathering-place for St. Clair's expedition was, as in the case of Harmar, Fort Washington. According to the plan adopted he was to have here three thousand effective troops by

267 For Harmar's expedition see Winsor, *op. cit.*, 417–20; Roosevelt, *op. cit.*, III, 304–10.

268 Roosevelt, *op. cit.*, IV, 19–20.

269 *Ibid.*, 28–30.

July 10, 1791. But not until July 15 did the first regiment of three hundred men arrive, and it was October before he could count two thousand effective men.[270] From beginning to end, this first great military enterprise of the new government was woefully mismanaged. The supplies provided were poor, the commissary department was both inefficient and corrupt, the commander was sick and incapable, and the troops themselves were "wretched stuff."[271] Aside from two small regiments of infantry, the army was composed of six months' levies, and of militia enrolled for this particular campaign. In its desire to economize Congress had fixed the net pay of the soldiers at two dollars and ten cents a month. The judgment passed by one who observed the force that "men who are to be purchased from prisons, wheelbarrows, and brothels at two dollars a month will never answer for fighting Indians" was amply justified by the sequel.[272]

Early in October the advance began.[273] St. Clair's instructions required him to establish a permanent fort at the Miami village and to maintain such a garrison in it as would enable him to detach five or six hundred men for special service as occasion should require. He advanced at a snail's pace, the army marching but five or six miles a day. In this way, stopping now and then to build a fort or delayed by lack of food, the commander sick, the troops disorderly and demoralized, with almost no effort to prevent surprise, the army stumbled northward through the wilderness. At the end of October, with the enemy in striking distance, some sixty of the militia deserted in a body, and the unfortunate commander made the fatal blunder of sending back one of his two regiments of regulars after them.

Perhaps it was just as well, for a larger force would have resulted only in a greater slaughter. On November 3 the army encamped on a branch of the Wabash near the middle point of the

[270] Winsor, *op. cit.*, 428.

[271] Roosevelt, *op. cit.*, IV, 30.

[272] Winsor, *op. cit.*, 426.

[273] Roosevelt (*Winning of the West*, IV, 30–52) gives a detailed and graphic account of St. Clair's campaign, with references to much of the important source material. For St. Clair's official reports see *American State Papers, Indian Affairs*, I, 136–38.

western boundary of Ohio. The main body of the army huddled together on the eastern bank of the stream, while the militia camped on the opposite side. Shortly after sunrise the next morning the Indians fell in fury upon this exposed detachment, and a battle ensued similar in character and in magnitude of horror and disaster to the defeat of the ill-fated Braddock. Concealed behind logs and trees the savages poured a steady fire upon the doomed army. The troops drawn up in close array, unable even to see their foe, fired vain volleys into the forest. A heavy pall of smoke soon overhung the army, under cover of which the agile savages darted again and again into the lines of the troops, tomahawking their chosen victims and slipping deftly away before the enraged but slower soldiers could retaliate. The officers displayed conspicuous bravery, encouraging their men and leading them again and again in bayonet charges against their tormenters. But the savages only retired before their advance to fall upon them the moment they turned; and at times the charging parties, isolated from the main body, fought their way back with difficulty.

A more terrible scene can scarcely be pictured. The bravery and exertions of the troops were all in vain against such a foe. For two hours the slaughter went on, while the wounded were gathered to the center and the officers strove to keep the lines intact. At last the men became demoralized. In ever larger numbers they deserted their posts to huddle terror stricken among the wounded. Seeing that all was lost and that the army could be saved from complete destruction only by an immediate retreat, St. Clair gathered such fragments of battalions as he could and ordered a charge to regain the road by which the army had advanced.

A vigorous charge drove the Indians back beyond the road, and through the opening the demoralized troops pressed, to use the expressive phrase of an eyewitness, "like a drove of bullocks."[274] The pursuit was delayed for a short time, apparently because the Indians failed at once to grasp the significance of the

[274] Roosevelt, *op. cit.*, IV, 44.

new movement; they soon fell upon the rear, however, and slaughtered without hindrance the terror-stricken fugitives, whose only thought was to get away. In the mad rout the soldiers, crazed by fear, threw away their weapons as they ran; the stronger and swifter rode down the weak; while the slower and the wounded fell to the rear, and by furnishing occupation for the tomahawk and the scalping knife purchased temporary respite for their more fortunate comrades. The savages drew off after they had followed the fleeing mob in this way for about four miles, possibly because for once they were satiated with slaughter, more probably because lured by the plunder of the camp. The soldiers continued their flight for twenty-five miles pursued only by the terrors evoked by their superheated imagination. At nightfall they streamed into Fort Jefferson; here some of the wounded who had escaped were left, and the army continued to flee till Fort Washington, the starting-point of the campaign, was reached.

Thus terminated the most disastrous campaign ever waged by an American army against the Indians. St. Clair had lost in killed and wounded over nine hundred men. There were no prisoners, practically, for the savages slew all but a few of those who fell into their hands. Only about one-third of St. Clair's men actually engaged in the battle of the fatal fourth of November escaped uninjured. Yet during the battle the Americans had scarcely seen the foe. St. Clair, judging from the destructive rifle fire poured in upon his ranks, reported that he had been overwhelmed by numbers, but this may well be doubted. Neither the number nor the loss of the red men is known with any certainty; that the latter was slight is, however, apparent, and Roosevelt's estimate that it may not have amounted to one-twentieth that of the whites seems not at all improbable.[275]

Fighting with the victors were two men whom we shall meet again in the annals of early Chicago. The one was Little Turtle, the famous Miami chieftain, who is generally supposed to have been the leader of the Indians this day; the other, his son-in-law,

[275] Roosevelt, *op. cit.*, IV, 47.

Captain William Wells, member of a prominent Kentucky family, who had been taken prisoner by the Indians in boyhood and adopted into the tribe. In this battle he is said to have slain several of the Americans with his own hand.[276] Soon after this he abandoned the Indians, and henceforth fought valiantly in behalf of his native race until he fell gloriously, over twenty years later, in the Fort Dearborn massacre.

The overthrow of St. Clair's army made necessary another campaign against the triumphant tribesmen unless the United States was to surrender her pretensions to that sovereignty over the Northwest which had been recognized in the treaty of 1783. Yet three years now elapsed before the final blow was struck against the Indian power in this region. Their easy triumph over St. Clair resulted in a great accession both to the number and spirit of the warring bands. Encouraged by the British, whose attitude toward the Americans during this period, as manifested by such officials as Simcoe and Lord Dorchester, became increasingly hostile, they maintained the attitude that they had not by any valid treaty surrendered any portion of the territory north of the Ohio, and continued to send their war parties in ever-increasing numbers against the "deluded settlers" of the northwestern frontier. The United States again tried vainly to secure peace by negotiation. The sanctity which hedges an ambassador about, familiar even to savages, was violated in the murder of Colonel Hardin and Major Trueman, who were sent as envoys to the hostile tribes in the spring of 1792. Despite this, the effort to bring about a peace was vainly continued throughout the year 1792 and the spring of 1793.[277] At last, there being no other alternative, the government made definite plans for a new campaign.

The preparations had already been begun and Anthony Wayne had been chosen by Washington, though with great reluctance, to succeed St. Clair as commander.[278] In Washington's

[276] *Ibid.*, 79.

[277] *Ibid.*, 52 ff.

[278] On the selection of Wayne to succeed St. Clair see Winsor, *Westward Movement*, 439–40.

opinion he was vain, open to flattery, easily imposed upon, and "liable to be drawn into scrapes." In spite of this he was considered the best man available, and his conduct following his appointment brilliantly refuted the prevalent opinion of his lack of judgment. If there ever had been ground for Washington's low opinion of Wayne's prudence, certain it is that he afforded none by his measures in this crisis in the history of the Northwest. His bravery was questioned by no one, and he had long been recognized as the most active and enterprising officer in the army.

In the autumn of 1792 Wayne established a camp on the Ohio about seven miles below Pittsburgh, and began the difficult task of organizing the remnant of St. Clair's army and the new recruits that were being enlisted into an efficient "legion," which should be able to face the red foe with some prospect of success.[279] During the winter his troops, which by springtime numbered twenty-five hundred men, were drilled incessantly. In May, 1793, he moved down the Ohio to Fort Washington, near which place he established a camp and called on the Kentucky volunteers to come to his assistance. The government was still carrying on futile negotiations with the hostile tribes, and not until October was Wayne given permission to launch the campaign. He then advanced about eighty miles north of Cincinnati to a place six miles beyond Fort Jefferson, where a second winter camp was established to which he gave the name of Greenville. From this place a detachment was sent forward to occupy the site of St. Clair's defeat and there build a post, to which the significant name of Fort Recovery was given.

The winter was spent in further drill, and in perfecting the preparations for a decisive conflict in the spring. The Indians harassed the posts, attacking convoys, and killing the commander of Fort Jefferson within three hundred yards of the fort.

[279] For standard secondary accounts of Wayne's campaign see Winsor, *op. cit.*, chap. xx; Roosevelt, *op. cit.*, IV, chap. ii. Original documents pertaining to the campaign, including Wayne's report of the attack on Fort Recovery and the battle of Fallen Timbers, are printed in *American State Papers, Indian Affairs*, I, 487–95. Wayne's Orderly Book, covering the period from 1792 to 1797, is printed in the *Michigan Pioneer Collections*, xxxiv, 341–734.

Ere spring the regular troops had developed into a finely drilled army, with confidence in their leader and in themselves. The natural contempt of the frontiersman for a regular force, heightened as it was by the disasters of the army in the last few years, gave way to genuine admiration for Wayne's troops. The cavalry had been trained to maneuver over any ground, and the infantry to load while on the run. By constant practice the soldiers had become as good marksmen as were the frontier hunters themselves, and Wayne, who had become famous in the Revolution for his reliance on the bayonet, had imbued his men with his own zeal for coming to close quarters with the enemy.

Prominent among the causes which had contributed to St. Clair's overthrow was the absence of an efficient corps of scouts to bring him information of the enemy's movements and protect his own army against surprise. The preparation of Wayne in this respect, and the skilful use which he made of his force of scouts, was in marked contrast to the course of his unfortunate predecessor. One of the leaders of this force was William Wells, the son-in-law of Little Turtle, who three years before had assisted his dusky relative to overthrow St. Clair. Since then he had rejoined the whites, to whom by reason of his long life on the frontier, and his intimate acquaintance with the very Indians against whom Wayne was marching, his services were invaluable. His scouts covered Wayne's front so effectively that the Indians were unable to obtain any correct information concerning his numbers or movements.

On June 30 an assault was made on Fort Recovery by two thousand Indians, but they were beaten off with considerable loss, which caused some of them to leave for their homes in despair.[280] On the other hand, Wayne's forces were augmented by the arrival of General Scott at the head of sixteen hundred Kentucky mounted volunteers. Having further deceived the enemy as to his intentions by making demonstrations to right and left, Wayne marched by a devious route to the Indian villages at the junction of the Glaize and the Maumee rivers, in

[280] *Wisconsin Historical Collections*, XVIII, 444–45.

the heart of the hostile country.[281] Here he had hoped to strike a telling blow, but the timely information of a deserter enabled the Indians to flee before his arrival. But their villages, stretching for several miles up and down the river, with cornfields more extensive than Wayne had ever seen before, "from Canada to Florida," fell into his hands without striking a blow. He spent some time in building here a strong stockade fort, which he grimly named Defiance, and in sending a last futile overture to the Indians for peace. It was now the middle of August, and on learning of the failure of his embassy, Wayne set forth on the final stage of his campaign.

The defiance to which his fortress gave expression was not directed against the Indians alone, for the British officials in the Northwest were now co-operating almost openly with the natives. In February, 1794, in the course of a speech to an Indian delegation, Lord Dorchester asserted that he would not be surprised if war between his country and the United States should begin during the year. This speech caused an immediate furore at Montreal, where it was construed to indicate that Dorchester had private intelligence which rendered him confident that such a war would shortly begin.[282] During the ensuing weeks it was actively circulated among the western tribes,[283] who were incited to collect their forces and assured that in the event of war they would have an opportunity to make a new boundary line. At the same time Simcoe, acting under Dorchester's orders, proceeded from Detroit to the Rapids of the Maumee, a few miles above the modern city of Toledo, with three companies of British regulars, and constructed a fort to serve as an outpost for the defense of Detroit against Wayne's advance. There is nothing improbable in the assertion that the Indians were given to understand that its gates would be open to shelter them, in case of

[281] Wayne to the Secretary of War, August 14, 1794; *American State Papers, Indian Affairs*, I, 490.

[282] *Michigan Pioneer Collections*, XX, 331. For an account of Dorchester's speech and its results see Roosevelt, *op. cit.*, IV, 57–60, 62.

[283] See, for example, Lieutenant-colonel Butler's speech to the chiefs of the Six Nations at Buffalo Creek, in April, 1794, printed in *Michigan Pioneer Collections*, XX, 342–43.

need, from Wayne's army, and it is clear that both the Indians and the Americans believed that the British were to all intents and purposes co-operating with the former. Wayne had learned of Simcoe's advance early in June, and since then he had received information from his scouts that the British had participated in the attack on Fort Recovery. It was therefore with the expectation of having a double foe to deal with that he planted and named Fort Defiance, preparatory to beginning the descent of the Maumee to the Rapids, where the British fort was located and near which the Indians had taken their stand.

The advance from Fort Defiance was begun on August 15, and three days later Wayne's army was within striking distance of the enemy. Here a halt was made and a temporary fortification thrown up. The savages had elected to defend a place known as Fallen Timbers, where the ground was thickly strewn with tree trunks as the result of a former tornado. This furnished an ideal covert for their mode of warfare, and at the same time, as they believed, rendered it impossible for Wayne's dreaded cavalry to act. Behind this shelter about two thousand warriors lay on the morning of August 20 awaiting Wayne's approach. The Indians were far from confident of repeating their success of three years before against St. Clair. Little Turtle, the leader on that occasion, had urged the acceptance of the peace overtures of "the chief who never sleeps," but in this he was overruled. Already some of the northern tribes had slunk away, disheartened by their discomfiture at Fort Recovery. The southern Indians had sent encouraging messages, but had failed to back them up with their warriors, and the sole hope of assistance rested with the British, who in similar crises in times gone by had failed them.[284]

In the ranks of the two armies, about to join combat, were a number of men who are famous in the history of the Northwest. General Wayne had acquired fame in the Revolution as a daring leader of men, but this campaign furnishes the climax of his military career and his surest claim upon the grateful remem-

[284] Winsor, *Westward Movement*, 457.

brance of posterity. From the most unpromising of raw material he had fashioned an army fit to cope with the red man in his lair, and had imbued it with his own dauntless confidence and enthusiasm. He had transformed such men as St. Clair had with difficulty held together in the absence of the enemy, and who had proved so helpless in his presence, into the peers of the frontiersmen themselves in marksmanship and dexterity in the saddle; and had made them submissive to an iron discipline which rendered them immeasurably superior to the latter for the conduct of a campaign or battle.

On the other side were a score or more of chieftains of varying degrees of importance and influence. If Little Turtle had favored a fight his rank and reputation would probably have given him the position of chief importance. Blue Jacket's advice had prevailed in the council before the battle, however, and as the result he occupied the position of commander. Two young men, one in either army, possess a peculiar interest for us by reason of their later careers. The one, a lieutenant in Wayne's army and aide-de-camp to the General, William Henry Harrison; the other, the warrior Tecumseh. Each distinguished himself according to the fashion of his race for bravery in the battle; each rose shortly to the position of leader of his race in the Northwest, and this leadership involved them in a deadly rivalry. In the long contest between them the red man went down to defeat; his projects for the resuscitation of his people were forever blasted at Tippecanoe, and two years later the battle of the Thames marked another victory for Harrison and Tecumseh's final defeat. For the one the reward was the Presidency, for the other a ruined people and a nameless grave. Yet who shall say that, measured by the standards of his race, Tecumseh was not the equal in greatness and ability of his victorious rival?

At eight o'clock on the morning of August 20 Wayne's legion advanced in columns in open order, its front, flanks, and rear protected by detachments of the Kentucky mounted volunteers and of Indians. After traveling a distance of five miles the mounted battalion in advance encountered the Indians, disposed in three lines stretching a distance of two miles at right angles to the river. The Kentuckians were driven back and the firing became general, but they had accomplished their purpose of giving the army timely notice of the position of the savages. Wayne's dispositions were quickly made. The infantry was drawn up in two lines. The whole force of mounted volunteers was sent by a circuitous path to turn the right flank of the savages, and the legionary cavalry under Captain Campbell was ordered to fall upon their left. At the same time the infantry moved forward with trailed arms to a bayonet charge, with orders to deliver their fire at close range after the Indians had been roused from their coverts, and then continue the charge, so as to give them no opportunity to reload.

The value of the months of careful drilling was now quickly manifested. Campbell's dragoons plunged forward over the difficult ground and fell upon the astonished savages, who delivered a single volley and fled. Campbell was slain and a dozen of his men killed or wounded, but the cavalry swept on, Lieutenant Covington, who succeeded to the command, cutting down two of the red men with his own hand. The infantry moved forward with equal impetuosity, driving the dismayed savages before them through the thick woods a distance of two miles in less than an hour. So quickly was the combat over that the second line of infantry and the Kentucky volunteers, despite their "anxiety" for action, were unable to reach their positions in time to share in the fight. The surviving savages and their Canadian allies scattered in flight, the Americans pursuing them as far as the walls of the British fort. Wayne reported a loss of one hundred and thirty-three in killed and wounded and estimated the loss of the enemy at more than double his own. The woods were strewn for some distance with the dead bodies of the Indians and their white auxiliaries, the latter armed with British muskets and bayonets.

The battle over, three days were spent in ravaging the surrounding fields and villages. The houses and stores of the British traders and agents shared the fate of the Indian villages, while the garrison looked on in impotent rage. Fortunately a conflict between the two armies, the danger of which was very real, was averted, the commanders contenting themselves with an exchange of verbal hostilities. A week after the battle the victorious army moved leisurely back to Fort Defiance, laying waste the villages and cornfields of the savages for a distance of fifty miles on either side of the Maumee. After two weeks spent in strengthening the fort, while waiting for supplies from Fort Recovery, the army moved up the river to the Miami villages at the mouth of the St. Mary's where Harmar's force had been rebuffed four years before. Here some weeks were spent in destroying the surrounding villages and fields and in building a fort which was named for the commander, Fort Wayne. At the end of October the army retired to Greenville where it went into winter quarters. Since the opening of the campaign it had performed "one of the most weighty and important feats in the winning of the West."[285]

The Indians were discouraged by their defeat and their abandonment by the British. The agents of the latter strove to reanimate them and prolong hostilities,[286] and for some time the issue was doubtful. Some of the savages were in favor of continuing the war, but the majority finally inclined to peace, and in February, 1795, Wayne entered into a preliminary agreement with a number of the tribes for the negotiation of a permanent peace on the basis of the terms of the treaty of Fort Harmar of January, 1789. The tawny diplomats straggled slowly in to the place appointed for the council. The council fire was kindled on June 16, [287] but owing to the tardiness of the various delegations a month elapsed before the formal negotiations were begun. Three weeks later, on August 10, the treaty was concluded. In all eleven hundred and thirty warriors had assembled. To the torrent of savage oratory which their spokesmen poured forth

[285] Roosevelt, *Winning of the West*, IV, 91.

[286] Winsor, *op. cit.*, 460–61; *American State Papers, Indian Affairs*, I, 547–58, 568.

[287] For Wayne's report of the proceedings attending the negotiation of the treaty see *American State Papers, Indian Affairs*, I, 562–83.

during the weeks of discussion Wayne replied in kind, showing himself as much at home in the council chamber as when on the field of battle.

On July 3 Wayne called the chiefs together to explain to them the significance of the impending celebration of Independence Day, so that they might not be alarmed when the roar of the big guns should "ascend into the heavens." Twelve days later the council was formally opened. Wayne displayed his credentials to the assembled chiefs, explained the occasion of the meeting, and closed by suggesting an adjournment of two or three days "to have a little drink" and consider the situation. The chief issue of the conference was immediately raised by Little Turtle, who professed ignorance of the treaty of Fort Harmar and denied that the Miamis had had any part in it. As the negotiations proceeded this chief strenuously opposed the cessions demanded by Wayne. In a speech delivered July 22 he expressed his regret over the division of opinion manifested by the assembled Indians, and claimed for his tribe all of the territory bounded on the east by a line from Detroit to and down the Scioto River to its mouth, on the south by the Ohio from this point to the mouth of the Wabash, and on the west by a line from the mouth of the Wabash to Chicago. He questioned the good faith of the Americans, saying they claimed the land in dispute now by cession by the British in 1783, now by that of the tribes who took part in the treaty of Fort Harmar. When, five days later, Wayne read the list of reservations which he proposed to embody in the treaty, including a tract six miles square "at the Mouth of Chikago River . . . . where a Fort formerly stood," Little Turtle answered that his people had never heard of it. On this particular point the facts of history favored the red man, for there is no satisfactory evidence that the French had ever had a fort here. But force and the logic of events favored the white leader, and in the final draft of the treaty was included the cession of "One piece of Land Six Miles square at the Mouth of Chickago River emptying into the Southwest end of Lake Michigan where a fort formerly stood."

Among those most disposed to accept the terms offered by Wayne were the Wyandots, to whom was intrusted one of the two copies of the treaty that were engrossed on parchment. Their leader, Tarke, responded to Little Turtle's reflections upon the cession made at Fort Harmar and upon those who disagreed with him, with a burst of eloquence characteristic of Indian oratory and of the figurative language which it habitually employed. Addressing his "Elder Brother," General Wayne, he said:

"Now listen to us: The Great Spirit above has appointed this day for us to meet together. I shall now deliver my sentiments to you, the Fifteen Fires. I view you lying in a gore of blood; it is me, an Indian, who has caused it. Our tomahawk yet remains in your head; the English gave it to me to place there.

"Elder Brother: I now take the tomahawk out of your head; but with so much care, that you shall not feel pain or injury. I will now tear a big tree up by the roots, and throw the hatchet into the cavity which they occupied, where the waters will wash it away where it can never be found. Now I have buried the hatchet and I expect that none of my color will ever again find it out. . . . .

"Brothers: Listen! I now wipe your body clean from all blood with this white soft linen [white wampum], and I do it with as much tenderness as I am capable of. You have appointed this house for the chiefs of the different tribes to sit in with you, and none but good words ought to be spoken in it. I swept it clean; nothing impure remains in it. . . . .

"Brother: I clear away yon hovering clouds, that we may enjoy a clear, bright day, and easily see the sun, which the Great Spirit has bestowed on us, rise and set continually. . . . ."

The negotiations were at length satisfactorily concluded, and all professed themselves satisfied with Wayne's demands. The treaty recognized the American title to the lands north of the Ohio bounded by a line drawn from the mouth of the Kentucky River to Fort Recovery, thence in a general easterly direction to the Muskingum, and along this river and the Cuyahoga to Lake Erie; in addition various reservations, aside from the one at Chicago, were made, most of them for the establishment of forts, and the free passage of the rivers and portages connecting the proposed chain of forts was guaranteed. In Illinois the grant included reservations at Chicago, at Lake Peoria, and at the mouth of the Illinois, and the free use of the Chicago Harbor, River, and Portage, and the Illinois River. On the other hand the Indian title to the soil was recognized, some twenty thousand dollars worth of presents were distributed, and the payment to the Indians of annuities aggregating nine thousand five hundred dollars was promised.

The treaty brought to an end forty years of warfare in the valley of the Ohio, during which it is estimated five thousand whites were killed or captured.[288] For three years past the war had cost the government of the United States over a million dollars a year. The peace which Wayne brought to the frontier endured for fifteen years, being broken only by Tecumseh's war, which shortly merged into the greater struggle between Great Britain and the United States in 1812. By that time the in-rush of settlers and the passing away of the older generation had wrought a material change in the condition of the Northwest; so that the Treaty of Greenville may fairly be said to have endured until the conditions which called it forth had passed away.

While Wayne was pushing his campaign against the northwestern Indians, which the British officials feared would end in their overthrow at Detroit, Washington dispatched John Jay on a diplomatic mission to England which was to result in the peaceable surrender of the northwestern posts. The differences between the two countries which had arisen from the unfulfilled treaty of 1783 had now become so serious that there was grave danger of a warlike termination. In the hope of preventing this calamity, therefore, Washington appointed Jay, in the spring of 1794, as a special envoy to England to treat of the matters in dispute.

[288] Winsor, *op. cit.*, 494.

During the summer the negotiations with the British government went slowly forward and in November a treaty was concluded. By the Americans its terms were received with bitter disgust, and there is even yet a difference of opinion among students over the question of the wisdom of Jay's conduct of the negotiations. The western Americans were especially loud in their denunciation of Jay and the treaty.[289] Yet they obtained by it the surrender of the British posts in the Northwest, a measure which constituted the logical completion of Wayne's work and was absolutely essential to the permanence of the peace so recently established on the frontier. It was stipulated that the posts should be evacuated on June 1, 1796, and Washington appropriately appointed Wayne to superintend the taking possession of them by the United States. As the appointed time drew near the British were more ready to make the surrender than were the Americans to receive it. At our own request, therefore, possession was retained until the arrival of the relieving forces at the various posts. During the summer and fall the transfers were made, the last post which was taken over by the Americans being Mackinac in October. Our boundaries in the Northwest, nominally established by the Treaty of Paris of 1783, were at last achieved in reality. The Indians had been conquered and Great Britain had retired; the Northwest was won for the United States.

[289] Roosevelt, *op. cit.*, IV, 194–97.

CHAPTER VI

THE FOUNDING OF FORT DEARBORN

The strategic value of Chicago as a center of control for the region between the Great Lakes and the Mississippi had been recognized long before our government took the step of establishing a fort there. On more than one occasion during the French régime recommendations were made to the French government in favor of a fort at Chicago. As early as 1697 two Frenchmen, Louvigny and Mantet, conceived the project of making a combined trading and exploring expedition from Canada toward Mexico by way of the Mississippi River, and to this end petitioned the French minister of war for a post at Chicago to serve as an entrepôt for their enterprise.[290] The importance of Chicago in the struggle between the British and the Americans during the Revolution has already been shown. After Wayne's triumph at Fallen Timbers in August, 1794, the British officer, Simcoe, proposed to the Lords of Trade a plan for shutting American traders out of the Mississippi Valley by establishing British depots along the portages leading to it, particularly at the Chicago Portage.[291] The British control of the Northwest which Simcoe was striving to perpetuate was, however, about to cease, and nothing came of his project. Wayne's appreciation of the importance of Chicago was shown by his demand in the Treaty of Greenville that the Indians cede to the United States a tract of land six miles square at the mouth of the Chicago River, to serve as the site for a future fort.

Two facts, both of them of great importance in American history, account for the establishment of Fort Dearborn, eight years after Wayne thus acquired from the Indians the title to its site. One was Wayne's victory over the northwestern tribes, the results of which were registered in this same Treaty of

[290] Margry, IV, 9 ff.

[291] Winsor, *Westward Movement*, 461.

Greenville; the other, the acquisition of Louisiana by the United States in 1803. Probably the first of these would alone have been sufficient to determine the establishment ere long of a fort at Chicago, but the influence of the two combined rendered delay impossible.

The victory of Wayne, by removing the menace of Indian hostilities, made possible the rapid settlement of the region northwest of the Ohio. During the next few years a veritable flood of immigration poured into this Northwest Territory, the portion nearest at hand being, as was natural, first occupied. Within five years of the Treaty of Greenville this portion of the territory was ready for statehood. In 1800, therefore, Congress provided for the separation of the Northwest Territory into two parts, and two years later the eastern section was admitted into the Union as the state of Ohio. The remaining portion became the territory of Indiana with William Henry Harrison, then a young man of twenty-seven, as governor. During the following years the line of white settlement advanced steadily, though more slowly, into the North and West. The two military posts farthest advanced in this direction were Detroit and Mackinac. Neither of these was advantageously situated for the administration of the country stretching from the upper lakes to the Mississippi.

With every passing year the necessity of exercising a firmer control over this region became greater. The settlers must be protected from Indian depredations, and the lawlessness of the traders and other frontiersmen must be curbed. One fact of great importance pertained to the British control of the Indian trade of the Northwest. The surrender of the posts in 1796 had not broken the grip of the traders on this region. Until the close of the War of 1812—and in the remoter portion of the Northwest, for some years after this—the influence of the Canadian traders over the Indians was paramount. It was impossible, therefore, for the United States to exercise an effective control over them, and a garrison to the west of Lake Michigan was needed to assist in wresting this commercial supremacy from the British traders.

The acquisition of Louisiana advanced our western boundary from the Mississippi to the crest of the Rocky Mountains. If before it had been difficult to control our westernmost frontier from Detroit and Mackinac, with this advance it became utterly impossible. New outposts must be established in order to keep pace with both the advancing boundary and the swelling wave of settlement. Chicago, still far in advance of the latter, was the logical place for the new establishment. A garrison here in the heart of the Indian country would serve to protect the settlements of Indiana and lower Illinois, would perfect the communication between the latter and the posts of Detroit and Mackinac, and constitute a convenient center of control for the region between Lake Michigan and the Mississippi.[292]

Rumors of a purpose to establish a post at Chicago preceded by some years its actual consummation. In the winter of 1797–98 William Burnett, a French trader on the St. Joseph River, informed the Montreal house from which he obtained his supplies for the Indian trade of the expectation that a garrison would be established at Chicago the following summer.[293] What the basis for this expectation was does not appear, but evidently Burnett considered it probable, for in August, 1798, he wrote that he now had reason to expect the garrison would arrive in the fall. The shrewd trader's interest in the matter was due to the fact that, having already a house at Chicago, and "a promise of assistance from headquarters," he would have occasion for "a good deal of liquors," and some other articles, for that post. Thus rum attended the birth, and, as we shall see, was prominent at the downfall, of old Fort Dearborn.

The "promise of assistance from headquarters" furnishes a possible clue to the source of Burnett's information. Though five years were yet to elapse before the project materialized, the letter is of some importance as showing that among those most interested it had long been regarded as a probability of the near

[292] See on this point the letter from Mackinac, September 6, 1803, printed in *Relf's Philadelphia Gazette and Commercial Advertiser*, November 19, 1803.

[293] Hurlbut, *Chicago Antiquities*, 66.

future. Early in 1803 the matter was at last determined. A letter from the Secretary of War,[294] dated March 9, to Colonel Hamtramck of the First Infantry, who was then stationed at Detroit, directed that an officer and six men be sent to make a preliminary investigation of the situation at Chicago and the route thither from Detroit. The party was to go by land from Detroit to the mouth of the St. Joseph River, marking a trail and noting suitable camping-places for the company which was to follow. Inquiry was to be made concerning the supplies of provisions which Burnett and the other traders could furnish, and a suitable "scite" was to be selected at St. Joseph for a temporary encampment of the company until preparations could be made at "Chikago" for its reception. In case the overland route should be found to be practicable for a company with packhorses for carrying provisions and light baggage, Colonel Hamtramck should order it to go, under command of a "discreet, judicious captain," and should send around the lakes the necessary tools and other equipment for the erection and maintenance of a strong stockade post at Chicago, together with two light fieldpieces and the necessary supply of ammunition.

Six weeks later the appointment of Captain John Whistler as commander of the new post had been made and, soon after, he departed with six men to examine the route and report to Major Pike.[295] At the same time the firm of Robert and James Abbott of Detroit was considering the advantages of the post as a possible trading center. They report that Whistler desired them to establish a store there, and it is possible that the sentiment the culmination of which is recorded in the quaint announcement of Whistler to Kingsbury in November, 1804, of the marriage of his eldest daughter to a "gentleman of my old acquaintance (James

[294] Copy, by Daniel O. Drennan, of letter of Inspector-general Cushing to Hamtramck, March 14, 1803, in Chicago Historical Society library. Mr. Drennan, as agent of the society, made exact copies of a large number of documents in the files of the War Department at Washington pertaining to Hull's campaign and to Fort Dearborn and early Chicago. These will be cited henceforth as the *Drennan Papers*.

[295] Letter of Robert and James Abbott of Detroit to Abbott and Maxwell of Mackinac, April 30, 1803, copied in *Chicago from 1803 to 1812*, by James Grant Wilson, MS in the Chicago Historical Society library.

Abbot)"[296] was already blossoming. If, as seems likely, Hamtramck was responsible for Whistler's appointment to the new command it must have been almost his last official act, for he died on April 11, less than a month after the issuance by the Inspector-general at Cumberland, Maryland, of the order for the establishment of the fort.[297]

At half-past five o'clock on the morning of July 14, 1803, the troops set out from Detroit under command of Lieutenant James Strode Swearingen of the artillery, then a youth of twenty-one.[298] Swearingen had volunteered to lead the troops to Chicago for Captain Whistler, on account of the infirm state of the latter's health. Whistler and his family, together with his son Lieutenant William Whistler and his young wife, embarked on the schooner "Tracy," commanded by Lieutenant Dorr, which had been ordered to proceed around the lakes with provisions and military stores for the new post. We have the journal which Swearingen kept on the trip, containing observations on the country, timber, camping-places, and water courses.[299] The daily march varied greatly in length. Sometimes the start was made before five in the morning and the march ended by two in the afternoon; at other times bad weather or other obstacles necessitated a late start and a march of only a few miles. The route followed was that of the old Chicago Trail, later known as the "Chicago Road." It led the troops across the Rouge and Huron rivers, past the site of the modern city of Ypsilanti to the upper waters of Grand River, which flows into Lake Michigan. Thence the route lay across country to the St. Joseph and down this river to its mouth.

[296] *Kingsbury Papers*, Whistler to Kingsbury, November 3, 1804.

[297] Hamtramck was a veteran soldier, having joined Montgomery's army before Quebec in 1776. He served throughout the remainder of the Revolution, and at its close continued in the army, rising by successive promotions to the rank of colonel. He was stationed on the northwestern frontier for many years prior to his death. At the battle of Fallen Timbers he commanded the left wing of the legion, and received special mention in Wayne's official report of the battle.

[298] For an account of Swearingen's career see report of an interview with him in 1863, together with his own sketch of his life, preserved in the MS volume of *Proceedings* of the Chicago Historical Society, 1856-64, 348.

[299] Printed as Appendix I.

On July 25 we find Swearingen at "Kinzie's improvement" on the St. Joseph. The site today is occupied by the sleepy hamlet of Bertrand, a short distance south of Niles, and the highway that crosses the river here is still called the Chicago Road. Here the party was detained for a day while boats were being procured. On July 27 the expedition proceeded down the river, the baggage and seventeen of the men in the boats, the remainder of the men marching by land. From July 28 to August 12 the troops were encamped at the mouth of the St. Joseph, awaiting the arrival of the "Tracy" with needed provisions. Swearingen estimated the distance from Detroit to the mouth of the St. Joseph at two hundred and seventy-two miles. The distance by rail today is considerably less, but the expedition had followed the tortuous Indian trail and then the course of the meandering St. Joseph. The remainder of the march around the lake to Chicago was accomplished in three days, the troops marching along the lake shore. The distance according to Swearingen's estimate was ninety miles, and in this he was not far astray. Probably the rapidity of the march, averaging thirty miles each day, may be explained by the supposition that the baggage continued to be transported by boat, for the journal records that the start from St. Joseph was delayed two days by the roughness of the lake. Unless the boats continued on to Chicago this would, apparently, have been of no concern to the expedition.

While the land detachment was thus marching across the wilderness of southern Michigan and northern Indiana, the "Tracy" was conveying the artillery, provisions, and heavy baggage around the lakes. A short stop was made at the mouth of the St. Joseph where the troops were supplied with provisions. Here the Whistlers, father and son, disembarked, and continued their journey to Chicago in a row-boat.[300] We have several accounts, each of them more or less fragmentary, of what happened upon the arrival of the troops at Chicago. Some of them are of contemporary origin, while two which will demand

[300] This circumstance was related over seventy years later by the wife of Lieutenant William Whistler (Hurlbut, *Chicago Antiquities*, 25). The reason for such a proceeding is not apparent.

consideration were written over half a century later by two surviving participants in the founding of the first Fort Dearborn.[301] Of these Swearingen's Journal is easily the most authoritative, but unfortunately it confines itself largely to describing the physical situation. The other reports help out the story by the addition of various details. The troops reached the Chicago River at two o'clock on the afternoon of August 17, after a march of twenty-four miles from their last camping-place on the Little Calumet. They found the Chicago a sluggish stream thirty yards in width at the bend where the fort was to be constructed. The river was eighteen feet or more in depth, but a sand bar at its mouth rendered the water dead and unfit for use. The existence of the bar made it possible for the troops to cross the river "dry shod" and encamp on the other side a short distance above its mouth. The river bank was eight feet high at the point where the fort was to be built, a half-mile above the mouth of the stream. The opposite bank was somewhat lower, while farther up the stream both banks were very low.

Swearingen's Journal says nothing of the Indians, but in the sketch of his life written sixty years later he records that the troops were greeted on their arrival by many Indians, all of whom were friendly. The wife of Lieutenant Whistler, who came a matron of sixteen summers to the site of the future metropolis, relates that while the schooner was here some two thousand natives gathered to see the "big canoe with wings." Doubtless their souls were stirred at the sight by emotions even stronger than those which today animate their more sophisticated successors at sight of the schooners of the air. Three weeks later a Mackinac letter-writer reported to the eastern press that the natives opposed the commander's design of building a fort and threatened to collect their warriors and prevent it.[302] The

[301] Swearingen's Journal, Appendix I; his statements made in 1863 preserved in the *Chicago Historical Society, Proceedings*, 1856–64, 348; letter from Mackinac, September 6, 1803, printed in *Relf's Philadelphia Gazette*, November 19, 1803; letter of Dr. William Smith from Fort Dearborn, December 9, 1803, to James May of Detroit, MS in Detroit Public Library; story of the wife of Lieutenant Whistler in 1875, Hurlbut, *Chicago Antiquities*, 23–28.

[302] *Relf's Philadelphia Gazette*, November 19, 1803.

writer's source of information was evidently someone on board the "Tracy," which touched at Mackinac on its return voyage to Detroit.[303] Since a hostile attitude on the part of the Indians is not mentioned by Mrs. Whistler, and is expressly denied by Swearingen, we may safely ascribe the statement to the desire of someone to tell an interesting story.

The construction of the stockade and a shelter for the troops was the commander's first care. Mrs. Whistler relates that there were no horses or oxen at hand, so that the soldiers were compelled to perform the work of dragging the timbers to their required positions. It seems likely, however, that there were some animals, though their number was probably inadequate. The original order for the establishment of a fort contemplated the use of packhorses by the troops on their overland march, and Whistler, writing to Kingsbury in July, 1804, complains of the scarcity of corn.[304] The public oxen had had none all summer, and when he first came here he could obtain but eighteen bushels. Evidently, then, the commander had oxen before many months elapsed, if not from the beginning. There was, however, another source of annoyance. If the natives did not threaten to prevent the building of the fort, we may be sure they made life a burden to the troops by their begging and petty thievery. The Illinois Indians had an ancient reputation, dating back to the early French period, for being expert thieves. When the second Fort Dearborn was built a dozen years later, begging and stealing by the Indians became such an intolerable nuisance that if we are to credit the assertion of Moses Morgan, who aided in its construction, it required more men to mount guard by day to keep the squaws and papooses away than at night.[305]

[303] Swearingen's statements in 1863, in *Chicago Historical Society, Proceedings*, 1856–64, 348.

[304] *Kingsbury Papers*, Whistler to Kingsbury, July 27, 1804.

[305] Moses Morgan's narrative, preserved by William R. Head, MS in Chicago Historical Society library. Head was, until his death in 1910, a worker in the local historical field. Most of his papers have been destroyed, but a few of them are in the Chicago Historical Society library, and a considerably larger number are owned by his widow. They will be cited henceforth as the *Head Papers*.

We have no such detailed account of the building of the first fort, but at least one characteristic incident has been preserved for us by Thomas G. Anderson. Anderson, who later fought on the British side in the War of 1812, was at this time a fur trader at Milwaukee. In his old age he prepared a long narrative of his life in the West.[306] It is vainglorious and unreliable in many respects, but with proper care one may glean much of interest and something of value from it. He relates that on learning of the coming of the troops to Chicago, he mounted his horse and went to pay a neighborly call.[307] He found Captain Whistler's family ensconsed temporarily in one of the wretched log huts which belonged to the traders, while his officers and men were living under canvas. Anderson accepted an invitation to dine with Whistler. The table was spread and the guests were seated, when through the door strode a band of painted warriors. The women shrieked and fled, leaving the men to play the rôle of hosts alone. The leader of the savages, unperturbed by this reception, proceeded to help himself to the bread on the table and distribute it among his warriors. Anderson berated him for his conduct and succeeded in inducing the band to leave; whereupon the doughty trader assumed to himself the credit of having averted a massacre of the garrison. It may seem hazardous to attempt to extract the kernel of truth in this tale from the chaff which surrounds it; however, the opinion may be ventured that some such scene may have occurred, but that the element of danger, and therewith the credit which Anderson assumes for his action, was wholly lacking.

The work of construction progressed but slowly. Soon after their arrival the troops suffered much from bilious fevers.[308] These abated with the coming of cold weather, but in December the garrison was still sheltered in small, temporary huts, and the

[306] For Anderson's narrative, together with a biographical sketch of the author, see *Wisconsin Historical Collections*, IX, 137 ff. The narrative is unreliable in many ways, and its statements should be used with caution.

[307] *Wisconsin Historical Collections*, IX, 154–55.

[308] Letter of Dr. William Smith to James May, December 9, 1803.

fort was described as "not much advanced." Fortunately the autumn persisted long. On December 9 the surgeon wrote to a friend in Detroit that there was neither snow nor ice, there had been but little rain or frost, and the season had been "remarkably fine."[309]

Before leaving the subject of the building of Fort Dearborn, it may be well to refer to another tale in connection therewith which has often been repeated.[310] It is to the effect that the government, having decided to establish a fort on Lake Michigan, sent commissioners to St. Joseph with a view of locating it there; they selected a site and began preparations for erecting a fort, when the Indians objected, and so the commissioners passed on to Chicago, where Fort Dearborn was constructed. No evidence has been offered in support of this story, notwithstanding its improbability. In the light of documents discovered in recent years it is possible to suggest an explanation of its origin. We have seen that Colonel Hamtramck was directed to send a detail to explore the route and select a site at the mouth of the St. Joseph for a temporary camp; and that Swearingen's company halted here for two weeks on its way to Chicago. It is possible that the natives, not knowing that the camp was but a temporary one, protested against it and believed their protest responsible for the removal of the troops to Chicago.

We may now turn our attention to the civilian population of Chicago at the time of the establishment of Fort Dearborn, and in this connection to what is known of the first white man who settled at this point. Here as elsewhere, in connection with the history of early Chicago, the truth has been obscured by a mass of tradition, fostered in large part by family pride. The effort to fix upon any certain person the distinction of being the first resident of Chicago is idle. Traders and other travelers passed through the place more or less frequently from the time of Marquette on, and at various times individuals, ordinarily

[309] Letter of Dr. William Smith to James May, December 9, 1803.

[310] The earliest publication of the story which I have found occurs in the *Michigan Pioneer Collections*, I, 122.

traders, established themselves here for a shorter or longer period. The story of Father Pinet's mission of the Guardian Angel at Chicago near the close of the seventeenth century has already been noted.[311] After this there are several more or less shadowy traditions of dwellers on the banks of the Chicago River during the second half of the eighteenth century. The earliest of these deals with a remarkable woman, whose career as painted for us by Reynolds would be difficult to parallel elsewhere in history.[312] Born of French parents of the name of La Flamme at St. Joseph on Lake Michigan in 1734, she first migrated to Mackinac. From thence with her husband, Pilette de Sainte Ange, she removed to Chicago about the year 1765. After some years' residence here her husband died and she removed to the French settlement of Cahokia, where she married a Canadian named La Compt and reared a large family of children. Widowed again, she became in due time the wife of Tom Brady. No issue resulted from this union, and Mrs. Brady was destined to still another widowhood, dying at Cahokia in 1843 at the age of one hundred and nine years.

Governor Reynolds knew Mrs. La Compt, as she was commonly known after Brady's death, for thirty years, and describes her as a woman of strong mind and an extraordinary constitution, and endowed with the courage and energies of a heroine. The Indians were her neighbors from her infancy until extreme old age; she became familiar with their language and their character, and over the Pottawatomies and other tribes she developed a remarkable influence. This she frequently exerted during the stormy days of the Revolution to protect the French settlers from attack by the hostile warriors, and later, in the early days of American domination in Illinois, she continued to shield the white settlers. Reynolds avers that on numerous occasions she was awakened in the dead of night by her Indian friends to give her warning of an impending attack in order that she might leave

[311] *Supra*, pp. 38-42.

[312] Reynolds, *Pioneer History of Illinois*, 168–69. The story is told, also, with certain variations and additional details, by Wm. R. Head (*Head Papers*, owned by his widow).

Cahokia. Instead of seeking her own safety, however, she would set out alone to meet the hostile war party, and never failed to avert the storm and prevent bloodshed. She sometimes remained with the warriors for days, appeasing their anger and urging wise counsels upon them. In due time the anxious villagers, who had been watching meanwhile with arms in their hands for the expected attack, would see Mrs. La Compt approach at the head of a band of warriors, their angry passions stilled and their war paint changed to somber black to manifest their sorrow for having entertained hostile designs against their friends. A feast would usually follow, cementing the reconciliation which Mrs. La Compt had been instrumental in effecting, and the warriors would disperse.

That tradition has exaggerated the influence and services of Mrs. La Compt is quite probable. But making due allowance for this, the impression remains that she was a woman of unusual vigor and strength of character. and it seems appropriate that her name should head the ever-lengthening list of white women who have been residents of Chicago. The next tangible tradition of white occupation of Chicago is contained in a story told to Gurdon S. Hubbard by the trader, Antoine De Champs.[313] He pointed out to the youthful Hubbard the traces of corn hills on the west side of the North Branch, and related that as early as 1778 a trader by the name of Guarie had lived here, from whom the river had taken its name. Hubbard gives further details concerning Guarie's trading house, taking pains to point out, however, that the statements are based on oral tradition. But this tradition is corroborated in one respect at least, for as late as 1823 the North Branch was called the "Gary" river by the historian of Major Long's expedition.[314]

Our only knowledge of Guarie's residence at Chicago is contained in the story recorded by Hubbard, but with the mixed-breed negro, Baptiste Point Du Sable, we reach more solid ground. The traditional account of his Chicago career, first

[313] For it see Blanchard, *Discovery and Conquests of the Northwest*, 757–58.

[314] Keating, *Narrative of an Expedition to the Sources of the St. Peter's River . . . . in 1823*, I, 172.

recorded by Mrs. Kinzie[315] and afterward repeated and enlarged upon by others,[316] must be regarded as largely fictitious and wholly unauthenticated. But by assembling the information contained in a number of documents widely scattered as to date and origin it is possible to learn much about him.[317] The usual accounts, following Mrs. Kinzie, represent Du Sable to have been a native of San Domingo. Matson, on the other hand, states that he was a runaway slave from the vicinity of Lexington, Kentucky, and describes his coming to Chicago and his supposed doings here with much circumstantial detail.[318] Much of this is obviously imaginary, and the two accounts are probably equally unworthy of credence. In general, Du Sable's occupation seems to have been that of a trader, though according to his own testimony he had improved a thirty-acre farm at Peoria as early as 1780.[319]

As a trader he moved from place to place and the date of his settlement at Chicago and the regularity of his stay here are alike uncertain. De Peyster says that he was here in 1779, and also darkly hints at some punishment meted out to him by Langlade, the reputed "father of Wisconsin."[320] In the summer of that year, however, we find him established with a house on the River

[315] Mrs. John H. Kinzie, *Wau Bun, the "Early Day" in the Northwest*, Caxton Club edition. This work has been reprinted several times since its first appearance in 1856. Page references to it in this work are to the Caxton Club edition of 1901.

[316] See, for example, Mason, "Early Visitors to Chicago," in *New England Magazine*, VI, 205–6.

[317] The following sources, on a study of which the accompanying account of Du Sable is based, contain practically all the information I have been able to collect concerning him: Kinzie, *Wau Bun*, 146; De Peyster's allusion, in speech to the Indians at l'Arbre Croche July 4, 1779, in *Wisconsin Historical Collections*, XVIII, 384; McCulloch, *Early Days of Peoria and Chicago*, 91–92; "Recollections of Augustin Grignon," in *Wisconsin Historical Collections*, III, 292; Lieutenant Bennett's report of arrest of Du Sable, August, 1779, in *Wisconsin Historical Collections*, XVII, 399; inventory of goods taken from Du Sable by Bennett, in *Michigan Pioneer Collections*, X, 366; Journal of Hugh Heward (MS original owned by Clarence M. Burton of Detroit; I have used the copy in the Chicago Historical Society library); Schoolcraft, *Personal Memoirs*, 478; Draper Collection, S, Vols. XXI and XXII, *passim;* McCulloch, "Old Peoria," in *Illinois State Historical Society, Transactions*, 1901, 46.

[318] Matson, N., *French and Indians of Illinois River*, 187–91. Matson's information purports to have been obtained from a grandson of Du Sable.

[319] McCulloch, *Early Days of Peoria and Chicago*, 91.

[320] *Wisconsin Historical Collections*, XVIII, 384; see also in this connection *ibid.*, 399, note 98.

Chemin, later known as Trail Creek, probably on the site of Michigan City, Indiana. Here he was arrested by Lieutenant Bennett, who had been sent by De Peyster toward Vincennes to forestall an anticipated attack on Mackinac by George Rogers Clark.[321] Du Sable's offense seems to have consisted only in his attachment to the American cause, and even his captor speaks highly of him. Curiously enough, he was in the employ of a British trader, Durand, at Mackinac, who this same summer had undertaken to guide a British war party to the Illinois country to co-operate with Bennett. The goods which Bennett seized from Du Sable belonged to Durand, who proceeded to file a claim with his government for their value. Because of this circumstance there is preserved an itemized inventory of Du Sable's stock in trade.[322] Perhaps the most interesting entry, aside from the quaint designation of Du Sable as a "naigre Libre," is the rum, ten barrels of twenty gallons each, with a value nearly twice as great as all of the remainder of the stock.

Whatever his nativity may have been, Du Sable proved, at least to the satisfaction of a government commission, that he was a citizen of the United States. In pursuance of a series of congressional acts and resolutions providing for grants in the Illinois country to citizens of the United States who had made improvements or who were heads of families, Du Sable made proof that both before and after 1783 he had resided at Peoria, that he was the head of a family, and that he had improved a farm of thirty acres at Peoria as early as 1780.[323] The commission therefore reported that he was entitled to eight hundred acres of land. How long after 1783 he continued to reside at Peoria does not appear, but in 1790 we find him established at Chicago near the mouth of the river. Whether, as Mrs. Kinzie suggests, he went into politics and sought election as a chief of the Pottawatomies is dubious,[324] but when Heward passed through Chicago

[321] *Wisconsin Historical Collections*, XVIII, 399.

[322] *Michigan Pioneer Collections*, X, 366.

[323] McCulloch, *Early Days of Peoria and Chicago*, 91.

[324] Mrs. Kinzie's brief statement on this point is greatly enlarged and improved upon by Matson, *French and Indians of Illinois River*, 188–91.

in the spring of 1790, he was entertained by Du Sable. The traveler exchanged some cotton cloth with him for a supply of food, and also borrowed his boat. Four years later he was still here, if Grignon's recollections are to be trusted. Alexander Robinson in his old age related that Du Sable, who had long lived at Chicago and was prominent among the Indians, came to Mackinac about the year 1796, accompanied by quite a band of Indians in several birch-bark canoes. The British greeted him on his arrival by the discharge of cannon.[325]

The accounts we have of the personality and character of Du Sable are for the most part highly creditable to him. Robinson describes him as tall and of commanding appearance. Another observer, Stephen Hempstead, who was acquainted with him in his old age, describes him as quite gray and venerable, about six feet in height, with a well-formed figure and a very pleasant countenance.[326] De Peyster, himself a rhymster and a friend of Robert Burns, calls him "handsome" and well educated. Doubtless in this case allowance should be made for poetic license and for the fact that the poet probably never actually saw the subject of his verse. Grignon recalled that Du Sable "drank pretty freely," and Robinson stated that he danced and caroused with the Indians and "drank badly." By way of palliation of this charge it may be noted that drinking was a habit common alike to Du Sable's age and his profession. There is a much larger mass of testimony in Du Sable's favor to offset this venial habit. Hempstead, who has already been quoted, says that he was not degraded, and that he appeared to be respected by those who knew him. Long years after his death the observant Schoolcraft recorded the information received from Mrs. La Framboise, an aged *métif* lady at Mackinac, that he was "a respectable man."[327] But the strongest praise comes from Lieutenant Bennett, Du Sable's captor in 1779. He reported to De Peyster that since his imprisonment Du Sable had behaved

[325] Interview with Lyman C. Draper, Draper Collection, S, XXI, 276.

[326] Interview of Lyman C. Draper with Hempstead, Draper Collection, S, XXII, 177.

[327] Schoolcraft, *Personal Memoirs*, 478.

in every respect as became a man in his situation, and that he had many friends who gave him a good character.

According to the tradition preserved by Mrs. Kinzie, Du Sable withdrew from Chicago to the home of a friend in Peoria, where he terminated his career. Alexander Robinson stated that he went off to the region of St. Louis and died there, probably before the beginning of the War of 1812.[328] A more specific and, apparently, reliable account of his last years is furnished by Hempstead.[329] He states that Du Sable had no goods in these last years, but spent his time hunting and fishing and lived by himself. He had a hut near the mouth of the Osage River, and here he died, probably about the year 1811.

When the troops came to Chicago in 1803 they found four huts or cabins here, belonging to some French Canadian traders.[330] One of these was occupied by Le Mai, who had bought out Du Sable, one by Ouilmette, and a third by Pettle. The fourth, apparently, belonged to Kinzie and was at this time vacant. Doctor Smith, the first surgeon at Fort Dearborn, and John La Lime shortly secured possession of it for the winter and fitted it up in a comfortable manner for their joint occupancy.[331]

Our information concerning Pettle is meager. According to Mrs. Whistler he was a French Canadian living here with an Indian wife when the garrison came in 1803.[332] The entries in John Kinzie's account books show that his first name was Louis, and that he either dealt in furs or himself hunted them.[333] His name occurs at intervals down to 1812, showing that he was a resident of Chicago during the entire period. With the last entry of his name in Kinzie's account book he disappears from history. Possibly it may have been his fate to fight and die with the Chicago militia at the baggage wagons on the fatal day of evacuation in the summer of 1812.

[328] Interview with Lyman C. Draper, Draper Collection, S, XXI, 276.

[329] *Ibid.*, XXII, 177.

[330] Hurlbut, *Chicago Antiquities*, 25.

[331] Letter of Dr. Smith to James May, December 9, 1803.

[332] Hurlbut, *Chicago Antiquities*, 25. [333] *Barry Transcript*.

Ouilmette claimed to have come to Chicago in 1790.[334] He was illiterate, and the statement, uncorroborated as it is, must be accepted with caution. We know, however, that when the soldiers came to establish the fort he was living with his Indian wife in one of the four huts which they found here.[335] When Doctor Cooper came to Fort Dearborn as post surgeon five years later, there were still but four houses on the north side of the river, of which Ouilmette's was one.[336] Ouilmette's chief dependence for a livelihood, apparently, was on the transportation of travelers and their baggage across the portage. It has already been shown that the French settlers at Chicago carried on this business in the first quarter of the nineteenth century.[337] That Ouilmette was engaged in this work was stated by Mr. Bain to Rev. William Barry, founder and first secretary of the Chicago Historical Society.[338] An entry in Kinzie's account book charges him for the use of a wagon and oxen to transport goods over the portage to the "Fork" of the Illinois River.[339]

In the summer of 1820 John Tanner, who had been for thirty years a captive among the Indians, passed through Chicago with his family, going by canoe from Mackinac to St. Louis.[340] His progress was halted here for a time by the low stage of water in the Illinois River. During this time he suffered greatly from illness and destitution; he was rescued from his plight by a Frenchman who had been to carry some boats across the portage. His wife, who was an Indian, usually accompanied him on such expeditions. Although his horses were much worn from their long journey, he agreed for a moderate price to transport Tanner and his canoe sixty miles, and, if his horses should hold out, twice this distance, the length of the portage at this stage of the river. In addition he lent Tanner, who was weak from illness, a young horse to ride. Before the sixty miles had been traversed the

[334] Ouilmette to John (H.) Kinzie, June 1, 1839, in Blanchard, *The Northwest and Chicago*, I, 574.

[335] Hurlbut, *Chicago Antiquities*, 25.

[336] Wilson, *Chicago from 1803 to 1812.*

[337] *Supra*, p. 19.

[338] *Barry Transcript.*

[339] *Ibid.*, entry for June 14, 1806.

[340] *Tanner's Narrative*, 257–58.

Frenchman was himself taken sick, and as there was now some water in the river Tanner dismissed him and attempted to descend the river in his canoe. That this Frenchman was Ouilmette seems probable. If so, the narrative throws an interesting light upon both his business and his character. It shows that the transporting of travelers over the portage was a common occupation of Ouilmette, and further that he was not inclined to take an unfair advantage of a weak and destitute traveler.

Mrs. Kinzie represents that in 1812 Ouilmette was "a part of the establishment" of John Kinzie, and relates a remarkable story of the rescue by his family of Mrs. Helm and Sergeant Griffith from impending slaughter at the hands of the Wabash Indians.[341] That Ouilmette may have been employed more or less by Kinzie is not unlikely; but the details of the rescue story, however creditable to his family, are so improbable as to challenge belief. It has been said that Ouilmette remained in Chicago after the massacre, being the only white inhabitant during the next few years.[342] However this may be, the new garrison which came in 1816 found him living here in serene possession.[343] With him, too, was the half-breed chief, Alexander Robinson, and the two were engaged by the soldiers to harrow the ground for a vegetable garden for the garrison. That Ouilmette continued to reside here after this time is shown by the occasional mention of his name by travelers and others as one of the inhabitants of the place.[344] In 1825 he was credited with taxable property to the amount of four hundred dollars, according to the earliest known Chicago assessment roll, and his name is found the following year on the first Chicago poll list.[345]

But little can be said of the character of Ouilmette. His dealings with Tanner, which have already been recounted, argue well

[341] Kinzie, *Wau Bun*, 182–86.

[342] Hurlbut, *Chicago Antiquities*, 452; Andreas, *History of Chicago*, I, 184. I have found no indication of the authority on which these statements rest.

[343] *Head Papers*, Narrative of Moses Morgan.

[344] See, for example, Hubbard, *Life*, 37; John H. Fonda, "Recollections," in *Wisconsin Historical Collections*, V, 216.

[345] Blanchard, *The Northwest and Chicago*, I, 516–17.

for his fairness and humanity. That he was possessed of more thrift than was the typical frontier French habitant of this period would seem to be attested by the facts already noted. Moses Morgan, who was employed in the construction of the second Fort Dearborn, had a poor opinion of Ouilmette and described his appearance as that of a "medium sized half starved Indian." He was a Roman Catholic and signed the petition for the establishment of the first Catholic church in Chicago.[346]

We are now ready to consider the reputed "father of Chicago," John Kinzie. According to Mrs. Kinzie, the family historian, he was born at Quebec in 1763. Shortly afterward his parents moved to Detroit, where the father died while John was still in infancy. His mother later married William Forsyth, who removed to New York City, where the boy's early childhood was passed. At the age of ten or eleven he ran away from home, and, making his way to Quebec, fell into the hands of a silversmith from whom he learned enough of the trade to enable him to make the ornaments which so delighted the simple red man. Meanwhile his mother's family returned to Detroit where, later, it was rejoined by the runaway son. In time he engaged in the Indian trade, carrying on operations in various places. The same authority states that his earlier establishments were at Sandusky and Maumee,[347] and this is confirmed by two independent sources. About the time of St. Clair's defeat Joseph Brant, the famous Iroquois chieftain, purchased a horse and other supplies from "Mr. Kinzie, Silver Smith at the Miami."[348] Henry Hay, who passed the winter of 1789–90 at the Miami settlement, makes frequent mention of Kinzie in the journal which he kept of his travels.[349] According to the journal Kinzie had both a house and a shop and "apprentices." Hay draws an interesting picture of the life of the little settlement. Neither social nor

[346] Andreas, *History of Chicago*, I, 289. For additional data about the Ouilmette family see Grover, *Some Indian Landmarks of the North Shore*, 277 ff.

[347] Kinzie, *Wau Bun*, 149.

[348] *Michigan Pioneer Collections*, XX, 336.

[349] *Journal from Detroit to the Miami River*, MS in the Detroit Public Library. The journal is anonymous, but Mr. Clarence M. Burton, who has a typewritten copy of it, ascribes it to Henry Hay.

religious consolation was lacking, and Hay played his flute and Kinzie his fiddle indifferently for drinking bout and mass. At times the two classes of entertainment followed each other so closely that the musicians went reeling from one to the other. "Got infernally drunk last night with Mr. Abbot and Mr. Kinzie," wrote the journalist on one occasion. "Mr. A. gave me his daughter Betsy over the bottle. Damnation sick this morning in consequence of last night's debashe—eat no breakfast. Kinzie & myself went to mass and played as usual. Mrs. Ranjard gave us a Cup of Coffee before mass to settle our heads."

During these years Kinzie was, of course, in league with the enemies of the United States. Hay makes frequent mention of the bringing in of American prisoners by the Indians, and of the presence of Little Turtle, Blue Jacket, and other chiefs hostile to the Americans, at the village. In the autumn of 1793 Kinzie was still at the Maumee Rapids, where he incurred the suspicion of the Indians by his communications with Wells, one of Wayne's chief scouts.[350] Probably his establishment was destroyed, along with those of the other British traders, by the American army following the battle of Fallen Timbers. The family historian states that he removed to the St. Joseph River about the year 1800,[351] but he must have located there at an earlier date, for William Burnett in 1798 speaks of him as "Mr. McKenzie of this place."[352] Apparently, however, while carrying on trade with the Indians at these places Kinzie retained some connection with Detroit. Hurlbut found evidence in the Wayne County records that he was doing business there in 1795 and again in 1797.[353] In 1798 he married Mrs. Eleanor McKillip,[354] the

[350] *Michigan Pioneer Collections*, XX, 342, 347. [351] Kinzie, *Wau Bun*, 349.

[352] Hurlbut, *Chicago Antiquities*, 67. Kinzie is a corruption of the Scotch name Mackenzie, which was the name of Kinzie's father.

[353] Hurlbut, *Chicago Antiquities*, 469.

[354] Kinzie had formed an earlier connection with a woman of the same family name as his own, Margaret McKenzie. The story that has been handed down to us of her career, while doubtless idealized through dint of repetition, well illustrates the possibilities for adventure of life on the American border a century and a quarter ago. In the course of Lord Dunmore's war, Margaret and Elizabeth McKenzie were carried away from their Virginia home into captivity among the Indians. The children were adopted by a Shawnee

widow of a Detroit militia officer in the British Indian service who had been slain on the Maumee during Wayne's campaign against the northwestern tribes. Mrs. McKillip had a daughter, Margaret, whom we shall meet later as the wife of Lieutenant Helm of the Fort Dearborn garrison.

In the spring of 1804 Kinzie became a resident of Chicago. The last entry in his account book at St. Joseph bears date of April 30, 1804, while the first at Chicago occurs on May 12. The hut which Du Sable and Le Mai had in turn occupied now became the habitation of Kinzie. His business prospered and he conducted trading "adventures" at Peoria, on the Kankakee, and elsewhere, in addition to the main establishment at Chicago.[355] By the massacre and the train of events brought on

chief who lived near the Indian town of Chillicothe in western Ohio. Years later, when they had grown to womanhood, Margaret, the elder, accompanied her foster parent on a hunting expedition to the vicinity of the modern Fort Wayne, Indiana. Here a young brave sought to force her to marry him. Spurning his attentions, she mounted a horse by night and fled through the forest a distance of seventy-five miles to her Indian home. The horse is said to have died from the effects of the wild ride, but the maiden was made of sterner stuff. At length Margaret McKenzie became the wife of John Kinzie, and her sister, Elizabeth, the wife of a Scotchman named Clark. Whether the two white men rescued the women from captivity and were rewarded for this service by their respective hands, or the old chief voluntarily brought them to Detroit on a visit, where the marriages were brought about in the usual way, depends upon which faction of Kinzie's descendants tells the story. So, too, it is still a matter of dispute whether or not the union was cemented by a formal marriage ceremony. Whatever the truth in these respects may be, the unions endured for a number of years, two children being born to the Clarks and three to the Kinzies. With the restoration of peace to the northwestern frontier in 1795 Isaac McKenzie, the father, learned of the whereabouts of his long-lost children. He journeyed to Detroit to see them, and when he returned to his home in Virginia his daughters with their children accompanied him, leaving their woodland husbands behind.

Conflicting explanations, colored in each case by partisan pride, have been given of the reasons for this untimely breaking-up of the two families. Since the only evidence in the premises is family tradition, it seems vain to seek to determine where the truth lies. Margaret Kinzie later married Benjamin Hall, while her sister became the wife of Jonas Clybourne. Two of the former's children by Kinzie, James and Elizabeth, in later years came to Chicago; so, too, did the Halls and the Clybournes; and these various family groups comprised a considerable proportion of the population of Chicago in the later twenties. On the subject of this footnote see Blanchard, *The Northwest and Chicago;* Hurlbut, *Chicago Antiquities;* Andreas, *Chicago;* Gordon, *John Kinzie, the "Father of Chicago."* For obvious reasons the Kinzie family historian makes no mention in *Wau Bun* of this feature of her father-in-law's career. Mr. Clarence M. Burton has a genealogy (MS) of the Kinzie family to which descendants respectively of John Kinzie's first and second families have contributed their views concerning the legitimacy of the former.

[355] *Barry Transcript;* Kinzie, *Wau Bun,* 150.

by the War of 1812, however, Kinzie's property was largely destroyed and his business was ruined. After his return to Chicago in 1816 the formidable competition of the American Fur Company combined with other causes to prevent him from achieving the degree of success which he had attained during the years from 1803 to 1812.

The propriety of designating Kinzie the "father of Chicago" is dubious. No one individual can properly claim exclusive right to this title. The event which, more adequately than any other, signalizes the beginning of modern white settlement here was the founding of Fort Dearborn; and the man who with more propriety than any other may be regarded as the "father" of the modern city is Captain John Whistler, who built the first fort and for seven years dominated the life within and around its walls. He came in obedience to an order, of course, as an officer in the army. Kinzie, on the other hand, came nearly a year later to conduct the usual Indian tradinghouse. There is no reason to suppose that he would have come to Chicago at all, but for the prior establishment of the garrison. Yet several other traders had established themselves here, not only before Kinzie, but also before the garrison came.

It has been stated that for nearly twenty years Kinzie was the only white inhabitant of northern Illinois outside the military.[356] So far is this from being true that there was never a moment of time during his residence at Chicago when he was the only civilian here. Particularly during the latter years of his life, a number of civilians were living in Chicago and in the immediate vicinity. The undue prominence in this period of Chicago history which Kinzie has come to hold in the popular mind is due to the fact that he gained, after his death, a daughter-in-law who possessed the literary skill to weave a romantic narrative celebrating the family name and deeds.

The name of Kinzie is unpleasantly associated with two other characters of these early years, John La Lime and Jeffrey Nash. La Lime was at St. Joseph in 1787, apparently in the employ of William Burnett.[357] Whether he located at Chicago before the

[356] Kinzie, *Wau Bun*, 146–47.

[357] Hurlbut, *Chicago Antiquities*, 55.

garrison came is not apparent; if not, he came the same year. Shortly after the arrival of the garrison he and Doctor Smith, the surgeon, began living together; they secured Kinzie's house for the first winter and fitted it up "in a very comfortable manner."[358] The fourth name entered in Kinzie's account book after his removal to Chicago in May, 1804, is that of La Lime.[359] In the same month he signed as witness the articles of indenture of Jeffrey Nash to Kinzie and Forsyth, "Merchants of Chicago."[360] When Cooper came to Fort Dearborn as surgeon in 1808, La Lime was living in one of the four houses on the north side of the river and acting as government Indian interpreter.[361] He continued to serve in this capacity until his death shortly before the massacre in the summer of 1812.

But for a single exception, all the reports concerning La Lime's character which have come to light are highly creditable to him. His few remaining letters show him to have been a man of some education. The esteem in which Jouett held him is shown by his naming a son after him.[362] Doctor Smith, who was living with him in the winter of 1803-4, described him as "a very decent man and a good companion."[363]

In the summer of 1812, a few weeks before the massacre, La Lime was stabbed to death by Kinzie in a personal encounter just outside the entrance to Fort Dearborn. Unless new sources of information shall come to light, the responsibility for this affray will never be determined. La Lime's side of the story has not been preserved, except in the form of unreliable verbal tradition, which pictures Kinzie in the light of aggressor and murderer.[364] The Kinzie family tradition represents that La Lime, insanely jealous over Kinzie's success as a trader, treacherously attacked him, armed with a pistol and dirk, and was

358 Letter of Dr. William Smith to James May, December 9, 1803.

359 *Barry Transcript.*

360 This document is preserved in the Draper Collection, *Forsyth Papers,* I, Doc. No. I.

361 Wilson, *Chicago from 1803 to 1812.* 362 Hurlbut, *Chicago Antiquities,* 108.

363 Letter of Dr. William Smith to James May, December 9, 1803.

364 *Head Papers.* Head was acquainted with various pioneer Chicagoans, and his statements purport to be drawn from such sources. His methods of work were such, however, that but little confidence can be had in his statements.

stabbed to death by Kinzie in self-defense.[365] Practically all writers on Chicago history hitherto have accepted this version,[366] but it is as little worthy of credence as the contrary one. The interest in the killing of La Lime must, in the nature of things, have soon given place to the general anxiety over the situation produced by the hovering war cloud which was now about to burst. Within four months came the massacre,[367] as the result of which over half of the inmates of the frontier settlement were slain and the remainder scattered far and wide. But few of them ever returned to Chicago, and these, like Rip Van Winkle, drifted back after the passage of years, as to a new world. That the fate of La Lime should be obliterated by the horrors and confusion of a three years' war was only natural. When in a later generation interest in his fate was revived only the version of it originating with the relatives and friends of the slayer gained the public ear, and this, for obvious reasons, put the onus of the affray on the slain. The fact of La Lime's death at the hands of Kinzie is clear; the responsibility for it cannot, in the light of existing information, be determined.

On May 22, 1804, articles of indenture were entered into which bound Jeffrey Nash, a "Negro man," to serve John Kinzie and Thomas Forsyth, "Merchants of Chicago," for the term of seven years.[368] The instrument describes Nash as an inhabitant of Wayne County, although it was executed, apparently, at

[365] The details of the affair vary, naturally, in the different accounts. For the Kinzie family tradition see Eleanor Kinzie Gordon, *John Kinzie, the "Father of Chicago,"* 8-9; letter of Gurdon S. Hubbard, in Wentworth, *Early Chicago*, Fergus Historical Series, No. 16, 83; Mrs. Porthier's narrative in Andreas, *History of Chicago*, I, 105. Hubbard procured his information from the members of Kinzie's family. Mrs. Porthier, who in old age claimed to have been an eyewitness of the killing of La Lime, was an inmate of the Kinzie household for several years following 1816.

[366] See for example Wentworth, *Early Chicago;* Kirkland, *The Chicago Massacre;* Andreas, *History of Chicago.*

[367] I have not been able to determine the exact date of the death of La Lime. It could not have been earlier than April 13, however, since on this date he wrote to Captain Wells of Fort Wayne an account of the murders at the Lee farm on April 6 (*Louisiana Gazette*, May 30, 1812, copied by Lyman C. Draper, Draper Collection, S, Vol. XXVI).

[368] Draper Collection, *Forsyth Papers*, I, Doc. No. 1.

Chicago.[369] The Chicago of 1804 was located in Wayne County, Indiana Territory, whose county seat was Detroit, over three hundred miles away. In return for meat, drink, apparel, washing, and lodging "fitting for a Servant," Nash bound himself to the maintenance of an utterly impossible standard of conduct.[370] Doubtless the quaint language of the indenture simply followed the customary form of such documents; it can scarcely have been expected that the bound man would live up to its numerous stipulations.

Nash signed the instrument by making his mark. It might reasonably be concluded, even in the absence of other information concerning him, that this indenture practically reduced him to slavery. That Kinzie and Forsyth chose to so regard Nash's status is shown by their treatment of him. He was taken to Peoria, Forsyth's place of residence from 1802 until 1812, and for many years held by the latter as a slave.[371] At length he ran away from his bondage and made his way to St. Louis, and eventually to New Orleans, where he was said to have had a wife and children. Forsyth and Kinzie sought to recover possession of him and to this end a suit was instituted in the parish court; the case went ultimately to the Supreme Court of Louisiana, where an interesting decision was rendered.[372]

[369] That the indenture was entered into at Chicago I infer from the facts that Kinzie opened his account books here on May 12, and numerous entries in them were made during the ensuing ten days, and that the name of John La Lime, one of the witnesses of the indenture, occurs among the entries for May 12.

[370] Among the other things it was agreed that for the space of seven years "the said servant his said Masters shall faithfully serve their Secrets keep their lawfully Command everywhere gladly Obey. He shall do no damage to his said Masters. He shall not wast his Masters goods nor lend them unlawfully to others. He shall not commit Fornication nor contract Matrimony within said Term. At dice Cards or any unlawful game he shall not play where by his said Masters may be damaged with his own goods or the goods of others during the said Term without licence of his said Masters he shall neither buy nor sell he shall not absent day nor night from his said Masters Service without their leave nor haunt Taverns or any place or places without permission from said Masters but in all things behave as a faithful Servant ought to do during the said Term."

[371] Draper Collection, *Forsyth Papers*, Vol. I, copy of decision of the Supreme Court of Louisiana, June 5, 1816, in the case of *Kensy and Forsyth, plaintiffs*, versus *Jeffrey Nash, defendant*.

[372] The summary given here is based on the manuscript copy of the decision in the *Forsyth Papers*. The case is reported in Martin, *Louisiana Reports*, II, 180.

The plaintiffs submitted two lines of evidence in support of their contention that Nash was their lawful slave. A number of witnesses testified that for a term of years he had lived at Peoria as Forsyth's slave, being "known and reputed" as such by the villagers. Furthermore the plaintiffs produced a bill of sale of Nash to them, dated at Detroit, September 5, 1803, and there recorded and duly authenticated. In view of the fact that the articles of indenture whereby Nash bound himself "voluntarily as a servant" to Kinzie and Forsyth for a term of seven years were executed in May, 1804, there seems to be no escape from the conclusion that the bill of sale was a forgery, fabricated for the use to which it was now put. Although it deceived the court, the fraud brought no profit to the plaintiffs. The judges declared that since the Ordinance of 1787 prohibited slavery in the Northwest Territory unless under two exceptions, the plaintiffs' "alleged possession" of Nash could only have been lawful at the time the bill of sale was produced on two grounds. There could be complete ownership and slavery only in case the person claimed had been convicted of a crime by which his freedom was forfeited. Or, if the defendant were a fugitive from involuntary servitude in another state, he might be seized and returned to servitude there.

The plaintiffs did not claim Nash on this latter ground, however. Their contention was for the absolute right to hold Nash during his natural life and dispose of him as they pleased. Their conduct toward him showed that they unlawfully attempted to, and did successfully, exercise for years the right of absolute control over him, until he at last sought safety in flight. Since no evidence had been produced to show that Nash had forfeited his freedom because of conviction for crime, the decision was given for him with costs. Thus did the Supreme Court of the slave state of Louisiana uphold the free character of the soil of Illinois, and rescue a free man from bondage, at a time when slavery openly flourished here, and slaves were bought and sold and held in bondage even by such prominent characters as the governor of the territory.

CHAPTER VII

NINE YEARS OF GARRISON LIFE

The privations and loneliness of life at the new post on the Chicago River in the years following 1803 can be imagined by most readers only with difficulty. Only those who have experienced the deadly dulness of military routine at an isolated station can appreciate it properly. All witnesses agree in testifying to the overpowering loneliness of life under such conditions as prevailed at Fort Dearborn from 1803 to 1812. "In compassion to a poor devil banished to another planet," wrote Governor St. Clair, from Cincinnati, to Alexander Hamilton, in 1795, "tell me what is doing in yours, if you can snatch a moment from the weighty cares of your office."[373] One day in October, 1817, a year after the establishment of the second Fort Dearborn, Samuel A. Storrow, who was making a tour through the Northwest, appeared on the north bank of the Chicago River, and shortly after entered the fort, where he was received "as one arrived from the moon."[374] A British officer, writing from Mackinac in 1796, laments as follows: "You talk of your place being duller than ever, &c, believe me it cannot be put in competition with ours for dullness, jealousy, and envy, with all the etceteras mentioned in yours."[375] And Captain Heald, writing from Fort Dearborn in June, 1810, within a few days of his taking command there, announces that unless he can obtain a leave of absence to go to New England the coming autumn he will resign the service, and leave the command to another. It is a good place for a man with a family, who can be content to "live so remote from the civilized part of the world."

[373] Smith, *The St. Clair Papers*, II, 318.

[374] *Wisconsin Historical Collections*, VI, 179.

[375] *Michigan Pioneer Collections*, XII, 211.

The little establishment at Fort Dearborn constituted a miniature world, with interests and ambitions quite detached from those of the larger world outside. The principal means of contact with the latter was afforded by the traders who passed through Chicago, proceeding with their merchandise to the Indian country or returning therefrom with the fruits of their barter. They brought the news of the outside world to the inmates of the garrison and surrounding cabins. Each year a vessel from Detroit or Mackinac brought a supply of merchandise to the traders at Milwaukee, Chicago, and St. Joseph, and took back the stock of furs accumulated by them.[376] Aside from these visits there were official communications from time to time between the commanding officers of the little group of northwestern posts, to which Fort Dearborn belonged, and advantage was taken of the opportunity thus presented to transmit letters and items of private import. Occasionally, too, the brig, "Adams," constituting the chief part of Commodore Brevoort's "navy of the lakes," would pay a visit to Chicago. It must have been an occasion of rare excitement in the lives of the inmates of Fort Dearborn when Kingsbury passed through Chicago with a company of troops in the spring of 1805, on his way to superintend the establishment of Fort Belle Fontaine near the mouth of the Missouri River.[377]

Only belated rumors of the events of the outside world ordinarily penetrated the seclusion of Fort Dearborn. From November until May it was as isolated as though on another planet. We have in epitome the story of the failure of one attempt, made by Captain Whistler in December, 1809, to break this isolation. He obtained a month's leave of absence to journey to Cincinnati.[378] Today the round trip may be made and a fair day's business transacted in twenty-four hours. Whistler left Chicago the last of November and reached Fort Wayne December 10, "much fatigued after 11 days wairy travel-

[376] Antoine le Claire's statement in *Wisconsin Historical Collections*, XI, 239–40.

[377] For the facts concerning this expedition see the *Kingsbury Papers*, letter book, *passim*.

[378] *Ibid.*, Whistler to Kingsbury, December 12, 1809.

ing through rain and snow." The water was so high that his further progress was prevented. Finding it impossible, should he proceed, to be back at his post by the end of the month, he prepared to return to Fort Dearborn, grateful to his superior for the opportunity accorded him as though he had succeeded in making the journey.

Kingsbury's letter books, whose contents relate to the several northwestern posts in general, are the best source of information upon the conditions that prevailed at Fort Dearborn in this period. In October, 1804, Kingsbury writes from Mackinac to an eastern correspondent urging him to reply immediately, in which case the answer will reach Mackinac by the first vessel in the spring, which will probably arrive in May or June.[379] The answer is to be directed to Detroit, the postmaster there having agreed to forward his mail to him at Mackinac. A year later, when Kingsbury is at Fort Belle Fontaine, a St. Louis friend sends him a bundle of newspapers, but requests him to preserve them in order that the writer may have a file of "Steady Habits" to peruse in a "Hypochrondichal hour."[380] How the inmates of Fort Dearborn sometimes received their mail is shown by a letter of William Burnett, the St. Joseph trader, to his Detroit correspondent in January, 1804, in which, among other things, he mentions the receipt of the letters and newspapers for "the doctor at Chicagou" and promises to forward them at the first opportunity.[381]

The observations of the frontier officers upon the public news of the outside world constitute an interesting part of their correspondence. In August, 1805, Kingsbury is informed by a Mackinac correspondent that the French and English fleets have not met, "which we consider an Unfortunate Circumstance," as no doubt is felt of the triumph of the British in the event of a combat.[382] The French have captured a rich American ship near Charleston, and the public prints are full of complaints

[379] *Ibid.*, Kingsbury to Benjamin Ellis, October 16, 1804.

[380] *Ibid.*, E. Hempstead to Kingsbury, October 17, 1805.

[381] *Michigan Pioneer Collections*, VIII, 547.

[382] *Kingsbury Papers*, David Mitchell to Kingsbury, August 24, 1805.

against the President for suffering such depredations upon American commerce. Bonaparte has gone to Italy "to extort much money from the Italians." Another correspondent of Kingsbury sends news late in February, 1805, of the election of Jefferson to the presidency.[383] An item which has a familiar ring relates that "Congress have done nothing since in Session worth mentioning that have come to our knowledge."[384]

Thus the public news items run. Bonaparte has been proclaimed "Emperor of the Gauls";[385] the death of Hamilton is announced, with regret. Burr has fled from New York, fearing assassination. The probabilities of a war with Spain and of a revolt in Louisiana are gravely discussed. The traders, too, had their disputes. Shortly before Kinzie removed to Chicago, he became involved in a business dispute with an associate named Pattinson. The latter addressed an acrid letter to him "dictated in such terms of impertinency that he pointly brings in question Kenzie's character, relative to their concerns. In a word he calls him everything but a gentleman."[386] Burnett of St. Joseph who, though not directly implicated in the Pattinson-Kinzie quarrel, seems to have sympathized with the latter, also became involved in the dispute. Pattinson claimed that Burnett had insulted him by speaking disrespectfully to his brother of his government, and by calling his house a "hog-sty." Burnett replied that it was not his intention to have "hurted their tender feelings," but that in the course of an argument over the relative greatness of Great Britain and America, in which Pattinson had made extravagant claims for the former, he took it upon himself to contradict "this high flier." It is refreshing to discover that at a time when our government was humiliating itself before those of Great Britain and France, the honor of America was thus valiantly upheld in an obscure corner of the northwestern frontier.

383 *Kingsbury Papers*, Clemson to Kingsbury, February 24, 1805.

384 *Ibid.*

385 *Ibid.*, Kingsbury to Whistler, September 10, 1804.

386 *Michigan Pioneer Collections*, VIII, 546–47.

The garrison at Chicago made what progress it might to complete the fort and prepare for the coming winter. The work of construction was seriously impeded, however, by the lack of necessary tools, and even the supplies of provisions and clothing for the men were inadequate. In July, 1804, a year after the arrival of the troops, Kingsbury learned from Major Pike and Doctor Smith that Whistler's men were almost destitute of clothing.[387] That the destitution extended to other things as well is shown by his letter to Whistler informing the latter that he has ordered a supply of clothing, kettles, stationery, hospital stores, a whip-saw, and other things to be sent to Chicago by the brig, "Adams." At the same time Kingsbury congratulates Whistler upon having accomplished so much with his meager resources, with "no clothing for the men," and without the necessary tools with which to work.

That the construction of the fort was not yet completed would seem to be indicated by numerous entries in Kinzie's account book during the summer of 1804 of the names of men who are designated as sawyers.[388] Two weeks after Kingsbury's letter informing Whistler of the shipment of supplies, the latter writes that they have been received.[389] But the whip-saw can be of little use without files, for oak is the only saw timber available at Chicago. There is clothing for the sergeants, but no invoice of it has been sent, and until this arrives the clothing cannot be used. Fifty-six suits of clothing have been received, but he has sixty-six men to supply. He has two fifers but the only fife has been lost. Watch coats are needed very badly. There has been no corn for the public oxen all summer and none can be procured here. All of these things may be sent by Kinzie, who is coming from Detroit in about a month.

Along with these homely details of toil and privation are others of more private interest, ranging in character from grave to gay. On the first of November, 1804, occurred the first

[387] *Kingsbury Papers*, Kingsbury to Whistler, July 12, 1804.

[388] *Barry Transcript*.

[389] *Kingsbury Papers*, Whistler to Kingsbury, July 26 and 27, 1804.

recorded wedding of white people at Chicago. It was, too, a society affair, for the contracting parties were Sarah, the eldest daughter of Captain Whistler, and James Abbott, the Detroit merchant. The proud father-in-law in announcing the event, states that he has long known and "had a great opinion of" the bridegroom.[390] The family genealogist records that the marriage ceremony was performed by John Kinzie, and that the bridal couple indulged in an overland wedding journey to Detroit, traveling on horseback and tenting at night.[391]

The next day after Chicago's first wedding the family of Kingsbury at Mackinac was gladdened by the appearance of a new daughter.[392] In announcing the event to Colonel Hunt at Detroit, the happy father hopes to hear of the latter being in a similar situation, unless he happens to prefer that Mrs. Hunt should present him with a son. Shortly afterward Kingsbury ordered from Detroit, by the first vessel in the spring, some walnut and cherry boards and a cow and calf.[393] He had already requested Whistler to send him some walnut planks from Chicago.[394] Whistler responded by sending him two, but explained that these were all he could procure and that he had not yet made a single table for himself.[395]

Less pleasing than the marriages and births are the reports of fever and other ills which beset the occupants of the garrisons in the new country. Fort Dearborn was only a year old when Whistler reported that more than half of his men had been ill. Whipple at Fort Wayne, writing in September, 1804, praises his new surgeon; since his arrival the sick list which had numbered twenty-five has been materially reduced.[396] "We have all been sick since you left this," wrote Clemson from Detroit in October of the same year.[397] The writer had not yet recovered from the

[390] *Kingsbury Papers*, Whistler to Kingsbury, November 3, 1804.

[391] Whistler family genealogy, MS in the Chicago Historical Society library.

[392] *Kingsbury Papers*, Kingsbury to Hunt, November 11, 1804.

[393] *Ibid.*, Kingsbury to Clemson, November 21, 1804.

[394] *Ibid.*, Kingsbury to Whistler, October 16, 1804.

[395] *Ibid.*, Whistler to Kingsbury, November 3, 1804.

[396] *Ibid.*, Whipple to Kingsbury, September 1, 1804.

[397] *Ibid.*, Clemson to Kingsbury, October 27, 1804.

severe attack of the fever, but expected with the assistance of the frosty nights to regain his strength. At the same time Lieutenant Rhea's little garrison on the Maumee was in a desperate condition. On July 31 he reported that in addition to himself ten men out of his force of twenty-one were ill.[398] A month later the number of sick men remained about the same; the wife of a corporal was at the point of death, and Rhea had sent to the River Raisin for a physician, expecting to pay the expense himself.[399] He appeals urgently for help and for removal. The "musketoes" are so thick that a well person cannot sleep at night; the place was never intended "for any Christian to be posted at."

A year later, in July, 1805, a pathetic letter from Whistler at Fort Dearborn announces that Mrs. Whistler is at the point of death.[400] She is in constant pain, and frequent bleeding is the only thing that affords her any relief. The anxious husband bravely reflects that while there is life there is hope, but laments his unhappy state, with so large a family of children, should he lose "so good a companion."

In Captain Heald's journal[401] occurs the entry, "On the 4th of May, 1812, we had a son born dead for the want of a skilful Midwife." The picture of the sorrow and tragedy concealed behind these few words may appropriately be left, as it has been by the parent, to the imagination. Three months later the young Kentucky bride, still grieving we may well believe over the loss of her first-born, conducted herself with such spirit during the terrible scenes of the massacre as to arouse the admiration of even the savage foe.

The diversions of the garrison were, naturally, but few. Fishing and hunting, and an occasional athletic contest with the Indians who visited the fort were the chief outdoor amusements. From its first discovery by the French until well into the nineteenth century the region around Chicago was a perfect hunter's

[398] *Ibid.*, Rhea to Kingsbury, July 31, 1804.

[399] *Ibid.*, Rhea to Kingsbury, August 31 and September 8, 1804.

[400] *Ibid.*, Whistler to Kingsbury, July 12, 1805.

[401] For it see Appendix III.

paradise. When Cooper came to Fort Dearborn in 1808 the officers and most of the civilians possessed horses, cows, and dogs.[402] Cooper himself had two good saddle horses, two cows, and a hunting dog. There was an abundance of game in the immediate vicinity. Within a week of Cooper's arrival, his dog and several others chased three deer past the post into the river. A young soldier who was in a canoe without any weapon sprang into the water as the deer were swimming past, caught one by the neck, and held its head under water until it was drowned. Cooper's dog seized the second, but the third, a large stag, gained the north bank and escaped.

Not long after this Cooper and Captain Whistler, while riding out together, came upon a large wolf within half a mile of the fort. Their dogs took up the chase and soon brought him to bay. The officers had no pistols, and the dogs manifested a wholesome respect for the formidable looking teeth of the wolf, and so they were called off and the animal allowed to go his way without further molestation. The howling of wolves at night was a common occurrence during these years. Grouse and other game birds were abundant, as were fish in the river and lake, so that in the hunting season the officers spent much of their leisure time with gun and rod.

We are indebted to Surgeon Cooper for the story of a notable athletic contest at Chicago, the description of which stirs the blood, even after the lapse of a hundred years.[403] Lieutenant William Whistler was a splendid specimen of physical manhood, over six feet in height and famous for his strength and powers of endurance. Among the visitors at Fort Dearborn was a Pottawatomie chief of similar physique and about the same age as Whistler. He was a great runner and enjoyed the reputation of never having been defeated in a race. A five-mile foot race between the two men was arranged, Whistler wagering his horse and accouterments against the horse and trappings of the chief. Both the red men and the soldiers of the garrison were

[402] Wilson, *Chicago from 1803 to 1812*. [403] *Ibid.*

confident of the prowess of their respective champions. The Indians staked their ponies and other available property on the chief and the soldiers accepted the wagers as fast as offered. The contest, which was witnessed by several hundred Indians and the entire garrison, was won by Whistler, after a superb struggle, by a margin of a few yards.

The final sequel of the race, according to the same authority, came some years later and was even more thrilling. During the War of 1812 the same chief, now serving with the British, sent a challenge to individual combat to Lieutenant Whistler or any officer or soldier in his command. It was promptly accepted by Whistler himself, and as the result of the ensuing hand-to-hand combat with knife, sword, and tomahawk, firearms not being allowed, the red man departed for the happy hunting ground.

An account of the garrison life at Fort Dearborn in this period would be incomplete without some reference to a drearier subject than any yet mentioned. The personnel of the army at this time was far from high. A considerable proportion of the men were foreigners,[404] and a far larger number were illiterate.[405] The life at the frontier posts was monotonous, drinking and desertions were common, and the punishment for infractions of discipline was atrocious. We have no record of the court martial proceedings at Fort Dearborn, but the records for some of the other northwestern posts are painfully abundant, and a sketch of their contents will answer as well for Fort Dearborn. The orderly book of Anthony Wayne, who has been well described as a "furious disciplinarian,"[406]

[404] Of the fifty-nine men in Captain Whistler's company at Fort Detroit in 1812 eighteen were foreigners. Of the fifty men in Captain Rhea's company at Fort Wayne in 1810 fourteen were foreigners (*Kingsbury Papers*, quarterly returns of the companies in question).

[405] Approximately 60 per cent of the members of Captain Heald's company at Fort Dearborn at the close of the year 1811 were unable to sign their names to the payroll receipts (payroll receipt of Fort Dearborn garrison for last quarter of the year 1811, in *Heald Papers*, Draper Collection, U, VIII, 92).

[406] *Detroit Tribune*, April 5, 1896.

presents a picture of corporal punishments meted out to the soldiers at Detroit in 1797, worthy of the palmiest days of the army of Frederick the Great.[407]

The commonest offense charged was drunkenness, the usual penalty for which was the public infliction of from twenty-five to one hundred lashes, and in the case of petty officers reduction to the ranks. Occasionally resort was had to other methods to punish and humiliate the guilty one. One culprit, a corporal, charged with desertion, was sentenced to walk the gauntlet six times between double ranks of soldiery, both ranks striking at the same time.[408] Two camp followers, a man and a woman, charged with selling liquor to a soldier were sentenced to be drummed out of camp to the tune of the Rogues' March, with a bottle suspended around the neck of each and the man's left hand tied to the woman's right. In this plight they were to be paraded past the citadel and through the barracks of the soldiery and the principal streets of the town.[409] The man's sentence was remitted, but that against the woman was carried into execution the same afternoon. Still another culprit, guilty of enticing a soldier to desert, was ordered to be given fifty lashes with "wired Catts," to have the left side of his head and his right eyebrow close shaved, and to be drummed with a rope around his neck through the citadel and fort and the principal streets of the town.[410]

It may be supposed that the punishments inflicted under Wayne's command were severer than those meted out at Fort Dearborn a few years later. Yet they show what might be done by an army officer at that time in the maintenance of discipline. The records of courts martial at Fort Detroit under Kingsbury's régime, after Whistler's removal thither from Fort Dearborn

[407] The orderly book is printed in *Michigan Pioneer Collections*, XXXIV, 341–734. It covers the five-year period from 1792 to 1797. The cases which I have chosen for illustration all occurred at Detroit in the last-mentioned year.

[408] *Ibid.*, 704.

[409] *Ibid.*, 701–9.

[410] *Ibid.*, 715.

in 1810, probably reflect fairly the state of affairs at Fort Dearborn.[411] In general the punishments are milder than those formerly meted out under Wayne. The common crimes were still drunkenness and desertion. For the former sentences of from twenty-five to fifty lashes on the "bear back" were commonly decreed. It should be noted that Whistler and Helm, both of whom served at Fort Dearborn, were often members of the court by which these sentences were imposed.

Two specific instances will be cited, in both of which Captain Whistler acted as president of the court martial. On May 23, 1811, Peter Sendale, a private soldier, was tried for drunkenness. The accused pleaded guilty, but advanced the ingenuous excuse by way of extenuation that he had worked hard all day in the Colonel's garden, that he had the latter's permission to go and get a drink, and that he "took a little too much." Notwithstanding this plea he was sentenced to receive twenty-five lashes on the "bear back." In the other case two men were charged with desertion. They admitted the offense, but pleaded in mitigation of it that they had repented of the act and were returning to their post of duty when arrested. The testimony given satisfied the court of the truth of this, yet the prisoners were sentenced to pay the cost of their apprehension and to be confined at hard labor with ball and chain for a period not to exceed one year. The court took occasion to observe that the punishment was not proportioned to the heinousness of the offense, and that its mildness was due solely to the testimony concerning the prisoners' belated repentance.

We may now direct our attention to Fort Dearborn itself and to those persons who composed its official family from 1803 to 1812. There exist two contemporary pictures of the fort and its surroundings in the year 1808, one the verbal account of Surgeon Cooper as recorded by James Grant Wilson,[412] the other a diagram carefully drawn to scale by Captain Whistler,

[411] *Kingsbury Papers*, records of court martial proceedings, *passim*.

[412] Wilson, *Chicago from 1803 to 1812*.

and accompanied by a summary verbal description.[413] The river at that time made a sharp turn about an eighth of a mile from the lake, and after running in a general southerly direction lost itself in the lake a mile south of its present mouth. The fort was built on a slight elevation close to the bend of the river, which enveloped it on its northern and eastern, and to some extent on its western, sides. The barracks and other structures for the accommodation of the garrison were built around the four sides of a quadrangle, facing inward toward the center. Two blockhouses, one containing two small cannon, the other containing one, stood at the northwestern and southeastern corners of the quadrangle, and the whole was inclosed within a

[413] The original is in the files of the War Department at Washington. Because of its historical value the verbal description which accompanies the drawing is reproduced here:

INDEX ANNEXED TO THE DRAUGHT OF FORT DEARBORN &c.

No.		No.	
1	Block Houses	17	Agents House
2	Port Holes for Cannon	18	Factors House
3	Loop Holes for small arms	19	Interpreters House
4	Magazine	20	Armerers Shop
5	Inward Row of pickets	21	Merchants Shop
6	Outward Row of pickets	22	Bake House
7	Main Gate	23	House in Factors Dept.
8	Wicket Gate	24	Stables
9	Guard House	25	River Cheykago
10	Comm'g Officers Barracks	26	Banks of said River
11	Officers Barracks	27	Wharf of said River
12	Soldiers Barracks	28	Low ground between said bank & River.
13	Contractors Store	29	Beach between Sd. River and Lake.
14	Hospital Store	30	John Kinzie Esq. House on the opisite side River
15	Asst. Military Agt. Store	31	Oather Dwelling Houses on opisite side River
16	Small Houses in the garrison	32	Old Grist Mill Worked by Horses

N. 33 Covered Way to procure Water }
N. 34 Gutters to carry off the Water } Omited in their places

NOTE. the Barracks are two storeys high with shingled Roofs and Galliaries fronting the parade. The measurement of the Garrison including the Block Houses And Barrick are laid down at twenty feet to the Inch the Cupolas are not yet built on the Block Houses as laid down. The Dwelling houses mentioned in the Indian Department are laid down at forty feet to the Inch, the oather houses without any Regular rule. The River is not regularly surveyed but still gives a strong Idea of Its Courses it is about six miles in length, except in high water, at which time there is no portage to the Illinois River.

The distances from the defirant places to the Garrison as mentioned with Red Ink on & red lines, are accurately measured, but not laid down by a scale. The woodland on the reserve Lyes on the north, & west, sides of the Garrison except a small strip of woods about one mile in length and two hundred yards in breadth, Lying on the bank of the river south west of the Garrison. Along the Margin of Said Woods, is good medow and supplyes the Garrison with hay. On the North and west sides of the Garrison there has been a quantity of underwood and shruby Bushes such as prickly Ash &c. they are now cut down and cleared off, all within one Fourth of a Mile of the Garrison.

On the south and southwest sides of the Garrison is a large parraria on which stands The aforesaid strip of woods as laid down in the Draught, and the distance from the Garrison three fourths of a Mile. On the East side is the Lake. There has been A picket fence on the Opisite side of the river, northwest of the Garrison as laid Down. this fence might serve as a Barrier against the Garrison as the pickets were five feet in length, sufficient in thickness to prevent a Musket Ball from doing execution to an Enemy lying behind them. I thought it proper for the safety of the Garrison to have them taken up and replaced with a common rail fence. At this time the Garrison (except the Houses on the Opisite side of the river being somewhat in the way) is perfectly secure from any ambuscade or Barrier.

The Branch that emptys into the Cheykag is considerably the longest, and has the greatest current. The parraria on the south and southwest as already mentioned is of great extent.

Fort Dearborn 20.th Feb.y 1808. J. Whistler Capt.

double row of palisades, so arranged that the blockhouses commanded not only the space without the four walls, but also that inclosed between the two rows of palisades. Thus if an enemy should scale the first row he would only find himself within a narrow inclosure between that and the second which was swept at every point by the fire from the blockhouses. From the northwest corner of the stockade to the river was a distance of eighty feet, and from a point midway of the eastern side it was sixty yards.

Within the stockaded inclosure were the barracks for the officers and men. They were two stories in height, with shingled roofs and covered galleries, and occupied the middle of each side of the inclosure facing toward the parade ground, in the center of which stood a lofty flagstaff. The commanding officer's quarters stood on the east side, and directly opposite were those for the subordinate officers. The main gateway of the stockade was at the middle of the south side and was flanked on either side by the main barracks for the common soldiers. The building opposite was in part devoted to barracks for the soldiers and in part to housing the contractor's store of supplies. Between this building and the northwestern blockhouse stood the magazine, a small structure made of brick. This alone defied the fire which destroyed the fort at the time of the massacre. Two small houses, one near the northeast corner of the inclosure and the other in the corner diagonally opposite, completed the list of structures within the stockade. The parade ground was surrounded by gutters for carrying off the water. A small wicket gate in the stockade gave ingress and egress near the northwestern blockhouse. From the northeast corner of the stockade a covered way led to the river, securing thus to the garrison access in safety to the water in time of attack.

To the south of the fort were the commanding officer's gardens in which, in Cooper's time, melons and other small fruit and vegetables were raised. Somewhat to the east, between the fort and the mouth of the river, was a smaller garden and an Indian graveyard. A short distance to the southwest were two log houses, one occupied by Matthew Irwin, the United States factor, and the other by Charles Jouett, the Indian agent. On the north side of the river, almost directly opposite the fort, was the house of John Kinzie, with outbuildings and a "Kitchen" garden. Whistler's diagram represents three houses to the westward of Kinzie's establishment, but omits the names of their owners. The omission is supplied by Cooper, however, who says that in his time there were four houses on the north side, occupied by Kinzie, Ouilmette, La Lime, and Le Mai. La Lime and Ouilmette were Frenchmen; Le Mai was a half-breed, married to a Pottawatomie squaw.

In addition to these houses Whistler's drawing represents a considerable number of houses and outbuildings ranged around the fort devoted to various purposes. Among these are houses for the interpreter and for the factor's department, an armorer's shop, a merchant's shop, and a bake shop, besides several stables on the south side; and on the north side, near Kinzie's place, a "Grist Mill Worked by Horses."

In the rear of the group of houses on the north side, the space between the lake and the north branch of the river was covered with timber. Along the east side of the South Branch, stretching southward from the forks of the river, was another strip of timber, two hundred yards in width and a mile long. Except for this strip of woodland, the area to the south and southwest of the fort constituted what Whistler quaintly designates as "a large Parraria." Along the inner margin of this woodland lay a good meadow which supplied the garrison with hay. Close to the forks on the south side of the main river a small field of eight or nine acres had been reduced to cultivation and made to serve as the company gardens and public cornfield.

It is evident from Whistler's description that he took careful measures to prepare the fort against the possibility of a hostile attack. The ground to the north and west was clear as far as the woodland mentioned, which lay at a distance of three-fourths of a mile from the fort. The east side was protected, of course, by the river and the lake. To the west and the north the ground had originally been covered with an undergrowth of prickly ash and other scrubby bushes, but this had been cleared away to a distance of a quarter of a mile from the stockade. On the north side there had been erected a heavy picket fence, four feet in height and sufficiently strong to afford an enemy protection against musketry fire from the fort. This Whistler caused to be removed and replaced by a common rail fence. At the time of making this diagram, in the winter of 1808, Whistler announced with satisfaction that the garrison was now perfectly secure from an ambuscade or barrier, except for the houses on the north side, which were somewhat in the way.

It is evident that the number of civilians clustered around the fort in the years prior to the massacre was considerably greater than has ordinarily been supposed. Cooper says there was a house a mile to the southeast of the fort, owned by a farmer who supplied the garrison with butter and eggs, and one near the forks of the river occupied by a man named Clark who was a cattle dealer. Whistler's drawing represents two houses at the forks, one occupied by a discharged soldier, and a house and inclosed field north of the river, belonging to Mr. "Coursoll." There were two Courselles, one of them a well-known trader, but the only other record of either of them being at Chicago is the recurrence of their names in Kinzie's account books. The farmer mentioned by Cooper was probably Lee, at whose farm on the South Branch the preliminary massacre of April, 1812, occurred. But Cooper does not mention the Burns family, which Mrs. Kinzie describes as living on the North Side at the time of the massacre. In addition to these were the houses which Whistler shows belonging to the Indian agent's and the factor's departments. The conclusion drawn from these various bits of evidence concerning the number of dwellers around Fort Dearborn is confirmed by the fact that after the murders at the Lee farm, Captain Heald enrolled fifteen militiamen from the civilian population outside the fort. It should be noted, too, that three of the long-time residents of Chicago, La Lime, Ouilmette, and Kinzie, were not included in this number.

Of the officers stationed at Fort Dearborn before the massacre, the régime of Captain John Whistler was the longest and in many respects the most important. Whistler was descended from an old English family, but he himself was born in Ireland, whither his immediate ancestors removed, in 1758.[414] In a youthful freak he ran away from home and joined the army, coming to America during the Revolution with the troops under Burgoyne. He was thus one of the members of that general's ill-fated army captured by the Americans at Saratoga. On his return to England Whistler received his discharge from the army, and soon after, forming an attachment for the daughter of one of his father's friends, eloped with her, coming a second time to America and settling at Hagerstown, Maryland. He entered the American army in 1791 and served continuously on the northwestern frontier under St. Clair, Wayne, and others, from that time until the breaking out of the War of 1812. He was commander at Fort Dearborn from 1803 to 1810, when he was transferred to Fort Detroit, under circumstances which will shortly demand our attention. He served under Hull in 1812 and, if family tradition is to be credited, was so enraged over the capitulation that he broke his sword rather than surrender it to the enemy.

The founder of Fort Dearborn thus enjoyed the unique experience of having been captured, along with the British army in which he served, by the Americans, and thirty-five years later, as a member of Hull's army, of being taken by the British. His connection with Chicago history is not limited to building and commanding Fort Dearborn. His eldest son served under him here as lieutenant for several years; his eldest daughter, as we have seen, became Chicago's first bride; and another daughter married Lieutenant Joseph Hamilton, who also served under Whistler at Fort Dearborn.

William Whistler came with his father to Fort Dearborn as second lieutenant in 1803, accompanied by his bride of a year. She was even now but sixteen years of age, and was destined to

[414] Whistler family genealogy, MS in Chicago Historical Society library.

be the last surviving witness of the building of the first Fort Dearborn. After several years of service here, Lieutenant Whistler was transferred to Fort Wayne. His term of service in the army lasted sixty years, during which time he had, according to Mrs. Whistler, but six short furloughs.[415] Like his father he was captured along with Hull's army at Detroit. In 1845 he became colonel of the Fourth Infantry, the regiment to which General Grant belonged during the Mexican War; and in after life the famous general told many anecdotes concerning his former commander.[416]

Two other descendants of Captain John Whistler demand attention at this point. George Washington Whistler was a toddling child three years of age when the commander brought his family to the new home in the summer of 1803. Here, on the banks of the Chicago River, during the next few years the child developed into sturdy boyhood. At the age of nineteen he graduated from West Point and was assigned to the artillery branch of the service. Until 1833, when he resigned his commission, he was engaged largely in engineering and topographical enterprises. After his resignation from the army he rose to eminence as an engineer, and during the remainder of his life was engaged in many important enterprises. In 1842 he went to Russia to enter the service of the Czar in the construction of the railroad from St. Petersburg to Moscow. In recognition of his services in this and other engineering enterprises in Russia Emperor Nicholas in 1847 conferred upon him the decoration of the Order of St. Anne.[417]

A son of the famous engineer, James Abbott McNeil Whistler, achieved in the realm of art an even greater reputation than had his father in that of engineering. Whistler's artistic achievements are so well known that there is no need to discuss them here. His connection with Fort Dearborn is not so commonly

415 Hurlbut, *Chicago Antiquities*, 27.

416 Heitman, *Dictionary of the United States Army*, I, 470, 1026; Wilson, *Chicago from 1803 to 1812*.

417 On George Washington Whistler see Vose, *Sketch of the Life and Works of George W. Whistler, Civil Engineer*.

understood, although the very names he bore served constantly to advertise it. James Abbott was Chicago's first bridegroom, who, as we have seen, married Sarah Whistler here in the fall of 1804. The artist himself never saw Chicago, but with the exception of West Point there was no other place in the United States in which he was so much interested.[418] He regarded his grandfather as the founder of Chicago, and more than once lamented his failure to visit the place.

The connection of James Strode Swearingen, the youthful second lieutenant who conducted the troops from Detroit to Chicago in the summer of 1803, with Fort Dearborn was but brief. Because of the physical infirmity of Captain Whistler, Swearingen offered to lead the troops from Detroit to Chicago for him, and this made it possible for Whistler to proceed around the lakes on the sailboat, "Tracy."[419] With the arrival of the troops at Chicago Swearingen's duty was discharged. He accordingly returned to Detroit on the "Tracy" and there rejoined his company. He retired from the army in 1815, owing to the importunity of his wife, and settled at Chillicothe, Ohio, where he lived in affluence until his death in 1864.[420]

Doctor William C. Smith, the first surgeon at Fort Dearborn, was succeeded in 1808 by John Cooper, who was sent here immediately after he entered the service. Cooper's grandfather fought under Wolfe at Quebec, and was near his leader when he fell.[421] The grandson was born at Fishkill, New York, in 1786. He came to Fort Dearborn by way of Albany and Buffalo, where he boarded the brig, "Adams," commanded by Commodore Brevoort. The voyage across Lake Erie consumed a week, and another week, including stops, was spent in passing through the River and Lake St. Clair and on to Mackinac. After several

[418] Statements of General James Grant Wilson, January 7, 1908, in letter to Chicago Historical Society library. Wilson was a personal acquaintance of Whistler.

[419] Swearingen's account of the expedition from Detroit to Chicago in 1803, MS in Chicago Historical Society library, *Proceedings*, 1856–64, 348.

[420] Heitman, *Dictionary of the United States Army*, I, 939; Wilson, *Chicago from 1803 to 1812*.

[421] Wilson, *op. cit.*

days' delay at the latter place the brig proceeded by way of Green Bay to Chicago, which was reached in three days. After three years' service at Fort Dearborn, Cooper resigned from the army and returned to the East by way of the overland route to Detroit, which had been followed by the troops under Swearingen eight years before. The journey to Detroit required fourteen days. From Detroit he went by way of Fort Wayne and Pittsburgh to Poughkeepsie, New York, where he made his home and practiced his profession for over half a century, dying in 1863.[422]

The year 1810 saw the culmination at Fort Dearborn of a garrison quarrel which resulted in the dispersion of the official family far and wide and the appearance of a new set of officials at the post. It might be supposed that the sense of isolation and the need of mutual assistance would bind together the little group of inmates of a frontier post, such as Fort Dearborn, as with bands of steel. But, alas for erring human nature, all too often conditions quite the contrary prevailed. "When society is thin," wrote the same British officer from Mackinac whose complaint in 1796 of the dulness, envy, and jealousy in existence there has already been noted, "I agree with you. They should make the most of it, but I don't know how it is. I have always found it the reverse. . . . ."[423] "The Amusements have not been general this Winter in Detroit. Indeed there has been none worth mentioning, Society a good deal divided," runs a letter to Kingsbury in the winter of 1805.[424]

As early as the autumn of 1804 a quarrel developed among the garrison officers of Fort Dearborn. The details left us are meager, but we know that Lieutenant Campbell raised charges against Doctor Smith,[425] who in turn preferred charges against Lieutenant Whistler,[426] and that Captain Whistler placed Smith

[422] *Ibid.* [423] *Michigan Pioneer Collections*, XII, 211.

[424] *Kingsbury Papers*, Clemson to Kingsbury, February 24, 1805.

[425] *Ibid.*, Smith to Kingsbury, November 3, 1804; Clemson to Kingsbury, October 27, 1804.

[426] *Ibid.*, Clemson to Kingsbury, October 27, 1804.

under arrest.[427] Thus, to quote from a contemporary letter, "a flame" was "kindled at Chicago."[428] Unfortunately for the historian, Captain Whistler found the affair "to disagreeable" for him to report, further than the bare announcement of the surgeon's arrest.[429] Possibly the difficulty was settled by the elimination of Lieutenant Campbell, for he resigned from the army a few months later,[430] while both Smith and the Whistlers continued to serve at Fort Dearborn for several years.

The feud which culminated in 1810 was far more serious. Our sources of information are scanty as to the origin of the quarrel, but fuller and more satisfactory for its course and conclusion. That there existed a rivalry at Fort Dearborn over the garrison trade, and that this rivalry was the cause of the feud, is clear. As early as the summer of 1807 Kinzie and John Whistler, Jr., a younger son of the commander, entered into a partnership for the purpose of supplying this trade.[431] The connection lasted until August 21, 1809, when for some reason not now known it was dissolved.[432] That some discord had developed is, however, reasonably apparent from what followed. Six weeks after the dissolution, Doctor Cooper, who had become the firm friend of Captain Whistler,[433] sought and obtained permission from the Secretary of War to suttle for the garrison.[434]

[427] *Kingsbury Papers*, Whistler to Kingsbury, November 3, 1804.

[428] *Ibid.*, Clemson to Kingsbury, October 27, 1804.

[429] *Ibid.*, Whistler to Kingsbury, November 3, 1804.

[430] Heitman, *Dictionary of the United States Army*, I, 276.

[431] *Barry Transcript*, entry for July 26, 1807; *Kingsbury Papers*, Matthew Irwin to Kingsbury, April 29, 1810. That it was John Whistler, Jr., who was Kinzie's partner is apparent from the county records at Detroit cited by Hurlbut, *Chicago Antiquities*, 469.

[432] *Barry Transcript*, entry for August 21, 1809.

[433] Wilson, *Chicago from 1803 to 1812*. On leaving Fort Dearborn in 1810, Whistler presented Cooper a pistol and a copy of Shenstone's poems. The latter was given by Cooper to General James Grant Wilson, and he in turn presented it to the Chicago Historical Society. Cooper wrote to Kingsbury at the time of the quarrel that he was willing to sell his life to prove Whistler's innocence of the charges against him (*Kingsbury Papers*). The date and salutation of this letter have been cut off, but it was evidently written soon after May 26, 1810.

[434] *Drennan Papers*, Nicoll to Whistler and Cooper, November 1, 1809.

To "suttle" meant to supply the soldiers with articles not furnished them by the government. Shortly after Cooper's arrival at Fort Dearborn Matthew Irwin had been appointed Government factor, to conduct the Indian trading establishment at Chicago.[435] He seems also to have held, as did Varnum, the former factor, the appointment of Government contractor for supplying the garrison with such provisions as were furnished the soldiers by the government.[436] The privilege which Cooper had obtained of suttling for the garrison interfered not only with Irwin's profits but also with those of Kinzie, who, until the dissolution of the partnership with the younger Whistler, had enjoyed this trade. Irwin and Kinzie soon drew together in opposition to Captain Whistler, whom they seem rightly to have regarded as the real power behind Cooper. For some reason Jouett, the Indian agent, and Lieutenant Thompson joined the Irwin-Kinzie coalition; Lieutenant Hamilton, who was Whistler's son-in-law, of course sided with the latter, and the quarrel soon became furious.

Irwin claimed that Whistler and his adherents combined in a policy of persecution calculated to force him to give up his position as contractor in order that Whistler's son might regain it.[437] Whistler, on the other hand, asserted that the "malignant wretches" opposed to him, particularly Jouett, were guilty of defrauding the public; as for Lieutenant Thompson, he was a mere tool in the hands of his associates, who despised him even while they used him.[438] Jouett had told of his running away to escape paying his landlord, and Whistler stated he had acknowledged himself a "Liar" in the presence of all the gentlemen of the fort and its vicinity. Cooper bore a challenge to a duel from Lieutenant Hamilton to Kinzie, which the latter declined

[435] *Wisconsin Historical Collections*, XIX, 326.

[436] That Irwin held this appointment is shown by his letters to Kingsbury; e.g., see letter of April 29, 1810, in *Kingsbury Papers*. My conclusion that Varnum had been contractor as well as factor is based on certain entries in the *Barry Transcript*.

[437] *Kingsbury Papers*, Irwin to Kingsbury, April 29, 1810. The obnoxious conduct of Whistler, Hamilton, and Cooper is detailed at considerable length in this letter.

[438] *Ibid.*, Whistler to Kingsbury, May 27, 1810.

to accept, contenting himself with roundly cursing both principal and second.[439] Half a century later Cooper described the trader as a man of ungovernable temper, who frequently engaged in bitter quarrels.

The opposition to Whistler, determined to drive him from Chicago if not from the army, preferred charges against him to Kingsbury and demanded a court martial. Among other things, aside from the claim that he had conspired with Hamilton and Cooper to force Irwin to give up his office, it was claimed that he had beaten a soldier for not trading with his son,[440] and had defrauded the government by raising ten acres of corn,[441] apparently by the labor of soldiers. On the other hand Cooper preferred charges against Thompson which he believed would inevitably "brake" him.[442] It is not possible with the information available to decide the question of right between the two warring parties, but it is significant that Whistler and later Captain Heald, both of whom incurred the enmity of Kinzie, repeatedly received testimonials of confidence from their brother officers. Captain Heald, who succeeded Whistler at Fort Dearborn, reported that he had found everything in good condition and believed that Whistler had paid "particular Attention to every Part of his duty" during the time he had commanded there.[443] He also refuted the charge of Whistler's enemies that he had been in the habit of raising large quantities of corn. Kingsbury, Whistler's immediate superior, also testified to his belief in his integrity, and in the falsity of the charges against him, and Varnum, who had been factor at Fort Dearborn from 1805 to 1808, expressed approval of Whistler's conduct during that time.[444] In harmony with this favorable

[439] Wilson, *Chicago from 1803 to 1812.*

[440] *Drennan Papers,* Kingsbury to Nicoll, February 15, 1811.

[441] *Kingsbury Papers,* Heald to Kingsbury, May 31, 1810; Kingsbury to Heald, June 11, 1810.

[442] *Kingsbury Papers,* letter of Cooper to Kingsbury cited in note 433.

[443] *Ibid.,* Heald to Kingsbury, May 31, 1810.

[444] *Drennan Papers,* Kingsbury to Nicoll, February 15, 1811.

testimony are the observations of William Johnston,[445] who journeyed from Fort Wayne to Chicago in the spring of 1809. He recorded that Fort Dearborn was "the neatest and best wooden garrison in the United States," a fact which did "great honor to Capt. John Whistler who planned and built it." The observant visitor also records that Whistler had under him, at the time of his visit, the same men as when he built the fort. Although their term of enlistment had expired they had all re-enlisted—a sure sign that Whistler was a good officer.

The outcome of the quarrel was, on the whole, a triumph for Whistler's enemies. Rather than bring Whistler and Thompson to trial on the charges preferred against them, the War Department decided on a general scattering of the officers at Fort Dearborn. In April, 1810, Whistler was sent to Detroit, and Hamilton to Fort Belle Fontaine. Captain Rhea, whose company at Detroit was given to Whistler, was sent to Fort Wayne to relieve Captain Nathan Heald, who, in turn, succeeded Whistler at Fort Dearborn.[446] Thompson and Cooper remained at Fort Dearborn, but the latter's privilege to suttle was withdrawn by special order of the Secretary of War.[447] Jouett and Irwin, the Indian agent and the factor, remained at Fort Dearborn. The atmosphere was now thoroughly uncongenial to Cooper, who soon resigned from the army in disgust, being unwilling to remain in a service where one could be so easily injured in the opinion of the heads of the department.[448]

Thus in gloom and defeat departed the man who, with more propriety than any other, may be called the father of Chicago. That he felt keenly the blow that had been dealt him is shown by his letters to Kingsbury.[449] He was old and infirm, his wife

[445] "Notes of a Tour from Fort Wayne to Chicago, 1809," MS in Chicago Historical Society library.

[446] *Kingsbury Papers*, Kingsbury to Irwin, June 11, 1810; *Drennan Papers*, Nicoll to Heald, April 11, 1810; Nicoll to Whistler, April 11, 1810; Nicoll to Kingsbury, April 11, 1810; Nicoll to Gansevoort, April 12, 1810.

[447] *Drennan Papers*, Nicoll to Whistler, March 30, 1810.

[448] *Kingsbury Papers*, letter of Cooper to Kingsbury cited in note 433.

[449] *Kingsbury Papers*, Whistler to Kingsbury, May 27, 1810; *Drennan Papers*, Kingsbury to Nicoll, February 15, 1811.

was ill, and he had a large family of young children to support, with little property, and burdened with debt.

Nathan Heald, the new commander at Fort Dearborn, was born at Ipswich, New Hampshire, in 1775.[450] He entered the army as an ensign in 1799, serving continuously at various places on the frontier and in the recruiting service until January, 1807, when he was promoted to the rank of captain and given command at Fort Wayne. That he was chosen to succeed Whistler at Fort Dearborn under the circumstances which have been described may fairly be regarded as an indication of confidence on the part of his superiors in his ability and good judgment. Rhea, who succeeded him at Fort Wayne, reported that he found everything had been going on "very correct" there, and that he intended to "take the Track of Captain Heald" as nearly as possible.[451] Rhea was much pleased with his new post and expressed the hope he might continue there. Heald, on the contrary, was dissatisfied with Fort Dearborn, and at once announced his intention of spending the coming winter in New England.[452] If the necessary leave of absence were not granted him he would resign the service rather than remain at Fort Dearborn.

Unfortunately for Heald the furlough was granted,[453] and thus he returned to Chicago to participate in the massacre two years later. After spending the winter in Massachusetts, Heald returned to the West by way of Pittsburgh and the Ohio River, stopping at Louisville to marry Rebekah Wells, the daughter of Colonel Samuel Wells and the niece of Captain William Wells, with whom Heald had long been associated at Fort Wayne.[454] The wedding occurred on May 23, 1811, and in June the com-

[450] Nathan Heald's Journal printed as Appendix III. The original is among the Heald papers in the Draper Collection.

[451] *Kingsbury Papers*, Rhea to Kingsbury, May 17, 1810.

[452] *Ibid.*, Heald to Kingsbury, June 8, 1810.

[453] Heald's Journal; *Kingsbury Papers*, Heald to Kingsbury, December 31, 1810, and May 1, 1811; Wentworth, *Early Chicago*, 88.

[454] Heald's Journal; Darius Heald's narrative of the Chicago massacre, in *Magazine of American History*, XXVIII, 114.

mander reached Chicago with his bride, after an absence of seven months. The bridal journey was made from Louisville to Chicago on horseback through the wilderness which lay between the two places. Mrs. Heald's slave girl, Cicely, accompanied them on their journey, and was an inmate of Fort Dearborn from this time until the massacre the following year. The statement preserved in the Heald family chronicle that the bridal party was received by the garrison with all the honors of war may well be believed, for the addition of a woman like Mrs. Heald to the garrison circle was an event of rare interest in the life of the little community.

In March, 1811, George Ronan, a young cadet direct from West Point, was given the rank of ensign and ordered to repair at once to Fort Dearborn.[455] On the fourth of the same month Lieutenant Thompson died. With him the last military officer involved in the quarrel of the preceding year disappeared from Fort Dearborn. Three months later his place was filled by the transfer of Lieutenant Linai T. Helm from Detroit to Fort Dearborn. The transfer was made at Helm's own request, the reasons for his desiring it being, apparently, his straitened financial circumstances and the cheaper cost of living at Fort Dearborn as compared with Detroit.[456] During the summer the place made vacant by Doctor Cooper's resignation was filled by the appointment of Isaac Van Voorhis, like Cooper a native of Fishkill, New York, born a few years after his predecessor, but a member of the same class in college.[457] The officers of Fort Dearborn were now the same as on the fatal day of evacuation, August 15, 1812.

[455] *Drennan Papers*, Nicoll to Ronan, March 27, 1811; Nicoll to Heald, March 27, 1811; Heitman, *Dictionary of the United States Army*, I, 844.

[456] *Drennan Papers*, Kingsbury to Nicoll, April 18, 1811; Nicoll to Kingsbury, May 24, 1811; *Kingsbury Papers*, Helm to Kingsbury, March 16, 1811.

[457] Van Voorhis, *Notes on the Ancestry of Wm. Roe Van Voorhis*, 143.

CHAPTER VIII

THE INDIAN UTOPIA

Meanwhile time and the fates were weaving a fatal web about the almost defenseless frontier. The western Indians, awed into submission for a time by the masterful hand of Wayne, were again stirred by a great unrest. There were, among others, three important causes for this condition: the rapid occupation of their hunting-grounds and the deterioration of the natives by contact with civilization; the steadily increasing influence of the British, to secure advantages in trade or help in case of war; and finally, a patriotic movement toward race unity among the Indians themselves, which had for its object a revival of the older and happier existence of their forefathers. This movement was full of danger for the West and of hope for the British.

In the first place, the red and white races were totally different in physical habits and in processes of thought by which perceptions become opinions. The Indian had an incomplete and indefinite notion of a treaty when he signed it, and was utterly unable to comprehend its final effect; the white man exacted to the utmost all possible advantages from these agreements. The ideas of the two races with respect to the ownership and transmission of title to land differed markedly. The white man appeased his omnipresent land hunger by inducing representatives of the tribes to make a cession, usually for a paltry consideration, of the land which was at the moment desired. The usual method of procuring such cessions was to call the leaders of the tribe affected together in solemn conclave, where they were plied with whisky and cajolery, and by alternate threats and appeals to their cupidity the bargain was extorted from them.[458] If the government did not itself directly supply

[458] For an excellent description of the scenes attending a typical treaty see Latrobe, *Rambler in North America*, II, chap. xi.

the liquor which befuddled the brain and weakened the will of the red man, it was at least guilty of permitting its subjects to do so.[459] How the transaction appeared to the Indian, when he had had time to reflect upon it, is well shown by an appeal of the Wyandot tribe in 1812 to be allowed to retain possession of the lands they were then cultivating, which had been ceded to the United States by a prior treaty. Their description of the process of obtaining cessions from the tribes can scarcely be improved upon for clarity and succinctness. "When the United States want a particular piece of land, all our natives are assembled; a large sum of money is offered; the land is occupied probably by one nation only; nine-tenths have no actual interest in the land wanted; if the particular nation interested refuses to sell, they are generally threatened by the others, who want the money or goods offered to buy whisky. Fathers, this is the way in which this small spot, which we so much value, has been so often torn from us."[460]

Thus the land hunger of the white man and the discord produced by the operation of two totally divergent conceptions of land ownership and alienation furnished the basis for a conflict between the two races which was probably inevitable under any circumstances. To the shame of the more enlightened race, however, it must be said that its relations with its less civilized neighbor were marked by a policy of persistent abuse and a disregard of justice and treaty obligations which operated time and again to goad the red man into impotent warfare, and this, in turn, became the excuse for further spoliation. No government ever entertained more enlightened and benevolent intentions toward a weaker people than did that of the United States toward the Indian, but never in history, probably, has a more striking divergence between intention and performance been witnessed.

[459] There is practically no limit to the number of sources which might be cited in support of this statement. See for example Latrobe, *op. cit.*, II, chap. xi. At the second Treaty of Greenville, July, 1814, the government agents seem to have deliberately adopted the policy of intoxicating the Indians in order to bend them to their wishes (Dillon, "The National Decline of the Miami Indians," in *Indiana Historical Society, Publications*, I, 136–37).

[460] *American State Papers, Indian Affairs*, I, 795–96.

The failure was due partly to ignorance, but also, in large part at least, to the inability or unwillingness of the government to restrain its lawless subjects, who, filled with an insatiable cupidity and animated by a wanton disregard of justice, hesitated at no means to possess themselves of the land and other property of the Indians.

The truth of these statements is so notorious as scarcely to require demonstration, were it not for the fact that with the passing of the relations that prevailed between the two races on the frontier a century ago our knowledge of them threatens to disappear. Almost any number of witnesses of unimpeachable authority might be cited to show the unjust administration of the regulations governing the intercourse between the two races. Said Hamtramck to St. Clair in 1790: "The people of our frontiers will be the first to break any treaty. The people of Kentucky will carry on private expeditions and will kill Indians whenever they meet them, and I do not believe there is a jury in all Kentucky who would punish a man for it."[461] This opinion was substantially repeated by Washington, who affirmed that the "frontier settlers entertain the opinion that there is not the same crime (or indeed no crime at all) in killing an Indian as in killing a white man."[462]

No man understood better the conditions that prevailed on the northwestern frontier than did General Harrison. His letters and messages abound in accounts of acts of violence and other crimes committed against the Indians, and of the impossibility of obtaining justice for them. By the treaties the Indians guilty of murder were to be surrendered to the whites, and whatever the form of trial were practically certain of punishment, while, as Hamtramck observed, western juries almost invariably acquitted white men guilty of the same offense. "The Indian always suffers, and the white man never," said Harrison to the Indiana legislature in 1806, in a message appealing for a redress of this grievance.[463] A year later, in discussing the subject of

[461] Winsor, *Westward Movement*, 421.

[462] *Ibid.*

[463] Dillon, *History of Indiana*, 424.

Indian unrest, the Governor returned to the same theme, expressing the opinion that the utmost efforts of the British to incite the Indians to make war upon the Americans would be unavailing "if one only of the many persons who have committed murders on their people, could be brought to punishment."[464] It had even come to pass from the partiality shown the whites in the enforcement of the laws that the Indians proudly compared their own observance of the treaty stipulations with that of their boasted superiors.[465]

An event reported by General Harrison in 1802 well illustrates the workings of the prejudice which rendered persons guilty of acts of violence against the Indians immune from punishment.[466] An Indian was barbarously murdered by a white man. The offender was a man of infamous character for whom no sympathy was felt, and the evidence of guilt was incontestable. Yet the jury, in obedience to the sentiment that no white man ought to suffer for the murder of an Indian, in a few minutes brought in a verdict of acquittal. A case which attracted a good deal of attention and served to embitter the minds of the Indians occurred about the beginning of the century. An entire party consisting of several persons, men, women, and children, was foully murdered by three white villains for the sake of a paltry fifty dollars' worth of peltry which they owned. The murder was revealed through the boasting of the murderers themselves. Governor Harrison made strenuous efforts to secure their punishment, but because of the active sentiment against punishing white men for killing Indians these were rendered of no avail.[467] In a similar manner in 1812 a trader who had killed an Indian at Vincennes was acquitted by the jury almost without deliberation.[468]

[464] Dawson, *Historical Narrative of the Civil and Military Services of Major-General William H. Harrison*, 97.

[465] Governor Harrison to the Indiana legislature, printed in Dillon, *History of Indiana*, 424. In a letter to Harrison from the War Department (unsigned), July 17, 1806, relative to the murder of an Indian occurs the following: "It is excessively mortifying that our good faith should so frequently be called in question by the natives who have it in their power to make such proud comparison in relation to good faith."—Indian Office, Letter Book B, 240.

[466] Dawson, *Harrison*, 45.

[467] *Ibid.*, 7–8, 31–32.

[468] Drake, *Life of Tecumseh*, 134.

Shortly after this the house of a white man was robbed by a Delaware Indian. To the demand that the culprit be given up for trial the chiefs of the tribe replied that they would never surrender another man until some of the white murderers of their own people had been punished; they would, however, punish him themselves, and this promise they kept by putting him to death.[469] Another illustration of the sense of injustice felt by the Indians over the one-sided administration of justice as between the two races, is afforded by the spirited speech of Main Poc, the Pottawatomie chief who lived near the junction of the Des Plaines and the Kankakee rivers, to the agent of Governor Edwards in 1811. To the latter's demand for the surrender of certain red men accused of committing murders among the whites Main Poc replied: "You astonish us with your talk. When you do us harm nothing is done, but when we do anything you immediately tie us by the neck."[470]

Thus to the native mind there were two kinds of justice, one red and the other white, and moreover the red man was keen enough to observe that most of the faults for which he was visited with punishment had been learned from the palefaces. In particular the white man's fire-water had for him a fatal fascination, leading him into depths of degradation and crime which beggar description. There is no more mournful picture in English literature than that of the steady destruction of the Indian race by this poison dealt out to the red man by the white trader for the sake of paltry gain. The efforts of Catholic and Protestant missionaries, and of the governments of France, Great Britain, and the United States to suppress the accursed traffic were all alike in vain. The narratives of travelers and the letters and reports of government officials abound in portrayals of shocking scenes of debauchery indulged in by the Indians while under the influence of liquor.[471] "I have witnessed the evils caused by that

[469] Dawson, *Harrison*, 178.

[470] Edwards, *Life of Ninian Edwards*, 49.

[471] For examples see Volney, *View of the Soil and Climate of the United States of America*, 354; Latrobe, *Rambler in North America*, II, chap. xi; Keating, *Narrative of an Expedition to the Sources of the St. Peter's River*, I, 124–27; Charlevoix, *Letters to the Duchess of Lesdiguières*, 228–29; and citations collected by Dillon, in *Indiana Historical Society, Publications*, I, 131–38.

liquor among the Indians," wrote Denonville, governor of New France, in an official memoir in 1690.[472] "It is the horror of horrors. There is no crime nor infamy they do not perpetrate in their excesses. A mother throws her child into the fire; noses are bitten off; this is a frequent occurrence. It is another Hell among them during these orgies, which must be seen to be credited. . . . . Those who allege that the Indians will remove to the English, if Brandy be not furnished them do not tell the truth; for it is a fact that they do not care about drinking as long as they do not see brandy; and the most reasonable would wish there had never been any such thing; for they set their entrails on fire and beggar themselves by giving their peltries and clothes for drink." "This passion for drink," said General Cass to the chief, Metea, at the Chicago Treaty of 1821, "has injured your nation more than any other thing—more than all the other causes put together. It is not a long period since you were a powerful independent tribe—now, you are reduced to a handful, and it is all owing to ardent spirits."[473] And Governor Harrison, pleading for a law to protect the Indians against the liquor traffic, thus addressed the Indiana legislature in 1805: "You are witnesses to the abuses; you have seen our towns crowded with furious and drunken savages, our streets flowing with their blood, their arms and clothing bartered for the liquor that destroys them, and their miserable women and children enduring all the extremities of cold and hunger. So destructive has the progress of intemperance been among them, that whole villages have been swept away. A miserable remnant is all that remains to mark the names and situation of many numerous and warlike tribes. In the energetic language of one of their orators, it is a dreadful conflagration, which spreads misery and desolation through their country, and threatens the annihilation of the whole race."[474]

At an earlier date than the foregoing, in an official communication to the Secretary of War, Harrison described the general

[472] O'Callaghan, *New York Colonial Documents*, IX, 441.

[473] Schoolcraft, *Travels in the Central Portions o the Mississippi Valley*, 351.

[474] Dawson, *Harrison*, 73.

effect upon the Indians of their intercourse with the whites in these words:

"Killing each other has become so customary amongst them that it is no longer thought criminal. They murder those whom they have been most accustomed to esteem and regard—their chiefs and their nearest relatives fall under the stroke of their tomahawks and their knives. . . . . All those horrors are produced to those unhappy people by their too frequent intercourse with the white people. This is so certain that I can at once tell, upon looking at an Indian whom I chance to meet, whether he belongs to a neighboring, or to a more distant tribe. The latter is generally well clothed, healthy, and vigorous; the former, half-naked, filthy, and enfeebled by intoxication; and many of them without arms, except a knife, which they carry for the most villanous purposes."[475]

The red men were not unconscious of the evils of intemperance, and often made pathetic appeals to the whites to protect them from temptation. "The Indian Chiefs complain heavily of the mischiefs produced by the enormous quantities of whisky which the traders introduce into their country," wrote Harrison to the Secretary of War in 1801.[476] In 1810 the Fox nation requested General Clark, Indian agent at St. Louis, to prevent whisky from coming among them as it made them "verry poor."[477] In a speech to the President of the United States in 1802 Little Turtle dwelt on the demoralization wrought among his people by liquor, and urged that its sale be prohibited. "Your children are not wanting in industry," he said, "but it is the introduction of this fatal poison which keeps them poor. Your children have not that command of themselves which you have, therefore, before anything can be done to advantage, this evil must be remedied."[478]

[475] Dawson, *Harrison*, 10–11.

[476] *Ibid.*

[477] *Edwards Papers*, MSS in Chicago Historical Society library, L, 77; Maurice Blondeau to Clark, August 25, 1810.

[478] *American State Papers, Indian Affairs*, I, 655.

The conditions which were working the ruin of the tribes were borne by the Indians with astonishing patience.[479] "They will never have recourse to arms," said Harrison in 1806, "unless driven to it by a series of injustice and oppression."[480] Yet often there were pathetic protests. "I had not discovered," wrote Black Hawk of the spring of 1812, "one good trait in the character of the Americans that had come to the country. They made fair promises, but never fulfilled them. . . . . Why did the Great Spirit ever send the whites to this island to drive us from our homes, and introduce among us poisonous liquors, disease, and death?"[481]

With the government demanding more lands and the advancing line of white settlement pressing ever forward, the game upon which the Indians subsisted became scarcer, and many of the tribes were reduced to destitution. Then came the remarkable attempt of Tecumseh, the Indian Moses, and his brother, the Prophet, to rescue their people from the impending doom. The story of Tecumseh, the greatest man of the native race, begins with the birth of three boys to the Cherokee squaw of a Shawnee warrior about the year 1770, in an obscure village near the present site of Springfield, Ohio.[482] In the nature of things not much can be known with certainty of his earlier years. His brother, the Prophet, has spun a fanciful tale of his descent from the union of a Creek warrior with the daughter of one of the colonial governors, but both this and the stories of his youthful precocity and prowess may be regarded with equal suspicion. In the same light must we view the story of the effect produced upon Tecumseh by the first spectacle, for him, of the burning of a prisoner, and his persuading his associates to abandon the custom,[483] though it is true his later career was marked by a humanity toward the vanquished foe quite unusual in an Indian.

479 Statement of Harrison to the Secretary of War, July 15, 1801, Dawson, *Harrison*, 9.

480 Dillon, *History of Indiana*, 423.

481 Black Hawk, *Life*, 34–35.

482 Drake, *Tecumseh*, chaps. i and ii.

483 *Ibid.*, 68–69.

The young warrior doubtless participated in various warlike forays during the stormy years prior to Wayne's victory at Fallen Timbers in 1794. He fought in that battle, but refrained from attending the council which resulted in the Treaty of Greenville.[484] During the next few years he assumed the dignity of a chief and gradually attracted to himself a considerable following. Before long his fame as an orator and a man of influence among his fellows had spread even to the white settlers. In 1805 several scattered bands of the Shawnee tribe, Tecumseh's among the number, united and settled at Greenville, where Tecumseh's brother began the career which has caused him to be known in history as the "Prophet."

Tecumseh was always an enemy of the Americans, but he based his enmity upon the losses and ills suffered by his people. Evidently the Great Spirit was angry with his red children, for they were being driven from their hunting-grounds, were losing their health and vigor, and sinking into the lowest depths of poverty and depravity. For all these evils there were two remedies; the first to recover the lost hunting-grounds, the second to reform the conduct of the warriors; and no European statesman ever faced an impossible task with greater courage or used his resources with greater skill than did Tecumseh.

The leading rôle was taken for some time by Tecumseh's brother the Prophet, who now took upon himself the name Tenskwautawau, meaning the "Open Door," signifying that he would point out to the Indians the new mode of life they should pursue.[485] From the village of the assembled bands near Greenville was sent out far and wide to the tribes in the year 1806 this revelation by the Prophet of the will of the Great Spirit: "I am the father of the English, of the French, of the Spaniards, and of the Indians. I created the first man, who was the common father of all these people, as well as yourselves; and it is through him, whom I have awaked from his long sleep, that I now address you. *But the Americans I did not make. They are not my children, but the children of the evil spirit.* They grew from

[484] Drake, *Tecumseh*, 81–83.

[485] *Ibid.*, 86.

the scum of the great water where it was troubled by the evil spirit, and the froth was driven into the woods by a strong east wind. They are numerous, but I hate them. . . . . I am now on the earth, sent by the Great Spirit to instruct you. Each village must send me two or more principal chiefs to represent you, that you may be taught. . . . . Those villages which do not listen to this talk, and send me two deputies, will be cut off from the face of the earth."[486]

A religious enthusiasm was thus enkindled which soon developed into a frenzy. The Prophet's teachings in the main were sound, from the red man's point of view, but they were attended by the excesses inevitable to such a movement.[487] Witchcraft, drunkenness, and intermarriage with the whites were declared against, and community of property, respect for the aged and infirm, and adherence to the native dress and customs were advocated. To all who would adopt these precepts the recovery of the comforts and happiness enjoyed by their forefathers before they were debased by their connection with the whites was promised. Among the first manifestations of the influence of the new teachings was the outbreak of a witchcraft delusion, similar in all essential respects to that in Massachusetts in 1692.[488] Under the influence of torture those accused confessed the possession of supernatural powers, and to aerial journeyings by night; but where staid and civilized Salem had been content to hang her victims, the untutored red man burned his at the stake.

This delusion was soon ended, partly by the good sense of the Indians reasserting itself, partly through the influence of Governor Harrison, who sent a ringing protest against it.[489] But the influence of the Prophet continued to wax, and by the summer of 1807 hundreds of Indians from far and near had come to visit him and to listen to his instruction.[490] The British, who feared an

[486] *American State Papers, Indian Affairs*, I, 798.

[487] For a statement of the Prophet's teachings at this time see Drake, *Tecumseh*, 87–88.

[488] *Ibid.*, 88–89; Dawson, *Harrison*, 82–83.

[489] Dawson, *Harrison*, 83–84.

[490] Captain Wells at Fort Wayne estimated that up to May 25, 1807, fifteen hundred Indians had passed that point going to visit the Prophet (Dawson, *Harrison*, 91).

outbreak of war and an invasion of Canada by the Americans following the Chesapeake affair of 1807, sought to foster the excitement and to turn it to their own ends by attaching the Indians to their cause in the impending conflict. Messengers were sent to all the tribes to summon them to Malden,[491] where for years presents of guns, ammunition, and other supplies had been distributed to the Indians with a prodigal hand.[492] Hull at Detroit did his best to counteract the effect of the meetings at Malden, but with indifferent success.[493] The British urged the Indians to join actively in the expected war with the Americans. Hull, on the other hand, tried to win them to a policy of neutrality, a rôle entirely foreign to their savage nature. Many of them stopped at Detroit on their return from Malden, and showed great readiness in inventing excuses for their conduct. "When you first sent for us," said one, "we immediately prepared to come to see you. Captain McKee prevented us from coming then; he renewed his promise of presents to us, and gave us a keg of spirits; that fatal keg stopped us. We were stopped a second and a third time; at last, without his knowledge, we crossed the river. We are now happy on your shore and safe under your protection."[494]

Meanwhile Tecumseh's plans steadily developed. In June, 1809, he established himself with his brother, the Prophet, and a considerable number of warriors gathered from various tribes on the "Great Clearing," where Tippecanoe Creek empties into the Wabash.[495] For three years this town was the center of Indian intrigue and turbulence in the Northwest. One hundred miles to the northwest was Fort Dearborn; about the same distance to the northeast Fort Wayne guarded the approach to the Maumee;

[491] *Michigan Pioneer Collections*, XV, 44–45, 47–48; *American State Papers, Indian Affairs*, I, 797 ff.

[492] For a description by a British partisan of the distribution of goods to the Indians at Malden, see Weld, *Travels through the States of North America*, II, Letter 34.

[493] *American State Papers, Indian Affairs*, I, 745–46; *Michigan Pioneer Collections*, VIII, 568–71.

[494] *American State Papers, Indian Affairs*, I, 745.

[495] Dawson, *Harrison*, 106–7.

while one hundred and fifty miles to the south Vincennes protected the Illinois frontier. The new Indian town occupied the center of the triangle formed by these three posts. Here was to be worked out, for weal or woe, the great experiment on the outcome of which depended the future of the red race. That Tecumseh's was the master mind which guided the enterprise cannot be doubted, although he made clever use of the influence wielded by his brother, and at times seemed to shrink into the background in comparison with the latter. Here at Tippecanoe the Indians proceeded to exemplify the Prophet's teachings, which shall be given in his own words.

"The Great Spirit told me to tell the Indians that he had made them and made the world—that he had placed them in it to do good, and not evil. I told all the redskins that the way they were in was not good, and that they ought to abandon it. That we ought to consider ourselves as one man, but we ought to live agreeable to our several customs, the red people after their mode, and the white people after theirs; particularly, that they should not drink whisky, that it was not made for them, but the white people, who alone know how to use it; and that it is the cause of all the mischiefs which the Indians suffer; . . . . Determine to listen to nothing that is bad. Do not take up the tomahawk, should it be offered by the British, or by the Long Knives. Do not meddle with any thing that does not belong to you, but mind your own business and cultivate the ground, that your women and your children may have enough to live on."[496]

The extent to which this advice was followed is astonishing, in view of the fact that it necessitated a complete revolution in the lives and habits of the natives. The influence of the Prophet's religious teachings was felt from Florida to Saskatchewan. Most marvelous of all, the love of liquor which had been the bane of the Indians from the beginning of their intercourse with the whites was for a time completely exorcised.[497] Seeking to test the strength of the Prophet's influence over his

[496] Speech to Governor Harrison, August, 1808; Dawson, *Harrison*, 108–9.

[497] *Wisconsin Historical Collections*, XIX, 322.

followers, Harrison tempted them with whisky in vain.[498] Even among the distant tribes to which the Prophet's emissaries came, drunkenness and warfare fell into disfavor.[499] The Ottawas of l'Arbre Croche were reported in 1807 to be adhering strictly to the "Shawney Prophet's" advice. The whisky and rum of the traders had become a drug on the market, not a gallon a month being purchased. Even when the white men sought to tempt the natives by urging liquor upon them as a present they refused it "with disdain."[500]

The settlers on the frontier were filled with apprehensions of danger from Tecumseh's movement, and protests and appeals for protection poured in upon Harrison. Yet the brothers protested that they had no hostile designs against the Americans. In the summer of 1808 the Prophet visited Harrison at Vincennes and succeeded in convincing him, apparently, that he desired only peace and the upbuilding of his race.[501] Meanwhile Tecumseh was conducting missions far and wide among the Indians, urging upon them his design of a confederation of all the tribes. In the famous Vincennes Council of 1810[502] he frankly informed Harrison that his purpose was to form a combination of all the Indian tribes of the surrounding region, to put a stop to the encroachments of the whites, and to establish the principle that the lands should be considered the common property of all the tribes, never to be sold without the consent of all. There was nothing original in this, for exactly the same design and contention had been advanced by the northwestern tribes in their general council at the mouth of the Detroit River in 1786.[503] The American government had, of course, ignored their pretensions. Much dissatisfaction was expressed by the tribes with the treaties of Fort McIntosh and Fort Harmar, subsequent to their enact-

[498] Drake, *Tecumseh*, 107.

[499] For evidence on this point see *Tanner's Narrative*, 155–58; *Wisconsin Historical Collections*, XIX, 322–23.

[500] *Wisconsin Historical Collections*, XIX, 322–23.

[501] Dawson, *Harrison*, 107–9.

[502] For an account of this council see *ibid.*, 155–59.

[503] *Michigan Pioneer Collections*, XI, 467–69.

ment, many of them refusing to recognize the validity of the cessions made by these treaties until compelled thereto by Wayne, in 1795. At the Treaty of Greenville in that year most of the northwestern tribes were represented; but many individuals belonging to them held aloof, and among these Tecumseh himself was numbered.

With the rapid advance of white settlement following Wayne's victory, new cessions of land were from time to time demanded. That the red man must go down before this advancing tide of invasion was inevitable. That he should struggle against his impending fate was but natural. The plan advanced in 1786 offered the only prospect of even temporarily holding back the whites, and this the more far-sighted among the Indians were shrewd enough to perceive. Harrison reported in 1802 the existence among them of an agreement that no proposition relating to their lands could be acceded to without the consent of all the tribes.[504] Nevertheless several treaties carrying large cessions of land were made during the next few years. One of these, in particular, made by the Piankeshaws and Delawares in August, 1804, excited the anger of the other tribes.[505] Others negotiated by Harrison in 1808 and 1809 again aroused them. To an agent of Harrison Tecumseh stated, in the summer of 1810, that the continuance of friendship with the United States was impossible unless the encroachment should cease.[506] "The Great Spirit," he said, "gave this great island to his red children, he placed the whites on the other side of the big water; they were not contented with their own, but came to take ours from us. They have driven us from the sea to the lakes, we can go no farther." This was repeated to Harrison himself a few weeks later at the Council of Vincennes, and the determination was proclaimed to put to death all the chiefs who had been parties to the late treaties, and to take away from the village chiefs the management of their tribal affairs and place it in the hands of the warriors.[507]

[504] Dawson, *Harrison*, 19.

[505] *Ibid.*, 61–3.

[506] *Ibid.*, 153.

[507] *Ibid.*, 155.

The Council of Vincennes closed with an ultimatum on the part of Tecumseh that the President must either agree to give up the lands recently purchased and promise never to make another treaty without the consent of all the tribes, or else prepare for war. Harrison agreed to transmit Tecumseh's demands to the President, but assured him there was no probability of their acceptance; to which the red leader's grim rejoinder was that in that event "you and I will have to fight it out." A year passed, however, and war was not yet begun. In 1811 another council was held between the leaders of the rival races.[508] Some murders had been committed in Illinois for which Harrison demanded satisfaction. Tecumseh professed himself unable to afford it. At the same time he informed the Governor that he had succeeded in uniting the northern tribes, and at the close of the council would set out for the south to bring the southern tribes also into union.

Tecumseh departed on his mission, but returned to find his hopes of realizing the red man's Utopia forever blasted. The settlers of Indiana, frantic with fear of the threatened destruction, demanded that the government take steps effectually to avert it.[509] Equipped at last with an adequate military force, Harrison determined to forestall the anticipated blow by striking first. The fight of Tippecanoe followed in November, 1811, and the Prophet's shrill battle song on that field was at once the death song to Indian unity and to peace on the frontier. Henceforth, if the dream of Tecumseh was to be realized, the Indians must, as he had threatened, throw in their lot with the British, and improve the opportunity afforded by a war between the two white nations.

Thus the agitation fostered by Tecumseh kept the northwestern frontier in a turmoil for several years, and constitutes for that region the prelude to the War of 1812. At Chicago there were no actual hostilities during this time, but the Indians of this vicinity shared the unrest which existed among their fellows on the Wabash. In June, 1805, representatives from several of the

[508] For an account of this council see *ibid.*, 182–85.

[509] *Ibid.*, 187–90.

northwestern tribes journeyed to Malden to solicit the assistance of their British Father against the encroachments of the Americans. Among the speakers were two chiefs from Chicago, one of them the notorious Black Bird to whom Captain Heald seven years later surrendered the survivors of the Fort Dearborn massacre. The burden of their complaint was that the Long Knives were pressing on them so that they deemed it time to take up the hatchet. Both the Chicago chiefs professed an attachment to peace hitherto, but seeing "the White Devil with his mouth wide open" ready to take possession of their lands by any means whatever, they had determined to join with their fellows in opposition.[510]

A year later, in June, 1806, a French trader informed Captain Wells at Fort Wayne that a plot had been formed by the Chippewas, Ottawas, and Pottawatomies to surprise Detroit, Mackinac, Fort Wayne, and Chicago.[511] In 1808 Jouett, the agent at Chicago, reported that the neighboring Indians were planning a visit to the Prophet.[512] He feared that the meeting would be attended with serious consequences, and advised that it be forestalled by the apprehension of the Prophet. About this same time the followers of Main Poc made threatening demonstrations at Fort Dearborn, stirred up, as Doctor Cooper was told, by some act of alleged injustice on the part of the government contractor.[513]

From threatened hostilities to the commission of acts of violence was a step easily taken. In 1810 the Indians of Illinois committed a series of depredations and murders along the Mississippi border.[514] In July four white men were killed near Portage des Sioux by a band of marauding Indians engaged in a horse-stealing expedition. Two of the murderers shortly took refuge with the Prophet.[515] Both Governor Edwards and Governor Harrison endeavored to secure the surrender of the offenders, but without success.[516] One of the culprits was

[510] *Michigan Pioneer Collections*, XXIII, 39–42.

[511] Dawson, *Harrison*, 85.

[512] *Ibid.*, 105.

[513] Wilson, *Chicago from 1803 to 1812.*

[514] Edwards, *Life of Ninian Edwards*, 37.

[515] *Edwards Papers*, 56–57; Edwards, *Life of Ninian Edwards*, 37.

[516] Dawson, *Harrison*, 182–84; Edwards, *Life of Ninian Edwards*, chap. iii.

Nuscotnemeg, who later bore a prominent part in the Chicago massacre.[517] Main Poc, who had made the demonstration against Fort Dearborn in 1808, seems to have been the most active marauder during the next few years. In May, 1811, La Lime, the interpreter at Fort Dearborn, reported that two of Main Poc's brothers had been engaged in stealing horses from the settlements of southern Illinois.[518] In August Gomo informed Governor Edwards' representative that Main Poc had gone to Detroit where he would remain until fall.[519] The nature of his mission is revealed by a letter of Captain Wells the following February.[520] He had been stationed near Malden since August, visiting the British headquarters there every few days. He had with him one hundred and twenty warriors, disposed in bands of ten or fifteen each to allay the suspicion of the Americans, ready to take the warpath the moment hostilities between the British and Americans should begin. Thus alarming reports poured in upon the government from every part of the frontier.[521] British agents in Canada co-operated with those in the West to secure the allegiance of the Indians, and early in the year 1812 attacks were proposed upon the border settlements of Louisiana and Illinois.[522] It was due mainly to Robert Dickson, one of the most astute and influential British traders in the Northwest, that these plans were not fully carried out, and that the hostile bands were transferred to the territory about Detroit and the Canadian frontier.[523] The Americans urged upon the Indians a policy of neutrality in the impending war between the whites,[524] while the British, with greater success, sought to enlist them actively in their support. The opening of the year 1812 found the Indians only awaiting the co-operation of the British to devastate the frontier with blood and slaughter.

[517] *Edwards Papers*, 57; *Wisconsin Historical Collections*, XI, 320.

[518] Kirkland, *Chicago Massacre*, 187; Edwards, *Life of Ninian Edwards*, 286–87.

[519] Edwards, *Life of Ninian Edwards*, 39.

[520] *American State Papers, Indian Affairs*, I, 805.

[521] For further examples see *ibid.*, 797–811.

[522] *Edwards Papers;* Edwards, *Life of Ninian Edwards, passim.*

[523] *Michigan Pioneer Collections*, Vol. XV, *passim;* Black Hawk, *Life*, 30–35.

[524] Black Hawk, *Life*, 34 ff; *Michigan Pioneer Collections*, XV, 196–98; Edwards, *Life of Ninian Edwards*, 57.

CHAPTER IX

THE OUTBREAK OF WAR

The indecisive outcome of the battle of Tippecanoe seemed to necessitate the continuation of the war which Harrison's campaign had precipitated. But Tecumseh's plans were not yet matured, and his British advisers steadily warned him against the mistake of making a premature beginning of the struggle with the Americans, which would permit them to crush the Indians before the British should be ready to come to their assistance. He chose, therefore, to make light of the affair at Tippecanoe, and continued to protest that there would be no war with the Americans unless they themselves forced it.[525] One thing had, however, been rendered certain by the Tippecanoe campaign: sooner or later the Americans must renew the attack upon the Indians; and a war with the British would bring an Indian war also upon the Northwest.

Finally after long debate the country blundered hesitantly and half-heartedly into the War of 1812. The people of New England were so bitterly opposed to this step, and to the party in power, as to give rise to suspicion of their loyalty to the Union. The middle and southern states were, on the whole, favorably disposed toward the war. But in no other section were the people as eager for war to begin as in the West. Here, on the frontier, the traditional enmity toward England was comparatively untouched by the commercial advantages which committed New England to a policy of peace. Revival of commerce had little effect upon the West with its desultory cultivation and

[525] In a speech delivered at a council of the tribes at Massassinway on the Wabash, in May, 1812, Tecumseh disclaimed responsibility for the fight of Tippecanoe, referring to it as "the unfortunate transaction that took place between the white people and a few of our young men at our village." He stated that the trouble between his followers and Governor Harrison had been settled, and further that had he been at home there would have been no bloodshed (Dawson, *Harrison*, 266–67).

crude and inadequate means of transportation, but the spirit of expansion was strong and the greed for land was unappeased. To this sentiment was added the belief, firmly held by the westerner, that the British were primarily responsible for the insecurity of the frontier. In part this was justified by the facts of the situation, but not to the extent which the American frontiersmen believed it was. Whether well founded or not, the belief filled them with resentment toward the British and rendered them keen for war. "I cannot but notice," wrote Surgeon Van Voorhis from Fort Dearborn in October, 1811, in a letter to a friend, "the villainy practiced in the Indian country by British agents and traders; you hear of it at a distance, but we near the scene of action are sensible of it. They labor by every unprincipled means to instigate the Savages against the Americans, to inculcate the idea that we intend to drive the Indians beyond the Mississippi, and that in every purchase of land the Government defrauds them; and their united efforts aim too at the destruction of every trading house and the prevention of the extension of our frontier. Never till a prohibition of the entrance of all foreigners, and especially British subjects, into the Indian Country takes place, will we enjoy a lasting peace with the credulous, deluded, and cannibal savages."[526]

The West looked forward to war, not only as a solution of the Indian problem, but also as the means of securing Canada. Yet greater danger threatened the Northwest, in the event of war, than any other portion of the United States. Of the territories Michigan was the most defenseless and exposed to attack. There were in all ten settlements scattered over a wide extent of country, the distance between the closest of them being thirty miles and that between the two extremes over ten times as great.[527] The entire population, counting British, French, Americans, negroes, and the troops of the garrison at Detroit,

[526] Van Voorhis, *Ancestry of Major Wm. Roe Van Voorhis*, 144–45.

[527] Memorial of the inhabitants of Michigan Territory to the President and Congress, December 8 and 10, 1811, in *American State Papers, Indian Affairs*, I, 780–82; *Michigan Pioneer Collections*, XV, 61–63.

was less than five thousand, four-fifths of them being of French-Canadian descent. The chief source of danger arose, however, from the exposed situation of the settlements, rather than from lack of numbers. Ordinarily the frontier was the extreme line of white occupation and was backed by settlements whose population became denser in proportion to their distance from it. Michigan, however, presented the phenomenon of a double frontier, open on one side to the British and on the other to the savages; furthermore the settlements were so scattered as to render effectual co-operation between them in case of attack out of the question.

Separated from even the southernmost of the Michigan settlements by a wide extent of wilderness, which contained the stronghold of the budding Indian confederacy, were the white settlements of Indiana. They had a population of about thirty thousand, clustered principally in two groups, the one around Vincennes, the other on the Ohio opposite Louisville, with one hundred miles of wilderness between them.[528] From the Wabash to the Illinois and Kankakee, stretching far to the southward, was the great wedge of lands still held by the Indian tribes. Beginning with the old French town of Vincennes, then Harrison's headquarters, the line of the frontier followed the Wabash River nearly fifty miles to Fort Harrison, opposite the present city of Terre Haute. Extending north from Fort Harrison to the Michigan settlements and westward to the Mississippi were the Indian villages and hunting-grounds. The principal settlements of Illinois were still, as in the old French days, clustered along its lower Mississippi border. A line drawn from Vincennes to the mouth of Rock River on the Mississippi would have had south of it practically all of them. The total white population of the territory was probably less than half that of Indiana.

To protect this extensive northwestern frontier the United States had, in the early part of 1812, some half-dozen feeble garrisons, with an average strength of about seventy-five men.

[528] Henry Adams, *History of the United States*, VI, 68.

At Detroit, the largest and most important military station in the Northwest, were ninety-four men;[529] at Mackinac, three hundred miles away, were seventy-nine; at the opposite end of Lake Michigan and about an equal distance from both Mackinac and Detroit was Fort Dearborn with a garrison of fifty-five men; at Fort Wayne and at Fort Harrison, the new stockade on the Wabash, were about as many. All of these were one-company posts except Detroit, which had two companies. The fortifications had not been designed for, nor were they expected to be capable of, defense against the forces of a civilized nation. They were supposed to possess sufficient strength to withstand an attack by Indians alone, and, providing the supply of provisions held out, this expectation would ordinarily have been realized. Even so, however, they could do nothing toward defending the scattered settlements against the attacks of the Indians, and the sequel showed that the garrisons were not even able to defend themselves. Mackinac surrendered without resistance to a combined force of Indians and Canadian traders; Fort Dearborn was abandoned, and the garrison was destroyed while seeking to escape; and Fort Wayne was saved from impending capture only by the approach of a large force of militia under General Harrison.

Against this frontier could be launched, in the event of an Indian war alone, several thousand warriors.[530] If war were joined with Great Britain at the same time, it was believed by both sides, and with good reason, that several thousand men employed in the Indian trade and in sympathy with the British would co-operate in the attack on the American frontier.[531] Potentially the Americans possessed in the population of Ohio and Kentucky resources vastly greater than those their opponents could bring to bear on the Northwest; and in the end the superiority of population made itself manifest in the triumph of

[529] *American State Papers, Indian Affairs*, I, 781.

[530] In the memorial cited above (note 527) of the inhabitants of Michigan Territory to the President and Congress, December 8 and 10, 1811, the number of warriors that might be brought against Detroit was estimated at five thousand.

[531] *Michigan Pioneer Collections*, XV, 61–63, 70–72; *Drennan Papers*, Hull to Eustis, March 6, 1812. The Americans estimated the number of traders who would assist the British at four thousand.

the American cause in this region. But this triumph came only after more than a year of fighting, during the greater part of which the Americans met with disaster after disaster. For the immediate present the northwestern frontier was practically undefended while in the traders and Indians the British possessed a force immediately available for action which constituted to all intents and purposes a formidable standing army.

That this force was not such as could safely be despised both the words and actions of the frontiersmen gave testimony. In more recent years on the western plains the forces of the regular army of the United States have time and again manifested their superiority over the Indians in open battle; and only rarely, when the advantage of numbers or position was greatly in their favor, have the red men won a victory over them. But in the old Northwest, where advantage could be taken of the heavy timber which covered so much of the country, the Indian warriors fighting on their own ground were superior, man for man, to any regular force that could be sent against them. In fifty years of warfare with the whites the northwestern Indians had never been defeated in open battle where the strength on both sides was nearly equal,[532] while time and again the forces of the whites had succumbed to inferior numbers. The one decisive American victory over these tribes down to the War of 1812 was that of Fallen Timbers in 1794. But this victory was won by a largely superior force under the command of the ablest general, with the possible exception of Clark, that the Americans had ever sent into the Northwest, and after two years of arduous preparation for the contest.

The battle of Tippecanoe afforded the most recent illustration of the prowess of the native warriors. Harrison was probably better fitted to command in a campaign against the Indians than any other man in the Northwest, and in this campaign he had a force of one thousand soldiers[533] of as high quality, on the whole,

[532] Adams, *op. cit.*, VI, 100; Dawson, *Harrison*, 216, 250.

[533] The number of Harrison's troops cannot be stated with entire precision. For a discussion of this point see Adams, *op. cit.*, VI, 96, and note 534 below.

as America could produce. In the actual battle his force outnumbered the Indians in the proportion of two to one.[534] Yet it was only with extreme difficulty and at the cost in killed and wounded of one-fourth of his army that the Indian attack was beaten off. Even this success was due in part to good fortune for the savages had purposely neglected far more favorable opportunities for attacking Harrison than the one they finally embraced. Furthermore, even Harrison's advocate grants that they fought with inferior arms and under circumstances which sacrificed the advantages which their style of fighting ordinarily afforded.[535] But for the absence of Tecumseh and the reluctance of the Indians to fight at all, it is not improbable that Harrison's army would have been overwhelmed.[536]

An indecisive blow had thus been struck, after which Harrison's forces were disbanded or scattered, and the frontier again became as defenseless as before the Tippecanoe campaign. With the series of depredations and murders which marked the spring of 1812 the settlers became panic-stricken. Large numbers abandoned their farms and either took refuge in temporary stockade forts or fled to a safer retreat in the older settlements.[537] The peril from which they fled was graphically painted by the citizens of Detroit in their appeal to the government for protection, in December, 1811. "The horrors of savage belligerence, descrip-

[534] Harrison himself stated his number in the battle as "very little above seven hundred men," aside from sixty dragoons whom he omitted from consideration because they were "unable to do us much service." They were present in the battle, however, and it is obvious that the mere fact of Harrison's failure to make effective use of them does not justify their omission from a statement of the strength of his army. The statement of Dawson, his biographer, therefore, that on the day before the battle he had "something more than eight hundred men," may be regarded as approximately correct. The number of the Prophet's followers can only be estimated. Harrison was "convinced that there were at least six hundred," but he admits that he had no data from which to form a correct statement. Henry Adams, allowing for "the law of exaggeration," concludes that there were not more than four hundred Indians in the battle. On the size of the two armies see *American State Papers, Indian Affairs*, I, 778; Dawson, *Harrison*, 216; Adams, *op. cit.*, VI, 104–5.

[535] Dawson, *Harrison*, 211–12, 236–37.

[536] See in this connection the account of the campaign, and particularly of the plight of the army after the battle, in Dawson, *Harrison*, 233, 238–39; see also, Adams, *op. cit.*, VI, chap. v.

[537] Adams, *op. cit.*, VI, 110; Dawson, *Harrison*, 236.

tion cannot paint. No picture can resemble the reality. No effort can bring the imagination up to the standard of fact. Nor sex, nor age, have claims. The short remnant of life left to the hoary head, trembling with age and infirmities, is snatched away. The tenderest infant, yet imbibing nutrition from the mamilla of maternal love, and the agonized mother herself, alike await the stroke of the relentless tomahawk. No vestige is left of what fire can consume. Nothing which breathes the breath of life is spared. The animals reared by the care of civilized man are involved in his destruction. No human foresight can divine the quarter which shall be struck. It is in the dead of the night, in the darkness of the morn, in the howling of the storm, that the demoniac deed is done."[538]

The nation entered upon the war in June, 1812, with a large portion of its best citizens and one entire section of the country bitterly opposed to the measure. Apathy and opposition combined with the incompetence of the administration at Washington to produce a state of unpreparedness which, in view of the seriousness of the situation, seems today incredible. Congress voted men for the army, but there was little disposition on the part of the country to supply them. The money that was no less essential to the conduct of a war not even Congress was willing to vote, except to a ludicrously inadequate degree.[539] Great Britain had stood undaunted for years between Napoleon and the realization of his ambition of European if not of world supremacy. Through generations of warfare her people had become habituated to devoting their treasure to this end, and had developed a strong military tradition. Both government and army had been brought to the greatest possible state of efficiency for the conduct of war by the experience gained in the two decades of practically constant warfare which the French Revolutionary era had opened. That the greater part of this schooling had been gained in combat with Napoleon, the greatest

[538] *American State Papers, Indian Affairs*, I, 781.

[539] On this whole subject see Adams, *op. cit.*, Vol. VI, *passim;* Babcock, *Rise of American Nationality*, chaps. iv and v.

military genius of modern times, did not detract from its value. On the sea the power of England was superior to that of all the rest of the world combined.

The contrast presented by the United States in 1812 in all that pertained to military affairs could hardly have been more striking. That the Americans were brave and potentially capable of making good soldiers does not, of course, admit of question. But this is equally true of the members of the mob which flees in terror before a detachment of regulars one-tenth as numerous as itself. The lack of a well-trained army was less serious, however, than was the absence of a disposition to submit to the labors and discipline necessary to create one. Of capable military leaders we had none. Yet this, while deplorable enough, was not so serious, probably, as was the contempt which all Americans outside the army itself evinced for regular military training and experience. Even after the bitter lessons taught us on land by the War of 1812, a sixteen-year-old runaway boy could convince as intelligent a man as Calhoun that he had a greater claim to preferment in the army than had the graduate of West Point.[540] And in the early stages of our next war with a civilized nation the President of the United States deliberately determined to appoint all of the officers of a newly created regiment from civil life, on the double ground that since he could not promote all of the officers of the existing army he would not promote any of them, and that it was "generally expected that they should be selected from citizens."[541]

On the sea we opposed sixteen ships,[542] excellent enough for their class, to the eight hundred odd of England. Their showing in the ensuing war is worthy of all praise. Yet it was probably as genuinely a matter of surprise to the Americans as it was to the British themselves. The glamor which resulted from the

540 Andrews, *Biographical Sketch of James Watson Webb*, 5–7.

541 *Diary of James K. Polk*, I, 412. The same contempt for trained military leaders, and preference for political appointees, was manifested during the early years of the Civil War.

542 Adams, *op. cit.*, VI, 362. This statement omits from consideration the gunboats of Jefferson's mosquito fleet.

success of the Americans in a number of single-ship duels has blinded the eyes of later generations to the facts that during the greater part of the war the British vessels maintained a close blockade of the American coast, insulting our sea ports with impunity, and that the navy committed blunders almost as serious as those of the army on land.

The army, when war was declared, was partly in the field and partly on paper.[543] The former portion consisted of ten old regiments with ranks partly filled, scattered in numerous garrisons from New England to New Orleans. The latter consisted of thirteen new regiments which had been authorized by Congress in January, but although recruiting began in March, only four thousand men had been secured by the middle of June. Shortly after the declaration of war Congress fixed the regular establishment at thirty-two regiments with a strength of thirty-six thousand seven hundred men, yet at this time, including the four thousand new recruits, there were but ten thousand men under arms. In February the raising of fifty thousand volunteers for one year was authorized, and in April the President was given power to call out one hundred thousand state militia. But in June less than one-twelfth of the volunteers had been enrolled, and whether the states would heed the call upon them for militia, or whether the militia when raised would serve beyond the frontier, no one yet knew.

The main reliance of the Americans must obviously be the militia. Fighting within their own boundaries, under competent officers of their own choosing, and in their own way, they were capable of excellent, and at times even brilliant service; Bennington, King's Mountain, and New Orleans are sufficient evidence of this. But for prolonged service in a national and offensive war they were of very little account. In subservience to impulse and impatience of discipline they rivaled the Indian himself. Said Amos Kendall, after witnessing a temporary muster in Kentucky in the summer of 1814: "The soldiers are under no

[543] On the state of the army at this time see McMaster, *History of the People of the United States*, III, chap. xxiii; Adams, *op. cit.*, VI, chap. xiv; Babcock, *op. cit.*, chap. v.

more restraint than a herd of swine. Reasoning, remonstrating, threatening, and ridiculing their officers, they show their sense of equality, and their total want of subordination."[544] Even so popular and experienced a frontiersman as Harrison, leading the citizens of his own territory in defense of their own homes, found great difficulty in controlling the militia in the short Tippecanoe campaign. His biographer repeats with evident pride that he relied upon his persuasive eloquence, rather than his authority, to prevent a general desertion.[545]

Equally typical of the volunteer militia of this period was the action of the Ohioans on receipt of the news, in the summer of 1812, that Fort Wayne was in imminent danger from the Indians. Their ardor to serve was such that "every road to the frontiers was crowded with unsolicited volunteers."[546] Yet this zeal, praiseworthy as it was in itself, only resulted in the consumption of the provisions which by General Hull's orders had been accumulated at the outposts for his use. When Harrison was finally ready to start upon the expedition for the relief of Fort Wayne he paraded his troops, "read several articles of war, prescribing the duty of soldiers, and explained the necessity for such regulations," and gave those who were unwilling to submit to them an opportunity to withdraw from the force. The enthusiasm of the troops was such that only one man availed himself of this opportunity; and he was conveyed astride a rail by his disgusted associates to the banks of the Big Miami, "in the waters of which they absolved him from the obligations of courage and patriotism." Yet not all of Harrison's eloquence sufficed ten days later to prevent the Ohio militia from abandoning his army in a body and returning to their homes with the campaign but half completed.[547]

However excellent the quality of the rank and file may have been, it still would have availed little in the absence of competent leaders. The painful experience of the government in the early

[544] Quoted in Babcock, *op. cit.*, 79–80.

[545] Dawson, *Harrison*, 230–31.

[546] *Ibid.*, 288.

[547] McAfee, *History of the Late War in the Western Country*, 128.

years of the Civil War has burned this lesson deeply into the consciousness of the American people. Though the War of 1812 was waged on a far smaller scale, the lack of competent generals in the earlier years is even more painfully apparent. The officers appointed by the President to command the army in 1812 have been well described as "old, vain, respectable, and incapable."[548] Of the two major generals and five brigadiers the youngest was fifty-five years of age, and the average age was fifty-nine. Most of them were veterans of the Revolutionary War, and only one had ever commanded a regiment in the face of an enemy.

The general plan proposed by Dearborn for the campaign provided for a main expedition against Montreal by way of Lake Champlain, flanked by invasions of Canada from Detroit, Niagara, and Sackett's Harbor. Such a plan vigorously pushed with proper forces would have compelled the British forces to stand strictly on the defensive, the Indians would have had no encouragement to rise, and the northwestern frontier might have been spared the horrors of the warfare that soon broke upon it. But while a force was sent to Detroit under Hull to begin the campaign in that quarter, elsewhere hostilities lagged. Hull's campaign, therefore, on the issue of which hung the fate of the Northwest, may receive our undivided attention.

Hull had neither sought nor desired the appointment to the command of the army in the Northwest. As a soldier of the Revolution and in various capacities since that war he had acquitted himself with credit, when, in 1805, he was appointed by Jefferson governor of the newly created Michigan Territory. In this office he remained when the War of 1812 began, notwithstanding the fact that his career as governor had been marked by discord and disappointment, due largely to Hull's inability to adjust himself to the environment, new to him, of the frontier.[549] He had urged upon the government the desirability of rendering Michigan defensible from a military point of view, advocating as essential to this end the control by armed vessels of Lake

548 McMaster, *United States*, III, 546.

549 On Hull's career as governor see Cooley, *Michigan*, chap. viii.

Erie.[550] In the early part of 1812 he was in Washington urging the same subject again upon the government. While thus engaged the military appointment of commander of the forces in that quarter was tendered to him by Madison and declined.[551] Colonel Jacob Kingsbury, who had commanded at Detroit, Mackinac, and Belle Fontaine from 1804 to 1811, and was now on leave of absence, was ordered to the West to resume his old command. He was, however, incapacitated by illness, whereupon Hull, urged a second time by the administration, accepted the appointment.

From every point of view this was a calamity. Hull's opinion that the control of the lakes was essential to the safety of Detroit and the Northwest had been repeatedly expressed, the last time as recently as March 6, 1812. Since that control had not been gained, it followed that Hull believed himself at the mercy of the enemy in the event of war. Holding such views it was impossible for him to enter upon the invasion of Canada with any confidence or determination. Kingsbury had seen much of the Northwest. Having had years of military service there, he was familiar with Heald, Whistler, and the other post commanders, and was possessed of energy and decision of character. Under him, even though the invasion of Canada had not been carried out, it is not likely t iat Detroit would have surrendered without a fight, and Fort earborn have been left to its fate.

The force put at Hull's disposal consisted of three regiments of Ohio militia, the Fourth United States Infantry, which had constituted the nucleus of Harrison's force at Tippecanoe, a troop of Ohio dragoons, and some scattering companies of volunteers, amounting in all to about two thousand men. With this force he must cut a road through the wilderness of northern Ohio, establish blockhouses to protect his line of communication for two hundred miles through the Indian country, protect the settlements, and, according to the expectations of the government, conquer Upper Canada. The mere statement of the task is

[550] Cooley, *Michigan*, 164; Hull, *Campaign of 1812*, 19–21; *Drennan Papers*, Hull to Eustis, March 6, 1812.

[551] Cooley, *Michigan*, 167; Hull, *Campaign of 1812*, 14–18.

sufficient to demonstrate the impossibility of executing it with the means at his disposal.

On April 25 Hull reached Pittsburgh on his way to the West,[552] and twelve days later was at Cincinnati, having come from Baltimore, a distance of over eight hundred miles, in sixteen days.[553] Meanwhile Governor Meigs with praiseworthy expedition was recruiting and organizing the regiments of militia. On May 25 he turned them over to Hull with a spirited speech, worthy of Napoleon's best style and containing withal much good advice.[554] The failure of the dragoons and the regiment of regulars to arrive was causing Hull much anxiety, but he announced his intention to proceed without them.[555] At last, on June 10, the regulars joined him at Urbana.[556] The whole army marched out a mile to meet and escort them ceremoniously into camp. A triumphal arch had been erected near the camp, with the American eagle displayed on the keystone, and inscribed in capitals on one side the word "Tippecanoe," and on the other "Glory." In the place of honor at the head of the army, preceded only by the troops of mounted dragoons, the regulars made their way into camp. Arrived at the arch, the cavalry opened out, allowing them to pass beneath it, while the militia regiments passed by on the outside, "hoping soon to be entitled to similar honors."

This pleasing ceremony ended, and permission having been gained from the Indian chiefs to open a road through their country and protect it with blockhouses,[557] the advance was pressed with vigor. The obstacles to be overcome were many: a new road fit for the passage of an army must be cut, blockhouses were to be erected at intervals of twenty miles through the Indian country, and the provisions needed for the army must be brought

552 *Drennan Papers*, Hull to Eustis, April 26, 1812.

553 *Ibid.*, Hull to Eustis, May 8, 1812.

554 *Ibid.*, Meigs's address to the "First Army of Ohio," May 25, 1812; Hull to Eustis, May 26, 1812.

555 *Ibid.*, Hull to Eustis, May 17, 1812.

556 *Ibid.*, Hull to Eustis, June 11, 1812.

557 The agreement entered into is given in *Drennan Papers*, Hull to Eustis, June 9, 1812

forward from the settled portion of Ohio. The equipment of the army was notably deficient in certain important respects. On reaching Cincinnati, Hull had found the supply of powder so inadequate as to necessitate sending at once to Lexington for more.[558] The guns were in such poor condition that to render them fit for use Hull was compelled to carry a traveling forge and create a company of artificers to repair them as the army advanced. In this way they were rendered serviceable at the rate of fifty a day.[559]

Hull reported the spirit of the army as excellent, yet a serious case of insubordination occurred at Urbana over a grievance, real or fancied, on the part of the militia with respect to their pay.[560] The officers had promised the men an advance for the year's clothing, which was not forthcoming. Papers were accordingly posted on trees the night before the departure from Urbana, warning Hull not to march until the army had been paid. He announced his determination to proceed, and when the assembly beat all but one company obeyed the order. A detachment from the Fourth Regiment of regulars was immediately marched toward it, which cowed the mutineers into submission. Three of the ringleaders were tried by a court martial which sentenced them to have one-half their heads shaved, their hands tied behind their backs, to be marched around the lines with the label "Tory" between the shoulders, and be drummed out of the army.

This exhibition of firmness on Hull's part seems to have had the desired effect. The culprits felt the disgrace keenly, considering the punishment worse than death, and at the solicitation of their officers Hull consented to pardon them.[561] Heavy and incessant rains, combined with the other obstacles, prevented the army from making the progress the commander desired.[562] On June 26, when Hull received a message warning him of the impending hostilities and urging him to press forward with all

558 *Drennan Papers*, Hull to Eustis, May 8, 1812.

559 *Ibid.*, Hull to Eustis, June 11, 1812.

560 *Ibid.*, Hull to Eustis, June 18, 1812.

561 *Ibid.*

562 *Ibid.*, Hull to Eustis, June 24 and 26, 1812.

possible speed, he had covered only about seventy-five miles from Urbana and was still thirty-five miles from the Maumee Rapids.[563] He reached this point four days later, and thereupon committed his first blunder. To save transportation, his personal baggage, papers, hospital stores, and other material were embarked on a schooner for Detroit. Meanwhile war had been declared by Congress on June 18; and the British forces at Malden, receiving prompt notice of this, seized the schooner with all it contained. Thus they became apprised of Hull's strength and of his instructions from his government.

On July 5 Hull reached Detroit, and four days later received word from Washington to begin the invasion of Canada.[564] His reply expressed confidence in his ability to drive the British from the opposite bank of the river, but he did not believe he could take Malden. A week later he crossed the river and occupied Sandwich, the British retiring before him without a blow. From Sandwich a proclamation was issued to the Canadians, designed to secure their acquiescence in the American conquest.[565] To some extent this hope was realized, and numbers of the Canadian militia deserted to the Americans. Instead, however, of pressing the attack on Malden at once, from this time Hull delayed until, with the enemy growing stronger and his own position more precarious, he lost all hope of success and retreated to Detroit. The factors responsible for this decision were the news of the capture of Mackinac with the prospect of the approach of a large number of traders and Indians upon Detroit in his rear, and the attacks by Tecumseh's Indians upon his line of communications with Ohio.

While Hull had thus been conducting affairs at Detroit, Dearborn, who had command of the army in New York, was dallying at Boston and Albany, doing nothing to engage the British by pushing the attack upon Canada from New York, a measure which was essential to Hull's success. On August 9 he even entered into an armistice with the British which bound him

[563] Adams, *United States*, VI, 298–99; *Drennan Papers*, Hull to Eustis, June 26, 1812.

[564] Adams, *op. cit.*, VI, 302.

[565] *Ibid.*, VI, 303–4.

to act only on the defensive until the government at Washington should decide upon the effect of the repeal of the obnoxious orders. This inactivity in the East left Brock, the British commander in Upper Canada, entirely free to direct his attention to Hull; and the attack upon Niagara on which Hull on July 19 had declared all his own success would depend was not made. Moving with a vigor and daring conspicuously wanting in the American generals, Brock transferred all of his available forces from the Niagara frontier to Malden. On arriving there he quickly determined to cross the river and assail Hull in Detroit. Although Hull's force was the larger, the audacity of Brock, combined with the senility displayed by Hull, rendered the movement a complete success. Without awaiting the assault, Hull surrendered his entire army, together with Detroit and Michigan Territory, to the British.

STARVED ROCK, THE SITE OF FORT ST. LOUIS

(By courtesy of the Chicago Historical Society)

THE FIRST FORT DEARBORN, 1803–1812

From the model owned by the Chicago Historical Society, after Captain Whistler's drawing of January 25, 1808

CAPTAIN JAMES STRODE SWEARINGEN

As a youthful lieutenant of twenty-one he led the troops to Chicago in 1803

(By courtesy of the Chicago Historical Society)

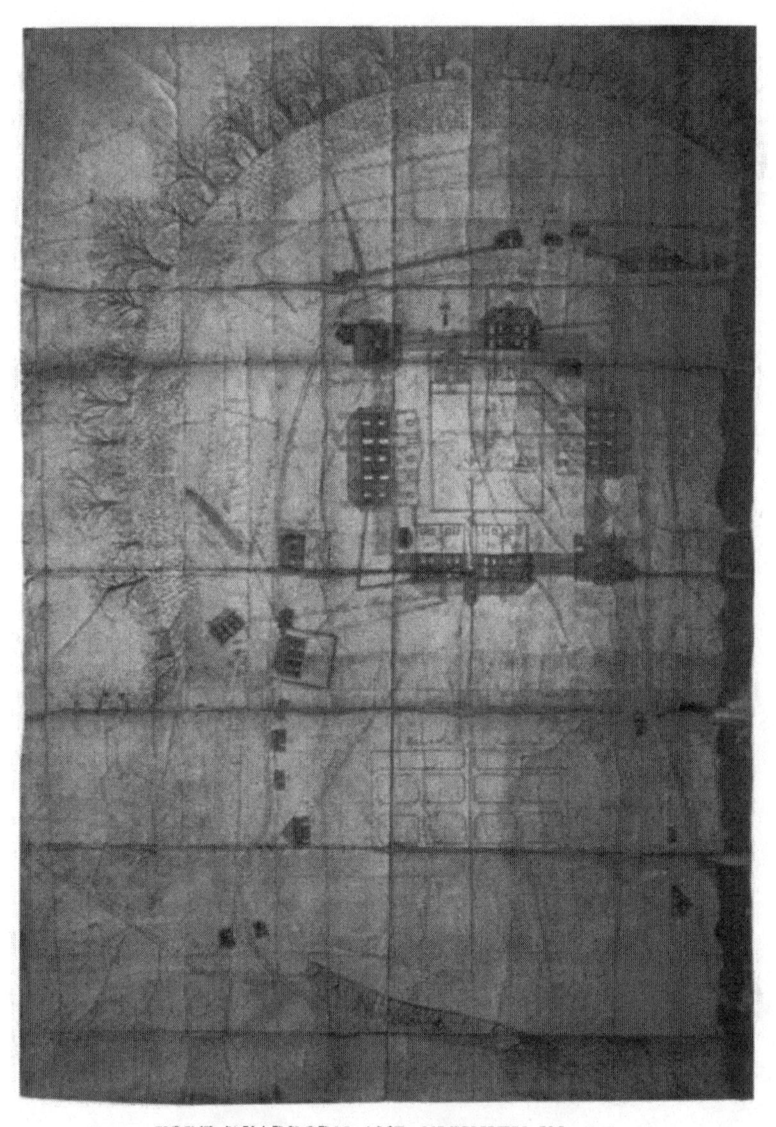

FORT DEARBORN AND VICINITY IN 1808

From the original draft by Captain Whistler in the archives of the War Department at Washington

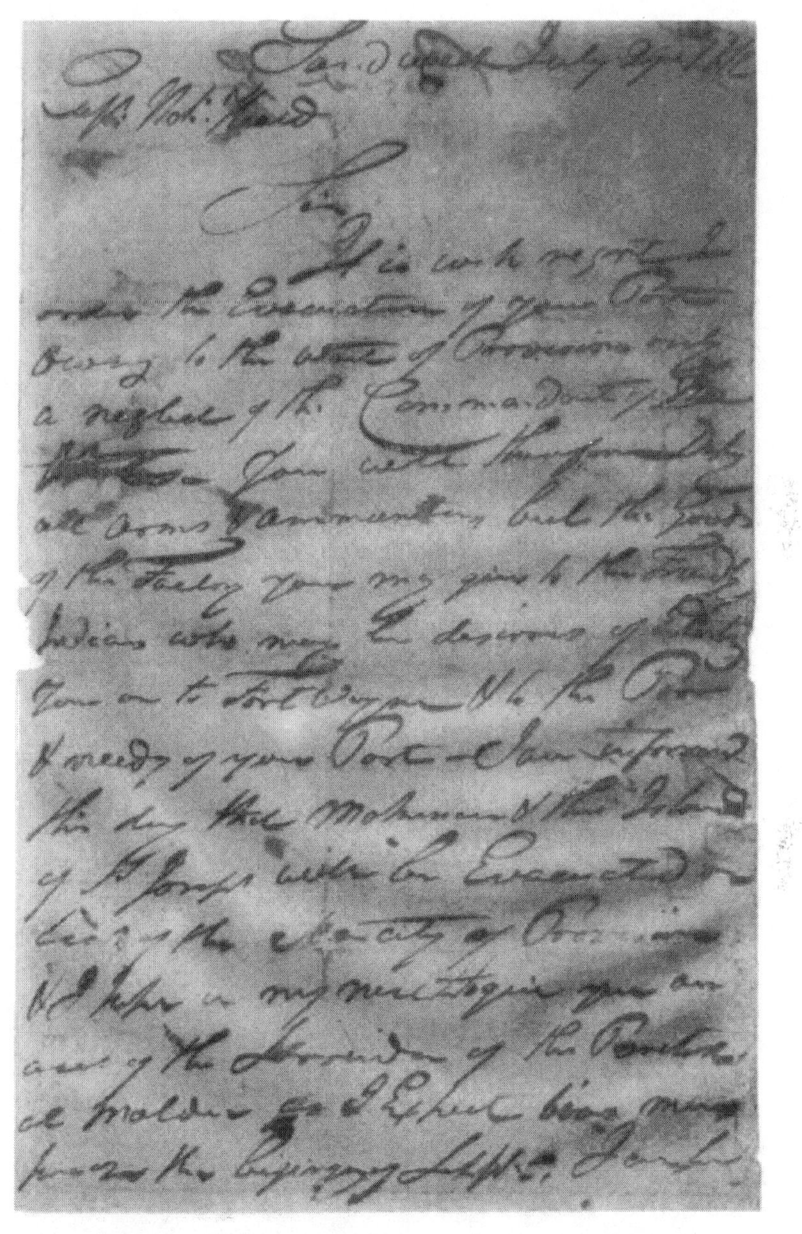

Sir

It is with regret I order the Evacuation of your Post owing to the want of Provisions only a neglect of the Commandant [illegible] You will therefore destroy all Arms & ammunition but the goods of the Factory you may give to the friendly Indians who may be desirous of [illegible] you on to Fort Wayne & to the Poor & needy of your Post — I am informed this day that Mackinac & the Island of St Joseph will be Evacuated [illegible] the scarcity of Provisions [illegible] I hope in my next to give you an account of the surrender of the British at Malden as I expect [illegible] from the beginning [illegible]

GENERAL HULL'S ORDER FOR THE EVACUATION OF FORT DEARBORN

(By courtesy of the Wisconsin State Historical Society)

THE HEALD HOME NEAR O'FALLON, MISSOURI

(From photograph taken in 1912; reproduced by courtesy of the grandchildren of Major Heald)

MRS. REBEKAH HEALD

From a daguerreotype taken in later life

(By courtesy of Mrs. Lillian Heald Richmond, St. Louis, Missouri)

THE TRANSFORMATION OF A CENTURY

Grant Park and Michigan Avenue, where the Fort Dearborn garrison marched to destruction one hundred years ago

Some time in [illegible] forty of Winnebagoes came to Chicago and murdered 2 Men this gave a different [illegible] for to suppose the Indians hostile as they had [illegible] by [illegible] having a weapon [illegible] as a [illegible]

in June Mr Kinzie [illegible] a Letter from the Interior of the Indian country to inform Capt Heald that the Indians were hostile inclined & only waited the declaration of War to commence Hostilities this they told Kinzie in confidence on the 10th of July Capt Heald got the information of War being declared & on the 9 of August got Genl Hulls order to Evacuate the Post of Fort Dearborn by the route of Detroit or Fort Wayne if practicable this Letter was brot by a Potowatomie chief [illegible] he informed Capt Heald through Kinzie to evacuate immediately the next day if possible as the Indians were hostile & that the troops should change the usual Route to go to Fort Wayne

[illegible]

Capt William Wells arrived from Fort Wayne with 27 Miamis [illegible]

[illegible]

[illegible]

LIEUTENANT HELM'S NARRATIVE OF THE FORT DEARBORN MASSACRE

(By courtesy of the Chicago Historical Society)

CHAPTER X

THE BATTLE AND DEFEAT

On the issue of Hull's campaign hung the fate of Fort Dearborn. With the Indian, war was a passion, at once his greatest pleasure and his chief business in life. He could not remain an idle spectator of such a war as had now been joined between the white races, but must be a participant on one side or the other. The exhortations of the Americans that the red man hold aloof from the war, which did not concern him, and let the whites fight out their own quarrel, would be heeded only on one condition. The Americans must manifest such a decided superiority over the British as to convince him that theirs was the successful cause. Both disposition and self-interest urged the Indian to take his stand on the winning side. As long as appearances led him to believe that this was the American, he would hold aloof from the war, since the United States did not desire his assistance. In the contrary event both inclination and self-interest would lead him to side with the British.

There were exceptions, of course, to these generalizations. Tecumseh's hostility to the Americans was independent of any such adventitious circumstances. But with Hull triumphant at Malden the tribes to the west of Lake Michigan would have possessed neither the courage nor the inclination to rise against the Americans; with the British flag waving over Detroit the whole Northwest as far as the Maumee River and the settlements of southern Indiana and Illinois would, as Hull pointed out to the government before the war began, pass under British control.[566]

Alarming reports of Indian hostility and depredations came to Chicago during the winter of 1812. Early in March Captain Heald received news from a Frenchman at Milwaukee of hos-

[566] *Drennan Papers,* Hull to Eustis, March 6, 1812.

tilities committed by the Winnebagoes on the Mississippi.[567] On April 6 a band of marauders who were believed to belong to the same tribe made a descent upon Chicago.[568] Shortly before sunset eleven Indians appeared at the farm of Russell and Lee some three or four miles from the fort up the South Branch. Lee is said to have settled at Chicago about the year 1805, having received the contract to supply the garrison with provisions.[569] He lived with his family a short distance southwest of the fort, and carried on his farming operations at the place on the South Branch which was later known as Hardscrabble. Russell was evidently the partner of Lee, but aside from this fact nothing is known about him. The farm was under the immediate superintendence of an American named Liberty White, who had lived at Chicago for some time.[570] At the time of the descent of the marauding war party there were three other persons, in addition to White, at the farm house, a soldier of the garrison named John Kelso,[571] a boy whose name no one has taken the trouble to record, and a Canadian Frenchman, John B. Cardin, who had but recently come to Chicago.

Soon after the arrival of the visitors Kelso and the boy, not liking the aspect of affairs, "cleared out" for the fort. White and Cardin, less apprehensive of a hostile disposition on the part of the Indians, remained and were shortly murdered. The former was "shockingly butchered." He was tomahawked and

[567] *American State Papers, Indian Affairs*, I, 806.

[568] Short reports of the attack by Matthew Irwin and by Captain Heald are printed in Wentworth, *Early Chicago*, 49–50. Longer and more valuable accounts are contained in the letters of Heald and John La Lime to Captain William Wells, dated April 15 and 13 respectively, printed in the *Louisiana Gazette* for May 30, 1812. I have made use of the copies of these letters made by Lyman C. Draper, in the Draper Collection, S, Vol. XXVI. The best known account is Mrs. Kinzie's narrative in *Wau Bun*, 155–60, but its statements require verification.

[569] Statement of William R. Head in his *Annals of Chicago*, MS owned by his widow. I have not been able to verify it.

[570] *Wau Bun*, 157. That his first name was Liberty is stated by Heald. That he had lived at Chicago for some time is evident from the occurrence of his name in Kinzie's account books.

[571] La Lime's letter to Wells, as printed in the *Louisiana Gazette*, May 30, 1812, gives the name of John Kelson. From the similarity of names I infer that the man was John Kelso, a private in Heald's company.

scalped, his face was mutilated and his throat cut from ear to ear, and he received two balls through his body and ten knife stabs in his breast and hip. It was with reason that Heald declared him to be "the most horrible object I ever beheld in my life." Cardin was shot through the neck and scalped, but his body was not otherwise mutilated. It was Heald's belief that the Indians "spared him a little" out of consideration for his nationality.

Following the murder of White and Cardin, the garrison and the civilian residents of Chicago endured for some time what may fairly be described as a state of siege.[572] The murderers were supposed to belong to the Winnebago tribe, but the efforts of the commander to learn from the neighboring Indians whether the supposition was correct were in vain. Accordingly he forbade the Indians to come to the place until he should learn to what nation the murderers belonged. Kinzie moved his family into the fort, and all of the other residents of the place outside the garrison fortified themselves in the house formerly occupied by Jouett, the Indian agent. Those able to bear arms, fifteen in all, were organized by Heald into a militia company and furnished with arms and ammunition from the garrison store.[573] Parties of savages lurked around, and the whites were forced to keep close to the fort to avoid the danger of losing their scalps. A few days after the murders three of the militia, two half-breeds and a Frenchman, deserted, thus reducing the membership of the company to twelve, the number present at the time of the massacre. The deserters were believed to have gone in the direction of "Millewakii," taking ten or a dozen horses with them.

On May 1 Francis Keneaum, a British subject who lived at Malden, reached Chicago attended by two Chippewa Indians, en route for Green Bay.[574] The party was arrested on suspicion that Keneaum was a British emissary, and he subsequently made

[572] The narrative at this point is based on the letters of La Lime and Heald to Captain Wells, April 13 and 15, 1812.

[573] Letter of Heald to Captain Wells, April 15, 1812; letter of Sergeant William Griffith to Heald, June 13, 1820, Draper Collection, U, VIII, 88.

[574] Edwards, *Life of Ninian Edwards*, 324.

an affidavit showing that he had been engaged by the brother-in-law of Matthew Elliot, the British Indian agent, to go on a secret mission to Robert Dickson, the most active and influential British emissary among the tribes west of Lake Michigan. The Indians had taken the precaution to conceal the letters intrusted to them in their moccasins and to bury them.[575] After their release from detention they proceeded on their way and delivered them to Dickson, who was passing the winter at the Fox-Wisconsin Portage. The message which Captain Heald thus failed to intercept was from no less a person than General Brock, who was seeking to establish communication with Dickson; and it was due to the communication thus established that Dickson led his northwestern bands to St. Joseph's to co-operate in the attack on Mackinac, and in that descent upon Detroit which had such a fatal effect upon Hull's campaign.[576]

We have seen already[577] how that campaign progressed to its disastrous close, and that on its issue hung the fate of Fort Dearborn and the Northwest. With so much of importance in the immediate vicinity of Detroit to demand his attention, Hull had little time or thought to devote to the remote posts at Mackinac and Chicago. News of the declaration of war was received at Fort Dearborn toward the middle of July.[578] The tradition was current at Chicago long afterward that the news was brought by Pierre Le Claire, a half-breed who figured in the negotiations for the surrender of the garrison on the day of the massacre, who walked from the mouth of the St. Joseph River to Fort Dearborn, a distance of ninety miles, in a single day.[579]

On July 14 Hull wrote to Eustis, the Secretary of War, that he would cause the brig, "Adams," which had been launched ten days before, to be completed and armed as soon as possible for

[575] Edwards, *Life of Ninian Edwards*, 333.

[576] This conclusion is based on the letters, in addition to those already cited, of Captain Glegg to Dickson printed in *Michigan Pioneer Collections*, XV, 180–82, 193–95, and the communications between Glegg and Dickson printed in *Wisconsin Historical Collections*, XII, 139–40.

[577] *Supra*, chap. ix.

[578] Lieutenant Helm's narrative of the massacre says July 10.

[579] Hubbard, *Life*, 126–27.

the purpose of supplying the posts of Mackinac and Fort Dearborn with the necessary stores and provisions, if they could be obtained at Detroit.[580] Exactly two weeks later, however, two Chippewa Indians reached Hull's camp at Sandwich bringing news of the surrender of Mackinac. The report seemed so improbable that at first Hull refused to believe it, but close questioning brought forth so many circumstantial details as to remove his doubt. On the same day, July 29, he wrote to the Secretary of War, "I shall immediately send an express to Fort Dearborn with orders to evacuate that post and retreat to this place or Fort Wayne, provided it can be effected with a greater prospect of safety than to remain. Captain Heald is a judicious officer, and I shall confide much to his discretion."[581]

With the evacuation impending, we come upon some of the most important questions in the history of Fort Dearborn. The nature of Hull's order for the evacuation, the demeanor of the savages around the fort immediately prior to the evacuation, the relations subsisting between Captain Heald and the officers and men under his control, the degree of sanity and sense displayed by the commander in dealing with the difficult situation which confronted him—all these things require careful consideration. In the accounts of the massacre that have been written hitherto, these matters have commonly been presented in such a way as to place the responsibility for the tragedy solely on Captain Heald's shoulders, and to represent his administration of affairs as stupid and incompetent to the verge of imbecility. But there is abundant reason for suspecting that these accounts, which all proceed, directly or indirectly from a common source, do Heald grave injustice.[582] If an examination of the available sources of information confirms this suspicion it is quite time, a century after the massacre, to correct the popular impression of the affair and do belated justice to the leader of civilization's forlorn hope on that day of savage triumph.

[580] *Drennan Papers*, Hull to Eustis, July 14 and 19, 1812.

[581] *Ibid.*, Hull to Eustis, July 29, 1812.

[582] See, on this point, Appendix II.

Hull's letter to Eustis of July 29 expressed an intention to confide much to Heald's discretion in the matter of the evacuation. But his letter to Heald, although written on the same day, does not fulfil this intention. The order to evacuate was positive,[583] and the reason assigned for this step was a want of provisions. Heald was also peremptorily enjoined to destroy the arms and ammunition. The only thing confided to his discretion was the disposition of the goods of the government factory, which he was authorized to give to the friendly Indians, and to the poor and needy of the settlement.

Unfortunately for Captain Heald's reputation with posterity, the evacuation order was lost to sight for almost a century. Lieutenant Helm's labored account of the massacre, written in 1814, states that the order to Heald was "to Evacuate the Post of Fort Dearborne by the route of Detroit or Fort Wayne if Practicable."[584] Helm's narrative, like the evacuation order, was unknown to the public for almost a century; his version of Hull's order, however, was preserved in the form of tradition in the family of Kinzie, the trader, to which Mrs. Helm belonged, and thus after the lapse of a third of a century it appeared in print in Mrs. Juliette Kinzie's account of the massacre[585] which was afterward incorporated in her book, *Wau Bun.*

[583] Lost to the world for almost a century, Hull's order was brought to light a few years since among the Heald papers in the Draper Collection at Madison, Wisconsin. It was first published by the author in "Some Notes on the Fort Dearborn Massacre," in the *Mississippi Valley Historical Association, Proceedings* for 1910–11, 138. The order reads as follows:

SANDWICH July 29th 1812

Capt. Nat. Heald.

Sir:—It is with regret I order the Evacuation of your Post owing to the want of Provisions only a neglect of the Commandant of [word illegible-possibly Detroit].

You will therefore Destroy all arms & ammunition, but the Goods of the Factory you may give to the Friendly Indians who may be desirous of Escorting you on to Fort Wayne & to the Poor & needy of your Post. I am informed this day that Makinac & the Island of St. Joseph will be Evacuated on acct of the scarcity of Provision & I hope in my next to give you an acct. of the Surrender of the British at Malden as I Expect 600 men here by the beginning of Sept.

I am Sir

Yours &c

Brigadier Gen. Hull.

Addressed; Capt. Nathan Heald, Commander Fort Dearborn by Express.

[584] Appendix VI.

[585] According to Mrs. Kinzie the order was "to evacuate the fort, if practicable, and in that event, to distribute all the United States' property contained in the fort, and in the United States' factory or agency, among the Indians in the neighborhood." *Wau Bun*, 162.

The evacuation order closed with the expression by Hull of the hope, destined never to be realized, of being able to announce in his next communication the surrender of the British at Malden. Instead of this, on August 8 he abandoned Sandwich and recrossed the river to Detroit. The next day the Indian runner, Winnemac, delivered to Captain Heald at Fort Dearborn his order for the evacuation.[586] Hull also sent word of the intended evacuation to Fort Wayne, ordering the officers there to cooperate in the movement by rendering Captain Heald any information and assistance in their power.[587] In consequence of this Captain William Wells, the famous Indian scout, set out for Fort Dearborn at the head of thirty Miami warriors to assist in covering Heald's retreat.

The days following the ninth of August were, we may well believe, filled with care and busy preparation for Captain Heald and all the white people in and around Fort Dearborn. Their situation in the heart of the wilderness was an appalling one, well calculated to tax the judgment and abilities of Heald, on whose wisdom and energy the fate of all depended, to the utmost. Apparently Kinzie sought to dissuade Heald from obeying Hull's order to evacuate. There must be powerful reasons to justify him in taking this step, yet if sufficiently convincing ones pertaining to the safety of the garrison existed, it is clear that Heald should have assumed the responsibility on the ground that the order had been issued in ignorance of the facts of the situation confronting the Fort Dearborn garrison.

There were several reasons to be urged against an evacuation. The fort was well situated for defense. With the garrison at hand it could probably be held indefinitely against an attack by Indians alone, providing the supply of ammunition and provisions held out. The surrounding Indians outnumbered the garrison ten to one, it is true, but success against such odds when the whites were sheltered behind a suitable stockade was not

[586] Heald's Journal, Appendix III; his report of the massacre, Appendix IV; Lieutenant Helm's narrative of the massacre, Appendix VI.

[587] Heald's report, Appendix IV; Brice, *History of Fort Wayne*, 206.

unusual in the annals of border warfare. The red man possessed little taste for besieging a fortified place, and if the first assault were beaten off, his lack both of artillery and of resolution to persevere in such a contest rendered his success improbable, unless the odds were overwhelmingly in his favor, or the provisions of the besieged gave out. Moreover, whatever the odds might be at Fort Dearborn, the probability of making a successful defense behind the walls of the stockade was immeasurably greater than it would be in the open country. Both Governor Edwards of Illinois and Harrison of Indiana were vigorous executives, and if the fort were held, relief might reasonably be expected before long from the militia which was then being collected in southern Illinois and Indiana, or even from Kentucky.

The situation was complicated, too, by the private interests at stake. Evacuation would mean financial ruin to Kinzie, the trader, and Lee, the farmer. These considerations Heald properly ignored of course. But the danger to the families of the soldiers and of the civilians clustered around the fort was greater and more appalling than to the garrison itself. There could be no thought of abandoning these helpless souls, yet the attempt to convey them away with the garrison would render the retreat exceedingly slow and cumbersome. Kinzie at Chicago and Forsyth at Peoria were well known and esteemed by the resident natives, and many of these were well disposed toward the Americans; the hostile bands might be expected to disperse after a period of unsuccessful siege, and the property of the settlers and the lives of the garrison would be saved.

On the other hand, most of these things were as familiar to Hull as to Heald himself. Practically the only feature of Heald's situation about which Hull's knowledge might be presumed to be deficient was that concerning the number and demeanor of the Indians around Fort Dearborn. But in the provision of his order authorizing Heald to distribute the goods of the factory "to the Friendly Indians who may be desirous of escorting you on to

Fort Wayne" was a clear indication of the commanding general's will in case this contingency should be realized. Obedience to orders is the primary duty of a soldier. He may not refrain from executing the order of his superior, however ill advised it may appear to him, unless it is evident that it was issued under a misapprehension of the facts of the situation, and that the commander himself, if aware of these facts, would revoke it. The truth of this proposition is so obvious that it would scarcely be worth while to state it, were it not for the fact that there has been a practically unanimous chorus of condemnation of Captain Heald on the part of those who have hitherto written of the Fort Dearborn massacre because he acted in accordance with it and obeyed his superior's order. Heald's own view of his duty is clear, both from the course he followed and from the narratives of himself and of his detractors. The latter shows that he paid no attention to the protests against the evacuation made by Kinzie and such others as the trader was able to influence; while in his own official report of the massacre Heald does not even discuss the question of holding the fort or of his reason for evacuating it, further than to recite the order received from Hull to do so.

The time until the thirteenth of August was doubtless spent in preparation for the wilderness journey, though actual details are for the most part wanting. Some slight indication of the commander's labors is afforded by an affidavit he made in 1817 in behalf of Kinzie and Forsyth's claims against the government for compensation for the losses sustained by them in the massacre. In this Heald stated that, being ordered to evacuate Fort Dearborn and march the troops to Fort Wayne, he employed sundry horses and mules, with saddles, bridles, and other equipment, the property of Kinzie and Forsyth, to transport provisions and other necessities for the troops.[588] On August 13 Captain Wells arrived from Fort Wayne with his thirty Miami warriors to act as an additional escort for the troops in their retreat. Probably on this day a council was held with the Indians at which Heald

[588] Affidavit of December 2, 1817, Draper Collection, *Forsyth Papers*, Vol. I.

announced his intention to distribute the goods among them and evacuate the fort, and stipulated for their protection upon his retreat.[589] On the fourteenth the goods in the factory were delivered to the Indians, together with a considerable quantity of provisions which could not be taken along on the retreat. The stock of liquor was destroyed, however, as were also the surplus arms and ammunition. The one was calculated to fire the red man to deeds of madness, while for the whites to give him the other would have been to furnish him with the means for their own destruction.

To the resentment kindled among the Indians by the destruction of these stores the immediate cause of the attack and massacre on the following day has often been ascribed. That the disappointment of the red man was keen is self-evident. Yet that but for the destruction of the powder and whisky there would have been no attack on the garrison seems most improbable. Heald stated under oath several years later that prior to the evacuation the Indians had made "much application" to him for ammunition, and expressed the opinion that but for the destruction which took place not a soul among the whites would have escaped the tomahawk.[590]

All was now ready for the departure, which was to take place on the morning of the fifteenth. At this juncture there came to the commander a belated warning. Black Partridge, a Pottawatomie chief from the Illinois River, came to him with the significant message that "linden birds" had been singing in his ears and they ought to be careful on the march they were about to make. At the same time he surrendered his medal,

[589] Heald's report does not mention the holding of a council; Helm's narrative represents that Wells held the council with the Indians. This is probably correct as to the main fact that a council was held, but untrue in representing Wells, rather than Heald, as the principal participant in it on the part of the whites. A few months after the massacre the Superintendent of Indian Trade was initiating measures for recovering from the War Department indemnity for the goods of the Chicago factory destroyed at the time of the massacre on the ground that they were delivered by Heald to the Indians "under a kind of treaty" between the two (Indian Office, Letter Book C, Mason to Matthew Irwin, February 9, 1813).

[590] Affidavit of December 2, 1817, Draper Collection, *Forsyth Papers*, Vol. I.

explaining that the young warriors were bent on mischief and probably could not be restrained.[591]

It was now too late to withdraw from the plan of evacuating the fort, even if the commander had desired to do so. The next morning dawned warm and cloudless. Inside the stockade the last preparations for the toilsome journey had been made. No chronicler was present to preserve a record of the final scenes, but the imagination can find little difficulty in picturing them. With all its rudeness and privation, the Chicago they were leaving was home to the members of the little party—for some the only one they had ever known. Here the Lees had lived for half a dozen years; here their children had been born, and had passed their happy childhood. Here the Kinzies had lived for an even longer time, and had long since attained a relative degree of prosperity. Here the soldiers had hunted and skated and fished, and gone through their monotonous routine duties until they had become second nature to them. Here the talented young Van Voorhis had dreamed dreams and seen visions of the teeming millions that were to compose the busy civilization of this region in the distant future. Hither in the spring of 1811 the commander had brought his beautiful Kentucky bride, the niece of Captain Wells; here, true to her ancestry, she had fallen in love with the wilderness life; and here, three months before, her life had been darkened by its first great tragedy, the loss of her first-born son, "born dead for the want of a skilful Midwife." We may not know the thoughts or forebodings that filled the mind of each member of the little wilderness caravan, but doubtless home was as dear, and anxiety for the future as keen, to the humbler members of the party as to any of those whose names are better known.

Without, in the marshes and prairies and woods that stretched away from the fort to south and west and north, the representa-

[591] There are two contemporary versions of this incident; one is contained in Lieutenant Helm's narrative of the massacre, the other in McAfee's *History of the Late War*, 98. McAfee's informant was Sergeant Griffith of Heald's company. Both of the accounts are very brief. They agree in the main fact that Black Partridge gave the warning to the interpreter, but Helm alone mentions the surrender of the medal.

tives of another race were encamped. Several hundred red warriors, many of them accompanied by their squaws and children, had gathered about the doomed garrison. For them, doubtless, the preceding days had been filled with eager debate and anticipation. The former had concerned the momentous question whether to heed the advice of the Americans to remain neutral in the war between the white nations, or whether to follow their natural inclination to raise the hatchet against the hated Long Knives and in behalf of their former Great Father. The latter had hinged about the visions of wealth hitherto undreamed of to flow from the distribution of the white man's stores among them; or about the prospect, equally pleasing to the majority, of taking sweet if belated revenge for the long train of disasters and indignities they had suffered at the hands of the hated race by the slaughter of its representatives gathered here within their grasp. As day by day the runners came from the Detroit frontier with news of the ebbing of Hull's fortunes and with appeals from Tecumseh to strike a blow for their race, the peace party among them dwindled, doubtless, as did the hope of Hull's army. Now, at the critical moment, on the eve of the evacuation when, if ever, the blow must be struck, had come a final message from Tecumseh with news of Hull's retreat to Detroit and of the decisive victory of August 4 over a portion of his troops at Brownstown. With this the die was cast, and the fate of the garrison sealed. The war bands could no longer be restrained by the friendly chiefs, to whom was left the rôle of watching what they could not prevent and saving such of their friends as they might from destruction.

And now the stage is set for Chicago's grimmest tragedy. Before us are the figures of her early days. Let us pause a moment to take note of some of the actors before the curtain is lifted for the drama. John Kinzie, the trader, vigorous and forceful and shrewd, with more at stake financially than anyone else in the company, but, of vastly greater importance, with a surer means of protection for the lives of himself and family in the friendship of the Indians. Chandonnai, the half-breed, staunch friend of the Americans, whom all authorities unite in crediting with noble exertions to save the prisoners. The friendly Pottawatomie chiefs, Alexander Robinson, who was to pilot the Healds to safety at Mackinac, and Black Partridge, who had warned Captain Heald of the impending attack, and who soon would save the life of Mrs. Helm. Among the hostile leaders were Black Bird, probably the son of the chief who had assisted the Americans in plundering St. Joseph in 1781; and Nuscotnemeg, or the Mad Sturgeon, already guilty of many murders committed against the whites.[592] There were, of course, many other chiefs of greater or less degree and reputation. Then there were the officers and their wives. Heald, the commander, old in experience and responsibility if not in years; his beautiful and spirited young wife, whose charm could stay the descent of the deadly tomahawk, and whose bravery extort the admiration of even her savage captors; Lieutenant Helm and his young wife, who preferred to meet the impending danger by the side of her husband. Of the younger men, Van Voorhis and Ronan, the former has left of himself a winning picture sketched in a letter a fragment of which has been preserved;[593] the latter is painted in the only description we have of him, in the pages of *Wau Bun*, as brave and spirited, but rash and overbearing and lacking a due sense of respect for his superiors in age and responsibility. These faults of youth, if in fact they existed, were soon to be atoned by the bravery with which he met his fate, fighting desperately to the end.

Sadder, however, than any of these was the situation of some of the humbler members of the party. That a soldier and officer should face death with composure was to be expected; that a soldier's wife should brave danger by his side was not an unknown thing in the annals of the frontier. But the officers' wives were mounted, and whatever might happen on the weary march, they were certain to receive the best care and attention the resources of the company could afford. There were, too, in their case no

[592] *Wisconsin Historical Collections*, XI, 320; Washburne, *Edwards Papers*, 57.

[593] For it see pp. 196, 387.

children for whom to provide or worry. But what of the state of mind of those members of the Chicago "militia," who in addition to abandoning their homes were burdened with wives and children, and with inadequate means of providing for them? What of Mrs. Burns and Mrs. Simmons with their babes of a few months and the hardships of the march before them? What of the other mothers' forebodings for their loved ones? What of the wife of Fielding Corbin, with the pangs of approaching maternity upon her and the prospect of the dreary journey before her? Perhaps it was a mercy a period was so soon to be put to her trials. Finally, what of the innocent babies whose bright eyes were looking out, doubtless, in uncomprehending wonder, upon the unwonted scene of bustle and excitement around them?

With them but not of them was William Wells, the famous frontier scout, the true history of whose life surpasses fiction.[594] Member of a prominent Kentucky family, the brother of Colonel Samuel Wells of Louisville, he was kidnaped at an early age by the Indians and adopted into the family of Little Turtle, the noted Miami chieftain. He became a noted warrior and fought by the side of his red brothers in the campaigns of 1790 and 1791, when they defeated the armies of Harmar and St. Clair. Afterward, whether because of a belated consciousness of his true race identity or of the solicitations of his white relatives and the pleading of his beautiful niece, Rebekah Wells, he threw in his lot with the whites. His fame as a scout and fighter soon became as great among them as it had formerly been with the Indians. He was a perfect master of woodcraft and of the Indian mode of warfare, and as head of a special force of scouts he rendered most efficient service in Wayne's campaign.

Perhaps the most notable tribute to his character is the fact that despite this change of allegiance he continued to retain the

[594] On the career of Wells see Kirkland, *Chicago Massacre*, 173–78; Roosevelt, *Winning of the West*, IV, 79 ff.; Wentworth, *Early Chicago*, 45–46, 56–57; speech of Little Turtle in *American State Papers*, *Indian Affairs*, I, 583; letter of Governor Harrison to the War Department, October 3, 1809, MS copy in Chicago Historical Society library.

esteem of his former associates; and that in this period of fierce rivalry between the two races he enjoyed at one and the same time the esteem and confidence of such men as Little Turtle on the one side and Anthony Wayne and William Henry Harrison on the other. At the conclusion of the Treaty of Greenville Little Turtle made a speech on behalf of the Indians, expressing his satisfaction with it; in the course of which, adverting to the subject of the traders, he especially requested that Wells be stationed by the government at Fort Wayne as resident interpreter, saying that he possessed the confidence of the Indians as fully as he did that of the whites. Fort Wayne remained his place of residence for the remainder of his life and during most of the time he was serving in the government Indian Department. In 1807 Nathan Heald came to Fort Wayne as commander of the post, and here met and wooed Rebekah, the daughter of Samuel, and favorite niece of William Wells. Now at the summons of love and duty, heedless of the danger to himself, the latter had hastened with his friendly Miamis from Fort Wayne to rescue her and assist in the retreat of the garrison. He alone of all the company, therefore, was present from choice rather than from necessity. His arrival at Fort Dearborn on the thirteenth must have afforded the only ray of cheer and hope which came to the settlement in this time of trial and danger.

All preparations being complete, about nine o'clock the stockade gate was thrown open and there issued forth the saddest procession Michigan Avenue has ever known.[595] In the lead were a part of the Miamis, and Wells, their leader, alert and watching keenly for the first signs of a hostile demonstration. In due array followed the garrison, the women and children who were able to walk, and the Chicago militia, the rear being brought up by the remainder of the Miamis. Most of the children, being too young to walk, rode in one of the wagons, accompanied,

[595] The account of the battle and the massacre which follows is the result of a study of all the known available sources of information. Since Appendix II is devoted to a consideration of the principal sources of our knowledge of the massacre, I have deemed it unnecessary to cite my authority in each instance for the statements made here.

probably, by one or more of the women. Mrs. Heald and Mrs. Helm were mounted and near or with their husbands though each couple became separated early in the combat. The other women and children were on foot around the baggage wagons, which were guarded by Ensign Ronan, Surgeon Van Voorhis, the soldiers who had families, and the twelve Chicago militia.

The route taken was due south, parallel with the river until its mouth was reached and then along the beach, not far, probably, from the present Michigan Avenue, for most of the land to the east has been filled in since the beginning of modern Chicago. On the right of the column moved an escort of Pottawatomies. Below the mouth of the river began a row of sand hills, or ridges, which ran between the prairie and the beach, parallel to the latter and distant from it about one hundred yards. When these were reached the soldiers continued along the beach, while the Pottawatomies disappeared behind the ridges to the right. The reason for this soon became apparent. When a distance of about a mile and a half had been traversed by the soldiers Captain Wells, who with his militia was some distance in advance, discovered that the Indians had prepared an ambush for the whites and were about to attack them from their vantage point behind the bank. Aware of a favorable position for defense a short distance ahead, he rode rapidly back toward the main body to urge Heald to press forward and occupy it, swinging his hat in a circle around his head as he went, as a signal that the party was surrounded. The heads of the warriors now became visible all along the line, popping up "like turtles out of the water." The troops immediately charged up the bank, and with a single volley followed home with a bayonet charge scattered the Indians before them. But this move proved as futile as it was brave. The Indians gave way in front only to join their fellows in another place, on the flank or in the rear, and the fight went on.

Meanwhile a deadlier combat, which we may perhaps think of as a separate battle, was raging around the wagons in the rear. Here it was that the real massacre occurred. Apparently in the charge up the sand hills and in the ensuing movements the main division of the regulars under Heald became separated from the rear division, and yet it was precisely here, where the provisions and the helpless women and children were placed, that protection was most urgently needed. The Indians, outnumbering the whites almost ten to one, swarmed around, some, apparently, even coming from the front to share in the easier contest at this point. Here were the junior officers, Ronan and Van Voorhis, and here, apparently, Kinzie had elected to stay. Around the wagons too were the militia, twelve in number, comprising the male inhabitants of the settlement capable of bearing arms, who had been organized and armed by Heald at the time of the April murders. The combat here was furious, being waged hand to hand in an indiscriminate mêlée. Fighting desperately with bayonet and musket-butt the militia were cut down to a man. But one, Sergeant Burns, escaped instant death, and he, grievously wounded, was slaughtered an hour after the surrender by an infuriated squaw. Ronan and Van Voorhis shared their fate as did the regular soldiers, Kinzie being the only white man at the wagons who survived. Even the soldiers' wives, armed with swords, hacked bravely away as long as they were able. In the course of the mêlée two of the women and most of the children were slain.

The butchery of these unfortunate innocents constitutes the saddest feature of that gory day. The measure which had been taken to insure their welfare was responsible for their destruction; for while the conflict raged hotly, a young fiend broke through the defenders of the wagons and climbing into the one containing the children quickly tomahawked all but one of them. Of the women slain one was Mrs. Corbin, the wife of a private soldier, who is said to have resolved never to be taken prisoner, dreading more than death the indignities she believed would be in store for her. Accordingly she fought until she was cut to pieces. The other was Cicely, Mrs. Heald's negro serving-woman. She and her infant son, who also perished, afford two of the few instances of which we have authentic record of negroes being held in slavery at Chicago.[596]

While this slaughter was going on at the wagons Captain Wells, who had been fighting in front with the main body of troops, seems to have started back to the scene to engage in a last effort to save the women and children. His horse was wounded and he himself was shot through the breast. He bade his niece farewell, when his horse fell, throwing him prostrate on the ground with one leg caught under its side. Some Indians approaching, he continued to fire at them, killing one or more from his prostrate position. An Indian now took aim at him, seeing which Wells signed to him to shoot, and his stormy career was ended. The foe paid their sincerest tribute of respect to his bravery by cutting out his heart and eating it, thinking thus to imbibe the qualities of its owner in life. Wells was the real hero of the Chicago massacre, giving his life voluntarily to save his friends. The debt which Chicago owes to his memory an earlier generation sought to discharge by giving his name to one of the city's principal streets. But to its shame a later one robbed him in large part of this honor, by giving to that portion of the street which runs south of the river the inappropriate and meaningless designation of Fifth Avenue.

The close of another brave career was dramatic enough to deserve separate mention. During the battle Sergeant Hayes, who had already manifested the greatest bravery, engaged in

[596] The printed sources of information concerning Cicely and her child are Darius Heald's narrative of the massacre in *Magazine of American History*, XXVIII, 111 ff., and the Heald petition to the Court of Claims for compensation for property lost in the massacre, in *Chicago Tribune*, December 8, 1883. The author has a memorandum prepared by Mrs. Heald for the guidance of her son, Darius, on the occasion of his visit to Chicago in 1855 for the purpose of procuring testimony in support of the claim for compensation for the Heald property lost in the massacre. It contains the following allusions to Cicely and her son: "John Kinzie at Chicago . . . . he knew the negro girl Cicely. He came to buy the negro girl offered me $600. he probably knows about the horses three in number. He knows about the negro woman being killed and also her male infant killed in the battle by the Indians. . . . . Mrs. Baubee [Beaubien]. . . . . Knew Capt. Heald and his wife and the negroes and horses which they had in possession at the time of the defeat. knows of the killing of the negroes. . . . . Mrs. Hellum [Helm]. . . . . Get these two Ladies to relate all their knowledge as regards the loss of the two slaves the horses and other personal property in their possession. . . . ."

individual combat with an Indian. The guns of both had been discharged, when the Indian ran up to him with uplifted tomahawk. Before the warrior could strike Hayes ran his bayonet into his breast up to the socket, so that he could not pull it out. In this situation, supported by the bayonet, the Indian tomahawked him, and the foemen fell dead together, the bayonet still in the red man's breast.[597]

Meanwhile what of Captain Heald and the troops under his immediate direction? The Miamis had abandoned the Americans at the first sign of hostilities. After a few minutes of sharp fighting Heald drew off with such of his men as still survived to a slight elevation on the open prairie, out of shot of the bank or any other cover. Here he enjoyed a temporary respite, for the Indians refrained from following him, having no desire, apparently, to grapple with the regulars at close range in the open. The fight thus far had lasted only about fifteen minutes, yet half of the regulars had fallen, Wells and two of the officers were dead and the other two wounded, and the Americans were hopelessly beaten. The alternatives before them were to die fighting to the last, or to surrender and trust to the savages for mercy. After some delay the Indians sent a half-breed interpreter, who lived near the fort and was friendly with the garrison, and who in the commencement of the action had gone over to the Indians in the hope of saving his life, to make overtures for a surrender. Heald advanced alone toward the Ind'ans and was met by the interpreter and the chief, Black Bird, who requested him to surrender, promising to spare the lives of the prisoners. The soldiers at first opposed the proposition, but after some parleying the surrender was made, Captain Heald promising, as a further inducement to the Indians to spare the prisoners, a ransom of one hundred dollars for every one still living. The captives were now led back to the beach and thence along the route toward the fort over which they had passed but an hour or so before. On the way they passed the scene of the massacre around the wagons.

[597] Schoolcraft, *Narrative Journal of Travels from Detroit . . . . to the Sources of the Mississippi River in the Year 1820*, 392.

Helm records his horror at the sight of the men, women, and children "lying naked with principally all their heads off." In passing the bodies he thought he perceived that of his wife, with her head severed from her shoulders. The sight almost overcame him, and we may readily believe that he "now began to repent" that he had ever surrendered. He was happily surprised, however, on approaching the fort to find her alive and well, sitting crying among some squaws. She owed her preservation to the friendly Black Partridge, who had claimed her as his prisoner.

In the action the white force numbered fifty-five regulars and twelve militia in addition to Wells and Kinzie, the latter of whom did not participate in the fighting.[598] Against these were pitted about five hundred Indians. The white men were better armed, but the Indians had the advantage of position and of freedom from the incumbrance of baggage and women and children to protect. Under the circumstances the odds were overwhelmingly in their favor, and their comparatively easy victory was but a matter of course. Their loss was estimated by Heald at about fifteen. The Americans killed in the action comprised twenty-six regular soldiers, the twelve militia[599] and Captain Wells, with two of the women and twelve children. A number of the survivors, too, were wounded.

Following the surrender came the customary scenes of savage cruelty. The friendly Indians could answer only for the prisoners in their possession. Some of the wounded were tortured to death, and it is not improbable that some of the prisoners were burned at the stake. The more detailed story of their fate, along with that of the other survivors of the battle, is reserved for the following chapter. For the remainder of the day and the ensuing night the victors surfeited themselves with the plunder and the torture. The following day the plundering of the fort and the distribution of the prisoners were completed, the buildings were fired, and the bands set out for their several

[598] On the number of the regulars and others engaged in the combat see Appendix IX.

[599] Including Burns, who was wounded in the action and killed by a squaw about an hour afterward.

villages. The corpses on the lake shore, bloody and mutilated, were left to the buzzards and the wolves, and over Chicago silence and desolation reigned supreme. In March, 1813, Robert Dickson passed through Chicago on a mission to rouse the northwestern tribes against the Americans. He reported[600] that there were two brass cannon, one dismounted, the other on wheels but in the river. The powder magazine was in a good state of preservation and the houses outside the fort were well constructed. He urged the Indians not to destroy them, as the British would have occasion to use them if they should find it necessary to establish a garrison here.

[600] *Michigan Pioneer Collections*, XV, 262.

CHAPTER XI

THE FATE OF THE SURVIVORS

Twenty-nine soldiers, seven women, and six children remained alive at the close of the battle among the sand dunes to face the horrors of captivity among the Indians. These figures do not include Kinzie, the trader, and the members of his family, who were regarded as neutrals and were not included by the Indians in the number of their prisoners. Concerning the fate of some of the survivors we have full information, but of others not even the names can be given with certainty, and of their fate we can speak only in general terms.

The student of the Fort Dearborn massacre finds himself hampered by a notable dearth of official records. This is due in part to the destruction, at the time of the massacre itself, of such as existed at Chicago; to an even greater extent, perhaps, to the destruction of the records of the War Department at the time of the looting of the Capital by the British in 1814. Finally, by a departmental ruling promulgated in 1897, the historical investigator has in recent years been denied the cold comfort of access to such fragmentary records as do in fact exist in the files of the War Department.[601] For such official documents as have been available for this study, therefore, the writer is indebted to other sources. Some of them were copied by earlier investigators in the field, before the War Department files were sealed to the student, and have been printed in various places. Others have been found in manuscripts or in printed works existing outside the government archives.

The last existing muster-roll of the Fort Dearborn garrison prior to the massacre has hitherto been supposed to be that for

[601] This prohibition was removed in 1912, too late, however, to be of any advantage to the author in the preparation of this work. For this reason the statements made have been allowed to stand unchanged.

December, 1810.[602] However, the Heald papers belonging to the Wisconsin State Historical Society include the muster-roll for the period ending May 31, 1812.[603] It shows a garrison strength of fifty-five men, which was probably the number present at the time of the massacre. No list of those slain in the massacre has ever been made, nor is there any comprehensive account of the names and fate of the survivors. The attempt to construct one[604] from the various fragmentary sources of information in existence has proved more successful than could perhaps have been reasonably anticipated. Yet it reveals certain discrepancies which cannot be harmonized until additional sources of information shall be uncovered. This is not surprising in view of the confusion attendant upon the massacre, and the scattering far and wide of the survivors following it. The passage of time and the absence of records make it impossible at this date to check up the errors and fill in the gaps in our information. The hardships endured or the adventures encountered by those whose experiences have been recorded may have been no greater or more noteworthy than by those whose fate is now buried in oblivion. Yet the historian must deal with the information he can obtain, and this chapter of necessity concerns itself largely with a comparatively small number of the survivors whose story has been preserved.

The battle and the massacre proper had barely ended when the dreary work of torture began. It had been stipulated by Captain Heald that the lives of the prisoners should be spared, but this agreement was promptly violated. We cannot speak with much assurance of the details of the tortures, but concerning the main fact there is no doubt. One man, Burns, who had been wounded in the battle, was killed by a squaw about an hour after its conclusion.[605] Possibly this is the man whom Mrs. Helm

[602] Printed in Wentworth, *Early Chicago*, 88.

[603] The muster-roll is printed for the first time as Appendix VIII.

[604] For it see Appendix IX.

[605] Letter of Sergeant Griffith to Heald, January 13, 1820, Draper Collection, U, VIII, 88; Judge Woodward to Proctor, October 7, 1812, Appendix VII.

refers to as having been stabbed to death with a stable fork in her presence.[606] In Judge Woodward's letter to General Proctor upon the survivors of the massacre, Burns is spoken of as a "citizen," and he is similarly designated in Helm's account of the massacre. A letter of Sergeant Griffith to Captain Heald in 1820 clears up the question of his identity.[607] It shows that he was a sergeant in the Chicago militia, enrolled by Heald after the murders at the Lee farm in April, 1812. It confirms the fact of his death at the hands of his captors after the surrender, and incidentally throws a pleasing light upon his character, recalling to Heald's mind "the Soldierlike conduct of . . . . Burns while engaged with an unequal force of Savages, and the manner in which he was inhumanly murdered (in your presence) after he was a prisoner." The *Wau Bun* narrative represents the Burns family as living at the time of the massacre on the north bank of the river some distance above the Kinzie house.[608] Apparently Burns was a discharged soldier who had made Chicago his permanent home, for the Fort Dearborn muster-roll for November, 1810, shows that he was then a member of the garrison and that his term of enlistment would expire in June, 1811.

The various accounts generally agree that a number of the prisoners were put to death during the night following the massacre. Judge Woodward's letter to Proctor, which, written October 7, 1812, and based on information given by Heald and Sergeant Griffith, is the most reliable source of information on this particular point, states that five soldiers were known to have been put to death at this time. The *Wau Bun* narrative, written many years later, makes the same statement. The Darius Heald narrative states that the Indians were believed to have gone off down the lake shore on the evening of the massacre day to have a "general frolic," torturing the wounded soldiers. Woodward gives the names of two of these victims, Richard Garner and James Latta, both private soldiers. By a process of comparison of all the sources concerning those who perished in

[606] Kinzie, *Wau Bun*, 176.

[607] Cited *supra*, note 605.

[608] Kinzie, *Wau Bun*, 155, 159.

captivity we get the names of the other three, Micajah Denison, John Fury, and Thomas Poindexter.[609] But one account attempts to tell us how they died, and this, of more than dubious validity, suggests rather than describes their fate. A half-breed Frenchwoman, who had remained in her hut on the north side of the river during the battle and massacre, made her way after its conclusion to a point opposite the Indian village north of the fort. Here she could see the "torture ground" where the squaws had three men, and the warriors one white woman, undergoing the most fearful torture and indignities, "such as she had never heard of in Canada."[610] Perhaps after all it is just as well that we have no more detailed description. The fate of the victims was no more awful than that customarily meted out to the vanquished white man in the course of his contest with the red man for the possession of this continent and it is better that the gory details should sink into oblivion.

On the day after the massacre, the fort having been burned and the plunder and the prisoners divided, the bands began to scatter to their various homes. The dreary story of the hardships endured by the captives and the indignities and cruelties meted out to them by their masters is relieved, happily, now and then by some act of kindness or generosity calculated to prove that gentleness and humanity were qualities not entirely unknown, even to the savage red man. Ultimately the majority of the prisoners were to find their way back to civilization, but for several death offered the only avenue of escape from their captivity. For some, indeed, death must have come as a welcome relief from sufferings far more dreadful.

Such must have been the case with Mrs. Needs, the wife of one of the soldiers. Her husband, her child, and herself all survived the massacre, only to die in captivity. The husband died in January, 1813; the brief record left us contains no indication of the cause of his death.[611] Annoyed by the crying which

609 For the way in which these names are determined see Appendix IX.

610 *Head Papers,* in Chicago Historical Society library.

611 *Niles' Register,* June 4 1814.

hunger forced from the child, the savages tied it to a tree to perish of starvation or to become the prey of some wild beast. Still later the wretched mother perished from cold and hunger. Another prisoner, William Nelson Hunt, was frozen to death.[612] Hugh Logan, an Irishman, unable to walk because of excessive fatigue, was tomahawked; such, also, was the fate of August Mortt, a German, and for a similar reason.[613]

With relief we turn from these tragic details to the story of the efforts which were making to restore the captives to civilization. On September 9 Proctor communicated to General Brock the news of the massacre at Fort Dearborn, expressing regret over its occurrence and denying that the British had known anything of the intended attack, or that the superintendent of the Indian Department had any influence over the Indians.[614] At the time of writing this letter Proctor believed that Captain Heald and his wife and Kinzie were the only survivors of the massacre, and no suggestion was made by him of measures for the relief of the

[612] *Niles' Register*, June 4, 1814. The name is printed as Nelson; it does not occur in any of the other accounts of the massacre, nor on the muster-roll of Heald's company of May 31, 1812. The latter does contain the name of William Nelson Hunt, however, and he is probably the man designated as Nelson in the newspaper account.

[613] The following letter written by Thomas Forsyth to Nathan Heald, April 10, 1813, suggests a different reason for the killing of Mortt. The letter is reproduced in full for the sake of the information it gives concerning the massacre and the affairs of some of the participants in it. The original manuscript is the property of Mrs. Lillian Heald Richmond, of St. Louis, Mo.

ST. LOUIS 10th April 1813.

SIR: I had the honor to receive from the hand of Gov. Howard, your letter to him of the 24th February last, in answer to his to you respecting Kinzie & Forsyth Claims for losses sustained 1st August at Chicago. in your letter you mention that you gave Mr. Kinzie a quantity of gunpowder for hire of horses to carry provisions, &c to Detroit, in that case, the gunpowder was from you to us, for hire of horses for public use and of course the gunpowder became our property. after the delivery of the gunpowder to Mr. Kinzie, I understood from him (K-) that either you or the late Captain Wells, and perhaps both, told him, that if he, (K) would destroy all his gunpowder and Whiskey, that he should be paid for his losses by the U. States all of which was certainly destroyed; in your letter to Gov. Howard, you say you seen the Whiskey destroyed and that you have no doubt but the gunpowder was also destroyed; In that case I would thank you if you would forward on to me at this place, a certificate of what you know about the destruction of those articles, also the prices of gunpowder, Whiskey, mules & horses, at Chicago. I have claimed for each horse $60—Mules $90—Whiskey $2 per gallon, gunpowder $2 per lb. this you know was the current price for Whiskey and Gunpowder; I paid myself, this price for Gunpowder bought out of the Factory of that place, as for the horses and Mules they are by no means high; our losses in horn cattle, hogs, merchandise &c are very great for which we demand nothing for. Depain and Buisson wintered at Chicago last winter with goods from Mackinaw, they have bought of[f] Mrs. Leigh and her younger child, and another woman which I expect is Mrs. Cooper or Burns, Old Mott was a prisoner, and became out of his head last Winter and was killed by the Indians.

Please give my respects to Mrs. Heald.

And Remain your most Obedt Servt

T. FORSYTH

[614] *Michigan Pioneer Collections*, XV, 144.

captives. Soon, however, Captain and Mrs. Heald and Sergeant Griffith reached Detroit, bringing information that nearly half of the garrison and a number of women and children were captives among the Indians. Detroit and Michigan being in the hands of the British, in the absence of any official representative of the American government Judge Woodward assumed the duty of procuring the initiation of measures for the relief of the prisoners. On the strength of the information furnished by Heald and Griffith he addressed a letter to Proctor, representing that over thirty Americans had been taken by the Indians.[615] He urged that immediate measures be taken for their relief, suggesting the sending a special messenger overland to Chicago, charged with the duty of collecting the captives who still survived and information of those who had perished, and supplied with the means of conveying the former to either Detroit or Mackinac. He further urged that Captain Roberts, the commander at Mackinac, be instructed to co-operate in the efforts to rescue the Americans, and assured Proctor that the funds necessary for the work would be repaid either by the American government or by private individuals.

In consequence of this bold and manly appeal, tardy measures were instituted by Proctor which resulted in the rescue of a number of the captives. Woodward was assured that all possible measures would be taken to secure their release, and two weeks later Proctor, in reporting the correspondence to his superior, announced that the chiefs of the tribe concerned in the massacre had been informed of his desire that the captives be brought to him.[616] Weeks passed, however, and it was not until the departure of Robert Dickson for the West in February, 1813, that any active measures were taken to recover them.

Dickson, as we have already seen,[617] had led a motley band of northwestern Indians to the assault on Mackinac in the summer

[615] The original draft of this letter is printed in Appendix VII; the statements in the text are based on the letter as actually sent. This differed in some respects from the rough draft.

[616] Proctor to Woodward, October 10, 1812, *Michigan Pioneer Collections*, XV, 163; Proctor to Evans, October 28, 1812, *ibid.*, 172.

[617] *Supra*, p. 214.

of 1812. In November he proceeded to Montreal and Quebec to lay before the authorities there a plan he had conceived for securing the active co-operation of the northwestern tribes in the prosecution of the war against the Americans.[618] He proposed that large stores of supplies be sent to Chicago and Green Bay in the spring of 1813, which points were the most convenient for rendezvous. He himself, if given the necessary authority and assistance, would proceed by way of Detroit and Chicago to the Mississippi and collect the warriors at these points, whence they could be led to the seat of war around Detroit in time to participate in the operations of 1813.

This plan was accepted by the military authorities and Dickson set out for the West. On February 15 he was at Sandwich and a month later was among the Pottawatomies of St. Joseph.[619] Here he was informed that the Fort Dearborn captives still in the hands of the Indians numbered seventeen men, four women, and several children. He at once took steps to secure them, and expressed confidence that he would succeed in getting them all. On March 22 he was at Chicago, and here penned the description of the fort to which reference has been made in a preceding chapter.[620] From this point he hastened on toward the Mississippi. Early in June he was back at Mackinac at the head of six hundred warriors, and in addition to these he reported the dispatch of eight hundred by land to Detroit.[621] That, in the face of such exertions as these achievements imply, he should have found any time to bestow on the Fort Dearborn captives, speaks well for both his energy and his humanity.

Apparently in the press of other matters Dickson neglected to report further as to his measures for the relief of the captives. In May, 1814, however, nine surviving members of the Fort Dearborn garrison arrived at Plattsburg, New York, from Quebec.[622] The story they told was that after the massacre they

[618] For Dickson's project see *Michigan Pioneer Collections*, XV, 180–82, 202–4, 208–11, 216–21 *et passim*.

[619] *Ibid.*, XV, 250, 258.

[620] *Supra*, p. 631.

[621] *Michigan Pioneer Collections*, XV, 321–23.

[622] *Niles' Register*, June 4, 1814.

had been taken to the Fox River country and there distributed among the Indians as servants. In this situation they remained about nine months, when they were brought to Chicago, where they were purchased by a "French trader" acting under the instructions of General Proctor. Doubtless the "trader" was Dickson, whose arrival at Chicago, March 22, 1813, falls in the ninth month after the massacre. From Chicago the captives were sent on to Amherstberg, or Malden, and thence to Quebec, where they arrived November 8, 1813.

The names of the nine men who were thus restored to their countrymen almost two years after the massacre deserve a place in our narrative. They were James Van Horn, Dyson Dyer, Joseph Noles, Joseph Bowen, Paul Grummo, Nathan Edson, Elias Mills, James Corbin, and Fielding Corbin. With the exception of Grummo, no record has been found of the further career of these men. His story, written down over four score years after the massacre, possesses considerable interest, and contains, moreover, certain details not preserved elsewhere.

In later life Grummo, or De Garmo, as he seems to have been known, settled at Maumee City, a few miles from Toledo, Ohio. Here on a small reservation in the early thirties was the gathering-place and council house of the surviving remnants of the Pottawatomie, Wyandot, and other tribes. Here, too, gathered various traders, among others Robert Forsyth, and James Wolcott, whose brother, Alexander, was Indian agent at Chicago until his death in 1830. From 1837 until about the year 1841 Charles A. Lamb, to whom we are indebted for the preservation of the story, was the nearest neighbor of Grummo at Maumee City.[623] He describes him as a tall, well-built man, who always insisted that he was a participant in the Fort Dearborn massacre.

As Lamb remembered his story, Grummo represented that he was employed as a scout in the summer of 1812, carrying dispatches between Fort Dearborn and Fort Wayne. After the battle he was adopted by a chief whose son he had killed in the

[623] Letter of Charles A. Lamb, August 24, 1893, MS in Chicago Historical Society library.

contest. His new-found father took him, in company with others, in a northwesterly direction. After traveling many days, they crossed the Mississippi above the Falls of St. Anthony, the object of their journey being to induce the tribes to join them in the war against the Americans. Returning from this mission, Grummo's captors sold him to the British at Detroit, "or somewhere around there." By them he was taken to Louisburg where he was kept till the close of the war, when he found his way to New York.

Such, in brief, was Grummo's story as recorded by Lamb a half-century after he had heard it. In some respects it is perplexing, and many of its details are untrustworthy. There is no reason to question Lamb's sincerity. He frankly admits his liability to error in telling it after the lapse of so great a time. It is evident, too, that Grummo drew a long bow in relating his own experiences. This, however, is so common a characteristic of old soldiers' stories that it need occasion no particular surprise. Lamb further records that though Grummo, whose story he has related only briefly, added many things to prove his veracity, yet he was never able to secure a pension. Both General Cass and General John E. Hunt exerted their influence in his behalf, but on the records of the War Department he had been set down as a deserter, and this charge could not be disproved.

The fortunes of the officers, Heald and Helm, and their wives, may be followed with less difficulty, though even here we encounter at times perplexing contradictions. The Indians who secured possession of Captain Heald and his wife at the close of the battle belonged to different bands. Owing to the entreaties of Mrs. Heald, however, and the efforts of Chandonnai, the two were brought together.[624] On the day after the battle their captors set out with them for the St. Joseph River, coasting around the southern end of Lake Michigan in

[624] The details as to Chandonnai's agency in the matter vary somewhat in the different accounts; it is clear that he exerted his influence, whether by purchasing Mrs. Heald from her captives or otherwise, to bring the Captain and his wife together, and that the Healds afterward regarded him in the light of a benefactor.

a canoe.[625] The trip consumed, according to Heald's journal, three days, although the distance is only about one hundred miles.

Practically the only details recorded of this journey are contained in the narrative of Darius Heald to Kirkland in 1892. That these details, based on second-hand information and written down at so late a date, cannot be relied upon is obvious. Yet they are of sufficient interest to merit inclusion here. Both Heald and his wife were badly wounded, the former being shot in the thigh and through the right forearm, and the latter having a half-dozen wounds in all, no one of which, apparently, was dangerous. After the party had traveled for many hours around the end of the lake a young deer was seen, coming down to the water in a clump of bushes to get a drink. The travelers drew close to the shore and the deer was shot by an Indian. They then pitched camp and dressed the animal. Using the hide as a kneading board Mrs. Heald stirred some flour which they had brought along in a leather bag into a stiff paste which she wound around sticks and toasted over the fire. Captain Heald afterward declared that this was the best bread he ever ate.

At the mouth of the St. Joseph, which was reached on August 19, the party halted. The Healds were permitted to stay in the house of Burnett, the trader, and their wounds were dressed and given medical attention by an Indian doctor.[626] After a few days most of the Indians trooped off to participate in the attack on Fort Wayne. In their absence an avenue of escape opened to the captives. A friendly Indian, Alexander Robinson, was prevailed upon to conduct them to Mackinac in his birch-bark canoe.

[625] The principal sources for the captivity of the Healds are the following: Heald's official report of the massacre (Appendix IV); his Journal (Appendix III); the Heald papers in the Draper Collection; the Darius Heald narrative of the massacre as reported, first, to Lyman C. Draper (Appendix V); and second, to Joseph Kirkland (*Magazine of American History*, XXVIII, 111–22). A brief account gained from Sergeant Griffith, the companion of the Healds until they reached Pittsburgh, is contained in McAfee, *History of the Late War*, 100–101.

[626] Among the Heald papers in the Draper Collection is a certificate of Captain Heald "on honor" that he paid ten dollars to an Indian for attendance and medicine while sick of his wounds at the St. Joseph River.

He was assisted by his squaw and, possibly, by one or two half-breeds, and for the service Heald paid him one hundred dollars.

The distance to Mackinac was three hundred miles along the eastern shore of Lake Michigan, and the journey consumed sixteen days. The treatment accorded to the fugitives by Captain Roberts on their arrival there forms one of the bright spots in the story of the wearisome captivity. He extended them every kindness within his power to render their condition as comfortable as possible. Both Captain Heald and Captain Roberts were Masons, and, as Mrs. Heald told the story in after-years, they retired to a private room together, when Heald told his story and asked for help and for protection from the Indians, who, he feared, were in pursuit of him. Roberts felt doubtful of his ability to protect the fugitives, but Heald was given his parole and permission to proceed to Detroit. Sergeant Griffith was permitted to attend him, and Heald agreed to deliver him up to the British officer in command upon reaching Detroit. It is of interest to note that one of the witnesses of Heald's parole was Robert Dickson, the vigilant and enterprising foe of the Americans in the Northwest. Probably due to the influence of Captain Roberts, the captives secured passage to Detroit on a small sail-boat, paying to Robert Irwin, the master, seventeen dollars for their transportation thither. Before parting from Captain Roberts the latter took out his pocket-book and urged Heald to help himself, saying he might repay the money if he ever reached home; if not it would not matter. It was not necessary to accept the generous offer, however, for before the evacuation Mrs. Heald had taken the precaution to sew a sum of money in her husband's underclothing, and this he had succeeded in retaining when stripped of his uniform by his captors.

On reaching Detroit at the close of September, Heald reported to General Proctor and was permitted by him to rejoin his countrymen. Griffith, also, was allowed to continue to attend him "to the U. States," on Heald's promise to do all in his power to prevent his serving in arms against the British until regularly exchanged. The party left Detroit October 4 for Buffalo, to which place they had been provided with transportation by Proctor. Curiously enough the vessel which bore them was the "Adams," Kingsbury's erstwhile "navy of the lakes," which had often journeyed to Chicago on friendly missions during the life of the first Fort Dearborn. In July Hull had attempted to fit it out for one more trip to carry provisions to Mackinac and Fort Dearborn. The successful execution of this project might have rendered Heald's present journey unnecessary. With the capture of Detroit the "Adams" had fallen into the hands of the British, and, as a British vessel, bore the defeated commander to Buffalo. From Buffalo the party journeyed by land to Erie, and thence by water to Pittsburgh, which was reached October 22. The movements of Griffith from this time are unrecorded. The Healds remained here sixteen days, during which time the commander wrote his official report of the massacre and of his subsequent movements. Resuming their journey down the Ohio on November 8 they reached Louisville, the girlhood home of Mrs. Heald, eleven days later. In their captivity and flight three months of time had been consumed, and a circuit of nearly two thousand miles had been traversed, almost all of it by water, much of the way in a canoe or open boat.[627] The distance from Chicago to Louisville by rail today is less than one-sixth as long as Heald's route, and can be traversed in thrice as many hours as the number of months he required.

At the home of Mrs. Heald's parents the fugitives were greeted as people risen from the dead. Part of the booty captured by the Indians at the time of the massacre had been taken down the Illinois River and sold to the whites. It chanced that Colonel O'Fallon, an old friend of the Healds, saw and recognized certain articles which had been their personal property. He had ransomed them and sent them to Samuel Wells at Louisville, as a memento of his brother and daughter who were both supposed to have been killed. Most of these articles, including Heald's sword, a comb, finger ring, brooch, and

[627] The estimate of the distance made by Heald in his Journal was nineteen hundred and seven miles. Of this only ninety miles, from Buffalo to Erie, were traveled by land.

table spoons of Mrs. Heald, are still in the possession of her descendants.

Captain and Mrs. Heald spent the winter at her father's home, and in the spring of 1813 went to Newport where the ensuing summer was passed. They shortly returned to the vicinity of Louisville, where in 1814 they purchased some land and began the erection of farm buildings, into which they moved late that fall. Three weeks after the massacre, while he was pushing his weary flight in an open canoe along the desolate eastern shore of Lake Michigan to Mackinac, Heald had been promoted to the rank of major.[628] His wounds, which never ceased to trouble him, incapacitated him for further service, and at the consolidation of the army in 1814 he was discharged. In 1817 he was granted a pension of twenty dollars a month, to date from the time of his discharge from the army in 1814.[629] During this year he removed to Stockland, now O'Fallon, Missouri. Here he purchased a farm from Jacob Zumwalt which had been granted to the latter by the Spanish government toward the close of the eighteenth century.[630] Here Major Heald continued to reside until his death in 1832, and Mrs. Heald until her demise a quarter of a century later. Shortly before Heald's death his old

[628] *Drennan Papers*, Cushing to Heald, November 9, 1812.

[629] The following letter from William Turner regarding the granting of Heald's pension discloses a creditable aspect of the latter's character. The original letter is the property of a granddaughter of Heald, Mrs. Edmonia Heald McCluer.

WASHINGTON CITY
25th January 1817

DEAR MAJ: I have taken the liberty without your approbation or knowledge with the assistance of my friend General Parker to procure you a full pension as Capt. We were at first in hopes to procure it as full pay for a Maj. but on examining the list of Officers we found that your promotion as Maj. took place eleven days after you received your wound.

It will take effect from the 10th June 1814 at twenty dollars per month which will be six hundred dollars up to the 31st Dec 1816.

You will excuse me for the liberty I have taken in procuring this pension without your knowledge and will explain that I always feel it my indisputable duty to render assistance to my fellow citizens in all cases but more particularly to a brother officer who has served his country as faithfully as you have and whose increasing friendship for myself & family have been so conspicuous.

Should you feel any delicacy in receiving the pension which I trust you will not as you are so greatly entitled to it, permit me to suggest the propriety of bestowin[g] it on your child or children, which will be of service to them at some future period.

General Parker will enclose to you the warrant or certificate for the pension with instructions how you are to obtain the money already due.

. . . .

WM. TURNER

MAJ. N. HEALD
LOUISVILLE, KENTUCKY

[630] Letters of Mrs. Rebecca Heald McCluer, granddaughter of Nathan Heald, to the author, May 7 and June 1, 1912.

benefactor, Chandonnai, paid him a visit, accompanied by a chief and a number of other Indians. The members of the party were on their way to Kansas to view the country and report to their people upon its desirability. They visited with Major Heald, who caused a sheep and a beef to be killed for their entertainment and talked over with them the story of the captivity. The Heald estate is still intact in the hands of the grandchildren. The old homestead, built by the original proprietor of hewn walnut logs, with the flooring held in place by wooden pegs, still stands. Within its walls the first Methodist sacrament in Missouri is said to have been administered in 1807, by Rev. Jesse Walker, the pioneer of Methodism in Chicago. For many years the house has been unoccupied, but it is still in a partial state of repair. Recently two of its rooms have been fitted up to serve as the meeting-place of local chapters of the society of Daughters of the Revolution.

The fortunes of the Kinzie family after the massacre are recounted with much detail in the family narrative, *Wau Bun*. Unfortunately, however, the details are untrustworthy. Some of the incidents recited undoubtedly possess a certain basis of fact, and the broader outlines of the itinerary of the family may in the main be accepted as correct; but these things aside, accuracy of statement is no more to be looked for than in a mediaeval historical romance.[631] Several days after the battle

[631] Probably there was a kernel of fact around which the story of the rescue of the family by Billy Caldwell from impending slaughter at the hands of the Wabash band of Indians was developed. Forsyth's letter to Heald, January 2, 1813 (*infra*, note 632), recounts the disappointment of "them murdering dogs from the Wabash," who reached Chicago shortly after Heald's departure therefrom. It is not improbable that they sought to vent their displeasure upon the Kinzies, nor, if so, that Caldwell, who was a firm friend of Kinzie, intervened to protect them. That Mrs. Helm may have sought refuge with Ouilmette's family is equally consonant with probability; but here as elsewhere it is evident from a critical reading that the bulk of the narrative is the product of the author's literary imagination. The account of the rescue of Sergeant Griffith must be regarded in a similar light. A careful reading of the story, accompanied by the reflection that Griffith was an experienced frontiersman and soldier, suffices to convince one of this. Instead of being on the north side of the river during the battle, Griffith was a participant in it. Necessarily then, the greater part of the narrative is invalid. Yet Helm's brief entry concerning Griffith, "Supposed to be a Frenchman and released," seems to indicate that Mrs. Kinzie's narrative had some incitement in fact.

the family proceeded by boat to the St. Joseph River[632] where it remained some weeks with the friendly Pottawatomies, when Mrs. Kinzie and her children journeyed to Detroit under the escort of Chandonnai, while John Kinzie remained behind for a time in the hope of collecting some of his scattered property.

Mrs. Helm shared the fortunes of her mother's family as far as Detroit. Meanwhile her husband, Lieutenant Helm, was taken by his captors down the Illinois River. Before leaving Chicago, apparently, Mrs. Kinzie interceded with her son-in-law's captors in his behalf; her speech had "the desired effect," and within a few weeks Thomas Forsyth succeeded in ransoming Helm by the payment of two mares "and a keg of stuff when practicable."[633] After spending some time with his rescuer at Peoria, Helm proceeded down the river, arriving at St. Louis October 14, two months after the massacre. Thence he made his

[632] According to the family narrative on the third day after the battle. The following letter from Thomas Forsyth to Heald, January 2, 1813, shows that in fact it was the fifth day. The letter is primarily concerned with the property losses of Forsyth and Kinzie, but incidentally it supplies some interesting data concerning the massacre and certain of the survivors. The original manuscript is owned by Mrs. Lillian Heald Richmond of St. Louis, Mo.

St. Louis, 2nd Jany. 1813

Sir: I have forwarded on to the City of Washington our Claims against the U. States for our Whiskey Gunpowders and horses that was lost at Chicago in August last. Lt. Helm (who I got off from the Indians) has proven by affidavit, to the Quantity of Gunpowders and Whiskey, but by a neglect in drawing up his affidavit it does not say that Lt. Helm saw the Gunpowder and Whiskey destroyed, say 850 Lbs. gunpowder and 1,200 Gallons Whiskey. I therefore would thank you if you would forward on to the City of Washington, to Gov. Howard of this place, who is gone on to that City, and has our claims with him, a Certificate or affidavit stating simply the destruction of the Gunpowder and Whiskey, (as Lt. Helm has proven that he saw the Horses and Mules in possession of the Indians when he was a prisoner) will be sufficient.

The day after the horrid affair, and I believe the very day you left Chicago for St. Joseph's I arrived there (Chicago) I remained four days with Kinsie and his family, and I left Chicago the same day Kinsie left it for St. Joseph's, and I have not heard of him since, you was certainly very fortunate in getting of from Chicago the moment you did, as I can assure you that a very few days longer and probably you would never have left Chicago, as them murdering dogs from the Wabash, was very much displeased when they you was gone, and said it would be needless to follow you, as the wind was fair and they could not overtake you, was they to follow the boat.

Lynch & Suttenfield was badly wounded, and were both killed before the Indians arrived at River Aux Sable. Crosier was taken off from River Aux Sable to Green Bay by a Chipeway Indian, an old friend of his, and therefore he is free. When you send on the deposition to Gov. Howard, direct your letter to him at Lexington Kentucky and should he not be there his friends will forward it on to the Seat of Government.

Please give my respects to Mrs Heald.

And remains
Sir
Your most Obedient
Servt. Thomas Forsyth
Sdg.

Capt. N. Heald
Louisville

[633] Helm's narrative of the massacre, Appendix VI; letter of Forsyth to Heald, January 2, 1813, *supra*, note 632; Forsyth to John Kinzie, September 24, 1812, in *Magazine of History*, March, 1912, p. 89.

way to his father's home in New York, where he rejoined Mrs. Helm, who had arrived there shortly before. For some reason not now in evidence, five months elapsed between Helm's arrival at St. Louis and the conclusion of his journey, the reunion with Mrs. Helm occurring in March, 1813, seven months and one week after their separation.[634]

The story of Mrs. Simmons and her infant daughter is in some respects the most interesting and heroic of the narratives of the Fort Dearborn captives.[635] Her husband was one of the little band of soldiers who died fighting in defense of the wagons. Among the children in the wagon was his son, David, two years of age, who perished beneath the tomahawk of the young fiend who slaughtered the children collected there. Mrs. Simmons on foot survived the massacre and succeeded in preserving her daughter, Susan, a babe of six months, whom she carried in her arms. Perceiving the delight which the savages derived from tormenting their prisoners, she resolved to suppress any manifestation of anguish. If the family narrative may be credited, her resolution was promptly put to a terrible test. The slain children were collected in a row, among them the gory corpse of

[634] In *Wau Bun*, p. 187, occurs a moving story of Mrs. Helm's journey from Detroit to Fort George on the Niagara frontier. It represents that Helm rejoined his wife in Detroit, where both were arrested by order of the British commander and sent on horseback in the dead of winter through Canada to Fort George. No official appeared charged with their reception, and on their arrival they were forced to sit waiting outside the gate for more than an hour, without food or shelter, notwithstanding the fact that Mrs. Helm was a delicate woman and the weather was most cold and inclement. When Colonel Sheaffe learned of this brutal inhospitality he expressed his indignation over it, and treated the prisoners kindly until they were exchanged, when they made their way to their friends in New York. Aside from the improbability that Helm, finding himself safe among his own countrymen at St. Louis, would voluntarily go to Detroit to become a prisoner of the British, the truth of Mrs. Kinzie's detailed narration is disproved by the explicit statement of Helm in his narrative of the massacre that after separating from his wife near the fort on the day of the massacre they met again at his father's home in the state of New York, "she having arrived seven days before me after being separated seven months and one week."

[635] For the story of the captivity of Mrs. Simmons the principal source is the family narrative, *Heroes and Heroines of the Fort Dearborn Massacre. A Romantic and Tragic History of Corporal John Simmons and His Heroic Wife*, by N. Simmons, M.D. The book is of value only for its story of the experiences of Mrs. Simmons and her daughter. The Fort Dearborn muster-roll for May, 1812, shows that Simmons was not a corporal as stated, but only a private. In general the book must be used with great caution.

her son, and she was led past them in the effort to discover from her bearing whether any of them had belonged to her. She passed through the ordeal without a sign of recognition, and according to the same account, endured the long months of her terrible captivity without once shedding a tear.

In the division of the captives Mrs. Simmons fell along with others into the hands of some savages from the vicinity of Green Bay. On the morning after the massacre they crossed the Chicago River and began the homeward march. The weather was warm and the hardship of the journey for Mrs. Simmons, aside from the fatigue of the travel, consisted mainly in being compelled to do the drudgery of her captors, such as gathering fuel and building fires. On the march she walked, carrying her baby the entire distance, two hundred miles or more. The hardships of the march were as nothing in comparison with the reception which awaited its conclusion. Runners were sent in advance to announce the approach of the war party to the members of the tribe in camp, and as it drew near the women and children streamed forth to meet it. They saluted the captives with a fusillade of insults, kicking and otherwise abusing them. Arrived at the village, they were put under close guard until the following day.

In the morning the village was early astir, and preparations were made for subjecting the captives to the ordeal of running the gauntlet. A long double line was formed by the women and children in an open space before the wigwams, and each of the soldiers was compelled to run between the lines, receiving the blows dealt out with sticks and clubs by those composing them. Mrs. Simmons' hope of being spared this ordeal proved vain, and she was led to the head of the line. Wrapping her babe in her blanket, and enfolding it in her arms to shield it, she ran rapidly down the path of torment and reached the goal, bleeding and bruised, but with the infant unharmed.

At this stage of her persecutions the mother encountered an unexpected act of kindness. An elderly squaw led her into her wigwam, washed her wounds, and gave her food and an opportunity to rest. The new-found friend continued her kindly services as long as Mrs. Simmons remained in the same camp with her; and the captive ever afterward spoke of her as her "Indian mother," and regretted her inability to repay the favors received from her.

Meanwhile Robert Dickson was collecting the western tribes to lead them to the scene of war on the Lake Erie frontier. The warriors rendezvoused at Green Bay, from which place the chieftain, Black Hawk, destined to play a prominent rôle in the Northwest twenty years later, led a party of five hundred southward around Lake Michigan, past the slaughtered garrison of Fort Dearborn, and onward to the frontier.[636] The band to which Mrs. Simmons belonged seems to have participated in this movement of the western tribes. The captive retraced her weary way from Green Bay to Chicago and the bones of her murdered husband, carrying her baby as before. From Chicago her captors led her around the lake to Mackanic; the length of the entire journey was about six hundred miles, and winter closed in before it was completed. Scantily clad, suffering from cold, weariness, and hunger, the mother strove desperately to save her child, and accomplished the almost incredible exploit of carrying it in safety to Mackinac.

Here she was cheered by the prospect of ransom or exchange; but the sequel proved that her trials were as yet but half surmounted. To accomplish her release she was sent to Detroit. The terrible march was again resumed, this time in the dead of winter. The route led through three hundred miles of wilderness; deep snows with occasional storms impeded the progress; her clothing was in rags, and food was so scarce that she was often constrained to appease her hunger by eating roots, acorns, and nuts, found under the snow. The child, now a year old, had much increased in weight, while the mother's strength was diminishing. But the prospect of release at the end of the journey buoyed up her hopes and she continued to struggle on.

[636] Black Hawk, *Life*, 40–42.

From Detroit to her parental home near Piqua, Ohio, the journey was comparatively easy. The first stage took her to Fort Meigs, then in command of General Harrison, where she arrived late in March, 1813. Here she learned that a supply train which had recently come from Cincinnati was about to return, and that it would pass within a few miles of her father's home. She accordingly secured passage in one of the government wagons. She still had over a hundred miles to travel over wet and swampy roads in early spring time; but in comparison with her earlier travels this stage of the journey must have seemed luxurious enough. About the middle of April she left the train at a point within four miles of her home, walked to the blockhouse where her parents had taken refuge from marauding Indians, and rejoined the family circle which had long mourned her as dead. Three years before, with husband and baby son, she had set out for her new home at Fort Dearborn. Both husband and son were dead and she now returned a widow, but with another child, who had been born at Fort Dearborn in February, 1812. Safe among her former friends, the brave woman at last broke down; to use her own language she "did nothing but weep for months."

There were still other dangers and trials, however, for Mrs. Simmons to pass through. In August a murderous attack was made by some marauding Indians upon the family of Henry Dilbone, who had married the sister of Mrs. Simmons. Mr. and Mrs. Dilbone were working together in the flax field, with their four young children close at hand. Near the close of the day's work their dog raised an alarm, and at almost the same instant the husband fell shot through the breast. The savage sprang forward from his place of concealment to take his victim's scalp. But the latter though mortally wounded was not dead, and gathering his remaining strength he rose, ran to the edge of the field, and leaped the fence which separated it from an adjoining swamp, where he fell among the bushes. The Indian abandoned the pursuit and turned back after Mrs. Dilbone, who had fled for concealment into the neighboring corn. Her flight was vain, however, for she was soon overcome, tomahawked, and scalped. The slayer now turned his attention to the four children, the eldest of whom was ten years of age and the youngest seven months. They, meanwhile, had been making what progress they could toward the house. Instead of pursuing them the warrior made off into the forest, fearing probably that the noise caused by the discharge of his gun and the screams of Mrs. Dilbone would attract rescuers to the spot.

The neighbors were quickly aroused and a company went in search of Mr. and Mrs. Dilbone. The corpse of the latter was found and carried together with the children to the blockhouse of the Simmons family. The search for Mr. Dilbone was given over for that night, through fear of an ambuscade. In the morning it was resumed and he was soon found, too weak to move or even to cry out. He, too, was borne to the blockhouse, where he expired the following day. Thus after her own escape from captivity and death at the hands of the savages, Mrs. Simmons found herself once more in the midst of bloodshed and slaughter —her sister and brother-in-law slain, her nephews orphaned. To such perils were the people on the northwestern frontier exposed during these troublesome and bloody years.

The story of the later career of Mrs. Simmons and her daughter can quickly be told. The latter in due course of time grew to womanhood and became the wife of Moses Winans. The couple first settled in Shelby County, Ohio, but in 1853 they removed to Springville, Iowa. Mrs. Simmons, who had previously taken up her abode in her daughter's family, removed with them to Iowa, and died at Springville in 1857.[637] Mrs. Winans' husband died in 1871, and seventeen years later she went to Santa Ana, California, to make her home with her younger daughter. She lived to become the last survivor of the Fort Dearborn massacre, dying at Santa Ana, April 27, 1900.[638]

637 For this and the following facts concerning Mrs. Winans see the letters and affidavits pertaining to the securing of a pension for Susan Simmons Winans in the Chicago Historical Society library.

638 Gale, *Reminiscences of Early Chicago*, 133.

An interesting although necessarily incomplete narrative of the fortunes of the surviving members of the Burns family may be constructed by assembling the facts contained in several widely scattered sources of information. The killing of the husband, Thomas Burns, an hour after the surrender has already been described.[639] A son of Mrs. Burns by a former marriage, Joseph or James Cooper, was also a member of the slaughtered militia.[640] To complete the tale of the mother's bereavement, her two children next in age perished in the massacre. The mother with two children, one of them an infant, alone survived to undergo the horrors of captivity among the Indians.[641] Concerning this captivity we have two accounts, both of them brief and unsatisfactory. Mrs. Kinzie relates in *Wau Bun* that Mrs. Burns and her infant became the prisoners of a chief, who carried them to his village. His wife, jealous of the favor shown by her lord and master to the white woman and her child, treated them with the greatest hostility, and on one occasion sought unsuccessfully to brain the infant with a tomahawk. Soon after this demonstration the prisoners were removed to a place of safety. The author further relates that twenty-two years after the massacre she encountered a young woman on a steamer, who, hearing her name, introduced herself and raising the hair from her forehead displayed the mark of the tomahawk, which so nearly had been fatal to her.[642]

The other narrative was given to John Wentworth in 1861 by the son of Abraham Edwards, who was hospital surgeon in Hull's army at Detroit in 1812.[643] He settled at Detroit in 1816, and there the family made the acquaintance of Mrs. Burns. Her daughter, Isabella Cooper, became an inmate of the Edwards home, and thus the younger Edwards became familiar with the story. Together with her mother and sister she had been an

[639] *Supra*, pp. 227, 234.

[640] Letter of Griffith to Heald, January 13, 1820, Draper Collection, U, VIII, 88.

[641] Griffith speaks of three children of Mrs. Burns. Helm's account of the massacre and the letter of Abraham Edwards to John Wentworth, which will be considered presently, mention only two, and this harmonizes with Heald's list of the survivors.

[642] Kinzie, *Wau Bun*, 188–89.

[643] Wentworth, *Early Chicago*, 54–60.

occupant of one of the wagons when the evacuation of Fort Dearborn took place. A young Indian pulled her out of the wagon by her hair, but the child, though only about nine years of age, fought him to the best of her ability, biting and scratching. Finally he threw her down, scalped her, and was about to tomahawk her, when an old squaw who had frequently visited at her father's house intervened and saved her life. The rescuer later took the child to her wigwam where she cared for her and healed her wound, although a spot on the top of her head the size of a silver dollar remained bare. She and her mother and sister remained among the Indians two years, when they were taken to Mackinac, purchased by some traders, and sent to Detroit.

The narrative thus told by Edwards to Wentworth fifty years after the massacre is confirmed in part by a letter of Sergeant Griffith to Captain Heald in 1820.[644] Griffith had recently been to Detroit, and wrote to Heald, then living on his farm in Missouri, to enlist his support in procuring a pension for Mrs. Burns. She was then living in Detroit, supporting herself and her three surviving children by her own labor. A number of officers and others had interested themselves in the project of obtaining a pension for her. Her husband had been enrolled by Heald as a sergeant in the militia, in which capacity he had served for several months and finally given up his life. Of all this the government had no record or knowledge, however, and so Heald's certificate as to the nature of Burns's services was needed. In the absence of any knowledge concerning the success of the pension project, we may hope that the government ministered to the needs of the widow who had suffered so grievously in the Fort Dearborn massacre. Edwards records that Mrs. Burns died at Detroit about the year 1823. He also states that the daughters were living as late as 1828, at which time he left Detroit, and that he had since heard they were living in Mackinac. With this, except for the brief notice by Mrs. Kinzie of a meeting with one of them, which has already been mentioned, our knowledge of them comes to an end.

[644] Letter of Griffith to Heald, January 13, 1820, cited *supra*, note 640.

Hovering on the border between myth and history are a number of stories concerning the fate of others who went through the massacre. Some of these may be true, while some are certainly without foundation in fact; they are grouped together here because of the impossibility of confirming their claim to validity. The story of little Peter Bell will probably forever remain an unsolved mystery. In September, 1813, a British officer, Captain Bullock, addressed an inquiry from Mackinac to General Proctor concerning the disposition to be made of certain prisoners whom the Indians had surrendered to the British at that post.[645] Among others he mentioned Peter Bell, a boy of five or six years of age, "whose Father and mother were killed at Chicagoe." He had been purchased from the Indians by a trader and brought to Mackinac in July, 1813, in accordance with the orders of Robert Dickson. The mystery concerns the identity of the child. The time and manner of his rescue harmonizes with what is known of Dickson's work for the relief of the Chicago captives. But in none of the accounts of Fort Dearborn and the little settlement around its walls prior to 1812, is there any mention of a Bell family. The various accounts of the massacre establish conclusively the proposition that there were nine women among the whites on that day. Two of these were killed; the names of all of them are known, and the list contains no Mrs. Bell. Moreover, it is clear from the sources that six children survived the massacre. The names of all these are known, but that of Peter Bell is not among them. The only explanation of the child's identity which suggests itself is that he was taken captive at some other place than Chicago and that his captors for some reason, perhaps because of the ransom offered, saw fit to surrender him as one of the children taken at Fort Dearborn. Whatever the true explanation may be, a mournful interest attaches to the forlorn little waif who thus appears for a moment amidst the wreck of battle, only to sink again into oblivion.

The fate of the Lee family is recorded in the pages of *Wau Bun*.[646] All of its members except the mother and an infant

[645] *Michigan Pioneer Collections*, XV, 392. [646] Kinzie, *Wau Bun*, 189–91.

child were killed during the battle. The fate of the girl, twelve years of age, was particularly pathetic. On leaving the fort, she had been placed upon horseback, but being unused to riding she was tied to the saddle for greater security. During the battle her horse ran away and the rider, partially dismounted yet held by the bands, hung dangling as the animal ran. From this predicament she was rescued by Black Partridge, with whom she had been a great favorite; but finding her badly wounded, he terminated her sufferings with a blow of the tomahawk.

The mother and her infant child were taken by Black Partridge to his village. There the infant fell ill and Black Partridge fell in love, instituting a campaign for the hand of his captive. Unable to cure the sick child, he took it during the winter to Chicago, where a French trader had established himself since the massacre. The trader, M. Du Pin, not only prescribed for the child, but learning of Black Partridge's designs upon its mother, proceeded to ransom her and then in turn to marry her.[647] This story is repeated with embellishments by Matson, who, with curious disregard for consistency, includes an important feature not found in the original. He avers that the child who was dragged by the horse and afterward tomahawked was Lillian Lee, ten years of age; and that she had a sister two years older who escaped unharmed, was taken by her captors to the Kankakee, and the following spring was carried to St. Louis, where she married a man named Besson, and was still living in East St. Louis at the time Matson's book was written.[648]

The story of David Kennison, a survivor of the Fort Dearborn garrison, is worthy of preservation, if only because of the remark-

[647] In his letter to Heald, April 10, 1813 (*supra*, note 613), Forsyth stated that "Dupain and Buisson wintered at Chicago last winter with goods from Mackinaw, they have bought of[f] Mrs. Leigh and her younger child, and another woman which I expect is Mrs. Cooper or Burns."

[648] Matson, *Pioneers of Illinois*, 257–62. The book was published in 1882. Notwithstanding the author's statement that he had interviewed Mrs. Besson and "listened to her thrilling narrative," there is much in his account to excite distrust. It recites many details which are obviously purely imaginary, and for the rest follows, in the main, the account in *Wau Bun*.

able career of the man.[649] Born in New Hampshire in 1736, if his own story of his age is to be accepted, a member of the Boston Tea Party, a participant in Lexington and Bunker Hill and many another battle of the Revolution, he had reached the respectable age of seventy-one when, in March, 1808, he enlisted in the army for the regular term of five years. Probably this was a re-enlistment, for Kinzie's account books show that he was at Chicago as early as May, 1804. The garrison muster-roll for May, 1812, shows that he was present for duty at that time. The supposition that he was a participant in the massacre three months later rests upon inference, for his name is nowhere expressly mentioned in connection with that event. Presumably he was one of the small number of survivors who returned from captivity concerning whom no definite record is left. In his old age Kennison told of further service in the War of 1812, but it is evident that his memory had become confused upon the subject.

After the war Kennison settled in New York, and in the ensuing years of peace met with physical injuries far more numerous and serious than in all of his years of warfare. A falling tree fractured his skull and broke his collar bone and two ribs; the discharge of a cannon at a military review broke both of his legs; and the kick of a horse on his forehead left a scar which disfigured him for life. Notwithstanding these accidents, Kennison succeeded in becoming a husband four times and a father twenty-two, and in living to the mature age of one hundred and fifteen. Late in life he became separated from all his children, and in 1845 he came to Chicago where his last years were spent. He drew a pension of eight dollars a month for his Revolutionary services, and until 1848 eked out this means of support by manual labor.

[649] The account given here of Kennison is drawn from the following sources: the *Chicago Democrat*, November 6 and 8, 1848, and February 25, 26, 27, 1852; the *Chicago Daily News*, December 19, 1903; the Fort Dearborn garrison payroll for the quarter ending December 31, 1811, and the muster-roll for the period ending May 31, 1812, both among the Heald papers in the Draper Collection (for the latter see Appendix VIII); the garrison muster-roll for December, 1810, printed in Wentworth, *Early Chicago*, 88. Many of the details concerning the career of Kennison are, of course, of doubtful validity.

Becoming incapacitated for the latter, however, he entered the Chicago Museum; in his card to the public announcing this step he explained that the smallness of his pension obliged him to take it to provide himself with the necessary comforts of life. For the last twenty months of his life the veteran was bedridden, but his sight and hearing, which for a time had been deficient, became perfect again, and he retained his ordinary faculties to the end. His death occurred February 24, 1852.

It was fitting that such a character should receive an imposing funeral. On the day before his death, in response to a request presented in his behalf that he be saved from the potter's field, the City Council had voted that a lot and a suitable monument be provided for him in the City Cemetery. The funeral was held from the Clark Street Methodist Church, and several clergymen assisted in the services. At their conclusion a procession moved in two divisions from the church to the cemetery, to the accompaniment of cannon booming at one-minute intervals. In the procession were the mayor and the councilmen, a detachment of the United States army, the various military companies and bands of the city, companies of firemen, and others. Upon this spectacle and that of the interment, which was marked by the usual military honors, a large proportion of the population of the city gazed. The cemetery occupied a portion of the ground now included in Lincoln Park. When the use of this for burial purposes was abandoned a number of years later, nearly all of the bodies interred in it were removed. Kennison's was one of the few left undisturbed. For many years the site of his grave had practically been forgotten, when, in 1905, with appropriate ceremonies it was marked by a massive granite monument, erected by a number of patriotic societies. Thus it has come to pass that Kennison's burial place possesses a prominence of which the humble soldier in life can hardly have dared to dream. Veteran of our two wars against Great Britain, participant in the Boston Tea Party and the Fort Dearborn Massacre, he enjoys the unique distinction of a grave in Chicago's most famous park, overlooking the blue waters of Lake Michigan.

Another massacre story, concerning the mythical character of which there can be no doubt, is noticed here because of the use that has been made of it by a historian of acknowledged worth and ability. Among the beautiful sheets of water which dot the surface of the Lower Peninsula of Michigan is Diamond Lake near the town of Cassopolis. In its midst lies Diamond Lake Island, a wooded expanse of perhaps forty acres in extent. This was occupied in the early days of white settlement in Cass County by an aged recluse who bore the prosaic name of Job Wright, but who was often more romantically designated as the hermit of Diamond Lake Island. The hermit eked out a living by fishing, hunting, trapping, and basket-weaving. Since he was of an uncommunicative disposition, his neighbors were free to give rein to their imagination in constructing the story of his past, and the scars upon his face furnished a visible support for the rumor that he had been a soldier.[650]

Another character of note in Cass County three-quarters of a century ago was Shavehead, the erstwhile leader of a band of renegade Indians. Shavehead's peculiar cognomen was due to his fashion of dressing his head; the hair at the base of the head was shaved off, and the rest gathered in a bunch and tied at the top. He had been throughout his lifetime the persistent foe of the whites, and among the early settlers of Cass County he enjoyed a reputation for knavery and villainy which must, if he was aware of it, have delighted his heart.

With old age Shavehead fell upon evil days. His followers disappeared, and with the advance of white settlement and the disappearance of game the old chief was reduced to sore straits for food. At times, however, he succeeded in securing a supply of firewater sufficient to obliterate for the time being the memory of his troubles. On one occasion the hermit, visiting Cassopolis to dispose of his wares, had his attention attracted by a group of men and boys on the village street who were being harangued by an Indian. Shavehead, for it was he, partially intoxicated, was

[650] For the story of Job Wright see Mathews, *History of Cass County, Michigan*, 65–66; *Michigan Pioneer Collections*, XIV, 265–67.

gesticulating wildly, relating the warlike exploits of his stormy past. As the white man paused to listen, the old chief was describing the massacre at Fort Dearborn, and the slaughter of the women and children around the baggage wagons. As he proceeded with his boastings the hermit muttered words of recognition, and involuntarily drew his gun from his shoulder as though to terminate Shavehead's recital together with his life; he, too, had fought near the baggage wagons. Changing his mind, however, he listened patiently to the end, but when at sundown the Indian left the town the soldier followed on his track. "The red man and the white passed into the shade of the forest; the soldier returned alone. Chief Shavehead was never seen again. He had paid the penalty of his crime to one who could, with some fitness, exact it."[651]

Such is the story of Shavehead and the hermit of Diamond Lake Island. So complete is it in its tragic fitness that one would fain believe it. Yet, though it received the approval of Edward G. Mason, it must be pronounced purely mythical, at least so far as its connection with Fort Dearborn is concerned. That Shavehead and Job Wright are historical characters in the early settlement of Cass County is clear. That the former took part in the Fort Dearborn Massacre is possible, and even probable. But that he met his death at the hands of Job Wright there is no proof whatsoever. Various other accounts exist, in fact, having apparently an equal claim on our credulity with the one already cited, of the manner in which Shavehead met his end.[652] Furthermore there is no evidence that Job Wright was a member of the Fort Dearborn garrison in 1812. On the contrary, that he was not may be stated with a positiveness bordering on certainty. That he was not a member of Heald's company is shown by the muster-roll of the garrison for May 31, 1812, while the possibility of his belonging to the militia is negatived by the positive statements of both Heald and Helm that all of the latter were slain.

[651] Mason, *Chapters from Illinois History*, 321.

[652] *Michigan Pioneer Collections*, XIV, 266–67.

It remains to relate what is perhaps the strangest tale of all, concerning the survivors of the massacre. For it we are indebted to Moses Morgan, whose share in the building of the second Fort Dearborn has already been explained.[653] In October, 1816, two of the men detailed to select timber for the work of construction proceeded in a skiff far up the North Branch, when they came upon a half-concealed Indian hut. They were first apprised of its proximity by the shrill shrieks of the squaws, who had seen their boat as it approached. As they turned their skiff to retreat they heard the voice of a white man, imploring them to stop and talk with him. The man spoke good English, indifferent French, and poor Winnebago. He informed them that he was one of the members of Heald's company. He had been wounded in the battle, but was mercifully saved by an elderly squaw, whom he had often provided with something to eat. She prevented the Indians from scalping him, and with the help of her girls moved him across the river and put him under some bushes. Here they cared for him, attending to his wounds, although both they and he suffered much from lack of food. As soon as he could be moved the women tied him onto a flat piece of timber taken from the burnt fort, and dragged him to a small lake some forty miles to the northward. Here he found himself compelled to take the old squaw for a wife or perish from starvation. Upon her sudden death, a year before the visit of the sawyers, he had taken the two oldest girls to be his squaws. There was a third girl, younger than these, and the three women and himself comprised the inmates of the hut.

When the sawyers reported their discovery at the encampment it was feared the squaws would spirit away their common husband. On the following day the surgeon, Doctor Gale, accompanied the sawyers to the hut, taking a boat load of presents for the squaws. It appeared that the inmates were about to change their location, and as a preliminary step the soldier had taken the youngest girl to be his third wife. She was then one hundred and fifty moons, or thirteen years old, but had

[653] *Supra*, p. 134.

desired to be married before leaving the vicinity of her mother's burial place.

Doctor Gale examined the man's wounds and found that they had healed, but with unnecessarily poor results, one leg being shortened and one arm of little use. The doctor took down his name and other personal details, and listened to his story of the massacre. He refused to return to civilization as long as the squaws would live with him and care for him; but he promised to bring them to visit the encampment, exacting, however, a promise that the little squaw should not be ridiculed by the soldiers. Nothing more was ever seen of the man, a fact not much to be wondered at. The surgeon wrote out his account of the interview and handed it, together with the memoranda he had made, to the adjutant, by whom in some manner it was lost. That the story did not, like the wounded soldier, pass into complete oblivion is owing to the quite accidental circumstance of its narration by Moses Morgan to Head, whose interest in Chicago history led him to preserve it.

CHAPTER XII

THE NEW FORT DEARBORN

The British negotiators of the Treaty of Ghent which brought the War of 1812 to a close made strenuous efforts to compel the renunciation by the United States of its sovereignty over all of that portion of the old Northwest not included within the line drawn by the Treaty of Greenville of 1795. The avowed object of this provision was to erect a permanent barrier between the United States and the possessions of Great Britain in that region by forever securing the territory thus surrendered by the former to the Indians. The American representatives refused even to consider this proposition, however, and in the end the British were compelled to abandon it. Their contention that the Indian should be admitted as a party to the treaty was also abandoned, and, as finally agreed upon, it provided for a better definition of the boundaries between the two nations, but for no surrender of territory on either side.

The counterpart for the Northwest of the Treaty of Ghent was the negotiation during the summer of 1815, by two commissions representing the United States, of over a score of treaties with the various tribes of that region.[654] One commission, consisting of Governor Edwards of Illinois and Governor Clark of Missouri Territory and Auguste Chouteau, the St. Louis Indian trader, met the diplomats of the red race at Portage des Sioux near the mouth of the Illinois River; the other, composed of General Harrison, General Duncan McArthur, and John Graham, conducted its negotiations at Spring Wells near Detroit. Except for the Sacs and Foxes, who manifested a belligerent attitude for some months longer, the autumn of 1815 witnessed the conclusion of treaty making and the formal restoration of peace to

[654] For the treaties and accompanying documents see *American State Papers, Indian Affairs*, II, 1–26.

the harassed northwestern frontier. But the British influence over the tribes was still powerful, despite the bitterness of the red men over their desertion, as they chose to regard it, by their former ally. The American influence over the tribes of Wisconsin and the territory farther west was as yet but slight.[655] Though nominally this region had long acknowledged the sovereignty of the United States, in fact it had remained commercially dependent upon Great Britain; and the British possessed, as a matter of course, the sympathy and affection of the red man.

With the restoration of peace, therefore, it remained for the Americans to establish an effective control over the northwestern tribes. The dominance of the British trader over them must be broken, and to this end garrisons must be scattered throughout the country to overcome the tribes and give countenance to the American traders in their efforts to compete successfully with their British rivals.

How the situation was viewed by well-informed Americans may be learned from a letter written by Lewis Cass to the Secretary of War in the spring of 1816.[656] Calling attention to the indications of a renewal by the British Indian Department of its old aggressive attitude with reference to the Indians of the United States, Cass pointed out the existence of three great channels for carrying on trade between Canada and the Indians of the Mississippi and Missouri country. These were, first, by way of Chicago and the Illinois River; second, by Green Bay and the Fox-Wisconsin waterway; third, from Lake Superior to the headwaters of the Mississippi. Of these the great channel at that time was the second. Through it great quantities of goods were smuggled into the Indian country of the United States. This practice could be cut off, Cass urged, so far as the Illinois and the Fox-Wisconsin river routes were concerned, by the establishment of garrisons at Green Bay and Chicago. To stop smuggling altogether, however, there must also be a post near the Grand Portage.

[655] *Wisconsin Historical Collections*, XVIII, xii.

[656] *Ibid.*, XIX, 376–79.

Almost a year before this John Kinzie had transmitted to Cass an argument in favor of the re-establishment of a garrison at Chicago to take the place of the one that had been destroyed in the massacre of 1812.[657] Kinzie was, of course, greatly interested in the adoption of this proposal, for it would make possible the renewal by him under favorable conditions of the pursuit of a livelihood at Chicago. He pointed out that the hostility for the Americans of the tribes around Lake Michigan, between Mackinac and the southern end of the lake, was mainly due to their intercourse with the traders of the Southwest Company, who were hostile to the American traders. Because of lack of game these tribes were forced to migrate at certain seasons to the waters of the Fox, Chicago, and Illinois rivers, and as an incident to this migration they generally rendezvoused at Chicago in the spring. For this reason a garrison there was necessary to preserve order among the Indians and to restrain the British traders, whose influence would ever keep them hostile to the United States.

Before the close of the summer of 1815 the government determined not only to establish garrisons at Chicago and Green Bay, but to reoccupy Prairie du Chien and erect a new fort at Rock Island on the Mississippi, and another in the vicinity of the Falls of St. Anthony.[658] At the same time it was planned to restore the government factory at Chicago for the conduct of the Indian trade, and to establish new factories at Green Bay and Prairie du Chien.[659] To the Third Infantry under Colonel Miller, then stationed at Detroit, was allotted the duty of garrisoning the forts at Mackinac, Green Bay, and Chicago.[660] Colonel Miller with his station at Mackinac was to have command of the three posts. Two companies, Bradley's and Baker's, were destined for Chicago. In the absence of Major Baker, the

[657] Kinzie to Cass, July 15, 1815; Indian Office, Book 204, Letter Book I, 90.

[658] Flagler, *History of the Rock Island Arsenal*, 14–16; *Wisconsin Historical Collections*, XIX, 376–89. The decision to restore Fort Dearborn was reached at least as early as June, 1815 (*ibid.*, 384).

[659] *Wisconsin Historical Collections*, XIX, 380–84.

[660] *Drennan Papers*, Department orders dated Detroit, June 7 and 8, 1816.

ranking officer, Captain Hezekiah Bradley, commanded the detachment. The companies comprising the Green Bay contingent were ordered to embark June 9.[661] Whether the Chicago detachment accompanied them on their way does not appear, but on June 30 it was on board the schooner "General Wayne" off the "Manitoo" Island in Lake Michigan. Here the first inspection was held, and a roster of the companies was made.[662] Of the one hundred and thirty-three men enrolled in the two companies one hundred and twelve were present on this expedition.

On July 4 the expedition arrived at Chicago. The public buildings were found to have been entirely destroyed with the exception of the magazine, which was badly damaged.[663] Numerous small parties of Indians visited the soldiers during the first few weeks, but no hostility was manifested by them. But one account preserves the details of the events attending the construction of the new Fort Dearborn, and this one is rambling and unreliable.[664] It relates that some Detroit traders, foreseeing a demand for vegetables upon the arrival of the garrison, had sent some Canadian half-breeds to Chicago in the spring of 1816 to start a truck garden. Upon the arrival of the "General Wayne" the troops landed and a temporary camp for the protection of themselves and the stores was established in a pasture near the old fort. Some garden seeds had been brought along, and one of the first tasks was to prepare a garden. Two half-breeds, Alexander Robinson and Ouilmette, and their squaws with their ponies were engaged to prepare the ground. With the aid of the soldiers the task was soon accomplished; but whether from the lateness of the season or for some other reason, the gardening experiment was not a success. The Canadian gardeners, who had planted in May about four miles

[661] For a short account of the establishment of the fort at Green Bay see Neville, *Historic Green Bay*, chap. vi.

[662] *Drennan Papers*, Fort Dearborn post returns.

[663] *Ibid.*, Bradley to Parker, August 3, 1816.

[664] *Head Papers*, narrative of Moses Morgan.

up the South Branch, brought in vegetables for sale to the garrison at high prices.

Meanwhile the construction of the fort was being prosecuted. In addition to the garrison, pit-sawyers and other workmen had been brought from Detroit. A grove of pine trees near the lake shore about four miles north of the river was selected, and the logs were rolled into the lake and rafted down to the mouth of the river and up the stream to a point opposite the site of the fort. Bands of Indians straggled around the buildings to gaze at the work of construction, beg for tobacco, and pilfer any unguarded tools that might be concealed under their blankets. The visits of the squaws and their papooses to the camp became so frequent and obnoxious that a heavier detail was required to mount guard by day to keep them away from the tents than was necessary by night. A detail of soldiers guarded the pit-sawyers at the pine grove on the north shore, who were engaged in cutting out the sawn lumber for roofs and floors. The Indians remained peaceable, but the sawyers' fears of them were easily excited. From this unpromising situation a real romance shortly developed. The disappearance of two of the Canadian pit-sawyers, who when last seen were in the company of an Indian, intensified the fears of their associates. Their anxiety was soon relieved by the reappearance of the men accompanied by two young squaws whom they had taken to wife. They had determined to take up their abode with a band of Indians residing on the Calumet, and had returned to demand their saws and the wages that were due them. Their requests were satisfied and they were allowed to depart, but not until the adjutant had read the marriage service to them and the garrison and workmen had celebrated the occasion with a holiday.

A few months after the arrival of the garrison Major Long of the engineer department of the army, who was to acquire fame several years later as an explorer, came to Chicago in search of information for a topographical report which he was preparing on the region roughly corresponding to the modern states of

Illinois and Indiana.[665] He found that the construction of the fort had been pushed with commendable industry, and reported that it would probably be brought to completion in the course of the following season. It was on a point of land formed by a bend in the river about eight hundred yards from its mouth. Curiously enough he reported that a more eligible site for the fort was afforded on the opposite side of the river, on the point of land between it and the lake. This location would more completely command the entrance to the river, and would also command the anchorage to a considerable extent. Perhaps the reason for this dissent from the judgment of the officers who had located the first and second forts may be inferred from Long's recommendation that the position he approved should be fortified in a manner calculated to resist any naval force that might be brought against it. Evidently he had in contemplation the possibility of another war with Great Britain, while both the first and second Fort Dearborn were designed to afford protection against Indian attacks only.

With the fort constructed and the garrison re-established, life at Chicago assumed in the main the aspects which it had borne before the massacre. Fort Dearborn was no longer, as in the old days, the farthest outpost of the United States in the Northwest, but it was still only an isolated wilderness station. Fort Wayne was the nearest post-office, and between this place and Chicago the mail was carried by foot soldiers once or twice a month.[666] Other agencies for maintaining connection with the outside world were few and irregular. The conduct of the business pertaining to the garrison and the operations connected with the prosecution of the fur trade were responsible for most

[665] The report is printed in full in the *National Register*, III, 193–98.

[666] In describing Chicago in 1818 Hubbard says (*Life*, 38) once a month. A report of the Post-Office Department, January 14, 1825 (*American State Papers*, Vol. XV, Post-Office Department, 136), shows that at that time the mail was carried between Fort Wayne and Green Bay once a month. J. Watson Webb, who was post adjutant at Fort Dearborn in 1821–22 states (Letter to John Wentworth, October 31, 1882) that he sent a sergeant and a private to Fort Wayne fortnightly to bring the mail for Chicago and Green Bay, and that a similar detail from the latter place was always on hand to receive and carry forward the mail destined for that place.

of them. The provisions for the garrison were for the most part brought around the lakes in schooners, although the live stock destined to supply the soldiers with fresh meat was sometimes driven overland to Chicago.[667] The historian of Major Long's expedition reported in 1823 that the total annual lake trade of Chicago, including the transportation of supplies for the garrison, did not exceed the cargo of five or six schooners.[668]

The existence of war interrupted but did not entirely prevent the conduct of the Indian trade at Chicago. The business of the American traders was broken up, but their lives were safe, even in the midst of the slaughter which attended the massacre.[669] The winter following the massacre two French traders, Du Pain and Buisson, established themselves with a stock of goods in the abandoned house of John Kinzie.[670] What success they met with, or whether they returned in the following years, does not appear, but the needs of the Indians were supplied to some extent by Robert Dickson, whose plans for stirring up the northwestern tribes against the Americans necessitated the sending of large quantities of goods to Chicago to distribute among his red allies.[671] The restoration of Fort Dearborn was the signal for the return of the American traders to Chicago. Among the early arrivals was John Crafts, the representative of a Detroit

[667] Keating, *Expedition to the Source of St. Peter's River*, I, 183. A letter from Captain Bradley of Fort Dearborn in the winter of 1816 (*Drennan Papers*, Bradley to McComb, December 3, 1816) announces that "a drove of hogs consisting of about three hundred recently arrived here for the contractor." At the time of the Chicago Treaty of 1821 two hundred head of cattle were driven from Brownstown to Chicago to supply fresh meat for the Indians in attendance on the negotiations (Schoolcraft, *Travels in the Central Portions of the Mississippi Valley*, 375). In June of this same year Rev. Isaac McCoy, while traveling from the mouth of the St. Joseph River to Fort Wayne, met a party engaged in driving cattle through the wilderness to Chicago (McCoy, *History of Baptist Indian Missions*, 108–9).

[668] Keating, *op. cit.*, I, 164.

[669] Kinzie and all his family passed through the massacre unscathed. Thomas Forsyth came to Chicago the day after the massacre and remained with the Kinzies several days (*supra*, note 632).

[670] *Supra*, note 613. Mrs. Kinzie gives the name as Du Pin (*Wau Bun*, 190). Her story of his rescue of Mrs. Lee and her baby from captivity and threatened matrimony at the hands of Black Partridge has already been told (p. 255).

[671] For a list of the goods to be sent from Mackinac to Chicago for Dickson at the opening of navigation in the spring of 1813 see *Michigan Pioneer Collections*, XV, 224.

firm, who is said to have established himself at Chicago some time during the year 1816.[672] His trading house was on the South Branch, not far from the Lee Cabin, where the murders of April, 1812, occurred. Crafts pursued his calling with success for several years, but the competition of the American Fur Company at last proved too strong, and in 1822 his establishment passed into its possession. Crafts became its employee at the same time, and continued to reside at Chicago until his death, several years later.

John Kinzie's interest in the restoration of Fort Dearborn has already been noted. The exact date of his return to Chicago is uncertain, but it apparently occurred during the latter half of the year 1816. In an affidavit made September 14, 1816, Kinzie described himself as "of the city of Detroit."[673] The last entry in his account book at Detroit bears date of June 16, 1816, and the first entry at Chicago occurs on January 10, following.[674] From the same source we learn that the revival of Kinzie's commercial activities at Chicago was coincident with the return of the garrison; for under date of June 13 occurs the invoice of a "Chicago Adventure," followed three days later by a second. The principal items of the first invoice are butter and whisky—four kegs and ten pounds of the former, and two barrels, containing sixty-eight gallons, of the latter. The contents of the second invoice pertain wholly to live stock, the principal items being five head of oxen and a mare and colt.

The Kinzie family was again established in the old home and the trader resumed his calling. He seems never to have recovered, however, the leading position as a trader which he held before the war. Within a few months after his return to Chicago he arranged with Varnum and Jouett to act as interpreter for both the factory and the Indian agency, and relin-

[672] On Crafts see Hurlbut, *Chicago Antiquities, passim;* Andreas, *History* of *Chicago*, Vol. I, *passim*. It is usually said that he was in the employ of Mack and Conant of Detroit, but Hurlbut suggests (*Chicago Antiquities*, 409) that Abraham Edwards was his employer.

[673] Copy of affidavit concerning the wounds received by Heald in the Chicago massacre, MS in possession of Mr. Wright Johnson of Rutherford, New Jersey.

[674] *Barry Transcript.*

quished his trade with the Indians.[675] He continued to act as interpreter for some time, and several years later, when Wolcott had succeeded Jouett as Indian agent at Chicago, Kinzie was appointed subagent, receiving separate compensation for each appointment.[676] In addition to his services with the government he again entered into the Indian trade during these years, part of the time on his own account, and later, according to Hubbard, as an employee of the American Fur Company.[677]

An important part of the life at Chicago in this period centered in the government Indian establishment, the restoration of which was coincident with the return of the garrison to Fort Dearborn. During the year 1815 Charles Jouett received the appointment of Indian agent, and Jacob B. Varnum was designated as factor.[678] Jouett had been agent at Chicago for several years prior to the War of 1812, but had resigned in the year 1811 and settled in Mercer County, Kentucky.[679] He now returned to the government service and to his old position at Chicago. His residence during this second incumbency was a log house on the north side of the river, possibly the same house which had sheltered the Burns family in the period before the massacre. It was far from adequate to the needs of Jouett's family, and in 1817 he complained bitterly of it and of the indifference of the officers of the garrison concerning his plight.[680] The house he described as "a little hut that a man of humanity would not suffer his negroes to live in." It was fourteen feet square, with but a single chair, which Jouett had brought with him from Kentucky, and there were nine persons in the family,

[675] Indian Department, Letter Book, Cass Correspondence, Kinzie to Cass, January 25, 1817; Jouett to Cass, January 25, 1817. All of the Indian Department letter books to be cited are preserved in the Pension Building at Washington.

[676] *American State Papers, Indian Affairs*, II, 365.

[677] Hurlbut, *Chicago Antiquities*, 31.

[678] *Wisconsin Historical Collections*, XIX, 380–95. Jouett was first appointed agent at Green Bay and Colonel John Bowyer agent at Chicago; at Jouett's request, however, a change was made in the appointments, Jouett going as agent to Chicago and Bowyer to Green Bay (*Wisconsin Historical Collections*, XIX, 391–92, 399).

[679] On Jouett see Hurlbut, *Chicago Antiquities*, 102 ff.; Andreas, *History of Chicago*, 87.

[680] Indian Department, Letter Book, Jouett to Cass, February 1, 1817.

including servants, to be accommodated. Jouett's indignant appeal produced little result, however. When Wolcott succeeded him as agent in 1819 he found the agency house a "mere shell," which necessitated rebuilding entirely to make it habitable.[681]

Jouett was a lawyer by training, and both before and after his second residence at Chicago he held the office of judge, the first time in Kentucky, the second in Arkansas Territory. He was a man of remarkable physique, six feet three inches in height, broad-shouldered and muscular. Among the Indians he was known as "the White Otter," and it is said that he possessed a commanding influence over them. His daughter recalled in after years that the red men were frequent visitors at her father's home, and that the dusky callers were especially kind to the children, her sister and herself. Their nurse was an Indian girl, a faithful and devoted servant, who afterward married a soldier of the garrison. In 1819 Jouett again resigned the Indian agency and returned to Kentucky. His place was filled by the transfer to the Chicago agency of Doctor Alexander Wolcott, who had been appointed "Agent to the Lakes," in April, 1818.[682]

Jacob B. Varnum, Chicago's only government factor after the War of 1812, belonged to an old and prominent New England family.[683] Through the family influence Varnum secured, when but twenty-three years of age, the appointment as government factor at Sandusky, Ohio.[684] He remained there until the news of Hull's surrender at Detroit, causing the precipitate retreat of the Ohio militia from Sandusky, compelled the abandonment of the factory. Varnum thereupon entered the army and served until the close of the war. On the return of peace, finding himself without an occupation, he applied for a position in the

[681] Indian Department, Cass correspondence, Wolcott to Cass, January 1, 1820.

[682] Indian Office, Letter Book D, 241, Calhoun to Wolcott, April 22, 1818; *ibid.*, 277, Calhoun to Wolcott, March 27, 1819.

[683] For it see Varnum, *The Varnums of Dracutt.* James Mitchell Varnum was a brigadier-general during the Revolution. His brother, Joseph B. Varnum, was speaker of the lower house of Congress from 1807 to 1811, and United States senator from Massachusetts, from 1811 to 1817.

[684] The account which follows is based upon the journal of Jacob B. Varnum.

Department of Indian Trade, and in the summer of 1815 was appointed factor at Chicago.

At this time it was the expectation of the department to establish the factory before the winter set in.[685] On receiving the news of his appointment Varnum set out for Erie by way of Buffalo, where he met Matthew Irwin, who had been factor at Chicago before the war and was now en route to establish the new factory at Green Bay. After a rough passage from Buffalo to Erie, in "a miserable apology for a schooner," the officials learned that the goods for the Indian trade, which were to have preceded them thither, had not arrived, and that the movement of the military to Chicago and Green Bay had been postponed to the following year. This involved the postponement of the establishment of the factories as well; nevertheless the naval commander at Erie resolved to take the goods, should they arrive in time, on to Mackinac that season, there to await the departure of the military expedition in the spring. Irwin thereupon returned to his home, while it was agreed that Varnum should go on to Mackinac in charge of the goods.

Varnum's narrative of the autumn voyage through the lakes from Erie to Mackinac presents a vivid picture of the discomforts and dangers of travel on the Great Lakes a century ago. The expedition consisted of two government vessels, the "Porcupine" and the "Ghent." The naval officers considered themselves insulted and degraded by the menial service of transporting merchandise. They therefore took no pains to protect the goods from ruin by water, and but little, apparently, to promote the comfort of the luckless factor. At Detroit a lady was given passage to Mackinac. In order to make room for her Varnum had to surrender the berth he had occupied thus far, and received in exchange for it one so near the bottom of the vessel that in rough weather the bilge water would spurt into it, keeping it wet most of the time.

The commander was a "perfect tyrant," as far as his power extended, and Varnum avers that during the four weeks they

[685] *Varnum's Journal;* Mason to Varnum, August 20, 1815, *Wisconsin Historical Collections,* XIX, 391–95.

were together he witnessed the infliction of more severe and often undeserved punishments than during all the remainder of his life. The stories of the floggings meted out by the commander's orders sicken the reader, after the lapse of a century, as they did the helpless witness at the time. On the second day out the negro cook, with whom the commander professed he would not part for his weight in gold, was given a dozen lashes because his master conceived the meat was not sufficiently cooked. A sailor possessed of an undue propensity for liquor had been unmercifully flogged for getting drunk, and threatened with a hundred lashes upon a repetition of the offense. Notwithstanding this the offense was repeated. The delinquent was ordered stripped and lashed to the shrouds. Varnum went below to escape witnessing the scene. In due time the commander came down, raging because the culprit had borne the torture so stoically. After receiving a hundred lashes without uttering a groan the tyrant demanded of him a promise not to repeat the offense, under pain upon refusal of receiving a second hundred on his now raw and bloody back. The torture proceeded and seventeen lashes had been administered when the victim gave in, making the promise required and begging for mercy. At the entrance to Lake Huron the rapid current made it difficult for sailing vessels to steer an even course. Dissatisfied with the helmsman's efforts the commander ordered a fresh man to the wheel, and the one who had been relieved received a dozen lashes. The new steersman promptly encountered the same difficulty and was as promptly relieved and flogged; and this routine was kept up until every seaman on board had taken his turn at the wheel and received his quota of lashes before the vessel got into the lake.

At Mackinac Varnum opened and dried the goods which had been wet, and then settled down to pass the long winter. Despite the extreme cold, and the desolation produced by the recent war, the winter's confinement proved to be one of the pleasantest periods of his whole life. He had a comfortable room with a good stove and plenty of firewood. The days were spent in reading, or, in pleasant weather, in excursions to the nets of the fishermen or elsewhere. The evenings were devoted to social amusements participated in by the merchants and the officers of the garrison. Among the latter were two brothers of Franklin Pierce, afterward President of the United States, one of whom, Captain Benjamin K. Pierce, wooed and married a half-breed French and Indian girl.[686]

Among the arrivals on the first vessel in the spring was a beautiful young woman from Detroit who came to visit her aunt. Varnum became enamored of her, and a romance began which was to culminate sadly enough at Chicago only a year later. The impression which the fair stranger made upon him was thus graphically set forth after the lapse of half a century: "She was a girl of polished manners, tall and graceful in her walk, and of striking symmetry of form. Her hair was auburn; her eyes dark blue, and remarkably transparent skin blended with a due proportion of red. I thought her in point of beauty quite equal to any lady I had seen."

That the young girl's beauty had a real existence, apart from the imagination of the fond lover, is shown by the reminiscences of Mrs. Baird of her childhood days at Mackinac. After a lapse of seventy years she alluded to her as "a beautiful woman, who was married at Mackinac."[687] Three months after the first meeting the beautiful girl became Varnum's bride, the marriage being solemnized by Major Puthuff in the absence of any minister of the gospel at Mackinac. A few days later the couple embarked with the factory goods on the "Tiger" bound for Chicago, whither the troops under Captain Bradley had recently preceded them. On their arrival the skeleton of a log hut on the south side which had survived the destruction in 1812 was assigned to Varnum to serve both as a store and as a dwelling. It was about twenty feet square, a story and a half in height, and without a floor. Varnum caused a floor of puncheons to be laid, made of logs split out four or five inches thick and roughly hewed on the face, and procured the erection of a lean-to for a kitchen. A

[686] Varnum's Journal; *Wisconsin Historical Collections*, XIV, 36, 40–41.

[687] *Wisconsin Historical Collections*, XIV, 26.

large portion of the goods were stored in the loft, the remainder being deposited with Kinzie for retail purposes.

In this hovel the brief period of the wedded life of the young couple was passed. According to the chronicler the winter passed "pleasantly enough." But for him there was the diversion of his business, and for recreation he indulged in frequent hunting excursions. For the young wife no relief from the lonely monotony and the grinding hardship of such an existence was possible. With the coming of spring she fell ill from approaching maternity. They had no servants, and there was no possibility of procuring any, but fortunately Mrs. Varnum's sister came on a visit and afforded assistance during the time of trouble. In June, 1817, the birth occurred, but the child was stillborn, and the trial killed the mother. The simple words of the husband written long afterward may well be permitted to terminate our recital of the pathetic tragedy: "Its long suffering mother survived but a few moments. Thus was I bereft of a beloved wife and the anticipated hope of a family. The mother with the child in her arms was buried a few yards from my house, where they rested when I left Chicago, 1822."

Two years passed, when Varnum joined a horseback party on a trip to Detroit. With the hot season the Indian trade ceased and the recreation of hunting was suspended. Diversions wholly failed, and the principal occupation consisted in fighting mosquitoes. The journey would involve a ride of seven hundred miles in fly time, yet Varnum gladly entered upon it to escape the deadly monotony of life at Chicago. Aside from Varnum the party consisted of Major Baker, John Dean, who had come to Chicago as an army contractor in 1816, and a guide. The route taken was by way of Fort Wayne and thence down the Maumee River and on to Detroit. The destination was reached after eleven days of travel, Varnum making his entry into Detroit after nightfall, covered with mud from head to foot as the result of being thrown from his horse into a swamp almost at the end of the journey.

Detroit was at that time a small village where each person interested himself in the affairs of all the rest. Upon the arrival of Varnum with no ostensible business the ready conclusion was reached that he had come in search of a wife. Although he denied such an intention, within two months he confirmed the expectation of the villagers by contracting a second marriage alliance. In the autumn of 1819 he embarked with his wife and her sister on a schooner for Chicago. The weather was pleasant and the company jovial. Arrived at Chicago the new wife began housekeeping under more favorable circumstances than her predecessor had done. The soldiers had constructed a new dwelling for the factor, under Varnum's superintendence; Mrs. Varnum had brought with her two servants, and the society of the place had improved somewhat. Several of the officers had brought on their families, and a spirit of friendliness and sociability prevailed, evening parties with dancing and other amusements being frequently held.

Among the inhabitants of Chicago during this period were several who had figured prominently in the massacre of 1812. About the time of Kinzie's return came Lieutenant Helm and his wife.[688] In 1817 they were living on the south side of the river in a small square house without a floor.[689] In lieu of this a tarpaulin was spread down, and tarpaulin was also hung about the walls. No one has taken the trouble, apparently, to record the duration of this domestic establishment. Mrs. Helm continued a resident of Chicago for many years, and frequent mention of her later doings is made by the family historian in the pages of *Wau Bun*. No mention of Lieutenant Helm occurs, however, and even the fact of his existence is ignored. The reason for this silence is perhaps revealed by certain court records of Peoria County, within whose boundaries Chicago was for a time included. These show that in 1829 Helm was still living, residing, apparently, in Clay County, Illinois.[690] In October of this year Mrs. Helm received a divorce from him together with alimony and the custody of their child.

[688] Helm's name appears in Kinzie's account book in January, 1817, and again in January, 1818.

[689] Recollections of Mrs. Baird, *Wisconsin Historical Collections*, XIV, 26.

[690] McCulloch, *Early Days of Peoria and Chicago*, 108.

To what extent Jean Baptiste Chandonnai made Chicago his home in the period of the second Fort Dearborn is also somewhat uncertain. It is related by Mrs. Baird that he was here in the employ of Kinzie shortly after the return of the troops, and his wife, coming to join him, was a passenger from Mackinac on the same schooner which brought Mrs. Baird and her mother to Chicago. The date of this visit is given as 1816, though it seems probable it actually occurred the following year. During the next few years Chandonnai was engaged in the fur trade in the region tributary to Chicago.[691] What the Indians received from him in exchange for their furs is perhaps sufficiently indicated by a consignment of goods sent to him from Mackinac, September 19, 1818, consisting of four barrels of whisky and six barrels of flour. Evidently the order had called for a larger quantity of fire-water, for the consignment was accompanied by the explanation that no more liquor could be promised because of its dearness and "uncommon scarcity." The next year Chandonnai betrayed the confidence reposed in him by the American Fur Company, by selling his furs to John Crafts and refusing to pay the company for the merchandise with which he had procured them.[692] The latter appealed to Kinzie to exert his influence in its behalf. That he did so with good effect seems evident from a later letter expressing gratitude for his exertions in securing the payment of a portion of the claim against Chandonnai. The writer urges a continuance of these efforts, and asks if a mortgage cannot be secured on the lands granted to Chandonnai by the Indians. What was, apparently, the sequel to this claim appeared fourteen years later in a clause of the Chicago Treaty of 1833. Among the grants of money made to individuals was the sum of two thousand five hundred dollars to Chandonnai, one thousand of which "by the particular request" of the latter was to be paid to Robert Stuart, agent of the American Fur Company.

[691] See on this point the letters of Ramsey Crooks printed in Andreas, *History of Chicago*, I, 94–95.

[692] *Ibid.*, I, 95.

Perhaps the most picturesque character in the little group of civilian residents of Chicago in the decade which began with the restoration of Fort Dearborn was Jean Baptiste Beaubien. He was descended from an old Canadian family, one of whose members is said to have been a follower of La Salle. About the middle of the eighteenth century a branch of the family established itself at Detroit, where the future citizen of Chicago was born in the year 1787.[693] He early engaged in the Indian trade, and according to the custom of the time married a squaw. He is said to have had a daughter born at Chicago as early as 1805, but the details both of his early migrations and of his marriage alliances are rather hazy. In 1814 he married Josette La Framboise, who was a servant in the family of John Kinzie at the time of the massacre. How soon after this Beaubien made Chicago his permanent place of residence is not certainly known, but in 1817 he purchased a house of John Dean, the army contractor, and thenceforth continued to reside on the Fort Dearborn reservation until, in the early thirties, his attempt to gain title to it precipitated the struggle over the Beaubien Land Claim which became famous in the annals of early Chicago.

An interesting feature of the life of Chicago and the adjoining region during the period under consideration was afforded by the periodical visits of the Illinois "brigade" of the American Fur Company. From its headquarters at Mackinac each autumn a number of trading outfits departed for the various trading posts scattered throughout the Northwest. Each brigade was composed of voyageurs organized into boat crews, the number of the latter varying with the importance of the station which constituted the destination of the brigade.[694] The goods were transported in bateaux, each manned by half a dozen men and carrying about three tons of merchandise. The Illinois brigade consisted of a dozen boats carrying, including the families of the traders, about a hundred persons.

[693] Beaubien family genealogy, MS in Chicago Historical Society library.

[694] On the operations of the American Fur Company see Hubbard, *Life, passim.*

Each autumn for a number of years this fleet made its way from Mackinac down the eastern shore of Lake Michigan and around its southern end to Chicago. From the south branch of the river the boats and goods were forced at the expense of much toil and hardship across the portage and down the Des Plaines until navigable water was reached on the Illinois River. Here the brigade broke up, small parties going to the various trading stations of the Illinois and its tributaries, and the winter was passed in bartering the goods for the furs of the Indians. With the opening of navigation in the spring the outfit reassembled and the return journey to Mackinac was begun. The boats, now laden with furs, were forced up the Illinois and the Des Plaines, the difficulty on the latter stream arising now from the excess of water, rather than from its scarcity, and the labor of stemming the raging current of the swollen stream. The remainder of the journey from Chicago, around the lake to Mackinac, was made with comparative ease.

We are indebted to the recollections of Gurdon S. Hubbard for an intimate picture of the life and activities of the traders who composed the Illinois brigade. Hubbard first visited the Illinois country as a youth of sixteen in the autumn of 1818. Approaching Chicago, the brigade spent the night at the mouth of the Little Calumet River. At dawn the party set out, in holiday attire and with flags flying, upon the last twelve miles of the lake voyage. At Douglas Grove young Hubbard landed, and climbing a tree gazed in wonder upon the first prairie he had ever beheld. In the foreground was a sea of waving grass, intermingled with a profusion of wild flowers; in the distance the groves of timber at Blue Island and along the Des Plaines River. A herd of wild deer appeared in view, while a pair of red foxes emerged from the grass within gunshot of the enraptured youth. To the northward could be seen the whitewashed walls of Fort Dearborn sparkling in the sunlight, while on the blue surface of the lake the brawny voyageurs urged onward the fleet of bateaux, their flashing oars keeping time with the music of the boat song.

Descending from his observation point, Hubbard made his way toward the fort, and found the traders encamped on the north side of the river to the west of Kinzie's house. Here he was entertained and a firm friendship between him and the Kinzie family soon developed. The young visitor was to return to Chicago frequently during the following years, until in 1834 he made it his permanent home and shortly became one of the foremost citizens of the struggling but optimistic young city.

Interesting glimpses of the manner of life in and around the new Fort Dearborn are afforded by the accounts of travelers who occasionally visited this frontier station. The reception of Storrow at Fort Dearborn in 1817, "as one arrived from the moon," has already been mentioned.[695] Storrow was greatly impressed with the strategic advantages possessed by Chicago, which he thus early pointed out marked it as the future place of deposit for the whole region of the upper lakes.[696] He described the climate and soil as excellent, although not all visitors of this early period agree with him in this opinion. At the time of his visit traces of the massacre yet remained, and Storrow encountered one of the "principal perpetrators," Nuscotnemeg, or the Mad Sturgeon.

From the pen of Mrs. Baird, whose visit to Chicago was probably made in the same year as that of Storrow, we get a more detailed description.[697] The vessel which transported her from Mackinac had for its cargo "the familiar load of pork, flour, and butter." There were no ports of call on the western side of Lake Michigan, and the master after seeking in vain at Chicago for a return cargo had finally to take on a ballast of sand and gravel. Mrs. Baird draws a pleasant picture of the household of her host, John Kinzie. The establishment included a number of "men and women retainers." There was as yet no bridge across the river, the only means of passage being a canoe or dugout, as in the days before the massacre. In this craft, with the two Kinzie

[695] *Supra*, p. 153.

[696] *Wisconsin Historical Collections*, VI, 183–84.

[697] *Ibid.*, XIV, 25 ff.

children, eight and ten years of age, acting as her crew, Mrs. Baird first crossed the Chicago River.

In the summer of 1820 Governor Cass of Michigan Territory, returning from a voyage of exploration to the sources of the Mississippi River, arrived in mid-August at Chicago with a party of sixteen men in two canoes.[698] At Chicago the party separated. Cass with several attendants proceeded on horseback along the Indian trail to Detroit, while the scientists of the expedition, Captain Douglas and Henry R. Schoolcraft, completed the circuit of Lake Michigan by continuing around its eastern shore to Mackinac. Schoolcraft, like Storrow, was greatly impressed with the natural advantages possessed by Chicago, and predicted for it a glowing future. With the extinguishment of the Indian title to the surrounding country immigration would flow in, and Chicago would become the dèpôt for the inland commerce between the northern and southern sections of the Union, and "a great thoroughfare for strangers, merchants, and travelers."

No little discernment was requisite thus to perceive the future destiny of the rude frontier hamlet which according to Schoolcraft's estimate contained, exclusive of the military, but ten or a dozen houses and a population of sixty souls. Quite different from Schoolcraft's description was that of the historian of Major Long's expedition to the sources of the St. Peter's River three years later.[699] He described the climate as inhospitable, the soil sterile, and the scenery monotonous and uninviting. The village consisted of a few huts of log or bark, low, filthy, and disgusting, displaying not the least trace of comfort, and inhabited by "a miserable race of men," scarcely equal to the Indians from whom they were descended. Nor could the chronicler perceive the brilliant future in store for Chicago which Schoolcraft had foretold. He granted that "at some distant day," when the country between the Wabash and the Mississippi

[698] For an account of the expedition see Schoolcraft, *Narrative Journal of Travels from Detroit . . . . to the Sources of the Mississippi River in 1820.*

[699] Keating, *Expedition to the Source of St. Peter's River*, I, 163–65.

should become populated, Chicago might become a point in the line of communication between the Great Lakes and the Mississippi; but even the intercourse which would be carried on through this channel would, he thought, be at all times a limited one.

From September, 1821, until June, 1823, the commander of Fort Dearborn was Lieutenant-colonel John McNeil.[700] Colonel McNeil was a man of interesting personality in many ways. Physically he was the rival of General Scott for being the tallest and heaviest man in the army, and the equal in size of "Long John" Wentworth, Chicago's well-known editor, mayor, and congressman.[701] He was a soldier of the War of 1812, during the course of which he was twice brevetted for gallant conduct, the first time in the battle of Chippewa and the second in the battle of Niagara.[702] Mrs. McNeil was a half-sister of Franklin Pierce, later President of the United States. She was described over half a century later, by one who as a young soldier had come under her influence, as a "most estimable woman," whose kindness and wise counsels had had a beneficial influence on his whole life.[703] For a daughter born to Mrs. McNeil at Fort Dearborn the father subsequently claimed the distinction of having been the first child born in the new fort.[704] Their only son, Lieutenant J. Winfield Scott McNeil, who died in 1837 of wounds received in a battle with the Seminole Indians,[705] was a young boy during the time his father was stationed at Fort Dearborn.

James Watson Webb, who later acquired national renown as editor, politician, and diplomat, was stationed at Fort Dearborn as a young lieutenant during a part of the period of McNeil's incumbency as commander. The descendant of an old New

[700] *Drennan Papers*, Fort Dearborn post returns.

[701] Wentworth, *Early Chicago*, 24–25. In 1857 Wentworth was said to be the tallest man in Chicago, measuring about six feet and a half and weighing two hundred and thirty pounds (*Chicago Magazine*, I, 399).

[702] Heitman, *Dictionary of the United States Army*, I, 679.

[703] Van Cleve, *Three Score Years and Ten*, 31.

[704] Wentworth, *Early Chicago*, 24.

[705] *Ibid.*, Heitman, *op. cit.*, I, 679.

York family, Webb ran away from home at the age of seventeen, and going to Washington secured as the result of a personal interview with Calhoun, then Secretary of War, a commission in the army. In October, 1821, he joined the Fort Dearborn garrison and remained here until the following June. Webb's service at Fort Dearborn was marked by a bold and arduous exploit. Toward the end of January, 1822, John Kinzie, who was then acting as sub-Indian agent, communicated to Colonel McNeil information which he had received from a friendly Chippewa chief of a plot on the part of the Sioux and Fox Indians to overwhelm the garrison at Fort Snelling on the upper Mississippi the following spring.[706] It was desirable to send word to Fort Armstrong of the plot, from which place the news could be forwarded up the Mississippi to Fort Snelling. Lieutenant Webb, though barely twenty years of age, volunteered for this service. Accompanied by a sergeant and a Pottawatomie guide, he set out on February 4, intending to proceed to the post of a French trader on the Rock River and there secure a Winnebago guide for the remainder of the trip. Upon reaching there, however, he found the Winnebagoes celebrating their war dance. To secure a guide from them was out of the question. During the night Webb and his companion set out, ostensibly to return to Chicago, but in reality to make their way across the prairie to Fort Armstrong. The weather was bitterly cold and they were exposed to the double danger of death from freezing and of being intercepted by the Indians. Neither materialized, however, and in due time Webb's message was delivered to the commander at Fort Armstrong.

In May, 1823, an order was issued from Washington for the evacuation of Fort Dearborn, and the following autumn the garrison departed.[707] Doctor Alexander Wolcott, who had succeeded Jouett as Indian agent at Chicago, continued to serve

[706] For Webb's account of the affair see his letter to John Wentworth, October 31, 1882, in Chicago Historical Society library, and Andrews, *Biographical Sketch of James Watson Webb*, 11–15. For Kinzie's report of the plot to Cass, February 1, 1822, see Indian Department, Cass correspondence.

[707] Wentworth, *Early Chicago*, 47; *Drennan Papers*, Fort Dearborn post returns.

in this capacity until his death in 1830. In July, 1823, he married Ellen Marion, the eldest daughter of John Kinzie's second family,[708] and upon the removal of the garrison took up his residence in the fort. The circumstances of Wolcott's marriage well illustrate the primitive conditions which prevailed at Chicago in this period. There was no justice of the peace, minister of the gospel, or other person at Chicago authorized to solemnize marriages. It chanced that William S. Hamilton, son of the famous statesman, Alexander Hamilton, who had adopted a roving life in the wilderness of northern Illinois, had taken a contract to supply the garrison at Fort Howard with beef cattle. John Hamlin, one of the early residents of Peoria who held a commission as justice of the peace, had accompanied Hamilton on a trip to Green Bay with a drove of cattle. On the return journey he reached Chicago about July 20, and advantage was taken of his presence by the prospective bride and groom to have their marriage ceremony performed.

With the garrison departed most of the life at Chicago. During the next few years little occurred to interrupt the monotonous course of existence. Rarely a new settler, attracted by the presence of relatives who had gone before, or lured westward by the hope of improving his material condition, would direct his steps to Chicago. Periodically the Indians, who still held possession of the country tributary to Chicago, would assemble to receive their annuities, the payment of which had been stipulated in various treaties. At such times the place teemed with savages and excitement for a few days, during which the traders reaped a golden harvest. Finally in 1827 occurred the Winnebago War, which for a time furnished plenty of excitement for Chicago, and led eventually to the reoccupation of Fort Dearborn by a garrison of United States troops.

[708] McCulloch, *Early Days of Peoria and Chicago*, 99.

CHAPTER XIII

THE INDIAN TRADE

To omit from the history of early Chicago an account of the Indian trade would be like giving the play of *Hamlet* with the principal character left out. Its origin is coeval with the advent of the white man in this region; and until almost the close of the period covered by this volume it constituted the basis of the commerce of the region tributary to the upper Great Lakes and the Mississippi Basin. With the advance of the settler into the Northwest the wild game receded before him; and its disappearance marked the passing of the Indian trade, soon to be followed by the red man himself. As a rule, the first white man to penetrate the wilderness was the trader, and the Indian's conception of the white race was based upon his intercourse with the traders, the class of whites with whom he was most familiar. Upon these he was dependent for the gun, ammunition, and other supplies which quickly became essential to his existence; and most of the problems which grew out of the contact of the two races centered around the conduct of the Indian trade.

As early as 1675, Marquette found French traders had entered Illinois and established themselves below Chicago, in the vicinity, apparently, of the junction of the Des Plaines River with the Kankakee.[709] Thus early, too, certain of the Indians themselves had turned traders, and Marquette was attended, on his second visit to Illinois, by a party of Illinois Indians who were returning from Canada with merchandise to trade with the members of their own race for furs.[710] One of the party, named Chachagwessiou, was "greatly esteemed" among his nation because, in part at least, he was engaged in the fur trade; and this, in spite of the fact that he and his associates subjected their kinsmen to the same extortion as did the white traders. That it

[709] *Jesuit Relations*, LIX, 175 ff.

[710] *Ibid.*, LIX, 165, 167, 175 *et passim*.

was primarily for the sake of the fur trade that the French valued the country is a fact easily demonstrable. The economic foundation of La Salle's colony was the Indian trade which he expected to develop. For its exclusive possession he sought and obtained the royal license, and against interlopers upon his privileged monopoly he waged relentless warfare. With his death the license to carry on trade at Fort St. Louis passed to his faithful lieutenant, Tonty. For many years from his lofty stronghold he continued to trade with the Indians of the surrounding region. But the French government looked upon the enterprise with a jealous eye, and early in the eighteenth century at its request Tonty's establishment at the rock of St. Louis was abandoned and he himself departed for lower Louisiana, where he shortly met his death.

During the greater part of the eighteenth century there was, as far as known, no civilized establishment at Chicago. That traders may have established themselves here for a shorter or longer time is entirely possible, but there was no regular French post here as has often been stated. Until the end of the French régime the trade of the territory around Chicago found outlet at the neighboring posts. The nearest of these was St. Joseph, but there were others at Mackinac, Green Bay, Ouiatanon, and in the French settlements of lower Illinois.[711]

The first trading establishment at Chicago of which we have any certain knowledge was that of Baptiste Point du Sable in the latter years of the eighteenth century. Hugh Heward, who in 1790 passed from Lake Michigan by way of the Chicago Portage to the Illinois, tarried at Chicago a day to prepare for the further journey. He exchanged his canoe for a pirogue belonging to Du Sable, and bought from him a quantity of flour and pork, for which he gave in exchange thirteen yards of cotton cloth.[712] How long Du Sable continued to reside here or how extensive was his trade is somewhat conjectural. It is evident that during the

[711] For the posts of the interior and their trade, toward the close of the French régime, see Bougainville's memoir in *Wisconsin Historical Collections*, XVIII, 167 ff.

[712] Heward, *Journal*.

closing years of the century the St. Joseph traders, Burnett and Kinzie, at times extended their trading operations around the lake as far as Chicago. It is evident, too, from the fact that when the garrison came in 1803 there were four traders' huts here, that still other traders had established themselves at Chicago for a shorter or longer period.[713]

So far as existing records are concerned, the first quarter of the nineteenth century marks the heyday of the Indian trade at Chicago. The establishment of the garrison here not only attracted traders and others, as in the case of Kinzie, but it also resulted in the handing down of more numerous and extensive accounts of the trading activities of this region than had ever been done before. Perhaps the most important private source of information for the period prior to 1812 is the transcript of names in Kinzie's account books.[714] Far overshadowing this in importance for the whole period from 1805 to 1822, however, are the records of the Department of Indian Trade, which maintained a government factory at Chicago.

The trading operations of Kinzie during the first period of his residence at Chicago were evidently of considerable importance. An entry at St. Joseph in April, 1804, less than a month before the removal to Chicago, shows that the sum of two hundred and forty-five pounds was invested in a single "adventure" at Peoria. That similar enterprises were being simultaneously conducted appears from an entry a week later concerning "Billy Caldwell's adventure." At Chicago, in addition to the trade he himself conducted and the "adventures" he financed, Kinzie was in partnership with his half-brother, Thomas Forsyth, during the entire period prior to 1812. Although the articles of indenture of Jeffrey Nash describe Kinzie and Forsyth as "Merchants of Chicago,"[715] Forsyth was stationed at Peoria until his establishment was broken up by Captain Craig's militia in the late autumn of 1812. In Kinzie's account book under date of June 13,

[713] See in this connection the letters of William Burnett, the St. Joseph trader, in Hurlbut, *Chicago Antiquities*, 49–70, *passim*.

[714] *Barry Transcript*.

[715] *Supra*, p. 150–52.

1806, settlements with four individuals, amounting in all to fourteen hundred and thirty-one pounds, are noted. The names of these men, Sigrain, Bourbonnais, LaVoy, and Maisonneuf, furnish a typical illustration of the nationality of the men who conducted the Illinois fur trade in the first decade of the nineteenth century.

Some individual entries taken at random from Kinzie's account books may be of interest as showing the prices that prevailed at Chicago a century ago. Thirty bushels of corn sold in 1805 for forty-five dollars. The same year, however, two bushels were sold by Kinzie to Ramsey Crooks for five dollars. Another entry for 1806 states that tobacco sold at fifty cents a pound; whisky at fifty cents a quart; powder at $1.50 a pound; and shot at thirty-three cents a pound. In May of this year butter was quoted at fifty cents, the same price which Kinzie paid at Detroit ten years later for a shipment of ten pounds sent on his first Chicago adventure after the return of the garrison to Fort Dearborn. This same "adventure" included two barrels of whisky invoiced at ten shillings or $1.25 a gallon. A comparison of this with the selling price already noted of fifty cents a quart would seem to indicate that the profit from the sale of firewater proceeded mainly from the dilution of it with water, which the traders customarily practiced. Returning to 1806, flour is priced at ten cents a pound, while the pay of six boatmen, hired to assist in pulling a trader's craft up the river, is fifty cents a day. In 1810 raisins sold for four shillings and tea for twenty shillings a pound; while the price of "1 tyson" which Jouett ordered was thirty shillings. "A silver brooch for six rats," "2 large silver crosses, $7.50," and "Francis Bourbonnaé Dr. to 1 negro wench sold him by Indenture £160" are entries which suggest their own explanation.

It seems evident that the fur trade of Illinois in the period under consideration was of considerable magnitude. "I had no idea of there being so extensive a trade carried on in that quarter," wrote Colonel Kingsbury to Captain Whistler in the fall of 1804, in reply to an inventory which the latter had sent him of peltries passing Fort Dearborn the preceding spring.[716] The operations of Kinzie and Forsyth could have constituted but a small part of the fur trade of Illinois at this period. In the spring of 1805 Kingsbury was himself at Chicago, seeking to conduct a company of soldiers down the Illinois River to establish a new fort near the mouth of the Missouri.[717] Whistler had been ordered to secure suitable boats for the transportation of the detachment, but his efforts to do so had been unavailing. Upon Kingsbury's arrival at Chicago, however, he succeeded in securing two traders' bateaux on condition that the goods, amounting to one hundred packs of peltry and ten bags, should be transported to Mackinac in the brig "Adams," which had brought the troops to Chicago. A few entries from Kinzie's account book will serve further to show the extent of the trade which passed through Chicago. June 14, 1806, Ouilmette is charged with the hire of a wagon and oxen to transport a trader's goods to the forks of the Illinois River. Three weeks later Hugh Pattinson and Company become indebted to Kinzie for the labor of four men for six days each pulling boats up the river, and at the same time for the portage of one hundred and fifty-six packs of peltries. In July, 1807, Kinzie transported forty-six packs across the portage for James Aird, and in the same month on two occasions transported enough for Auguste Chouteau to incur charges of almost forty pounds. A similar entry in July, 1808, charges Chouteau with two hundred and fifty-six dollars for carrying one hundred and twenty-eight packs from Mount Joliet to Chicago.

The government factory or trading house constituted a notable feature of the Indian trade at Chicago after 1805. The policy of the government toward the red man which found expression in the factory system was fraught with such significance, not only for the Indian trade, but also for the larger subject of the relations between the two races, that it seems desirable at

[716] *Kingsbury Papers*, Whistler to Kingsbury, August 14, 1804; Kingsbury to Whistler, September 10, 1804.

[717] For this expedition see *ibid.*, Cushing to Kingsbury, February 20, 1805; Kingsbury to Smith, June 2, 1805; Smith to Kingsbury, June 1, 1805; Kingsbury to Brevoort, June 2, 1805; Kingsbury to Williamson, July 10, 1805, *et passim.*

this point to present a somewhat comprehensive account of it. The origin of the policy of government trading houses dates from the early colonial period. In the Plymouth and Jamestown settlements all industry was at first controlled by the commonwealth, and in Massachusetts Bay the stock company had reserved to itself the trade in furs before leaving England.[718] In the last-named colony a notable experiment was carried on during the first half of the eighteenth century in conducting "truck houses" for the Indians. About the close of this period Benjamin Franklin, whose attention had been called to the abuses which the Indians of the Pennsylvania frontier suffered at the hands of the private traders, investigated the workings of the Massachusetts system and recommended the establishment of public trading houses at suitable places along the frontier.[719]

The first step toward a national system of Indian trading establishments was taken during the opening throes of the Revolution. The establishment of friendly relations with the Indians appeared to the second Continental Congress a matter of the "utmost moment."[720] Accordingly it was resolved, July 12, 1775, to establish three Indian departments, a northern, a middle, and a southern, with appropriate powers for supervising the relations of the United Colonies with the Indians. In November of the same year a committee, of which Franklin was a member, was directed to devise a plan for carrying on trade with the Indians, and ways and mean for procuring the goods proper for it.[721]

Acting upon the report of this committee, in January, 1776, the Congress adopted a series of resolutions outlining a general system of governmental supervision of the Indian trade, and appropriating the sum of forty thousand pounds to purchase goods for it.[722] These were to be disposed of by licensed traders, acting under instructions laid down by the commissioners, and

[718] Turner, *Indian Trade in Wisconsin*, 58.

[719] Franklin, *Works*, II, 221. The letter is not certainly by Franklin, but he is supposed to have been its author. See *ibid.*, 217, footnote.

[720] *Journals of the Continental Congress*, II, 174.

[721] *Ibid.*, III, 350, 365, 366.

[722] *Ibid.*, IV, 96–98.

under bond to them to insure compliance with the prescribed regulations. The following month Congress further manifested its good intentions toward the native race by passing resolutions expressing its faith in the benefits to accrue from the propagation of the gospel and the civil arts among the red men, and directing the commissioners of Indian affairs to report suitable places in their departments for establishing schoolmasters and ministers of the gospel.[723] Owing to the exigencies of the war, however, these plans for the establishment of a trading system and for the civilization of the Indians were alike frustrated. The struggle with the mother country absorbed all the energies and resources of the Revolutionary government. How this affected the prosecution of the plans for the Indian Departments, which had been entered upon so hopefully in the beginning of the war, is sufficiently shown by the fact that the expenses of the government in behalf of the Indians fell from two hundred and sixty-one thousand dollars in 1776 to thirty-five hundred dollars in 1779; and the total amount for the five years from 1779 to 1783 inclusive was less than one-tenth the sum spent in the single year 1776.[724]

During the period of the Confederation the subject of the Indian trade was frequently acted upon by Congress, but no systematic effort was made to regulate it until 1786. In that year an ordinance was passed dividing the Indian Department into two districts and appointing a superintendent and a deputy for each.[725] They were to execute the regulations of Congress relating to Indian affairs, and to grant licenses to trade with the Indians. Only citizens of the United States whose good moral character had been certified to by the governor of a state were eligible to licenses; they were to run for one year and to be granted upon the payment of fifty dollars and the execution of a

723 *Ibid.*, IV, 111.

724 *American State Papers, Indian Affairs*, II, 210. The sum spent in 1776 was $261,783.44; for the five years from 1779 to 1783 inclusive it was $25,641.34.

725 For a sketch of the relations of the government with the Indians see the report of Calhoun, Secretary of War, to Congress in 1816 (*American State Papers, Indian Affairs*, II, 181 ff.); for the act of 1786 see *ibid.*, I, 14.

bond to insure compliance with the established regulations. To engage in trade without a license incurred a penalty of five hundred dollars and forfeiture of goods.

This was, apparently, a judicious system, but the government of the Confederation had about run its course, and the general paralysis which overtook it, and the confusion incident to the change to a new form of government, prevented the new policy toward the Indians from being carried into effect. Prominent among the problems which the new national government found pressing upon it for solution was the subject of Indian relations and, in this connection, the question of the regulation of the Indian trade. In 1790 the licensing system of 1786 was temporarily adopted, but shorn of some of its valuable features. There was no prohibition against foreigners and no fee was required for a license. This system was continued without essential change until 1816, when an act was passed prohibiting foreigners from trading with Indians of the United States, except by special permission of the President and under such regulations as he should prescribe.

The young government shortly entered upon the most serious Indian war in all its history, and not until one of its armies had been repulsed and another destroyed did Anthony Wayne succeed, in 1795, in bringing the hostile red men to recognize the superior might of the nation he represented. At the close of this war Congress, at the instigation of Washington, determined to experiment with another system of conducting the Indian trade. In the session of 1795, stirred up by the repeated recommendations of Washington, that body debated a bill for the establishment of Indian trading houses.[726] Though the bill was defeated at this time its purpose as stated by its supporters is worth noting. It was regarded as constituting a part only of a comprehensive frontier policy; this policy embraced the threefold design of the military protection of the frontier against Indian invasions, the legal protection of the Indian country against predatory white incursions, and the establishment of trading

[726] *Annals of Congress*, 3d Congress, 1262–63.

houses to supply the wants of the Indians and free them from foreign influence. It was believed that these three things embraced in one system would bring about the great desideratum, peace on the frontier; but that without the last the other parts of the plan would prove totally ineffectual.

The defeat of the advocates of the system of government trading houses in 1795 was neither final nor complete. Their principal measure had failed of passage, but at this same session Congress appropriated the sum of fifty thousand dollars to begin the establishment of public trading houses,[727] and two were accordingly started among the Cherokees, Creeks, and Chickasaws of the Southwest. The next year a second act was passed, carrying an appropriation of one hundred and fifty thousand dollars, in addition to an annual allowance for the payment of agents and clerks.[728] The President was authorized to establish trading houses at such places as he saw fit for carrying on a "liberal trade" with the Indians. The agents and clerks employed were prohibited from engaging in trade on their own account, and were required to give bonds for the faithful performance of their duties. The act was to run for two years, and the trade was to be so conducted that the capital sum should suffer no diminution.

Notwithstanding the appropriation and act of 1796, for several years no extension of the system of trading houses beyond the two experimental establishments of 1795 was attempted; nor did the government avail itself, to any considerable extent, of the money appropriated for this purpose. The total amount appropriated in 1795 and 1796 was two hundred thousand dollars. In December, 1801, the Secretary of War reported that only ninety thousand dollars of this amount had been drawn upon, and that the number of trading houses was still limited to the two that had been first established.[729] Even the act authorizing

[727] *Ibid.*, 4th Congress, 1st session, 152; *American State Papers, Indian Affairs*, I, 583.

[728] *Annals of Congress*, 4th Congress, 1st session, 282–85; for the act itself, see *ibid.*, 4th Congress, 2d session, 2889–90.

[729] *American State Papers, Indian Affairs*, I, 653–55.

the system had expired in 1799, and in spite of repeated recommendations to Congress in the matter no action had been taken to renew it.

In the debates over the passage of the Act of 1796 it was made evident that even the supporters of the measure regarded it in the light of an experiment.[730] The recent war had cost one and a half million dollars annually; it was worth while to try another method of securing peace on the frontier. Since the Canadian trading company was too powerful for individual Americans to compete successfully with it the government must assume the task. If upon trial the plan should prove a failure, it could be abandoned. On the other hand it was objected that public bodies should not engage in trade, which was always managed better by individuals; fraud and loss could not be guarded against; nor should the people be taxed for the sake of maintaining trade with the Indians. In spite of these objections and prophecies, the report of 1801 showed that the original capital had suffered no diminution, but had, in fact, been slightly increased; this, too, despite losses that had been incurred through the failure of the sales agent, to whom the peltries had been assigned, to dispose of them before many had become ruined.

It remains to speak of the degree of success achieved in the broad objects for the attainment of which the system had been inaugurated. Concerning this the report of the Secretary of War in 1801 was entirely favorable.[731] As far as it had been established the effects of the system upon the disposition of the Indians had been very salutary. The several tribes were desirous of participating in its advantages, and no doubt was felt that its extension would be attended by all the good effects originally contemplated by the government, and this without any diminution of the original fund.

Two years later, in January, 1803, Jefferson stated in a message to Congress that private traders, both foreign and domestic, were being undersold and driven from competition,

[730] *Annals of Congress*, 4th Congress, 1st session, 229–32.

[731] *American State Papers, Indian Affairs*, I, 653–55.

that the system was effective in conciliating the good will of the Indians, and that they were soliciting generally the establishment of trading houses among them.[732] At the same time the Secretary of War reported the establishment of four new stations, at Detroit, Fort Wayne, Chickasaw Bluffs, and among the Choctaws, to which the remainder of the money appropriated in 1796 had been applied.[733] This remained the number until 1805, when four more were established: at Arkansas on the Arkansas River, at Nachitoches on the Red River, at Belle Fontaine near the mouth of the Missouri, and at Chicago.[734] The following year a trading house was established at Sandusky on Lake Erie, and in 1808 three more, at Mackinac, at Fort Osage, and at Fort Madison.[735] Meanwhile the two original houses had been removed to new locations and two others, those at Detroit and at Belle Fontaine, had been abandoned.

From 1808 until the beginning of the War of 1812 there were thus twelve factories in operation. At each was stationed an agent, or factor, and at most an assistant, or clerk, as well. The salaries of the former prior to 1810 ranged from $750 to $1,250, in most cases not exceeding $1,000; the pay of the latter from $250 to $650; in both cases subsistence was granted in addition.[736] In 1810 the superintendent of the trade estimated that of the total amount of $280,000, which had been invested in the business, $235,000 still remained; the loss in the capital invested to this date was therefore, in round numbers, $45,000.[737] The four-year period ending in 1815, on the other hand, in spite of the disturbance to trade which attended the operations of the War of 1812, produced a profit of almost $60,000.[738] Approximately three-fourths of this gain was swallowed up in the destruction, during the war, of the factories at Chicago, Fort Wayne, Sandusky, Mackinac, and Fort Madison; but

[732] *Ibid.*, I, 684. [733] *Ibid.*, I, 683.

[734] Report of John Mason, Superintendent of Indian Trade, April 12, 1810, *ibid.*, I, 768 ff.

[735] *Ibid.* [736] *Ibid.* [737] *Ibid.*

[738] Report of Crawford, Secretary of War, March 13, 1816, *ibid.*, II, 26–28.

this was the fortune of war and not in any way the fault of the system.

The establishment of a factory at Chicago was determined upon in the spring of 1805, and on March 19 Ebenezer Belknap of Connecticut was commissioned as factor.[739] The factory at Detroit was to be abandoned and the goods and furniture for the factor's dwelling to be removed to Chicago.[740] To supplement the stock of goods for the Indian trade removed from Detroit an initial invoice of new goods to the value of eight thousand dollars was ordered to be sent to Detroit for the Chicago factory.[741] Belknap's instructions shed much light upon the practice followed when a new factory was to be established. He was to receive a salary of $1,000 a year and in addition to this $365 in lieu of subsistence.[742] He was empowered to employ, if necessary, a "principal clerk" at a salary not to exceed $500; if a young man could be procured for the place at a salary of $200 or $300, this was to be done. When a new factory was established an allowance to the factor of $200 for household furniture and domestic utensils and $25 yearly for the same purpose after the first year was made. Since Belknap was to take over the outfit of the Detroit factory his initial allowance for this purpose was reduced to $100.

The establishment of the Chicago factory was not unattended with difficulties. Munroe, the Detroit factor, was indisposed to surrender the public property in his possession, and much embarrassment was experienced on this account.[743] Scarcely had Belknap had time to proceed to his destination when warning

739 Belknap's commission, Indian Office, Letter Book B, 69. In some cases two or more of these letter books are designated in the same way. In such cases the volume in question can be determined by taking account of the dates of the contents.

740 *Ibid.*, 72, War Department (unsigned) to Belknap, April 12, 1805; *ibid.*, 438, Dearborn to John Johnston, June 3, 1805.

741 *Ibid.*, 68, John Smith to William Davy, April 12, 1805.

742 Belknap's commission, *ibid.*, 69; his instructions, April 12, 1805, *ibid.*, 72.

743 Various letters in the Indian Office letter books refer to this difficulty, particularly one from the War Department (unsigned) to William Davy, Superintendent of Indian Trade, May 17, 1805 (Letter Book B, 76). I have not been able to learn how the trouble was finally settled.

came to the War Department that his character was not what it should be.[744] Our information concerning the difficulty is but scanty, but the outlines of the situation are clear. An investigation into the fitness of Belknap for the position was instituted,[745] and as a precautionary measure it was decided to appoint a "suitable character" as his assistant, with instructions to report faithfully to the War Department concerning the character and conduct of his superior.[746] Apparently the investigation confirmed the charges against Belknap, for before the end of November the choice of a successor to him was being considered,[747] and on December 31, 1805, the luckless factor's services at Chicago terminated.[748] He was superseded by Thomas Hayward, who had been acting as his assistant since the third of the preceding October. Belknap proceeded to Washington, and in a preliminary interview with his superiors gave such an account of himself as to imbue them with the belief that partisan rancor had been responsible for the charges preferred against him.[749] With this our information concerning the matter abruptly terminates, and we can only hope that the fuller investigation established his innocence of the charge against him.

Thomas Hayward continued in charge of the Chicago factory until the spring of 1807, when he resigned his appointment. No successor could be found at once, and accordingly Jouett, the Indian agent, was asked to take temporary charge of the factory.[750] A few weeks later the President of the United States "approbated" the appointment of Joseph B. Varnum, a clerk in the War Department, to the vacant position.[751] Varnum came

744 Indian Office, Letter Book B, 104, War Department to William Davy, August 31, 1805.

745 *Ibid.*, 104, War Department to Davy, August 31, 1805; *ibid.*, 136, War Department to Davy, November 22, 1805.

746 *Ibid.*, 104, War Department to Davy, September 26, 1805.

747 *Ibid.*, 136, War Department to Davy, November 22, 1805.

748 Indian Office, Letter Book A, 94, John Mason to Davy, March 10, 1808.

749 Indian Office, Letter Book B, 218, War Department to Davy, May 12, 1806.

750 *Ibid.*, 304, War Department to General John Shee, Superintendent of Indian Trade, May 12, 1807; *ibid.*, 314, War Department to Jouett, May 19, 1807.

751 *Ibid.*, 318, War Department to Shee, June 6, 1807.

highly recommended by his superiors, and his services as factor gave equal satisfaction to his new employer. "No young man possess[es] more purity of morals or integrity of Character," wrote his superior at the time he was appointed to his new position, and he further expressed the conviction that Varnum would perform his new duties with "perfect fidelity."[752]

Varnum took up his new work at Chicago the last of August. The invoice of the household furniture belonging to the factory made on this date by Jouett and Kinzie is still preserved.[753] His predecessors had not made use of the full $200 allowed for this purpose, apparently, for the invoice shows the total original cost of the equipment to have been $142.87. The appraisers estimated the present value of the articles at about 80 per cent of the original cost. The meager equipment included six chairs, one table, and one camp and two cot bedsteads; the most prominent items among the kitchen utensils being two brass and four tin kettles, valued at fifteen dollars.

In 1808 it was decided to establish a factory at Mackinac. Under the impression that Varnum preferred this station to the one at Chicago the appointment was made, and Matthew Irwin of Philadelphia was designated to succeed Varnum at Chicago.[754] Varnum, too late, protested against his transfer, preferring to remain at Chicago, but the appointment of Irwin had already been made, and it was decided that the arrangement could not be altered. Irwin's salary and subsistence was fixed at $1,165, $200 less than his predecessor had been given.[755] He was expected to proceed to Chicago at once, and to arrive there in time to permit Varnum to open the factory at Mackinac the same season. This plan miscarried, however. Irwin in charge of a consignment of goods went as far as Albany; here the goods were stored and the factor returned to Philadelphia to pass the winter. In the spring

[752] Indian Office, Letter Book B. The letter is unsigned but probably was written by Dearborn.

[753] Department of Indian Trade, Chicago invoice book.

[754] Indian Office, Letter Book A, 196, John Mason to Matthew Irwin, August 8, 1808; Letter Book B, 436, War Department to Irwin, May 6, 1809.

[755] Indian Office, Letter Book A, 196, Mason to Irwin, August 8, 1808.

of 1809 he again started for Chicago.[756] His tenure as factor lasted three years. The outbreak of war in 1812 terminated the usefulness of the factory for the time being, and Irwin proceeded to wind up its affairs. The stock of furs on hand was sent by vessel to Mackinac, only to fall into the hands of the British. On July 5 Irwin left Chicago, having closed the storehouse and delivered the keys to Doctor Van Voorhis.[757]

With the plans for the restoration of the Chicago factory after the war Irwin was again appointed factor, but before the factory had actually been established his appointment was changed from Chicago to Green Bay. His was the only incumbency of the latter factory, his service there continuing from its establishment in 1816 to the abandonment of the factory system six years later. Irwin returned to Pennsylvania, his native state, where he died in 1845.[758] He was of medium height, well proportioned, "of pleasing deportment, and quite interesting and popular in his address."

From the records of the Department of Indian Trade, and the reports of the Superintendent printed in the volumes of the American State Papers devoted to Indian affairs, considerable information concerning the operations of the Chicago factory can be gleaned. The buildings of the factory cost $1,000, and the value of the furniture prior to the war was placed at $134.31.[759] The operations for the four-year period ending September 30, 1811, produced a profit of $3,454.24.[760] This favorable showing was due to the fact that the peltries received at the Chicago factory consisted chiefly of hatters' furs on which a profit was made, and shaved deer skins, which deteriorated comparatively little in handling.[761] For the year ending April 1, 1812, the business done at Chicago showed a profit of $1,773.94, a larger gain than for any similar period thus far.[762] At the last mentioned

[756] *Ibid.*, 348, Mason to Irwin, May 6, 1809.

[757] Indian Office, Letter Book C, 131, Mason to Irwin, February 9, 1813.

[758] For a sketch of Irwin's life see *Wisconsin Historical Collections*, VII, 269–70.

[759] *American State Papers, Indian Affairs*, I, 770, 792.

[760] *Ibid.*, 792. [761] *Ibid.*, 788, 792. [762] *Ibid.*, II, 40.

date the stock on hand amounted to almost $12,500, and the total value of the stock, buildings, peltries, and other assets was $13,727.15. When Fort Dearborn was evacuated in the following August, Captain Heald distributed the merchandise of the factory, amounting in value to more than $6,000, among the Indians. Prior to this nearly $5,000 worth of peltries and furs had been shipped to Mackinac, all of which, like the peltries belonging to Kinzie and Forsyth, fell into the hands of the British. Together with the loss incurred through debts owed by the Indians or by members of the Fort Dearborn garrison, and the destruction of the buildings and furniture of the factory, the total loss of the Chicago factory was $13,074.47.[763]

That the operations of the Chicago factory prior to the War of 1812 were, on the whole, successful, can scarcely be doubted. The realization of a profit from the Indian trade had never entered into the calculations of the founders of the factory system, yet, as has been shown, a steady profit was realized from the Chicago factory, at least from the year 1807 on. How well the factory fulfilled its primary function of regulating the prices of the private traders is significantly shown by the unconscious testimony of Black Partridge and Petchaho, the latter the brother and successor of Gomo, the head chief of the Illinois River Pottawatomies. In 1814 they complained to Thomas Forsyth, who visited them as a representative of the United States Indian Department, of the high prices of goods in the sutler's store at Fort Clark. They pleaded that the United States take pity on them and establish a factory at Fort Clark, and expressed the hope that they would be able to get goods as cheap in this way "as they formerly did in the factory at Chicago."[764] At another time Forsyth himself, than whom no one was more familiar with the conditions affecting the Indian trade in Illinois, stated that no one who bought his goods in this country could sell them as cheaply as the factories. The British traders only could oppose the factories, and this was

763 *American State Papers, Indian Affairs*, II, 59.

764 *Wisconsin Historical Collections*, XI, 337.

possible because of their extensive credit, and the superior quality of their goods.[765]

From the time of its re-establishment in 1816 the factory was conducted at Chicago until the abolition of the government trading-house system in 1822; but the Chicago factory did not acquire during this time the trade and influence enjoyed by the first factory in the period before the War of 1812. The reasons for this failure to recover the old-time influence will be set forth in connection with the consideration of the failure and abolition of the factory system as a whole.

We have seen that the system of government trading houses was entered upon as an experiment, and that as such it was renewed from time to time. Congress never abolished the earlier system of licensed private traders, and never gave a whole-hearted support to the competing system. Herein lay the chief cause of the ultimate failure of the experiment, and here, too, is to be found the principal reason for the limited degree of influence and success achieved by the government trading houses during its continuance. Upon the formation of the American Fur Company by John Jacob Astor, that powerful corporation, operating from Mackinac as a center, undertook to monopolize the Indian trade of the Northwest. There ensued for a few years the most vigorous exploitation of the fur trade which this region ever witnessed. The American Fur Company, in connection with other private traders, was antagonized by the government factory system, and consequently left no stone unturned to overthrow it. Partly because of this, but in part from the operation of other factors, to be noted in their place, the trade of the Chicago and Green Bay factories largely disappeared prior to 1820; and it had been decided, in fact, to discontinue them and establish a new one on the St. Peter's River when Congress, under the urging of Senator Benton, decided in 1822 to abolish the entire factory system.

The system of government trading houses had been established under the influence of a twofold motive. The primary

[765] *Ibid.*, XI, 344.

consideration of the government's Indian policy was the maintenance of peace on the frontier. This could best be accomplished by rendering the Indian contented, and by freeing him from the influence of foreigners. Not merely his happiness, but his very existence depended upon his securing from the whites those articles which he needed but which he himself could not produce; and since the private traders took advantage of his weakness and ignorance to exploit him outrageously in the conduct of the Indian trade, it was argued that the welfare of the Indian would be directly promoted, and indirectly the peace of the frontier be conserved, by the establishment of government trading houses upon the principles that have been indicated.

The theory underlying the government factory system seemed sound, but in practice several obstacles to its successful working, powerful enough in the aggregate to cause its abandonment, were encountered. Not until 1816 was an act passed excluding foreigners from the trade, and even then such exceptions were allowed as to render the prohibition of little value.[766] The amount of money devoted to the factory system was never sufficient to permit its extension to more than a small proportion of the tribes. However well conducted the business may have been, this fact alone would have prevented the attainment of the larger measure of benefit that had been anticipated.

Another and inherent cause of failure lay in the difficulty of public operation of a business so special and highly complicated in character as the conduct of the Indian trade. Great shrewdness, intimate knowledge of the native character, and a willingness to endure great privations were among the qualifications essential to its successful prosecution. The private trader was at home with the red man, his livelihood depended upon his exertions, and he was free from the moral restraints which governed the conduct of the government factor. Above all he was his own master, free to adapt his course to the exigencies of the moment; the factor was hampered by regulations prescribed by a super-

[766] See report of the Committee on Indian Affairs to Congress in 1817, in *American State Papers, Indian Affairs*, II, 127; Irwin-McKenney correspondence and report of Jedediah Morse in *Wisconsin Historical Collections*, VII, 269 ff.

intendent who resided far distant from the western country; and he, in turn, by a Congress which commonly turned a deaf ear to his repeated appeals for amendment of the act governing the conduct of the trade. The factor's income was assured, regardless of the amount of trade he secured; nor was he affected by losses due to errors of judgment on his part, as was the private trader. Too often he had, at the time of his appointment, no acquaintance with the Indian or with the business put in his charge. To instance a single case, Jacob Varnum at the time of his appointment to the Sandusky factory was a native of rural New England, who had neither asked for nor desired such an appointment. It is doubtful whether he had ever seen an Indian, and he was certainly entirely without mercantile experience; yet he had for competitors such men as John Kinzie, Thomas Forsyth, and Antoine De Champs, men who had spent practically their whole lives in the Indian trade.

The goods for the government trade must be bought in the United States, and the peltries secured in its conduct must be sold here. This worked disaster to the enterprise in various ways. From their long experience in supplying the Indian trade the English had become expert in the production of articles suited to the red man's taste. It was impossible for the government, buying in the United States, to match, in quality and in attractiveness to the Indian, the goods of the Canadian trader. Even if English goods were purchased of American importers, the factory system was handicapped by reason of the higher price which must be paid. On the other hand the prohibition against the exportation of peltries compelled the superintendent of the trade to dispose of them in the American market. Experience proved that the domestic demand for peltries, particularly for deer skins, did not equal the supply; so that the restriction frequently occasioned financial loss. But there were further restrictions in the act of 1806 which narrowed the choice of a market even within the United States.[767] That these restrictions

[767] Report of the Superintendent of Indian Trade, January 16, 1809, *American State Papers, Indian Affairs*, I, 756; for the act of 1806 see *Annals of Congress*, 9th Congress, 1st session, 1287–90.

would operate to diminish the business, and accordingly the influence of the government trading houses, is obvious.

Another group of restrictions worked injury to the factory system through their failure to accommodate the habits and desires of the Indian. To trade with the government the Indian must come to the factory. The private trader took his goods to the Indian. The red man was notably lacking in prudence and thrift, and was careless and heedless of the future. He was, too, a migratory being, his winters being devoted to the annual hunt, which frequently carried him several hundred miles away from his summer residence. Before setting out on such a hunt he must secure a suitable equipment of supplies. Since he never had money accumulated, this must be obtained on credit and be paid for with the proceeds of the ensuing winter's hunt. The factor was prohibited, for the most part, from extending such credit; the private trader willingly granted it, and furthermore he frequently followed the Indian on his hunt to collect his pay as fast as the furs were taken. In such cases as the factor did extend credit to the Indian, the private trader often succeeded in wheedling him out of the proceeds of his hunt, leaving him nothing with which to discharge his debt to the factor.

The greatest advantage, perhaps, enjoyed by the private trader involved at the same time the most disgraceful feature connected with the Indian trade. From the first association of the Indian with the white race his love of liquor proved his greatest curse. The literature of the subject abounds in narrations of this weakness, and the unscrupulous way in which the white man took advantage of it. For liquor the Indian would barter his all. It constituted an indispensable part of the trader's outfit, and all of the government's prohibitions against its use in the Indian trade were in vain, as had been those of the French and British governments before it. The Indians themselves realized their fatal weakness, but although they frequently protested against the bringing of liquor to them, they were powerless to overcome it. The factor had no whisky for the Indian, and consequently the private trader secured his trade.

The remedy for this state of affairs is obvious. Either the government should have monopolized the Indian trade, at the same time extending the factory system to supply its demands; or else the factory system should have been abandoned and the trade left entirely to private individuals under suitable governmental regulation. The former course had been urged upon Congress at various times, but no disposition to adopt it had ever been manifested. The time had now arrived to adopt the other alternative. Soon after Thomas Hart Benton entered the Senate he urged upon Calhoun, then Secretary of War, the abolition of the factory system. Calhoun's opinion of the Superintendent of Indian Trade, Thomas L. McKenney, was such that he did not credit Benton's charges of gross mismanagement, and accordingly he refused to countenance the proposition.[768] This refusal led Benton to make an assault upon the system in the Senate.[769] In this two advantages favored his success: as the inhabitant of a frontier state he was presumed to have personal knowledge of the abuses of the system he was attacking; and as a member of the Committee on Indian Affairs he was specially charged with the legislative oversight of matters pertaining to the Indians.

Benton believed and labored to show that the original purpose of the government trading houses had been lost sight of; that the administration of the system had been marked by stupidity and fraud; that the East had been preferred to the West by the Superintendent of Indian Trade in making purchases and sales; in short that the factory system constituted a great abuse, the continued maintenance of which was desired only by those private interests which found a profit therein. In view of all the circumstances of the situation his conclusion that the government trading houses should be abolished was probably wise; but the reasons on which he based this conclusion were largely erroneous. His information was gained from such men as Ramsey Crooks,

[768] Benton, *Thirty Years View*, I, 21.

[769] For the debate see *Annals of Congress*, 17th Congress, 1st session, I, 317 ff. For the documents see *American State Papers, Indian Affairs*, II, *passim*.

then and for long years a leader in the councils of the American Fur Company. This organization had a direct interest in the overthrow of the factory system. Its estimate of the value of the latter was about as disingenuous as would be the opinion today of the leader of a liquor dealers' organization of the merits of the Prohibition party. In view of the charges of Crooks it is pertinent to inquire why, if the factory system was so innocuous, the American Fur Company was so eager to destroy it; and if a monopoly of the fur trade was so repugnant to the sense of fairness why was Crooks willing to see his company replace the government of the United States in the enjoyment of that monopoly?[770]

Benton's charge of fraud on the part of the superintendent and the factors failed to convince the majority of the senators who spoke in the debate, and the student of the subject today must conclude that the evidence does not sustain them. There was more truth in his charges with respect to unwise management of the enterprise; but for this Congress, rather than the superintendent and factors, was primarily responsible. It is evident, too, that in spite of his claim to speak from personal knowledge, Benton might well have been better informed about the subject of the Indian trade. One of his principal charges concerned the unsuitability of the articles selected for it by the superintendent. But the list of items which he read to support this charge but partially supported his contention.[771] Upon one item, eight gross of jews'-harps, the orator fairly exhausted his powers of sarcasm and invective. Yet a fuller knowledge of the subject under discussion would have spared him this effort. Ramsey Crooks could have informed him that jews'-harps were a well-known article of the Indian trade. Only a year before this tirade was delivered the American Fur Company had supplied a single trader with four gross of these articles for his winter's trade on the Mississippi.[772]

[770] Chittenden, *American Fur Trade of the Far West*, I, 18.

[771] *Annals of Congress*, 17th Congress, 1st session, I, 319.

[772] American Fur Company invoices of goods sold to traders, MSS in the Detroit Public Library. For similar invoices see *Wisconsin Historical Collections*, XI, 377–79; *Michigan Pioneer Collections*, XXXVII, 309–11. Mr. Lewis Beeson of Niles, Michigan, has several dozen jews'-harps in his collection of relics from the site of old Fort St. Joseph.

Although Benton's charges so largely failed of substantiation, yet the Senate approved his motion for the abolition of the factory system. The reasons for this action are evident from the debate.[773] Even his colleagues on the Committee of Indian Affairs did not accept Benton's charges of maladministration. They reported the bill for the abolition of the trading-house system in part because of their objections to the system itself. It had never been extended to more than a fraction of the Indians on the frontier; to extend it to all of them would necessitate a largely increased capital, and would result in a multiplication of the obstacles already encountered on a small scale. The complicated nature of the Indian trade was such that only individual enterprise and industry was fitted to conduct it with success. Finally the old argument which had been wielded against the initiation of the system, that it was not a proper governmental function, was employed. The trade should be left to individuals, the government limiting itself to regulating properly their activities.

Benton's method of abolishing the factory system exhibited as little evidence of statesmanship as did that employed by Jackson in his more famous enterprise of destroying the second United States Bank. In 1818 Calhoun, as Secretary of War, had been directed by Congress to propose a plan for the abolition of the trading-house system. In his report he pointed out that two objects should be held in view in winding up its affairs: to sustain as little loss as possible, and to withdraw from the trade gradually in order that the place vacated by the government might be filled by others with as little disturbance as practicable.[774] Neither of these considerations was heeded by Benton. He succeeded in so changing the bill for the abolition of the system as to provide that the termination of its affairs should be consummated within a scant two months, and by another set of men than the factors and superintendent.[775]

[773] See, for example, the arguments of Johnson and Lowrie, *Annals of Congress*, 17th Congress, 1st session, I, 339-44.

[774] *American State Papers, Indian Affairs*, II, 181-85.

[775] *Annals of Congress*, 17th Congress, 1st session, I, 318, 351, 354.

That considerable loss should be incurred in winding up such a business was inevitable. Calhoun's suggestions would have minimized this as much as possible. Benton's plan caused the maximum of loss to the government and of confusion to the Indian trade. According to a report made to Congress in 1824 on the abolition of the factory system, a loss of over 50 per cent of the capital stock was sustained.[776]

The journal of Jacob Varnum sheds some light upon the losses sustained at the Chicago factory, by reason of the operation of Benton's amendments. Varnum relates that A. B. Lindsay, "a hanger-on about the offices for an appointment for years," superseded him in charge of the factory. "After remaining in Chicago as long as his instructions would permit without making any sale or collecting the debts, he packed all the goods and shipped them to Detroit, where they were again offered for sale; and were finally auctioned off without a guarantee of any kind as to payment. They sold at good prices—the purchasers, not intending to pay, were indifferent as to the prices offered, and, what was foreseen in Detroit, no satisfaction of value was received by the government, and Lindsay, a man without a single business qualification, got credit for the prompt and satisfactory manner with which he had closed the business, and subsequently received an appointment in the Custom service."

These statements, coming from an interested source, should, of course, be subjected to due scrutiny; but in at least one respect they receive confirmation from Lindsay himself. In 1823 in the course of a congressional investigation into the closing up of the Indian trading houses, under cross-examination at the hands of McKenney, the deposed superintendent, Lindsay stated that he had never been engaged in the Indian trade, and that he did not know the proper weight of a three-point northwest blanket, nor what its dimensions should be.[777] It further appears from the financial statement rendered by him that though the property at Chicago invoiced nearly $16,000 he turned over to the government less than $1,250 in cash, the two principal items in his

[776] *American State Papers, Indian Affairs*, II, 513. [777] *Ibid.*, 420.

account consisting, in round numbers, of bills receivable to the amount of $5,000 and losses on sales of $7,000.[778]

The failure of the trading-house system constitutes but one chapter in the long and sorrowful story of the almost total failure of the government of the United States to realize in practice its good intentions toward the Indians. The factory system was entered upon from motives of prudence and humanity; that it was productive of beneficial results cannot be successfully disputed; that it failed to achieve the measure of benefit to the red race and the white for which its advocates had hoped must be attributed by the student, as it was by Calhoun, "not to a want of dependence on the part of the Indians on commercial supplies but to defects in the system itself, or in its administration."[779] The fatal error arose from the timidity of the government. Instead of monopolizing the field of the Indian trade, it entered upon it as the competitor of the private trader. Since its agents could not stoop to the practices to which the latter resorted, the failure of the experiment was a foregone conclusion. Yet it did not follow from this failure that with a monopoly of the field the government would not have rendered better service to the public than did the private traders. Lacking the courage of its convictions, it permitted the failure of perhaps the most promising experiment for the amelioration of the condition of the red man upon which it has ever embarked.

[778] *Ibid.*, 518.

[779] *Ibid.*, 181–85.

CHAPTER XIV

WAR AND THE PLAGUE

Almost a dozen years had passed since the coming of Captain Bradley's troops to Chicago to plant again the banner of civilization on the spot where savagery had triumphed in 1812, and nearly half as many since the garrison had been withdrawn from Fort Dearborn in 1823, when the humdrum quiet of the little settlement was broken by new rumors of war. Two Indian wars and a visitation of war's twin scourge of humanity, the plague, coming in quick succession, served to relieve the monotony of life at Chicago during the next few years.

The first of the Indian outbreaks, the Winnebago War, occasioned little actual fighting, but it filled the frontier settlements with alarm, caused the movement of several hundred soldiers, many of them for hundreds of miles, and was concluded by a formal treaty between the United States and the disaffected tribes. That it was not attended by more bloodshed was due to the prompt display by the government of an overwhelming military force which awed the red man into submission.

Driven to desperation by the encroachments and aggressions of the whites, and encouraged, possibly, by the removal of the garrisons from Chicago and Prairie du Chien, the Winnebagoes in the summer of 1827 were in a mood for war. The first outbreak occurred on the upper Mississippi toward the end of June. A keelboat, returning from a trip to Fort Snelling with provisions for the garrison at Fort Crawford, was attacked by the Winnebagoes near the mouth of the Bad Axe River. On the same day a murderous assault was made upon the family of a Canadian half-breed named Gagnier, living a short distance from Prairie du Chien.[780] The nature of the immediate provocation for the attack upon the keelboat is a matter of dispute. The assault

[780] On these events see *Wisconsin Historical Collections, passim.*

upon the family of Gagnier, however, was deliberately planned by a band of Winnebagoes, which had suffered great indignities at the hands of the whites.[781] The leaders of the band deliberated over their wrongs and resolved to enforce the native law of retaliation. The choice of the agent to commit the act fell upon Red Bird, a chief who was beloved by the Indians and respected and admired by the whites. Noted for his friendly disposition toward the whites, Red Bird undertook the commission of his band with the intention of pretending to fulfil it and reporting to his tribe that he had been unable to find a victim.

This plan, unfortunately, miscarried. Being upbraided for his conduct and taunted as a coward, Red Bird resolved to redeem his reputation and set out for Prairie du Chien, accompanied by WeKau and a third Indian, determined to execute his commission in grim earnest. The chance presence of an old trader at the house of Mr. Lockwood, which the party first visited, caused them to refrain from committing there the intended violence.[782] Crossing the prairie they came to the house of Gagnier, about three miles from the town. Here they found the husband, his wife, a babe of eleven months, and a discharged soldier named Lipcap. The presence of the visitors at first excited no particular comment. They asked for food and Mrs. Gagnier had turned to provide it when the bloody work began. Gagnier was shot by Red Bird and Lipcap by the third Indian, while Mrs. Gagnier engaged in a struggle with WeKau in which she succeeded in wresting from him his gun. He turned and ran and she pursued him, but overcome by excitement or fear, and finding herself powerless to fire the gun, she made her way to the village and gave the alarm. Meanwhile WeKau again entered the cabin and scalped the babe, apparently executing the horrible task with deliberation in order to secure as much hair with the scalp as possible. When a posse arrived from Prairie du Chien the murderers had departed; the babe was still alive and, strangely enough, recovered from its ghastly wounds and grew to womanhood.

781 *Ibid.*, V, 201 ff.

782 *Ibid.*, II, 161; V, 199.

In the same month of June, 1827, Governor Cass and Colonel Thomas L. McKenney were sent to negotiate on behalf of the United States a treaty with the Winnebagoes and other tribes of Wisconsin respecting the boundaries which had been provided for in the Treaty of Prairie du Chien of 1825.[783] On reaching Butte des Morts on Fox River, the place designated for the council, the commissioners found but a single band of Winnebagoes represented, and learned at the same time of the hostile disposition of the tribe and of the outrages committed on the Mississippi.

In this emergency Cass decided on a bold and energetic course. Leaving the camp at Butte des Morts in charge of Colonel McKenney, he himself set out in a large canoe manned by a dozen boatmen for the seat of trouble.[784] The route to Prairie du Chien led through the midst of the disaffected tribe. In his descent of the Wisconsin River Cass came upon the Winnebago encampment. Undaunted by the manifest signs of hostility which were displayed on his approach he landed and harangued the savages and persuaded them to smoke the calumet. As he turned to leave, a young brave sought to assassinate him, but the attempt was frustrated by an older man striking his gun aside.

On reaching Prairie du Chien on the morning of July 4 Cass did what he could to encourage the terrified settlers, who were gathered in the abandoned Fort Crawford in momentary expectation of an attack, and took into the service of the United States the impromptu military company which had been organized.[785] He then passed quickly down to Galena, the center of the lead-mining district. The news from Prairie du Chien of the Indian hostilities had spread terror and dismay among the

[783] Smith, *Life and Times of Lewis Cass*, 185; Young, *Life of General Cass*, 93; Schoolcraft, *Personal Memoirs*, 265–67.

[784] On Cass's trip see Schoolcraft, *Personal Memoirs*, 266; Smith, *Cass*, 185–90; Young, *Cass*, 93–96; Hubbard, *Life*, 150–51; *Wisconsin Historical Collections*, II, 166, 330; V, 156–57.

[785] For the occurrences at Prairie du Chien see James H. Lockwood's narrative, *Wisconsin Historical Collections*, II, 157 ff.

miners, who with one accord fled in wildest panic to Galena.[786] The roads were lined with men, women, and children in momentary fear of the dread tomahawk or scalping-knife, and the encampment of the fugitives on Apple River on the first night of the alarm was said to have extended four miles and numbered three thousand persons. Such was the state of confusion and panic when Cass arrived at Galena on July 6. Quickly enrolling a company of riflemen, it was dispatched on a keelboat for Prairie du Chien, while Cass's canoemen sped onward in the opposite direction to carry the news to St. Louis and set the regulars under General Atkinson's command at Jefferson Barracks in motion. The destination was reached in record time,[787] and soon Atkinson at the head of seven hundred troops was proceeding up the Mississippi River by steamer to the scene of hostilities.

Instead of returning with the regulars, Cass and his party ascended the Illinois River to Chicago. Fortunately for them heavy rains had raised the Des Plaines to such a height that it was possible to pass up it and across the portage to Chicago without disembarking from the canoe. In the course of this passage nightfall overtook the party in Mud Lake. Fearful of staving a hole in their birch-bark canoe, the boatmen anchored it by thrusting their paddles into the mud on either side. In this dreary spot, tormented by mosquitoes and with the rain descending in torrents to the accompaniment of intense thunder and lightning, the future senator, cabinet officer, and presidential candidate passed the hot July night.

The arrival of Cass at Chicago the following morning has been described by Gurdon S. Hubbard, who chanced to be in Chicago at this time, at the home of his friend, John Kinzie.[788] The inmates of the household were at breakfast when the sound

[786] *Ibid.*, II, 329.

[787] On the rapidity of Cass's descent of the Mississippi see Young, *Cass*, 96; Smith, *Cass*, 189–90; Schoolcraft says (*Personal Memoirs*, 267) that the entire circuit from Butte des Morts to Saint Louis, and back again by way of the Illinois River and Chicago, was made "in an incredible short space of time."

[788] Hubbard, *Life*, 150–51; *Caldwell and Shabonee*, in "Fergus Historical Series," No. 10, 41–46; *Wisconsin Historical Collections*, VII, 341–43.

of the Canadian boat song was heard, faintly at first, but gradually growing louder. Kinzie recognized the leading voice as that of his nephew, Robert Forsyth, private secretary to Governor Cass, and made his way to the front porch, followed by the rest of the company. Looking up the river they beheld Cass's canoe bearing rapidly down upon them, the boatmen keeping time with their paddles to the music of the song. It was soon at hand and during the brief stay which Cass made the Chicagoans learned for the first time of the outbreak of war and the outrages on the Mississippi. They learned, also, the reason of the unusual conduct of Big Foot's band of Indians at Chicago a few days before.[789] The buildings of the abandoned Fort Dearborn were at this time under the custody of the Indian agent, Doctor Alexander Wolcott. With his family he was living in one of them, while the others were occupied by several French and American families. The annual payment to the Pottawatomies had drawn to Chicago a large number of Indians. Upon receiving their annuity all had departed except a portion of Big Foot's band, who lived at the modern Lake Geneva. In the night following the payment, during a violent storm of wind and rain, the soldiers' barracks were struck by lightning and destroyed, together with the storehouse and a portion of the guardhouse.

The alarm of fire soon roused the little settlement, and men and women to the number of about forty turned out. The barracks and storehouse were seen to be doomed and so the attention was devoted to saving the remaining structures. Robert Kinzie, wrapped in a wet blanket, mounted to the roof of the guardhouse, which was already on fire, while the others formed a line to the river along which water was passed to him in buckets and other available utensils. Despite his burns and the danger he ran, Kinzie maintained his position until, about dawn, the fire was subdued. During all this time Big Foot's followers idly viewed the struggle, ignoring the appeals made to them for assistance. The next day they started for their homes,

[789] *American Historical Collections, loc. cit.*

but the subject of their strange behavior furnished food for discussion at Chicago, until the information brought by Cass a few days later explained it and their disaffection.

With the departure of Cass the inhabitants of Chicago assembled for consultation.[790] It was determined to send the chiefs, Shabbona and Billy Caldwell, to Big Foot's village to gather information concerning the plans of the Winnebagoes and the intentions of Big Foot's band. The friendly chiefs at once departed upon their mission. On reaching Lake Geneva they separated; Caldwell secreted himself near the town, while Shabbona entered it, and was promptly imprisoned on the charge of being a spy and a friend of the Americans. This he denied, pretending that having heard of the threatened hostilities with the whites he had come to take counsel with Big Foot's followers concerning the course of his own people. By dint of argument and dissimulation he finally obtained permission to return, accompanied by a number of Big Foot's band, to his village. Both Caldwell and Shabbona separately made their way back to Chicago and reported the result of their mission.

Their report plunged the settlement into a state of panic akin to that which had earlier seized upon the inhabitants of Prairie du Chien and Galena. A consultation was held, in the course of which Hubbard suggested that a messenger be sent to the settlements on the Wabash for assistance. Volunteers for this service were called for, but no one except Hubbard himself appeared desirous of undertaking it; against his going the objection was raised that in his absence no one else could control the voyageurs, most of whom were in his employ. Notwithstanding this, it was finally decided that Hubbard should go. He left Chicago in the afternoon and reached Danville, one hundred and twenty miles away, on the following day, having changed mounts about midnight at his trading house on the Iroquois River. The news of his mission was spread abroad, and a force of fifty men or more was quickly raised to march to the relief

790 *Ibid.*

of Chicago.[791] Before starting five days' rations were cooked. Many of the volunteers were without horses of their own. Most of these were supplied with mounts by neighbors who were to stay at home, but the number of horses available was insufficient to supply all the men and five set forth on foot. In other respects the company's equipment was even more inadequate. The food supply was insufficient and the arms were most heterogeneous in character. Squirrel rifles, flintlocks, old muskets, "or anything like a gun" that could be found had been seized, and some of the men had no guns at all. The latter, as well as those whose arms were insufficient, were supplied by Hubbard, who also issued flour and salt pork, from his trading house on the Iroquois River.

The march to Chicago was completed, after numerous vicissitudes, near the close of the fourth day. The Vermilion River was up, running bank full and with a strong current. The men and saddles were taken across in a canoe and an effort was made to compel the horses to swim. When the force of the current struck them, however, they would circle about and return to the bank. Provoked at the delay Hubbard mounted "old Charley," a large, steadygoing horse, and plunged in, the other horses being driven in after him. In the swift current "Charley" became unmanageable, when Hubbard dismounted on the upper side, and seizing him by the mane with one hand and swimming with the other guided him toward the opposite shore. During the march rain fell most of the time. The condition of the streams and the intervening country compelled some of the footmen to turn back, and two of the men with horses also abandoned the expedition.

The company reached Chicago in the midst of a tremendous thunder storm. The welcome extended by the settlers, who had been in momentary expectation of an attack, was naturally most hearty. If the narrator's reminiscences may be trusted,

[791] *Wisconsin Historical Collections*, narrative of Hezekiah Cunningham, in "Fergus Historical Series," No. 10, 47 ff. Cunningham, who was a member of the Danville company which marched to Chicago, says it numbered fifty men, while Hubbard gives the number as one hundred.

a touch of genuine burlesque was now added to the warlike scenes of the last few days. During Hubbard's absence the settlers had organized a military company composed of a few Americans interspersed among a considerable number of Canadian half-breeds. The former, perceiving that the Danville company was a better-looking crowd than their own, proposed to abandon their associates and join it. This feeling stirred up a quarrel, but the officers quelled the disturbance and the discontented men remained with their own command. The Danville company remained at Chicago a number of days, keeping guard day and night, until news arrived from Green Bay that a treaty of peace had been made with the Winnebagoes. In their joy over the good news the citizens brought forth barrels of whisky and other liquors and a general drinking bout ensued.

Thus hilariously ended Chicago's part in the Winnebago War. Its speedy and bloodless conclusion was due primarily to the energetic measures of Governor Cass. From Chicago he had passed up the western shore of Lake Michigan to Green Bay, and entering the Fox River had come again to the place of council at Butte des Morts, after a circuit of eighteen hundred miles. The prompt movement of troops from every direction upon the country of the Winnebagoes quickly convinced them of the hopelessness of resistance. From Jefferson Barracks, Fort Snelling, and Fort Howard, detachments of regulars converged upon the disaffected tribesmen, while a force of volunteers from Galena under General Dodge marched overland toward the Wisconsin Portage. On August 11 Cass concluded with the tribes concerned the treaty of Butte des Morts, which settled, for the time being, the boundary questions which had grown out of the Treaty of Prairie du Chien of 1825.[792] Although the Winnebagoes were parties to the treaty, the liberty was reserved by the United States of punishing the perpetrators of the recent outrages and exacting from them guaranties of good conduct in the future.

[792] *Treaties between the United States of America and the Several Indian Tribes, from 1778 to 1837*, 412–15.

The treaty concluded, Cass returned to Detroit, while the military continued its task of running down the culprits wanted. On September 1 the troops from Fort Howard under command of Major Whistler encamped at the Fox-Wisconsin Portage.[793] The following day three separate messages arrived from the hostile Winnebago encampment announcing that the murderers, WeKau and Red Bird, would be surrendered the day after, and begging the military not to strike. The murders at Prairie du Chien had been committed deliberately in accordance with the Indian law of retaliation. From their standpoint the murderers had perpetrated no crime, but had performed a meritorious and public-spirited act. Yet now that the white man's armies were at hand, they voluntarily surrendered themselves to save their countrymen from further punishment.

About noon of the following day a body of Indians was descried approaching Whistler's camp. As they drew nearer the voice of Red Bird singing his death song could be heard. The military was drawn out in line to receive the delegation and a dramatic ceremony ensued. On the right and slightly advanced was the band of musicians. In front of the center, at a distance of a few paces, stood the murderers, Red Bird and WeKau; on their right and left, forming a semicircular group, were the Winnebagoes, who had accompanied them. All eyes were fixed on the magnificent figure of Red Bird: six feet in height, erect, and perfectly proportioned, his very fingers "models of beauty"; on his face the most noble and winning expression; his every movement imbued with grace and stateliness; his dress of barbaric splendor, consisting of a suit of white deer skin appropriately fringed and decorated, and over the breast and back a fold of scarlet cloth; no wonder he seemed to the spectators, even of the hostile race, "a prince born to command and worthy to be obeyed."

The effect of Red Bird's presence was heightened by the contrast, in all outward respects, presented by the miserable WeKau. "Meagre—cold—dirty in his person and dress—

[793] Thomas L. McKenney's narrative, *Wisconsin Historical Collections*, V, 178 ff.

crooked in form—like the starved wolf, gaunt, hungry, and bloodthirsty," his entire appearance accorded with the conception of a fiend who could scalp a babe in the cradle.

Red Bird stood erect without moving a muscle or altering the expression on his face. The music having ceased and all being seated except the speakers, the latter began their address. Its substance was that two of the murderers had voluntarily surrendered themselves in response to the white man's demand; as their friends they had come in with them, and hoped their white brothers would agree to accept the horses they had brought in satisfaction of the offense. They asked kind treatment for their friends, and urged that they should not be put in irons. The spokesman for the whites replied with much advice, which was doubtless excellent from the white man's point of view. They were told that the prisoners should be tried by the same laws as the white man, and the promise was given that for the present they should not be put in irons.

At the conclusion of the harangue Red Bird stood up facing Major Whistler. In physique and bearing the latter—the same magnificent athlete who had bested the champion of the natives in the Fort Dearborn foot race a score of years before—was a worthy representative of his race. After a moment's pause the words, "I am ready," came from the lips of Red Bird. Advancing a step or two he paused, saying, "I do not wish to be put in irons. Let me be free. I have given away my life—it is gone"—stooping and taking some dust between his fingers and thumb, and blowing it away—"like that. I would not take it back, *It is gone.*" Throwing his hands behind him to indicate that he was leaving all things behind, he marched briskly up to Major Whistler, breast to breast. A platoon wheeled backward from the center of the line of soldiery, Whistler stepped aside, Red Bird and WeKau marched through the line, and were conducted by a file of men to a tent prepared for them in the rear, and the ceremony was concluded.

The fate of Red Bird may quickly be told. Together with seven others of his tribe who had surrendered themselves to the whites he was taken to Prairie du Chien and imprisoned to await trial on the charge of murder.[794] Their imprisonment was regarded by the Indians as a punishment worse than death itself. Red Bird bore his confinement hardly and at length sickened and died. WeKau and another of his associates were finally brought to trial, in September, 1828. They were found guilty and sentenced to be hung on December 26, but before the time set for the execution arrived both were pardoned by President Adams. The other prisoners were discharged for lack of evidence to convict them.

Although the Winnebago War was thus easily ended, it was not without important consequences. The Indians had been cowed, but not conciliated. The original cause for their dissatisfaction had not been removed; the aggressions of the lead miners continued, and the specter of white domination still menaced them as before the uprising. The confinement and death of Red Bird, whom they believed to have been poisoned by the Americans,[795] did not tend to alleviate their dissatisfaction, while the withdrawal of the troops after the brief summer campaign of 1827 emboldened them again. At the close of the year 1827 Joseph Street, the Indian agent at Prairie du Chien, reported to Governor Edwards of Illinois that the Winnebagoes were greatly dissatisfied, and would, in his opinion, resist the execution of Red Bird if they could induce any other tribe to join them.[796] The following spring news was carried to the British post at Drummond's Island, to which place many of the American Indians resorted annually for presents, that several of the northwestern tribes were planning an uprising against the Americans.[797]

To restrain the dissatisfied tribes between Lake Michigan and the Mississippi by the presence of an adequate military

[794] *Wisconsin Historical Collections*, XI, 366–68; VIII, 264–65; Smith, *History of Wisconsin*, I, 250–51.

[795] Speech of Nayocantay at Drummond's Island, June 30, 1828, *Michigan Pioneer Collections*, XXIII, 146.

[796] *Wisconsin Historical Collections*, XI, 366–68.

[797] *Michigan Pioneer Collections*, XXIII, 144–51.

force, it was determined permanently to regarrison Fort Crawford and Fort Dearborn, and in addition to establish a new post at the Wisconsin Portage.[798] To the latter was given the name of Fort Winnebago, and its garrison muster-rolls during the next few years contain the names of many men who later won national fame and reputation.[799] Our primary interest, however, is centered in Chicago. On October 3, 1828, after an interval of five years, Fort Dearborn was reoccupied by a regular garrison of about sixty men, comprising companies A and I of the Fifth Infantry, under command of Major John Fowle.[800] The Fifth Regiment had been stationed at Jefferson Barracks prior to the Winnebago outbreak. In connection with the general shifting of troops and the re-establishment of garrisons occasioned by that trouble, to which allusion has already been made, the garrisons at Sault Ste. Marie, Mackinac, and Fort Howard, consisting of detachments of the Second Infantry, were moved down the lakes to Fort Gratiot and Fort Niagara, while the Fifth Regiment relieved the Second in garrisoning the places named and in addition sent two companies to reoccupy Fort Dearborn.[801] The latter probably came up the Illinois River route. The remaining eight companies moved up from St. Louis by way of the Wisconsin and Fox Rivers, with the expectation that the march of so large a body of soldiery through the heart of their territory would produce a quieting effect upon the minds of the Winnebago and other tribes.[802]

For two and one-half years companies A and I of the Fifth Infantry continued to garrison Fort Dearborn. Major Fowle remained in command until December, 1830, when he was granted six months' leave of absence and Lieutenant Hunter

[798] *Wisconsin Historical Collections*, XIV, 70–71.

[799] Among others may be mentioned Jefferson Davis, David E. Twiggs, William J. Worth, E. V. Summer, and E. Kirby Smith. See on this the "History of Fort Winnebago" in *Wisconsin Historical Collections*, XIV, 75 ff.

[800] *Drennan Papers*, Fort Dearborn post returns, October, 1828.

[801] *Wisconsin Historical Collections*, XIV, 70; Wentworth, *Early Chicago*, 27.

[802] On the movement of the troops see *Wisconsin Historical Collections*, XIV, 70; Wentworth, *Early Chicago*, 27; statement of General Hunter in Hurlbut, *Chicago Antiquities*, 490.

succeeded to the command. He later became prominent in his profession and during the Civil War rose to the rank of major-general. At this time he was a West Point graduate of eight years' standing, who since his arrival at Fort Dearborn in the autumn of 1829 had wooed and married Maria Indiana, the daughter of John Kinzie. Captain Martin Scott, another member of the little group of officers in this period, was noted for his eccentricities.[803] He was famous for his skill as a marksman and passionately fond of hunting. Probably because of this trait, he maintained a numerous array of dogs. Both Scott and Hunter had been stationed at Fort Snelling, where each acquired a reputation for firmness, not to say obstinacy, in adhering to views which had once been formed. Upon one occasion they determined to find out by actual experiment which could abstain the longer from eating. At the end of two days Scott surrendered unconditionally; it was the general opinion of the garrison that Hunter would have perished rather than yield.

Notwithstanding the scare which had caused the regarrisoning of Fort Dearborn, the months passed into years without any occasion for the actual services of the soldiers arising. In the spring of 1831 the fort was again abandoned, the garrison being ordered to Green Bay.[804] Less than a year later, however, Major Whistler, who had seen the first Fort Dearborn built in 1803, was ordered from Fort Niagara to Chicago with two companies of the Second Infantry.[805] He arrived on June 17, 1832, and for the third time since its rebuilding, less than a score of years before, Fort Dearborn housed a garrison. The order for its reoccupation was issued in February, but before Whistler's force arrived the Black Hawk War had begun and Chicago and Fort Dearborn were crowded with panic-stricken settlers. The disaffected Sac leader, Black Hawk, on April 6, at the head

[803] For an intimate characterization of Captain Scott see Van Cleve, *Three Score Years and Ten,* chap. iii.

[804] Wentworth, *Early Chicago,* 30. An account of the breaking-up of the garrison is given by Mrs. Kinzie in *Wau Bun,* chaps. xxiii and xxiv.

[805] Wentworth, *Early Chicago,* 30.

of five hundred warriors and their squaws and children, had crossed the Mississippi River and begun the invasion of the state of Illinois. Therewith began for Illinois her last Indian war, and for Chicago and Fort Dearborn a period of excitement and activity on a greater scale than the place had ever known.

The Black Hawk War constitutes one of the saddest chapters in all the long story of the spoliation of the red race at the hands of the white. Notable for the number of men of national prominence in American history who participated in it, it is no less notable for the blundering and unworthy course pursued by the whites, first in bringing it on and second in waging it to a conclusion. The names of two Presidents of the United States, Abraham Lincoln and Zachary Taylor; of the only President of the Southern Confederacy, Jefferson Davis; of a presidential candidate, and for a full generation the most notable soldier in America, Winfield Scott; of senators and governors and generals in profusion—A. C. Dodge, Henry Dodge, John Reynolds, George W. Jones, Sidney Breese, Henry Atkinson, Albert Sydney Johnston, Joseph E. Johnston, David E. Twiggs, S. P. Heintzelman, John A. McClernand, E. D. Baker, William S. Harney, and Robert Anderson, among others—furnish ample evidence that no other Indian war in American history was participated in by so many notable men.[806]

The history of the war may be found in many places, and the design of the present narrative is limited to a recital of it from the point of view of its bearing upon Chicago and the results for Chicago's development which proceeded from it.[807] Black Hawk had planned his return to Illinois under the belief that the Winnebagoes, Pottawatomies, and other tribes and even the

[806] This list of participants is drawn from the *Drennan Papers*, Fort Dearborn post returns, and Stevens, *Black Hawk War, passim.*

[807] Many contemporary narratives are printed in the volumes of the *Wisconsin Historical Collections;* for the most part they should be used with discrimination. For a sane and useful brief account of the war see Thwaites, "Story of the Black Hawk War," in *Wisconsin Historical Collections*, XII, 217–65. Stevens, *Black Hawk War*, is a detailed and valuable narrative. In using it due allowance must be made for the author's too evident anti-Indian bias

British would ally with him against the Americans.[808] Before the actual crossing he was partly disabused of this idea, but only in part. His immediate purpose was to raise a crop of corn on Rock River, with the Winnebagoes of that locality, and prepare for active warfare in the fall. This design was frustrated by the action of the whites. Governor Reynolds promptly called out the Illinois militia, and early in May four regiments, numbering sixteen hundred men, accompanied by Governor Reynolds himself, were at Fort Armstrong, ready to co-operate with the small force of regulars under Atkinson in the pursuit and overthrow of Black Hawk's band.[809]

Meanwhile Black Hawk had learned in a council with the Pottawatomies that while Big Foot and some others were hot for war, the bands of Shabbona and Wabansia were determined to remain at peace with the whites. The news of Black Hawk's incursion spread rapidly among the scattered settlements, carrying in its train confusion and panic. Many of the settlers abandoned their homes and fled for protection to the larger settlements; some left the country never to return; others gathered for mutual protection within rude stockade forts, which were hastily improvised. On May 14 an advance division of the pursuing army under Major Stillman encountered Black Hawk and a small number of his warriors, and in the engagement that ensued the whites sustained a disgraceful defeat.[810] The raw Illinois militiamen, filled with zeal for the killing of Indians, rushed headlong into the contest, regardless of the efforts of their officers to restrain them. Although they outnumbered the Indians in the proportion of eight or ten to one,[811] their flight, upon receiving the first fire of the latter, was no less precipitate. For all but a handful, who fell fighting bravely to cover the retreat, the flight continued to Dixon's Ferry, twenty-five miles

[808] *Wisconsin Historical Collections*, XII, 227, 231.

[809] *Ibid.*, XII, 232–34.

[810] On the battle of Stillman's Run see *ibid.*, XII, 236–39; Stevens, *op. cit.*, chap. xix

[811] Stillman's force numbered three hundred and forty-one men; Black Hawk stated that he had forty followers, and Reynolds credited him with not to exceed fifty or sixty (*Wisconsin Historical Collections*, XII, 235, 237).

away, and many did not pause even here, but pressed madly on to their homes.

In comparison with the panic which ensued upon the news of Stillman's overthrow, the earlier panic of the settlers, from which they had already recovered in a measure, seemed trivial.[812] The terror excited by the exaggerated stories of the militia spread consternation, not only throughout the frontier immediately affected, but eastward into Indiana and southern Michigan.[813] Rumor multiplied many fold the number of Black Hawk's followers. From Dixon's Ferry, on the day after the defeat of Stillman, Governor Reynolds "by the light of a solitary candle" penned a call for two thousand more volunteers.[814] Shabbona and his friends, at the risk of their own lives, set forth to warn the settlers of their danger.[815] Most of them fled to cover. At Chicago, where the citizens had organized a militia company early in May, the whole surrounding population gathered within Fort Dearborn, with two hundred armed men on guard. Yet in the terror of the first panic an appeal was dispatched to the acting governor of Michigan for assistance.[816]

Of the scenes of wild confusion and fear which attended the flight of the settlers to Chicago and other points, and the hardships endured at Chicago, a graphic description has been left by one of the participants, Rev. Stephen R. Beggs.[817] He had recently settled at Plainfield, Illinois, when "the inhabitants came flying from Fox River, through great fear of their much dreaded enemy. They came with their cattle and horses, some

812 *Ibid.*, XII, 238–40; Beggs, *Early History of the West and Northwest*, 97 ff.

813 For a semi-humorous account of the panic in southwestern Michigan see Henry Little, "A History of the Black Hawk War in 1832," in *Michigan Pioneer Collections*, V, 152 ff. On the scare in Indiana see, e.g., [Banta] *History of Johnson County, Indiana*, 126 ff.

814 Stevens, *op. cit.*, 139.

815 *Ibid.*, 148; *Wisconsin Historical Collections*, XII, 39; Matson, *Memories of Shaubena*, 114 ff.

816 The muster-roll of the Chicago company is printed in Wentworth, *Early Chicago*, 64–65. For the appeal to the acting governor of Michigan for assistance see letter of Thomas Owen, Indian agent at Chicago, May 21, 1832, printed in the *New York Mercury*, June 6, 1832.

817 Beggs, *op. cit.*, 97 ff.

bareheaded and others barefooted, crying, 'The Indians! The Indians!'" Those of the adjoining settlements who were able fled with all speed for Danville, only a few of the men remaining behind to look after their property as best they might. Some friendly Indians shortly came to allay their fears, but believing them to be hostile, without allowing them an opportunity to explain, the settlers mounted horses and fled after those who had gone before. The Indians pursued, seeking vainly to correct the mistake, but this served only to increase the terror of the whites.

The residents of Plainfield at first determined to defend themselves. The house of Beggs was turned into a fort, the outbuildings being torn down to furnish logs for the construction of a breastwork. Here one hundred and twenty-five people, old and young, assembled. Ammunition was scarce, however, and they had but four guns among them. As the next best means of defense a supply of axes, hoes, forks, and clubs was requisitioned. A few days later the Chicago militia to the number of twenty-five, hearing of their plight, came, accompanied by an equal number of friendly Indians, to the rescue. The next day militia and Indians in separate companies set forth to reconnoiter along the Fox. At nightfall one of the whites and a few of the Indians returned, bringing "fearful stories" of having been captured by the Indians, and the warning that Fort Beggs would be attacked that night or the next at the latest.

This information precipitated a fresh panic. "The stoutest hearts failed them, and strong men turned pale, while women and children wept and fainted, till it hardly seemed possible to restore them to life, and almost cruel for them to return from their quiet unconsciousness to a sense of their danger." Immediate flight, either to Ottawa or Chicago, was debated, but after discussion was dismissed as impracticable, and the resolution was reached to remain in the fort and sell their lives as dearly as possible. Two days passed with occasional alarms, when every man was ordered to his post to prepare to meet an attack. Instead of the enemy, however, the Chicago militia appeared.

The joy of the inmates of Fort Beggs was tempered by the news they brought of the terrible Indian Creek massacre a dozen miles north of Ottawa.[818] The Chicagoans advised the immediate abandonment of Fort Beggs and retirement either to Ottawa or Chicago. The latter destination was decided upon, and the ensuing night was spent in busy preparation for the march. Early the next morning the company set out, escorted by the Chicago militia, and by sunset had completed the forty-mile journey to Chicago and safety.

Although Chicago afforded the fugitives a safe refuge, there was for them no cessation of hardship. The place was crowded to overflowing. Beggs and his wife were compelled to take up their abode in a room fifteen feet square, already occupied by several other families. The plight of the inmates under such conditions may easily be imagined. One afternoon in the midst of a violent thunderstorm a stroke of lightning broke open the end of their room and passed down the wall to the room beneath, leaving a charred seam within a few inches of a keg of gunpowder. The next morning Mrs. Beggs gave birth to a child. If the chronicler's statistics are accurate, fifteen infants were born during their stay at the fort.

Whatever apprehensions of danger the refugees at Chicago were still under must have been materially relieved by the arrival on June 12 of a force of Michigan militia under General J. R. Williams. Assembled at Detroit and other points in the latter part of May, they had finally pushed forward, after numerous vicissitudes arising from incompetent leadership, to Chicago, where they assumed for a short time the responsibility of the defense of Fort Dearborn.[819] This service was terminated by the arrival successively, on June 17, of the two companies of regulars under Major Whistler from Fort Niagara, and five days later of a regiment of three hundred mounted militia from

[818] This occurred on Tuesday, May 20, 1832. Beggs states (*op. cit.*, 101) that the Chicagoans brought the news of it to Plainfield on Wednesday evening. For an account of the massacre and the narrative of the captivity of the Hall girls, the only prisoners taken, see Stevens, *op. cit.*, 146 ff.

[819] On the movements of the Michigan militia see Stevens, *op. cit.*, chap. xxxvii.

Indiana. The Michigan troops were thereupon ordered to embark on board the "Napoleon" for transportation across the lake to St. Joseph, whence they were to be marched to Niles and mustered out of the service. Many of the settlers who had taken refuge at Fort Dearborn shortly began to depart, some of them under armed escort, for their homes.[820] Meanwhile from the seat of government at Washington the military had been set in motion for the scene of war, and Chicago became the appointed rendezvous for a larger body of soldiery than had ever yet been gathered here. From Fortress Monroe, Fort McHenry, Fort Columbus, Fort Niagara, Fort Gratiot, Fort Brady, and other places infantry and artillery to the number of one thousand men were started for Chicago, and General Winfield Scott was ordered from the seaboard to take charge of the operations against Black Hawk.[821] Three weeks after the arrival of Major Whistler's detachment General Scott arrived. With him, too, came a peril before which the menace of the hostile Indians paled into insignificance. Instead of peace and tranquillity, the settlers were plunged anew into panic by the appearance in their midst of the dreaded Asiatic cholera.

From Europe where it had prevailed for many weeks the cholera crossed the ocean, making its first appearance in America at Quebec in the early part of June.[822] From here it quickly passed up the St. Lawrence to Montreal and then southward to Albany. The legislature of New York met in special session, June 21, to devise measures for preventing the spread of the disease, but less than two weeks later it reached New York City, and by July 4 eleven deaths from it had occurred there. The next day was observed as a day of fasting and prayer by many of the churches of the city but the plague rapidly increased in virulence and in the two weeks ending July 28 over fourteen hundred deaths occurred. By the end of August the disease

[820] Beggs, *op. cit.*, 104.

[821] *Drennan Papers*, copies of orders to the various detachments, and post returns of the troops sent to Chicago; *Wisconsin Historical Collections*, XII, 241.

[822] *New York Mercury*, June 20, 1832, November 21, 1832, *et passim*.

had practically spent its force in New York, but meanwhile the pestilential wave was passing southward and westward over the country. By late autumn it was estimated that one thousand deaths from cholera had occurred at Philadelphia and an equal number at Baltimore, and at New Orleans over a hundred persons a day were dying from cholera and yellow fever combined, a rate which, if continued, would depopulate the city in a year's time.[823]

During the latter part of June the various detachments of regulars from the Atlantic Coast were proceeding toward Chicago.[824] At Buffalo the troops embarked on board the steamers, "Henry Clay," "Superior," "William Penn," and "Sheldon Thompson."[825] While passing up the lakes the cholera made its appearance among the soldiers. More potent than the hostile red man, it disrupted the expedition.[826] Two of the vessels got no farther than Fort Gratiot, where the virulence of the pestilence compelled the soldiers to land.[827] The others continued, after a period of delay, to Chicago, where the troops were compelled to halt until the pestilence had spent its force and the survivors were again fit for the field.

The ravages among the men of the detachment of Colonel Twiggs which was landed at Fort Gratiot were so awful as to banish discipline to the winds.[828] Those of the command who

[823] *Ibid.*, November 21, 1832.

[824] *Drennan Papers*, Fort Dearborn post returns. Six companies of artillery from Fortress Monroe left New York June 26, and on June 30 were at Clyde in that state. Company E, Fourth Artillery, started from Fort McHenry, June 18. The route followed by the seaboard companies was by way of New York City to Buffalo and thence by vessel around the lakes.

[825] Letter of Captain A. Walker, October 30, 1860, in *Chicago Weekly Democrat*, March 23, 1861.

[826] For an account of Scott's expedition and the cholera outbreak see Stevens, *op. cit.*, chap. xxxvi; Scott's own narrative is given in his *Memoirs*, I, chap. xviii; additional material occurs in Wentworth, *Early Chicago*, *passim*; *Niles' Register*, Vols. XLII and XLIII, *passim*; the *New York Mercury* for 1832, *passim*.

[827] Letter of Captain A. Walker in *Chicago Weekly Democrat*, March 23, 1861; letter from an officer on the *Henry Clay*, in *New York Mercury*, July 18, 1832.

[828] Letters of John Nowell in *Niles' Register*, July 28, 1832; of Captain A. Walker in *Chicago Weekly Democrat*, March 23, 1861; letters from Detroit (unsigned) in *New York Mercury*, July 18, 1832.

were not stricken dispersed in every direction. Many, stricken later, died in the woods or along the roadway, the terrified inhabitants refusing them shelter or assistance. According to a letter from an officer of the Second Infantry, dated July 11, of Twiggs' three hundred and seventy men, twenty or thirty had died and about two hundred had deserted.[829] From another contemporary newspaper report it appears that the detachment consisted of both infantry and artillery, and that the great majority of desertions occurred in the former branch of the service.[830] Of two hundred and eight recruits, thirty had died and one hundred and fifty-five had deserted; while of one hundred and fifty-two artillerymen, twenty-six had died and but twenty had deserted.

No fatalities occurred on the "Sheldon Thompson," the steamer on which General Scott had embarked, until Mackinac had been passed and Lake Michigan entered. Before setting out for the Northwest Scott, anticipating an outbreak of the plague, had taken lessons from Surgeon Mower, stationed in New York, upon its character and treatment.[831] On Scott's particular steamer the disease broke out suddenly and with fatal violence. The only surgeon on board became panic-stricken, drank a bottle of wine, and went to bed sick, and, to quote the commander's grim comment, "ought to have died." In this crisis Scott himself turned doctor, applying as best he could the medicine and treatment suggested by Surgeon Mower. He himself states that his principal success consisted in preventing a general panic. From beginning to end of the cholera visitation he set the example to his subordinates of exhibiting no sign of fear concerning it, visiting and personally attending to the wants of the afflicted. In comparison with this exhibition of fearlessness, the courage required on the field of battle seems trivial.[832]

829 *New York Mercury*, July 18, 1832.

830 *Niles' Register*, August 11, 1832.

831 Scott, *Memoirs*, I, 218 ff.

832 The terror of the troops and of the citizens in the vicinity of Detroit has already been noticed. A concrete instance of the dread which the cholera inspired is given by Mrs. Kinzie, who was at Green Bay when the news of the approach of the plague reached

Some time after the Mexican War, Scott told John Wentworth that he had often been in the midst of danger and suffering, but "he had never felt his entire helplessness and need of Divine Providence as he did upon the lakes in the midst of the Asiatic Cholera. Sentinels were of no use in warning of the enemy's approach. He could not storm his works, fortify against him, nor cut his own way out, nor make terms of capitulation. There was no respect for a flag of truce, and his men were falling upon all sides from an enemy in his very midst."[833]

The "Sheldon Thompson" reached Chicago on the afternoon of July 10.[834] Since there was no harbor, and the bar at the mouth made it impossible for the vessel to enter the river, the troops must be landed in small boats, which was done the next day. The troops under Major Whistler, who had been occupying Fort Dearborn since June 17, were promptly moved out and on July 11 the fort was converted into a general hospital for the use of Scott's men.[835] During the night which elapsed between the arrival at Chicago and the landing of the troops the following morning three more of the company died and their bodies were consigned to the bottom of the lake. Years afterward the captain of the steamer recalled that their forms could plainly be seen through the clear water from the deck, exciting such disagreeable sensations in the minds of the beholders that it was deemed prudent to weigh anchor and shift the vessel a sufficient distance from the spot to shut out the gruesome sight.[836]

For several days the pestilence raged at Fort Dearborn with violence similar to that previously manifested at Fort Gratiot. The official medical report shows that two hundred cases were

that place. She relates (*Wau Bun*, 340) that the news was brought to her by a relative, "an officer who had exhibited the most distinguished courage in the battlefield, and also in some private enterprises demanding unequalled courage and daring." When he had broken the news he "laid his head against the window-sill and wept like a child." This effect was produced, not by the actual presence of the pestilence, but by the news of its ravages at Detroit and the fear of its advent at Green Bay.

833 Wentworth, *Early Chicago*, 37.

834 Scott to Governor Reynolds, July 15, 1832, in *Niles' Register*, August 11, 1832.

835 *Drennan Papers*, Fort Dearborn post returns, October, 1832.

836 Letter of Captain A. Walker, in *Chicago Weekly Democrat*, March 23, 1861.

admitted to the hospital in the course of six or seven days, fifty-eight of which terminated fatally.[837] The terror which the cholera inspired was due as much, apparently, to the rapid progress of the disease as to the high percentage of mortality which prevailed among its victims. The first soldier who perished on the "Henry Clay" was stricken in the evening of July 5 and died seven hours later.[838] On Scott's vessel, the "Sheldon Thompson," men died in six hours after being in perfect health. Sergeant Heyl "was well at nine o'clock in the morning—he was at the bottom of Lake Michigan at seven o'clock in the afternoon."[839] The author of the statement which has just been quoted gives a graphic description of his own illness, from which at the time of writing he was in process of recovering. He was serving as officer of the day when the "Sheldon Thompson" arrived at Chicago, and superintended the landing of the sick on board the vessel. "I had scarcely got through my task," he wrote two days later, "when I was thrown down on the deck almost as suddenly as if shot. As I was walking on the lower deck I felt my legs growing stiff from my knees downward. I went on the upper deck and walked violently to keep up the circulation of the blood. I felt suddenly a rush of blood from my feet upwards, and as it rose my veins grew cold and my blood curdled. . . . . My legs and hands were cramped with violent pain."[840]

Some interest attaches to the methods employed by physicians in treating the disease, especially in view of what transpired

[837] Hyde, *Early Medical Chicago*, 18–19. I have not had access to the original report on which this statement is based. Hyde says these two hundred cases occurred among "the Entire force of one thousand." This statement, which does not include Whistler's two companies, is evidently erroneous. The entire force ordered to Chicago numbered only a thousand men, and several hundred of these had already been dissipated through death and desertion, or by delaying at Fort Gratiot and elsewhere. I have not learned the number of men at Fort Dearborn at this time, but evidently it was much less than one thousand; the rate of sickness and mortality was, of course, correspondingly greater.

[838] *New York Mercury*, July 18, 1832.

[839] Letter from an officer of Scott's command, dated Fort Dearborn, July 12, *Niles' Register*, August 11, 1832.

[840] *Ibid.*

at Chicago. In general it may be said that on both sides of the ocean the medical profession was helpless to stay its course. In London over one-half of the twenty-three hundred and eighty-two cases which occurred prior to April 12 terminated fatally.[841] At the same time the deaths in Paris from cholera numbered several hundred daily. It was everywhere noted that persons addicted to intemperance were especially prone to fall before the disease. The first six victims among the soldiers on the "Henry Clay" were all intemperate men.[842] The surgeon who attended Scott's men at Fort Dearborn treated all cases with calomel and blood-letting. This proved so efficacious, according to his report, that he regarded the disease as "robbed of its terrors."[843] In view of the nature of the remedies employed, and the fact that fifty-eight of the two hundred cases admitted to the hospital terminated fatally, in addition to the deaths which occurred on board the steamer, the grounds for his satisfaction are not entirely clear. But few fatalities occurred among the men of Major Whistler's two companies, who had been removed some distance from the fort and were attended by another physician, Doctor Harmon.[844] Strangely enough he attributed his success to the fact that he did not employ calomel in the treatment of the disease. That some of the soldiers who came with Scott to Chicago were subjected to other treatment than the blood-letting and calomel described in the surgeon's report seems evident from the statements of the officer whose sudden seizure on board the "Sheldon Thompson" has been described. The doctor administered eight grains of opium to him and made him rub his legs as fast as he could; he was also made to drink a tumbler and a half of raw brandy. At the time of writing the patient described himself as "out of danger," but whether because of this treatment would be hazardous to affirm.

[841] *New York Mercury*, May 23, 1832.

[842] Letter from Fort Gratiot dated July 7, 1832; *ibid.*, July 18, 1832.

[843] Hyde, *Early Medical Chicago*, 19.

[844] *Ibid.*, 14.

The spread of the contagion at Chicago was checked before the end of July, and on the twenty-ninth of the month Scott set out, accompanied by a few officers, along the Chicago-Galena trail for the seat of war, leaving orders for Lieutenant-colonel Eustis to follow him with all of the troops who should be able to move by the third of August. Scott reached Prairie du Chien and assumed command of the army on August 7, only to find that the war had been brought to a close. The Illinois militia under Henry and Dodge and the regulars under Atkinson had roused Black Hawk's band from the wilderness fastness to which it had retired in the neighborhood of Lake Koshkonong, and hotly pursued it across southern Wisconsin, through the beautiful Four-Lakes country where the capital of the state has since been located, to the Mississippi River about forty miles above the mouth of the Wisconsin. Here on August 2 in the battle of the Bad Axe, which shortly degenerated into a massacre, Black Hawk's band was practically destroyed, and the war concluded. The red leader himself, seeing the end at hand, had deserted his party the night before the battle, and with a few followers had fled eastward to the Dalles of the Wisconsin.[845] About three hundred of his deserted band succeeded in escaping across the Mississippi, either before or during the affair at the Bad Axe, but half of these were shortly slaughtered by a party of one hundred Sioux, whom General Atkinson had sent after them. Of the band of nearly one thousand persons who had crossed the Mississippi in April not more than one hundred and fifty lived to tell the tragic story of the Black Hawk War, "a tale fraught with dishonor to the American name."[846]

General Scott's first act after assuming command of the army was to order the discharge of the volunteers.[847] On August 10 he started down the Mississippi by steamer to Fort Armstrong, intending there to bring the war to a formal close by the negotiation of a treaty of peace. The troops from Chicago, who were

[845] Thwaites, "Story of the Black Hawk War," in *Wisconsin Historical Collections*, XII, 258.

[846] *Ibid.*, XII, 261.

[847] Stevens, *op. cit.*, 247–48.

making their way, meanwhile, across Illinois to the seat of war in obedience to Scott's orders, were met at Dixon's Ferry by news of the termination of the war, and orders to change their destination to Fort Armstrong. Here, while awaiting the bringing-in of the prisoners, and examining those brought in to determine their share of responsibility for the war, Scott was once more confronted by the enemy that had wrought such havoc among the troops in the journey around the Lakes and at Chicago. About August 26 the cholera again broke out among his troops with all the virulence of a first attack.[848] Four companies of United States Rangers had been enlisted, one from Illinois, two from Indiana, and one from Missouri.[849] The Illinois company, while proceeding to the seat of war, had been, like Eustis' detachment of regulars from Chicago, directed to make its way to Rock Island. On the way down Rock River from Dixon's Ferry, the soldiers were attacked by cholera; some were left behind, ill, on the march, and others died after reaching camp near Rock Island. Whether or not it was brought by these troops, the disease soon made its appearance in Rock Island, the first death occurring August 27.[850]

The outbreak of the plague halted, for the time being, the progress of arrangements for the treaty. The Indians who had not yet assembled were directed to remain away until a new summons should be sent them, and those at hand were permitted to disperse. In this connection there occurred a striking exhibition of the red man's devotion to his code of honor. Among the prisoners whose cases were awaiting disposition were three Sacs who were accused of having murdered some Menominees in accordance with the Indian law of retaliation. Scott set them at liberty to seek safety in the prairies from the pestilence, having first exacted a promise that in response to a prearranged signal, to be hung out from a dead tree on the subsidence of the pest, they would return to stand their trial. The cholera having

[848] Scott, *Memoirs*, I, 221; *Wisconsin Historical Collections*, X, 231.

[849] *Wisconsin Historical Collections*, X, 231.

[850] Scott's Order No. 16, August 8, 1832, printed in Stevens, *op. cit.*, 248–49.

passed away the signal was displayed, and a day or two later the murderers presented themselves.[851] It is pleasing to be able to add that an appeal which Scott had already dispatched to Washington in their behalf met with a favorable response and that it was not necessary to take the lives of the men who esteemed their honor so highly.

Scott's measures for coping with the cholera at Rock Island were no less energetic and courageous than those he had already taken in dealing with the earlier outbreak of the plague. In a characteristic order to his troops, issued the day after the first death occurred, he recited the facts of the situation and commanded a strict observance of the proper sanitary regulations.[852] He stated that having himself seen much of the disease, he knew the generating cause of it to be intemperance. Every soldier, therefore, who should be found intoxicated after the issuance of this order would be compelled, as soon as his strength should permit, to dig a grave large enough for his own reception, as such grave could not fail soon to be wanted "for the drunken man himself or some drunken companion." This order was given, it was added, as well to serve for the punishment of drunkenness as to spare good and temperate men the labor of digging graves for their worthless companions.

The troops were camped in tents in close order exposed for several days to cold rains.[853] The groans and screams of the afflicted, audible to everyone, added to the horror of the scene. In the face of this situation the hearts of the stoutest quailed. Through it all General Scott ministered personally to the wants of the afflicted, officers and privates alike, freely exposing himself to disease and death in the most terrible form, and by his example exciting confidence and courage in all.[854] The ravages of the cholera were finally checked by removing the troops from

[851] Stevens, *loc. cit.*, Scott, *Memoirs*, I, 221–23.

[852] Stevens, *op. cit.*, 248–49.

[853] Captain Henry Smith's narrative, in *Wisconsin Historical Collections*, X, 165. The author was himself an officer in General Atkinson's brigade during the war.

[854] *Ibid.;* Scott, *Memoirs*, I, 230–32.

their camp on Rock Island to small camps on the bluffs on the Iowa side of the Mississippi.[855]

On September 15 and 21, 1832, treaties were concluded by General Scott and Governor Reynolds, acting on behalf of the United States, with the Winnebago and the Sac and Fox Indians respectively, which formally terminated the war.[856] The former were compelled to cede their lands in southern Wisconsin to the United States, and accept in their stead a new home west of the Mississippi in the modern state of Iowa; the latter surrendered an important tract of their territory on the western side of the Mississippi, extending northward from the northern boundary of Missouri. Thus was punishment meted out by the victors—to the Sacs and Foxes for their active participation in the war, to the Winnebagoes for the sympathy and covert assistance extended by them to the former. Black Hawk, the leader of the forlorn red hope in this disastrous foray, was taken, after several months' imprisonment, upon a tour of the East, with the design of imbuing him with a conviction of the futility of further resistance to the whites. Upon his return, shorn of all political power, he was permitted to live out the remainder of his life in retirement, the quiet and peace of which contrasted strangely with the tempestuousness of his active career. No better defense of his action in going to war with the whites can be made than he himself offered in the course of a Fourth of July speech shortly before his death: "Rock River was a beautiful country. I loved my towns, my cornfields, and the home of my people. I fought for it."[857]

Upon the conclusion of peace the troops which had been gathered at Rock Island were dispersed in various directions. The survivors of the six companies of artillery which had left Fortress Monroe in June for the seat of war returned to that place in November. Their return route from Rock Island was down the Mississippi and up the Ohio and the Kanawha to

[855] Flagler, *Rock Island Arsenal*, 22; *Wisconsin Historical Collections*, X, 166.

[856] *Treaties . . . . from 1778 to 1837*, 503 ff.

[857] Stevens, *op. cit.*, 271.

Charleston and thence across Virginia to the final destination.[858] On September 23 six companies of infantry of the Second and Fifth Regiments under Lieutenant-colonel Cummings left Rock Island for Chicago.[859] Seven days later the detachment was in camp, on the east branch of the "River du Pagan" near Chicago.[860] Evidently the "Du Pagan" was the modern Du Page. The next day Major Whistler's two companies of the Second Infantry, which were included in the detachment, moved into Chicago and once more took up their quarters in Fort Dearborn. Two days later, October 3, Lieutenant-colonel Cummings left Chicago for Fort Niagara with the two companies of the Fifth Infantry which had come from that place four months before to take part in the war. The destination of the remaining companies of the detachment which had marched from Rock Island to Chicago is not in evidence.

Thus the Black Hawk War passed into history. It remains to speak of the momentous results for Chicago and the country west of Lake Michigan which accrued from it. By the war the beautiful region of northern Illinois and southern Wisconsin was first fairly made known to the whites. "The troops acted as explorers of a large tract of which nothing had hitherto been definitely known among white men."[861] It has even been said that portions of the country which the armies traversed had previously been as little known to the Indians themselves "as the interior of Africa was to Stanley when he first groped his way across the Dark Continent." One of the Illinois militiamen wrote of the Four-Lakes country that if these lakes were anywhere else they would be regarded as among the wonders of the world.[862] On the shores of one of them stands today the capital of Wisconsin, and on the very spot over which the troops of

[858] *Niles' Register*, November 17, 1832.

[859] *Drennan Papers*, Fort Dearborn post returns for 1832.

[860] *Ibid.*

[861] Thwaites, "Story of the Black Hawk War," in *Wisconsin Historical Collections*, XII, 264.

[862] Wakefield, quoted in *ibid.*, XII, 252.

Dodge and Henry pressed in hot pursuit of the fleeing red men has grown up one of America's greatest universities. With the close of the war the East was flooded with books, pamphlets, and newspaper articles describing the newly discovered paradise. The result of this thorough advertising was a rush of immigrants to take possession of it. No other point in all the West profited by this as did Chicago. Her position at the foot of Lake Michigan, on the great highway of trade and travel between the lakes and the Mississippi, which it was expected the construction of the canal from the Chicago River to the Illinois, long under agitation, would shortly open up, secured to her commercial advantages which no other point in the Northwest could rival. Chicago became, therefore, the great entrepôt for the onrushing tide of immigrants. In turn the development of her hinterland provided the substantial basis for a trade, growing ever vaster, of which Chicago constituted the natural outlet and center. The fulfilment of the prophecy made by Schoolcraft a dozen years before that Chicago would become the dépôt for the inland commerce between the northern and southern sections of the Union, and "a great thoroughfare for strangers, merchants, and travellers," was at hand. The lethargy of a century and a half was about to be thrown off, in the birth of a new Chicago whose name was to become the synonym for energy, enthusiasm, and progress.

CHAPTER XV

THE VANISHING OF THE RED MAN

The Treaty of Paris of 1783 which closed the Revolutionary War gave the new nation whose birth it marked the Mississippi River for its western boundary, and a line through the middle of the Great Lakes and extended thence to the Mississippi, as its boundary on the north. Until Wayne's victory over the northwestern tribes in the battle of Fallen Timbers, in August, 1794, however, the grip of the red man upon the territory north of the Ohio River was practically unbroken. Certain treaties had been made, it is true, carrying cessions of land to the whites in this region,[863] but their validity was contested by powerful tribes and factions among the Indians, and the tide of white settlement was still confined to the country closely bordering upon the Ohio River. By the Treaty of Greenville, a year after his victory over the Indians, Wayne secured the cession by them to the United States of about twenty-five thousand square miles of land, comprising roughly the southern half of the present state of Ohio together with a long and narrow strip of land in southwestern Indiana.[864] At the same time, however, the Indian ownership of the remainder of the Northwest, aside from certain reservations which were specially excepted, was conceded. The extinguishment of the Indian title, thus formally recognized, to the soil of the Northwest required two score years of time and the negotiation of dozens of treaties. Its consummation marked the passing of the red man from the imperial domain of the old Northwest.

From the beginning of his term as governor of Indian Territory, Harrison pursued the policy of procuring by treaties of cession the Indian lands. This policy was pressed by him, and later by other representatives of the national government in the

[863] See *supra*, pp. 109–10.

[864] For a further account of the terms of the treaty see pp. 124–25.

Northwest, at every suitable opportunity. To the omnipresent land hunger of the whites the development of the agitation led by Tecumseh, and his brother, the Prophet, was primarily due. The treaties negotiated by Harrison at Fort Wayne in September, 1809, by which almost three million acres of land was conveyed to the whites, especially angered Tecumseh, who threatened to put to death the chiefs who had signed them.[865] His purpose to form an Indian Confederacy to stay the farther advances of the whites and the alienation of the lands belonging to the Indians was boldly avowed to Harrison at Vincennes in August, 1810. He viewed the policy pursued by the United States of purchasing the red man's lands as "a mighty water ready to overflow his people," and the confederacy he was forming among the tribes to prevent any individual tribe from selling without the consent of the others was the dam he was erecting to resist this mighty water.[866]

Tecumseh's dam, however, proved ineffectual to accomplish its purpose. As well might he seek to turn back the waters of the Mississippi as to stay permanently the westward tide of white settlement. By treaty after treaty the red man's birthright was pared away, until he had lost possession of practically all of the old Northwest. The methods pursued in the negotiation of all these treaties were similar. They will be sufficiently illustrated in the account of the two Chicago treaties of 1821 and 1833.

About the middle of the year 1804 the Sac Indians murdered three Americans who had settled above the mouth of the Missouri River.[867] Governor Harrison journeyed to St. Louis to demand from the representatives of the tribe to which the murderers belonged satisfaction for the offense. Advantage was taken of the situation to obtain from the Sacs and Foxes a cession of lands. By a treaty concluded November 3, 1804, in return for an insignificant consideration,[868] the two tribes ceded over fifty

[865] *Supra*, p. 191.

[866] Drake, *Tecumseh*, 129.

[867] Dawson, *Harrison*, 58 ff.

[868] Goods to the value of $2234.50 were given to the Indians, and the payment of an annuity of $1,000 was promised.

million acres of land in Missouri, Illinois, and Wisconsin to the United States. The portion of the cession east of the Mississippi included all the land between that stream and the Illinois River and its tributary, the Fox, extending northward to a line drawn from the latter stream to a point on the Wisconsin, thirty-six miles above its mouth. But this magnificent cession was ultimately to cost the Americans far more than the paltry sum stipulated in the treaty. Black Hawk and others of his faction among the Sacs protested that the chiefs who made the cession had acted without the authorization or knowledge of their people,[869] and the disputes engendered over the terms of the cession furnished the principal cause of the Black Hawk War.

In August, 1816, the Indian title to that portion of the Sac and Fox cession lying north of a line drawn due west from the southern extremity of Lake Michigan was revived.[870] At the same time the United States secured possession of a strip of land lying along Lake Michigan ten miles north and ten miles south of the mouth of the Chicago River, and extending thence in a general southwesterly direction to the Fox and Illinois rivers, so as to give the whites control of the route by the Chicago River and Portage to the Illinois. Control over this strip of land was desired to facilitate the building of the proposed canal. "Of all the Indian treaties ever made, this will be remembered when all others, with their obligations, are forgotten."[871] The sectional surveys of the country lying on either side of the zone included in this cession of 1816 were made at different times. The section lines were not made to meet each other, and diagonal offsets along the entire length of the Indian grant resulted. So long as the present system of land surveys endures, all sectional maps of this portion of Illinois will be disfigured by the triangular fractions which resulted from this error in the original surveys.

The various treaties by which the United States acquired the Indian title to the land of the Northwest were held at such places

869 Black Hawk, *Life*, 27–28.

870 Treaty of August 24, 1816, *Treaties . . . . from 1778 to 1837*, 197.

871 Blanchard, *The Northwest and Chicago*, I, 491.

as best suited the convenience of the parties to the transaction. Two notable ones were concluded at Chicago, the first in 1821, the second twelve years later. Fortunately for the historian the scenes attending the negotiation of each of these treaties have been described by witnesses possessed of unusual narrative skill.

The purpose of the Treaty of 1821 was to secure from the Pottawatomies a considerable tract of land in southern Michigan extending from Grand River southward to the northern boundary of Indiana. The United States Commissioners, Governor Cass and Solomon Sibley, accompanied by Henry R. Schoolcraft as secretary, left Detroit for Chicago July 3, 1821.[872] The route from Detroit to Chicago usually followed at this time was the overland trail, which necessitated a journey of about three hundred miles; the alternative was to go by schooner or other vessel around the lakes, which entailed a journey twice as long. Cass's party pursued neither of these routes, however. Partly because of business on the Wabash, partly from a desire to explore the country, it was decided to travel in a large canoe by way of the Maumee and the Wabash rivers to the Ohio and thence to and up the Illinois to Chicago.[873]

Several weeks later the party was at Starved Rock on the Illinois. Here the canoe was abandoned because of the impossibility of proceeding farther by water and the journey was continued on horseback. The last few miles of the way the travelers were almost constantly in the company of parties of Indians, dressed in their best attire and decorated with medals, feathers, and silver bands; all, like Cass's party, were making their way to Chicago to participate in the negotiations over the treaty.[874] The gaudy and showy dresses of the Indians, with their spirited manner of riding and the jingling caused by the striking of their ornaments, created a novel and interesting scene. Since they were converging upon Chicago from all parts of an extensive circle of country, the nearer Cass and his associates approached the more compact the assemblage became, and they found their

[872] Schoolcraft, *Travels in the Central Portions of the Mississippi Valley*, 15 ff.

[873] *Ibid.*, 9.

[874] *Ibid.*, 335.

cavalcade augmented and the dust, confusion, and noise increased at every bypath which intersected their way.

In all three thousand Indians gathered at Chicago to attend upon the work of treaty making. To accommodate this assemblage an "open bower" had been erected on the north side of the river under the guns of the fort to serve as the council house.[875] At the first formal session of the council, which occurred on August 17, Cass set forth in a short speech, the delivery of which was punctuated at every point by the "hoah," indicative of attention, the object of the government in calling the red men together. Without in any way indicating their attitude, the chiefs adjourned for deliberation. Two days later they were ready with their answer, which was delivered by the Wabash chieftain, Metea, the greatest orator of the Pottawatomies. With a mixture of boldness and humility he advanced a number of reasons for aversion on the part of the red men for making the cession desired, and concluded with a flat refusal of Cass's proffer. Speech-making in profusion followed, interspersed with frequent adjournments, in the course of which day after day passed away. From the point of view of the Indians there was no reason for hurry. They were being entertained and fed at the expense of the government, and it was natural that they should improve the opportunity to the utmost. Not only was the occasion an enjoyable one, but by assuming a recalcitrant attitude and prolonging the council a better bargain might be driven.

Some misapprehensions concerning the terms of a former treaty were effectually dispelled by the commissioners, the wavering and the stubborn were won over, and on August 29 the treaty was concluded.[876] The Ottawa tribe was to receive an annuity of one thousand dollars forever, while the Pottawatomies were to be paid five thousand dollars annually for twenty years. On behalf of the Ottawas the government agreed, also, to expend fifteen hundred dollars annually for ten years for the support of a blacksmith and a teacher and the promotion of the

[875] Schoolcraft, *op. cit.*, 337 ff.

[876] For it see *Treaties . . . . from 1778 to 1837* 297 ff.

arts of civilization. In similar fashion the sum of one thousand dollars was to be expended annually for fifteen years for the maintenance of a teacher and a blacksmith among the Pottawatomies.

The foregoing provisions were of general application. The treaty contained in addition a list of special reservations of tracts of land which were granted to individuals, usually of mixed descent. The story of the influences responsible for these provisions of the treaty afford a view of the methods by which the terms of such cessions in the Indian treaties of this period were ordinarily devised. The provisions for supporting the work of instructing and civilizing the Indians were due to the exertions of Rev. Isaac McCoy, the founder of Carey's Mission among the Pottawatomies, near the modern city of Niles. Unable himself to come to Chicago, he sent a representative to urge upon both the commissioners for the United States and the Indians the recognition of his project for establishing a mission among the latter.[877] Of more importance, he enlisted the support of Colonel William A. Trimble, who had recently resigned his office in the army and become a United States senator from Ohio. On his way to Chicago to attend the council he stopped at Carey's, and having listened to McCoy's unfolding of his plans and his need of aid to realize them, promised to exert his influence in the missionary's behalf at Chicago. Largely because of this championship, apparently, the provisions already recounted for the support of blacksmiths and teachers among the tribes involved in the cession were made. Shortly afterward McCoy received the appointment as teacher of the Pottawatomies, and his associate, Mr. John Sears, the similar appointment among the Ottawas, while the selection and control of the blacksmiths was also confided to McCoy.[878]

"To bring about such an arrangement as this," wrote McCoy, "had cost us much labor, watchfulness, and anxiety. Others, in their intercourse with the Indians, had money and goods with

[877] McCoy, *History of Baptist Indian Missions*, 113.

[878] Cass to McCoy, July 16, 1822, *ibid.*, 145 ff.

which to purchase their consent to measures to which they otherwise felt disinclined; but we had neither money nor consciences that could be thus used."[879] The significance of this statement becomes evident upon examination of the list of special reservations provided for by the treaty. The traders and their half-breed families and their descendants, shrewder and more influential than the full-blooded Indians, provided for their future welfare by procuring the reservation to themselves of generous tracts of land. That these special grants of land were obtained by the use of improper methods and influences, as McCoy has charged, can scarcely be doubted.[880] One of the witnesses to the treaty was Jean Baptiste Beaubien, the Chicago trader. It can hardly be deemed a mere coincidence that among the grants to individuals are included one half-section of land to each of his sons, Charles and Madore, by his Ottawa squaw, Mahnawbunnoquah, who had by this time been dead for many years. To the chieftain Peeresh, or Pierre Moran, who guided Cass's party from Starved Rock to Chicago,[881] and whose racial affiliations are sufficiently indicated by his name, was granted one section of land at the mouth of the Elkhart River, while two more sections were reserved for his children. "To William Knaggs, or Waseskukson, son of Chesqua, one-half of a section of land," reads another clause of the treaty. Reference to the list of witnesses who signed it reveals the name of "W. Knaggs, Indian Agent," and this individual acted as interpreter during the negotiation of

[879] McCoy, *op. cit.*, 113–14.

[880] The policy of bribing the leaders among the Indians was deliberately adopted by the agents of the government, including such men even as Lewis Cass. On January 1, 1821, Alexander Wolcott, the Chicago agent, thus addressed Cass relative to the contemplated Indian treaty and the expenses of his agency for the ensuing year: "To induce the Pottawatomies to sell their lands, particularly the district of Saint Joseph's to which they are much attached it will be requisite to bribe their chief men by very considerable presents and promises; and that should be done, in part at least, before the period of treating arrives, so that time may be given for its effects to spread through the body of the nation. . . . . In short, it appears to me that a small portion of the sum appropriated to the treaty can be disposed of in the best and most efficient manner in conciliating and securing before hand the principal men of the nation" (Indian Department, Cass Correspondence, Wolcott to Cass, Jan. 1, 1821). Cass in reply expressed his approval of the proposal.

[881] Schoolcraft, *op. cit.*, 321.

the treaty.[882] Pierre Le Clerc, or Le Claire, the half-breed who had assisted in negotiating the surrender of the defeated Fort Dearborn garrison in August, 1812, now received a section of land on the Elkhart, and his brother, Jean B. Le Clerc, half as much. Another participant in the Fort Dearborn massacre, Jean Baptiste Chandonnai, whose activities as a trader at Chicago and elsewhere have already received our attention,[883] was granted two sections of land.

Among the most highly favored recipients of special grants by this treaty were the traders Burnett and Bertrand, and their families. Burnett had married KawKeemee, the sister of the Pottawatomie chieftain, Topinabee, and Bertrand had also married a squaw. The success of these families in securing special favors for themselves from the Indians and the government is evidenced by the recurrence of their names in many treaties. Both Burnett and Bertrand were present at Chicago and exerted their influence in support of the commissioners at a critical stage in the negotiations.[884] John Burnett received by the treaty two sections of land, and four of his children one section each, near the mouth of the St. Joseph River. To the wife of Bertrand was given one section of land, and to each of her five children one half-section. To John La Lime, son of Nokenoqua, a half-section of land was granted. Presumably he was the son of the Fort Dearborn interpreter slain by John Kinzie in 1812. The latter was now sub-Indian agent, and assisting in the negotiation of the treaty. Whose influence was responsible for the special grant to young La Lime can only be conjectured.

The fatal love for liquor which was working the ruin of the Indians was significantly manifested during the course of the negotiations over this treaty. To their honor the commissioners determined not to supply the Indians with liquor until the negotiations should be concluded. This did not meet the approval of the latter, however, and in his speech of August 22 Metea gave expression to their dissatisfaction.[885] Cass

[882] *Ibid.*, 365.

[883] *Supra*, p. 277.

[884] Schoolcraft, *op. cit.*, 352–53.

[885] *Ibid.*, 350.

answered him with a spirited rebuke, repelling the implication of parsimony and showing that the liquor had been denied the Indians out of regard for their own welfare, that they might be able to keep sober and protect their interests in the negotiations. He concluded by painting the baneful influence of whisky upon them, and appealing to them to wait, if they were determined to drink, until a proper time. The rebuke was effective in quieting their importunities upon the subject until the negotiations were concluded a week later. Then their pent-up thirst for the liquor, which they had stipulated should accompany the distribution of goods, overcame their power of self-control. The aged Topinabee pleaded with Cass for the "milk" he had brought for them, but was told that the goods were not yet ready to be issued. "We care not for the land, the money, or the goods," he rejoined; "it is the whisky we want—give us the whisky." The whisky was shortly provided, and within twenty-four hours ten shocking murders had been committed.[886]

The inrush of white settlers which followed the close of the Black Hawk War made necessary the early removal of the Indians from northern Illinois. The Pottawatomies and allied tribes still held title to a large tract of land between Lake Michigan and Rock River and extending northward from the line drawn due west through the southernmost point of Lake Michigan. With a view to securing the cession of this land and the removal of its owners to some point west of the Mississippi, the last and greatest Indian council ever held at Chicago was convened in September, 1833. It was meet that every warrior of the tribes concerned in the proposed negotiation should attend the grand pow wow, bringing his squaws, papooses, ponies, and dogs with him, and accordingly several thousand Indians assembled.[887] From far and near, too, gathered "birds of

[886] Schoolrcaft, *op. cit.*, 387–88; McCoy, *op. cit.*, 116, 146–47.

[887] Latrobe (*Rambler in North America*, II, 201) says the number was estimated at five thousand. Shirreff says (*Tour through North America*, 227) "it was supposed nearly 8,000 Indians were assembled." Porter says (*Earliest Religious History of Chicago*, 71) that on the appointed day "Indians began to pour in by thousands." All three writers were in Chicago while the treaty was being negotiated.

passage" of the white race, representing every gradation of character from rascality to respectability.

The Chicago of September, 1833, was "a mush-room" village of a few score houses.[888] Most of them had been hastily erected since the preceding spring and were small and unsubstantial.[889] "Frame and clapboard houses were springing up daily," wrote Latrobe, the English traveler, who visited Chicago while the council was in progress, "under the active axes and hammers of the speculators, and piles of lumber announced the preparation for yet other edifices of an equally light character."[890] The one business street of the place was South Water Street, along which a row of one-story log houses sprawled westward from the reservation, its monotony only slightly broken by the two or three frame stores which the village at this time boasted.[891] The unwonted concourse of visitors in attendance upon the treaty taxed the accommodations of the place to the utmost. There were "traders by scores and hangers-on by hundreds."[892] According to one observer, a stranger to America, a "general fair" and "a kind of horse market" seemed to be in progress.[893] Large wagons drawn by six or eight oxen and heavily loaded with merchandise were arriving and departing. In the picturesque language of Latrobe there were "emigrants and land speculators numerous as the sand, horse dealers and horse-stealers—rogues of every description, white, black, brown, and red—half-breeds, quarter-breeds, and men of no breed at all; dealers in pigs, poultry, and potatoes; men pursuing Indian claims, some for tracts of land, others for pigs which the wolves had eaten;—creditors of the tribes, or of particular Indians, who know they have no chance of getting their money if they do not get it from the government agents; sharpers of every degree; peddlers,

[888] Shirreff (*op. cit.*, 226) gives the number of houses as about one hundred and fifty. Latrobe (*op. cit.*, II, 206) speaks of "the half a hundred clapboard houses."

[889] Latrobe, *op. cit.*, II, 209; Hoffman, *Winter in the West*, I, 199, 202; letter of Charles Butler in Andreas, *History of Chicago*, I, 129–30.

[890] Latrobe, *op. cit.*, II, 209.

[891] Porter, *Earliest Religious History of Chicago*, 70.

[892] *Ibid.*, 71.

[893] Shirreff, *op. cit.*, 228.

grogsellers; Indian agents and Indian traders of every description, and Contractors to supply the Pottawatomies with food."[894]

The few primitive hotels were, of course, utterly unable to accommodate comfortably the crowds of strangers who clamored for board and lodging. Latrobe characterizes his hotel, which was, apparently, the Sauganash, kept by Mark Beaubien, as "a vile, two-storied barrack," within which "all was in a state of most appalling confusion, filth and racket."[895] The public table was such a scene of confusion that the traveler felt compelled to avoid it. The French landlord was "a sporting character" and "everything was left to chance, who in the shape of a fat housekeeper, fumed and toiled around the premises from morning to night."

The character of the impression which the traveler forms is determined as much by his standard of judgment as by the conditions he actually encounters. Latrobe was a cultivated English gentleman, habituated to another manner of life than that which prevailed upon the American frontier. The picture drawn by Shirreff, himself a sturdy farmer, of Chicago's inns in September, 1833, is perhaps fairer than that of Latrobe; yet even when measured by his more lenient standards the conditions described seem crude enough.[896] His hotel was so disagreeably crowded that the landlord could not positively promise a bed, although he would do his best to accommodate his guests. His house was "dirty in the extreme, and confusion reigned throughout," but the traveler temperately observes that the extraordinary circumstances of the village went far to extenuate this. The table was amply supplied with substantial provisions, although they were indifferently cooked and served "still more so." At bedtime the guest was assigned to a dirty pallet in the corner of a room ten feet square which contained two small beds already occupied. But he was not to enjoy even this poor retreat without molestation. Toward morning he was aroused from a sound sleep by "an angry voice uttering horrid imprecations,"

[894] Latrobe, *op. cit.*, II, 206.

[895] *Ibid.*, II, 209.

[896] Shirreff, *op. cit.*, 228–29.

accompanied by a demand to share the bed. The lighted candle in the hands of the speaker showed that the intruders were French traders. Shirreff checked their torrent of profanity with a dignified rebuke, which caused them to withdraw from the room, leaving him in undisturbed possession of the bed.

The thousands of savages congregated to barter away their birthright presented an extraordinary spectacle.[897] Although several different tribes were represented, their dress and appearance depended upon individual caprice and the means of gratifying it, rather than upon tribal customs and distinctions. Those who possessed the means generally attired themselves in fantastic fashion and gaudy colors. As a rule the warriors were attired more gaily and were more given to dandyism than were the squaws. All of the men, except a few of the very poorest, wore breechclouts and blankets. Most of them added to these articles leggings of various colors and degrees of ornamentation; while those who were able disported themselves in loosely flowing jackets, rich sashes, and gaudy shawl or handkerchief turbans. The squaws wore blue or printed cotton cloths and the richer ones had embroidered petticoats and shawls. The various articles of clothing of both men and women were covered with gewgaws of silver and brass, glass beads, and mirrors, such as had from time immemorial been supplied to the Indians by the traders. The women wore ornaments in their ears and occasionally in their noses, while the faces of both sexes were bedaubed with paint, blue, black, white, and vermilion, applied according to more or less fanciful designs.

On every hand the camps of the natives were to be seen. The woodlands and prairies surrounding the village, and the sand hills along the lake shore, were studded with their wigwams, while herds of ponies browsed in all directions. Along the river were many groups of tents, constructed of coarse canvas, blankets, and mats, surrounded by poles supporting meat, moccasins, and rags. The confined area within was often covered

[897] For the picture that follows I have drawn on the works of Latrobe, Shirreff, and Porter, already cited.

with half-rotten mats or shavings, over which men, women, children, and baggage sprawled promiscuously.

The treaty-making offered to the red man an opportunity of indulging in an extended carousal. Supplied with food by the commissioners and with liquid refreshment by the traders, for the present his cup of contentment overflowed. Gossiping, gambling, racing, and loafing were the order of the day. "Far and wide the grassy Prairie teemed with figures; warriors, mounted or on foot, squaws, and horses. Here a race between three or four Indian ponies each carrying a double rider, whooping and yelling like fiends. There a solitary horseman with a long spear, turbaned like an Arab, scouring along at full speed; groups of hobbled horses; Indian dogs and children, or a grave conclave of grey chiefs seated on the grass in consultation."[898]

Of one of these "grave conclaves" a story has been handed down which smacks strongly of the age of chivalry.[899] Two finely built young men who were the best of friends, the sons of two chiefs, Seebwasen and Sanguanauneebee, were courting the same young squaw, the daughter of Wampum, a Chippewa chief from Sheboygan. The lovers had proposed to decide the question as to which should possess the girl by fighting a duel. Their fathers had submitted this proposition to a council for decision. The result of the weighty deliberation was that the youths should fight to the death, the survivor to take the girl. They were brought before their elders and informed of this decision. Their ponies were brought forth, their manes and tails were decked with ribbons, and the saddles and the duelists themselves with beads, brooches, and other ornaments. After the ponies had been driven once or twice around the council place, the duelists and their friends set out for the place of encounter, swimming their horses across the river, and drew up at an open spot on the north side. Crude flags attached to poles stuck up in the sand gave notice that a fight to the death was impending, while guards

[898] Latrobe, *op. cit.*, II, 210.

[899] For it see *Wisconsin Historical Collections*, XV, 460–63. The story as at present preserved was told to the secretary of the Wisconsin Historical Society by the son of the Milwaukee trader, Jacques Vieau, who attended the negotiation of the treaty.

were placed to clear a ring for the encounter. Outside the ring, alone, her arms akimbo and her attitude one of indifference, stood the girl over whom the duel was to be waged. The time was an hour before sundown, and four or five hundred spectators, Indians and white men, were gathered around.

One of the duelists wheeled to the right and the other to the left. Then their horses were brought sideways together, head to tail and tail to head. As the signal was given each fighter drew his long-bladed knife. A hubbub arose among the spectators as they clashed, the squaws rending the air with their cries. Thrust followed upon thrust, the blood spurting forth as each blow was given. The bloody work could not continue long, of course. Soon Sanguanauneebee's son cried out in his death agony and toppled over backward, his arm raised for a blow, his opponent's knife in his spine. A moment later Seebwasen's son fell over and died. The girl, bereft of both her lovers, at last manifested some concern, and wrung her hands in frenzy. The assemblage dispersed and the primitive tragedy was ended.

It is painfully evident from a study of the treaty and of the descriptions of the scenes attending its negotiation which have come down to us, that the public sentiment of the frontier had become demoralized by the opportunities for dishonest gain afforded by the cession of the lands belonging to the red man. Unscrupulous individuals were never lacking to take advantage of these opportunities, and others, who under a proper system of administration of affairs pertaining to the Indians would have scorned corrupt practices, permitted their honesty to be undermined by the influence of the example of their fellows in the mad scramble for plunder. The Treaty of 1833 afforded the last, and at the same time the greatest, opportunity at Chicago for individuals to enrich themselves at the expense of the Indians or of the government of the United States. Since both the red man and the government submitted meekly to the process, a carnival of greed and graft ensued.

A set of temporary plank huts had been erected on the north side of the river for the accommodation of the commissioners and their dependents, and a "spacious open shed" had been constructed, also on the north side, to serve as the council house.[900] The commissioners were Governor George B. Porter of Michigan, Thomas J. V. Owen, Indian agent at Chicago, and William Weatherford. About the middle of September they assembled the chiefs in a preliminary council and Governor Porter explained the purpose of the assembly, urging upon them the wisdom of acceding to the government's wishes. The chiefs received the proposal without enthusiasm, disclaiming any desire to part with their lands. The request that they return a prompt answer to the government was negatived with equal decision. The next day they indulged in a "begging dance" through the streets of the town. Half a hundred painted Indians on horseback followed some thirty naked savages on foot, as they danced, whooped, and shouted from the fort down South Water Street, stopping before each door to receive whisky, tobacco, or bread. To the pioneer minister of the gospel who reports the scene they appeared like the very incarnation of evil. Several days passed. In vain the signal gun from the fort boomed out its daily notice of the assemblage of the council, for the chiefs would not assemble. At length, on the afternoon of September 21 they were induced to come together. The council fire was kindled and the commissioners and interpreters gathered at one end of the chamber, while twenty or thirty chieftains occupied the other. The relative positions of the groups of white and red men representing the two races seemed to typify their relation to each other: "The glorious light of the setting sun streaming in under the low roof of the council-house, fell full on the countenances of the former as they faced the West—while the pale light of the East hardly lighted up the dark and painted lineaments of the poor Indians whose souls evidently clave to their birth-right in that quarter."[901]

For a few days longer the Indians refused the proffered terms. At length, urged by the agents and traders, the chiefs one

[900] For the further account of the negotiations I have drawn upon the works of Latrobe, Shirreff, and Porter, as before; chiefly, however, upon Latrobe.

[901] Latrobe, *op. cit.*, II, 214.

after another submitted to the inevitable, until, on September 26, the treaty was concluded. The real significance of the submission cannot be better stated than in the words of the talented Latrobe, who was a keen-sighted spectator of the proceedings. "The business of arranging the terms of an Indian Treaty," he observed, "lies chiefly between the various traders, agents, creditors, and half-breeds of the tribes, on whom custom and necessity have made the degraded chiefs dependant, and the Government Agents. When the former have seen matters so far arranged that their self-interest, and various schemes and claims are likely to be fulfilled and allowed to their heart's content—the silent acquiescence of the Indian follows of course; and till this is the case the Treaty can never be amicably effected."[902]

The treaty[903] provided that the Pottawatomies and allied tribes should cede their lands to the west of Lake Michigan and their remaining reservation in southwestern Michigan, supposed to contain about five million acres, to the United States, and within three years' time remove beyond the Mississippi River. In return they were to receive five million acres of land in the West for their new home; the United States was to transport them thither and pay the cost of their support for one year after their arrival; and the expenditure in their behalf of sums of money aggregating almost a million dollars was agreed upon. These provisions were regarded as very liberal on the part of the United States.[904] In comparison with similar treaties of the time this view was doubtless justified; but an examination of the disposition of the money which the United States was to pay confirms Latrobe's account of the influence by which the terms of the treaty were shaped. Except for a few minor bequests the entire sum appropriated was devoted to six principal purposes

[902] *Ibid.*, II, 215. An editorial in the first number of the first newspaper published in Chicago, commenting on the difficulties encountered by the commissioners in the early stages of the negotiations, says: "The various and clashing interests of the Traders were powerfully operating, and altogether seeme d, for some days, to render doubtful the accomplishment of this great and vastly important object" (*Chicago Weekly Democrat*, November 26, 1833).

[903] For it see *U.S. Statutes at Large*, VII, 431 ff.

[904] Porter, *op. cit.*, 72.

which fall naturally into two groups of three each. The sum of three hundred and twenty thousand dollars was devoted to the payment for twenty years of an annuity of sixteen thousand dollars. For the erection of mills, blacksmith shops, and houses, the employment of physicians, blacksmiths, and mechanics, and the promotion of civilization generally, one hundred and fifty thousand dollars were set aside; while the sum of seventy thousand dollars was devoted to educational purposes and the encouragement of the domestic arts.

This group of provisions, which were calculated to redound to the advantage of the red man, requires no discussion. The second group, from which he derived little or no advantage, calls for extended consideration. It was agreed that goods and provisions to the value of one hundred and twenty-five thousand dollars should be distributed to the Indians, one portion at the conclusion of the negotiations, the residue during the ensuing year. The sum of one hundred and ten thousand dollars was devoted to the satisfaction of "sundry individuals in behalf of whom reservations were asked, which the Commissioners refused to grant." A list of the persons thus favored, together with the amount granted to each, was appended to the treaty as Schedule A. Finally, provision was made for the payment of one hundred and seventy-five thousand dollars to various individuals to satisfy claims made by them against the tribes concerned in the treaty, "which they have admitted to be justly due." The list of claimants with the amount allowed in each case constituted Schedule B of the treaty.

It was in connection with the contents of Schedules A and B that the most striking display of greed and dishonesty occurred. Judged by the standards of the time, some of the requests for reservations were doubtless proper; measured by the same standards, too, some of the claims advanced were probably valid; yet there is no room to doubt that a large proportion of the grants to individuals under these two heads were improperly made. "It was an apportionment," remarks Andreas of the one hundred and seventy-five thousand dollars granted under Schedule B, "of the ready money of the tribes among all the whites who could bring a claim against an Indian. The honest debtor and the unjust and dishonest claimant absorbed the fund. How large a portion of it represented robbery, theft, and perjury will never be known until the great book is opened at the last day."[905]

Doubtless this is true, yet the impropriety of many of the claims allowed is patent even today. The story of "Snipe" and his claim for pay for hogs which the wolves had eaten is probably fairly typical of the groundlessness of most of these claims. "Snipe," whose real name, unfortunately, has not been recorded, was a farmer from the St. Joseph country, who came to Chicago in the same stage which brought Latrobe and Shirreff, to prosecute a claim against the Indians, which on his own statement of the case was improper.[906] He had intended to make a great deal of pork that season, but upon collecting his hogs from the woods, where they had run for five months, he could number only thirty-five instead of fifty-five. The Indians had been hunting hogs, he stated, and he expected the government agents to allow his claim for the twenty which were missing.

Due provision was, of course, made for the influential chiefs, who were frequently half-breeds, and either themselves engaged in the Indian trade or the descendants of traders. To Billy Caldwell and Alexander Robinson life annuities of four hundred and three hundred dollars respectively were granted. In addition, each was to be given ten thousand dollars, although before payment this sum was cut in half in each case. Besides these provisions Caldwell's children were granted six hundred dollars, and the children of Robinson four hundred. Pokagon, the St. Joseph River chieftain, received two thousand dollars. The families of Burnett and Bertrand, the St. Joseph traders, were well provided for. The various members of the latter family alone received grants aggregating thirty-nine hundred dollars. Jean Baptiste Chandonnai received one thousand dollars under schedule A, and two thousand five hundred under

[905] Andreas, *History of Chicago*, I, 126–27.

[906] For the story of "Snipe" see Latrobe, *op. cit.*, II, 188–89; Shirreff, *op. cit.*, 220.

Schedule B. Joseph La Framboise, a Chicago half-breed who ranked as chief, was the recipient of numerous favors. By the Chicago Treaty of 1821 he had been granted a section of land. Now, aside from a life annuity of two hundred dollars, he received one grant of three thousand dollars and he and his children another of one thousand. Numerous other bequests were made to individuals bearing the name of La Framboise, whose precise relation to Chief Joseph it does not seem worth while to attempt to determine.

Another pioneer Chicagoan whose Indian affiliations now proved valuable to him was Antoine Ouilmette. By the Treaty of Prairie du Chien of July, 1829, he had been given eight hundred dollars for losses sustained at the time of the Chicago massacre, and by the same treaty his wife and children were granted two sections of land a few miles north of Chicago.[907] Now he again received the sum of eight hundred dollars. Whether this was in payment of the same damages already recompensed by the Treaty of Prairie du Chien is not recorded, but in view of the identity of the sums involved, and the way in which the claims of others against the Indians which had long since been settled were repaid at this treaty, the supposition that such was the case does not seem at all improbable. To one daughter, Mrs. Mann, was given one thousand dollars and to another, Mrs. Welch, two hundred dollars; a third daughter, Josette, also received two hundred dollars, although this was probably at the instigation of John H. Kinzie. Finally, still another allowance of two hundred dollars was made to Ouilmette's "children."

Since the identity of "Snipe" is unknown, it is not possible to say whether his effort to secure compensation for his hogs "which the wolves had eaten" was successful. That a large number of traders and other persons were influential enough to gain more than generous recognition at the hands of the commissioners, however, is quite apparent from a study of Schedules A and B. Thus Jean Baptiste Beaubien obtained recognition on more than

[907] *U.S. Statutes at Large*, VII, 321, 604.

one count. His sons, Madore and Charles, were granted three hundred dollars each under Schedule A. His wife, Josette, received five hundred dollars under the same schedule, and her children, of whom, presumably, he was the father, received one thousand dollars. In addition to these grants, both Madore and his father received sums of money in payment of claims against the Indians.

But few of the traders who shared in the distribution of the public funds can receive individual mention. The disappointment of James Kinzie over the denial of his request for a reservation might be supposed to have been measurably assuaged by the five thousand dollars granted him in lieu thereof. Since Kinzie was of pure American descent, it is difficult to justify this grant on any ground of recognized propriety. The same may be said of the aspiration of Robert A. Forsyth for a reservation, which he was forced to forego for the more paltry donation of three thousand dollars. A claim which he preferred for the same amount under Schedule B was allowed, however, as well as another claim for thirteen hundred dollars, and in addition to all this he was made trustee of grants to various individuals amounting to many hundred dollars more.

It can hardly be regarded as a mere coincidence that the names of many of those who signed the treaty as witnesses on behalf of the United States should be enrolled in the list of beneficiaries under it. Thus, of those already mentioned, Robert Forsyth, James Kinzie, and Jean Baptiste Beaubien were witnesses of the treaty. William Ewing was secretary of the commission, and to him and G. W. Ewing a claim of five thousand dollars was allowed. Luther Rice and James Connor acted as interpreters. Rice received two thousand five hundred dollars under Schedule A, while various sums were granted to individuals bearing the name of Rice, whose relation to the interpreter there is now no means of determining. Connor was allowed a claim of twenty-two hundred and fifty dollars; and in conjunction with another man of the same name received seven hundred dollars under Schedule A. Thomas Forsyth witnessed the treaty and was allowed payment of a claim of fifteen hundred dollars. "J. C. Schwarz Adj.M.M." likewise witnessed the treaty, and "John C. Schwarz," who was doubtless the same person, received forty-eight hundred dollars by it. In like manner "Laurie Marsh" signed the treaty and a claim of "Lowrian Marsh" for thirty-two hundred and ninety dollars was recognized by it. George Hunt, another witness, who had been engaged in the Indian trade at Chicago a short time before, was given nine hundred dollars in satisfaction of a claim and seven hundred and fifty dollars in lieu of a reservation which he had requested. B. B. Kercheval, still another signer of the treaty, secured fifteen hundred dollars. Gholson Kercheval, who was the sub-Indian agent at Chicago, was one of the few witnesses, aside from the commissioners and the officers of the garrison, who received nothing from it. A year later, however, October 1, 1834, by an amendatory treaty signed at Chicago by a small number of chiefs he was granted two thousand dollars for services rendered the Indians in the Black Hawk War.[908]

It is, of course, conceivable that this payment was a proper one, even though the propriety of requiring the friendly Pottawatomies to pay for the services of the captain of the Chicago militia company in the Black Hawk War is not at this late day apparent. The largest single beneficiary by the treaty under Schedule B was the American Fur Company. Robert Stuart had come on from Mackinac to attend the negotiations and look out for the interests of his company in connection therewith.[909] Of the success of his mission some indication is afforded by the fact that over one-tenth of the total sum of one hundred and seventy-five thousand dollars awarded to individuals in payment of claims against the Indians went to the American Fur Company.[910] In addition to this, of the sum allotted to Jean Baptiste

[908] *U. S. Statutes at large*, VII, 447.

[909] Stuart was among those who signed the treaty. For his attendance upon it see Porter, *op. cit.*, 72; also Porter (Mary), *Eliza Chappell Porter*, 100.

[910] Robert Stuart, as agent of the company, received seventeen thousand dollars, and James Abbott, also on behalf of the company, twenty-three hundred dollars.

Chandonnai under Schedule A, one thousand dollars were, by his "particular request," to be paid to Robert Stuart, agent of the American Fur Company. While engaged in the Indian trade at Chicago fourteen years before, Chandonnai had received goods from the American Fur Company on credit, for which he afterward refused to pay. A part of the debt thus repudiated had been secured through Kinzie's influence. Apparently advantage was now taken of the opportunity presented by the cession of the Pottawatomie lands to secure payment of the remainder, ostensibly from the Indians but in reality from the government. The impropriety of requiring either party to pay the debts of Chandonnai is self-evident. Notwithstanding his "particular request," Chandonnai evidently could not be trusted himself to pay the debt, with the money of the government given into his possession, and so it was arranged it should pass directly from the agent of the United States to the American Fur Company.

The dubious character of the claims presented and allowed at this treaty is still further exemplified by the rôle played in it by the heirs of John Kinzie. Both of his sons, John H. and Robert A. Kinzie, attended the negotiation and signed the treaty as witnesses. The latter was at the time proprietor of a trading establishment at Chicago. John H. Kinzie, the elder brother, had a wide acquaintance throughout the Northwest, with the Indians and whites alike. He had been at different times in the employ of Robert Stuart of the American Fur Company, secretary to Governor Cass, and sub-Indian agent at Fort Winnebago.[911] He had recently resigned the latter position, laid out the land pre-empted by the family into town lots, and thrown in his fortune with that of the nascent Chicago. The interests of the Kinzie heirs, therefore, were advocated by influential spokesmen. Even the welfare of numerous half-breed dependents of the family was provided for. To the old family servant of John Kinzie, Victoire Porthier,[912] and her children, the sum of seven

[911] A sketch of Kinzie's career written by his widow is printed in Andreas, *op. cit.*, I, 97–99.

[912] For her connection with Kinzie see *ibid.*, I, 105.

hundred dollars was given under Schedule A. Her brothers, Jean Baptiste and Thomas Mirandeau, and her sisters, Jane and Rosetta, received among them the sum of twelve hundred dollars with the provision that John H. Kinzie should act as trustee of the fund. Thomas is the "Tomah" of *Wau Bun*, the lad who had been taken by Kinzie to Fort Winnebago the preceding winter to become a member of his household.[913] That Jean Baptiste had also been a servant of the Kinzies at Chicago is stated by the author of *Wau Bun*.[914] Another member of John Kinzie's household for whom a grant of money was secured was Josette, the daughter of Antoine Ouilmette. Like "Tomah" she was a mere child.[915] She had been a member of Kinzie's household since the spring of 1831. She was granted two hundred dollars and Kinzie was appointed trustee of the fund.

Of the one hundred and seventy-five thousand dollars paid out under Schedule B, over one-eighth was given to the four sons and daughters of John Kinzie and to his stepdaughter, Mrs. Helm. To the latter the sum of two thousand dollars was granted, while twenty thousand dollars were divided in equal portions among the former. In addition to all this, a second claim of Robert A. Kinzie for twelve hundred and sixteen dollars was allowed. Although there is no record in the treaty of the grounds on which the various demands presented were based, the improper character of these claims seems obvious. Whatever the basis of the smaller claim of Robert Kinzie may have been, the twenty thousand dollars apportioned in equal amounts among the four brothers and sisters must have been claimed by virtue of some inheritance from the father. The facts that two of the claimants were women, who of course had never engaged in the Indian trade, and each of whom had been for some years the wife of a government official; that the claims of all were equal in amount; and that Robert Kinzie presented a second claim,

[913] Andreas, *op. cit.*, I, 105; Kinzie, *Wau Bun*, 376.

[914] Kinzie, *Wau Bun*, 376.

[915] She was ten years old in 1831 (*ibid.*, 233).

which was allowed, all point to this conclusion. A claim for damages at the hands of the Indians inherited from John Kinzie must necessarily have been based on the losses he sustained in connection with the Chicago massacre. The losses of Kinzie and Forsyth at that time had been severe, and Forsyth at least had made strenuous efforts to obtain compensation from Congress for them.[916] Whatever ground there may have been for compensation from this source, there was none whatever for claiming it from the Indians in connection with the cession of their lands. The losses sustained were due to acts of war, for which, at the close of the War of 1812 mutual forgiveness and oblivion had been pledged in the treaties between the United States and the various northwestern tribes.[917] John Kinzie lived until 1828, and was for several years interpreter and sub-Indian agent at Chicago. He assisted in negotiating various treaties,[918] yet notwithstanding ample opportunity he apparently made no effort to secure compensation from the Indians for his losses. In the space of a few months after his death, however, his family twice secured from the government, through the medium of an Indian treaty, the sum of thirty-five hundred dollars. By the treaty with the St. Joseph River Pottawatomies negotiated at Carey's Mission in September, 1828, Robert Forsyth was granted the sum of twelve hundred and fifty dollars and the widow and heirs of John Kinzie thirty-five hundred. The allowance to the latter, it was stated, was "in consideration of the attachment of the Indians to her deceased husband, who was long an Indian trader, and who lost a large sum in the trade by the credits given to them and also

[916] See, e.g., his letters to the Secretary of War in *Wisconsin Historical Collections*, XI, 351–55; also his letters to Captain Heald, January 2 and April 10, 1813, *supra*, notes 613 and 632.

[917] See, e.g., the Treaty of Portage des Sioux, July 2, 1815, with the Illinois River Pottawatomies. Article I provides that "every injury or act of hostility by one or either of the contracting parties against the other shall be mutually forgiven and forgot." About a dozen treaties concluded at this time with the various tribes contain this same provision. *American State Papers, Indian Affairs*, II, 2 ff.

[918] Treaty with the Wyandots and other tribes concluded at St. Mary's, September 17, 1818; treaty with the Delawares at the same place, October 3, 1818; treaty with the Miamis October 6, 1818; treaty with the Pottawatomies at Chicago in 1821.

by the destruction of his property."[919] It was further explained that this money was in lieu of a tract of land which the Indians gave to John Kinzie, and upon which he lived.

It is unnecessary to speculate upon the question of the location of this land, for the Indians were powerless to alienate their land to individuals, a fact which was, of course, well known to the commissioners who negotiated the treaty. It is worth noting, however, that two of the signers of the treaty were Alexander Wolcott, son-in-law of Kinzie, and Robert Forsyth, the beneficiary of the smaller grant. Less than a year later, at the treaty concluded at Prairie du Chien with the Ottawas, Pottawatomies, and Chippewas, in July, 1829, the heirs of Kinzie again claimed and received the sum of thirty-five hundred dollars. The claim this time was "for depredations committed on him [Kinzie] by the Indians at the time of the massacre of Chicago and at St. Joseph's, during the winter of 1812."[920] The treaty stipulated that the sums paid to claimants were "in full satisfaction" of the claims brought by them against the Indians. Alexander Wolcott assisted in negotiating this treaty also, and both he and his brother-in-law, John H. Kinzie, signed it. Thus in 1829 the heirs of Kinzie obtained "full satisfaction" from the Pottawatomies and allied tribes for the losses sustained in 1812, despite the fact that by solemn treaty between the United States and the Indians mutual forgiveness and oblivion for the hostile acts of each had been decreed. But the payment in full in 1829 was as little successful in disposing of the matter as the treaty of 1815 had been, for the self-same claimants utilized the opportunity presented by the Pottawatomie cession of 1833 to raise themselves to comparative affluence by extracting, ostensibly from the Indians but in reality from the government, the sum of twenty thousand dollars more.

Nor is the grant of two thousand dollars to Mrs. Helm by the Treaty of 1833 less dubious in character. Lieutenant Helm had

[919] For the treaty see *U.S. Statutes at Large*, VII, 317–19. For the schedule of sums granted to individuals see *ibid.*, 603–4.

[920] For the treaty see *ibid.*, 320–22; for the schedule of claims see *ibid.*, 604.

come to Fort Dearborn in the summer of 1811 in straitened financial circumstances.[921] Since his pay was but twenty-five dollars a month, he can scarcely have increased his fortune materially in the ensuing period of a little over a year. In fact, during this time, his account with the government factory steadily increased, and when the store was closed by Irwin in July, 1812, was one of the largest on the factor's books.[922] In the nature of things he could not have lost any great amount of property at the time of the massacre. Whatever it was, however, Mrs. Helm had already been compensated for it. By the Treaty of Prairie du Chien of July, 1829, she received eight hundred dollars "for losses sustained at the time of the capture of Fort Dearborn, in 1812," with the stipulation, of course, that this payment was "in full satisfaction" of all claims. Like her half-brothers and sisters, however, she now again received compensation, and her claims, like theirs, had waxed greater with the passage of time and the increase of opportunity for collecting them. The ignoring of Lieutenant Helm's interest in the money collected for the destruction of his property was due to the fact that in the summer of 1829 Mrs. Helm obtained a divorce from him.[923] The decree provided that she should hold in her own right, as a part of the alimony allowed her, all of the money or other property granted to her as one of the heirs of John Kinzie in the late treaty of Prairie du Chien. Although the latter antedates the granting of the divorce decree by almost eleven weeks, it is evident that Mrs. Helm's spokesmen at the negotiation of the treaty had arranged its terms, as far as they related to her, with this provision of the decree in view.

A few days after the treaty had been concluded the distribution of goods to the Indians for which it made provision was begun. Of the one hundred and twenty-five thousand dollars' worth of goods which the Indians were to receive, eighty thousand dollars' worth were distributed at this time, in addition to the

[921] See *supra*, p. 177.

[922] Indian Trade Department, Chicago Petty Ledger, MS volume in Pension Building.

[923] McCulloch, *Early Days of Peoria and Chicago*, 108.

payment of the annuity in cash. But little reflection is required to show that the Indians themselves profited little by the wealth bestowed upon them. The greater part of it quickly passed from their hands to the coffers of the traders, much of it in exchange for bad whisky; and the red man was probably more injured than benefited by the mess of pottage for which he had surrendered his birthright.

Jeremiah Porter, the pioneer preacher, has left a vivid description of the proceedings which accompanied the payment to the Indians.[924] The money and goods were paid to heads of families according to the number in each household. The money was paid in silver half-dollars, and some heads of families received four hundred of these coins, which were thrown into the corner of their dirty blankets and "carried off in triumph." The scenes attending the payment were full of excitement. The distribution was continued on Sunday the same as during the week. "Thousands of human beings—some sitting, some standing, others lying on the grass in all imaginable positions, some riding, some fighting, and one bleeding to death, the main artery of his arm being cut off, while his murderer stood a prisoner, struggling in the arms of a female avenger of blood"—such were the scenes enacted that Sabbath day. Meanwhile the minister preached to his little flock from the text, "And he kneeled down and cried with a loud voice, Lord, lay not this sin to their charge, and fell asleep."

In preparation for the payment the traders had ordered large quantities of whisky, anticipating a golden harvest. To their chagrin, however, a strong south wind prevailed for many days, so that no vessels could come up the lake while the Indians were here. Temperance men and Christians rejoiced, while the traders were correspondingly disappointed. In consequence of this "Divine protection" of the Indians, they carried away from Chicago a large amount of the silver which, but for the contrary wind, would have been wasted in revelry and debauchery.[925]

[924] Porter, *Earliest Religious History of Chicago*, 72-74.

[925] Porter, who wrote many years after the event, states that the amount paid in silver was fifty thousand dollars, and estimates that the savages took away thirty thousand dollars among them.

Two years passed when in the summer of 1835 the natives assembled at Chicago to receive the last payment of their annuity and to prepare for the long journey to their new home beyond the Mississippi. Chicago had long been a favorite resort with the Pottawatomies. Here they had come to hold their councils and to receive their annuities. Here almost a quarter of a century before they had gained their most signal triumph over the race that was crowding them ever westward. Since the last great gathering two years before, the sprawling village had developed into what, to the unsophisticated red man, must have seemed a veritable metropolis. The signs of civilization which it presented to their wondering gaze, although crude enough from the point of view of the twentieth century, must have brought home to them the realization that their birthright had passed into the possession of a mightier race; already they were strangers in the land of their nativity.

As on happier occasions of meeting, however, the Indians danced and sang and drank and fought. Several thousand had assembled,[926] and much the same picturesque and motley scenes were presented as had attended the gathering of 1833. "Some were well dressed, well mounted, and dignified," wrote Porter. "These were, I suppose, civilized and Christianized Indians from St. Joseph. Others were ragged, dirty, half-naked, and drunk, singing their fiendish songs. . . . . Thousands are around us. I can hardly raise my eyes to my window without seeing them in some form—men racing on horseback or women riding by with their heavy panniers full of flour, or beef, or children. Many of the horses have bells on them that are ringing all day. Some of the men and some of the women also have bells on their limbs which ring with each step they take."[927] "A more motley group eye never beheld," wrote the reporter for Chicago's only newspaper, the *Weekly Democrat*. "Their clothing is of every color,

[926] Jeremiah Porter wrote in his journal at the time, "thousands are around us" (*Chicago Times*, December 19, 1875). The *Chicago Weekly Democrat*, August 19, 1835, estimated the number present at from two thousand to four thousand. John Dean Caton, who was a resident of Chicago and deeply interested in the Indians, puts the number (*Miscellanies*, 139) at five thousand.

[927] Journal of Jeremiah Porter, in *Chicago Times*, December 19, 1875.

bright red predominating, and bedizened with bracelets, ribbons, and feathers." The reporter dismisses the entire subject of the gathering in a single paragraph, however, in the course of which he nonchalantly imparts the information that "On Monday, we understand that one was tried by his tribe for the murder of a squaw, and sentenced to death. He was shot by the chief a short distance from town."[928]

Before quitting forever their ancient council ground the warriors indulged in a last great war dance. The matchless charm of Irving has immortalized the Moor's farewell to his beloved land. More dramatic in its picturesque savagery, and worthier far of the life he had led, was the Pottawatomie's farewell to Chicago. Driven westward by the advancing tide of civilization, in the final moments of their expiring tenure of their homeland the warriors gave a demonstration of their devotion to their ancient ideals, by staging before their conquerors such an exhibition of savagery as appalled the stoutest hearts.

As many warriors as could be mustered, about eight hundred in number, assembled in the council house on the north side of the river.[929] Their only covering was a strip of cloth about the loins and a profusion of paint of brilliant colors with which the face and body were hideously decorated. Their hair, long, coarse, and black, was gathered into a scalp lock on top of the head and profusely decorated with hawk and eagle feathers, some strung together so as to extend down the back nearly to the ground. Led by a band of musicians, the procession moved westward from the council house along the bank of the river until the North Branch was reached. Crossing this on the old bridge, it turned to the south along the West Side to the bridge across the South Branch, not far from Lake Street. This was crossed in turn, and the procession moved eastward on Lake Street and came to an end in front of Fort Dearborn.

Every effort was made to render the dance, which to the participants was "a funeral ceremony of old associations and

[928] *Chicago Weekly Democrat*, August 19, 1835.

[929] For the ceremony I have drawn upon the graphic description of Caton (*Miscellanies*, 141–45), who was an eye-witness of the proceedings.

memories," impressive and solemn. The procession moved slowly, the warriors advancing with a continual dance. In front of every house along their course a stop was made and extra feats were performed. The musicians produced a discordant din of hideous noises by beating on hollow vessels and striking sticks and clubs together.

The Sauganash Hotel at that time stood on the corner of Lake and Market Streets, where a quarter of a century later Abraham Lincoln received that nomination for the presidency which involved the nation in civil war. From its second-story parlor windows a group of spectators, chiefly ladies, gazed out upon the strange exhibition. From this vantage point John D. Caton, a future chief justice of the Supreme Court of Illinois, looked down upon the dance. It was mid-August, the morning was very warm, and the exertions of the warriors caused the perspiration to pour forth almost in streams. "Their eyes were wild and blood-shot," writes Caton, "their countenances had assumed an expression of all the worst passions which can find a place in the breast of a savage; fierce anger, terrible hate, dire revenge, remorseless cruelty, all were expressed in their terrible features. Their muscles stood out in great hard knots, as if wrought to a tension which must burst them. Their tomahawks and clubs were thrown and brandished about in every direction with the most terrible ferocity, and with a force and energy which could only result from the highest excitement, and with every step and every gesture they uttered the most frightful yells, in every imaginable key and note, though generally the highest and shrillest possible. The dance, which was ever continued, consisted of leaps and spasmodic steps, now forward and now back or sideways, with the whole body distorted into every imaginable unnatural position, most generally stooping forward, with the head and face thrown up, the back arched down, first one foot thrown forward and then withdrawn, and the other similarly thrust out, frequently squatting quite to the ground, and all with a movement almost as quick as lightning. Their weapons were brandished as if they would slay a thousand enemies at every blow, while the yells and screams they uttered were broken up and multiplied and rendered all the more hideous by a rapid clapping of the mouth with the hand."

The impression produced upon the spectators by such an exhibition can readily be imagined. Many of those who had gathered at the Sauganash were recent arrivals from the East and knew nothing of the Indians but what they had been told of their butcheries and tortures. Others, like Caton himself, had been for some time familiar with the red men. But the spectacle tried the nerves of even the stoutest, and all felt that one such sight was sufficient for a lifetime. From the Sauganash parlors, whose windows faced the west, the parade was visible some time before it reached the North Branch bridge, and from this place all the way to the bridge across the South Branch and down Lake Street to the hotel itself. As they came upon the bridge, the wild band of musicians in front redoubled their blows to increase the noise. When the head of the column had reached the front of the hotel, "leaping, dancing, gesticulating, and screaming, while they looked up with hell itself depicted on their faces, at the *chemokoman* squaws in the windows, and brandished their weapons as if they were about to make a real attack in deadly earnest, the rear was still on the other side of the river, two hundred yards off; and all the intervening space including the bridge and its approaches, was covered with this raging savagery glistening in the sun, reeking with streamy sweat, fairly frothing at their mouths as with unaffected rage, it seemed as if we had a picture of hell itself before us, and a carnival of the damned spirits there confined, whose pastimes we may suppose should present some such scene as this."

Thus did the red man play his savage rôle to the end. It was a brave show which he enacted that summer morning, but it was nothing more. For him the scepter of power had departed, and this was his final farewell. A few weeks later he took up his weary journey toward the sunset, and Chicago knew him no more. The red man had vanished, and Chicago and Chicago's future were committed to the care of another and mightier race.

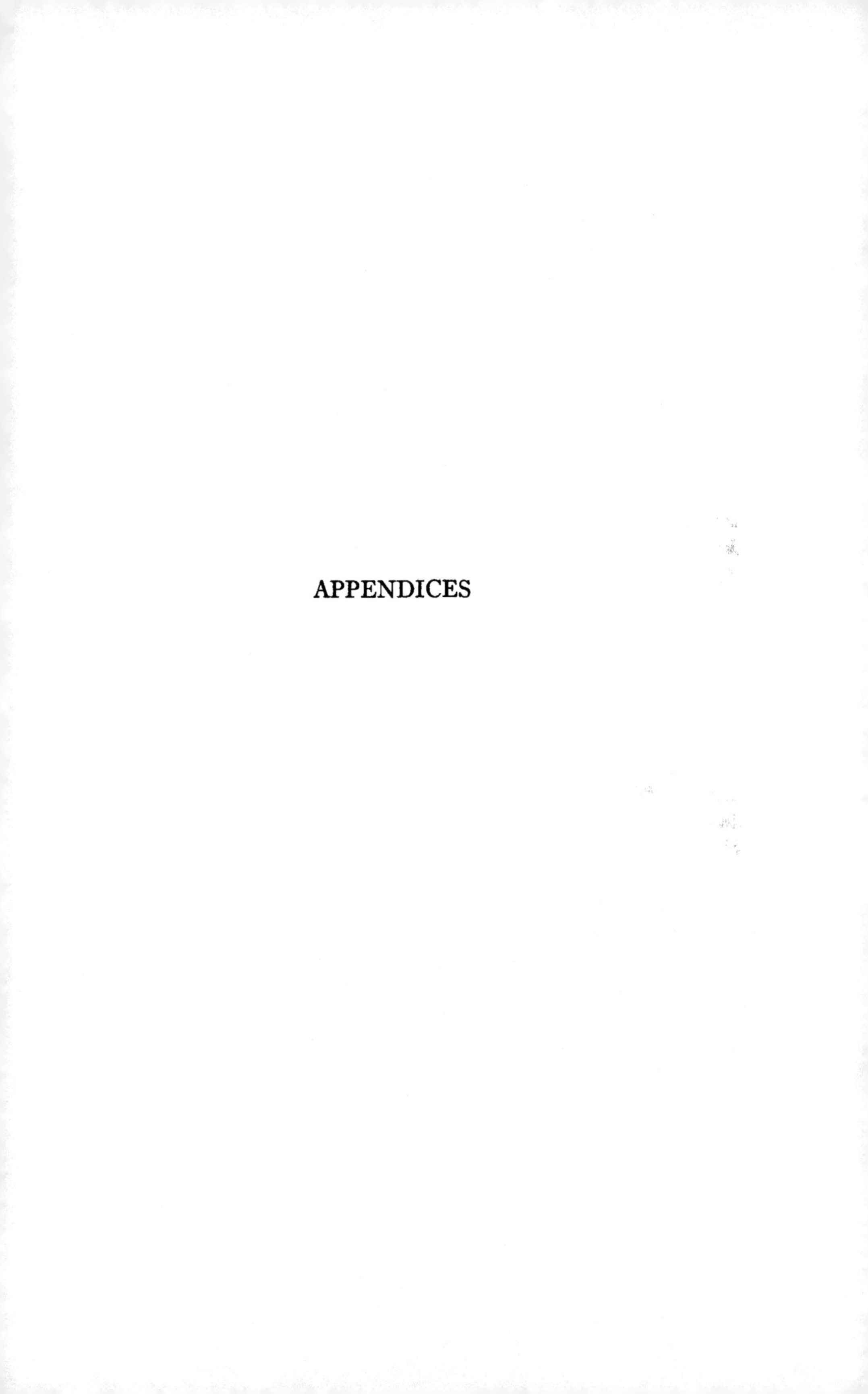

APPENDICES

APPENDIX I

JOURNAL OF LIEUTENANT JAMES STRODE SWEARINGEN, "REMARKS ON THE ROAD FROM DETROIT TO CHICAGO," JULY-AUGUST, 1803[930]

DETROIT, July, 14th, 1803.

Left this place this morning at half past five o'clock, for Chicago and proceeded about 26 miles and encamped at five o'clock p.m., on a small branch of bad water. The land is generally good timbered, with large oak, ash, and hickory. A great deal of underbrush. Crossed no waters except the river Roush.

FRIDAY, July, 15th.

Proceeded on our march at half past four a.m., 20 miles, and encamped at 1 o'clock P.M., on the river Huron, which is very low. The land is generally level and wet. Several swamps, badly timbered, and the road very bad on account of being so wet. Fine weather.

SATURDAY, July, 16th.

Proceeded on our march at 6 o'clock a.m., 18 miles, and encamped at a small Indian village near three small lakes and branch, at 2 o'clock, p.m. The land is generally level and poor, timbered with oak, several prairies, not of a good quality. The weather is warm. Clear days.

SUNDAY, July, 17th.

Proceeded on our march at 7 o'clock a.m., 20 miles, and encamped at 5 o'clock P.M., on a handsome branch of cool, good water, near a spring of clear, fine water. The land is generally poor and hilly. Passed a lake of about 2 miles in length and one half in breadth, and

[930] The Journal was kept by Swearingen while en route to Chicago in temporary command of the company of United States soldiers going to establish the first Fort Dearborn in the summer of 1803. The original manuscript is at present the property of a grandson of Swearingen, Mr. James S. Thatcher, of Dallas, Tex. Since access to it was impossible the text presented here is taken from a typewritten copy of the original made for the Chicago Historical Society in 1903 by another descendant of Swearingen, Miss Marian Scott Franklin, of Chillicothe, Ohio.

a spring and a handsome branch of fine water. At this branch, there is every appearance of a large bed of iron ore. Fine weather.

MONDAY, July, 18th.

Proceeded on our march at 15 minutes past 2 o'clock p.m., 18 miles and encamped on Grand river, at 7 o'clock, p.m., near a village. Crossed two small branches, passed several ponds of water. Grand river is about 30 feet wide and tolerably rapid. At this time it is shallow. The land is poor, hilly, and barren, except the river bottom, which is about a half mile wide and well timbered, with ash, oak, and beech. Weather fine and cool.

TUESDAY, July, 19th.

Proceeded on our march at 6 o'clock, a.m., 25 miles, and encamped on the river Kehanimasoo, at 15 minutes after 6 o'clock. The river is about 60 feet wide, tolerable rapid, and not deep. The banks are low, no bottoms. The land is hilly, poor and barren. About four and a half miles from the river, there is a handsome spring and large branch. This day we crossed several handsome branches of tolerable good water, several large swamps, praries, &c. &c. The weather is warm and fine.

WEDNESDAY, July, 20th.

Proceeded on our march at half past 6 o'clock, a.m., 27 miles and encamped on the river Kehanimasoo, at 6 o'clock p.m. This day we crossed Little Kehanimasoo, at 6 miles from our encampment, and several other small branches. The land is tolerably good in places, remainder open, oak land, soil thin. Fine weather.

THURSDAY, July, 21st.

Proceeded on our march at half past 6 a.m., 15 miles, and encamped on the river Kehanimasoo, at 3 o'clock, p.m. The land is broken and barren, timber generally small oak, except the last four miles, which is fine rich land well timbered. Crossed several small branches and passed near some handsome lakes and praries, some of which, are low and swampy. Fine, cool weather. 9 o'clock, p.m. smart shower.

FRIDAY, July, 22nd.

Proceeded on our march at 15 minutes past 7 o'clock a.m. The land in places, tolerably good. Most of this day's march, is through level barrens, large praries 9 miles through, soil not good. Crossed 2 branches in the morning. Fine weather.

Saturday, July, 23rd.

Proceeded on our march at 9 o'clock a.m., 12 miles and encamped near an Indian village at 2 o'clock, p.m., near the edge of a small lake of very bad water. The land in general, tolerably good, well timbered, with ash, oak, beech, sugar trees, etc. Several large grass swamps, roads very bad on account of fallen timber. 9 o'clock p.m., heavy storm of rain and wind.

Sunday, July, 24th.

Proceeded on our march at 7 o'clock a.m., 19 miles and encamped in a prarie near a creek at 6 o'clock p.m. The land is part very good, timber, ash, beech, and sugar trees. Greater part very poor and barren, several large creeks, praries, swamps. A handsome spring in the edge of a wet prarie, 12 miles from encampment.

Monday, July, 25th.

Proceeded on our march at 15 minutes past 8 o'clock a.m., 12 miles to the river St. Josephus and encamped on the bank near Kinzey's Improvement, at 1 o'clock p.m. The first mile is through a very handsome prarie, through a small piece of tolerable woodland. One mile to the river Limmonet, Crossed a handsome branch at the mouth and proceeded down this river about two miles, crossed it, 3 miles through tolerably good oak land, timber tall and handsome, to an Indian village, on the river near the mouth, crossed it at this village, and proceeded up the river St. Josephus, 5 miles, crossed several handsome branches. Several showers of rain. The land from the village is barren and poor.

Tuesday, July, 26th.

Detained her[e] on account of sending for [boats ?] to the Kenkakee river, which is 6 miles from this place. Portage 4 miles, from St. Josephus river to the Kenkakee river. Kenkakee is a branch of the Illinois and is navigable, a short distance above this, for small crafts. In the spring there is no portage, the two waters connect.

Wednesday, July, 27th.

Proceeded down the river, 15 minutes past 12 o'clock with 17 men and baggage, 36 miles, and encamped on the river bank, at half past 6 o'clock, p.m. The remainder of the men, marched by land. This river is generally very rapid and shoal bank very good.

THURSDAY, July, 28th.

Proceeded down the river at half past 6 a.m., 40 miles and encamped at the mouth, at 2 o'clock p.m. The bank at this place is about 60 feet high, level oak land back. From Kinzey's, to this place, by land, is 36 miles. Detained at this place until the 12th of August. The weather was generally very good. Distance from Detroit to this place is 272 miles.

FRIDAY, August, 12th, 1803.

Proceeded on our march up the lake at 6 o'clock a.m., 14 miles and encamped at 1 o'clock, p.m., on account of the roughness of the lake. Several very heavy showers of rain.

SATURDAY, August, 13th.

Detained on account of the roughness of the lake. High winds.

SUNDAY, August, 14th.

Still detained on account of the roughness of the lake and high winds.

MONDAY, August, 15th.

Proceeded on our march at 5 o'clock, a.m., 39 miles and encamped at half past 5 p.m. near an old fort. Heavy storm of wind and rain, in the night. 12 miles from encampment is a handsome Indian village, 3 miles to a river about 20 yards wide, shallow, 12 miles to a small river, then 12 miles to plain [place ?] of encampment.

TUESDAY, August, 15th.

Proceeded on our march at 15 minutes past 5 o'clock a.m. 33 miles, and encamped on the Little Calamac river, at 16 minutes past 5 o'clock, p.m. Crossed the Grand Calamac river, at 8 o'clock a.m., 12 miles from encampment.

WEDNESDAY, August, 17th.

Proceeded on our march at 6 o'clock a.m., 34 miles and encamped on the Chicago river, at 2 o'clock p.m. This river is about 30 yards wide where the garrison is intended, to be built, and from 18 feet and upwards, deep, dead water, owing to its being stopped up at the mouth, by the washing of sand, from the lakes. The water is not fit to use. The bank where the fort is to be built is about 8 feet high and a half mile above the mouth. The opposite bank is not so high, not being a difference, of more than two feet, by appearances. The banks above are quite low. The distance from Detroit, to the mouth of the St. Josephus, is 272 miles. From the mouth of the St. Josephus to Chicago, 90 miles, making in the whole 362 miles.

PORTAGE.

A portage from the Chicago river, so as to get into the Illinois river, which is 400 miles from the lakes, or the mouth of Chicago. This portage is 6 miles above the mouth and a short distance, across into a small creek, which discharges itself into the river, 16 miles from this place, at a village, from thence, into a small lakes and creeks, until intersected, by the Illinois river, from thence into the Mississippi. In the spring or time of high water, small crafts, may pass without any land carriage.

APPENDIX II

SOURCES OF INFORMATION FOR THE FORT DEARBORN MASSACRE

The history of lost manuscripts, even in so new a country as the United States, contains not only much of interest to the curious, but much of profit to the serious, who are genuinely interested in the work of preserving the records of the past. Various have the fortunes of these precious documents been. Some have been used by frugal housewives to cover jelly glasses or pack eggs, others have gone to feed the paper mill or the furnace; while all the time our libraries and historical societies are longing for the opportunity to secure such materials for preservation for the use of future generations. At times, however, the very measure of placing manuscripts within the protecting walls of an institution has been responsible for their oblivion. Either the document has been mislaid and its resting-place forgotten, or actual destruction has come upon it.

The history of manuscripts pertaining to the Fort Dearborn tragedy furnishes numerous illustrations of these various contingencies. One of the most important of them, a document of several hundred pages, disappeared, apparently for all time, from the home of the Heald family a half-century ago. Another, Lieutenant Helm's massacre narrative, after being lost to sight for three-quarters of a century, was discovered a few years since in the Detroit Public Library. A third, the fatal order of Hull to Captain Heald for the evacuation of the fort, long supposed to have been destroyed, has been for over forty years, unknown to historical workers, a part of the Draper Collection, now the property of the Wisconsin State Historical Society. Still other documents gathered with loving care within the walls of the local Historical Society by citizens of Chicago, by reason of this fact were doomed to perish in one or other of the fires which have twice consumed the Society's archives. Such was the fate of the papers of Lieutenant Swearingen, destroyed in the great fire of 1871, a few years after he had presented them to the Society. Such was the fate, also, of John Kinzie's account books with their unique picture of early Chicago in the years from 1804 to 1824.

Fortunately in both these instances a remnant of the original has been preserved to us through the very fact of its retention in private hands. Swearingen retained part of his private papers, and some of these, including the original journal of the march of the troops from Detroit to Chicago in 1803 to establish the first Fort Dearborn, are still in the possession of his descendants.[931] Of Kinzie's account books a transcript of the names together with some additional data is all that remains.[932] Its preservation is due to the fortunate circumstance that ten years before the Chicago Fire the list was copied for the use of a historical worker, who carried it with him when he left Chicago to enter the Union army. More than forty years later, on the occasion of the centennial of the founding of Fort Dearborn, the original books having been destroyed, it was returned to the Historical Society.

A source of equal regret to the investigator is the fact that many of the documents pertaining to the massacre which actually remain to us are a disappointment in one respect or another. Captain Heald, who of all men was best qualified to speak with authority, left a report of only a page to cover the entire period from the preliminary massacre at Chicago in April until his arrival in Pittsburgh late in October. Lieutenant Helm, who should have been the best qualified witness after Heald, labored long and arduously upon a narrative which goes into minute detail with respect to the massacre itself; on examination, however, it becomes evident that much of the author's labor was directed to the end of misstating rather than revealing the facts. McAfee, one of the best historians of the War of 1812, deriving his information from Sergeant Griffith, a participant in the massacre, saw fit to devote but three pages to his account of the fall of Fort Dearborn. Finally, in Mrs. Kinzie, the author of *Wau Bun*, the youthful Chicago gained a writer of more than usual charm, who from her position in the Kinzie family and her proximity to the massacre in point of time enjoyed an opportunity now gone forever to gain from eye-witnesses of the events attending the massacre information for an authoritative narrative; yet her account is perhaps the most disappointing, from the historical point of view, of any with which we have to deal.

[931] For the Journal see *supra*, Appendix I.

[932] The allusion is to the *Barry Transcript*, which has been cited in various footnotes.

It is our immediate task, however, to estimate the sources of information that remain to us for what they are worth. First in order must be placed the report of Captain Heald to the government. His official rank, the concise yet inclusive manner of expression, the early date, October 23, 1812, all unite to give it priority of consideration. Hull's terse compliment, "Captain Heald is a judicious officer, and I shall confide much to his discretion," Heald's record in the service, the peculiar circumstances under which he took command at Fort Dearborn, and the few papers of his in existence, show him to have been an officer of merit and of judgment. In striking contrast with the narratives of some of his detractors, Heald's report is marked by an air of candor and plain common sense. He gives not the slightest intimation of any feeling of prejudice or hostility toward anyone in the garrison or settlement. Kinzie, the trader, who looms so large in the *Wau Bun* narrative, is not even mentioned. No statements calculated to challenge the reader's credulity are made. From any point of view the report must be ranked as historical material of a high order of excellence, our only ground for disappointment proceeding from its brevity.

Heald's official report is supplemented to some extent by his journal, which sketches the main events of his life until after his retirement from the army, and by a number of letters and papers in the Draper Collection and in the possession of his descendants. The second important source is the narrative of Lieutenant Helm, written in the summer of 1814. It is approximately three times as long as Heald's report, and describes the actual battle with much detail. Written by the officer second in command of the troops, it would be of inestimable value to the student in supplementing Heald's report, were it not for the fact that in this instance the author's candor is as conspicuous by its absence as it is by its presence in the former one.

Further consideration of Helm's narrative is reserved for the present. After these accounts of the two ranking officers, who were also the only ones to survive the battle, must be placed the narratives of their wives as recorded by their descendants. These are the relation of Rebekah Heald as told to her son, Darius Heald, and his family, and the Helm-Kinzie account embodied in Mrs. Juliette Kinzie's *Wau Bun*.

Rebekah Heald was the only one, apparently, of those concerned in the massacre who took the trouble to write a comprehensive account of her life in Chicago. Before her death in 1856 she dictated to a niece a large number of facts connected with her early life. The manuscript was foolscap and contained, according to her son's recollection of it, several hundred pages.[933] During the Civil War the Heald residence in St. Charles County, Missouri, was ransacked from cellar to garret by a band of Union soldiers. Among other things which were taken by the marauders was Captain Heald's sword, and Mrs. Heald's manuscript. The sword was recovered by a negro boy, but the manuscript has never since been seen, and was probably destroyed at the time.[934].

Fortunately we have an indication of the character of its contents in the recital by Darius Heald of his mother's story as he remembered it from hearing her tell it "a hundred times." His narrative has been recorded in two forms, with an interval of many years between them. In 1868 he was interviewed by Lyman Draper, the famous collector in the field of western history, who at the time was on one of his tours in search of historical information. Draper's record of the interview was, however, buried away among his papers, and has until the present time been unknown to workers in the field of Chicago history.[935] In ignorance, therefore, of the Draper interview, Darius Heald was again interviewed, almost a quarter of a century later, by Joseph Kirkland, and the story which he obtained was considered by him sufficiently important to lead him to write his book, *The Chicago Massacre.*[936] A comparison of the two versions affords in some degree a test of the reliability of the Darius Heald narrative. It reveals, as might be expected, discrepancies in matters of detail, but the final impression left by the comparison is that neither Darius Heald nor his mother was animated by any conscious purpose to deceive. Produced under such circumstances as have already been described, the limitations of the narrative are obvious, and proper caution must be

[933] For the history of this manuscript, together with Darius Heald's recital to Kirkland of his mother's story of the massacre, see *Magazine of American History*, XXVIII, 111–22.

[934] Curiously enough, if Darius Heald's impression is correct, it was a Chicago regiment which perpetrated the act of destruction (*ibid.*, 122).

[935] The narrative is printed for the first time as Appendix V.

[936] The entire narrative is printed in the *Magazine of American History*, XXVIII, 111–22. For the use which Kirkland made of it see his book, *The Chicago Massacre.*

preserved and due allowance for error made in the use of it. Subject to these limitations it may be regarded as a valuable contribution to our knowledge of the massacre.

We may now direct our attention to the Kinzie family narrative of the tragedy as told by Mrs. Juliette A. Kinzie, the daughter-in-law of John Kinzie, the trader. Like the narrative of Rebekah Heald, as told by her son Darius, it comes down to us in two forms. Put forth at first anonymously in pamphlet form in 1844,[937] it appeared twelve years later as a part of the author's book *Wau Bun, or The Early Day in the Northwest.* It was published at a time when the consciousness of Chicago's future destiny was already dawning on its citizens. To a developing popular interest in the city's past was joined a general lack of information concerning her greatest tragedy. Mrs. Kinzie's narrative, claiming to be based on the testimony of eye-witnesses, spoke with assurance and precision on a subject about which all others were ignorant. Its statements have commonly been accepted without question or criticism, and have constituted the foundation, and usually the superstructure as well, of almost all that has been written upon the Fort Dearborn massacre. Sober historians and fanciful novelists alike have made it the quarry from which to draw the material for their narratives. Says Moses in his *Illinois*, published in 1889: "Without exception, historians have relied for their facts in regard to the massacre upon the account given of the event by Mrs. Juliette A. Kinzie . . . ."; and although he points out the possibility of an undue criticism of Captain Heald, he concludes that its statements "bear upon their face the appearance of truth and fairness."[938] While it is true that some dissent from the general chorus of confidence in Mrs. Kinzie's narrative has been voiced,[939] the statement made by Thwaites in 1901 that it "has been accepted by the historians of Illinois as substantially accurate,

[937] *Narrative of the Massacre at Chicago, August 15, 1812, and of Some Preceding Events* (Chicago, 1844).

[938] Moses, *Illinois, Historical and Statistical*, I, 251–52.

[939] Notably by Hurlbut, *Chicago Antiquities*, and Kirkland, *Chicago Massacre*. Carl Dilg and William R. Head, two recent workers in the local antiquarian and historical field, both repudiated it. Both men were unscientific in their methods and animated by violent prejudices, however. Dilg's papers are now owned by the Chicago Historical Society, while most of Head's were destroyed a few months after his death in 1910. A few fragments are in the Chicago Historical Society library, while a considerably larger number are still in the possession of the widow, Mrs. William R. Head, of Chicago.

and other existing accounts are generally based upon this,"[940] still stands as entirely correct.

A critical examination of Mrs. Kinzie's narrative is, then, essential to any study of the Fort Dearborn massacre. The author was born at Middletown, Conn., in September, 1806, and seems to have enjoyed educational advantages unusual for girls in her generation. Her uncle, Doctor Alexander Wolcott, was for almost a dozen years prior to his death in 1830 government Indian agent at Chicago. Through the circumstance of his having married the daughter of John Kinzie, the niece became acquainted with her brother, John Harris Kinzie, and in August, 1830, the young couple were married.[941] Shortly afterward the bride was brought by her husband to Wisconsin, where he held the position of sub-Indian agent at Fort Winnebago. Here they resided until 1834, when Chicago became their permanent home. Mrs. Kinzie, therefore, possessed no contemporary or personal knowledge of the Fort Dearborn massacre, her information being derived from members of her husband's family subsequent to her marriage. Of these the ones best qualified to give her first-hand information were her mother-in-law and her husband's half-sister, Mrs. Helm. Since the older woman did not witness the actual conflict, for this part of her narrative Mrs. Kinzie purports to quote directly the words of Mrs. Helm, though it is evident that not all that passes for direct quotation from the latter was actually derived from her.

In the preface to the pamphlet narrative of 1844 Mrs. Kinzie explained that the record had been taken many years since from the lips of eye-witnesses of the events described, and written down simply for the purpose of preserving to her children "a faithful picture of the perilous scenes through which those near and dear to them had been called to pass." Her record of the massacre is thus on a footing of equality with that of Darius Heald, in that each is based on information derived from participants in the events attending the massacre. From the point of view of the historian, however, it possesses at least one marked advantage over the latter. The Heald narrative was reduced to writing for the first time in 1868, over half a century after the occurrence of the events described. The pamphlet edition of the

[940] Kinzie, *Wau Bun*, Caxton Club edition, p. xix.

[941] A sketch of the early life of Mrs. Kinzie by her daughter is appended to the Rand-McNally 1903 edition of *Wau Bun*.

Kinzie narrative was published in 1844, almost a quarter of a century earlier. Aside from this priority in point of time, its author possessed, at the time she received her information, the conscious purpose of preserving it in written form, if not, indeed, of publishing it. Unfortunately, however, these obvious advantages possessed by Mrs. Kinzie are offset by qualities in her narrative which destroy, in large part, the historical value it might otherwise have possessed. The evident inability of the author to state the facts correctly is manifest throughout the work. It abounds in details that could not possibly have been remembered by Mrs. Kinzie's supposed informants; in others that could not have been known to them; and in still others that could never have occurred. Undaunted by the absence of records, Mrs. Kinzie repeats speeches and dialogues verbatim, as she, apparently, conceived they should have been recited. Thus the warning speech of Black Partridge, the order of Hull for the evacuation, and the speech of the Miami chieftain at the beginning of the fight are given with all the precision of stenographic reports. The Black Partridge incident is undoubtedly founded on fact, but Mrs. Kinzie's version of his speech is just as certainly the product of her own literary imagination.[942] That Hull sent an order for the evacuation was, of course, a matter of common knowledge; that Mrs. Kinzie possessed a copy of it or could pretend to report it literally is so improbable that even though the original order had never been recovered, we might reasonably regard her version of it as unreliable. Concerning the speech of the Miami chief, if delivered at all, it could not have been in the form which Mrs. Kinzie has recorded; nor could

[942] Mrs. Kinzie's version of this speech, which has frequently been quoted, affords a typical illustration of her practice of embellishing the narrative with details wholly imaginary. The two source accounts of the incident both agree that Black Partridge sought out the interpreter in order to deliver his warning. According to Helm the two waited upon Heald, to whom "the Indian gave up his medal & told Heald to beware of the next day that the Indians would destroy him & his men." Thus Helm, writing within two years of the event, did not attempt to do more than give the substance of Black Partridge's speech. Nor could he possibly have done otherwise, if there is any truth in his further statement that the warning was concealed from the other officers by Heald and that Wells alone knew of it. Despite this handicap and the equally serious one that the warning was uttered by Black Partridge in his native tongue, Mrs. Kinzie was able, over thirty years later, to report it as follows: "Father, I come to deliver up to you the medal I wear. It was given me by the Americans, and I have long worn it in token of our mutual friendship. But our young men are resolved to imbrue their hands in the blood of the whites. I cannot restrain them and I will not wear a token of peace while I am compelled to act as an enemy."

Mrs. Helm, from whom it purports to be reported, possibly have heard it uttered.

But a graver fault than the foregoing vitiates the narrative. The account of the events attending the massacre is highly partisan, manifesting throughout a bitter antipathy to Captain Heald and a corresponding idealization of Kinzie. Probably the author is herself responsible for the latter feature; the responsibility for the former must be shared with her informants. Their representations concerning the massacre, and the rôle played by Captain Heald therein, would obviously be similar to those of Lieutenant Helm. The extent of his antipathy for, and misrepresentations of, his commander will be set forth presently. It is probable that the younger Mrs. Kinzie never saw his narrative of the massacre, although her own account repeats many of the statements contained in it. The fact of their occurrence in the earlier narrative, however, does not of itself establish their reliability. It merely shifts the responsibility for them to Helm and compels an inquiry as to the character of his narrative; and the result of such an inquiry is to dispel all confidence in its reliability and in the candor of its author.

Finally the historical value of Mrs. Kinzie's book is lessened by the author's fondness for romance and for dramatic effect, which too often overshadow her zeal for the simple truth. It was this characteristic of the book, apparently, which led Kirkland to conclude that the author intended it to be regarded as a romance rather than as sober history. Whatever the truth may be as to her intention, there can be no gainsaying Kirkland's verdict that the book reads like a romance. In capacity for adventure its characters rival the traditional mediaeval knight; while over it all the author has thrown a glamor of romance which was strikingly absent from the crass materialism of life on the northwestern frontier a century ago.

It had been arranged by Kinzie that Mrs. Kinzie and her children should be taken across the lake to St. Joseph in a boat in charge of the servants and some friendly Indians. Kinzie himself went with the troops. The boat was detained at the mouth of the river, however, and here Mrs. Kinzie spent the time during the battle and massacre. Mrs. Helm had ridden out with her husband, and thus was actually present in the battle. She soon became separated from her husband and apparently was with the rear division around the wagons during the fighting there. According to her own story as told in *Wau Bun*, at the height of the fighting she drew aside and with philosophic calmness began to compose herself to meet her end. While thus engaged the surgeon, Van Voorhis, came up, wounded and panic-stricken, "every muscle of his face quivering with the agony of terror." Oblivious of the helplessness and inexperience of the young woman, he frantically sought some assurance of safety from her. While the battle raged around she strove to discourage his hope and to arouse him to meet his fate with manly firmness. She even pointed out the soldierly behavior of Ronan, who, though mortally wounded and nearly down, was fighting with desperation on one knee. This appeal to the example set by Ronan was, however, in vain, eliciting from the surgeon only the astonishing rejoinder "with a convulsive shudder," that he had "no terrors of the future—he is an unbeliever."

The remarkable dialogue was interrupted at this point by a young Indian who attempted to tomahawk Mrs. Helm. She dodged the blow, and closing with the warrior struggled to secure his knife. From this predicament she was suddenly snatched by Black Partridge, who bore her to the lake and plunged her into the water. Instead of drowning her as she expected, he held her in a position which permitted her to breathe, and she soon discovered that he had taken this way of saving her from the tomahawk. When the firing died down he bore her to the shore and up the sand bank, whence she was conducted back to the Pottawatomie camp west of the fort on the south side of the river.

Such is Mrs. Helm's narrative of her experience in the massacre itself, as reported by Mrs. Kinzie. It is evident that only a portion of the tragedy came under her own personal observation, although in *Wau Bun* all the remainder of the narrative, many pages in length, is represented as being quoted directly from her. If any portion of the *Wau Bun* account of the massacre is worthy of credence it should be this which recites Mrs. Helm's personal experience. Unfortunately the credibility of even this portion is dubious. That the actor should emphasize her own part in the affair is, of course, only natural. That the dialogue with Van Voorhis occurred as represented is, under all the circumstances, simply incredible. Unfortunately we have no other record of how Van Voorhis met his fate, and so for nearly three-quarters of a century his memory has been blackened by this cruel tale, thoughtlessly taken up and repeated in the numerous accounts of the massacre based on that contained in *Wau Bun*. The little we know of Van Voorhis tends to the belief that he was a young man of more than usual spirit and breadth of vision. His friend and college classmate, Surgeon Cooper, testified to his personal worth and bravery, and to the end of his life protested that the *Wau Bun* version of his death was a cruel slander.[943] More significant is the testimony of the fragment of a single letter of Van Voorhis, of which a copy has been preserved. Writing from his lonely station in October, 1811, he thus foretold the future destiny of this region: "In my solitary walks I contemplate what a great and powerful republic will yet arise in this new world. Here, I say, will be the seat of millions yet unborn; here the asylum of oppressed millions yet to come. How composedly would I die could I be resuscitated at that bright era of American greatness—an era which I hope will announce the tidings of death to fell superstition and dread tyranny."[944] The man who at the age of twenty-two could pen these lines is the only one of the whites present on the day of massacre who is represented as having behaved like a poltroon and a coward.

The story of the rescue of Mrs. Helm by Black Partridge has come to be regarded as a classic in the early history of Chicago. It has been made the dominant theme of the massacre monument, and has been accepted without question by practically all who have written upon the massacre. Yet it may well be doubted whether the event as described by Mrs. Kinzie in *Wau Bun* ever actually occurred. That Black Partridge saved Mrs. Helm is probably true, but that the affair possessed the romantic aspect which it has come to assume in the popular mind, or that Mrs. Helm distinguished herself by her heroism seems unlikely.

The evidence in support of this conclusion is largely negative. Lieutenant Helm's labored narrative, written in 1814, contains no mention of the Black Partridge rescue, or of any heroism displayed by his wife. Concerning her deportment in the massacre he simply records that, having believed her slain, he was astonished on coming to the Indian camp to see her "sitting among the squaws crying."

[943] Wilson, *Chicago from 1803 to 1812*.

[944] Van Voorhis, *Ancestry of Wm. Roe Van Voorhis*, 144.

In 1820 the careful and scholarly Schoolcraft passed through Chicago. He gives us an account of the massacre which he derived chiefly from John Kinzie, whose guest he was for several days.[945] He describes, among other things, the duel to the death between Sergeant Hayes and an Indian. The story is curious and interesting enough to justify him in recording and commenting upon it. But it is not more curious and thrilling than that of the Black Partridge rescue of Mrs. Helm, Kinzie's stepdaughter. Why did Kinzie relate the one and omit to relate the other to Schoolcraft? Or if Schoolcraft, who is always careful to make note of anything curious or unusual, was told of the rescue story, why did he fail to record it? Was there in fact no such rescue, or is the omission due to its commonplaceness?

We may now consider the narrative of Lieutenant Helm, sent to Augustus B. Woodward, of Detroit, in November, 1815.[946] Unfortunately it adds but little to our knowledge of the massacre—why will be apparent upon analysis. It is a partisan document for which the writer expects court martial. Its purpose is evidently to discredit Captain Heald. Helm's letter to Woodward shows that he had spent some time in preparing it. Yet the manuscript contains many erasures and alterations. It is strangely inaccurate with respect to dates, and as strangely precise in certain details not likely to be noticed or remembered on a battle field. It makes Hull's order arrive one day too early, the eighth of August. It also makes Winnemac advise Heald, through Kinzie's agency, to evacuate at once, the next day if possible, and urge him to change the usual route to Fort Wayne. Wells is represented as arriving on the twelfth with the report that the Indians about Fort Wayne are hostile and will probably interrupt the troops on the march.

On the day of his arrival Wells held a council with the Indians to the amount of "500 warriors 179 women and children," as a result of which he gave the opinion that they also were hostile and would attack the garrison on the march. On this date, August 12, Helm asserts that the fort had two hundred stand of arms, six thousand pounds of powder, four pieces of artillery, an adequate supply of shot and lead, and three months' supply of Indian corn, besides two

[945] Schoolcraft, *Narrative Journal of Travels from Detroit . . . to the Sources of the Mississippi River in the Year 1820*, 390–93.

[946] For the narrative, together with Helm's letter to Woodward, June 6, 1814, announcing it, see Appendix VI.

hundred head of horned cattle and twenty-seven barrels of salt. In addition, three months' provisions had been expended between August seventh and twelfth, how or why the writer does not say. After the survey had been made, Kinzie (here Kinzie is erased in the manuscript and Wells substituted)—Wells demanded of Heald if he intended to evacuate, and received an affirmative reply. Helm and Kinzie now urged Wells to ask Heald to destroy the ammunition and liquor. Wells declined, but offered to accompany Kinzie and Helm. To their representations Heald replied that he had received positive orders to deliver to the Indians "all the Public Property of whatsoever nature," that it was bad policy to tell a lie to an Indian, and that such a crime might irritate the natives and result in the destruction of his men. Kinzie thereupon offered to assume the responsibility by fabricating an order from Hull; to this scheme Heald assented; Kinzie wrote an order "as if from genl. Hull" and gave it to Heald, and the arms and ammunition were destroyed.

The account of the battle and massacre then follows. It contains some information of value, but unfortunately it is mingled with much that is evidently untrue. The attack began at ten o'clock in the morning, at a distance of a mile and a half from the fort. In a few minutes all but ten of the men were killed or wounded. Helm called upon his men to follow him to the prairie, then moved forward under heavy fire one hundred and five paces, when he wheeled to the left to "avoid being shot in the back." This careful enumeration, while under heavy fire, of the exact number of paces taken by the troops can hardly convince the student of the writer's sincerity. Waiving this point, however, it is apparent that the Indians on Helm's flank were gaining his rear and he wheeled to the south to intercept them. The Indians now stopped firing "and nevour more renewed it." Helm at once ordered the men to reload their guns. He now discovered Captain Heald, "for the first time to my knowledge during the battle. He was coming from towards the Indians and to my great surprise they nevour offered to fire on him." The inference which the writer wishes to convey is plain, but it is also evident that Heald had been engaged in battle farther south, and that he had already taken steps to stop further slaughter by bargaining for surrender. A futile attempt on the part of the soldiers to charge was followed by more parleying on Heald's part. Passing over the details,

Helm represents that while Heald was agreeing with Black Bird upon the terms of surrender he himself with the men who were left fell back to an elevation near at hand. For a reason hinted at but not explained the men now regarded Helm as their commander. Heald repeatedly inquires of his subordinate what he intends to do. The men on the other hand beg him not to surrender. He urges them not to be uneasy for he has already done his best for them and will not surrender unless they are willing.

Even the hostile savages now became aware of the quiet usurpation of the command by Helm during the heat of the battle. The half-breed interpreter who had conducted the negotiations between Captain Heald and Black Bird came running to warn Helm not to surrender until a general council of the Indians had agreed to the terms. Helm replied that he "had no Ideah of surrender." The interpreter now collected the Indians and after haranguing them returned with the promise that they would spare the lives of Helm and his men if they would surrender. He also informed them that the lives of Kinzie and some of the women and children had already been spared. This last news enlivened Helm and his men, for they "well knew Mr. Kinzie stood higher than anny man in that country" among the Indians, and that "he might be the means of saving us from utter destruction, which afterwards proved to be the case."

There follows a description of the scene of the massacre at the wagons which filled Helm with horror. There are a number of other details that need not be noticed here. The document is of great interest and of considerable value, but its partisan character is evident throughout. In his desire to cast discredit upon Captain Heald, Helm played fast and loose with the facts of the situation. The length to which he was willing to go in the effort to impugn Heald's judgment is perhaps sufficiently indicated by the story of the forged order for the destruction of the arms and ammunition. Even in the absence of positive evidence, the inherent improbability of the tale is such as to arouse grave suspicion of its validity. The discovery of Hull's order for the evacuation changes this suspicion to certainty. Since Heald was expressly enjoined to destroy the surplus arms and ammunition the whole tale concerning the forged order is obviously a sheer invention. Further misstatements occur in connection with the account of the supplies on hand at the time of the evacuation.

Instead of two hundred stand of arms, the last Fort Dearborn inspection return shows that there were approximately one-third this number;[947] and the number of surplus muskets destroyed did not exceed half a dozen. Instead of twenty-seven barrels of salt there were, according to a letter of Heald, written six weeks after the massacre, but seventeen barrels.[948] That there were seventy muskets instead of two hundred, and seventeen barrels of salt in place of twenty-seven, is of no particular consequence, for in each case the supply was more than sufficient. But the inaccuracy of Helm's statements is of some significance, as affording evidence of the untrustworthiness of his narrative, even in matters concerning which no adequate motive for misrepresentation is apparent. The connection between Helm's narrative of the massacre and that of Mrs. Kinzie in the pages of *Wau Bun* has already been pointed out. The two proceed from a common source, and have a common bias against Captain Heald. Helm was the original traducer of Heald. Almost a hundred years elapsed before his narrative appeared in print, and Mrs. Kinzie was probably unaware of its existence. Notwithstanding this its spirit is faithfully reflected in the latter's account, and through its agency passed into the literature of the Fort Dearborn massacre. Thus the partisan statements of a bitter enemy, who did not hesitate to pervert the truth in order to discredit his commander, taken up and reproduced by others, have been potent to blast the reputation of Heald to the present time, a century after the massacre.[949]

[947] *Heald Papers,* Draper Collection, U, Vol. VIII.

[948] Heald to Augustus Porter, contractor for the western posts, September 26, 1812. MS owned by the author.

[949] The issues raised by Helm's account of the massacre render it a matter of regret that but little authentic information is extant concerning him. Judge Woodward, in his letter to Proctor concerning the Chicago captives, speaks highly of Helm (Appendix VII); there is evidence, however, which tends to invalidate Woodward's estimate of Helm's character. The following sheds some light upon the characters respectively of Heald and his detractor. Heald was twice wounded in the battle of August 15, receiving a bullet in the hip and another through the arm. The former wound never ceased to trouble him (Physician's certificates, *Heald Papers,* in Draper Collection), and he carried the bullet which caused it to his grave. Helm received a slight flesh wound in the heel, from which he recovered so quickly that within six weeks Forsyth reported him "in good health and spirits" (letter of Thomas Forsyth to John Kinzie, September 24, 1812, printed in *Magazine of History,* XV, 89; see also, *infra,* letter of Heald to B. Roberts, December 1, 1825). Heald refrained from applying for a pension, and when one was procured for him by two of his friends without his knowledge, the latter, in breaking the news to him, thought it

After the sources of information derived from the two surviving officers and their wives follow a number of reports of distinctly lesser importance which found their way into the newspapers of the time. Several of these were preserved from oblivion by being reprinted during the few weeks following the massacre in that general repository of information, *Niles' Register*. The number of such reports which require consideration here is small. The news of the fall of Fort Dearborn was borne to the nearest American settlements more rapidly than might, in view of all the circumstances, have been expected. As early as August 28 a report of it was published in the *Western Courier*, of Louisville.[950] It consisted of an extract from a letter received at Louisville from an officer of the army who apparently was at or in the vicinity of Fort Wayne. It stated correctly enough the leading facts that the fort had been evacuated, the garrison attacked after marching "about one mile," and that Heald had surrendered on receiving

worth while to urge him not to decline it, and to suggest that he bestow it upon his children in case he felt any delicacy about accepting it himself (*supra*, note 629). It is apparent from the letter of Heald to B. Roberts, December 1, 1825 (printed below), that when Helm came to apply for a pension he not only made what he might of his wound, but also preferred a claim against the government for money advanced by him from his own funds to purchase articles for the troops at Chicago. This claim Heald denominated "entirely false & without the least foundation imaginable"; and further that any vouchers which Helm might submit in support of his claim were fraudulent. Heald's emphatic condemnation of Helm's assertions and claim find support in what we know of Helm's financial situation at the time. See on this *supra*, p. 365. In view of this it seems unlikely, without regard to Heald's testimony, that he was in a position to advance money to buy articles for the soldiers.

[*Letter of Heald to B. Roberts*]

ST. CHARLES MISSOURI
1 December 1825.

DEAR SIR, I have recd. your Letter from Russellsville on the subject of Capt Helms claims on the Government. As to his wound recd. at Chicago I know nothing that can be of service to him in order that he may procure a pension. all that I can say of my own knowledge is that I discovered he walked a little lame, soon after the action was over, but I had no opportunity to find out the cause of it, before we were seperated. I was told about 10 days after the action by Mr. Kinzie, the stepfather of Mrs. Helm, that Capt. Helm's wound was very trifling & could not injure him. I have since seen Mr. Thos. Forsyth with whom Capt. Helm resided for several mo[n]ths immediately after the action and he told me that Capt. Helms wound was of no consequence, & that it appeared to be nothing more than a small flesh wound in one of his heals & did not disable him in the least.

The statement he made to you respecting the articles he says he purchased for the troops & advanced the money out of his own funds to pay for them is entirely false & without the least foundation imaginable. And If he has any vouchers to support the claim, depend upon it Sir, they are fraudulent.

Should you wish for my deposition stating my own knowledge of Capt. Helms

Should you wish for my deposition to support Capt. Helms claim for a Pension, I am perfectly willing to give it, but I can say nothing more than I have said in this letter of my own knowledge.

THE HONBL. B.ROBERTS
Member of Congress.

The original manuscript from which the foregoing is taken is the copy of the letter retained by Heald, and is owned by his granddaughter, Mrs. Wright Johnson, of Rutherford, N.J.

[950] A copy of this paper is owned by the Chicago Historical Society.

assurances of mercy for the garrison. It erred, however, in reporting Heald and his wife among the slain, as well as all but three of Wells's Miamis. From these three survivors, it was stated, the information had been gained.

In similar fashion the news of the massacre was carried to Detroit, now in the hands of the British, about the first of September. The first printed account from this source is found in *Niles' Register* for October 3, copied from an earlier number of the *Buffalo Gazette.* Considering the source of the information, the brief narrative corresponds more closely to the facts as we know them than might be expected. A Pottawatomie chief had brought the news to Detroit, from which place it had been carried eastward by the British warship, the "Queen Charlotte"; a flag of truce sent ashore at Fort Erie conveyed the news to the Americans there, from which place, presumably, it was carried to Buffalo. The account places the number of survivors at ten or twelve, and, like the Louisville report, includes Captain Heald among the slain.[951]

More important than either of the foregoing is the report which appeared in the *Missouri Gazette* of September 19, 1812. It represents[952] Captain Wells as bringing the order from Hull for the distribution of the stores among the Indians and the evacuation of the fort. Heald prepared to comply with the order, but thought prudent to destroy all the powder and whisky before distributing the goods. The Indians suspected this, overheard the staving-in of the powder kegs, and charged Wells with the fact. He denied it, however, and the goods were distributed to about eight hundred Indians. Signs of discontent were already manifest among the Indians when on the fourteenth an Indian runner arrived with a large red belt. He had been sent by Main Poc, the inveterate enemy of the Americans, who lived on the Kankakee but who was now fighting with Tecumseh's forces near Malden. The message the runner bore acquainted the Indians around Fort Dearborn with the British successes and Hull's predicament on the Detroit frontier; it added that a vessel would be dispatched in a few days for Chicago with goods and ammunition for the Indians, and urged them to strike the Americans immediately.

951 For other early newspaper reports of the massacre see Hurlbut, *Chicago Antiquities*, 175-77.

952 I have not had access to the paper itself, but have made use of the copy of the article made by Lyman C. Draper, in the Draper Collection, S, XXVI, 76.

This message, added to the discontent over the destruction of the powder and whisky, precipitated the attack. The next day, about ten o'clock, the troops, fifty-four in number, with ten citizens, nine women, and eighteen children, evacuated the fort. After they had gone about a mile they were attacked by about four hundred Indians, and a general slaughter ensued. Thirty soldiers, including the doctor and the ensign, all of the citizens, two women, and twelve children were torn to pieces. The heart of Wells was torn out and divided among the different bands. In the midst of the carnage Mrs. Heald had sunk on the ground and an Indian had a war club raised to drive into her head, when she was rescued by a young Frenchman who purchased her with a mule. Heald's captors gave him his liberty, contrary to the wishes of the other savages. The commander and his wife were given protection in the house of a trader, where their wounds were dressed, and at the time of the report they were in process of recovery.

This early report is worthy of notice for several reasons. It is notably accurate in some respects, and as notably incorrect in others. The figures given for the participants in the massacre and for the slain are surprisingly accurate for so early an unofficial report. On the other hand, while the order for the evacuation is given with a fair degree of accuracy, the account of its transmission to Fort Dearborn and the date of its arrival is entirely wrong. It is to be noted that thus early to the destruction of the ammunition and liquor is ascribed a large degree of responsibility for the massacre, and that a version of the ransoming of Mrs. Heald with a mule appears. It is evident that this report must have come from someone familiar with the facts concerning the massacre. Although it is not susceptible of proof, the opinion may be hazarded that this person was Thomas Forsyth, of Peoria, Kinzie's half-brother. He came to Chicago the day after the massacre, and started to return to Peoria a few days later.[953] He was active and enterprising, and not long afterwards was acting as an agent of the government among the Illinois River Indians. He was well known at St. Louis, and it seems not unlikely that he would have forwarded thither at the earliest opportunity an account of what had occurred at Chicago.

Another report of the massacre, published in *Niles' Register* May 8, 1813, requires more extended consideration. It purports to be an

[953] Letter of Forsyth to Heald, January 2, 1813, *supra*, note 632.

extract from a letter of Walter Jordan, "a non-commissioned officer of the Regulars at Fort Wayne," to his wife, October 19, 1812. The writer claims to have been a member of Wells's relief expedition, and thus to have been a participant in the Fort Dearborn massacre. According to the letter Wells left Fort Wayne August 1, accompanied by Jordan and one hundred "Confute" Indians to escort Heald on his retreat from Chicago to Fort Wayne, "a distance of 150 miles." Wells reached Chicago August 10, and on the fifteenth all was in readiness for an immediate march, all the property that could not be removed having been burned. The force which evacuated the fort consisted of "Capt. Wells, myself and 100 Confute Indians, Capt. Heald's 100 men, 10 women, and 20 children—in all 232." After a ten-minute conflict, in the course of which the "Confute" allies deserted to the enemy, all but fifteen of the whites were killed. But "thanks be to God," Jordan was numbered among the survivors. If his escape was as miraculous as the narrative represents it to have been, his thankfulness was not inappropriate. First the feather was shot off his cap, then the epaulet from his shoulder, and finally the handle from his sword. Unwilling, apparently, to tempt Providence further, Jordan now surrendered to "four savage rascals." His good fortune did not desert him, however; the Confute chief, taking him by the hand, assured him his life would be spared, but invited him to "come and see what we will do with your Captain." Leading the way to Wells they cut off his head and put it on a pole, took out his heart, and, having divided it among the chiefs, "ate it up raw." After this the fifteen survivors were parceled out among the victors. The band to whom Jordan fell promised, if he would stay with them, to make a chief of him; if he tried to escape they would burn him alive. Despite this alternative, having gained their confidence with a "fine story," Jordan made his escape and reached Fort Wayne on August 26, two days before it was blockaded by the Indians.

If Jordan was in fact a member of Wells's party and this is an authentic account of the massacre by an eye-witness, it must be regarded as one of our most valuable sources of information. Its early date, the detailed description of events, and the precise enumeration of the forces engaged, combine with its first-hand character to give it this rank. If, on the other hand, the narrative is not to be accorded this high estimate, it must be dismissed as a mendacious and worthless fabrication. The circumstances of the case render the assumption of any middle ground between these positions impossible.

Turning to Jordan's letter, even a casual inspection compels the adoption of the latter position. Waiving the question whether such a person as Walter Jordan ever in fact existed, the complete silence of all other sources as to his presence in Wells's party and at the Chicago massacre is enough to rouse grave suspicion concerning the truth of his story. His misstatements concerning the expedition of Wells and the massacre itself change this suspicion into certainty. Neither lapse of time nor second-hand information can be urged in extenuation of his false statements about the number of Wells's followers and of Heald's party. Aside from this consideration, the misstatements as to the time of Wells's trip, the tribe to which his followers belonged, and the distance from Fort Wayne to Chicago can hardly be explained on any other hypothesis than that of deliberate fabrication. Surely "a non-commissioned officer of the Regulars at Fort Wayne" would not substitute for the Miamis a purely imaginary tribe of Indians, having no existence outside the pages of his letter. A more Falstaffian tale than that of Jordan's miraculous escape from death, or a more improbable one than that detailing the circumstances attending the death of Wells would be difficult to imagine. Further refutation of the narrative is unnecessary, nor would it deserve the space that has already been devoted to it but for the fact that some have been misled into a belief in its reliability.

The correspondence of Judge Woodward of Detroit with General Proctor relative to the survivors of the massacre constitutes a source of information of the highest quality.[954] With the massacre itself, however, it deals only incidentally, being limited to a consideration of the survivors and the means of rescuing them from captivity. Woodward was perhaps the most prominent citizen of Detroit and Michigan Territory, noted for his eccentricity and his ability. On the arrival of Captain Heald and his wife and Sergeant Griffith at Detroit early in October, Woodward set himself the task of gaining all the information they could give him concerning the losses in the battle and the survivors of the massacre, and this information he incorporated a few days later in a vigorous letter to Proctor, the British commander at Detroit, appealing to him to take all the measures in his power to

[954] For Woodward's letter to Proctor, October 7, 1812, see Appendix VII.

recover the unfortunate captives. It is probable that Heald and Griffith could not speak with entire accuracy concerning the losses sustained and the number of these survivors, but they were of course able to give Woodward valuable information on the subject; and his letter to Proctor constitutes one of our most valuable sources of information concerning it.

An account of the massacre drawn in large part from the same source as Woodward's information, but written a few years later, is contained in McAfee's *History of the Late War*, published in 1816. McAfee was a Kentuckian and himself a soldier in the war, having served as an officer in the regiment of Colonel Richard M. Johnson. Because of this, and because his information was largely gathered from participants in the events described, his history possesses much of the flavor of a first-hand narrative. McAfee gives a short account of the destruction of Fort Dearborn, based on information received from Sergeant Griffith, who was also a member of Johnson's regiment. The narrative, being thus second-hand, is open to criticism in certain respects, but the chief occasion for regret is that McAfee's purpose was satisfied with so brief an account; for the source of his information, the early date of the history, and the character of McAfee as a historian all tend to the belief that had it suited his purpose to enter more fully into the account of Fort Dearborn, a narrative of great value would have been produced.

We come, after these contemporary accounts, to the recollections and reminiscences told in old age by participants, or relatives or friends of participants, in the massacre. Some of these have proved to be of considerable value for the reconstruction of our story, but in most sources of this character the traces of time and of failing memory are plainly to be seen. Moreover, some of them are affected by the narrator's personal friendships or antipathies, and given in support or contradiction of some partisan account. Few of them are or pretend to be more than fragmentary accounts of the battle. Among such sources may be mentioned the testimony of Black Hawk,[955] of Shabbona,[956] of Joseph Bourassa,[957] and of Paul De Garmo.[958]

[955] Black Hawk, *Life*, 42.

[956] *Wisconsin Historical Collections*, VII, 416–18.

[957] Draper Collection, S, XXIII, 165 ff.

[958] De Garmo's story is contained in a letter of Charles A. Lamb, August 24, 1893, MS in the Chicago Historical Society library.

Logically belonging in the same class as the foregoing, but requiring in each case more extended consideration, are the narratives of Alexander Robinson, of Moses Morgan, and of Susan Simmons Winans. Robinson was one of the chiefs in the massacre who was friendly to the whites and did what he might to save them. He it was who piloted the Healds and Sergeant Griffith in their three-hundred-mile canoe voyage from the St. Joseph River to Mackinac. He was one of the last survivors of the massacre, living in the immediate vicinity of Chicago until 1872, and well known to the generation of Chicagoans before the great fire. For some reason the first generation of writers upon early Chicago history did not take the trouble to secure from Robinson his version of the massacre. A manuscript which purports to contain his story of the affair is, however, in the possession of the Chicago Historical Society. The information contained in it purports to have been secured by Carl A. Dilg in a series of interviews with the daughter of Robinson some time after the chief's death. Dilg considered it of great importance, but a careful study of it compels the conclusion that it possesses practically no historical value. It was not put in writing until three-quarters of a century had elapsed; more important, Robinson himself was illiterate, and the story, third-hand at best, was elicited from his daughter in a series of interviews extending over several years, by a man whose prejudices were so violent and methods of work so unscientific as to render confidence in its reliability impossible.

The account of Susan Simmons Winans, of great value from one point of view, must, for the actual affair of the massacre, be classed with the story of Robinson. Mrs. Winans, the infant daughter of John Simmons, was saved by her mother from the slaughter at the wagons. Both mother and child appeared as if from the dead in April, 1813, after a series of adventures which recall the age of miracles and providential protection. Mrs. Simmons lived until 1857, and her daughter, Mrs. Winans, until 1900, being the last known survivor of the massacre. Both mother and daughter frequently narrated to their relatives the story of their captivity, the daughter's knowledge having been derived, of course, from her mother. A relative, Doctor N. Simmons, the son of a brother of John Simmons, moved by family pride in the narrative and possessed of some slight literary ability, published in 1896 a small volume which contained, in addition to the story of his kinsfolk, a sketch of the massacre and of the Pottawatomie tribe of Indians.[959] The account of the massacre is a reprint of Edward G. Mason's narrative in his *Chapters from Illinois History*, and the volume is of value solely for the account it gives of the captivity and later life of Mrs. Simmons and her daughter.

Finally, we may consider the massacre narrative of Moses Morgan as preserved by William R. Head. Among the workmen who helped to build the second Fort Dearborn in 1816 was Moses Morgan, foreman of a gang of carpenters. He had served as a volunteer in Hull's army in 1812, and after his exchange from the captivity consequent upon the surrender of Detroit, had re-entered the service as a carpenter. He soon became a foreman, and in this capacity assisted in the building of Commodore Perry's fleet on Lake Erie. In 1816 he was ordered to accompany the troops sent to rebuild the fort at Chicago. In later life he became the neighbor at Carlinville, Ill., of William R. Head, who for many years before his death in 1910 was a resident of Chicago. Head early became interested in local history, and for a period of forty years was a tireless collector of data pertaining to early Chicago and Illinois. Among other things, he recorded the story told him by Moses Morgan. It contains many details not found elsewhere, and if it were of such a character that these could be relied upon, it would constitute an exceedingly valuable source of information.

Unfortunately, however, it exhibits many defects. The account was written out by Head late in life from notes taken and from recollections of his various conversations with Morgan many years before. Head, like Dilg, was lacking in historical training, while he held a number of theories concerning the massacre and possessed a violent antipathy for everything connected with the Kinzie family. In his old age he undertook a revision of his manuscript, which further militated against its reliability; finally, to complete the tale of defects, after his death the mass of notes and other material which he had accumulated, and by which the correctness of his statements might to some extent have been tested, was burned as rubbish by his family. Because of the unreliable character of the narrative but little dependence can be placed upon it, particularly in those portions which involve Head's theories or his prejudices. Yet it seems possible to

[959] Simmons, N., *Heroes and Heroines of the Fort Dearborn Massacre.*

trust some of its statements and accordingly some use has been made of it in the present work. There is no reason to question the character and integrity of either Morgan or Head, or to suppose that either consciously misrepresented the facts. The more reliable portion of the narrative has been utilized in the chapter on the fate of the survivors of the massacre. The part which deals with the tragedy itself is given here because of its human interest, in spite of a lack of confidence in its historical worth.

When the garrison came, in the summer of 1816, to rebuild the fort, many evidences of the massacre were still to be seen. Many attempts were made by the officers to get an exact account of the destruction of the first fort from the Indians and the half-breeds who knew the facts. No dependence, however, could be placed upon their statements. Previous to the coming of the troops some of these residents had boasted of the part they had taken in the slaughter. For obvious reasons their denials were now as strenuous as their former boasting had been loud. It was found that tales of the fight were being manufactured by the interpreters, and some of them were dismissed, but without any favorable results in the form of desired information.

One account was obtained by a soldier's wife from Okra, Ouilmette's wife, and a half-breed French woman. These women had, they said, watched the departure of the troops from the fort. From a favorable vantage point on the north side of the river where Ouilmette's hut stood they had watched the troops march out, the Captain and his wife being the last to leave. There were two army wagons, one containing the women and children and the personal baggage, drawn by Lee's horses; to the other, laden with ammunition and provisions, three pairs of steers were yoked. Soon the women heard the sound of firing and smelled the powder smoke, but from their position on the north side of the river they were unable to see the fight.

Another and fuller story was obtained from a wounded soldier of Heald's command who was found, under circumstances already described,[960] living a few miles up the North Branch. In presenting the details, it should be noted that they bear throughout the imprint of Head's theories and prejudices. There were not provisions enough

[960] *Supra*, pp. 260–61.

for a long siege. The garrison should not have left so soon. Kinzie was not faithful in his interpretations. Lieutenant Helm was so drunk on the morning of August 15 that he was not able to retain his place in line. There were two wagons, one of which was guarded by the militia and the soldiers who had children. The troops marched out close to the water's edge, and when the wagons had gone a short distance beyond the mouth of the river two half-grown Pottawatomie boys began shooting at the animals hitched to the wagons, wounding one of the horses and causing it to lie down. The steers attached to the army wagon turned quickly around, breaking the wagon-pole, and half overturning the wagon. For a time the men about the wagons stood patiently in line surrounded by a group of friendly Indians. Then the strange Indians, not finding the ammunition and provisions in the fort, came rushing down upon the wagons. As they came on the men gave three volleys, killing many of them. The surrender was made by the Captain to Black Bird, and the valuables and money were given under a promise of protection for the men. The Captain and a sergeant were turned over to Robinson to be saved for their money. The general opinion when Morgan left Chicago was that the delay caused by the Indian boys' attack upon the teams was the chief reason why the party did not escape; that the attack upon the wagons took place beyond the mouth of the river; and that the ensign made a mistake in commanding his men to fire so quickly.

APPENDIX III

NATHAN HEALD'S JOURNAL[961]

Nathan Heald, the son of Thomas Heald & Sibyl, his wife, was born in New Ipswich in the state of New Hampshire the 24th of September 1775, and entered the army of the U. States as an Ensign the 2nd of March 1799. In the spring of 1800 went to Springfield in Mass. on the Recruiting Service.

In the spring of 1801 left Springfield with a Detachment of Recruits under the command of Capt. Lyman to join the western Army, and arrived at Wilkinson Ville on the Ohio early in the fall of the same year. Left Wilkinson Ville late in the fall of the same year, with a Detachment of 4 Companies of Inf' under the Command of Capt. R. Bissell & went up Tennessee River 2 or 3 miles above the mouth of Bear Creek, built a cantonment &c.

In the spring of 1802, a part of the Army being disbanded, I went to Vincennes with a Detachment of Capt. Lyman's company to join that post.

In the spring of 1803, went on Command to Detroit with Gov'r Harrison, & returned to Vincennes the next fall, having been sick at Detroit all summer.

In the beginning of 1804, went to Chilicothe Ohio on the Recruiting service; spent the summer following at Maysville Ky on the same service & returned to Vincennes in the fall of the same year.

In the spring of 1805, went to Fort Massack where I commanded till late in the fall of the same year when I sat out on furlough for Concord Mass. and arrived there in January 1806. Attended a Genl. Court Martial as a Member on the seaboard in New Hampshire the same winter, and went to New London Conn. on the Recruiting service with Cap. Stoddard in the spring. Left New London late in the summer & went to New Brunswick N.J. on the same service, &

[961] Printed for the first time from the original manuscript among the Heald papers in the Draper Collection at Madison, Wis. The Journal was kept by Heald in a small blank book about 3X6 inches in size. It contains in addition to the autobiographical matter presented here a number of pages of memoranda consisting of military data, financial entries, medical and household recipes, and so forth.

in the fall, was ordered to Fort Wayne, by the way of Philadelphia where I joined Capt. Stoddard with a Detachment of Recruits & went with him to Newport on the Ohio, then by myself to Fort Wayne, where I arrived and took the command in Jan. 7 1807. On the 31st of that month & the same year was promoted to a Capt. in 1st Reg't Infantry.

In the spring of 1807 went to Detroit to sit on a Gen'l Court Martial & returned to Fort Wayne in the summer.

In June 1810 left Fort Wayne & went to Chicago to Command that Post. went on furlough to Massachusetts in the fall of the same year and returned by the way of Kentucky where I was married to Rebecca Wells the daughter of Gen'l Samuel Wells and Mary his wife, on the 23d of May 1811, and arrived at Chicago in June with Mrs. Heald.

On the 4th of May 1812, we had a son born dead for the want of a skilful Midwife.

On the 9th of Augt, 1812, rec'd orders from Gen'l Wm. Hull to evacuate the Post of Chicago and proceed with my Command to Detroit.

On the 15th Marched for Detroit & was attacked by about 500 Indians two miles from the Fort and there was killed in the action 1 Ensign, 1 Surgeon's Mate, 24 Non-Commissioned Officers Musicians & Privates, 12 Militia including Capt. Wells of the Indian Department at Fort Wayne, 2 Women & 12 Children. Myself, one Lieut. 25 Non-Commiss. Officers Musicians & Privates and eleven Women & Children were captured by the Indians. On the 16th, that is the day after [the] action, Mrs. Heald & myself were taken to the St. Joseph River by our new Masters. The journey was performed in three days by coasting the Lake (Michigan) and we remained with them (both being badly wounded & unable to help ourselves) till the 29 of the same Month when we took our departure for Michilimackinac in a Birch Canoe, with Sergeant Griffith, one of the unfortunate prisoners, and 3 Frenchmen & a Squaw. The 14th of Sept. we all arrived safe at Michilimackinac. I was there Paroled by Capt. Roberts, the British Comma[n]dant, & permitted to proceed to Detroit with Mrs. Heald & the Sergeant.

Left the Island on the 19th of the month (Sept.) and arrived at Detroit the 22nd—was there permitted by Capt. Proctor to proceed to the U. States on Parole. Left Detroit the 4th of October, and arrived at Buffalon the 8th in the old Brigg Adams. Left Buffalon the 10th and arrived at Pittsburg the 22nd.

Left Pittsburgh the 8th Nov. and arrived at Louisville the 19th. The distance from Chicago to Michilimackinac in coasting the Lake on the east side is .... 400 miles

Thence to Detroit	300
Thence to Buffalon	280
Thence to Erie by land	90
Thence to Pittsburgh by land but we travelled by water	132
Thence to Louisville by water	705
Total	1907

On the 26th of August 1812, I was promoted to a Major in the 4th Regt. Inf'y.

The winter of 1812–13 Mrs. Heald & myself spent at her father's, and went to Newport in the spring where we spent the summer following & returned to Mr. Jacob Geiger's near Louisville & spent the winter of 1813–14. The spring and summer following I was engaged in putting up buildings on a piece of Land I bought of Mr. Wand joining Jacob Geiger's Plantation & moved into the buildings late in the fall of 1814.

At the Consolidation of the Army in 1814 I was disbanded, being then a Major in the 19th Regt. of Inf'y.

Mary Sibyl Heald was born at her Grandfather's near Louisville on the 17th of Ap'l 1814.

Margaret Ann Heald born at my House near Louisville the 9th of Dec'r 1816 Kentucky.

Feb 15th 1817 sold my House & Lot near Louisville Ky to Mr. Jacob Geiger for $3000.

March 22nd 1817. Left Louisville with my family for St. Charles County Missouri Territory and arrived there the 15th of Apl. following.

Spent the summer of 1817 at Joseph Batys plantation.

Nov'r 1817 moved to a Plantation I bought of Jacob Zumwalt for $1000.

Rebecca Hackley Heald was born in St. Charles County the 7th January 1819.

21st September 1820. Mr. Geiger's family arrived from Kentucky.

Nov'r 2nd Mrs Geiger died of a consumption. (Nov) 6th Mr. Geiger with his Children sat out for Kentucky.

17th October (1820) Bought a House and lot in St. Charles of Antoine Ganis for the sum of $450. cash in hand.

Rebecca Hackley Heald Died 16th Jan'y 1821, between the hours of 8 & 9 P.M. Aged 2 Years & 10 days.

Darius Heald born on Sunday Jan'y 27th 1822, at 3 o'Clock in the morning. The Moon 5 days old, in the sign of (Aries) State of Missouri St. Charles County.

APPENDIX IV

CAPTAIN HEALD'S OFFICIAL REPORT OF THE EVACUATION OF FORT DEARBORN[962]

PITTSBURG, October 23d, 1812.

SIR: I embrace this opportunity to render you an account of the garrison of Chicago.

On the 9th of August last, I received orders from General Hull to evacuate the post and proceed with my command to Detroit, by land, leaving it at my discretion to dispose of the public property as I thought proper. The neighboring Indians got the information as early as I did, and came in from all quarters in order to receive the goods in the factory store, which they understood were to be given them. On the 13th, Captain Wells, of Fort Wayne, arrived with about 30 Miamies, for the purpose of escorting us in, by the request of General Hull. On the 14th, I delivered the Indians all the goods in the factory store, and a considerable quantity of provisions which we could not take away with us. The surplus arms and ammunition I thought proper to destroy, fearing they would make bad use of it if put in their possession. I also destroyed all the liquor on hand after they began to collect. The collection was unusually large for that place; but they conducted themselves with the strictest propriety till after I left the fort. On the 15th, at 9 o'clock in the morning, we commenced our march: a part of the Miamies were detached in front, and the remainder in our rear, as guards, under the direction of Captain Wells. The situation of the country rendered it necessary for us to take the beach, with the lake on our left, and a high sand bank on our right, at about 100 yards distance.

We had proceeded about a mile and a half, when it was discovered that the Indians were prepared to attack us from behind the bank. I immediately marched up with the company to the top of the bank,

[962] The report has been published in various places, usually with the opening sentence omitted. As presented here the report is taken from the Drennan Papers, copied from Brannan's *Official Military and Naval Letters* (Washington, 1823), 84.

when the action commenced; after firing one round, we charged, and the Indians gave way in front and joined those on our flanks. In about fifteen minutes they got possession of all our horses, provisions, and baggage of every description, and finding the Miamies did not assist us, I drew off the few men I had left, and took possession of a small elevation in the open prarie, out of shot of the bank or any other cover. The Indians did not follow me, but assembled in a body on the top of the bank, and after some consultations among themselves, made signs for me to approach them. I advanced towards them alone, and was met by one of the Potawatamie chiefs, called the Black Bird, with an interpreter. After shaking hands, he requested me to surrender, promising to spare the lives of all the prisoners. On a few moments consideration, I concluded it would be most prudent to comply with his request, although I did not put entire confidence in his promise. After delivering up our arms, we were taken back to their encampment near the fort, and distributed among the different tribes. The next morning, they set fire to the fort and left the place, taking the prisoners with them. Their number of warriors was between four and five hundred, mostly of the Potawatamie nation, and their loss, from the best information I could get, was about fifteen. Our strength was fifty-four regulars and twelve militia, out of which, twenty-six regulars and all the militia were killed in the action, with two women and twelve children. Ensign George Ronan and doctor Isaac V Van Voorhis of my company, with Captain Wells, of Fort Wayne, are, to my great sorrow, numbered among the dead. Lieutenant Lina T. Helm, with twenty-five non-commissioned officers and privates, and eleven women and children, were prisoners when we were separated. Mrs. Heald and myself were taken to the mouth of the river St. Joseph, and being both badly wounded, were permitted to reside with Mr. Burnet, an Indian trader. In a few days after our arrival there, the Indians all went off to take Fort Wayne, and in their absence, I engaged a Frenchman to take us to Michilimackinac by water, where I gave myself up as a prisoner of war, with one of my sergeants. The commanding officer, Captain Roberts, offered me every assistance in his power to render our situation comfortable while we remained there, and to enable us to proceed on our journey. To him I gave my parole of Honour, and came on to Detroit and reported myself to Colonel Proctor, who gave us a passage to Buffaloe; from that place I came by way of Presque Isle, and arrived here yesterday.

I have the honor to be yours, &c.,

N. HEALD,
Captain U.S. Infantry.

THOMAS H. CUSHING, ESQR.,
Adjutant General.

APPENDIX V

DARIUS HEALD'S NARRATIVE OF THE CHICAGO MASSACRE, AS TOLD TO LYMAN C. DRAPER IN 1868[963]

In a newspaper account preserved by D. Heald, somewhat fragmentary—evidently an obituary notice of Maj. Heald—is the following, supplying a few words toward the close in brackets:

"Maj. Heald was in command of Fort Dearborn, Chicago, in 1812, when an order was presented to him by a British officer [an Indian, Mr. D. Heald believes] from Gen. Hull to deliver up the post, with all the public property therein. The officer was accompanied by several hundred Indians who, after the troops had left the garrison, commenced an indiscriminate massacre of the men, women & children. The Major endeavored to rally the few who were armed, but was so severely wounded in the very outset as to be deprived of every means of resistance. In this situation he was about to be dispatched by some of the Indians and was only saved by the interference of a young man, a half-breed connected with the Indians by the name of *Jean Baptist Chandonnis*, through whose persuasions & the hope of a considerable reward which he held out to the savages, they were induced to desist from their murderous design, & to take him a prisoner. Mrs. Heald was in the early part of the action separated from her husband & fell in company with her uncle, the late *Maj. Wm. Wells*, formerly Indian Agent at Fort Wayne. In the running fight which this brave man kept up with a dozen of the Indians, & while dying of the wounds he had received, he killed three of their best warriors, two with his rifle & the third with his dirk. Mrs. Heald was wounded in the breast, in both arms and in the side. To her unshaken [firmness] is she indebted [for the preservation of her own life and that of] her husband [by the aid of] their friend Chandonis."

[963] For an account of the two Darius Heald narratives of the massacre see *supra*, p. 381. The earlier narrative of the two, which is presented here, was related in an interview with Lyman C. Draper in 1868. It is printed here for the first time, from the original manuscript in the Draper Collection. It has never been used by historical writers hitherto, nor, apparently, has the fact of its existence been known.

[*From Darius Heald*]

Maj. Heald resolved to retire for Detroit. Can't tell when nor where the militia came from who were killed. Wells thought there would be difficulty, yet thought they might effect their escape, & strongly advised the attempt, saying the longer they remained the more Indians there would be ready to intercept them when they should start, as they would have to do when starved out. Thinks there was no opposition to evacuation by any of the officers. Mrs. Heald used so to represent it. Capt. Wm. Wells got there perhaps three or four days before the evacuation, nothing was then destroyed; the secreting the ammunition in the well was after he came, as also the destruction of the whiskey, so the Indians should not have it to infuriate them.

The government Indian goods were distributed to the Indians, who were receiving them as the garrison left. Capt. Wells & the militia were half a mile in advance. The Indians had formed a half circle at the east end of the Lake, & the west end of which was left open for the Americans to enter. They did enter. This half moon trap was about three-fourths of a mile long. Wells discovered them as he neared their upper or western line, the advanced party were fired on, returned the fire & fell back to the main body. Wells gave a signal with his hat before reaching Maj. Heald & the main body. Wells & party yet some distance off, mounted on ponies, waving his hat, indicating that their march was intercepted. Indians' heads now began to pop up all along the line. Then Maj. Heald formed his men in battle line on a sand hill, the wagons were made part of the line of defence. The Indians would get up as near as they could, behind trees, bushes & sand banks to protect them, would fire upon Heald's band, who would repel these attacks. Discovering a short distance ahead a better position for defence, Maj. Heald got the wagons containing sick soldiers, women & children between the troops & the Lake, made a charge, drove the Indians & secured this more desirable position.

The Indians kept crowding up & a running fight took place, seemingly from the fort to where the wagons were. Mrs. Heald found herself in front & near her uncle, who rode up beside her, saying, "My child, I'm mortally wounded." The blood was oozing from his mouth & nose. Shot through the lungs. She inquired if he might not possibly recover. "No, I can't live more than an hour," and added, "My horse is also badly wounded & I fear cannot carry me to where the wagons are. I must hasten." His horse soon fell & caught one of the dying captain's legs under him; but Wells managed to disengage himself. Mrs. Heald now said to him, "See, there are Indians close by." He replied, "I care not. I cannot last but a few minutes; I will sell my life as dearly as possible; as there is no apparent hope for your escape, my dear child, I trust you will die as bravely as a soldier." He now fell to the ground & shot as he lay, with his rifle & then with his pistol, thus dispatching two Indians; while reloading several other Indians came up & laying as if dead he made a last effort, raised his rifle & killed another, then hastily bidding his niece farewell, adding that he had done all he could in his weakness, the advancing Indian host had now come up, readily recognized him, though painted black & dressed like an Indian, & while some of them, disingenuously, treacherously, spoke of saving him, one of their number pointed his gun at Wells' head, seeing which the dying man pointed his finger at his heart, & made a circular motion around the crown of his head, thus indicating where to shoot him, & take his scalp, in another instant he lay in death, when his heart was taken out, cut up into small bits, distributed & eaten, that they might prove as brave as he. His scalp was then torn off, his body well hacked & cut to pieces.

Mrs. Heald received her wo[u]nds while close by her brave uncle, three wounds in one arm, one in the other, one cut across her breast, one in her side, only one bone, & that in one of her arms, broken. She stuck to her horse, was surrounded by the savages & taken prisoner. She had no weapon of defense. Doesn't know what Indian took her, except that he was a young chief. She & her horse were led off and taken to where the squaws were. On the way the Indians charged her with being an *Ep-pi-con-yare*—a Wells. This, from supposed policy, she denied. The squaws came out to meet the approaching party, and one of these forest ladies at once commenced pulling out the blanket from under Mrs. Heald, which was spread over the saddle, & on which she sat, when she tried to see if she could use her right hand, which was the least disabled of the two, & plied her riding whip two or three times smartly over the adventurous squaw's bare neck and shoulders, who quickly relinquished her hold and retreated beyond the reach of this white squaw warrior. The young chief who had her in charge let go the bridle & raised a hearty yell of rejoicing at the daring intrepidity of his prisoner, exclaiming, "brave squaw! Epiconyare!" He seemed resolved on protecting & serving her, & appeared to admire her spirit. He would afterwards take the unfortunate squaw, who was supposed to be his wife, & exhibit to the Indians the marks on her shoulders & relate the circumstances of her receiving them, when they would all raise a hearty laugh, which the squaw herself seemed to enjoy as much as the others.

The chief gave directions to the squaws who lifted Mrs. Heald from her horse, to dress the wounds with poultices, which they did, & rendered her condition very comfortable.

In the fight she had observed one of the officers fall, perhaps her husband. She inquired as to Maj. Heald's fate, saying she was the white captain's squaw. They told her he was wounded & a prisoner to another band, & had not yet marched away. She then told them she wanted to see him & share his fate in company with him. They told her that she and her husband belonged to different parties, and she could not go with him. She insisted that she must see him or die. A squaw who had dressed her wounds now addressed her as Epi-con-yare, and she now frankly acknowledged the relationship, and said if she had been a man she would have fought as long as a red skin could have been found.

Now Jean Baptist Chandonnis made quite a speech to the Indians of the band who had her, appealing to them in their native language, saying that she was an Ep-i-con-yare, that she was not only related to a brave man, but was the wife of a brave officer, and had proved herself a brave & spirited woman, and ought to be permitted to see her husband, and closed with a noble appeal in her behalf. He obtained their promise to remain until he could go and see the Indian who had Captain Heald as his prisoner. He at once repaired to the other camp & informed [Captain Heald] about his wife; & prevailed on his Indian captor to mount him on a poney, though wounded, & conveyed him to where his wife was, when an affecting meeting took place. The good-hearted Chandonnis then tried to effect a trade, an arrangement by which the two prisoners should be kept together. At length Chandonnis purchased Mrs. Heald from her captor for an old mule captured there and a bottle of whiskey, and had her placed with her husband.

In the fight the Indians got in the rear & were killing sick soldiers, women and children when Heald & party commenced falling back, but they were overpowered, killed and taken. Capt. Heald also captured, all at last, in a hand-to-hand fight, all mixed up, whites & Indians.

The Indians used guns, spears, bows & arrows, in the fight.

Thinks the prisoners, Mr. & Mrs. Heald, were some thirty days reaching Mackinaw where Capt. Heald, being a mason, was befriended by the British officer in command there, one of the fraternity, & was treated very kindly, who offered to loan him any amount of money, tendering him his pocketbook even; adding that if he ever reached home he could return it—if not it would all be right.

It was believed by Mrs. Heald that it was her spirited conduct that induced the Indians to spare her & her husband, both badly wounded, & in such condition would be troublesome & cumbersome.

Mrs. Heald saw & read Mrs. Kinzie's Waubun & said it was exaggerated & incorrect in its relation of the Chicago massacre. Don't know the name of the Indian who took Capt. Heald.

Mrs. Heald said the Indians were not drunk.

Mr. D. Heald thinks the friendly Miamis who came with Wells to escort in the troops were what Maj. Heald speaks of as militia [which I doubt, as it seems that the friendly Indians took no part in the fight, whereas some of the "militia" were killed, as Heald's report shows. L.C.D.]

Thinks Wells painted himself as much to disguise his person as for anything else. Mrs. Heald said that she did not see the incident of Mrs. Helm (if it was her) being sent by her captor into the edge of the lake for safety.

In 1831, Chandonnis called & visited Maj. Heald & wife, accompanied by a chief, and spent two or three days there, they being cordially entertained, Maj. H. killing a beef & a sheep & gave them a feast of fresh meat, & talked over the story of the eventful captivity. Chandonnis & others were then on their way to Kansas as a deputation to view the country & report the result of their observations to their people.

Just before the evacuation of Chicago, Mrs. Heald had sewed into a wamus, or roundabout, several hundred dollars in paper money, & gave the since chief Alex. Robinson $100. for conveying Maj.

Heald & wife to Mackinaw, which he safely accomplished. This garment Maj. Heald wore under his regular military suit, & when his outside clothing was stripped from him, the old wamus & money were left untouched.

Page 615 of Peck's edition of *Annals of the West*, says Mrs. Heald was attacked in a boat, this is a mistake.

The Indians were not troublesome as represented in that work, as crowding into the fort before the evacuation.

Wells arrived the 13th, see Heald's official report in the "Annals."

Maj. Heald was so disabled that he was not engaged in any other active military service subsequently. After a few years his wounds gradually grew worse, so that he had to use a crutch & cane, & these wounds finally hastened his death, the ball was never extracted.

Can't say about Capt. Heald first going to Chicago in 1810, don't know whether there was then any garrison there or not.

Mrs. Heald was born in Jefferson Co., Ky., in 1790, was in her 21st year when married in May, 1811.

Mr. Heald has got a small water-color likeness of his grandfather, Gen'l Sam'l Wells, and a daguerreotype[964] of Mrs. Rebecca Heald. There is no likeness extant of Maj. Heald.

[964] Now owned by his daughter, Mrs. Lillian Heald Richmond, of St. Louis; for a reproduction of it see p. 300.

APPENDIX VI

LIEUTENANT HELM'S ACCOUNT OF THE MASSACRE. TOGETHER WITH THE LETTER[965] OF HELM TO JUDGE WOODWARD ANNOUNCING THE NARRATIVE

FLEMINGTON NEW JERSEY 6th June, 1814.

DEAR SIR: I hope you will excuse the length of time I have taken to communicate the history of the unfortunate massicree of Chicago it is now nearly finished and in two weeks you may expect it—as the history cannot possibly be written with truth without eternally disgracing major Heald I wish you could find out whether I shall be cashiered or censured for bringing to light the conduct of so great a man as many thinks him—You know I am the only Officer that has escaped to tell the news some of the men have got off but where they are I know not they could be able to testify to some of the principal facts—I have waited a long time expecting a court of inquiry on his conduct but see plainly it is to be overlooked—I am resolved now to do myself justice even if I have to leave the service to publish the history, I shall be happy to hear from you immediately on the receipt of this—

I have the honor to be
Sir—
with great respect
Your Obt Hb Servt
L. T. HELM.

AUGUSTUS B. WOODWARD ESQR.
Washington City.

[965] The letter as printed here is copied from the original manuscript in the Detroit Public Library. Notwithstanding Helm's statement that the narrative would be ready in two weeks, an endorsement on the back of it indicates that it was not received by Woodward until November 10, 1815. In the meantime Heald had severed his connection with the army, near the close of 1814. In view of Helm's apprehensions of being court-martialed for his story, it seems not unlikely that there is some relation between Heald's retirement and its long-delayed appearance. Words and phrases which have been crossed out in the original manuscript of the letter and of the massacre narrative are printed in italics and put within brackets.

[Addressed] Flemington [*Paid*] 17
Jun 6th.
Augustus B. Woodward, Esq.
Milton,
[*Washington City*]
Va.

[Endorsed]
Helm, Mr. Linah T.,
letter from
Dated Fleming-
ton New Jersey
June 6th. 1814.
Received at Washing-
ton.
June
14th
1814.

THE MASSACRE NARRATIVE[966]

Some time in [*March*] April, about the 7th–10, a party of Winnebagoes came to Chicago and murdered 2 Men this gave a Sufficient ground for to suppose the Indians Hostile as they had left every sign by scalping them & leaving a weapon say a war mallet as a token of their returning in June, Mr. Kinzie sent in a letter from the Interior of the Indian country to inform Capt. Heald that the Indians were Hostile inclined & only waiting the Declaration of War to commence Hostilities this they told Kenzie In confidence on the 10th of July Capt. Heald got the information of War being declared & on the 8th. of august got Genl. Hull's order to Evacuate the Post of Fort Dearborne by the route of Detroit or Fort Wayne if Practicable. This Letter was brot by a Potowautemie Chief Winnemeg & he informed Capt. Heald through Kenzie to evacuate immediately the next day if possible as the Indians were hostile & that the Troops should change the usual Route to go to Fort Wayne. [*The Evacuation took place on the 15 August prior to this*] Capt. William Wells arrived from Fort Wayne on the 12th August with 27 Miamis and after a council

[966] The narrative, like the letter (*supra*), is copied from the original manuscript in the Detroit Public Library. The tabular list of the survivors of the massacre which seems to have accompanied the narrative is written in pencil and on paper of a different size than that used for the narrative proper. The sheet is in such condition that a number of the names would be undecipherable but for the light shed by a comparison with the Fort Dearborn muster-roll of May 31, 1812.

being held by him with the tribes there assembled to amount of 500 warriors 179 women & children he after council declared them Hostile & that his opinion was that they would interupt us on our route. Capt. Wells enquered into the State of the arms, ammunition & Provisions [*of the fort*] we had 200 stand of arms [*over them*] four pieces of artillery 6000 lb of Powder & a sufficient quantity of shot Lead &c. 3 Months provisions taken in Indian Corn & all this on on the 12th. Of August having prior to this expended 3 month Provisions at Least in the interval between the 7th & the 12th of august, exclusive of this we had at our command 200 Head of Horned Cattle & 27 barrels of Salt—after this Survey [*Kinzie*] Wells demanded of Capt Heald if he intended to evacuate. his answer was he would. Kenzie then with Lt. Helm cald on Wells and requested him to call on Capt Heald and cause the ammunition & arms to be destroyed but Capt Wells insisted on Kenzie & Helm to join with him This being done Capt Heald Hestitated & observed that it was not sound Pollicy to tell a lie to an Indian that he had received a positive order from Gen. Hull to deliver up to those Indians all the public Property of whatsoever nature particularly to those Indians that would take in the Troops & that he could not alter it, & that it might irritate the Indians & be the means of the Destruction of his Men Kenzie Volunteered to take the responsibility on himself provided Capt Heald would consider the Method he would point out a safe one. He agreed, Kenzie wrote an order as if from Genl. Hull & gave it into Capt Heald it was supposed to answer & accordingly was carried into effect. The ammunition & Muskets were all destroyed the night of the 13th, the 15th. we evacuated the Garrison & about one and [a] half mile from the Garrison we were informed by Capt Wells that we were surrounded & the attack by the Indians began, about 10 of the Clock Morning the men in a few minutes were with the exception of 10 all killed and wounded the Ensign and Surgeons Mate were both killed the Capt and myself both badly wounded during the battle I fired my piece at an Indean and felt confident I killed him or wounded him badly, I immediately called to the men to follow me in the pirara or we would be shot down before we could load our guns we had proceded under a heavy fire about an hundred & 5 paces when I made a wheel to the left to observe the motion of the Indeans and avoid being shot in the back which I had so far miraculously escaped Just as I wheeled I received a ball through my coat pocket which struck the barrel of my gun and fell in the lineing of my coat in a few seconds I received a ball in my right foot which lamed me considerably the Indeans happened immediately to stop firing and nevour more renewed it I immediately ordered the men that were able, to load their guns and commence loadin for them that were not able, I now discovered captain Heald for the first time to my knowledge during the battle, he was coming from towards the Indeans and to my great surprise they nevour offered to fire on him he came up and ordered the men to form that his intentions were to charge the boddy of indeans that were on the bank of the Lake where we had just retreated from they appeared to be about 300 strong we were 27 including all the wounded he advanced about 5 steps and not atal to my surprise was the first that halted some of the men fell back instead of advanceing we then gained the only high piece of ground their was near, we now had a little time to reflect and saw death in every direction, at this time an interpiter from the In[d]eans advanced towards us and called for the Captain who immediately went to meet him (the interpiter was a half indean and had lived a long time within a few yards of the fort and bound to Mr. Kinzie he was allways very friendly with us all) a chief by the name of Blackbird advanced to the interpiter [*the capt*] and met the Capt who after a few words conversation delivered him his sword and in a few minutes returned to us and informed me he had offered 100 dollars for every man that was then liveing, he sayed they were then decideing on what to do, they however in a few minutes called him again and talked with him some time when he returned and informed me they had agreed if I and the men would surrender by laying down our arms they would lay down theirs meet us half way shake us by the hand as friends and take us back to the fort. I asked him if he knew what they intended doing with us then, he sayed they did not informe him he asked me if I would surrender, the men were at this time crouding to my back and began to beg me not to surrender. I told them not to be uneasy for I had already done my best for them and was determined not to surrender unless I saw better prospects of us all being saved and then not without [*their being*] they were willing the Capt asked me the [*third*] second time what I would doo without an answer, I discovered the interpiter at this time running from the Indeans towards us and when he came in about 20 steps the Capt put the Question the third time, the Interpiter called out Lieut dont surrender for if you doo they will kill you all for their has been no general council held with them yet you must wait and I will go back and hold a general council with them and return and let you know what they will doo. I told him to go for I had no Ideah of surrender he went and collected all the indeans and talked for some time, when he returned and told me [*if*] the Indeans sayed if I would surrender as before described they would not kill any [*of us*] and sayed it was his opinion they would doo as they sayed for they had already saved Mr. Kinzie and some of the women and children this enlivened me and the men for we well knew Mr. Kinzie stood higher than anny man in that country among the Indeans and he might be the means of saveing us from utter destruction which afterwards proved to be the case we then surrendered and after the Indeans had fired of our guns they put the Capt myself and some of the wounded men on horses and marched us to the bank of the lake where the battle first commenced when we arrived at the bank and looked down on the sand beach I was struck with horror at the sight of men women and children lying naked with principally all their heads off, and in passing over the bodies I was confident I saw my wife with her head off about two feet from her sholders tears for the first time rushed in my eyes but I consoled myself with a firm belief that I should soon follow her, I now began to repent that I had ever surrendered but it was two late to recall and we had only to look up to him who first caused our existence, when we had arrived in half a mile of the Fort they halted us made the men sit down form a ring round them began to take off their hats and strip the Capt they attempted to strip me but were prevented by a chief who stuck close to me, I made signes to him that I wanted to drink for the weather was very warm he led me off towards the Fort and to my great astonishment saw my wife siting among some squaws crying our feelings can be better judged than expressed they brought some water and directed her to wash and dress my wound which she did and bound it up with her pocket handkerchief, they then brought up some of the men and tommyhawked [*some*] one of them before us, they now took Mrs. Helm across the river (for we were nearly on its bank) to Mr. Kinzies, we met again at my Fathers in the state of New York she having arrived seven days before me after being sepe-rated seven months and one week she was taken in the direction of

Detroit and I was taken down the Illinois river and was sold to Mr. Thomas Forsyth half brother of Mr. Kinzies who a short time after effected my escape. this Gentleman was the means of saveing many lives on the Warring frontier I was taken on the 15th of August and arrived safe among the americans at St. Louis on the 14th. of October.

Captain Heald through Kenzie sending his two Negroes got put on board a Indean boat going to St. Joseph & from that place got to Makinac by Lake Michigan in a Birch Canoe—The night of the 14th the Interpreter and a Chief black patredge waited on Capt Heald the Indian gave up his medal & told Heald to beware of the next day that the Indians Would destroy him & his men this Heald never communicated to one of his officers there was but Capt Wells that was acquainted with it you will observe Sir that I did with Kenzie protest against Dest[r]oying the arms ammunition and Provisions untill that Heald told me positively that he would evacuate at all Hasards—

15 of August we evacuated the Fort the number of soldiers was 52 privates & musichn 4 officers & Physician 14 Citizens 18 children and 9 women, the baggage being in front with the Citizens Women and Children I [*could not*] & on the [*Beach*] Margin of the Lake we having advanced to gain the Prarie I could not see the massacre but Kinzie with Doctor Van Vorees being ordered by Capt Heald to take charge of the Women & children remained on the Beach & Kinzie since told me he was an Eye witness to the Horred scene the Indians came down on the baggage waggons for Plunder they Butchered every male citizen but Kenzie two women & 12 Children in the most inhuman manner Possible opened them cutting off their Heads & taken out their Hearts, several of the women were wounded but not dangerously.

[Endorsed on back] Mr. Helm. Nov. 10, 1815.

Nathan Heald	1.	Released.
Lina T. Helm	2	Do
Nathan Edson	3	....
Elias Mills	4	....
Thos. Point Dexter	5	....
August Mort	6	Died Natural
James Latta	7	Killed
Michael Lynch	8	Killed
John Suttinfield	9	Killed
John Smith Senr.	10	Released
John Smith Junr.	11	....

Nathan Hurt	12	Deserted
Richard Garner	13	Killed
Paul Grumo	14	....
James Vanhorn	15	....
Wm Griffiths	16	Supposed to be a
Joseph Bowen	17	frenchman and Released
John Fury	18	....
John Crozier	19	Deserted
John Needs	20	
Daniel Daugherty	21	
Dyson Dyer	22	Killed
John [Prestly] Andrews	23	Killed
James Starr	24	Killed
Joseph Noles	25	
James Corbin	26	
Fielding Corbin	27	
Citizens		
Jos. Burns	28	Mortally wounded since killed

[Names of women on reverse page]

Women taken prisoners.

Mrs. Heald — Released.
Mrs. Helm — Do

Mrs. Holt
Mrs. Burns
Mrs. Leigh
Mrs. Simmons
Mrs. Needs
— Prisoners.

....

Killed in the action
Mrs. Corbin
Mrs. Heald's Negro woman

Children yet in Captivity
Mrs. Leigh's 2 one Since Dead N D
Mrs. Burns 2
Mrs. Simmon[s] 1
13 Children Killed during the action
11 Citizens including Capt. Wells.

John Kinzie taken but not considered as a Prisoner of War

---

54 Rank & file left the Garrison

APPENDIX VII

LETTER OF JUDGE AUGUSTUS B. WOODWARD TO COLONEL PROCTOR CONCERNING THE SURVIVORS OF THE CHICAGO MASSACRE[967]

MICHIGAN, oct. 7, 12.

SIR, It is already known to you that on saturday the fifteenth day of August last, an order having been given to evacuate fort dearborn, an attack was made by the savages of the vicinity on the troops and persons appertaining to that garrison, on their march, and at the distance of about [*after before they had marched*] three miles from the fort [*three of the survivors of that terrible massacre*] and the greater part of the number barbarously and inhumanly massacred. Three of the survivors of that unhappy and terrible disaster having since reached this country I have employed some pains to collect the number and names of those who were not immediately slain and to ascertain whether any hopes might yet be entertained of saving the remainder. It is on this subject that I wish to interest your feelings and to solicit the benefit of your interposition convinced that you [*will ever*] estimate humanity among the brightest virtues of the soldier. [*On the policy of associating uncivilized men in the hostile operations of civilized powers, or on the rules and limitations on which a savage force if employed at all should be regulated, I will say nothing because I am impressed with a strong conviction that if any British officer had been present on this melancholy occasion the consequences would have been extremely different, infinitely less to be regretted.*]

I find, Sir, that the party consisted of ninety-three persons. Of these the [*regular*] military [*forces*] including officers, non-commissioned officers, and privates, amounted to fifty-four. The [*militia*] citizens not acting in a military capacity consisted of twelve. The number of women was nine and that of the children eighteen. The whole of the citizens were slaughtered, two women, and twelve children. Of

[967] Copied from the original rough draft of the letter in the Detroit Public Library. The letter as actually sent differed slightly from the rough draft. The latter is presented here with all its erasures and changes. Words and phrases crossed out in the original manuscript are printed in italics and placed within brackets.

the military twenty-six were killed at the time of the attack, and accounts have [*reached*] arrived of at least [*four*] five of the surviving prisoners having been put to death in the course of [*that*] the same night. There will remain then twenty-[*four*]three of the military, seven women and six children, whose fate with the exception of the three who have come in, and of two others who are known [*understood*] to be in safety at St. Joseph's, remains to be yet ascertained. Of these [*I will fur*]—amounting—[*to*] in all to thirty-one persons I will furnish you with the names of all that I have been able to identify. First. There is one officer a lieutenant, of the name of Linah T. Helm, with whom I have had the happiness of a personal acquaintance. His father is a [*respectable*] gentleman of Virginia & of the first respectability who has since settled in the state of New York. He is an officer of great merit and the most unblemished character. The lady of this gentleman a young and [*beautiful*] amiable victim of misfortune was separated from her husband. She was delivered up to her father-in-law, [*a British subject,*] who was present. [*but*] Mrs. Helm was transported into the Indian country a hundred miles from the scene of action and has not since been heard of at this place. Second. Of six non-commissioned officers four survived the action. [*Their names are*] John Crozier a sergeant, Daniel Dougherty a corporal, and one other corporal by the name of Bowen. The other is William Griffin a serjeant who is now here. [*In addition to*] With these may be included John Fifer Smith a fifer.

Third. Of the privates it is said that five, and it is not known how many more were put to death in the night after the action. Of those who are said to have thus suffered I have only been able to collect the names of two Richard Garner and James Latte. Mr. Burns a citizen severely wounded was killed by a squaw in the day time about an hour after the action. There will thus remain
to be accounted for of whom I can only give the following names—Micajah Dennison and John Fury were so badly wounded in the action that [*perh*] little hope was indulged of their recovery. Dyson Dyer, William Nelson Hunt, Duncan McCarty, Augustus Mott, John Smith Senior, father of John Smith before named as a fifer, James Van Horn.

Fourth. Of the [*six*] five women whose fate remains to be ascertained I am enabled to give the names of all. They were Mrs. Burns wife to the citizen before mentioned as killed after the attack. Mrs. Holt, Mrs. Lee, Mrs. Needs, Mrs. Simmons. Among these women were six children saved out of the whole number which was eighteen, part of them belonging to the surviving mothers & part to those who were slain. [*The*] As to the means of preserving them I can only suggest the sending a special messenger to that quarter charged with collecting the prisoners who may survive and transmitting them to Michillimackinac. A communication to Capt. Roberts at that place may co-operate.

[*The permis*]

[Endorsed] Chicago prisoners, Oct. 7. 1812.

APPENDIX VIII[968]

MUSTER-ROLL OF A COMPANY OF INFANTRY UNDER THE COMMAND OF CAPT. NATHAN HEALD IN THE FIRST REGIMENT OF INFANTRY COMMANDED BY COLONEL JACOB KINGSBURY FROM THE 20TH OF APRIL WHEN LAST MUSTERED TO THE 31ST OF MAY, 1812

No.	Names	Rank	Date of appointment or enlistment	To what time engaged or enlisted	Names Present	Remarks and alterations since last muster
1	Nathan Heald	Capt.	31 Jan'y 1807	....	Nathan Heald	
2	Lina T. Helm	2nd Lieut.	15 Dec'r 1808	....	Lina T. Helm	
3	George Ronan	Ensign	1 March 1811	....	George Ronan	
4	Isaac N. Van Voorhis	Surg'n Mate	1 March 1811	....	Isaac N. Van Voorhis	
1	Isaac Holt	Sergeant	22 Apl. 1811	22 Apl. 1816	Isaac Holt	
2	Otho Hays	"	23 Apl. 1811	23 Apl. 1816	Otho Hays	
3	John Crozier	"	2 July 1808	2 July 1813	John Crozier	
4	Wm. Griffith	"	1 May 1812	1 May 1817	Wm. Griffith	Joined by enlisting at this place 1 May 1812.
1	Thomas Forth	Corporal	6 July 1807	6 July 1812	Thos. Forth	
2	Joseph Bowen	"	22 Apl 1811	22 Apl 1816	Joseph Bowen	
1	George Burnett	Fifer	1 July 1811	1 July 1816	George Burnett	
2	John Smith	"	22 Apl. 1811	22 Apl. 1816	John Smith	
3	Hugh McPherson	Drumr	20 Oct. 1807	20 Oct. 1812	Hugh McPherson	
4	John Hamilton	"	5 July 1808	5 July 1813	John Hamilton	
1	John Allin	Private	27 Nov. 1810	27 Nov. 1815	John Allin	
2	George Adams	"	21 Aug. 1811	21 Aug. 1816	George Adams	
3	Prestly Andrews	"	11 Apl. 1811	11 Apl. 1816	Prestly Andrews	
4	James Corbin	"	2 Oct. 1810	2 Oct. 1815	James Corbin	

[968] Printed for the first time from the original manuscript among the Heald Papers in the Draper Collection.

MUSTER-ROLL OF A COMPANY OF INFANTRY UNDER THE COMMAND OF CAPT. NATHAN HEALD—*Continued*

No.	Names	Rank	Date of appointment or enlistment	To what time engaged or enlisted	Names Present	Remarks and alterations since last muster
5	Fielding Corbin	Private	25 Oct. 1811	25 Oct. 1816	Fielding Corbin	
6	Asa Campbell	"	26 Jan'y 1810	26 Jan'y 1815	Asa Campbell	
7	Dyson Dyer	"	1 Oct. 1810	1 Oct. 1815	Dyson Dyer	
8	Stephen Draper	"	19 Apl. 1811	19 Apl. 1816	Stephen Draper	
9	Dan'l Daugherty	"	13 Aug. 1807	13 Aug. 1812	Dan'l Daugherty	Re-enlisted 1st June 1812.
10	Micajah Denison	"	23 Jan'y 1811	23 Jan'y 1816	Micajah Denison	
11	Nathan Edson	"	6 Apl. 1810	6 Apl. 1815	Nathan Edson	
12	John Fury	"	19 March 1808	19 March 1813	John Fury	Sick.
13	Paul Grummo	"	1 Oct. 1810	1 Oct.. 1815	Paul Grummo	
14	Richard Garner	"	2 Oct. 1810	2 Oct. 1815	Richard Garner	
15	Wm. N. Hunt	"	8 Oct. 1810	8 Oct. 1815	Wm. N. Hunt	
16	Nathan A. Hurtt	"	29 Dec. 1811	29 Dec. 1816	Nathan A. Hurrt	
17	Rodias Jones	"	9 Dec. 1807	9 Dec. 1812	Rodias Jones	
18	David Kinison	"	14 March 1808	14 March 1813	David Kinison	
19	Sam'l Kilpatrick	"	20 Dec. 1810	20 Dec. 1815	Sam'l Kilpatrick	
20	John Kelso	"	3 May 1812	3 May 1817	John Kelso	Joined by re-enlisting at this place 3d May 1812.
21	Jacob Landon	"	28 Nov. 1807	28 Nov. 1812	Jacob Landon	
22	James Latta	"	10 Apl. 1810	10 Apl. 1815	James Latta	
23	Michael Lynch	"	23 Dec. 1810	23 Dec. 1815	Michael Lynch	
24	Hugh Logan	"	5 Feby. 1811	5 Feby. 1816	Hugh Logan	
25	Frederick Locker	"	13 Apl. 1810	13 Apl. 1815	Frederick Locker	
26	August Mortt	"	9 Apl. 1811	9 Apl. 1816	August Mortt	
27	Peter Miller	"	24 July 1811	24 July 1816	Peter Miller	
28	Duncan McCarty	"	31 Aug. 1807	31 Aug. 1812	Duncan McCarty	
29	Wm. Moffett	"	23 Jany. 1811	23 Jany. 1816	Wm. Moffett	
30	Elias Mills	"	26 Oct. 1811	26 Oct. 1816	Elias Mills	
31	John Needs	"	5 July 1808	5 July 1813	John Needs	
32	Joseph Noles	"	8 Sept. 1810	8 Sept. 1815	Joseph Noles	

33	Thos. Poindexter	Private	3 Sept. 1810	3 Sept. 1815	Thos. Poindexter	Sick.
34	Wm. Prickett	"	7 March 1811	7 March 1816	Wm. Prickett	
35	Frederick Peterson	"	7 June 1808	7 June 1813	Frederick Peterson	
36	David Sherror	"	1 Oct. 1810	1 Oct. 1815	David Sherror	
37	John Suttenfield	"	8 Sept. 1807	8 Sept. 1812	John Suttenfield	
38	John Smith	"	2 Apl. 1808	2 Apl. 1813	John Smith	
39	James Starr	"	18 Nov. 1809	18 Nov. 1814	James Starr	
40	John Simmons	"	14 March 1810	14 March 1815	John Simmonds	
41	James Vanhorn	"	2 May 1810	2 May 1815	James Vanhorn	

[The roll concludes with a table of recapitulation, a certificate as to its correctness, signed by Heald and Van Voorhis, and a certificate by Heald, dated Louisville, December 3, 1812, that the foregoing is a true copy of the original muster-roll.

APPENDIX IX

THE FATED COMPANY: A DISCUSSION OF THE NAMES AND FATE OF THE WHITES INVOLVED IN THE FORT DEARBORN MASSACRE

No comprehensive record of the names and fate of those who composed the company which marched out of Fort Dearborn under Captain Heald on the morning of August 15, 1812, has ever been made. Here for the first time, a hundred years after the massacre, an effort is made to supply such a record. Such success as has been achieved is due to a study, in addition to the sources of information which have been used by previous workers in the local historical field, of several new sources unknown to or unused by students hitherto. The most important of these is the Fort Dearborn muster-roll for May 31, 1812. This, together with the list of survivors given by Lieutenant Helm, the data left by Captain Heald,[969] and the letter of Judge Woodward to Colonel Proctor constitutes the basis of the present study.

At the outset of the effort to name and account for the members of the fatal company, a difficulty is encountered concerning the precise number of regular soldiers in Heald's company. In his official Report, Heald stated that his force of regulars numbered fifty-four. Whether he intended to include himself in this number is not clear. The tabular statement, preserved among his papers, of the composition of his force and its fate, which gives the total strength of his company as fifty-four, exactly one-half of whom were slain, would seem to indicate that he did. Yet the latter document disagrees with the Report in the number of slain, which the Report gives as twenty-six. Turning to Heald's Journal we find the number of soldiers slain in the battle placed at twenty-six, and the number of survivors at twenty-seven, which would give a total strength of fifty-

[969] Aside from the Fort Dearborn muster-roll for May 31, 1812, the papers left by Heald which are of chief importance for our subject are the following: the official report of the evacuation (Appendix IV); Heald's Journal (Appendix III); the Fort Dearborn quarterly returns for the quarter ending June 30, 1812; the monthly return for June, 1812; a tabular statement concerning the troops engaged in the massacre and their fate; a summary statement concerning the women, and concerning the men who perished in captivity. With the exception of the official report all of these papers are in the Draper Collection.

three. There is reason for believing that the number of regulars slain in the battle was in fact twenty-six, but it is manifestly impracticable to determine certainly, from the accounts left by Heald, the exact strength of his company on the morning of the massacre. Heald had, to the end of his life, the garrison muster-roll for May 31, 1812, and other contemporary records, and these are still preserved. An examination of them suggests an explanation of the reason for his conflicting statements. The garrison muster-roll for May 31 and the monthly return for June each show a strength of fifty-five men, while the quarterly return of June 30 and the inspection return of the same date show a strength of fifty-four. The first two agree in showing four officers and fifty-one non-commissioned officers, musicians, and privates present; the third shows three officers and fifty-one of lesser rank present, and the fourth four officers and fifty of lesser rank. There is disagreement, then, between the contemporary returns over the number of the garrison at the end of June; yet it is evident that its nominal strength at that time was four officers and fifty-one men of lesser rank, although one of the fifty-five may possibly have been absent. There is no reason to suppose that there was any alteration in this number between the end of June and the fifteenth of August. Without venturing to say that there is any unquestionable preponderance of evidence that the strength of Heald's company, including himself, on the latter date was fifty-five rather than fifty-four, from a consideration of all the factors involved I incline to believe that it was. In the calculations and statements that follow, therefore, it is to be understood that the total number of regular soldiers involved in the massacre is reckoned as fifty-five.

Including the commander, then, ninety-six persons comprised the doomed company which evacuated the fort on the morning of the fifteenth of August. These fall logically into several groups, varying greatly as to size: John Kinzie, a neutral and non-combatant; Wells, the leader of the Miamis; the nine women and eighteen children of the company; the twelve Chicago residents composing Heald's "militia" company; and finally the fifty-five regulars. The first two of these require but little consideration here, as the fortune of each has been discussed elsewhere. Wells was slain, while Kinzie passed unscathed even through the carnage around the wagons where not another white man escaped with his life.

There is no uncertainty respecting the fate of the women of the company. The subject has already been discussed at length and only a brief recapitulation need be given here.

No.	Name	Fate
1	Cicely, Mrs. Heald's negro slave	Killed in battle
2	Mrs. Fielding Corbin	Killed in battle
3	Mrs. Heald	Returned to civilization
4	Mrs. Helm	Returned to civilization
5	Mrs. Lee	Returned to civilization (Ransomed by Depain and Buisson at Chicago)
6	Mrs. Holt	Returned to civilization (Possibly the woman ransomed along with Mrs. Lee)
7	Mrs. Burns	Returned to civilization
8	Mrs. Simmons	Returned to civilization
9	Mrs. Needs	Died in captivity of exposure and hardship

Of the eighteen children in the massacre only a very incomplete record can be made from the sources that have come to light thus far. Neither Mrs. Heald nor Mrs. Helm had children; each of the remaining seven women, with the possible exception of Mrs. Corbin, had one or more. Mrs. Burns had several, some of whom bore her former name of Cooper; probably several belonged to Mrs. Lee. Black Cicely had one child, and Mrs. Simmons two. One child each at least, and perhaps more, belonged to Mrs. Needs and Mrs. Holt. Twelve of the children perished in the massacre, most of them in one wagon at the hands of a single fiend, and six survived it. One of these, the Needs child, met perhaps the saddest fate of all the company, being tied to a tree by the savages and left behind to die. The other five returned with their mothers to civilization. Two of them belonged to Mrs. Burns, and one each to Mrs. Simmons, Mrs. Holt, and Mrs. Lee.

Unless additional sources of information shall come to light, the names of most of the members of the Chicago "militia" will forever remain unknown. All of the twelve men were killed in the combat except the leader, Thomas Burns, who, badly wounded, was killed a short time later by a squaw. One of his followers was his stepson,

Joseph, or James, Cooper; Lee, the farmer, must have been another although there is no positive record to this effect. Of the others the names of but one or two can be conjectured even. If the boy who escaped from the April massacre was the son of Lee, he doubtless was one of the militiamen. Probably Louis Pettle, who lived at Chicago from 1803 to 1812 and then disappeared from recorded history, was still another. In this connection the conjecture may be hazarded that Pierre LeClaire, the half-breed interpreter, was one of the twelve. Griffith represents that he deserted at the beginning of the fight, for which Griffith at first intended to kill him, but relented when LeClaire pleaded that it was the only way to save his life. If the suggestion that LeClaire was one of the militiamen be accepted, the statements of Heald and others that all of them perished must be regarded as erroneous. This view, however, would explain Heald's statement in his Journal, otherwise erroneous, that twelve militia, including Wells perished.

I have reserved for consideration last the most perplexing problem, that concerning the regulars of the Fort Dearborn garrison. The names of the fifty-five men are preserved in the muster-roll of May 31, 1812. The only man who attempted to record the names of those who survived the battle was Helm, and his list, while incomplete, and inaccurate in various respects, furnishes the most convenient starting-point for determining the names of those slain in the battle, and the subsequent fate of the survivors. Excluding Burns, the militiaman, Helm lists the following twenty-seven survivors:

1. Captain Nathan Heald
2. Lieutenant Lina T. Helm
3. Sergeant John Crozier
4. Sergeant Wm. Griffith
5. Corporal Joseph Bowen
6. John Smith, fifer
7. Private Prestly Andrews
8. Private Fielding Corbin
9. Private James Corbin
10. Private Daniel Daugherty
11. Private Dyson Dyer
12. Private Nathan Edson
13. Private John Fury
14. Private Richard Garner
15. Private Paul Grummo
16. Private Wm. N. Hunt
17. Private James Latta
18. Private Michael Lynch
19. Private Elias Mills
20. Private August Mortt
21. Private John Needs
22. Private Joseph Noles
23. Private Thomas Poindexter
24. Private John Smith
25. Private James Starr
26. Private John Suttenfield
27. Private James Van Horn

As far as it goes the accuracy of this list is confirmed by other sources of information, except for Andrews and Starr, concerning whose fate there is no mention elsewhere. On the other hand Woodward, whose information was obtained from Heald and Griffith, names Denison and McCarty, the former badly wounded, among the survivors; the report of the nine survivors who arrived at Plattsburg, New York, in 1814, adds the name of Hugh Logan; while David Kennison, who was buried at Chicago with great civic pomp forty years later, evidently survived the massacre despite the fact that his name does not appear in any of the sources. We have, therefore, the names of thirty-one survivors, three more than there actually were. Probably two of the names in error are those of Andrews and Starr, mentioned above; possibly the third is that of Logan, although obviously there can be certainty respecting none of the three. A comparison of this list with the complete garrison roll discloses the names of those certainly slain in the battle, twenty-four in number, as follows:

1. Surgeon Isaac VanVoorhis
2. Ensign George Ronan
3. Sergeant Isaac Holt
4. Sergeant Otho Hays
5. Corporal Thomas Forth
6. George Burnett, fifer
7. John Hamilton, drummer
8. Hugh McPherson, drummer
9. Private John Allin
10. Private George Adams
11. Private Asa Campbell
12. Private Stephen Draper
13. Private Nathan A. Hurtt
14. Private Rhodias Jones
15. Private Samuel Kilpatrick
16. Private John Kelso
17. Private Jacob Landon
18. Private Frederick Locker
19. Private Peter Miller
20. Private Wm. Moffett
21. Private Wm. Prickett
22. Private Frederick Peterson
23. Private David Sherror
24. Private John Simmons

There were twenty-six slain, however, according to Heald's Report and Journal. The two names needed to complete the list are probably those of Prestly Andrews and James Starr.

We have thus reached, although not with absolute certainty in every case, the names of twenty-nine survivors and the twenty-six who lost their lives in the battle. It remains to follow the fortunes of the former and trace out those who perished in captivity and those who finally returned to their countrymen. Helm's list is of little assistance here, for his account of the fate of the survivors is both incomplete and inaccurate. The fate of twelve of the twenty-seven on his list is left a blank; opposite the names of five stands the word "released," and opposite two "deserted." In fact, eleven perished in captivity and eighteen returned to civilization. It is evident that Helm was ignorant of the arrival of the nine Fort Dearborn soldiers at Plattsburg in the spring of 1814, and of the news they brought of their comrades who had perished in the wilderness. One of the nine he records as killed, one as released, and leaves the fate of the others blank. Why Hunt and Crozier should have been set down as deserters is not apparent. In fact, the former froze to death in captivity, while the latter effected his release through the agency of a friendly Indian.

The most practicable starting-point for determining the names of those who perished in captivity and those who escaped from it is afforded by Heald's tabular statement. This indicates that twenty-seven survived the battle, nine of whom died in captivity, and eighteen returned to civilization. Our study, however, has already established the names of twenty-nine survivors of the battle. On the assumption, which there are strong reasons for making, that the two not included in Heald's statement perished in captivity, the names of all belonging to the latter class, and of all who were restored to freedom, can be determined. Elsewhere Heald gives the names of nine who died in captivity. They were:

1. Richard Garner
2. Wm. N. Hunt
3. James Latta
4. Michael Lynch
5. August Mortt
6. Hugh Logan
7. John Needs
8. Thomas Poindexter
9. John Suttenfield

The accuracy of this list is confirmed by other sources with respect to all except Poindexter, concerning whose fate there is no mention elsewhere. The two names wanting to complete the list of those who perished in captivity are Micajah Denison and John Fury, who according to Woodward were so badly wounded in the battle that but little hope was entertained of their recovery.

With this list of eleven as our basis it is possible to determine with reasonable assurance the names of the men who were tortured to death the night following the massacre. Forsyth's letter shows that Lynch and Suttenfield, badly wounded, were killed by the Indians, while en route to the Illinois River. The report of the Plattsburg group of survivors accounts for the death of four others. Hunt froze to death; Needs died about the middle of January, 1813, probably from the hardships of his captivity; Logan and Mortt were tomahawked because of their inability to keep up with their captors. The five remaining, Garner, Latta, Denison, Fury, and Poindexter, are evidently the men who were tortured to death at Chicago. Concerning the first two we have the positive statement of Woodward in his letter to Proctor. The belief that this was the fate of the others rests, obviously, on inference and deduction.

To determine the names of the eighteen who returned to civilization it is now necessary only to eliminate these eleven names from the list of the twenty-nine survivors already given. Concerning the return of twelve of the eighteen there are positive records, while that of Kennison may safely be inferred from our knowledge of his later life and death at Chicago. Of the other five no mention or record has been found, and their names are obtained only by the process of analysis which has already been gone through. In the list that follows these five are given last:

1. Captain Nathan Heald
2. Lieutenant Lina T. Helm
3. Sergeant Wm. Griffith
4. Corporal Joseph Bowen
5. Private James Corbin
6. Private Fielding Corbin
7. Private Dyson Dyer
8. Private Nathan Edson
9. Private Paul Grummo
10. Private Elias Mills
11. Private Joseph Noles
12. Private James Van Horn
13. Private David Kennison
14. Sergeant John Crozier
15. Private Daniel Daugherty
16. Private Duncan McCarty
17. John Smith, fifer
18. Private John Smith (father of the preceding)

Although some doubt necessarily attends the conclusions which have been reached concerning the fate of some of the members of the Fort Dearborn garrison, practical certainty attaches to the conclusion reached concerning the great majority, and it is believed that the present study is as accurate and complete as can be made with the sources of information at present available. The study may properly conclude with a tabular recapitulation, embodying the conclusions reached as to the names and fate of the regular soldiers of the Fort Dearborn garrison on the morning of August 15, 1812.

1.	Nathan Heald	Capt.	Returned to civilization
2.	Lina T. Helm	2nd Lieut.	Returned to civilization
3.	George Ronan	Ensign	Killed in battle near the baggage wagons
4.	Isaac Van Voorhis	Surgeon's mate	Killed in battle near the baggage wagons

1. Isaac Holt	Sergeant	Killed in battle
2. Otho Hays	Sergeant	Killed in battle in individual duel with an Indian
3. John Crozier	Sergeant	Returned to civilization
4. Wm. Griffith	Sergeant	Returned to civilization
1. Thomas Forth	Corporal	Killed in battle
2. Joseph Bowen	Corporal	Returned to civilization
1. George Burnett	Fifer	Killed in battle
2. John Smith	Fifer	Returned to civilization
3. Hugh McPherson	Drummer	Killed in battle
4. John Hamilton	Drummer	Killed in battle
1. John Allin	Private	Killed in battle
2. George Adams	Private	Killed in battle
3. Prestly Andrews	Private	Killed in battle
4. James Corbin	Private	Returned to civilization
5. Fielding Corbin	Private	Returned to civilization
6. Asa Campbell	Private	Killed in battle
7. Dyson Dyer	Private	Returned to civilization
8. Stephen Draper	Private	Killed in battle
9. Daniel Daugherty	Private	Returned to civilization
10. Micajah Denison	Private	Badly wounded in battle; tortured to death the ensuing night
11. Nathan Edson	Private	Returned to civilization
12. John Fury	Private	Badly wounded in battle; tortured to death the ensuing night
13. Paul Grummo	Private	Returned to civilization
14. Richard Garner	Private	Tortured to death the night after the massacre
15. Wm. N. Hunt	Private	Frozen to death in captivity
16. Nathan A. Hurtt	Private	Killed in battle
17. Rhodias Jones	Private	Killed in battle
18. David Kennison	Private	Returned to civilization; died at Chicago in 1852
19. Samuel Kilpatrick	Private	Killed in battle
20. John Kelso	Private	Killed in battle
21. Jacob Landon	Private	Killed in battle
22. James Latta	Private	Tortured to death the night after the massacre
23. Michael Lynch	Private	Badly wounded; killed by the Indians en route to the Illinois River

24. Hugh Logan	Private	Tomahawked in captivity because unable to walk from fatigue
25. Frederick Locker	Private	Killed in battle
26. August Mortt	Private	Tomahawked in captivity
27. Peter Miller	Private	Killed in battle
28. Duncan McCarty	Private	Returned to civilization
29. Wm. Moffett	Private	Killed in battle
30. Elias Mills	Private	Returned to civilization
31. John Needs	Private	Died in captivity
32. Joseph Noles	Private	Returned to civilization
33. Thos. Poindexter	Private	Tortured to death the night after the massacre
34. Wm. Prickett	Private	Killed in battle
35. Frederick Peterson	Private	Killed in battle
36. David Sherror	Private	Killed in battle
37. John Suttenfield	Private	Badly wounded; killed by the Indians while en route to the Illinois River
38. John Smith	Private	Returned to civilization
39. James Starr	Private	Killed in battle
40. John Simmons	Private	Killed in battle
41. James Van Horn	Private	Returned to civilization

BIBLIOGRAPHY

BIBLIOGRAPHY

Adams, Henry. *History of the United States of America, 1801-1817* (New York, 1903-4). 9 vols.

The standard general authority for the period it covers. Vol. VI, 1811-13, contains an account of the contest with Tecumseh, the opening of the War of 1812, and of Hull's campaign and surrender.

Alvord, Clarence W. "The Conquest of St. Joseph, Michigan, by the Spaniards in 1781," *Missouri Historical Review*, II, 195-210.

A critical study, presenting a new interpretation of the expedition. Condemns sharply the prior study of the same expedition by Mr. E. G. Mason, in his *Chapters from Illinois History.*

American Fur Company invoices (MS).

These papers, in the possession of the Detroit Public Library, are useful for the light they shed upon the operations of the American Fur Company.

American State Papers. Documents, legislative and executive, of the Congress of the United States, from the first session of the first to the third session of the thirteenth Congress inclusive.

The two volumes devoted to Indian affairs are the ones of principal importance to this work. They contain a large mass of material pertaining to the relations between the Indians and the United States during the early period of our national existence.

Andreas, A. T. *History of Chicago.* From the earliest period to the present time (Chicago, 1884). 3 vols.

One of the best of the type of commercial histories compiled for popular consumption. Volume I treats of the period covered by this work.

[Andrews, George H.] *Biographical Sketch of James Watson Webb* (New York, n.d.). Pamphlet.

Reprinted from the *Morning Courier and Enquirer*, September 16, 1858. A frankly laudatory sketch by an intimate friend and business associate of the subject.

Babcock, Kendric Charles. "The Rise of American Nationality, 1811-1819" (New York, 1906).

Constitutes Vol. XIII of *The American Nation: a History* (Albert Bushnell Hart, editor).

Banta, D. D. *History of Johnson County, Indiana.* From the earliest time to the present, with biographical sketches, notes, etc., together with a short history of the Northwest, the Indiana Territory, and the state of Indiana (Chicago, 1888).

Barry, Rev. Wm. Transcript of names in John Kinzie's account books kept at Chicago from 1804 to 1822 (MS).

The original account books, four in number, were burned in the destruction of the library of the Chicago Historical Society in the Chicago Fire of 1871. Before the outbreak of the Civil War James Grant Wilson conceived the project of writing a history of early Chicago and commissioned Rev. William Barry, founder and first secretary of the Chicago Historical Society, to make for his use a complete transcript of the names in Kinzie's account books. Wilson's project never materialized, owing to the disarrangement of his plans and occupation caused by the outbreak of the war. The transcript came into the possession of the Chicago Historical Society in 1902. It consists of about fifty closely written pages containing about two thousand names, with brief entries frequently concerning the commercial transaction in question. It was jealously guarded by Wilson, and since by the Historical Society, and has never been accessible to students hitherto. It is a unique and valuable source of information for the period with which it deals.

Beaubien family genealogy (MS).

Compiled by Clarence M. Burton of Detroit. I have used the typewritten copy presented by him to the Chicago Historical Society.

Beggs, Rev. S. R. *Pages from the Early History of the West and Northwest.* Embracing reminiscences and incidents of settlement and growth, and sketches of the material and religious progress, of the states of Ohio, Indiana, Illinois, and Missouri, with especial reference to the history of Methodism (Cincinnati, 1868).

Beggs was a pioneer Methodist preacher of northern Illinois in the early thirties. The book contains a vivid account by a participant of the scenes of excitement at Chicago and in northern Illinois in 1832 in connection with the Black Hawk War.

[Benton Thomas H.] *Thirty Years' View; or, a History of the Working of the American Government for Thirty Years, from 1820 to 1850. . . . .* By a senator of thirty years (New York, 1854). 2 vols.

Benton led the fight in the Senate on the government factory system. The book contains a brief partisan account of his activities in this connection.

Black Hawk. Life of Ma-ka-tai-me-she-hia-kiak or Black Hawk . . . . with an account of the course and general history of the late war . . . . (Boston, 1834).

The work, edited by J. B. Patterson, purports to have been dictated by Black Hawk to Antoine Le Clare, a half-breed interpreter. Its trustworthiness has been called in question, but for the purposes for which it has been cited in this work, at least, it seems worthy of credence.

Blanchard, Rufus. *Discovery and Conquests of the Northwest with the History of Chicago* (Wheaton, Ill., 1881).

A later edition of this work was brought out at Chicago in 1898 in two volumes. It is carelessly and uncritically written, but contains some information obtained by the author in interviews with pioneers which is not to be had elsewhere.

Brice, Wallace A. *History of Fort Wayne from the Earliest Known Accounts of this Point to the Present Period* . . . . (Fort Wayne, Indiana, 1868).

Carter, Clarence Edwin. *Great Britain and the Illinois Country, 1763–1774* (Washington, 1910).

One of the prize essays of the American Historical Association.

Caton, John Dean. *Miscellanies* (Boston, 1880).

Contains a description by a sympathetic and highly intelligent observer of the Pottawatomies' farewell to Chicago in 1835.

Charlevoix, P. de. *Histoire et description générale de la Nouvelle France, avec le journal historique d'un voyage fait par ordre du roi dans l'Amérique Septentrionale* (Paris, 1744). 6 vols.

One of the best of the seventeenth-century accounts of New France. The first four volumes comprise the *Histoire . . . . de la Nouvelle France;* the last two constitute the journal and bear the separate title *Journal d'un voyage fait par ordre du Roi dans l'Amérique Septentrionale; addresse à Madame la Duchesse de Lesdiguières.* The *Histoire* has been translated into English by John G. Shea (*q.v.*) and there are two English editions of the *Journal.*

Charlevoix, Father. *Letters to the Duchess of Lesdiguières; Giving an Account of a Voyage to Canada and Travels through That Vast Country, and Louisiana, to the Gulf of Mexico.* Undertaken by order of the present king of France (London, 1763).

Chicago Historical Society. Collections (Chicago, 1882–1910), Vols. I–IX.

Unlike the usual series of collections of historical societies, the contents of each of these volumes pertain in most cases to a single subject. Those which have been of use in the preparation of this work will be cited under their separate titles.

Chittenden, Hiram Martin. *The American Fur Trade of the Far West.* A history of the pioneer trading posts and early fur companies of the Missouri Valley and the Rocky Mountains and of the overland commerce with Santa Fe (New York, 1902). 3 vols.

The standard authority for the subject treated; contains a chapter on the abolition of the government factory system.

Cooley, Thomas McIntyre. *Michigan, a History of Governments* (Boston, 1895).

Craig, Oscar J. "Ouiatanon," in *Indiana Historical Society Publications,* Vol. II, No. 8.

Davidson, Alexander, and Bernard Stuvé. *A Complete History of Illinois, from 1673 to 1884* (Springfield, Ill., 1884).

Dawson, Moses. *A Historical Narrative of the Civil and Military Services of Major-general William H. Harrison, and a Vindication of His Character and Conduct as a Statesman, a Citizen, and a Soldier.* With a detail of his negotiations and wars with the Indians until the final overthrow of the celebrated chief Tecumseh, and his brother the Prophet (Cincinnati, 1824).

Although frankly partisan this is a source of prime importance for the relations between the Indians and the whites in the Northwest during Harrison's long régime as governor of Indiana Territory.

Dilg, Carl. Papers (MS).

Dilg was a Chicago archaeologist and antiquarian, full of industry and zeal, but with rather erratic methods of work and violently partisan in his advocacy of his theories. After his death his papers were purchased by the Chicago Historical Society. From the point of view of this work they contain a small amount of useful information, difficult to extract from the mass of chaff in which it is embedded.

Dillon, John B. *A History of Indiana from Its Earliest Exploration by Europeans to the Close of the Territorial Government in 1816 . . . . and a General View of the Progress of Public Affairs in Indiana from 1816 to 1856* (Indianapolis, 1859).

An excellent state history by a careful and scholarly worker, whose efforts to preserve the early history of his state were but little appreciated by the generation to which he belonged.

Drake, Benjamin. *Life of Tecumseh, and His Brother the Prophet; with a Historical Sketch of the Shawanoe Indians* (Cincinnati, 1856).

An unpretentious but creditable narrative, based to a considerable extent on source material. There were at least two earlier editions of the work than the one which I have used.

Draper, Lyman C. Collection (MS).

Lyman C. Draper was an indefatigable collector during a long lifetime of materials pertaining to western history. Upon his death his papers became the property of the Wisconsin State Historical Society, of which he had long been the secretary. The documents of chief importance in the preparation of the present work are the Heald Papers. For a fuller account of the Collection see Thwaites, *How George Rogers Clark Won the Northwest, and Other Essays in Western History* (Chicago, 1903), 335 ff.

Drennan, Daniel O. Papers (MS).

Drennan was employed by the Chicago Historical Society to search in the archives of the War Department at Washington for documents pertaining to Chicago and Fort Dearborn. The papers consist of attested copies of several hundred documents, chiefly military orders and communications, covering the years from 1803 to 1836.

Dunn, J. P., Jr. *Indiana, a Redemption from Slavery* (Boston, 1893).

Edwards, Ninian W. Papers (MS).

Edwards was the first and only territorial governor of Illinois, and later served as governor of the state. His papers, which comprise four bound volumes of letters and other manuscripts, were presented to the Chicago Historical Society by his son, Ninian Wirt Edwards. They constitute an indispensable source of information for the history of Illinois in the period covered by them. They have been of only minor assistance in the preparation of this work, however, owing to the fact that until practically the close of the period of which it treats Chicago was separated from the settled portion of southern Illinois by a broad expanse of wilderness, and both politically and commercially was much more closely affiliated with Michigan Territory and Detroit. Many of the manuscripts in the collection have been published in Edwards, *History of Illinois . . . . and Life and Times of Ninian Edwards*, and Washburne (editor), *The Edwards Papers*.

Edwards, Ninian W. *History of Illinois from 1778 to 1833; and Life and Times of Ninian Edwards* (Springfield, Ill., 1870).

Farrand, Livingston. *Basis of American History 1500–1900* (New York, 1904).

This constitutes volume II of *The American Nation: a History* (Albert Bushnell Hart, editor).

Fergus Historical Series.

This consists of thirty-five pamphlets, numbered consecutively, pertaining to the early history of Chicago and Illinois. They were issued by the Fergus Printing Company of Chicago. Those numbers to which reference has been made in the present work are cited under their separate titles.

Flagler, Major D. W. *A History of the Rock Island Arsenal from Its Establishment in 1863 to December, 1876; and of the Island of Rock Island, the Site of the Arsenal, from 1804 to 1863* (Washington, 1877).

The early pages of this work give a brief account of the island of Rock Island in the period beginning with 1804.

Franklin, Benjamin, The Complete Works of, Including His Private as Well as His Official Correspondence . . . . John Bigelow, editor (New York, 1887–89). 10 vols.

French, B. F. *Historical Collections of Louisiana, Embracing Many Rare and Valuable Documents Relating to the Natural, Civil, and Political History of That State* (New York, 1846–53). 5 vols.

Contains translations of many of the records of the early French explorers in the Mississippi Valley.

Gale, Edwin O. *Reminiscences of Early Chicago and Vicinity* (Chicago, 1902).

The recollections in old age of one who spent practically his entire life at Chicago. The book is written in familiar and entertaining style, but is quite uncritical and abounds in the faults common to this species of historical work.

Gordon, Eleanor Lytle Kinzie. *John Kinzie, the "Father of Chicago"; a Sketch* (1912). Pamphlet.

A fanciful and highly laudatory sketch by the granddaughter of Kinzie, drawn chiefly from her mother's book, *Wau Bun*. Contains the latest restatement by a member of the family of the Kinzie tradition.

Gordon, Nelly Kinzie (editor). *The Fort Dearborn Massacre, Written in 1814 by Lieutenant Linai T. Helm, One of the Survivors.* With letters and narratives of contemporary interest (Chicago, [1912]).

This volume contains the documents printed in Appendices VI and VII of the present work, chaps. xviii, xix, and xxii of Kinzie's *Wau Bun*, and a reprint of the author's sketch of her grandfather, John Kinzie, noted in the reference immediately above. The text of Helm's massacre narrative, the document of chief importance in the collection, has been freely emended without giving any notice to the reader of the fact. In similar fashion the composition of the chapters from *Wau Bun* has been liberally emended, and in at least one instance an important interpolation has been made, without warning to the reader.

Grover, Frank R. "Some Indian Landmarks of the North Shore" (Chicago, n.d.). Pamphlet.

An address read before the Chicago Historical Society, February 21, 1905.

———. "Father Francois Pinet S.J., and his Mission of the Guardian Angel of Chicago (L'Ange Gardien) A.D. 1696–1699" (Chicago, 1907).

A paper read before a joint meeting of the Chicago and Evanston Historical Societies, November 27, 1906. The author is uncritical and his works should be used with caution. In the present work he contends that "there is not the slightest doubt" that Pinet's Mission stood on the site of the present Skokie March within the limits of the village of Gross Point.

[Hay, Henry]. Journal from Detroit to the Miami River (MS).

This manuscript in the Detroit Public Library is the journal of a Detroit trader who spent the winter of 1789–90 at the French settlement near the Rapids of the Maumee. It gives an interesting and graphic picture of the life of this pro-British settlement during the winter. The chief importance of the journal to the present work consists in the information it gives about John Kinzie, whose convivial companion throughout the winter the journalist became. The journal does not contain the author's name; I have accepted tentatively the ascription of it by Mr. Clarence M. Burton to Henry Hay.

Head, Wm. R. Papers (MS).

Head was a Chicago antiquarian who for many years industriously collected data pertaining to the early history of Chicago and Illinois.

Most of his papers were destroyed, following his death in 1910. A few of them are in the possession of the Chicago Historical Society, however, and a somewhat larger number were until recently retained by his widow. For an estimate of their character, and their value to the present work see Appendix II.

Heald, Nathan, Papers (MS).

These papers, of prime importance for the reconstruction of the story of the Fort Dearborn massacre, and the fortunes of the Healds, are now widely scattered. Much the more important of those still in existence are in the Draper Collection, for which they were procured, apparently, at the time of Lyman C. Draper's interview with Darius Heald in 1868. Those which remained in the possession of the family were exposed to the vicissitudes of chance and the weather until a few years since, when an awakening realization of their historical importance led to a division of such as still remained among the various representatives of the family, the grandchildren of Nathan Heald, by whom they are now carefully preserved. Such as could be assembled were collected for the use of the writer in preparing the present work by Mr. Wright Johnson of Rutherford, New Jersey, a son-in-law of Darius Heald. There are a few Heald papers, also, among the Kingsbury Papers in the Chicago Historical Society library.

Hebberd, S. S. *History of Wisconsin under the Dominion of France* (Madison, 1890).

Important chiefly for its treatment of the long wars of the Fox Indians with the French. The author takes issue with the conclusions of Parkman in certain important respects.

Heitman, Francis B. *Historical Register and Dictionary of the United States Army, from Its Organization, September 29, 1789, to March 2, 1903* (Washington, 1903). 2 vols.

Hennepin, Father Louis. *Nouvelle découverte d'un tres grand pays situé dans l'Amerique entre le Noveau Mexique et le Mer Glaciale* . . . . (Utrecht, 1697–98). 2 vols.

Vol. II bears the title "Noveau voyage d'un pais plus grand que L' Europe . . . ."

———. *A New Discovery of a Vast Country in America.* Reprinted from the second London Edition of 1698 . . . . by Reuben Gold Thwaites (Chicago, 1903). 2 vols.

Heward, Hugh. Journal (MS).

This is the journal of a trader who made a trip from Michigan by way of the Chicago Portage to lower Illinois in 1790. The original manuscript is owned by Mr. Clarence M. Burton of Detroit. There is a verbatim copy of it in the Chicago Historical Society library.

[Hoffman, Charles Fenno]. *A Winter in the West.* By a New Yorker (New York, 1835). 2d ed., 2 vols.

Contains a graphic description of the village of Chicago at the time of the author's visit in the winter of 1834.

Hubbard, Gurdon Saltonstall. Autobiographical Sketch (MS).

Hubbard first visited Chicago as an employee of the American Fur Company in 1818. With the development of the modern city in the early thirties he became, and remained for half a century, one of its prominent citizens. This manuscript deals with his early career in the fur trade. It forms the basis of the published *Life* of Hubbard.

———. *Incidents and Events in the Life of; Collected from Personal Narratives and Other Sources and Arranged by His Nephew, Henry E. Hamilton* ([Chicago,] 1888).

This work, while written in the first person and largely drawn from the Hubbard manuscript cited above, is not strictly an autobiography, a fact sufficiently indicated by the title. Taken as a whole it constitutes a valuable and graphic picture of the methods of conducting the fur trade in the halcyon days of the American Fur Company, and of the manner of life incident thereto. It is of chief value to the present work for its account of the passing of the Chicago Portage. A new edition of the work was issued in Chicago in 1911 with the title *The Autobiography of Gurdon Saltonstall Hubbard: Pa-pa-ma-ta-be, "The Swift Walker."*

Hulburt, Archer Butler. *Portage Paths: the Keys of the Continent* (Cleveland, 1903).

This work constitutes Vol. VII of the series "Historic Highways of America."

Hull, William. *Memoirs of the Campaign of the Northwestern Army of the United States, A.D. 1812.* In a series of letters addressed to the citizens of the United States. With an appendix containing a brief sketch of the Revolutionary services of the author (Boston, 1824).

This work contains Hull's own exculpation to his countrymen for his course in the campaign of 1812.

Hurlbut, Henry H. *Chicago Antiquities.* Comprising original items and relations, letters, extracts, and notes pertaining to early Chicago (Chicago, 1881).

A useful collection of source material, arranged in discursive fashion, and of very uneven value.

———. *Father Marquette at Mackinaw and Chicago.*

Hutchins, Thomas. *A Topographical Description of Virginia, Pennsylvania, Maryland, and North Carolina.* Reprinted from the original edition of 1778; edited by Frederick Charles Hicks (Cleveland, 1904).

Hyde, James Nevins. *Early Medical Chicago.* An historical sketch of the first practitioners of medicine, with the present faculties, and graduates since their organization, of the medical colleges of Chicago (Chicago, 1879). Pamphlet.

This is No. 11 in the Fergus historical series. Of value for its account of the cholera outbreak and the methods of treatment employed at Chicago in 1832. Contains the only defense I have seen of Surgeon Van Voorhis against the charge of cowardice made in Kinzie's *Wau Bun*.

Illinois State Historical Library Collections (Springfield, 1903–11).

Illinois State Historical Society. *Transactions* (Springfield, 1901–1911). Nos. 1–15.

Indian Office. Letter books and other documents (MS).

These comprise a great mass of manuscripts and records pertaining to the relations between the United States and the various Indian tribes, preserved in the Pension Building at Washington. For the most part they have been used but little, if at all, by historical workers. Those which have proved of chief assistance in the preparation of the present work are the letter books and other records of the Department of Indian Trade. Among these are the daybook kept by Matthew Irwin as factor at Chicago, his petty ledger, the Chicago order book, and other volumes relating to the operations of the Chicago factory and of the government trading-house system in general.

Indiana Historical Society. *Publications* (Indianapolis, 1895–1905), Vols. I–III.

James, James Alton. "Indian Diplomacy and Opening of the Revolution in the West," in *Wisconsin State Historical Society, Proceedings*, 1909, 125 ff.

———. "Some Problems of the Northwest in 1779," in *Essays in American History, Dedicated to Frederick Jackson Turner*, Guy Stanton Ford, editor (New York, 1910).

———. "The Significance of the Attack on St. Louis, 1780," in *Mississippi Valley Historical Association Proceedings* for 1908–9, 199 ff.

———. "George Rogers Clark and Detroit 1780–1781," in *Mississippi Valley Historical Association Proceedings* for 1910–11, 291 ff.

Jesuit Relations and Allied Documents; Travels and Explorations of the Jesuit missionaries in New France 1610–1791, Reuben Gold Thwaites, editor (Cleveland, 1896–1901). 73 vols.

Valuable for the movements of the early missionary explorers and their work among the Indians of the Northwest in the early French period.

Johnston, William. "Notes of a Tour from Fort Wayne to Chicago, 1809." MS in Chicago Historical Society library.

A detailed description of the route between Fort Wayne and Chicago, together with brief observations on Fort Dearborn and the Chicago Portage. The MS is a copy, approximately contemporary, of the original.

Journals of the Continental Congress 1774–1789. Edited from the original records in the Library of Congress by Worthington Chauncey Ford, Chief, Division of Manuscripts (Washington, 1904–10). 18 vols.

Keating, William H. *Narrative of an Expedition to the Source of St. Peter's River, Lake Winnipeek, Lake of the Woods, etc, etc.* Performed in the year 1823, by order of the Hon. John C. Calhoun, Secretary of War, under the command of Stephen H. Long, Major, U.S. T.E. (Philadelphia, 1824). 2 vols.

The explorers passed through Chicago and the historian of the expedition has left an unusually doleful description of the place and of its prospects.

Kingsbury, Jacob. Papers (MS).

Kingsbury was an officer in the army in command of Detroit and other northwestern posts at various times from 1804 to 1812, and the officer first selected by the government to lead the northwestern army in the campaign of 1812. His papers, in the possession of the Chicago Historical Society, consist of letter books, original letters, and other documents, and shed much light upon conditions in the Northwest, particularly in the army, in this period. The Library of Congress possesses three bound volumes of Kingsbury's correspondence, but their contents are of comparatively slight importance for the present work.

Kinzie, John, Genealogy of the Descendants of (MS).

This is a typewritten manuscript in the Chicago Historical Society library, compiled by Mrs. Gordon, the granddaughter of Kinzie. It deals only with the descendants of the trader's second, or legitimate, family.

———. Family Genealogy (MS).

This is a portion of a lengthy typewritten genealogical record of the Kinzie, Lytle, and other families of early Detroit owned by Clarence M. Burton of Detroit. It was compiled by an advocate of the claims to legitimacy of the offspring of Kinzie's first family, and later submitted to the criticism of Mrs. Gordon, who believes that her grandfather's first family was an illegitimate one.

[Kinzie, Mrs. John H.] *Narrative of the Massacre at Chicago, August 15, 1812, and of Some Preceding Events* (Chicago, 1844). Pamphlet.

Aside from some scattered source material, this is the first printed account of the massacre, and it constitutes the basis of almost all the later accounts that have been written to the present time. The author was a daughter-in-law of John Kinzie, and her information was obtained chiefly from his wife and his step-daughter, the wife of Lieutenant Helm. The narrative is fanciful and unreliable, yet because of the use made of it by later writers a knowledge of it is now necessary to any understanding of the literature pertaining to the Fort Dearborn massacre.

———. *Wau Bun, the "Early Day" of the Northwest.* New edition, with an introduction by Reuben Gold Thwaites (Chicago, the Caxton Club, 1901).

The first edition of this work appeared in 1856. The author incorporated in it her earlier narrative of the Fort Dearborn massacre. For the rest the work deals with her experience in the West from 1830 to 1834, and with the early history of her husband's family. Although from some points of view the work possesses historical value, from the viewpoint of the present work the judgment of a recent correspondent of the writer that it "is interesting as fiction very slightly founded on fact, but worthless as a work of history" is scarcely too severe.

Kirkland, Joseph. "The Chicago Massacre in 1812," in *Magazine of American History*, XXVIII, 111 ff.

Kirkland interviewed Darius Heald in 1892, and this is his report of the latter's narrative of the Chicago massacre as told by his mother, Mrs. Rebekah Heald.

———. *The Chicago Massacre of 1812*. A historical and biographical narrative of Fort Dearborn (now Chicago). How the fort and city were begun, and who were the beginners (Chicago, 1893).

This little work was inspired by the author's rediscovery of the Darius Heald-Rebekah Heald narrative of the massacre. In it he strives to reconcile this narrative with that of Mrs. Kinzie in *Wau Bun*.

Lahontan, Baron de. *New Voyages to North America*, Reuben Gold Thwaites, editor (Chicago, 1905). 2 vols.

Latrobe, Charles Joseph. *The Rambler in North America, 1832–1833* (London, 1835). 2 vols.

One of the best of the series of descriptions by foreigners of their travels in the United States of which the first half of the nineteenth century was so prolific. Contains a graphic description of the scenes attending the negotiation of the Chicago Treaty of 1833, of which the author was an eyewitness.

Legler, Henry E. "Chevalier Henry de Tonty," in *Parkman Club Publications*, No. 3. (Milwaukee, 1896).

A sympathetic and scholarly summary of Tonty's career in America.

McAfee, Robert B. *History of the Late War in the Western Country*. Comprising a full account of all the transactions in that quarter, from the commencement of hostilities at Tippecanoe, to the termination of the contest at New Orleans on the return of peace (Lexington, Ky., 1816).

One of the best of the contemporary narratives of the War of 1812. Contains an account of the Fort Dearborn massacre drawn from Sergeant Griffith, a participant.

McCoy, Isaac. *History of Baptist Indian Missions*. Embracing remarks on the former and present condition of the aboriginal Indian tribes; their settlement within the Indian Territory, and their future prospects (Washington, 1840).

An account of the courageous and self-sacrificing labors of the founder of Carey's Mission among the St. Joseph Pottawatomies. Sheds some light on the Chicago Treaty of 1821.

McCulloch, David. *Early Days of Peoria and Chicago.* An address read before the Chicago Historical Society at a quarterly meeting held January 19, 1904 ([Chicago], n.d.). Pamphlet.

———. "Old Peoria," in *Illinois State Historical Society Transactions,* 1901.

McLaughlin, Andrew C. "The Western Posts and the British Debts," in *American Historical Association, Annual Report for 1894,* 413–44 (Washington, 1895).

The standard study of this subject.

McMaster, John Bach. *A History of the People of the United States from the Revolution to the Civil War* (New York, 1891–1906). Vols. I–VI.

Map: Bellin, M. *Carte de l'Amérique Septentrionale depuis le 28 degrê de latitude jusqu'au 72.* Par M. Bellin, Ingénieur de la marine et du depost des plans, ... (1755).

Shows an abandoned French post at Chicago.

Map: Homann, Johannes Baptista. *Totius Americae Septentrionalis et Meridionalis, novissima representatio quam ex singulis recentium geographorum tabulis collecta luci publicae accommodavit* (Nuremberg, [1700?]).

Shows La Salle's Fort Miami at Chicago.

Map: Moll, Herman. *Atlas Minor: or a New and Curious Set of Sixty-two Maps, in Which Are Shown All the Empires, Kingdoms, Countries, States in All the Known Parts of the Earth . . . .* (London, n.d.).

Map: Popple, Henry. *A Map of the British Empire in America with the French and Spanish Settlements Adjacent Thereto* (London, 1733).

Map: Rocque, John. *A General Map of North America: in Which Is Expressed the Several New Roads, Forts, Engagements, &c. Taken from Actual Surveys and Observations Made in the Army Employ'd There, from the Year 1754 to 1761;* drawn by the late John Rocque, topographer to his Majesty.

Margry, Pierre. *Decouvertes et etablissements des Français dans l'ouest et dans le sud de l'Amérique Septentrionale (1614–1754);* mémoires et documents orignaux (Paris, 1876–1886). 6 vols.

The early volumes contain a mass of source material pertaining to the work of La Salle in North America.

Martin. *Report of Cases Argued and Determined in the Supreme Court of the State of Louisiana,* comprising Louisiana Term Reports IV and V (New Orleans, 1852).

Contains the decision of the court in the case of *Kinzie and Forsyth* vs. *Jeffrey Nash.*

Mason, Edward G. *Chapters from Illinois History* (Chicago, 1901).

Contains several charmingly written chapters on Illinois in the early French period, based to a large extent on a study of the original sources; a study of the Spanish expedition against St. Joseph in 1781, which has until recently been regarded as the standard treatment of the subject; and the address of Mason on the occasion of the unveiling of the Fort Dearborn massacre monument. The historical value of the latter study is much inferior to that of the preceding ones.

———. "Early Visitors to Chicago," in *New England Magazine* (Boston), new ser., VI, 188 ff.

Matson, N. *French and Indians of Illinois River.* 2d ed. (Princeton, Ill., 1874).

———. *Memories of Shaubena with Incidents Relating to Indian Wars and the Early Settlement of the West* (Chicago, 1890).

———. *Pioneers of Illinois.* Containing a series of sketches relating to events that occurred previous to 1813, ... drawn from history, tradition, and personal reminiscences (Chicago, 1882).

The author of these three works was an Illinois pioneer possessed of more zeal for preserving the history of early Illinois than he was of critical insight. Despite the advantage he enjoyed of personal acquaintance and contact with many of the characters treated in his works, but little confidence can be had in the accuracy of his statements, while it is often obvious that they have no tangible basis in fact.

Michigan Pioneer and Historical Society. *Collections and Researches* (Lansing, 1887–1910). Vols. I–XXXVIII.

This series contains a vast number of documents, indifferently edited for the most part, bearing on the history of the Northwest.

Mississippi Valley Historical Association Proceedings (Cedar Rapids, 1909–12). Vols. I–IV.

The volumes in this new series are ably edited and their contents, relating to the history of the Mississippi Valley region, are in general of a high order of excellence.

Missouri Historical Review (Columbia, 1907–12). Vols. I–VI.

Moses, John. *Illinois, Historical and Statistical.* Comprising the essential facts of its planting and growth as a province, county, territory, and state . . . . (Chicago, 1889). 2 vols.

Neville, Ella Hoes, Sarah Greene Martin, and Deborah Beaumont Martin. *Historic Green Bay, 1634-1840* (Green Bay, Wis., 1893).

Niles' Register . . . . (Baltimore), 1811–49. 76 vols.

O'Callaghan, E. B. (editor). *Documents Relative to the Colonial History of the State of New York* (Albany, 1853–58). 10 vols.

Parkman, Francis. *A Half-Century of Conflict* (Boston, 1897). 2 vols.

This covers the first half of the eighteenth century, and includes an extensive account of the Fox wars. The series to which the work belongs has long ranked as a classic in American historical literature, yet the account of the Fox wars is now obsolete in many respects, and requires rewriting in the light of the mass of documents brought to light since Parkman's work was done.

———. *La Salle and the Discovery of the Great West* (Boston, 1897). 2 vols.

This work still remains the standard authority on the subject treated.

———. *The Conspiracy of Pontiac* (Boston, 1897).

Some of the conclusions expressed in this work have been challenged by Hebberd (*Wisconsin under the Dominion of France*), and other writers.

Peyster, Arent Schuyler de. *Miscellanies by an Officer* (Dumfries, 1813).

A reprint of the original edition of this work has been issued under the editorship of J. Watts de Peyster (New York, 1888).

Polk, James K. *The Diary of James K. Polk during His Presidency, 1845 to 1849* . . . . Edited and Annotated by Milo Milton Quaife . . . . (Chicago, 1910). 4 vols.

This constitutes Vols. VI to IX inclusive of the *Chicago Historical Society Collections.*

Porter, Rev. Jeremiah. *The Earliest Religious History of Chicago.* An address before the Chicago Historical Society in 1859 (Chicago, 1881). Pamphlet.

This work is No. 14 in the Fergus Historical Series.

Porter, Mary H. *Eliza Chappell Porter. A Memoir* (Chicago, 1892).

Quaife, Milo Milton. "Some Notes on the Fort Dearborn Massacre," in *Mississippi Valley Historical Association Proceedings* for 1910–11, 112 ff.

A critical estimate of the printed accounts of the Fort Dearborn massacre, more particularly of Mrs. Kinzie's *Wau Bun.*

Reynolds, John. *The Pioneer History of Illinois.* Containing the discovery in 1673, and the history of the country to the year 1818, when the state government was organized. 2d ed., with portraits, notes, and a complete index (Chicago, 1887).

Roosevelt, Theodore. *The Winning of the West* (New York, 1889–96). 4 vols.

Vols. III and IV of this work contain a good account of the Indian troubles in the Northwest and the campaigns of Harmar, St. Clair, and Wayne in the opening years of the new national government.

Schoolcraft, Henry R. *Narrative Journal of Travels from Detroit Northwest through the Great Chain of American Lakes to the Sources of the Mississippi River in the Year 1820* (Albany, 1821).

This volume has a second title-page with a somewhat longer title. The author was an observer of more than usual intelligence and zeal who spent a great many years in the Northwest as Indian agent at Sault Ste. Marie and Mackinac. The expedition described in this volume was sent out by the government under the leadership of Lewis Cass. The *Journal* contains a description of Chicago in 1820 and an account of the massacre based in part on information obtained from John Kinzie.

———. *Summary Narrative of an Exploratory Expedition to the Sources of the Mississippi River in 1820: Resumed and Completed by the Discovery of Its Origin in Itasca Lake, in 1832* . . . . (Philadelphia, 1855).

———. *Travels in the Central Portions of the Mississippi Valley: Comprising Observations on Its Mineral Geography, Internal Resources, and Aboriginal Population* (New York, 1825).

The "travels" which furnished the material for this work comprised a circuit by Schoolcraft from Detroit by way of the Maumee and Wabash rivers to the Ohio, across southern Illinois, up the valley of the Illinois River to Chicago, and thence around the lakes to Detroit. Most of the journey was made in a large canoe, the remainder on horseback. The occasion for making it was the Chicago Treaty of 1821 to which Schoolcraft came with Lewis Cass in the capacity of secretary. The work contains, therefore, the most valuable account in existence of the negotiations attending that treaty.

———. *Personal Memoirs of a Residence of Thirty Years with the Indian Tribes on the American Frontier, with Brief Notices of Passing Events, Facts, and Opinions, A.D. 1812 to A.D. 1842* (Philadelphia, 1851).

Shirreff, Patrick. *A Tour through North America; Together with a Comprehensive View of the Canadas and United States.* As adapted for agricultural emigration (Edinburgh, 1835).

The author of this work was a shrewd farmer, and his observations upon the people among whom he came are characterized by a degree of sanity and fairness all too rare, unhappily, in the works of English travelers in the United States in this period. Shirreff came to Chicago in 1833 in the same stage that brought Latrobe. His observations on the place, and on the proceedings attending the Indian treaty which was in process of negotiation may profitably be compared with those of Latrobe.

[Scott, Winfield]. *Memoirs of Lieutenant-General Scott, LL.D.* Written by himself (New York, 1864). 2 vols.

Valuable for the cholera epidemic of 1832, and for Scott's share in the Black Hawk War.

Shea, John Gilmary. "Chicago from 1673 to 1725," in *Historical Magazine* (New York, April, 1861).

A brief summary, now of little importance.

———. (editor). *History and General Description of New France.* By the Rev. P. F. X. de Charlevoix, S. J. Translated, with notes by John Gilmary Shea (New York, 1866–1872).

A reprint of this work has been issued (New York, 1900), edited by Noah F. Morrison.

———. *The Catholic Church in Colonial Days . . . . 1521–1763* (New York, 1886).

———. *History of the Catholic Missions among the Indian Tribes of the United States, 1529–1854* (New York, 1857).

———. *Early Voyages Up and Down the Mississippi, by Cavalier, St. Cosme, Le Seur, Gravier, and Guignas* (Albany, 1861).

Contains an English translation, abounding in numerous errors, of St. Cosme's letter describing the expedition of the party of Seminary priests to which he belonged to the lower Mississippi country in 1698–1699. Valuable for its account of Chicago and the Chicago Portage. The original manuscript is in the archives of Laval University at Montreal. There is an attested copy of the manuscript in the Chicago Historical Society library.

Simmons, N. *Heroes and Heroines of the Fort Dearborn Massacre. A Romantic and Tragic History of Corporal John Simmons and His Heroic Wife* (Lawrence, Kansas, 1896).

A slight work with many faults. It is, however, practically the only source of information concerning the captivity of Mrs. Simmons and her infant daughter.

Smith, William Henry (editor). *The St. Clair Papers.* The life and public services of Arthur St. Clair . . . . with his correspondence and other papers (Cincinnati, 1881).

Smith, W. L. G. *The Life and Times of Lewis Cass* (New York, 1856).

Smith, William R. *The History of Wisconsin* In three parts, historical, documentary, descriptive (Madison, 1854).

Smith, Dr. William. Letter of, to James May, dated Fort Dearborn, December 9, 1803.

Smith was the first surgeon at Fort Dearborn. This letter is the earliest contemporary document from Fort Dearborn that I have knowledge of. Contains some information about the founding of the fort not to be found elsewhere. The letter is in the Detroit Public Library.

Stevens, Frank E. *The Black Hawk War, Including a Review of Black Hawk's Life* (Chicago, 1903).

By far the most extensive and valuable account of the war. The author's sympathies are too strongly enlisted on the side of the whites, however, to entitle it to be ranked as an impartial history. The work is profusely illustrated.

Steward, John F. *Lost Maramech and Earliest Chicago* (Chicago, 1903).

Stiles, Henry Reed (editor). *Joutel's Journal of La Salle's Last Voyage 1684–1687* . . . . New edition with historical and biographical introduction, annotations, and index (Albany, 1906).

This is a reprint of the English edition of Joutel's *Journal* published in 1714. It is an incomplete and garbled translation of the original, which is printed in Margry, Vol. III.

Stoddard, Major Amos. *Sketches, Historical and Descriptive, of Louisiana* (Philadelphia, 1812).

The author was sent by the government of the United States to take possession of Louisiana in 1803, and he became the first territorial governor.

Swearingen, James Strode. Papers in the Chicago Historical Society library (MS).

These consist of three documents, copies, apparently, of the originals, which were loaned for this purpose by Lyman C. Draper. They comprise an interview with Swearingen by an agent of Draper in 1865; a letter of Swearingen's written at that time, concerning his share in bringing the troops from Detroit to Fort Dearborn in 1803; and a detailed account of his subsequent career. For a fuller account of these papers see Quaife, "That First Wilderness March to Chicago," in *Chicago Record-Herald*, August 11, 1912. Their existence has been unknown until recently, and no use has hitherto been made of them by students.

Tanner, John. *A Narrative of the Captivity and Adventures of John Tanner . . . . during Thirty Years Residence among the Indians of the Interior of North America.* Prepared for the press by Edwin James, M.D. (New York, 1830).

Tanner journeyed from Mackinac to St. Louis in 1820 by way of the Chicago Portage and Illinois River. The book contains a valuable account of the crossing of the portage in the dry season of the year.

Teggart, Frederick J. "The Capture of Saint Joseph, Michigan, by the Spaniards in 1781," in *Missouri Historical Review* (Columbia, 1911), V, 214–28.

This is the third and most recent critical study, that has been made of this subject. It is based in part on hitherto unused documents. The author dissents rather violently from the conclusions of Professor Alvord, and tends in the main to approve the earlier study of Edward G. Mason.

Thwaites, Reuben Gold. *How George Rogers Clark Won the Northwest, and Other Essays in Western History* (Chicago, 1903).

Among the "other essays" is an account of the Draper Collection in the possession of the Wisconsin State Historical Society.

Treaties between the United States of America and the Several Indian Tribes from 1778 to 1837 (Washington, 1837).

The use of the various collections of Indian treaties is attended with some perplexity. Some of the treaties made can be found only in this one; some others, printed elsewhere, are without one or more of the schedules and special provisions which were ordinarily an accompaniment of Indian treaties.

Turner, Frederick J. "The Character and Influence of the Fur Trade in Wisconsin," in *Wisconsin State Historical Society Proceedings* for 1889 (Madison, 1889), 52 ff.

This was an address delivered on the occasion of the annual meeting of the Society. It was afterward expanded by the author into the work cited immediately below.

———. "The Character and Influence of the Indian Trade in Wisconsin," in *Johns Hopkins University Studies in Historical and Political Science*, IX, 543–615 (Baltimore, 1891).

U.S. Congress, Debates and Proceedings in. Annals of the Congress of the United States . . . . (Washington, 1834–56). 42 vols.

This collection covers the period from 1789 to 1824; it was continued in the *Register of Debates in Congress* (1825–37). 14 vols.

United States of America vs. *the Economy Light and Power Company* (Chicago, 1912). 3 vols.

The evidence in this case, which involves the question of the physical character and the historical use of the Des Plaines River, constitutes one of the most exhaustive investigations ever made, probably, of a comparatively obscure historical question. The original testimony, of which the printed record is only an abstract, constitutes a vast storehouse of information and expert critical opinion concerning the Chicago area, given under oath and subject to cross-examination.

U.S. Public Statutes at Large. Vol. VII (Boston, 1853) bears the title, *Treaties between the United States of America and the Indian Tribes* (Richard Peters, Esq., ed.).

Van Cleve, Charlotte Ouisconsin. *Three Score Years and Ten. Life Long Memoirs of Fort Snelling, Minnesota, and Other Parts of the West* (Minneapolis, 1888).

This volume contains the reminiscences, charmingly written, of the author's life, first as daughter and later as wife of an army officer, at Fort Snelling, Fort Winnebago, and other posts. Some of the persons whose characters are sketched were stationed at Fort Dearborn, either before or after the author's acquaintance with them.

Van Voorhis, Elias W. *Notes on the Ancestry of Major Wm. Roe Van Voorhis, of Fishkill, Duchess County, New York* (privately printed, 1881).

Varnum, Jacob. Journal (MS).

Varnum was factor at Chicago from 1816 to 1822. This document is an account of his life to 1822, cast in the form of a journal. It was made up in 1865 from papers and other data in the writer's possession. The copy in the Chicago Historical Society library, a typewritten manuscript, was furnished by John Marshall Varnum, author of *The Varnums of Dracutt.*

Varnum, John Marshall. *The Varnums of Dracutt (in Massachusetts)*, Boston, 1907).

Virginia State Papers. Calendar of Virginia state papers and other manuscripts . . . . preserved in the capitol at Richmond (Richmond, 1875–85). Vols. I–V.

Volney, C. F. *A View of the Soil and Climate of the United States of America.* With supplementary remarks upon Florida; on the French colonies on the Mississippi and Ohio, and in Canada; and on the aboriginal tribes of America. Translated, with occasional remarks, by C. B. Brown (Philadelphia, 1804).

Contains an account of an extended interview, at Philadelphia in 1798, with Little Turtle and Captain William Wells.

Vose, George L. *A Sketch of the Life and Works of George W. Whistler, Civil Engineer* (Boston, 1887).

Walker, Charles I. *The Northwest during the Revolution* (Madison, 1871). Pamphlet.

This was delivered as the annual address before the Wisconsin State Historical Society, January 31, 1871.

Washburne, E.B. (editor). *The Edwards Papers.* Being a portion of the collection of the letters, papers, and manuscripts of Ninian Edwards, ... presented to the Chicago Historical Society, October 16th, 1883, by his son, Ninian Wirt Edwards (Chicago, 1884).

This work constitutes Vol. III of the *Chicago Historical Society Collections.*

Webb, James Watson, letter to John Wentworth, October 31, 1882 (MS).

This letter, in the Chicago Historical Society library, contains the narration in old age of the writer's recollections of life at Fort Dearborn, sixty years before.

Weld, Isaac Jr. *Travels through the States of North America, and the Provinces of Upper and Lower Canada, during the Years 1795, 1796, and 1797.* 4th ed. (London, 1800). 2 vols.

Contains an account of the distribution of goods at Malden to the Indians.

Wentworth John. *Early Chicago. Fort Dearborn.* An address delivered at the unveiling of the memorial tablet to mark the site of the block-house on Saturday afternoon, May 21, 1881 . . . . (Chicago, 1881).

This constitutes No. 16 of the Fergus Historical Series. As published it embraces a number of documents and other material not contained in the original address.

Whistler, John, Genealogy of the family of (MS).

This document, compiled by James Whistler Wood, a grandson of John Whistler, is in the Chicago Historical Society library.

Wilson, James Grant. "Sketch of the Life of Lieutenant James Strode Swearingen, Together with the Journal Kept by Him on the March from Detroit to Chicago in 1803," in *New York Herald*, October 4, 1903.

———. Chicago from 1803 to 1812 (MS).

A sketch based largely on information gained from Surgeon John Cooper, who was stationed at Fort Dearborn from 1803 to 1811.

Winans, Susan Simmons, Papers Pertaining to the Securing of a Pension for (MS).

These papers, in the Chicago Historical Society library, constitute the only available source of information concerning the life of the last known survivor of the Fort Dearborn massacre.

Winsor, Justin. *Cartier to Frontenac: Geographical Discovery in the Interior of North America in Its Historical Relations, 1534–1700* (Boston, 1894).

This and the two volumes which follow are standard authorities for their respective periods and subjects. They are particularly notable for the use made by the author of historical maps as a basis for his narrative.

———. *The Mississippi Basin: the Struggle in America between England and France 1697–1763* (Boston, 1895).

———. *The Westward Movement: the Colonies and the Republic West of the Alleghenies 1763–1798* (Boston, 1897).

———. *Narrative and Critical History of America* (Boston, 1889). 8 vols.

Wisconsin State Historical Society. *Collections of the State Historical Society of Wisconsin.* Vols. I–XIX (Madison, Wis., 1855–1910).

This constitutes one of the most valuable collections of material in print for the history of the Northwest.

Young, William T. "Sketch of the Life and Public Services of General Lewis Cass. . . . ." 2d ed. (Detroit, 1852).

INDEX

INDEX

Abbott, James, trading-post at Chicago, 130; marriage, 130–31, 158, 170.

Abbott, Robert, trading-post at Chicago, 130.

"Adams," sailing-vessel, visits Chicago, 154; Hull plans to equip, 214–15, 243; carries Heald to Buffalo, 243; carries furs to Mackinac, 289.

Adams, John Quincy, pardons Winnebago murderers, 320.

Aird, James, crosses Chicago Portage, 289.

Algonquin Indians, expedition against Iroquois, 51–52.

Allouez, Father, successor to Marquette, 29; at Chicago, 29.

Alvord, Clarence W., study of Spanish attack on St. Joseph, 100, 439.

American Bottom, settlements of, 82.

American Fur Company, Illinois brigade, 10, 14–15, 278–79; John Crafts employee of, 269; claim against J. B. Chandonnai, 277, 360–61; seeks monopoly of Indian trade, 301; hostility to factory system, 306; grants to, 360–61; invoices, 439.

American State Papers, 439.

Anderson, Robert, in Black Hawk War, 323.

Anderson, Thomas G., narrative of, 135.

Andreas, A. T., history, 439.

Apple River, camp on, 313.

Arkansas, factory at, 295.

Armstrong, Fort, J. Watson Webb's mission to, 283; Illinois militia at, 324; peace negotiations at, 334–35, 337; troops ordered to, 335. *See also* Rock Island.

Army, condition in 1812, 203–5.

Astor, John Jacob, founds American Fur Company, 301.

Atkinson, Henry, in Winnebago War, 313; in Black Hawk War, 323, 334.

Bad Axe, battle, 334.

Bad Axe River, keelboat attacked near mouth, 310.

Baird, Mrs., reminiscences, 274, 277; description of Chicago, 280–81.

Baker, Daniel, company ordered to Chicago, 264–65; horseback journey to Detroit, 275–76.

Baker, E. D., in Black Hawk War, 323.

Baltimore, cholera at, 329.

Barry, Rev. William, founder of Chicago Historical Society, 143; transcript of John Kinzie's account-books, 440.

Beaubien, Charles, grant to, 346, 359.

Beaubien, Jean Baptiste, career, 278; grants to, and family, 346, 358–59.

Beaubien, Josette, grant to, 359.

Beaubien, Madore, grant to, 346, 359.

Beaubien, Mark, keeps hotel, 350.

Beaubien family, genealogy, 440.

Beaubien land claim, 278.

Beauharnois, Charles, ancestry, 66; and Fox wars, 69–70, 76–77.

Beauharnois, Fort, evacuated, 66.

Beeson, Louis, collection of relics, 306.

Beggs, Rev. Stephen R., narrative of Black Hawk War, 325–27; history, 440.

Beggs, Fort, in Black Hawk War, 326–27.

Belknap, Ebenezer, factor at Chicago, 296–97.

Bell, Peter, story of, 254.

Belle Fontaine, Fort, established, 17, 154; factory at, 295.

Bennett, Lieutenant, operations against Americans, 92–94; arrests Du Sable, 140; praises Du Sable, 141–42.

Benton, Thomas H., author of Graham and Phillips' report, 16; attacks factory system, 301, 305–8; history, 440.

Bertrand, Kinzie's trading house at, 132.

Bertrand, trader, grants to, 347; grants to family. 357.

Big Foot, in Winnebago War, 314–15; favors war with whites, 324.

Biloxi, founded, 36.

Bird, Henry, attack on Clark, 95.

Black Bird, speech, 193; receives surrender of Heald, 229, 390, 401, 407, 418.

Black Hawk, leads Indians to Canadian frontier, 249; in Black Hawk War, 322–25, 334; later career, 337; on Fort Dearborn massacre, 397; *Life*, 440.

Black Hawk War, 322–29; cause, 342.

Black Partridge, warns Heald, 220–21, 223, 384, 420; rescues Mrs. Helm, 223, 230, 386–88; captor of Mrs. Lee, 255; asks for factory at Fort Clark, 300.

Black Watch Regiment, occupies Fort Chartres, 81.

Blanchard, Rufus, history, 440–41.

Blue Jacket, Indian leader at Fallen Timbers, 120; at Maumee Rapids, 146.

Board of Trade, reports to, 3, 44.

Boston Tea Party, David Kennison in, 256–57.

Bougainville, memoir, 47.

Bouquet, Henry, ends Pontiac War, 80.

Bourassa, Joseph, recollections, 397.

Bowen, Joseph, captivity, 238–39; survivor of massacre, 423.

Bowyer, John, Indian agent, 270.

Bradley, Hezekiah, company ordered to Chicago, 264–65.

Bradstreet, John, in Pontiac's war, 80.

Brady, Fort, troops sent to Chicago, 328.

Brant, Joseph, buys supplies of Kinzie, 145.

Breese, Sidney, in Black Hawk War, 323.

Brevoort, Commodore, commands "navy of the lakes," 154.

British, reports to Board of Trade, 3, 44; plans for campaign of 1779, 94–95; Cruzat's plans against, 98; raid Ohio River settlements, 103–4; policy in Northwest, 106–8; encourage Indians against United States, 108, 122, 181, 194, 196; hostility toward Americans, 115; build fort at Maumee Rapids, 118; aid Indians in battle of Fallen Timbers, 121; Wayne destroys houses and stores, 121; surrender Northwestern posts, 126; influence over Indians, 178, 263; fear war following Chesapeake affair, 187–88; seek Indian aid against Americans, 188, 194; warn Tecumseh against premature war, 195; strength in Northwest in 1812, 198–99; ask renunciation of portion of Northwest, 262; capture furs of Chicago factory, 299. *See also* English.

Brock, Isaac, operations against Hull, 210; letter to Proctor, 236.

Brodhead, Daniel, ordered to assist Clark, 113.

Brownstown, American defeat, 222.

Buffalo Gazette, report of Fort Dearborn massacre, 393.

Buisson, winters at Chicago, 236; trading establishment at Chicago, 268.

Bullock, Captain, letter to Proctor, 254.

Burnett family, grants to, 357.

Burnett, John, grant to, 347.

Burnett, William, expects fort at Chicago, 129; letter of, 155; dispute with Pattinson, 156; Healds stay with, 241, 407; extends trade to Chicago, 287.

Burns, Thomas, resident of Chicago before 1812, 167; in Fort Dearborn massacre, 227, 230, 234, 252, 423, 430; career, 233–34; in Chicago militia, 253.

Burns, Mrs. Thomas, in Fort Dearborn massacre, 224; ransomed, 236; captivity and later life of, 252–53; children, 252–53, 430.

Bushy Run, battle, 80.

Butte des Morts, treaty, 312, 317.

Cahokia, St. Cosme at, 42; Pinet at, 42; British garrison at, 81; population in 1778, 82; surrenders to Clark, 87; residents join Spanish expedition against St. Joseph, 100; Mrs. La Compt's career at, 137–38.

Caldwell, Billy, trading adventure, 287; mission to Big Foot's village, 315; grants to, 352.

Calhoun, John C., report on Indian trade, 291; confidence in T. L. McKenney, 305; plan for abolition of factory system, 307–9.

Calumet Portage, use, 24.

Campbell, Anthony, in garrison feud, 171–72.

Campbell, Robert, in battle of Fallen Timbers, 121.

Canada, England gains, 79; De la Balme's project against, 98; objects to terms of treaty of 1783, 107; invasion feared, 187–88; West desires conquest, 196; Dearborn's plans for invading, 205; Hull's invasion, 206, 209.

Canal, across Chicago Portage, 5–8, 12–14, 19–20, 339, 342.

Cardin, John B., murdered, 212–13.

Carey's Mission, founded, 345; treaty at, 363–64.

Cass, Lewis, crosses Chicago Portage, 12, 15–16, 19, 313; on evil of liquor to Indians, 183; aids Grummo, 240; proposals for garrisons in the Northwest, 263; party visits Chicago, 281; in Winnebago War, 312, 315, 317–18; negotiates Chicago Treaty of 1821, 343–48.

Cassopolis, and story of Job Wright, 258–59.

Caton, John D., account of Pottawatomie dance, 369–70, 441.

Cavelier, party crosses Chicago Portage, 18, 38–39; at Chicago, 38–39, 44.

Cerré, Gabriel, adventure on Chicago Portage, 18–19.

Chachagwessiou, trader, 285.

Chambolee, bribed to capture Siggenauk, 101.

Champlain, expedition against Iroquois, 51–52.

Chandonnai, Jean Baptiste, in Fort Dearborn massacre, 222–23; rescues Healds, 240, 409, 412; visits Healds, 245, 413; trading career, 277; grants to, 347, 357–58; claim of American Fur Company against, 277, 360–61.

Charlevoix, Father, tour, 11–12, 16; journal, 45–46; in Fox Wars, 63; writings, 441.

Chartres, Fort, Fox raids reach, 55; De Noyelles retires to, 75; English take possession, 81.

Chemin River, Michigan City at mouth, 100; Du Sable located on, 139.

Cherokee Indians, factory established among, 293.

Chesapeake affair, 188.

Chevalier, Louis, leads Pottawatomies against Americans, 90; aids Spanish against St. Joseph, 101.

Chicago, natural advantages, 1; strategic location, 2; Marquette's camp, 24–28; Allouez at, 29–30; Cavelier's party at, 37–38, 44; origin of name, 38; mission of Guardian Angel, 38–42; St. Cosme's party at, 40–42; French cease to visit, 42; Wayne secures cession of land at, 42–43, 123, 125; French fort at, 42–50, 123; rendezvous for campaign against Indians, 45, 59; for campaign against St. Louis, 95; for soldiers in Black Hawk War, 328; Illinois war party at, 60; Langlade's party at, 97; proposals for fort at, 127; rumors of fort at, 129; earliest resident, 136–37; first white woman resident, 137–38; "father" of, 145, 148; John Kinzie locates at, 147; slavery at, 148–52, 177, 228, 288; first wedding, 157–58; civilian residents before 1812, 167; militia company in Fort Dearborn massacre, 167, 224–25, 227, 407, 413, 430–31; in Winnebago War, 317; in Black Hawk War, 325–27; Indians plan visit to Prophet, 193; speech of chiefs from, at Malden, 193; Indian murders, 212–13; arrest of Francis Keneaum, 213–14; goods of factory distributed to Indians, 217–18; indemnity for loss of, 220; establishment of factory, 264, 272, 295; history of factory, 296–301, 308; operations of Robert Dickson, 237–39; residence of David Kennison at, 256–57; establishment of fort urged, 263–64; Indians gather at, 264; gardening enterprises, 265–66; life after establishment of second Fort Dearborn, 267–84; bringing of supplies to, 268; Indian trade at, 268–69, 285–309; John Kinzie's career at, after 1816, 269–70; residence of Jouett at, 270–71; visits of American Fur Company traders, 278–79; G. S. Hubbard's first visit, 279–80; S. A. Storrow's description, 280; Mrs. Baird's description, 280–81; visit of Cass in 1820, 281; Schoolcraft's description, 281; Schoolcraft's prophecy, 281, 339; Keating's description, 281–82; payments to Indians at, 284, 314, 366–67; marriage of Alexander Wolcott, 284; traders' huts at, 287; in Winnebago War, 313–17; in Black

Hawk War, 325–39; description in 1833, 349; Indian duel, 352–53; Pottawatomies' farewell to, 368–70. *See also* Fort Dearborn.

Chicago Portage, 3–20; war party passes, 65; builds fort at, 68; Americans to enjoy free use of, 125; travelers carried across, 143–44, 289; American Fur Company traders cross, 279; Hugh Heward crosses, 286; Lewis Cass crosses, 313; United States gains control over, 342; Swearingen's description, 377.

Chicago River, bar at mouth, 6, 133, 331, 376; Des Plaines empties into, 9; Americans enjoy free use of, 125.

Chicago Treaty of 1821, 183, 343–48.

Chicago Treaty of 1833, 277, 348–66.

Chicago-Detroit trail, 68, 131, 343.

Chicago-Galena trail, Scott traverses, 334.

Chickasaw Bluffs, factory established at, 295.

Childs, Ebenezer, crosses Chicago Portage, 10.

Chippewa Indians, Sacs and Foxes wage war on, 77; numbers of, 83; disloyal to British, 94; plot of, against Northwestern posts, 193; followers of Keneaum, 213–14; bring Hull news of surrender of Mackinac, 215; Indian rescues Crozier, 246; chief reveals plot against Fort Snelling, 283; treaty with, at Prairie du Chien, 364.

Choctaw Indians, factory established among, 295.

Cholera, epidemic, 328–37.

Chouteau, Auguste, negotiates treaties, 262; furs taken across Chicago Portage, 289.

Cicely, slave girl, 177; death, 227–28, 430.

Clark, cattle dealer, 167.

Clark, husband of Elizabeth McKenzie, 147.

Clark, Fort, appeal for factory at, 300.

Clark, George Rogers, operations in Revolution, 84–104; leads Kentuckians against Indians, 109.

Clark, William, appeal of Fox Indians to, 184; negotiates treaties, 262.

Clybourne, Jonas, marriage, 147.

Columbus, Fort, troops sent to Chicago, 328.

Confederation, Indian trade policy, 291–92.

Congress, Continental, Indian policy, 290–91.

Connor, James, grant to, 359.

Cooper, Isabella, in Fort Dearborn massacre, 252–53.

Cooper, John, surgeon at Fort Dearborn, 143, 149; reports of life at, 160–61; description of, 163; privilege to suttle at, 172–73, 175; resigns from army, 175; on death of Van Voorhis, 387.

Cooper, Joseph, death, 252; stepson of Burns, 431.

Cooper, Mrs. *See* Mrs. Burns.

Corbin, Fielding, captivity, 238–39.

Corbin, Mrs. Fielding, in Fort Dearborn massacre, 224; death, 227.

Corbin, James, captivity, 238–39.

Corn Island, Clark builds blockhouse on, 85–86.

Courselle, house at Chicago, 167.

Court martial, proceedings at Detroit, 161–63; of mutineers in Hull's army, 208.

Covington, Leonard, in battle of Fallen Timbers, 121.

Crafts, John, trading house at Chicago, 268–69.

Crawford, Fort, settlers take refuge in, 312; regarrisoned, 321.

Creek Indians, factory established among, 293.

Crespel, Father, shocked at tortures, 65.

Crevecoeur, Fort, built, 31–32; destroyed, 32.

Croghan, George, mission to western tribes, 81.

Crooks, Ramsey, buys corn of Kinzie, 288; charges of, against factory system, 305–6.

Crozier, John, captivity, 246; survivor of massacre, 423; fate, 433.

Cruzat, Antoine, plans against British, 98.

Cummings, Alexander, in Black Hawk War, 338.

Dablon, Father, report of Joliet's expedition, 4–5.
Danville, militia company in Winnebago War, 315–17; settlers flee to, 326.
Daugherty, Daniel, survivor of Fort Dearborn massacre, 423.
Davis, Jefferson, at Fort Winnebago, 321; in Black Hawk War, 323.
Dawson, Moses, on strength of Harrison at Tippecanoe, 200; biography of Harrison, 442.
Dean, John, horseback journey to Detroit, 275; J. B. Beaubien buys house, 278.
Dearborn, first Fort, establishment, 127–30, 134–36; John Whistler appointed commander, 130; John Cooper, surgeon, 143, 149; life at, 153–77; description of, and surroundings, 164–67; garrison feud, 171–76; Main Poc threatens, 193; Indian plot against, 193; strength of garrison in 1812, 198, 428–29; and Hull's campaign, 211; news of War of 1812 received, 214, 416; Hull plans to send supplies to, 214–15; Hull's order for evacuation, 215–17; 378, 393, 403, 406, 409, 416; evacuation of, 217–20; Wells reaches, 219, 225; ruins of, in 1813, 231; last muster roll, 232–33, 247, 256, 259, 425–29; measures for relief of captives, 237–39; Nathan Heald commander of, 403; supplies on eve of massacre, 388–91, 417.
Dearborn, second Fort, establishment, 264–67; John McNeil commander, 282; first white child born in, 282; garrison withdrawn, 283, 310, 322; burning of barracks, 314; regarrisoned, 321–22; settlers take refuge in, 325; converted into cholera hospital, 331–32.
Dearborn, Fort, massacre, preliminary, 212–13, 416; participants in, 222–25; forces and losses in, 230; fate of survivors, 232–61, 422–24; account of, in Heald's Journal, 403; Heald's official report, 406–8; Helm's narrative, 415–21; fate of women in, 421, 430; Woodward's letter concerning survivors, 422–24; names and fate of participants, 428–36; fate of children, 430. *See also* Chicago.
Dearborn, Henry, plans for campaign of 1812, 205; inactivity, 209–10.
De Champs, Antoine, trader, 138, 303.
Defiance, Fort, built, 118; Wayne retires to, 122.
De Garmo, Paul. *See* Grummo.
De la Balme, Augustin, project against Detroit, 98; sends detachment against St. Joseph, 99.
De Lery, report of siege of Detroit, 56, 58.
De Leyba, Francisco, friendly to Clark, 87; defense of St. Louis, 95–96; death, 98.
De Lignery, Marchand, expedition against Foxes, 65.
Denison, Micajah, death, 235, 433–34; wounded, 423.
Denonville, campaign against Iroquois, 38; on effects of liquor on Indians, 183.
De Noyelles, Nicolas, expedition against Foxes, 70–75.
Department of Indian Trade, records of, 287, 299, 447.
De Peyster, Arent Schuyler, proposes expedition against Illinois posts, 90; defies Clark, 91–92; verses, 93; succeeds Hamilton at Detroit, 94; efforts to capture Siggenauk, 100–101; sends force against Americans, 103; statement about Du Sable, 139.
De Quindre, Louis, defeats Hamelin's party, 99; efforts against Spaniards, 102.
Des Moines River, Fox post on, 72–73.
Des Plaines River, fluctuations, 6–8, 16–17; Thomas Tousey explores, 12–13. *See also* Chicago Portage.
Detroit, Fox siege, 55–58; war party at Chicago, 61; resists Indian attack, 80; center of British control of Northwest, 81, 84; defenses in 1776, 82; British expect assault, 91; De Peyster stationed at, 94; De la Balme's project against, 98; Clark's plans against, 103–4; outpost of Americans in Northwest, 128; court-martial proceedings at, 161–63; John Whistler transferred to, 175; Indian plot against, 193; Indian attacks diverted to frontier, 194; garrison in 1812, 198; appeal of settlers for protection, 200–201; invasion of Canada from, planned, 205; capture, 210; effect of capture on Northwest, 211;

Dickson sends warriors to, 238; journey of Mrs. Simmons to, 249; trip of Jacob B. Varnum and party to, 275-76; J. B. Beaubien born at, 278; factory discontinued, 295-96; goods of Chicago factory shipped to, 308.

De Villiers, Louis Coulon, captures George Washington, 66.

De Villiers, Nicolas Coulon, marches against Foxes, 66; commander at Green Bay, 69; slain, 70.

Diamond Lake Island, and story of Job Wright, 258-59.

Dickson, Robert, leads Indians to Detroit frontier, 194; Keneaum's mission to, 213-14; describes ruins of Fort Dearborn, 231; rouses Indians against Americans, 237-38; rescues Fort Dearborn captives, 238-39, 254; witnesses Heald's parole, 242; collects warriors at Green Bay, 249; sends goods to Chicago, 268.

Dilbone, Henry, assault upon, and family, 250-51.

Dilg, Carl, papers, 382, 442; rejects Mrs. Kinzie's narrative, 382; records Alexander Robinson's narrative, 398.

Dillon, John B., history, 442.

Dixon's Ferry, flight of Stillman's force to, 324; Governor Reynolds issues call for troops from, 325; orders to soldiers at, 335.

Dodge, A. C., in Black Hawk War, 323.

Dodge, Henry, in Winnebago War, 317; in Black Hawk War, 323, 334, 337-38.

Dorchester, Lord, hostility toward Americans, 115, 118.

Dorr, Lieutenant, commander of "Tracy," 131.

Douglas, Captain, companion of Schoolcraft, 281.

Draper, Lyman C., records Darius Heald's narrative of Fort Dearborn massacre, 381, 409-14.

Draper Collection, Heald papers in, 380, 442.

Drennan, D. O., papers, 130, 442.

Drummond's Island, distribution of presents to Indians at, 320.

Dubuisson, report of siege of Detroit, 55.

Du Page River, troops camp on, 338.

Du Pain (Depain, Du Pin), trader, at Chicago, 236, 268.

Durand, employer of Du Sable, 140.

Durantaye, fort of, 47-48.

Du Sable, Baptiste Point, De Peyster mentions, 93; career, 138-42; trading post at Chicago, 286.

Dyer, Dyson, captivity, 238-39.

Economy Light and Power Company, case of, 7, 456.

Edson, Nathan, captivity, 238-39.

Edwards, Abraham, narrative of Burns family, 252-53; employer of John Crafts, 269.

Edwards, Ninian, Main Poc's speech to agent of, 182; seeks to obtain Indian murderers, 193; negotiates treaties, 262; report to, 320; papers, 443, 457.

Elliot, Matthew, British Indian Agent, 214.

English, compete for fur trade, 53; overthrow French in America, 79.

Erie Indians, exterminated, 52.

Erie, Lake, Hull urges armed control of, 205-6.

Ewing, G. W., grant to, 359.

Ewing, William, grant to, 359.

Factory, to be re-established at Chicago, 264; system, 289-309; distribution of goods at Chicago, 406. *See also* Fur Trade; Indian Trade; Trade.

Fallen Timbers, battle of, 119-21; Hamtramck's part in, 131; Tecumseh in, 186; sole decisive victory over Indians, 199.

Fever, among Northwestern garrisons, 135, 158-59.

Fifth Infantry, movements, 321, 338.

Finney, Fort, Treaty of, 109.

Firearms, Iroquois gain, 52.

Forsyth, Robert, at Maumee City, 239; secretary to Lewis Cass, 314; grants to, 359, 363; signs treaty, 364.

Forsyth, Thomas, relations with Jeffrey Nash, 148-52; Heald employs horses of, 219; losses in Fort Dearborn massacre, 236, 246, 363-64; Indians esteem, 218; letter to Heald, 236, 255; ransoms Helm, 246; partner of John Kinzie, 287; on operations of factory system, 300–301; witnesses treaty, 359–60; author of narrative of Fort Dearborn massacre, 394.

Forsyth, William, marries Mrs. Kinzie, 145.

Fort, French, at Chicago, 42–50; French forts abandoned, 65; Pontiac plans to destroy English, 80; Cass urges establishment in Northwest, 263.

Fortress Monroe, troops in Black Hawk War, 328–29; 336–37.

Four-Lakes country, pursuit of Black Hawk through, 334; beauty of, 338–39.

Fourth Infantry, honors to, 207; quells mutiny, 208.

Fowle, John, commander at Fort Dearborn, 321.

Fox Indians, wars against French, 45–46, 51–78; request liquor be kept from, 184; plot against Fort Snelling, 283. *See also* Black Hawk War; Sacs and Foxes.

Fox-Wisconsin Portage, Dickson winters at, 214; Fort Winnebago at, 321.

Fox-Wisconsin waterway, 54, 263, 321.

Franklin, Benjamin, and government trading houses, 296.

Fraser, Lieutenant, mission, 80–81; report of, 82.

French, highways to Mississippi, 3; seek route to South Sea, 22; traders in Illinois, 25–27, 285; Iroquois hostility for, 51–52; wars with Foxes, 45–46, 51–78; compete with English for fur trade, 53; power in Northwest tottering, 76–78; overthrow in America, 79; negotiations in Treaty of 1783, 103; importance of fur trade to, 286.

Frontenac, Count, version of Joliet's report, 4–5; recalled, 35; breaks up Pinet's mission, 39.

Fur trade, death knell of, 20; English-French competition for, 53; Fox war hinders, 58–59; British desire to control in Northwest, 107; Indians engage in, 285; volume of, in Illinois, 288–89. *See also* Factory; Indian Trade; Traders.

Fury, John, death, 235, 433-34; wounded, 423.

Gage, Fort, British garrison at, 81.

Gagnier family, assault on, 310–11.

Gale, E. O., reminiscences, 443–44.

Gale, John, and story of Fort Dearborn captive, 260–61.

Galena, panic of settlers, 312–13; volunteers from, in Winnebago War, 317.

Galvez, Bernardo de, operations against British, 94.

Garner, Richard, death, 234, 423, 434.

Gary (Guarie), trader, 138.

Gary River, name of North Branch, 138.

Gautier, Charles, operations against Americans, 90–93.

Geiger, Jacob, relations with Heald, 404.

"General Wayne," carries troops to Chicago, 265.

Geneva, Lake, home of Big Foot's band, 314.

Ghent, Treaty of, 262.

Gibault, Father, assists Clark, 86–87.

Glaize River, Wayne destroys villages on, 117–18.

Gomo, gives news of Main Poc, 194.

Gordon, Eleanor, writings, 444.

Graham, John, negotiates treaties, 262.

Graham, R., report of, 16, 19.

Grand Portage, need of fort at, 263.

Grant, Ulysses S., serves under William Whistler, 169.

Gratiot, Fort, garrisoned, 321; troops from, sent to Chicago, 328; cholera at, 329–30.

Great Lakes, ice in, 7; New France extends to, 52; Jacob B. Varnum's voyage on, 272–73; northern boundary of United States, 272–73.

Green Bay, Foxes threaten, 54; abandoned, 65, 80; post reoccupied, 69, 80; Sacs refuse to return to, 76; Dickson plans to send goods to, 238; captivity of Mrs. Simmons at, 248–49; Dickson collects warriors at, 249; American fort established, 263–65; factory established, 264; French post at, 286; Fort Dearborn garrison ordered to, 322; cholera panic at, 330–31. *See also* Fort Howard.

Greenville, Wayne establishes camp at, 116; Wayne retires to, 123; Prophet begins career at, 186; Treaty of, 42–43, 122–25, 191, 225, 262, 340; second Treaty of, 179.

"Griffin," built, 30; lost, 31–32.

Griffith, William, letter of, 234, 253; captivity, 236, 242–43; informant of McAfee, 379, 397; survivor of massacre, 423; intends to kill Le Claire, 431.

Grignon, Augustin, statements about Du Sable, 141.

Grover, Frank R., on Pinet's mission, 40–41; addresses, 444.

Grummo (De Garmo), Paul, captivity, 238–40; account of Fort Dearborn massacre, 397.

Guardian Angel Mission, 37–42.

Guignas, Father, captivity, 66.

Hagar, Albert D., on Marquette's route, 24.

Hall, Benjamin, Margaret Kinzie marries, 147.

Hamelin, Jean Baptiste, expedition against St. Joseph, 99.

Hamilton, Alexander, letter to, 153; death, 156; son of, 284.

Hamilton, Henry, rouses Indians against Americans, 84; expedition against Vincennes, 87–88; captured, 89; orders of, for campaigns against Americans, 90–91; imprisonment of, 94.

Hamilton, Joseph, marriage, 168; in garrison feud, 173–74; sent to Fort Belle Fontaine, 175.

Hamilton, William S., contractor, 284.

Hamlin, John, performs marriage ceremony, 284.

Hamtramck, John, commander at Detroit, 130; death, 131; on injustice to Indians, 180.

Hardin, John, murder of, 115.

Harmar, Fort, Treaty of, 109–10, 122, 190–91.

Harmar, Josiah, expedition of, 111.

Harmon, Dr., treatment of cholera, 333.

Harney, William S., in Black Hawk War, 323.

Harrison, Fort, place in Northwestern frontier, 197; garrison in 1812, 198.

Harrison, William H., dealings with Tecumseh, 120, 190–92, 341; governor of Indiana Territory, 128; on liquor-drinking by Indians, 183–84; on injustice to Indians, 180–81; protests against witchcraft delusion, 187; seeks to obtain Indian murderers, 193; difficulty with militia, 204; commander of Fort Meigs, 250; negotiates treaties, 262, 340–42; biography, 442.

Hay, Henry, journal, 145–46, 444.

Hayes, Otto, death, 228–29, 388.

Hayward, Thomas, factor at Chicago, 297.

Head, William R., papers, 134, 149, 382, 444–45; preserves Moses Morgan narrative, 261, 399; rejects Mrs. Kinzie's narrative, 382.

Heald, Darius, narrative of massacre, 234, 241, 380–82, 384, 409–14, 449; birth, 405.

Heald, Nathan, desires leave of absence, 153, 176; birth of children, 159, 404–5; commends John Whistler, 174; transferred to Fort Dearborn, 175–76; visits New England, 175–76; marriage, 176–77; receives news of Indian depredations, 211–12; report of April murders, 212; organizes militia company, 213; Hull commends, 215, 380; Hull's order to, to evacuate Fort Dearborn, 215–17, 378, 393, 403, 406, 409, 416; responsibility for Fort Dearborn massacre, 215, 217–19; preparations for evacuation, 219–20; Black Partridge's warning to, 220–21, 223, 384, 420; in Fort Dearborn massacre, 223, 226, 229; stipulates prisoners to be spared, 233; letter of William Griffith to, 234, 253; letters of Thomas Forsyth to, 236, 246, 255; captivity, 240–3, 403–4, 407; wounds, 241, 244, 391, 403, 407, 414; later life, 244–45; pension, 244, 391–92; home of, 245; home looted, 381; gives factory goods to Indians, 300; report of massacre, 379–80, 406–8; antipathy of Mrs. Kinzie's narrative, 385; conduct in massacre, 389–90, 415–20; journal, 402–5; obituary, 409; papers, 428, 445. *See also* Chicago; Fort Dearborn.

Heald, Mrs. Rebekah, birth of children, 159, 404–5; marriage, 176–77; death of children, 159, 221, 405; in Fort Dearborn massacre, 223, 226, 394, 409–13; memorandum on property

losses, 228; captivity, 240–43, 403–4, 407; wounds, 241, 403, 407, 409, 411–12; later life, 244–45; narrative of massacre, 380–82, 410–14; birth, 414; daguerreotype of, 414.
Heintzelman, S. P., in Black Hawk War, 323.
Helm, Leonard, surrenders Vincennes, 87–88.
Helm, Linai T., member of courts-martial, 163; transferred to Fort Dearborn, 177; financial condition, 177, 365; version of evacuation order, 216; in Fort Dearborn massacre, 230, 401; captivity, 246–47, 419–20; later career, 276; narrative of massacre, 378–80, 385, 387–91; version of Black Partridge's warning, 384; wound, 391–92; pension, 392; letter to Judge Woodward announcing narrative of massacre, 415–16; list of survivors of massacre, 421, 431–33; survivor of massacre, 423.
Helm, Mrs. Linai T., in Fort Dearborn massacre, 223, 226, 385–88, 419; rescue of, 223, 230, 386–88, 413; captivity, 246–47; second residence at Chicago, 276; divorce, 276, 311; grants to, 362, 364–65; informant of Mrs. Kinzie, 383; survivor of massacre, 423.
Hempstead, Stephen, statements about Du Sable, 141–42.
Hennepin, Father, expedition planned, 32; *New Discovery*, 49–50.
Henry, James, in Black Hawk War, 334, 337–38.
Henry, Patrick, approves Clark's plans, 85; Fort Vincennes named after, 89.
"Henry Clay," carries troops to Chicago, 329; cholera on, 332–33.
Hesse, Emanuel, operations of, in 1780, 95.
Heward, Hugh, dealings with Du Sable, 140–41, 286; journal, 445.
Heyl, Sergeant, death, 332.
Hopson, John, crosses Chicago Portage, 10.
Horses, use of, on Chicago Portage, 11–13, 15–19; in building first Fort Dearborn, 134.
Howard, Fort, troops from, in Winnebago War, 317–18.
Hubbard, Gurdon S., crosses Chicago Portage, 10, 14–15; preserves story of Cerré, 18; preserves story of Gary, 138; first visit to Chicago, 279–80; describes arrival of Cass at Chicago, 313–14; brings militia from Danville, 315–17; writings, 446.
Hulbert, A.B., *Portage Paths*, 3, 7, 446.
Hull, William, seeks to counteract British machinations among Indians, 188; campaign of 1812, 205–10, 214, 222; order for evacuation of Fort Dearborn, 215–17, 378, 393, 403, 406, 409, 416; commends Heald, 380; memoirs, 446.
Hunt, George, grant to, 360.
Hunt, John E., aids De Garmo, 240.
Hunt, Thomas, commander at Detroit, 158.
Hunt, William N., death, 236, 433.
Hunter, David, commander at Fort Dearborn, 321–22.
Huron Indians, forays against Foxes, 46, 67–69; Iroquois ruin, 52; foray against Mascoutens, 61–62; defeat Foxes, 62; join De Noyelles' expedition, 70.

Iberville, expedition of, 36.
Illinois, British attempts to gain possession of, 80–81; plans against, in 1781, 97–98; Indian depredations in, 193–94; settlements in 1812, 197; fur traders in, 25–26, 285; operations of American Fur Company in, 278–79; volume of fur trade in, 288–89; militia in Black Hawk War, 324–25, 334.
Illinois Indians, village at Starved Rock destroyed, 33; Foxes wage war against, 55, 77; Foxes attack, 59; war party comes to Chicago, 60; war with Foxes, 63–64; abandon Starved Rock, 64; part in De Lignery's expedition, 65; thievery of, 134; engage in fur trade, 285.
Illinois Mission, founded, 28; Allouez appointed to, 29; success of, 39.
Illinois River, Joliet and Marquette on, 23–24; highway between Great Lakes and Mississippi, 51, 263; Americans to enjoy free use of, 125; Indians cede land at mouth of, 125; ascent of, by Cass, 313; by Fort Dearborn garrison, 321.

Independence Day, celebration, 123.

Indians, as carriers on Chicago Portage, 18; population in Northwest, 83, 198–99; neutrality in Revolution, 83; British policy toward, 84, 106–8; desert Lieutenant Bennett, 93–94; threaten Langlade, 97; relations with United States in Northwest, 108–9, 264; raid Ohio frontier, 111, 115; British encourage against United States, 108, 122, 181, 194, 196; and building of first Fort Dearborn, 133–34; ideas of land ownership, 178–79; failure of United States government policy toward, 179–84; use of liquor, 178–79, 182–84, 188–90, 304, 347–48; patient endurance of evils, 185; Americans urge to neutrality, 188, 194; Tecumseh and Prophet attempt to reform, 186–90; Tecumseh attempts to unite, 190–92; oppose cession of lands, 191; visit Malden, 193; plot against Northwestern posts, 193; murders in Illinois, 193–94; prowess as warriors, 199; horrors of warfare, 200–201; Dickson leads against Americans, 237–38; treaties with, in Northwest, 262–63; policy of Continental Congress toward, 290–91; of Confederation toward, 291; ask establishment of government trading houses, 294–95; plan rising against Americans, 320; code of honor, 335–36; title to land of Northwest, 340; bribery of, 345–46.

Indian Creek massacre, 327.

Indian trade, basis of, 53; competition for, 78; of Northwest, rivalry over, 107; at Chicago, 285–309; department, records of, 287, 299, 447; factory system, 289–309.

Indiana, territory created, 128; Harrison's messages to legislature, 180-81, 183; fears of settlers, 190–92, 325; settlements in 1812, 197; militia in Black Hawk War, 327–28.

Iroquois Indians, destroy Illinois village, 33; Denonville's campaign against, 38; war party attacks Foxes, 46; Champlain joins expedition against, 51–52; gain firearms, 52; encourage Foxes, 54; Christian, join foray against Foxes, 70; share in De Noyelles' expedition, 70, 73–75; Foxes ally with, 77; Butler's speech to, 118.

Iroquois River, Hubbard's trading house on, 316.

Irwin, Matthew, factor at Chicago, 166, 298–99; in garrison feud, 173; report of, on April murders, 212; factor at Green Bay, 272, 299.

Irwin, Robert, conveys Healds to Detroit, 242.

Jacques, companion of Marquette, 24, 26–7.

Jay, John, negotiates treaty, 103, 125–26.

Jefferson, Fort, St. Clair's army reaches, 114; commander killed, 116.

Jefferson, Thomas, resigns governorship, 103; message on trading-house system, 294–95.

Jefferson Barracks, troops from, in Winnebago War, 313, 317; Fifth Infantry at, 321.

Jesuit order, proselyting work, 38–39.

Jews'-harp, use of in Indian trade, 306.

Johnston, Albert Sidney, in Black Hawk War, 323.

Johnston, Joseph E., in Black Hawk War, 323.

Joliet, Louis, on Chicago Portage, 4–6, 8; proposes canal at Chicago Portage, 5–6, 19; expedition of, 22–24.

Jones, George W., in Black Hawk War, 323.

Jordan, Walter, report of Fort Dearborn massacre, 394–96.

Jouett, Charles, names son for La Lime, 149; Indian agent at Chicago, 166, 270–71; in garrison feud, 173–76; house fortified, 213; in charge of Chicago factory, 297; invoices furniture of factory, 293.

Joutel, narrative, 36–38.

Juries, western, refuse to convict of crimes against Indians, 180–81.

Kankakee River, Charlevoix follows, 11–12, 16, 45; not used by Marquette, 28–29; John Kinzie trades on, 147.

Kaskaskia, population in 1778, 82; Clark captures, 86.

Kawkeemee, wife of Burnett, 347.

Keating, William. H., narrative of Long's expedition, 10, 448; on Chicago's lake trade, 268; description of Chicago, 281–82.

Keith, Governor, memorial to Board of Trade, 44.

Kelso, John, escapes from April murders, 212.

Kendall, Amos, on character of militia, 203–4.

Keneaum, Francis, mission of, 213–14.

Kennison, David, career, 255–57; survivor of massacre, 432, 434.

Kentucky, G. R. Clark settles in, 85; county of, created, 85; inhabitants raid Indians, 109, 111; volunteers in Wayne's army, 116–17; people kill Indians, 180.

Kercheval, B. B., grant to, 360.

Kercheval, Gholson, grant to, 360.

Kickapoo Indians, allies of Foxes, 56; war parties against Foxes, 58; desert Foxes, 66.

Kingsbury, Jacob, papers, 17, 448; crosses Chicago Portage, 17, 289; establishes Fort Belle Fontaine, 154; contents of letter books, 155–56; birth of daughter, 158; court martial proceedings, 162–63; commends John Whistler, 174; offered command of Northwestern army, 206; letter to John Whistler, 288.

Kinzie, Elizabeth, comes to Chicago, 147.

Kinzie, Ellen Marion, marriage, 284.

Kinzie, James, comes to Chicago, 147; grant to, 359.

Kinzie, John, carries traders across portage, 16, 19; house at Chicago, 142, 166, 268; account books, 143, 149, 167, 256, 269, 287, 289, 378–79; career, 145–52; kills John La Lime, 149–50; relations with Jeffrey Nash, 151–52; dispute with Pattinson, 156; performs marriage ceremony, 158; in garrison feud, 172–74; moves family into Fort Dearborn, 213; and evacuation of Fort Dearborn, 218–19, 417, 420; Heald employs horses, 219; in Fort Dearborn massacre, 222, 227, 230, 232, 385, 420, 429; losses in massacre, 236, 246, 363–64; experiences of family after massacre, 246; urges re-establishment of fort at Chicago, 264; career at Chicago after 1816, 269–70; sub-Indian agent, 270, 363; goods of factory deposited with, 275; American Fur Company appeals to, 277; household, 280; learns of plot against Fort Snelling, 283; trading operations, 287–88; invoices furniture of factory, 298; recognizes Cass's party, 313–14; helps negotiate treaty, 347; claims of heirs, 361–65; tells story of death of Sergeant Hayes, 388; and story of forged order, 389, 417; influence over Indians, 390, 419; writes Heald of Indian hostility, 416; biography, 444; family, genealogy, 448.

Kinzie, Mrs. John, marriage, 145–46; intercedes for Helm, 246; in Fort Dearborn massacre, 385.

Kinzie, John H., share in Chicago Treaty of 1833, 358, 361–64; sub-Indian agent, 361, 383; signs Treaty of Prairie du Chien, 364; marriage, 383.

Kinzie, Mrs. Juliette A. (John H.), account of Du Sable, 139, 142; story of Ouilmette, 144; narrative of April murders, 212; version of evacuation order, 216; story of cholera panic, 330–31; narrative of Fort Dearborn massacre, 379, 382–88, 391, 413; writings, 448–49.

Kinzie, Maria Indiana, marriage, 322.

Kinzie, Robert, in Fort Dearborn fire, 314; grants to, 361–64.

"Kinzie's Improvement," 132, 375.

Kirkland, Joseph, interviews Darius Heald, 381; estimate of *Wau Bun*, 385; writings, 449.

Knaggs, William, grant to, 346.

Koshkonong, Lake, Black Hawk retreats to, 334.

La Barre, Lefevre de, hostile to La Salle, 35.

La Compt, Mrs., career, 137–38.

La Framboise, Joseph, grant to, 358.

La Framboise, Josette, marriage, 278.

La Framboise, Mrs., statement about Du Sable, 141.

Lahontan, Baron de, maps, 4; crosses Chicago Portage, 17–18; writings, 449.

La Lime, John, occupies Kinzie's house, 142; career, 148–50; house, 166; reports Indian depredations, 194; report of April murders, 212.

La Lime, John [son of above ?], grant to, 347.

Lamb, Charles A., story of Grummo, 239–40.

Land, process of obtaining cessions, 178–79; Tecumseh's contentions, 190–92, 341; hunger of whites for, 178, 341.

Langlade, Charles de, captures Pickawillany, 78, 90; operations against Americans, 90–93; in attack on St. Louis, 95, 97; and Du Sable, 139.

La Salle, description of Chicago Portage, 4–11; uses St. Joseph Portage, 5; early explorations, 21; at Chicago, 21–22; career, 30–36; survivors of Texan expedition, 37–38; followers build fort at Chicago, 47; colony founded on Indian trade, 286.

Latrobe, Charles J., account of Chicago Treaty of 1833, 349–57, writings, 449.

Latta, James, death, 234.

Laval, Bishop, Pinet appeals to, 39.

Le Claire (Le Clerc), Jean B., grant to, 347.

Le Claire (Le Clerc), Pierre, brings news of war to Fort Dearborn, 214; grant to, 347; member of Chicago militia, 431.

Lee, farmer at Chicago, 167; murders at farm of, 212–13; evacuation means financial ruin, 218; captivity of family, 254–55; member of Chicago militia, 431.

Lee, Lillian, death, 255.

Lee, Mrs., ransomed, 236, 255; captivity, 254–55.

Le Mai, resident of Chicago, 142; home of, 166.

Lincoln, Abraham, in Black Hawk War, 323; nomination, 370.

Lincoln Park, Kennison buried in, 257.

Linctot, expedition of, 92–93.

Lindsay, A.B., closes Chicago factory, 308.

Lipcap, murder of, 311.

Liquor, Burnett needs, 129; Du Sable's stock, 140; Indians plied with, at treaties, 178–79; efforts to suppress traffic vain, 182; effects on Indians, 182–84, 188–90, 304; given to Indians, 188; Prophet forbids use of, 189–90; destruction of, at Fort Dearborn, 220, 236, 246, 389, 393–94, 406, 410; drinking at close of Winnebago War, 317; drinkers victims of cholera, 333, 336; eagerness of Indians for, 347–48; Mrs. Heald ransomed with, 412.

Little Turtle, in St. Clair's defeat, 114; at Fallen Timbers, 120; contentions at Treaty of Greenville, 123; at Maumee Rapids, 146; on evils of liquor-drinking, 184.

Lockwood, James H., attack upon family averted, 311.

Loftus, Major, defeat of expedition, 80.

Logan, Hugh, death, 236, 404.

Logan, James, report of, 3–4, 44, 50.

London, cholera at, 333.

Long, Stephen H., topographical report, 8, 266–67; expedition of, 281.

Long River, story of, 17–18.

Louisiana, La Salle takes possession, 34; La Salle the father of, 36; France loses, 79; and establishment of Fort Dearborn, 128–29; court upholds free character of Illinois Territory, 151–52; revolt discussed, 156; attacks on settlements proposed, 194.

Louvigny, makes peace with Foxes, 58; expedition against Foxes, 59, 62–63; trading project, 127.

Loyalists, anger of patriots for, 106.

Lynch, Michael, death, 246, 433–34.

McAfee, Robert B., version of Black Partridge's warning, 221; account of Fort Dearborn massacre, 379, 397; history, 449.

McArthur, Duncan, negotiates treaties, 262.

McClernand, John A., in Black Hawk War, 323.

McCoy, Rev. Isaac, meets cattle drivers, 268; share in Chicago Treaty of 1821, 345–46; history, 449.

McHenry, Fort, troops from, sent to Chicago, 328–29.

McIntosh, Fort, treaty of, 109, 190–91.

McKee, Captain, gives liquor to Indians, 188.

McKenney, Thomas L., Benton's charges against, 305; cross examines Lindsay, 308; negotiates treaty, 312.

McKenzie, Elizabeth, story of, 146–47.

McKenzie, Isaac, recovers daughters, 147.

McKenzie, Margaret, story of, 146–47.

McKillip, Mrs. Eleanor, marries John Kinzie, 145–46. *See also* Kinzie, Mrs. John.

McKillip, Margaret, marries Lieutenant Helm, 147. *See also* Helm, Mrs.

McNeil, John, commander of Fort Dearborn, 282.

McNeil, Mrs. John, half-sister of Franklin Pierce, 282.

McNeil, J. W. S., son of John McNeil, 282.

Mackinac, rendezvous against Foxes, 59; captured in Pontiac's war, 80; English reoccupy, 80; expect assault, 91; Patrick Sinclair takes command, 94; last Northwestern post surrendered, 126; outpost of Americans in Northwest, 128; dulness of life at, 153; Indian plot against, 193; garrison in 1812, 198; Hull learns of surrender, 209, 215; Dickson's share in capture, 214, 237; Hull plans to supply, 214–15; Dickson leads warriors to, 238; experience of Healds at, 242; Jacob B. Varnum winters at, 273–74; headquarters of American Fur Company, 278; French post at, 286; factory at, 295, 298; garrison changed, 321.

Madison, Fort, factory at, 295.

Mahnawbunnoquah, wife of J. B. Beaubien, 346.

Main Poc, speech on injustice to Indians, 182; followers threaten Fort Dearborn, 193; marauding of, 194; sends news of Hull's reverses, 393.

Malden, distribution of goods to Indians, 188; Northwestern Indians visit, 193; Hull's operations before, 209; Brock reaches, 210; Hull hopes for surrender of, 217.

Mann, Mrs., grant to, 358.

Mantet, trading project, 127.

Maps, list of, 450.

Marest, Father, in Fox war, 58.

Marietta, founded, 109; settlements near, raided, 111.

Marquette, Father, crosses Chicago Portage, 9; interest in exploration, 22; founds mission of St. Ignace, 23; joins Joliet's expedition, 23; second expedition, 24–29; death, 28; Indian traders accompany, 285.

Marsh, Laurie, grant to, 360.

Mascouten Indians, allies of Foxes, 56; kill Miami squaws, 56–57; war parties against French, 58; Huron foray against, 61–62; desert Foxes, 66.

Mason, Edward G., credits French fort tradition, 43; describes fort at Chicago, 47; study of Spanish attack on St. Joseph, 100; credits story of Job Wright, 259; account of Fort Dearborn massacre reprinted, 399; writings, 451.

Massac, Fort, Heald commander of, 402.

Massachusetts, government trading houses, 290.

Matchekewis, joins in attack on St. Louis, 95.

Matson, N., account of Du Sable, 139; account of captivity of Lee family, 255; writings, 255, 451.

Maumee City, settlement at, 239.

Maumee Rapids, British build fort at, 118; settlement at, 145–46; Hull's army reaches, 209.

Maumee River, Wayne destroys villages on, 117–18; Cass and Schoolcraft ascend, 343.

Meigs, Fort, Mrs. Simmons reaches, 250.

Meigs, Governor, raises militia for Hull's campaign, 207.

Metea, speech of Cass to, 183; Pottawatomie orator, 344.

Miami, De la Balme captures, 98.

Miami, Fort, location, 4, 44, 49; La Salle builds, 31; captured in Pontiac's war, 80.

Miami Indians, Harmar's expedition against, 110–11; St. Clair to establish fort among, 112; villages ravaged, 122; followers of Wells in Fort Dearborn massacre, 217, 219, 225, 229, 406, 416.

Michigan, settlements in 1812, 196–97; Hull as governor, 205; Hull surrenders to British, 210; panic of settlers in Black Hawk War, 325; militia in Black Hawk War, 327–28.

Militia, character in 1812, 203–4.

Mills, Elias, captivity, 238–39.

Milwaukee, character of Indian population, 83; Indians join Spaniards against St. Joseph, 100.

Mirandeau, Jean Baptiste, grant to, 362.
Mirandeau, Thomas, grant to, 362.
Mississippi River, Joliet and Marquette descend, 22–23; Hennepin's exploration planned, 32; La Salle descends, 34; Spain seeks exclusive navigation, 105; Cass descends, 313; Black Hawk's followers cross, 323, 334; western boundary of United States, 340.
Missouri Gazette, report of Fort Dearborn massacre in, 393–94.
Moll, Herman, description of Chicago Portage, 3–4; maps, 4, 450.
Montgomery, John, pursues British, 97.
Montigny, threatens Foxes, 64.
Moreau, Pierre, courier de bois, in Illinois, 25–27.
Morgan, George, urges expedition against Detroit, 84.
Morgan, Moses, workman on second Fort Dearborn, 134; describes Ouilmette, 145; story of Fort Dearborn captive, 260–61; narrative of massacre, 399–401.
Mortt, August, death, 236, 334.
Moses, John, estimate of Mrs. Kinzie's narrative, 382; history, 451.
Mount Joliet (Monjolly), portage extends to, 11–12, 16; furs transported between, and Chicago, 289.
Mud Lake, La Salle describes, 6; passage of, by American Fur Company traders, 14–15; Cass passes night on, 313.
Murders, of Indians by whites, 180–82; by Indians in Illinois, 193–94.

Nachitoches, factory at, 295.
Nakewoin, joins Spaniards against St. Joseph, 100.
"Napoleon," transports Michigan militia, 328.
Nash, Jeffrey, case of, 148, 150–52, 450; articles of indenture, 287.
Navy, in War of 1812, 202–3.
Nayocantay, speech, 320.
Necessity, Fort, capture of, 66.
Needs, John, death, 433–34.
Needs, Mrs. John, fate, 235–36.
New Orleans, cholera at, 329.
Niagara, portage at, 4; council at, 109; invasion of Canada from, planned, 205.
Niagara, Fort, garrison changes, 321–22; troops from, sent to Chicago, 327–28; troops return to, 338.
Nicolet, Jean, exploration of, 52.
Niles, Fort St. Joseph at, 45; militia mustered out at, 328; Carey's Mission near, 345.
Niles' Register, reports of Fort Dearborn massacre in, 392–96.
Noles, Joseph, captivity, 238–39.
Nontagarouche, taunts De Noyelles, 73.
Northwest, Indian population at opening of Revolution, 83; French-Spanish efforts to gain, 105; posts held by British, 106–7; relations between Indians of, and United States after Revolution, 108; territorial government provided, 109; title to land of, 125, 340; posts surrendered to Americans, 126; Wayne's victory makes settlement possible, 127–28; unrest of Indians, 178; dangers to frontier, 196–97; defenses in 1812, 197–98; strength of British and Indian forces in, 198–99; panic of settlers, 200; effect of Hull's capture on, 211; United States asked to renounce portion of, 262; government to establish garrisons in, 264; American Fur Company attempts to monopolize trade of, 301; treaties closing War of 1812 in, 363.
Nuscotnemeg, murders white men, 193–94; in Fort Dearborn massacre, 223; Storrow meets, 280.

O'Fallon, John, ransoms property of Healds, 243.
O'Fallon (Missouri), Heald home at, 244–45.
Ohio, admission of, 128; conduct of militia in Fort Wayne campaign, 204; militia in Hull's army, 206–7; Hull's advance through, 207–9.
Ohio, Falls of, Clark builds blockhouse at, 85–86; Clark retires to, 94; expedition against Clark at, 95; British plan to attack Clark at, 104.
Ohio Company, founds Marietta, 109.
Ohio River, British raid settlements, 103–4.
Okra, tells story of Fort Dearborn massacre, 400.

Onontio, designation of French governor and king, 64.

Onorakinguiah, bravery of, 73–74.

Ordinance of 1787, prohibition of slavery in, upheld, 152.

Osage, Fort, factory at, 295.

Ottawa Indians, follow Prophet's advice, 190; plot of, against Northwestern posts, 193; and Chicago Treaty of 1821, 344–45; treaty with, at Prairie du Chien, 364.

Ottawa River, French follow route of, 52.

Ouashala, Fox chief, 63; nephew burned, 64.

Ouiatanon, population, 82; Linctot reaches, 93; French post at, 286.

Ouiatanon Indians, measles among, 59–60; visited by De Noyelles, 71.

Ouilmette, Antoine, transports travelers across portage, 13, 19, 143; career, 142–45; house of, 166; hired to prepare garden, 265; hires wagon, 289.

Ouilmette, Josette, grant to, 358, 362.

Owen, Thomas J. V., negotiates treaty, 354.

Paris, Treaty of, 79, 340; cholera at, 333.

Parkman, Francis, account of siege of Detroit, 55; writings, 452.

Patrick Henry, Fort, named, 89.

Pattinson, Hugh, dispute with John Kinzie, 156; hires furs carried across Chicago Portage, 289.

Peck, John M., *Annals of the West* corrected, 414.

Peoria, variations of name, 77; Du Sable at, 139–40; John Kinzie trades at, 147, 287; servitude of Jeffrey Nash at, 152; Helm at, 246. *See also* Fort Clark; Fort Crèvecoeur; Lake Peoria.

Peoria, Lake, Fort Crèvecoeur at, 31–33; Linctot at, 92; Montgomery reaches, 97; Spaniards leave boats at, 101; Indians cede land at, 125.

Pepin, Lake, French fort on, abandoned, 65.

Petchaho, asks establishment of factory at Fort Clark, 300.

Petite Fort, fight at, 99–100.

Pettle, Louis, trader, 142; member of Chicago militia, 431.

Phillips, Joseph, report of, 16, 19.

Pickawillany, capture of, 78, 90.

Pierce, Benjamin K., marriage, 274.

Pierce, Franklin, brothers at Mackinac, 274; Mrs. McNeil a half-sister, 282.

Pinet, Father, mission of, at Chicago, 38–42, 137; at Cahokia, 42.

Pitt, Fort, resists Indian attack, 80; importance of, 83.

Pittsburgh, Wayne establishes camp near, 116; Healds at, 243.

Plainfield (Ill.), panic of settlers, 325–27.

Poindexter, Thomas, death, 285, 434.

Pokagon, grant to, 357.

Pomme de Cigne River, Fox forts on, 72.

Popple, Henry, map, 44, 450.

Portage des Sioux, whites killed near, 193; treaties negotiated at, 262.

Porter, George B., negotiates treaty, 354.

Porter, Rev. Jeremiah, describes Indian gathering at Chicago, 366–67; writings, 452.

Porteret, Pierre, companion of Marquette, 24.

Porthier, Mrs. Victoire, version of La Lime's death, 150; grant to, 361–62.

Pottawatomie Indians, numbers at opening of Revolution, 83; plot against Northwestern posts, 193; Dickson among, at St. Joseph, 238; at Maumee City, 239; payment of annuity to, 314; in Black Hawk War, 323–24; treaties with, 343–66; Carey's Mission among, 345; farewell to Chicago, 367–70.

Prairie du Chien, factory and garrison at, 264; garrison withdrawn, 310; militia organized, 312; treaties of, 312, 317, 358, 364–65; Red Bird's imprisonment at, 319–20; General Scott at, 334.

Presque Isle, captured in Pontiac's war, 80.

Proctor, Henry A., disclaims responsibility for Fort Dearborn massacre, 236; orders Fort Dearborn captives ransomed, 239; letter of Woodward to, 239, 422–24, 428; letter of Bullock to, 254; paroles Heald, 403.

Prophet, The, career, 185–90; cause of agitation led by, 341.

Puthuff, Major, performs marriage ceremony, 274.

"Queen Charlotte," carries news of Fort Dearborn massacre, 393.

Ramezay, Claude de, recommends fort at Chicago, 44.

Rangers, protect Ohio frontier, 111; cholera among United States, 335.

Recovery, Fort, built, 116; assault on, 117.

Red Bird, attacks Gagnier family, 310–11; surrender and death, 318–20.

Revolution, in the West, 81–104.

Reynolds, John, story of Mrs. La Compt, 137–38; in Black Hawk War, 323–25, 337; negotiates treaty, 337; history, 452.

Rhea, James, troops fever stricken, 159; transferred to Fort Wayne, 175–76.

Rhone River, floods of, 7, 9.

Rice, Luther, grant to, 359.

Roberts, Charles, and recovery of Fort Dearborn captives, 237; treatment of Healds, 242, 403, 407, 413.

Robinson, Alexander, statements about Du Sable, 141–42; resident of Chicago in 1816, 144; in Fort Dearborn massacre, 223; conveys Healds to Mackinac, 241–42, 413–14; hired to prepare garden, 265; grants to, 357; narrative of massacre, 398; given charge of Heald, 401.

Rock Island, garrison to be established, 264; cholera at, 335–37; troops leave, 337–38. *See also* Fort Armstrong.

Rock River, Montgomery's expedition on, 97; Black Hawk plans to raise crop on, 324; march of troops along, 335; Black Hawk's speech on beauty of country, 337.

Ronan, George, ordered to Fort Dearborn, 177; account of, in *Wau Bun*, 223; in Fort Dearborn massacre, 226; death, 407.

Russell, April murders at farm of, 212–13.

Sac Indians, allies of Foxes, 56; shelter Foxes, 70; assist Americans, 91; murderers of Menominees, 335–36; murder Americans, 341.

Sac and Fox Indians, confederation, 70; wage war on Illinois and Chippewas, 77; part in attack on St. Louis, 95–96; maintain hostile attitude, 262; treaties with, 337, 341–42.

St. Ange, Jean de, commands Charlevoix's escort, 63; leads expedition against Foxes, 66.

Sainte Ange, Pilette de, early resident of Chicago, 137.

St. Clair, Arthur, governor of Northwest Territory, 109; negotiates treaty of Fort Harmar, 109–10; calls for troops, 110; expedition of, 111–14; letters of, 153, 180.

St. Cosme, Father, crosses Chicago Portage, 11, 17; letter of, 40; party of, at Chicago, 40–42; at Cahokia, 42.

St. Ignace, Mission of, 23.

St. Joseph, Linctot plans to attack, 93; Hamelin captures, 99; Spanish attack on, 100–103; studies of, 100, 102, 439, 451, 455; Fort Dearborn garrison camps at, 130, 132, 136; captivity of Healds at, 241, 403, 407; French post at, 286; Michigan militia at, 328.

St. Joseph, Fort, at Niles, 45; captured in Pontiac's war, 80; relics from, 306.

St. Joseph Portage, La Salle uses, 5; Hubbard uses, 15; description of, 375. *See also* Kankakee River.

St. Joseph River, Harmar destroys towns on, 111; Swearingen descends, 132; Kinzie removes to, 146; traders operate at Chicago, 287.

St. Lawrence River, gives French access to interior, 2.

St. Louis, British attack on, 95–97; preparations against in 1781, 100; treaty negotiated at, 341–42.

St. Louis, Fort, navigation begins at, 6; built, 35; Cavelier's party at, 37–38; ordered abandoned, 44: Tonty succeeds La Salle at, 286. *See also* Starved Rock.

St. Mary's River, Harmar destroys towns on, 111; Wayne ravages villages on, 122.

St. Peter's River, Long's expedition to, 281; factory to be established on, 301.
Sandusky, captured in Pontiac's war, 80; John Kinzie at, 145; Jacob B. Varnum at, 271, 303; factory at, 295.
Sandwich, Hull captures, 209; abandons, 217; Dickson at, 238.
Sauganash Hotel, 350, 369.
Sault Ste. Marie, English abandon, 80; reoccupy, 80; garrison changed, 321.
Schoolcraft, Henry R., crosses Chicago Portage, 12, 15-16, 19; records information about Du Sable, 141; description of Chicago in 1820, 281, 339; describes Chicago Treaty of 1821, 343; account of Fort Dearborn massacre, 388; writings, 453.
Schwartz, J. C., grant to, 360.
Scott, Charles, joins Wayne with Kentucky troops, 117.
Scott, Martin, eccentricities, 322.
Scott, Winfield, physical stature, 282; in Black Hawk War, 323, 328-37; *Memoirs*, 453.
Sears, John, teacher among Ottawas, 345.
Second Infantry, movements of, 321, 338.
Sendale, Peter, court martial of, 163.
Settlement, geographic factors, 2; rush of, west of Alleghenies, 109.
Shabbona, mission to Big Foot's village, 315; opposes war, 324; in Fort Dearborn massacre, 397.
Shavehead, story of, 258-59.
Shawnee Indians, employed on Chicago Portage, 18; Tecumseh a Shawnee, 185-86.
Shea, John G., translation of St. Cosme's letter, 40; writings, 454.
"Sheldon Thompson," carries troops to Chicago, 329; cholera on, 330-32.
Shirreff, Patrick, observations on Chicago, 348-51, 357; writings, 453.
Sibley, Solomon, negotiates treaty, 343.
Siggenauk, in Spanish attack on St. Joseph, 100; De Peyster tries to capture, 100-101.
Simcoe, John, hostility toward Americans, 115; builds fort at Maumee Rapids, 118; proposes fort at Chicago, 127.
Simmons, David, death, 247.
Simmons, John, death, 247.
Simmons, Mrs. John, in Fort Dearborn massacre, 224; captivity, 247-51; later career, 251.
Sinclair, Patrick, commander at Mackinac, 94; operations against Americans, 95-98; arrests Chevalier, 101.
Sioux Indians, French trade with, 54; and Foxes ally, 76-77; in attack on St. Louis, 95, 98; plot against Fort Snelling, 283; kill Black Hawk's followers, 334.
Smith, E. Kirby, at Fort Winnebago, 321.
Smith, William C., occupies Kinzie's house, 142; praises La Lime, 149; first Fort Dearborn surgeon, 170; part in garrison feud, 171-72; letter of, 454.
Snelling, Fort, plot of Sioux and Foxes against, 283; troops from, in Winnebago War, 317.
"Snipe," story of, 357-58.
South Water Street, only business street, 349; Indians dance down, 354.
Southwest Company, traders hostile to Americans, 264.
Spain, British plans against, 94-95; efforts to regain Northwest, 105; war with, discussed, 156.
Spanish, operations in lower Mississippi Valley, 94; defense of St. Louis, 95-96; expedition against St. Joseph, 100-103; king, on ownership of Northwest, 103.
Spring Wells, treaties negotiated at, 262.
Starved Rock, capital of La Salle's colony, 5; Tonty ordered to fortify, 32; Iroquois destroy village at, 33; Fort St. Louis built on, 35; Foxes destroyed near, 46, 66-67; French retire to, 60-61; Foxes capture, 64; Illinois abandon, 64. *See also* Fort St. Louis.
Stevens, Frank E., writings, 323, 455.
Stillman, Isaiah, defeat of, 324.
Storrow, Samuel A., reception at Fort Dearborn, 153; description of Chicago, 280.
Street, Joseph, report of, 320.
Stuart, Robert, agent of American Fur Company, 277; at Chicago Treaty of 1833, 360-61.

Sumner, E. V., at Fort Winnebago, 321.
"Superior," carries troops to Chicago, 329.
Suttenfield, John, death, 246, 433.
Swearingen, James S., leads troops to Chicago, 131–34; connection with Fort Dearborn, 170; journal, 373–77; papers, 378–79, 455.

Talon, Jean Baptiste, sends Joliet to explore Mississippi, 22–23.
Tamaroa Indians, St. Cosme stationed among, 42.
Tanner, John, crosses Chicago Portage, 13, 19, 143–44; narrative of, 455.
Tarke, speech of, 124.
Taylor, Zachary, in Black Hawk War, 323.
Tecumseh, protagonist of Harrison, 120; career, 185–92; repudiates Tippecanoe affair, 195; attacks Hull's line of communications, 209; sends to Chicago news of Hull's retreat, 222; cause of agitation led by, 341; biography, 442.
Teggart, Frederick J., study of Spanish attack on St. Joseph, 100, 102, 455.
Thompson, Seth, in garrison feud, 173–76; death, 177.
Thwaites, Reuben G., on Mrs. Kinzie's massacre narrative, 382.
"Tiger," carries Jacob B. Varnum to Chicago, 274.
Tippecanoe, battle, 192; Tecumseh repudiates, 195; forces engaged, 199–200.
Tippecanoe Creek, Tecumseh's town at mouth of, 188.
Tonty, Illinois career, 31–36; in Denonville's campaign, 38; trading license at Fort St. Louis, 44, 286; describes Durantaye's fort, 47–48.
Topinabee, brother-in-law of Burnett, 347; pleads for whisky, 348; Pottawatomie chief, 377.
Tousey, Thomas, explores Des Plaines River, 12–13.
"Tracy," voyage to Chicago in 1803, 131–32.
Trade, rivalry over, at Fort Dearborn, 172; channels of, 263; dependence of Indians upon, 285; Indian, at Chicago, 285–309. *See also* Indian Trade; Traders.
Traders, French, in Illinois, 25–26, 285; treachery of, to British, 96; influence of Canadian, in Northwest, 128; disputes of, 156; sympathize with British, 198; smuggle goods into Northwest, 263; carried across Chicago Portage, 289; interest of, in Chicago Treaty of 1833, 355.
Treaties, with Indians of Northwest, 108–10, 191, 262–63; Indian ideas concerning, 178; whites break, 180–81; Indian fidelity to, 181; collections of, 456; Treaty of Greenville, 42–43, 122–25, 191, 225, 262, 340; of Paris, 79; of Utrecht, 79; of alliance with France, 103; of 1789, 103, 105, 107, 340; of Fort Finney, 109; of Fort Harmar, 109–10, 122–23, 190–91; of Fort McIntosh, 109, 190–91; John Jay's treaty, 125–26; second, of Greenville, 179; Chicago, of 1821, 183, 343–48; of Ghent, 262; Chicago, of 1833, 277, 348–66; of Butte des Mortes, 312, 317; of Prairie du Chien, 312, 317, 358, 364–65.
Trimble, William A., at Chicago Treaty of 1821, 345.
Trueman, Alexander, murder of, 115.
Turkey River, British capture boat near mouth of, 96.
Turner, William, letter of, 244.
Twiggs, David E., at Fort Winnebago, 321; in Black Hawk War, 323; cholera among troops of, 329–30.

United States, discord with Great Britain, 106; relations with Northwestern Indians, 108, 263; reluctant to begin war, 110, 115; Indian policy, 179–84, 292–93; military power in 1812, 201–2; unreadiness for war, 202–5; navy in War of 1812, 202–3; army in 1812, 203–5; factory system, 289–309; rangers, cholera among, 335.
Urbana, Hull's army at, 207–8.
Utrecht, Treaty of, 79.

Van Cleave, Charlotte Ouisconsin, reminiscences, 456.
Van Horn, James, captivity, 238–39.
Van Voorhis, Isaac, stationed at Fort Dearborn, 177; letter of, 196, 223, 387; in Fort Dearborn massacre, 226, 420; given key of factory, 299; death 386–87, 407.

Varnum, Jacob B., career, 270–76; ignorance of Indian trade, 303; on abolition of Chicago factory, 308; journal, 457.

Varnum, Joseph B., commends John Whistler, 174; factor at Chicago, 297–98; at Mackinac, 298.

Venango, captured in Pontiac's war, 80.

Vermilion River, Danville militia cross, 316.

Vincennes, population, 82; Clark gains, 87; Hamilton captures, 87–88; Clark's expedition against, 88–89; position of, in frontier, 97; Council of 1810, 190–92; Heald stationed at, 402.

Wabansia, opposed to war, 324.

Wabasha, operations against Americans, 95, 98.

Walker, Rev. Jesse, pioneer preacher, 245.

Wapsipinicon River, Fox posts on, 72.

War of 1812, strength of contestants, 201–5; news of declaration, at Malden, 209; at Fort Dearborn, 214.

Washington, Fort, Harmar starts from, 110; St. Clair's expedition gathers at, 111; army flees to, 114; Wayne establishes camp near, 116.

Washington, George, captured, 66; favors Clark's projects, 103; opinion of Wayne, 115–16; sends Jay to England, 125; appoints Wayne to receive Northwestern posts, 126; on frontier violence toward Indians, 180; advocates government factory system, 292.

Wau Bun, account of Fort Dearborn massacre in, 216, 382–88, 413; of April murders, 212; of Ronan, 223; of Thomas Burns, 234; of captivity of Kinzie family, 245; of captivity of Mrs. Helm, 247; of captivity of Mrs. Burns, 252; of fate of Lee family, 254–55; ignores Helm, 276.

Wayne, Anthony, gains land at Chicago, 42–43, 123; expedition of, 115–22; negotiates Treaty of Greenville, 122–25; receives surrender of Northwestern posts, 126; appreciates importance of Chicago, 127; victory of Fallen Timbers, 119–21, 199, 292, 340; courts martial under, 162; generalship, 199.

Wayne, Fort, built, 122; garrison fever-stricken, 158; William Whistler transferred to, 169; Rhea transferred to, 176; Indian plot against, 193; garrison in 1812, 198; campaign, 204; officers at, ordered to assist Heald, 217; Heald commander at, 225, 403; St. Joseph Indians join in attack on, 241; mail between Chicago and, 267; factory at, 295.

Weatherford, William, negotiates treaty, 354.

Webb, J. Watson, letter of, 267, 457; Fort Dearborn career, 282–83; biography, 439.

WeKau, attacks Gagnier family, 310–11; surrender and fate of, 318–20.

Welch, Mrs., grant to, 358.

Wells, Rebekah, marriage, 176–77. *See also* Heald, Mrs. Rebekah.

Wells, William, in St. Clair's defeat, 115; leader of Wayne's scouts, 117; uncle of Rebekah Wells, 176; learns of plot against Americans, 193; reports movements of Main Poc, 194; leads force to relief of Heald, 217, 219, 395, 406, 416; career, 224–25; in Fort Dearborn massacre, 226–28; and council with Indians, 388; on destruction of liquor and ammunition, 389; death, 395, 403, 407, 409–11.

Wentworth, John, letter of Abraham Edwards to, 252–53; physical stature, 282; statements of Scott to, on cholera, 331; addresses, 458.

West, desires war with Great Britain, 195–96.

Western Courier, report of Fort Dearborn massacre in, 392.

Whisky. *See* Liquor.

Whistler, George W., career of, 169.

Whistler, James A. McNeil, and Fort Dearborn, 169–70.

Whistler, John, commander at Fort Dearborn, 130; marriage of daughter, 130–31, 158, 170; "father" of Chicago, 148; attempts journey to Cincinnati, 154–55; map of Fort Dearborn and vicinity, 163–67; career, 168; in garrison feud, 171–76; transferred to Detroit, 175; letter to, 288; family, genealogy, 458.

Whistler, John, Jr., partner of Kinzie, 172.

Whistler, Sarah, marriage, 130–31, 158, 170.

Whistler, William, journey to Chicago, 131; race with Indian, 160–61; career, 168–69; in garrison feud, 171; in Winnebago War, 318–19; in Black Hawk War, 322, 327, 331, 333, 338.

Whistler, Mrs. William, and founding of Fort Dearborn, 133, 168–69.

White, Liberty, murder of, 212–13.

"William Penn," carries troops to Chicago, 329.

Winans, Susan Simmons, career, 251; narrative of, 398–99.

Winnebago, Fort, established, 321; J. H. Kinzie sub-agent at, 361, 383.

Winnebago Indians, news of depredations, 211–12; commit April murders, 213, 416; celebrate war dance, 283; treaties with, 312, 317, 337; in Black Hawk War, 323–24.

Winnebago War, 284, 310–21.

Winnemac, brings evacuation order, 217, 416; advises Heald, 388, 416.

Winsor, Justin, description of Chicago Portage, 3; writings, 458.

Wisconsin, Nicolet explores, 52; abandoned to Indians, 65; British influence over Indians of, 263.

Wisconsin River, British assemble at mouth of, 95; Black Hawk flees to Dalles of, 334. *See also* Fox-Wisconsin Waterway.

Witchcraft delusion, 187.

Wolcott, Alexander, Indian agent at Chicago, 239, 270–71, 383; marriage, 383–84; in charge of abandoned fort, 314; urges bribery of Indian leaders, 346; signs treaty, 364.

Wolcott, James, at Maumee City, 239.

Woodward, Augustus B., letter to Proctor, 234, 237, 396–97, 422–24, 428; Helm narrative sent to, 388; letter of Helm to, announcing narrative, 415.

Worth, William J., at Fort Winnebago, 321.

Wright, Job, story of, 258–59.

Wyandot Indians, approve Treaty of Greenville, 124; appeal of, 179; at Maumee City, 239.

Zumwalt, Jacob, Heald buys plantation of, 244, 404.

University of Illinois Press
1325 South Oak Street
Champaign, IL 61820-6903
www.press.uillinois.edu